| | | |
|---|---|---|
| Standard Error of the Mean | $\sigma_{\overline{X}} = \dfrac{\sigma_X}{\sqrt{n}}$ | |
| General Formula for a $z$ Score | $z = \dfrac{\text{score} - \text{mean}}{\text{standard deviation}}$ | Sec. 13.5 |
| Estimate of the Population Standard Deviation | $s_X = \sqrt{\dfrac{SS_X}{n - 1}}$ | Sec. 13.9 |
| Estimate of the Standard Error of the Mean | $s_{\overline{X}} = \dfrac{s_X}{\sqrt{n}} = \dfrac{S_X}{\sqrt{n - 1}}$ | Sec. 13.9 |
| $t$ Test: Hypothesis about a Single Mean | $t = \dfrac{\overline{X} - \mu_{\text{hyp}}}{s_{\overline{X}}}$ | Sec. 13.10 |

Effect Size

One sample: $d = \dfrac{\mu_{\text{true}} - \mu_{\text{hyp}}}{\sigma}$ or $g = \dfrac{\overline{X} - \mu_{\text{hyp}}}{s_X}$     Sec. 14.2

Two samples: $d = \dfrac{(\mu_X - \mu_Y)_{\text{true}} - (\mu_X - \mu_Y)_{\text{hyp}}}{\sigma}$     Sec. 15.9

or $g = \dfrac{(\overline{X} - \overline{Y}) - (\mu_X - \mu_Y)_{\text{hyp}}}{\sqrt{\dfrac{SS_X + SS_Y}{(n_X - 1) + (n_Y - 1)}}}$

or $r = \sqrt{\dfrac{t^2}{t^2 + df}}$

| | | |
|---|---|---|
| Estimate of the Standard Error of the Difference between Two *Independent* Means | $s_{\overline{X} - \overline{Y}} = \sqrt{s_{\overline{X}}^2 + s_{\overline{Y}}^2} = \sqrt{\dfrac{s_X^2}{n_X} + \dfrac{s_Y^2}{n_Y}}$ | Sec. 15.5 |
| Estimate of the Standard Error of the Difference between Two Independent Means (Assuming Homogeneity of Variance) | $s_{\overline{X} - \overline{Y}} = \sqrt{\dfrac{SS_X + SS_Y}{(n_X - 1) + (n_Y - 1)} \left( \dfrac{1}{n_X} + \dfrac{1}{n_Y} \right)}$ | Sec. 15.5 |
| (Same as above when $n_X = n_Y$) | $s_{\overline{X} - \overline{Y}} = \sqrt{\dfrac{SS_X + SS_Y}{n(n - 1)}}$ | Sec. 15.5 |
| Test Statistic: Hypothesis about the Difference between Two *Independent* Means, $t$ Distribution Model | $t = \dfrac{(\overline{X} - \overline{Y}) - (\mu_X - \mu_Y)_{\text{hyp}}}{\sqrt{\dfrac{SS_X + SS_Y}{(n_X - 1) + (n_Y - 1)} \left[ \dfrac{1}{n_X} + \dfrac{1}{n_Y} \right]}}$ | Sec. 15.5 |
| Estimate of the Standard Error of the Difference between Two *Dependent* Sample Means | $s_{\overline{X} - \overline{Y}} = \sqrt{s_{\overline{X}}^2 + s_{\overline{Y}}^2 - 2rs_{\overline{X}}s_{\overline{Y}}}$ | Sec. 16.1 |
| $t$ Test: Hypothesis about the Difference between Two *Dependent* Means | $t = \dfrac{(\overline{X} - \overline{Y}) - (\mu_X - \mu_Y)_{\text{hyp}}}{\sqrt{s_{\overline{X}}^2 + s_{\overline{Y}}^2 - 2rs_{\overline{X}}s_{\overline{Y}}}}$ | Sec. 16.1 |

*(continued on back endpapers)*

# Statistical Reasoning in Psychology and Education

## Fourth Edition

Bruce M. King
Edward W. Minium

John Wiley & Sons, Inc.

SENIOR ACQUISITIONS EDITOR      Tim Vertovec
MARKETING MANAGER      Kevin Malloy
MEDIA EDITOR      Lisa Schnettler
PRODUCTION EDITOR      Sandra Russell
SENIOR DESIGNER      Kevin Murphy
PRODUCTION SERVICES MANAGEMENT      mb editorial services

This book was set in 11/12 Bembo by Matrix Publishing Services and printed and bound by R.R. Donnelley (Willard). The cover was printed by Lehigh Press.

This book is printed on acid free paper. ∞

King, Bruce M., Edward W. Minium
Statistical Reasoning in Psychology and Education, Fourth Edition
ISBN 0-471-21187-7

Printed in the United States of America

10   9   8   7   6   5   4

To Students Who Want To Learn
and Instructors Who Like to Teach

# PREFACE

*Statistical Reasoning in Psychology and Education*, fourth edition, is emphatically concerned with students' conceptual growth. The text develops in students an understanding of statistical logic and procedures, the properties of statistical devices, the importance of the assumptions underlying statistical tools, and an understanding of what happens when the strict requirements of statistical theory meet the circumstances of real-world data.

We try particularly to be clear on those points in inferential statistics that tend to be stumbling blocks. At the same time we give full treatment in the first half of the text to descriptive statistics in the belief that once inference is done, one must return to the descriptive measures to assess the meaning of the inquiry; both concepts must be fully understood.

We also stress the interplay between statistical questions and answers and research questions and answers so that students see that statistics really has significance for their discipline. Thus, throughout the text we interweave aspects of experimental design with the statistical topics to which they are closely related.

*Statistical Reasoning in Psychology and Education*, fourth edition, is appropriate for students at different levels of sophistication. It requires an understanding only of common arithmetic and an elementary knowledge of equations. To assist those students who once knew but whose memory has now grown dim, we provide an extended review of basic mathematical propositions in an appendix. It is preceded by a diagnostic pretest (with answers) to help students learn which sections they need to study. For those students competent in algebra, Mathematical Notes at the end of many chapters offer an enriched program, but the text is designed to stand without them.

In many introductory classes, the computer plays a role in the application of statistics. However, we do not attempt to teach computer skills in this text. We leave to the instructor the difficult choice of which computer and computational programs to teach, if any.

The text should serve very well for a one-semester course. Even so, there is more material than can be covered in most one-quarter of one-semester courses. The Instructor's Resource Manual offers suggestions for adapting the book to particular needs.

# Features New to the Fourth Edition

This fourth edition of *Statistical Reasoning in Psychology and Education* has major changes in content. Since the publication of the last edition, inferential statistics has been the focus of often heated debate. Several leading statisticians have called for a complete ban on traditional, null hypothesis significance tests. Others continue to strongly defend their use. For this edition, we have made every attempt to follow the recommendations of the APA Task Force on Statistical Inference (Wilkinson et al., 1999). This includes greater emphasis on effect size, power, and confidence intervals. Beginning with Chapter 14, measures of effect size (both *d* family and *r* family measures) are integrated with the material on hypothesis testing. Specific changes include:

- a separate chapter on random sampling and sampling distributions;
- a much earlier introduction of effect size and power, and thereafter, integration of this material with the discussion of new inferential tests;
- earlier presentation of the chapters on chi-square and inference about correlation; and
- greater emphasis on confidence intervals as an alternative to hypothesis testing.

Some texts present chapters on correlation and regression after the chapters on hypothesis testing. However, we firmly believe that the material on correlation should come first so that we may more fully develop the material on correlated-groups designs and the *r* family of measures of effect size.

# Pedagogy

In addition to text features, we have added new pedagogical features to the fourth edition to help students learn:

- learning objectives at the beginning of each chapter (to go along with a summary at the end of each chapter to reinforce what has been presented), and
- the presentation of definitions, symbols, and equations in the margins of the text so that the student may easily identify important new material.

Key terms and concepts are also boldfaced at their first occurrence in each chapter and listed again for review at the end of each chapter. Special boxed sections called Points of Controversy introduce students to topical and/or current issues to let them see that statistics is an evolving, vital area of inquiry. There are also numerous problems at the end of each chapter. Some give practice in problem-solving technique; others require the use of critical judgment. Answers to the odd-numbered problems are in an appendix at the end of the text.

# Supplements

The following supplements are available with *Statistical Reasoning in Psychology and Education*:

- **Instructor's Resource Guide and Test Bank**
  Written by text author Bruce King and available to instructors at www.wiley.com/college/king, this useful guide contains information on how to adapt the text to limitations of time and to personal preference, a list of useful books and films, and over 700 examination questions.

- **Computerized Test Bank**
  Featuring over 700 questions written by the author of the text, this software program allows the instructor to create a custom exam, within an easy-to-use interface.

- **eGrade**
  An online assessment system that contains skill-building problems and solutions that correspond to each chapter. Instructors can automate the process of assigning, delivering, grading, and routing all kinds of homework, quizzes, and tests while providing students with immediate scoring and feedback on their work. Wiley *eGrade* "does the math" . . . and much more. For more information, visit www.wiley.com/college/egrade.

# Acknowledgments

Many reviewers, mentors, colleagues, friends, and family members helped develop the text. To them we extend our lasting gratitude for debts that can never be fully repaid. In particular, Ed Minium acknowledges the encouragement and understanding of his wife, Juanita, and Bruce King thanks his wife, Gail, for her support during the seemingly never-ending time he juggled the demands of authorship, teaching, research, and administrative responsibilities. We are especially grateful for the leadership of Anne Smith, whose confidence and patience enabled us to complete the project. We both thank Gordon Bear for his contributions to the third edition.

In addition, we want to express our gratitude to the following reviewers for suggestions made during various stages of the manuscript. We may not have made every change the reviewers desired, but each suggestion caused us to stop and carefully reassess our goals and the needs of the students and instructors. The reviewers are

Robert W. Allan, Lafayette College

Razia Azen, University of Illinois at Urbana–Champaign

Frank M. Bagrash, California State University–Fullerton

Dr. D. K. Beale, Cerrito College

Dr. David M. Boynton, Western Connecticut State University

Shirley Brown, SUNY Albany

Jerry Cohen, University of Rhode Island

Jane Conner, SUNY Binghamton

Stephen S. Cooper

Donna Cruse

Ernest C. Davenport, University of Minnesota–Twin Cities

Janis W. Driscoll, University of Colorado at Denver

Bruce Dudek, SUNY Albany

Rick M. Gardner, University of Colorado at Denver

Sonia V. Gonsalves, Richard Stockton College of NJ

Shelia Kennison, Oklahoma State University

Dr. Melanie Kercher, Sam Houston State University

Donald L. Meyer, University of Pittsburgh

Frederick L. Oswald, Michigan State University

Robert R. Provine, University of Maryland–Baltimore County

Robert M. Pruzek, SUNY Albany

William P. Reich, Loyola University of Chicago

William M. Rogers, Grand Valley State University

Margaret G. Ruddy, The College of New Jersey

Ron Serlin, University of Wisconsin–Madison

Murray Singer, University of Manitoba

Gregory T. Smith, University of Kentucky

Alan Sockloff, Temple University

John E. Stecklein, University of Minnesota

Dr. Chehalis Strapp, Western Oregon University

Lawrence J. Stricker, The New School for Social Research

Ellen P. Susman, Metropolitan State College

Penelope G. Vinden, Clark University

Julia Wallace, University of Northern Iowa

William Yost, Loyola University of Chicago

Dr. Lynnette Zellezny, California State University at Fresno

# About the Authors

Edward W. Minium 1917–

Ed Minium earned his B.A. at Stanford University in 1939. After serving with the United States Air Force during World War II, he returned to earn his Ph.D. in psychology at the University of California at Berkeley in 1951. He was a faculty member at San José State University from 1948 to 1982 and served as chair of the Department of Psychology from 1961 to 1966. He was the only author for the first two editions of this textbook, which was first published in 1970.


Bruce M. King 1946–

Bruce King earned his B.A. in psychology at UCLA in 1969 and a Ph.D. in biopsychology at the University of Chicago in 1978. He is a Fellow in the American Psychological Society.

# CONTENTS

CHAPTER **3**

# Frequency Distributions, Percentiles, and Percentile Ranks   25

CHAPTER **4**

# Graphic Representation of Frequency Distributions   45

CHAPTER **5**

# Central Tendency   65

CHAPTER **13**

# Introduction to Statistical Inference:
# Testing Hypotheses about Single Means ($z$ and $t$)    231

CHAPTER **14**

# Interpreting the Results of Hypothesis Testing:
# Effect Size, Type I and Type II Errors, and Power    263

## CHAPTER 15

# Testing Hypotheses about the Difference between Two Independent Groups  287

## CHAPTER **19**

## Chi-Square and Inference about Frequencies    365

## CHAPTER **20**

## Testing for Differences among Three or More Groups: One-Way Analysis of Variance (and Some Alternatives)    387

# CHAPTER 21

# Factorial Analysis of Variance:
# The Two-Factor Design for Independent Groups    423

# APPENDIX E
# Statistical Tables   509

# CHAPTER 1

## Introduction

When you have finished studying this chapter, you should be able to:

- Define statistics as a specialization within the field of mathematics;
- Understand the difference between descriptive and inferential statistics;
- Explain the role of applied statistics;
- Understand the difference between a research question and statistical question, and the difference between a statistical conclusion and research conclusion;
- Understand that statistical techniques are tools that are only as good as the individual who uses them, but that sometimes even good researchers make incorrect statistical conclusions; and
- Appreciate that to learn statistics you may have to read and study differently than for other subjects.

In early 1987, the U.S. Food and Drug Administration (FDA) was faced with an unprecedented situation. Thousands of people were dying of acquired immunodeficiency syndrome (AIDS), a relatively new sexually transmitted disease caused by the human immunodeficiency virus. The virus that causes AIDS attacks and kills white blood cells called CD4+ lymphocytes that are part of the body's immune system. As the number of healthy CD4+ cells decreases, the body is increasingly unable to defend against diseases and tumors. The number of new cases of AIDS was increasing so rapidly that the Public Health Service was predicting that more than 50,000 Americans would soon be dying of the disease every year. Not only was there no known cure, but there was not even a drug available to slow the progression of the disease. However, early clinical trials of an experimental antiviral drug known then as azidothymidine (AZT) were promising. AIDS patients given AZT were displaying increased appetites, weight gains, and elevations in the number of CD4+ cells. Moreover, only 1 of 145 AIDS patients on AZT had died, compared to 19 of 137 patients in a control group given a placebo (a substance that is medically without effect).

The process of approval of a new drug is typically very slow (8.8 years, on average), and several more years of clinical trials were scheduled. There were medical questions remaining to be answered. What was the optimal dose? For how long would the drug continue to thwart the virus? Would it prove to have toxic side effects? There were ethical questions as well. Was it morally right to withhold from other patients a drug that seemingly prolonged lives? There was also an important statistical question, one that had to be answered before the medical and ethical questions could be addressed. Was the fewer number of deaths among AIDS patients using AZT the result of the drug, or was it due just to chance? Even if the FDA had given both groups of AIDS patients the placebo or both AZT, it would be unlikely that the same number of deaths would have occurred in both groups. One would expect a difference due to chance. Were the observed differences in deaths, CD4+ cell counts, and weight changes great enough to warrant early approval of the drug? Statistical tests showed that the differences between the two groups were so great that the probability of their having occurred by chance was less than 1 in 1,000 (Fischl et al., 1987). Armed with these statistics, the FDA gave final approval for the use of AZT in March 1987 after only 21 months of testing.

The FDA's decision to give early approval for AZT was an ethical one designed to prolong lives, but it was made only after statistical analysis. Statistics is not only used in making important decisions, as in the case of AZT, but also in our everyday lives. When your professor organizes test scores into a grade distribution and calculates the class average, he or she is using statistics. If you have ever kept track of the number of gold, silver, and bronze medals won by athletes in Olympic games competition, you have used statistics. Without statistics, data collected in our everyday observations or in carefully controlled experiments would have very little meaning.

**statistics**
the science of classifying, organizing, and analyzing data (for another meaning, see Chapter 2)

What do we mean when we use the word *statistics*? In ordinary language, most people use the term *statistics* to refer to any set of facts that involve numbers (e.g., "birth statistics," "crime statistics," "unemployment statistics"). Here, *statistics* is a plural word (e.g., "The crime statistics are going to be reported on Wednesday"). However, in this chapter we refer to *statistics* as a science, a specialization within the field of mathematics. **Statistics** is the science of classifying, organizing, and analyzing data. In this sense, the word is singular (e.g., "Statistics is a science"). We introduce yet another meaning of the term *statistics* in Chapter 2.

The goal of this book is to teach you the techniques of statistics used by researchers to analyze data. Some of these techniques will be very simple, and others will be more complex. In learning statistics, it is useful to divide the subject into two parts: descriptive statistics and inferential statistics. We introduce these topics in the next two sections.

# 1.1  Descriptive Statistics

In a new school, a biology instructor is thinking about what the first group of students will be like. How much biological information will they already have? She does not wish to bore them by underestimating their readiness, but she also does not want to lose them by assuming too much. Should she begin with a review of fundamentals? How extensive? In what areas? It would also be helpful to know if the students vary widely in the extent of their biological knowledge. If they do, the instructional method may need adjustment. Finally, she would like information about the students as individuals. Who will need special help during the initial weeks? Who is ready for special challenges?

Let us suppose that the biology instructor administers a nationally developed test of biological knowledge to her students at the first class meeting. Let us also assume that she is able to learn how students in similar educational circumstances perform on this test. With this knowledge, she discovers, for example, that Bob Beaver's score in zoology is better than that of 90% of students in the same grade and that only 15% of students get lower scores than Steve Smith's.

The biology instructor finds that there are too many scores to keep in mind at once. Because the names in her gradebook are in alphabetical order, the scores are not in numerical order. She needs a way to simplify consideration of the group, so she first organizes the scores in descending order and then finds the class average for each subtest and for the complete test. Then she compares the class averages with the performance data for other similar students. This comparison shows that as a group her students are approximately at the expected level in botany and that their performance is superior in zoology. This knowledge will help her go about teaching.

**descriptive statistics**
its purpose is to organize and summarize observations

In reorganizing and comparing her students' scores, our instructor is making use of techniques that are part of the body of descriptive statistics. The purpose of **descriptive statistics** is to organize and to summarize observations so that they are easier to comprehend.

# 1.2  Inferential Statistics

**inferential statistics**
its purpose is to draw a conclusion about conditions that exist in a population from study of a sample

What is the attitude of the voting public toward capital punishment? A second branch of statistical practice, known as inferential statistics, provides the basis for answering questions of this kind. Pollsters would find it impossible to put a question like the one about capital punishment to all voters, so they ask it of a small portion of voters and then use the answers to estimate the attitudes of the whole. The purpose of **inferential statistics** is to draw a conclusion (an inference) about conditions that exist in a population (the complete set of observations) from study of a sample (a subset) drawn from the population. Because of chance factors associated with drawing a sample, the outcome, like any estimate, is subject to error. However, if the sample of voters selected for study has been chosen according to statistical principles, it is possible to know what margin of error is involved.

Another application of inferential statistics is particularly suited to evaluating the outcome of an experiment. Is it possible that a certain drug has an effect on the speed of learning? Let us suppose that an investigator decides on the kind of subjects he wishes to study. As in the first example, it is impossible to administer the drug to everyone in the population, so the investigator selects at random two samples of 25

**random sampling**

a procedure that ensures that all samples of a particular size have an equal chance of being selected

subjects each. **Random sampling** is a procedure that ensures that all samples of a particular size have an equal chance of being selected and thus eliminates any bias when we draw a sample. The investigator then administers the drug to one of the groups and a placebo to the other group. He gives both groups a learning task and treats both alike in all ways. He finds that the average learning scores of the two groups differ by 5 points.

We would expect some difference between the groups even if both received the drug because of chance factors involved in the random selection of the groups. The question faced by the experimenter is whether the observed difference is within the limits of expected variation. If certain preconditions have been met, statistical theory can provide the basis for an answer. If the experimenter finds that the obtained difference of 5 points is larger than can be accounted for by chance variation, he will infer that other factors must be at work. If examination of his experimental procedures reveals no reasonable cause for the difference other than the deliberate difference in the experimental treatment, he may make an inference about the effects of the drug in the population. This is the same type of reasoning that the FDA investigators used to conclude that AZT prolonged the lives of AIDS patients. Their conclusion was not about just those patients in the study but about the effects of AZT if it were given to *all* persons with AIDS.

## 1.3 Relationship and Prediction

Experience tells us that there is some relationship between the intelligence of parents and that of their offspring but that the relationship is not perfect. We would expect that the parents of the brightest child in a class are also bright, but we would not expect that they are necessarily the most intelligent of all the parents of the children in this group. Can we describe with greater exactness the extent of this relationship?

Suppose that the personnel office of a company gives an aptitude test to its prospective clerical employees. Is there really any relationship between the score on this test and the subsequent level of job proficiency? How much? If there is a relationship, what percentage of applicants would we expect to succeed on the job if the company hires only those who score above a certain value on the test? How does this compare with what would happen if the company quit using the test?

These are examples of questions that ask about the existence and extent of a *relationship* between two (or more) factors and explore the possibility of *prediction* of the standing in one factor from knowledge of the standing in the other. These kinds of analyses are so frequently of interest that a considerable number of statistical techniques have been developed to deal with them.

# 1.4  Our Concern: Applied Statistics

Statistical theory is closely related to (and much of it is based on) the notion of probability. It is not surprising, therefore, that much of the development of statistics is owed to mathematicians and professional statisticians who are well grounded in mathematics. However, the mathematical development of statistics is not what this book is about.

Instead, we will be concerned with applied statistics. Our outlook will be that of investigators who need to know statistics to appreciate reports of findings in their professional fields or who must select and apply statistical treatment in the course of inquiry. We may think of ourselves as statistical technicians, therefore. Among our ranks will be the biologist, educator, psychologist, engineer, census taker, medical researcher, geologist, agriculturalist, physicist, personnel officer, counselor, businessperson, and city manager. All these professionals and many more regularly find that statistical procedures can be helpful in their work.

# 1.5  The Role of Applied Statistics

**research question**

a question of fact about the subject matter under investigation

**independent variable**

the variable that is systematically manipulated by the investigator

**dependent variable**

the variable that is measured

**confounding variables**

factors (other than the independent variable) that might affect the dependent variable

**statistical question**

a question about a numerical aspect of the observations

From the discussion so far, it is apparent that *applied statistics is a tool and neither a beginning nor an end in itself.* For any subject area, scientific study begins with an investigator posing a question based on the results of previous studies and theoretical considerations. This is the **research question**, a question of fact concerning the subject matter under investigation. Suppose, for example, that we are interested in whether reaction time depends on the intensity of a stimulus.

We must next decide on the specifics necessary to explore the question. We may decide to assign 50 available subjects at random to two groups of 25, one of which will receive a strong stimulus and the other a weaker one. Other designs are possible, but the experimental design will depend, for the most part, on the research question. For example, if we believe that reaction time decreases as stimulus intensity increases, we could test reactions to more than two intensities of the stimulus and assign fewer subjects each to a larger number of groups.

The variable that is systematically manipulated by the investigator is called the **independent variable** (e.g., stimulus intensity). The variable that is measured is called the **dependent variable** (e.g., reaction time). It is important that all other factors that might affect the dependent variable (**confounding variables**) be the same for all groups. For example, it would be important to see that the subjects have been tested at approximately the same time of day to avoid having one group fresh and alert while the other is weary and inattentive. Having designed our study, we are finally ready to make observations. We measure the reaction time of each subject and record it.

After recording our measurements, we calculate the average reaction time for each group, see that they differ, and raise a statistical question: Is the average reaction time under the two conditions so different that chance variation alone cannot account for it? A **statistical question** is a question about a numerical aspect of the observations. Often there are alternative statistical questions that can be applied to explore the research question under study. For instance, we might ask whether the proportion of subjects with high reaction times, say 50 milliseconds or more, differs under the two conditions beyond the limits of chance variation. Part of the study of statistics is to learn how to choose among alternative statistical approaches.

**statistical conclusion**
a conclusion about a numerical property of the data

After applying a statistical procedure, we arrive at a statistical conclusion. A **statistical conclusion** is a conclusion about a numerical property of the data. For example, as a result of applying the appropriate statistical procedures in our hypothetical experiment, we might be able to conclude that the average reaction times under the two conditions are so different that it is not reasonable to believe that chance alone could account for it.

Now we return to the research question. If we had carefully arranged the conditions of the study, it may be possible to conclude that intensity of the stimulus does make a difference, at least under the conditions that held in this experiment. This is our final step, and it is a research conclusion. A **research conclusion** is a conclusion about the subject matter. In our initial example about AZT, the statistical conclusion was that the number of deaths, CD4+ cell counts, and weight changes in the two groups differed by beyond what would have been expected by chance. The research conclusion was that the difference was due to AZT. Although the research conclusion derives partly from the statistical conclusion, we see that other factors must be considered. The investigator, therefore, must weigh both the statistical conclusion and the adequacy of the research design in arriving at the research conclusion.

**research conclusion**
a conclusion about the subject matter

**statistical procedures**
only a middle step in the investigation of a research question

It is important to understand that **statistical procedures** *are only a middle step in the investigation of a research question.* If an investigator has not carefully controlled for all confounding variables, it is possible to make a correct statistical conclusion but an incorrect research conclusion. Such was the case in a well-known study by Joseph Brady and some colleagues at the Johns Hopkins University (Brady, Porter, Conrad, & Mason, 1958). They investigated the effects of stress on the development of ulcers in four pairs of monkeys. Each pair was locked into adjacent chairs during testing. One monkey in each pair, designated the "executive" monkey, could avoid a strong electric shock by pressing a lever that postponed the shock for 20 seconds. Whenever the executive monkey did receive a shock, the other monkey in the pair, called the "yoked" control monkey, also received a shock (which it could not avoid). The investigators assigned monkeys to the executive group based on their high rates of lever pressing in previous studies.

The executive monkeys developed ulcers, but the yoked monkeys did not, even though they received identical shocks. The difference was so great that it was unlikely that the results occurred by chance (the statistical conclusion). Because they believed that they had controlled for all other factors, Brady and his colleagues concluded that it was the continuous stress of having to decide how often to press the lever to avoid shock that caused the ulcers in the executive monkeys (the research conclusion).

Later studies were unable to replicate the results. Moreover, it was found that animals selected for high rates of responding were more susceptible to developing ulcers than were other animals (Weiss, 1971). When monkeys that did not differ in activity level were tested together, the executive monkeys developed less severe ulcers (Foltz & Millett, 1964; Natelson, 1976). We now know that in general, control over an aversive event reduces the stress the event causes (Taylor, 1991). The original investigators had unknowingly biased the outcome of their experiment by not randomly assigning the monkeys to the two conditions and thus reached an incorrect research conclusion.

# 1.6 Do Statistics Lie?

> **There are three kinds of lies: lies, damned lies, and statistics.** Benjamin Disraeli, 19th-century British statesman

Do statistics really lie? In the experiment by Brady and his colleagues, the investigators reached an erroneous research conclusion, but there really was an observed difference between the executive and yoked monkeys in their susceptibility to developing ulcers. Is it possible to make an incorrect statistical conclusion which, of course, would lead to an invalid research conclusion? The answer is "yes." You may have noted in our previous examples that the statistical conclusions always made some statement about whether or not the observed result could have occurred by chance. We will discuss this in greater detail later, but accept for now that a statistical conclusion is always about a probability. When the average scores for two groups are found to be "statistically different," it means only that the numerical results had a low probability of occurring by chance alone. However, even events with a low probability (getting struck by lightning, for example) do occur sometimes, and when that happens with empirically obtained data, it results in an incorrect statistical conclusion.

Let us give an example. In the 1960s, a few investigators published results of studies in which they had trained planaria (small flatworms) on a simple task, then sacrificed them and fed their brains to naive (untrained) planaria. The "cannibal" planaria's subsequent average performance on the same task was much better than one would reasonably expect to have occurred by chance (the statistical conclusion). In fact, the results had only a 5% (1 in 20) chance or less of having occurred only by chance. The investigators concluded that memory was stored in the brain in discrete chemical units called engrams that the cannibal planaria had consumed, resulting in their "knowing" how to perform the task (the research conclusion).

Scientific journals generally publish only results that would have occurred by chance 5% of the time or less. As it turns out, many other scientists had attempted the same experiment and had not observed any improvement in performance by the cannibal planaria that was so unlikely that it could not have occurred by chance. Therefore, they had not submitted their results for publication. When they talked to each other and learned of each other's failures, 23 of them got together and published a rebuttal (Byrne et al., 1966). Even though there is apparently no chemical engram, with so many investigators attempting the experiment, it was to be expected that 1 in 20 would observe an average numerical difference between cannibal planaria and other planaria that would have occurred by chance only 5% of the time. It is a good thing that the original investigators' research conclusion was wrong. Otherwise, there would be a far easier way for students to learn statistics from their professor than having to sit through a course.

Although an incorrect conclusion was made in both the executive-monkeys and cannibal-planaria experiments, there was no intent on the part of the investigators to deceive anyone. The incorrect conclusions were honest mistakes. Unfortunately, there have also been cases of scientific fraud (see Roman, 1988). Some claim that one of the most notorious was that of Cyril Burt (Hearnshaw, 1979; MacKintosh, 1995; Samelson, 1996), who for years was recognized as one of the leading investigators of intelligence. Burt was a strong proponent of the view that intelligence is biologically determined. His numerous published results of similar IQ scores in identical twins

## Point of Controversy

### Are Statistical Procedures Necessary?

In a 1988 article, psychologist Robert Bolles makes a spirited attack against the use of statistics. He advises that "one should avoid statistics whenever possible . . . and get on with the business of science." Specifically, he suggests that scientists should measure things rather than test hypotheses. They should look for the obvious. (When you see it, why do you need statistics?) And they should look at the data rather than the statistics. (Your data "will tell you if you have found something, even while statistical tests are fibbing, lying, and deceiving you.") Another researcher has argued that a good graph is worth a thousand statistical tests (Loftus, 1993). Rather than consult a statistician, Bolles suggests that we "talk to Buddha or somebody like that," for if "one of the gods wants you to discover, you certainly do not have to do a statistical test."

Bolles is not the only researcher to reject statistics. B. F. Skinner (1966), Murray Sidman (1960), and many others who study operant conditioning (experimental analysis of behavior) abhor averaging data and the use of inferential statistics. In fact, besides Skinner, there are some other frequently cited individuals in psychology who never used inferential statistics. This includes Freud and Piaget (see Smith et al., 2000). Some researchers continue to defend the presentation of results without formal statistical tests (e.g., Hopkins, Cole, & Mason, 1998; Perone, 1999).

Bolles gives several examples from his own research in which there were near-perfect relationships between variables or where some experimental manipulations produced 100% change. In cases like these, statistics are, of course, superfluous. However, this does

raised apart provided the strongest evidence for this viewpoint. After his death, it was discovered that not only had Burt fabricated some of his data but that he may have put the names of fictitious coauthors on his papers as well. (We should mention that Burt still has his defenders; see Fletcher, 1991, and Joynson, 1989.) The statistical procedures used to analyze data cannot tell whether the numbers used are the result of empirical observations or someone's imagination. We might remember the old saying: "Figures never lie, but liars often figure."

Sometimes an individual can mislead others not by fabricating data but by presenting only part of them. For example, in a given state college, it may be that 80% of the courses are taught by instructors holding doctorate degrees, but that only 60% of all the instructors at the institution hold the degree. If a journalist's theme is the "rotten state of higher education," we can guess which figure is more likely to be mentioned. On the other hand, if an economy-minded representative of the taxpayers' association wishes to argue that higher salaries are unnecessary to attract a fully qualified faculty, a different choice will be made. Unfortunately, if we are presented in a telling way with only one of these approaches, the possibility of others may never occur to us.

The misuse of statistics is an important topic, but limitations of space prevent a

not mean that we should abandon statistics, for to do so would relegate us to areas of research where only large effects occur. At what point do you draw the line between that which is obvious and that which is not so obvious? Statistical procedures give us a way of answering this without resorting to complete subjectivity. Besides, not every research project can hope for dramatic effects, such as discovering that penicillin kills the bacteria that cause many diseases. In a rebuttal of Bolles, Patricia Cohen (1988), the editor of the journal in which Bolles's article was published, pointed out that often there are very subtle effects that, if they can be identified, may be of considerable importance. Knowledge of advanced statistical procedures can encourage sophisticated questions.

Most of the researchers who have opposed the use of statistics devoted their careers to extensive study of the behavior of individual subjects (e.g., Freud, Bolles, Skinner, Sidman). Statistical procedures are particularly useful when researchers wish to know if there is a difference among groups. For example, statistical procedures played an important role in allowing researchers to conclude that the drug AZT significantly helped patients with AIDS.

The criticisms by Bolles and others are not totally without merit. There are those who use statistics to lend apparent importance to trivial results. Statistics cannot tell whether a question is scientifically important or of practical use. As Cohen emphasizes, statistical techniques "can never produce high quality science in the absence of thorough consideration of basic questions."

Statistics are no substitute for judgment. Henry Clay, American statesman, 1777–1852

As you read this book, keep in mind that *statistical techniques are tools* that are only as good as the individual who uses them. With good questions at the beginning of a study and good common sense throughout, statistical procedures are very helpful tools in arriving at answers to those questions.

more detailed treatment here. For those who are interested, we refer you to Huff (1993) and Best (2001).

## 1.7 Some Tips on Studying Statistics

**A good teacher is a tough guy who cares very deeply about something that is hard to understand.** Norman MacLean, University of Chicago

Is statistics a hard subject? It is and it isn't. In general, learning how to do it requires attention, care, and arithmetic accuracy, but it is not particularly difficult. Learning the "why" of things may be harder. Look again at the title of your textbook. The emphasis in this book is *reasoning* (the logic of statistics), not mathematical formulas and proofs.

What about the expected reading rate for a book about statistics? A 4-page assignment in mathematics may require the same time as 40 pages in history. Certainly, one should not expect to read a statistics text like a novel, nor even like the usual history text. Some parts, like this chapter, will go faster, but others will require concentration and several readings. In short, don't feel stupid if you cannot race through a chapter and instead find that some absorption time is required. The logic of statistical inference, for example, is a new way of thinking for most people and requires getting used to.

Although the emphasis of this book is on reasoning, you will, of course, be required to work mathematical problems. Like many students, you may have anxieties about mathematics. However, you will need to know only ordinary arithmetic and simple algebra. For students who feel at home in elementary algebra, we include algebraic notes at the end of several chapters. They provide a supplementary "handle" to better understand statistical techniques. On the other hand, we provide a review of elementary mathematics in Appendix A for those who feel that their mathematics lies in the too distant past to ensure a sense of security. You may determine which elements, if any, you need to review by taking the pretest at the beginning of Appendix A.

We include questions and problems at the end of each chapter and suggest that you work enough of them to feel comfortable. They have been designed to give practice in how to do it, in the exercise of critical evaluation, in developing a sense of the link between real problems and methodological approach, and in comprehending statistical relationships.

When working problems, try constantly to see the big picture. Look at the result of each calculation. Does it make sense? Don't fail to be suspicious when you find the average to be 53 but most of the numbers are in the 60s and 70s. Remember Minium's First Law of Statistics: "*The eyeball is the statistician's most powerful instrument.*" You will benefit by trying to answer all questions and problems, even though your teacher may assign only a few.

## THE FAR SIDE® BY GARY LARSON

The Far Side® by Gary Larson. © 1982 FarWorks, Inc. All Rights Reserved. Used with permission.

**Early stages of math anxiety**

We need to say a word about the ladder-like nature of a course in elementary statistics. What you learn in earlier stages becomes the foundation for what follows. Consequently, it is very important that you keep up. If you have difficulty at some point, seek assistance from your instructor. Don't delay. Those who think matters may clear up if they wait may be right, but the risk is greater than in courses where the material is less interdependent. It can be like trying to climb a ladder with some rungs missing. Cramming usually does not work in statistics. Success in studying statistics depends on regular work, and if you do this, relatively little is needed in the way of review before examination time.

Finally, try always to relate the statistical tools to real problems. Imagine an inquiry of special interest to you, and consider which methods might be most suited to the hypothetical approach that you have designed in your mind. Statistics can be an exciting study, but only if you open your mind and reach out. It is a study with relevance to real problems.

## 1.8 Summary

Statistics is the science of classifying, organizing, and analyzing data. There are two main branches: descriptive statistics and inferential statistics. The techniques of descriptive statistics allow us to organize and summarize observations so they become easier to understand. Procedures in inferential statistics are used to draw inferences about conditions that exist in a population from study of a sample (a subset of the population).

It is important to distinguish between research matters and statistical matters. Research questions and conclusions concern the subject matter under investigation, whereas statistical questions and conclusions apply to the numerical characteristics of the data. There are often several statistical questions that we could apply to explore a given research question. Statistical procedures are only a middle step in arriving at a research conclusion. The typical steps of an investigation are

$$
\begin{array}{ccccc}
\text{Research} & & \text{Statistical} & & \text{Collection} & & \text{Statistical} & & \text{Research} \\
\text{question} & \rightarrow & \text{question} & \rightarrow & \text{of data} & \rightarrow & \text{conclusion} & \rightarrow & \text{conclusion}
\end{array}
$$

Although statistical theory is rooted in mathematics and probability, it is quite possible to acquire a good working understanding of elementary statistics without having to take advanced courses in math. You will only have to do ordinary arithmetic and follow what is happening in simple equations. The emphasis in this book will be on conceptual development.

## Key Terms, Concepts, and Symbols

| | | |
|---|---|---|
| statistics   (2) | research question   (5) | statistical question   (5) |
| descriptive statistics   (3) | independent variable   (5) | statistical conclusion   (6) |
| inferential statistics   (3) | dependent variable   (5) | research conclusion   (6) |
| random sampling   (4) | confounding variables   (5) | statistical procedures   (6) |

# Problems

1. An experimenter may "wear two hats," that of subject-matter expert and that of statistician. Is our experimenter wearing primarily the first hat, primarily the second, or both about equally when he or she: (a) Thinks up the problem? (b) Translates it into a statistical question? (c) Draws a conclusion that the average performance of experimental and control groups is really different? (d) Decides that the imposed difference in treatment was responsible for the difference in average performance? (e) Relates this finding to those of previous studies?

2. The subject of statistics is often divided into two parts: descriptive and inferential. Briefly describe each.

3. For the following examples, is the individual primarily using descriptive statistics, inferential statistics, or relationship and prediction? (a) A pollster asks a group of voters how they intend to vote in the upcoming election for governor. (b) A university official uses standardized test scores to admit or reject applicants to the freshman class. (c) A researcher tests a new diet drug on a group of overweight individuals. (d) A teacher organizes test grades into a distribution, from best to worst. (e) A sports fan ranks a team's players according to their batting averages. (f) A researcher esti-

mates the incidence of lung cancer from data on cigarette smoking.

4. A graduate student was entranced by the capabilities of a particular statistical tool and searched for a thesis problem that would allow him to use it. Is his enthusiasm misplaced? Explain.

5. Is it possible to draw a correct statistical conclusion yet reach an incorrect research conclusion? Explain your answer.

6. Is it likely to arrive at a correct research conclusion after making an incorrect statistical conclusion? Explain your answer.

7. Diabetes is a major health problem that affects millions of Americans. To counter this, many products now contain noncaloric sweeteners, such as saccharin. However, packets of saccharin have a warning in tiny print that saccharin causes cancer in lab animals. A 1992 study, for example, found that rats fed a high dose of saccharin (equal to about 1,000 packets a day to a human) developed bladder tumors. Mice fed the same amount did not. (a) What is the statistical conclusion? (b) What is the research conclusion? (c) What questions might you raise in generalizing these results to humans?

# CHAPTER 2

## Preliminary Concepts

When you have finished studying this chapter, you should be able to:

- Define what is meant by a population and a sample;
- Understand the difference between a parameter and a statistic;
- Describe a random sample and explain random sampling variation (sampling error);
- Understand the difference between variables and constants;
- Recognize measurements as being on one of four scales—nominal, ordinal, interval, or ratio—and understand that not all numbers can be treated alike; and
- Understand the difference between a discrete variable and a continuous variable.

**population**
the complete set of observations about which an investigator wishes to draw conclusions

**sample**
a subset of a population

We introduced the concepts of a population and a sample briefly in Chapter 1. Now the first thing that comes to mind in connection with the word *population* is that we must be talking about people. In statistics, that is not necessarily so. A **population** is the complete set of observations about which an investigator wishes to draw conclusions. A **sample** is a part of that population. Notice that a *population is defined in terms of observations rather than people*. This way of looking at things works better in statistics. Suppose, for example, that we want to know both the SAT scores and the high school grade point averages for the current crop of freshman students in our college. We are talking about two populations, despite the fact that they are attached to the same people. Or suppose our interest is in determining reaction time for one particular person. The population consists of the large number of possible reaction times that could be measured for this person. Note how confusing it would be if we insisted on thinking of a population as people rather than observations.

Notice also that *a population is defined by the interest of the investigator*. If pollsters are trying to take the pulse of the nation prior to an election, their target population consists of the preferences of those who will go to the polls and vote. The opinions of those persons actually interviewed constitute a sample of that population. (There is a potential problem here in that some of those polled may fail to vote.) Thus, we study a sample in the hope that it will lead to meaningful conclusions about the larger target population. Sometimes, of course, observations obtained from the group at hand are just what we want, and therefore they would constitute the population. If an instructor wants to know how the present class performed on the first midterm, the students' scores constitute the population and not a sample.

For convenience and to avoid awkward language, we often say "a sample of college seniors" or "a sample of laboratory rats" rather than "a sample of SAT scores obtained from college seniors" or (ugh!) "a sample of records of the number of trials required to learn a maze obtained from laboratory rats." But statistically speaking, both sample and population consist of measurements (observations) rather than the organisms or objects from which they were derived.

**statistic**
a descriptive index of a sample (for another meaning, see Chapter 1)

**parameter**
a descriptive index of a population

In Chapter 1, we defined statistics as a science. However, the term statistic has another meaning that we will use throughout the book. A **statistic** is a descriptive index of a sample. The same index, if descriptive of a population, is called a **parameter**. Thus, the average of a sample of scores is a statistic; the average of a population of scores is a parameter. *In inferential statistics, we will be interested in estimating population parameters from sample statistics.*

## 2.1 Random Samples

There is nothing in the definition of a sample that specifies how it is to be selected from a population. However, the method of selection matters very much in statistics. For example, in the 1936 American presidential election, the incumbent, Franklin D. Roosevelt, a Democrat, was being challenged by Republican Alf Landon. As in all election years, there was great interest in the outcome. One of the leading magazines of the day, the *Literary Digest*, surveyed voter preferences by mailing questionnaires to 10 million people whose names were gathered from lists of automobile and telephone owners. Over 2 million people responded, and the results indicated that Landon would beat Roosevelt by a landslide. In fact, Roosevelt beat Landon by one of the largest margins ever. This was one of the largest surveys ever taken. How could it have been so wrong? The United States was in the middle of the Great Depression in 1936 and only a minority of people were financially secure enough to own a car and a telephone. They tended to vote Republican. Most other Americans were worried about buying enough food to feed their families, and they tended to vote Democratic. In other words, the *Literary Digest* had surveyed an unrepresentative subgroup of the population (Kaplan & Saccuzzo, 1989).

An essential assumption in inferential statistics is that samples are drawn randomly from a particular population. A **random sample** must be obtained in such a way that each possible sample of the same size has an equal probability of being selected from the population. Essentially, a random sample is one where chance does the selecting, as in a properly conducted lottery. Suppose, for example, that we wish to select five persons at random from our current statistics class. We might write the name of each class member on a slip of paper, put those slips in a gallon jar, shake and tumble the contents of the jar well, and withdraw five slips from the lot. The observations based on the persons thus selected would be a random sample of observations for the entire class.

The election year surveys taken today by the CNN/*USA Today* and Gallup organizations poll only a few thousand registered voters, but because the opinions are sampled randomly, the survey results taken a day or two before election day are usually within a few percentage points of the actual outcomes. In fact, these organizations use a very sophisticated sampling technique called *stratified random sampling*. Based on the latest national census, the entire country is broken down by demographics, such as sex, age, race, educational level, and geographical location. The pollsters know, for example, what percentage of the U.S. population is white, Protestant, college educated, and living in the Northeast. They then randomly take a certain number of voter opinions from each demographic subgroup and combine the figures into one best estimate for the entire population.

Most people believe that a random sample is always highly representative of the population from which it is drawn, but that is not necessarily so (Tversky & Kahneman, 1971). There are two properties of random samples that you must keep in mind. First, if several random samples are drawn from the same population, the samples will almost always differ, and therefore their characteristics (statistics) will vary from sample to sample. Thus, if the CNN/*USA Today* and Gallup organizations each draw a random sample of responses from the voting population, the samples will not be identical, and so their projections of the final vote will usually not be exactly the same. Similarly, if the average midterm score of all students in our statistics course is 85, we would expect that the average of a randomly selected sample of five of these midterm scores would differ somewhat from 85. We would also expect it to differ from the average for another sample drawn in the same way. This chance variation from sample to sample is known as **random sampling variation**, or **sampling error**.

Second, we would expect that the larger the random samples from a given population, the less the variation in characteristics from sample to sample. This is of obvious importance in statistical inference, because it generally means that large random samples will provide a more precise estimate of what is true about the population than will small random samples. We will look at the concept of random sampling much more closely in Chapter 12.

---

**random sample**

sample obtained in a way that ensures that all samples of the same size have an equal chance of being selected from the population

**random sampling variation (sampling error)**

the variation among random samples due to chance

## 2.2 Variables and Constants

**variable**
a characteristic
that may take
on different
values

In conducting a study, we must often consider several variables and constants. A **variable** is a characteristic that may take on different values. Typical examples are intelligence test scores, height, number of errors on a spelling test, eye color, marital status, and sex.

The concept of a variable does not imply that each observation must differ from all the others. All that is necessary is the possibility of difference. Suppose, for example, that a school nurse is interested in the height of seventh-grade males in Lincoln Junior High School. If she selects a sample of three for study and finds that they are all the same height, it is still proper to refer to height as a variable because the possibility of getting students of different height existed.

**constant**
a characteristic
that can have
only one value
(other values are
not possible)

On the other hand, her decision to study height only among the seventh-grade students means that grade level is a constant rather than a variable in this inquiry. When, in terms of the particular study, it is not possible for a characteristic to have other than a single value, that characteristic is a **constant**. Constants limit the applicability of the results of a study. In the school nurse's situation, for example, the sex of the students (male), the school (Lincoln), and the grade level (seventh) are all constants. Even if the nurse had taken a sample of larger size, the conclusions that she would draw could apply for sure only to seventh-grade males in that school. The outcome might be different under other circumstances. The problem is one of generalization of results.

## 2.3 Scales of Measurement

**measurement**
the process
of assigning
numerals to
observations

**Measurement** is the process of assigning numerals to observations. This is not done arbitrarily, but in a way so that the numbers are meaningful. How do we do this? Variables do not all have the same numerical properties. In measuring weight, we are accustomed to the idea that 40 pounds is twice as much as 20 pounds, and that the difference between 10 and 20 pounds is the same as that between 60 and 70 pounds. Similarly, if a baseball team has won 40 games and another only 20, we can say that the first has won twice as many games as the second team. However, if we put baseball teams in order of their standing in the league, we should not think that the number one team is twice as good as the number two team, nor would we expect that the difference in merit between the first and second team is necessarily the same as that between the second and third team. It is apparent that numbers have a different significance in these two situations. To help distinguish different kinds of situations, the psychologist S. S. Stevens (1946) identified four different scales of measurement. You will find that numbers are treated differently depending on their scale of measurement.

### Nominal Scale

Some variables are qualitative in their nature rather than quantitative. For example, the two categories of biological sex are male and female. Eye color, types of cheese, and party of political affiliation are other examples of *qualitative variables*. The several

**nominal scale**

mutually exclusive and exhaustive categories differing in some qualitative aspect

categories of such a variable are said to constitute a **nominal scale** (the Latin root of *nominal* means "name"). The only requirements of a nominal scale are that the categories be *mutually exclusive* (the observations cannot fall into more than one category) and *exhaustive* (there must be enough categories for all the observations). Male and female are mutually exclusive categories for sex; but Ford, General Motors, Toyota, Chevrolet, and Honda are not mutually exclusive categories for types of cars (Chevrolets are made by General Motors). There is no question about one category having more or less of any particular quality; all categories are simply different. We may use numbers to identify the categories of a given scale. For example, we might identify three cheeses as Cheese No. 1, Cheese No. 2, and Cheese No. 3. Numbers used in this way are simply a substitute for names and serve only for purposes of identification. Numbers on football jerseys similarly indicate only the position of the player (e.g., offensive line, offensive backfield). If one football player wears the number 10 on his back while another wears the number 20, there is no implication that the second player is "more than" the other in some dimension, let alone that he has twice as much of something. A quarterback times a lineman does not give us a fullback (Stine, 1989).

## Ordinal Scale

**ordinal scale**

has the properties of a nominal scale, but in addition the observations may be ranked in order of magnitude (with nothing implied about the difference between adjacent steps on the scale)

At the next level of complexity is the **ordinal scale** (the Latin root means "order"). In this type of measurement, *the categories must still be mutually exclusive and exhaustive, but they also indicate the order of magnitude of some variable.* With a nominal scale, the outcome of classification is a set of unordered categories. With the ordinal scale, it is a set of ranks. A classic example is military rank. Sergeant is greater than corporal, which is in turn greater than private. Another example is academic standing—freshman, sophomore, junior, and senior. In yet another example, a supervisor may estimate the competence of seven workers by arranging them in order of merit. The only relation expressed in a series of numbers used in this way is that of "greater than." We may use numbers for the ranks but need not. Among persons ranked 1, 2, and 3, the first person has a greater degree of merit than the person ranked second, and the second person has greater merit than the third. However, nothing is implied about the magnitude of difference in merit between adjacent steps on the scale. Furthermore, nothing is implied about the absolute level of merit; all seven workers could be excellent, or they could be quite ordinary.

## Interval Scale

**interval scale**

has all the properties of an ordinal scale, and a given distance between measures has the same meaning anywhere on the scale

The next major level of complexity is the **interval scale**. This scale has all the properties of the ordinal scale, but with the further refinement that a *given interval (distance) between scores has the same meaning anywhere on the scale.* Thus, it could be better called an *equal-interval scale.* Examples of this type of scale are degrees of temperature on the Fahrenheit or Celsius scales. A 10° rise in a reading on the Celsius scale represents the same change in heat when going from 0° to 10° as when going from 20° to 30°. The limitation of an interval scale is that it is not possible to speak meaningfully about a ratio between two measurements. We illustrate this point in Figure 2.1. The top of this illustration shows three temperatures in degrees Celsius: 0°, 50°, and 100°. It is tempting to think of 100°C as twice as hot as 50°. However, the value of

**FIGURE 2.1**   Three temperatures represented on the Celsius and Kelvin scales.

zero on this scale is simply an arbitrary reference point (the freezing point of water) and does not imply an absence of heat. Therefore, it is not meaningful to assert that a temperature of 100° Celsius is twice as hot as one of 50° or that a rise from 90° to 99° Celsius is a 10% increase.

## Ratio Scale

**ratio scale**
has all the properties of an interval scale plus an absolute zero point

A **ratio scale** possesses all the properties of an interval scale and in addition *has an absolute zero point.* The bottom of Figure 2.1 shows the same three temperatures in degrees Kelvin. This scale uses the same unit for its intervals; for example, 50° of change in temperature is the same on both scales. However, the Kelvin scale has an absolute zero, the point at which a substance would have no molecular motion and, therefore, no heat. Thus, 100° is twice as hot as 50° on the Kelvin scale (100° is only 1.15 times as hot as 50° on the Celsius scale). Other examples of ratio scale

**TABLE 2.1**   *Scales of Measurement and Their Characteristics*

| SCALE | PROPERTIES | EXAMPLES |
|---|---|---|
| Nominal | Mutually exclusive and exhaustive categories differing in some qualitative aspect. | Sex, ethnic group, religion, eye color, academic major |
| Ordinal | Scale has the property of a nominal scale (mutually exclusive categories) and in addition has observations ranked in order of magnitude. Ranks, which may be numerical, express a "greater than" relationship, but with no implication about how much greater. | Military rank, academic standing, workers sorted according to merit |
| Interval | Scale has all the properties of an ordinal scale, and in addition numerical values indicate order of merit and meaningfully reflect relative distances between points along the scale. A given interval between measures has the same meaning at any point in the scale. | Temperature in degrees Celsius or Fahrenheit |
| Ratio | Scale has all the properties of an interval scale, and in addition has an absolute zero point. Ratio between measures becomes meaningful. | Length, weight, elapsed time, temperature in degrees Kelvin |

measurements are length, weight, and measures of elapsed time. Not only is the difference between 40 in. and 41 in. the same as the difference between 80 in. and 81 in., but it is also true that 80 in. is twice as long as 40 in.

Table 2.1 summarizes the characteristics of the four scales of measurement we have just discussed.

## 2.4 Scales of Measurement and Problems of Statistical Treatment

An understanding of the scales of measurement provides a framework for appreciating certain problems in the interpretation of data. The first thing we need to realize is that in psychology and education, there are many measuring instruments that lack equal intervals and an absolute zero point. Consider, for example, a spelling test. Easier items might be words such as *garden, baseball,* and *rowboat*. But we might also find *perceive, complacency,* and perhaps even some stumpers like *gauge, accede,* and *abscissa*. A score of zero on this test means that the person could not spell the simplest word on the list, but what if simpler words had been on the test, such as *cat, run,* and *bat*? Our spelling test, then, does not have an absolute zero point because zero on the spelling test does not indicate a total absence of spelling ability. The same is true of midterm tests, IQ tests, the SAT, and almost all other tests of mental performance.

What about equal intervals? To have equal intervals on our spelling test, we should be able to state quantitatively just how much more spelling ability is needed to spell *garden* than to spell *cat* and how much more is needed to spell *gauge* than to spell *rowboat*. So far, we have found no objective way to determine when equal numerical intervals on a mental test represent equal increments in performance. Realization of this situation caused a certain amount of concern in statistical circles about 30 years ago. Some people argued that calculating certain statistical variables (such as averages) on tests of mental abilities could be seriously misleading. Fortunately, the weight of the evidence suggests that in most situations, making statistical conclusions is not seriously hampered by uncertainty about the scale of measurement. We will consider this matter further in the Point of Controversy in Chapter 5.

There are, however, several areas where we need to be aware of scale problems to avoid taking tempting but erroneous positions. For example, we should not assert that a person with an IQ of 150 is twice as bright as one with an IQ of 75, or that the difference between 15 and 25 points on a spelling test necessarily represents the same increment in spelling ability as the difference between a score of 30 and 40 points on the same test. In psychological measurement, this problem may be particularly critical when a test does not have enough "top" or "bottom" to differentiate adequately among the group measured. For example, imagine a test of ability that has a maximum possible score of 50 points and that is too easy for the group measured. For two persons who score 50 points, the score for one may indicate the maximum level of attainment, but the second person may be capable of a much higher level of performance. The measuring instrument is simply incapable of showing this difference because it does not include items of greater difficulty.

# 2.5 Computational Accuracy with Continuous Variables

**discrete variable**

a variable that can take on only certain values

**continuous variable**

a variable that can take on any value (within the limits that its values may range)

Variables may be either discrete or continuous. A **discrete variable** can take on only certain values. If we count the people at a meeting, we might learn that 73 persons attended, or 74, but no value between these two figures is possible. The values are *exact numbers*. Other examples include the number of multiple-choice questions answered on an exam, the number of lever presses performed by a rat in a learning experiment, and the steps in a salary scale that changes only by 5% increments.

A **continuous variable** can take on any value (within whatever limits its values may range). In measuring length, for example, it is possible for an object to be 3 ft. 1 in. or 3 ft. 2 in. long, or any conceivable length in between. A continuous variable has no gaps in its scale. Other examples include weight, age, and temperature.

*Even though a variable is continuous in theory, the process of measurement always reduces it to a discrete one.* For example, if we measure weight to the nearest tenth of a pound, a weight of 18.3 pounds means that the object is closer to 18.3 pounds than it is to 18.2 pounds or 18.4 pounds. The value of 18.3 pounds is an *approximate number*. The actual weight is somewhere between 18.25 pounds and 18.35 pounds. In this example, our recorded measurements form a discrete scale in steps of one-tenth of a pound.

When measuring a continuous variable, our level of accuracy is limited in large part by our instrumentation and method of collecting data. Athletes in the 100-meter dash used to be timed by hand-held watches that were accurate to the nearest tenth of a second. Today, runners are electronically timed to the nearest hundredth of a second.

Within the limits of the recording equipment, it is up to the investigator to determine the degree of precision appropriate to the problem at hand. Sometimes, potential precision is discarded because keeping it is not worth the trouble. At a particular moment, your height may measure out at 67 and 7/16 in., but who cares? Measurement to the nearest half-inch will be quite adequate.

Typical statistical computations involve both exact and approximate numbers—for example, dividing the sum of the scores (usually the sum of approximate numbers and thus itself approximate) by the number of cases (an exact number) to produce an average. *In computations involving both exact and approximate numbers, the accuracy of the answer is limited by the accuracy of the approximate numbers involved.* For example, if weight is measured to the nearest tenth of a pound and the total weight of three objects is 67.0 pounds, it would be misleading to report the average weight (67.0/3) as either 22.333333 pounds (the output of the common eight-digit display calculator) or 22 pounds. Because the approximate number is reported to the nearest tenth of a pound, the reported average weight should be 22.3 pounds.

When working with a series of statistical computations involving approximate numbers, it is a good idea to keep a little more accuracy than we think is the minimum to which we are entitled (perhaps one extra decimal place) because in a sequence of computations it is possible to compound inaccuracy. Once the computation is completed, we should round back to the least accurate of the numbers used. If the last digit is greater than 5, round up; if it is less than 5, round down. *When rounding a number that ends exactly with the numeral 5, you should always round to the nearest even number.* This avoids introducing a bias in your calculations. (Sometimes you will round up and other times down rather than always in the same direction.) For example, if rounding to the nearest tenth, 1.35 becomes 1.4, as does 1.45.

## 2.6 Statistics and Computers

Computers and software for statistics have greatly eased the computations necessary to solve many statistical questions. In fact, your course may require that you learn how to use computerized statistical packages. There is a practical advantage to this real-life application. However, the emphasis of this book is on understanding statistics. Without a basic understanding of statistics, computer programs can be misused. Suppose, for example, an individual enters his or her data incorrectly. Garbage in always results in garbage out. Without a basic understanding of statistics, he or she will just accept the printout as correct. Another person knowledgeable in statistics will have some idea of what the result should look like and will check the way the data were entered. We know of a few cases, for example, in which investigators have ignored the obvious in their data when statistical results, done by computer, indicated something else. "After all," they insisted, "computers don't lie." With some difficulty, the investigators were persuaded to recheck their data, only to discover that they had entered them in the computer incorrectly.

In 1996, the American Psychological Association's Task Force on Statistical Inference issued the following initial report concerning the use of computers:

"Issues with computerized data analysis

Elegant and sophisticated computer programs have increased our ability to analyze data with substantially greater sophistication than was possible only a short time ago. The ease of access to state-of-the-art statistical analysis packages, however, has not universally advanced our science. Common misuses of computerized data analysis include:

a) reporting statistics without understanding how they are computed or what they mean,

b) relying on results without regard to their reasonableness, or without verification by independent computation, and

c) reporting results to greater precision than supported by the data, simply because they are printed by the program. The task force encourages efforts to avoid the sanctification of computerized data analysis."

The final report cautioned: "As soon as you have collected your data, before you compute *any* statistics, *look at your data*. . . . More important than choosing a specific

DON'T LOOK NOW, BUT HERE COMES 'OL "GARBAGE-IN" AGAIN.

Frank & Ernest ©
NEA Reprinted
by Permission.

statistical package in verifying your results, understanding what they mean, and knowing how they are computed. . . . Do not report statistics found on a printout without understanding how they are computed or what they mean. . . . There is no substitute for common sense" (Wilkinson & the Task Force on Statistical Inference, 1999).

In later chapters we will provide some problems that can be worked with a computer. However, be sure that you have an understanding of the statistical procedure *before* you enter your data.

## 2.7 Summary

The notions of population and sample are basic to statistics. A population is a group of observations about which the investigator wishes to draw conclusions; a sample is a part of that population. In statistics, it is better to think of these terms as applying to observations rather than to persons. An index that is descriptive of a population is called a parameter. If the same index is descriptive of a sample, it is called a statistic.

For a sample to be random, it must have been obtained in such a way that each possible sample of the same size has an equal probability of being selected from the population. Characteristics of random samples drawn from a given population will vary from sample to sample (due to chance), but the results obtained from larger random samples tend to vary less than those from smaller samples.

A variable is a characteristic that may take on different values. Constants, on the other hand, remain the same in a given study. Constants define the boundaries of a study and also limit the generalizability of the results.

Variables may be qualitative, expressing only differences in kind (nominal scale), or they may be quantitative, expressing differences in amount (ordinal, interval, and ratio scales). Numbers can be used to identify different values on any of the scales, but the meaning of these numbers differs with the nature of the scale.

Most psychological and educational tests lack equal intervals and an absolute zero point. Although these shortcomings do not ordinarily prevent us from using statistical procedures, scale problems can lead to erroneous research conclusions.

Discrete variables have exact values, like the number of subjects in an experiment. Continuous variables can take on any value, but the process of measurement always reduces them to discrete variables. Thus, measurement of a continuous variable gives us approximate values, like the length or weight of an object. When computations involve both approximate and exact numbers (as is typical in calculating an average), the approximate numbers dictate the accuracy of the outcome.

## Key Terms, Concepts, and Symbols

| | | |
|---|---|---|
| population  (14) | random sampling | nominal scale  (17) |
| sample  (14) | variation  (15) | ordinal scale  (17) |
| statistic  (2, 14) | sampling error  (15) | interval scale  (17) |
| parameter  (14) | variable  (16) | ratio scale  (18) |
| random sample  (15) | constant  (16) | discrete variable  (20) |
| | measurement  (16) | continuous variable  (20) |

# Problems

1. We are interested in this year's entering freshmen's choices of majors at our university. We randomly survey 10% of them. (a) What is the population? (b) What is the sample? (c) What is the parameter? (d) What is the statistic? (e) What kind of variable is being measured? Explain.

2. A baseball coach tests a switch hitter, Em B. Dexterous, to see whether he performs better as a rightie or a leftie. Mr. Dexterous bats against a machine that throws the same pitch every time. He tries 50 pitches batting right and 50 pitches batting left. For each pitch, the coach records whether or not Mr. Dexterous hit it. (a) How many samples are there? What are they? (b) From what population do the samples come? (c) What kind of variable is the coach recording? Explain.

3. A school psychologist determines the IQ score for every student in her school. The school nurse measures the current height of every student. Are the two studying the same population? Explain.

4. In the 2000 presidential election, George W. Bush beat Al Gore with 48.1% of the vote (Mr. Gore had 48.2%). A *New York Times/ CBS News* poll of 1,158 registered voters conducted 3 to 5 days before the election found that Mr. Bush was preferred by 46% of registered voters, Mr. Gore by 41%, Ralph Nader by 5%, Pat Buchannan by 1%, with 7% undecided. (a) What is the population? (b) What is the sample? (c) Why do the sample results differ? (d) What constant limits the generalizability of the results?

5. There have been numerous attempts to update Alfred Kinsey's pioneering surveys of Americans' sexual attitudes and behaviors conducted in the late 1940s and early 1950s. In 1982, *Playboy* magazine asked its readers to fill out and mail in a questionnaire that was in one of its issues. Over 100,000 people responded. Among the results was the finding that one-third had engaged in group sex. (a) What was the intended population? (b) What was the sample? (c) What was the parameter? (d) What was the statistic? (e) Is it safe to infer something about behaviors in the population from this sample? Explain.

6. You are starting a diet with the intention of losing weight. You decide to weigh yourself now and 1 month from now. To refine your study, what factors should you hold constant when you do the weighing?

7. We wish to compare the relative effectiveness of morning hours versus afternoon hours as a time for study. Name several factors that we should hold constant.

8. In one state, voters register as Republican, Democrat, or Independent and records of the total registration are kept. Which scale of measurement is used?

9. Instructor, assistant professor, associate professor, and professor form what kind of scale?

10. The low temperature in Billings, Montana, last January 14 was −25° Fahrenheit. Zero on this scale is the freezing point of salt water. What kind of scale is formed by degrees Fahrenheit?

11. With an interval scale, is it proper to consider that an increase of 20 points is twice as much as an increase of 10 points? Explain.

12. Assume that the following series of numbers form an interval scale: 0, 1, 2, 3, . . . , 19, 20. (a) Would it still be an interval scale if we added 10 points to each score? Explain. (b) Would it still be an interval scale if we multiplied each score by 10? Explain.

13. (a) If the numbers in Question 12 form a ratio scale, and 10 points are added to each, would we still have a ratio scale? Explain. (b) If we multiply each score by 10? Explain.

14. Dr. Jones, the history professor, administers a 30-item test the first day of class to ascertain his students' initial level of knowledge of American history. Bob got a 0, Joe a 10, Betty a 20, and Mark and Sheela each got a perfect 30. (a) In all likelihood, what kind of scale of measurement is this? Explain. (b) Can Dr. Jones conclude that Bob does not know anything about American history? Explain. (c) Is Betty's knowledge of American history twice as great as Joe's? Explain. (d) Can Dr. Jones conclude that Mark and Sheela have an equally good knowledge of American history? Explain.

**15.** If the effect of the act of measurement is disregarded, which of the following variables are best regarded fundamentally as forming a discrete series, and which a continuous series? (a) Temperature. (b) Time. (c) Sex. (d) Brands of orange juice. (e) Size of family. (f) Achievement score in mathematics. (g) Merit ratings of employees. (h) Score on an introversion–extroversion scale.

**16.** Temperature is considered to be an example of a continuous variable. What kind of variable is formed when we measure temperature to the nearest tenth of a degree? Explain.

**17.** The weights of nine children were recorded to the nearest tenth of a pound, and their total weight was found to be 812 pounds. What do you think about reporting the average weight (812/9) as (a) 90.22222 pounds? (b) 90.2 pounds? (c) 90 pounds? Explain.

**18.** In a study of the effect of alcohol consumption on driving skill, a psychologist observes 25-year-old men as they maneuver a car around an obstacle course. All of them operate the same car, which is unfamiliar to all, at the same time of day. Half have spent the previous hour drinking a pitcher of beer; half have spent it drinking a pitcher of fruit juice. The psychologist randomly assigned the subjects to the two groups. (a) What are the constants in this study? (b) What effects do the constants have on how widely the psychologist can generalize the finding of the study? (c) What are the variables in this study? (d) Which is the independent variable? (e) Which is the dependent variable? (f) Is random sampling variation at work here? Explain.

# CHAPTER 3

# Frequency Distributions, Percentiles, and Percentile Ranks

When you have finished studying this chapter, you should be able to:

- Organize scores into a frequency distribution in table form;
- Understand the difference between apparent limits and real limits;
- Organize scores into a relative frequency distribution;
- Construct a cumulative frequency distribution and a relative cumulative frequency distribution; and
- Compute percentiles and percentile ranks.

The professor of your history class has just returned the midterm exams. Aside from the primary question about your grade, you'd like to know more about how your score compares with others in the class. Professor Abelard, anticipating such interest, writes the 50 scores on the board. Because her gradebook is in alphabetical order, the scores are not in numerical order, so the result appears in the form shown in

**TABLE 3.1**    *Scores for 50 Students on a History Midterm Examination*

| | | | | |
|---|---|---|---|---|
| 84 | 82 | 72 | 70 | 72 |
| 80 | 62 | 96 | 86 | 68 |
| 68 | 87 | 89 | 85 | 82 |
| 87 | 85 | 84 | 88 | 89 |
| 86 | 86 | 78 | 70 | 81 |
| 70 | 86 | 88 | 79 | 69 |
| 79 | 61 | 78 | 75 | 77 |
| 90 | 86 | 78 | 89 | 81 |
| 67 | 91 | 82 | 73 | 77 |
| 80 | 78 | 76 | 86 | 83 |

Table 3.1. Imagine that your score was 84. What more can you learn by studying the scores on the board?

You note that there are some scores in the 60s and some in the 90s, but that most appear to be in the 70s and 80s. However, you are still uncertain about how your performance compares to that of the rest of the class, so you decide to place the scores in order. The best way to do this is to list all *possible* score values from the highest to the lowest. The highest score on the exam is 96 and the lowest is 61. Thus, the recorded sequence is 96, 95, 94, . . . , 61, as shown in Table 3.2.

**TABLE 3.2**    *Frequency Distribution of Possible Scores on History Midterm Examination (from Table 3.1), Organized by Order of Magnitude*

| SCORE | FREQUENCY | SCORE | FREQUENCY |
|---|---|---|---|
| 96 | 1 | 78 | 4 |
| 95 | 0 | 77 | 2 |
| 94 | 0 | 76 | 1 |
| 93 | 0 | 75 | 1 |
| 92 | 0 | 74 | 0 |
| 91 | 1 | 73 | 1 |
| 90 | 1 | 72 | 2 |
| 89 | 3 | 71 | 0 |
| 88 | 2 | 70 | 3 |
| 87 | 2 | 69 | 1 |
| 86 | 6 | 68 | 2 |
| 85 | 2 | 67 | 1 |
| 84 | 2 | 66 | 0 |
| 83 | 1 | 65 | 0 |
| 82 | 3 | 64 | 0 |
| 81 | 2 | 63 | 0 |
| 80 | 2 | 62 | 1 |
| 79 | 2 | 61 | 1 |

Returning to the unordered set of scores on the blackboard, you take them in order of occurrence and record a tally mark for each score in the new (ordered) list and then convert these tallies to numerical frequencies. The result, which shows the possible scores and their frequency of occurrence, is called a **frequency distribution**.

Once the data are organized in this way, you can make a variety of interesting observations. You can see, for instance, that your score of 84 is somewhat above the middle of the distribution. Although the scores range from 61 to 96, the bulk of the scores fall between 67 and 91. There is one student whose performance stands well above the rest, and two students who "aren't getting it." Your score of 84 is not far from being quite a good performance in this class.

# 3.1 Organizing Qualitative Data

**frequency distribution**

shows the number of observations for the possible categories or score values in a set of data

Observations, or data, occur in a variety of forms. They may be numerical scores, such as weights in pounds, daily temperatures, or scores on a history midterm, or they may be qualitative data, as in the case of eye color, type of cheese, or political party. Regardless of their nature, we must organize and summarize observations to make sense out of them. We can make a frequency distribution for qualitative data as well as for quantitative data. This is illustrated in Table 3.3, where students enrolled in the College of Science of a local university are organized according to the variable of academic major.

The same procedures used to construct Table 3.2 were used to construct Table 3.3. However, instead of possible scores, we have different categories. Thus, we must expand our definition of a frequency distribution: A **frequency distribution** shows the number of observations for the possible categories or score values in a set of data. In Table 3.3, the order in which we put the different types of academic majors does not matter because the categories form a nominal scale. Put them in whatever order you wish; often, arranging them in order of magnitude of frequency (as in Table 3.3) will make sense. With ordinally scaled observations, you should arrange the categories in order of rank.

# 3.2 Grouped Scores

With numerical data, combining individual scores or measurements to form a smaller number of groups of scores often makes it easier to display the data and to grasp their

TABLE 3.3  *Frequencies of Academic Majors in a College of Science*

| MAJOR | FREQUENCY |
| --- | --- |
| Biology | 529 |
| Chemistry | 221 |
| Physics | 106 |
| Geology | 58 |
| Mathematics | 41 |
| | Total = 955 |

**class
intervals**

in a frequency
distribution, a
range of values
that are grouped
together

meaning. This is especially true when there is a wide range of values. Suppose, for example, that after constructing a frequency distribution of the history exam scores (Table 3.2), you decide to group every three consecutive scores beginning with 60, 61, and 62 and ending with 96, 97, and 98. Rather than a distribution of original scores, you would now have a distribution of score **class intervals** from 60–62 to 96–98. Column A in Table 3.4 shows how the grouped frequency distribution would appear. With this distribution, you can quickly see that most of the exam scores were between 66 (the lowest score of the interval 66 to 68) and 92 (the highest score of the interval 90 to 92).

Although grouped frequency distributions can make it easier to interpret data, some information is lost. In Column A of Table 3.4, for example, we can see that more people scored in the interval 84–86 than in any other interval. However, unless we have all the original scores to look at, we would not know whether the 10 scores in this interval were all 84s, all 85s, all 86s, or were spread throughout the interval in some way. This problem is referred to as **grouping error.** The wider the class interval width, the greater the potential for grouping error.

**raw scores**

scores in their
original form

A set of **raw scores** (scores in their original form) does not result in a unique set of grouped scores. For example, had you decided to use a class interval width of 5 instead of 3, your grouped frequency distribution might have looked like that in Column B of Table 3.4. We say "might have looked like" because even for an interval width of 5, there are several (five, in fact) possible grouped frequency distributions for the data in Table 3.2. For example, instead of starting with the interval 60–64, you might have decided to start with the interval 61–65, in which case your grouped frequency distribution would have appeared as shown in Column C of Table 3.4.

If a given set of scores can be grouped in more than one way, what is the best way so that the data are most easily understood? Fortunately, there are some widely

**TABLE 3.4**    *Scores from Table 3.2 Converted to Grouped Frequency Distributions*

| A CLASS INTERVAL WIDTH = 3 | | B CLASS INTERVAL WIDTH = 5 | | C CLASS INTERVAL WIDTH = 5 | |
|---|---|---|---|---|---|
| *Scores* | *Frequency* | *Scores* | *Frequency* | *Scores* | *Frequency* |
| 96–98 | 1 | 95–99 | 1 | 96–100 | 1 |
| 93–95 | 0 | 90–94 | 2 | 91–95 | 1 |
| 90–92 | 2 | 85–89 | 15 | 86–90 | 14 |
| 87–89 | 7 | 80–84 | 10 | 81–85 | 10 |
| 84–86 | 10 | 75–79 | 10 | 76–80 | 11 |
| 81–83 | 6 | 70–74 | 6 | 71–75 | 4 |
| 78–80 | 8 | 65–69 | 4 | 66–70 | 7 |
| 75–77 | 4 | 60–64 | 2 | 61–65 | 2 |
| 72–74 | 3 | | *N* = 50 | | *N* = 50 |
| 69–71 | 4 | | | | |
| 66–68 | 3 | | | | |
| 63–65 | 0 | | | | |
| 60–62 | 2 | | | | |
| | *N* = 50 | | | | |

accepted conventions that can help us here. These are just guidelines and not hard-and-fast rules. Refer to Table 3.4 as you work down this list.

1. *Be sure that your class intervals are mutually exclusive.* That is, intervals should not overlap, so no score can belong to more than one interval.

2. *Make all intervals the same width.* This convention usually makes it easier to recognize the overall pattern of the data.

3. *Make the intervals continuous throughout the distribution.* In Column A of Table 3.4, there are no scores in the interval 63–65, but it appears anyway. To omit this interval and close the gap would create a misleading impression.

4. *Place the interval containing the highest score value at the top.* This convention saves the trouble of having to figure out how to read each new table when we come to it. If you can avoid it, your *highest and lowest intervals should not include any score values that are not possible.* For example, if the highest possible score on an exam was 100, it would be misleading to have 98–102 as your highest interval.

5. *For most work, use 10 to 20 class intervals.* In Table 3.4, the distribution in Column A meets this criterion; the distributions in Columns B and C do not. Fewer class intervals mean wider intervals and thus greater loss of accuracy. More class intervals result in greater complexity. The number of class intervals will, of course, be a function of sample size. When the number of cases is small, for example, a small number of intervals is often preferable.

6. *Choose a convenient interval width.* In choosing the interval width, the number of intervals desired is only one factor to consider; convenience is another. Values such as 2, 3, 4, 5, 10, 25, and 50 make both the construction and interpretation of a distribution easier, whereas values like 9, 19, or 33 should be avoided. If you are going to present your frequency distribution as a graph (Chapter 4), *selection of an odd-numbered interval width is advisable because the midpoints are whole numbers.*

7. *When possible, make the lower score limits multiples of the interval width.* This also makes construction and interpretation easier. The distributions in Columns A and B in Table 3.4 meet this criterion; the distribution in Column C does not.

## 3.3 How to Construct a Grouped Frequency Distribution

With these guidelines in mind, we will translate a set of raw scores to a grouped frequency distribution. We will illustrate the procedure with the history midterm scores from Table 3.1.

The first step is to find the lowest score (61) and the highest score (96). The difference between these two figures is the **range** of scores. Therefore, the range is $96 - 61 = 35$. Because there are to be 10 to 20 class intervals, we must find an interval width satisfying that condition. If we divide the range by 10, we get the interval width necessary to cover the range in 10 intervals ($35/10 = 3.5$). If we use 20 intervals, the class interval width would be exactly half of this amount ($35/20 = 1.75$). We should choose an interval width equal to some *convenient* number between 1.75 and 3.5, and the only possibilities are 2 and 3. Suppose we decide to use an interval width of 3. In statistical work, interval width is symbolized by the letter $i$; for this problem, we have selected $i = 3$.

**range**
the difference between the lowest score and the highest score

*$i$*
symbol for interval width

Next, we must determine the starting point of the bottom class interval. The lowest score is 61, thus the lowest interval could be 59–61, 60–62, or 61–63. We select 60–62 because 60 is a multiple of our interval width of 3. This gives us the set of class intervals shown in Table 3.5.

*f*

symbol for frequency

*n*

symbol for total number of cases in a sample

*N*

symbol for total number of cases in a population

Next, tally the raw scores one by one against the list of class intervals. Then convert the tally to frequency (symbolized by $f$), as shown in the last column of Table 3.5. The total number of cases in the distribution is found by summing the several values of $f$ and is symbolized by $n$ if the distribution is considered a sample, or by $N$ if it is a population. These steps are summarized as follows:

**Step 1:** Find the lowest score and the highest score.

**Step 2:** Find the range by subtracting the lowest score from the highest.

**Step 3:** Divide the range by 10 and by 20 to determine the largest and the smallest acceptable interval widths. Choose a convenient width ($i$) within these limits.

**Step 4:** Determine the score at which the lowest interval should begin. It should ordinarily be a multiple of the interval width.

**Step 5:** Record the limits of all class intervals, placing the interval containing the highest score value at the top. Make the intervals continuous and of the same width.

**Step 6:** Using the tally system, enter the raw scores in the appropriate class intervals.

**Step 7:** Convert each tally to a frequency ($f$).

## 3.4 Apparent versus Real Limits

In our example, we have treated the test score as if it were a discrete variable. We did not allow for the possibility of getting a fraction of a point. What would we have

TABLE 3.5   *Tallies for Determining the Frequency of Scores on the History Midterm Exam (Table 3.1)*

| SCORES | TALLY | $f$ |
|--------|-------|-----|
| 96–98 | | | 1 |
| 93–95 | | 0 |
| 90–92 | \|\| | 2 |
| 87–89 | ⅧⅠ \|\| | 7 |
| 84–86 | ⅧⅠ ⅧⅠ | 10 |
| 81–83 | ⅧⅠ \| | 6 |
| 78–80 | ⅧⅠ \|\|\| | 8 |
| 75–77 | \|\|\|\| | 4 |
| 72–74 | \|\|\| | 3 |
| 69–71 | \|\|\|\| | 4 |
| 66–68 | \|\|\| | 3 |
| 63–65 | | 0 |
| 60–62 | \|\| | 2 |
| | | $N = 50$ |

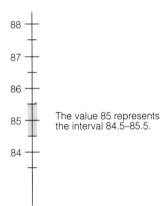

FIGURE 3.1    Real limits of a score on a history midterm.

**real limits of a score**
extend from one-half of the smallest unit of measurement below the value of the score to one-half unit above

done if one student had scored $86\frac{1}{4}$ points? Table 3.5 shows that this score does not fall in any class interval. It lies between the class intervals 84–86 and 87–89. How, then, do we deal with continuous variables?

In general, the **real limits of a score** are considered to extend from one-half of the smallest unit of measurement below the value of the score to one-half unit above. (Age is one common exception; when a man says he is 52, he means his age is between 52.0 and 53.0.) For example, consider three possible adjacent scores on the history midterm: 84, 85, and 86. It is reasonable to think that the score of 85 represents a level of knowledge closer to 85 than that indicated by a score of 84 or 86. Because the smallest unit of measurement on the exam was 1, the real limits of the score of 85 extend from 84.5 to 85.5. We illustrate this interpretation of a score in Figure 3.1.

**apparent limits of a score interval**
extend from the smallest unit of measurement in the interval to the largest

In Chapter 2, you learned that the process of measurement always reduces a continuous variable to a discrete one. If we record length to the nearest tenth of an inch, a measurement of 2.3 in. really represents the interval 2.25 in. to 2.35 in. If we weigh coal to the nearest 10 lb., a weight of 780 lb. represents 780 ± 5 lb., or from 775 to 785 lbs.

**real (exact) limits of a score interval**
extend from one-half the measurement unit below the lowest score to one-half the unit above the highest score

How do we determine real limits in a grouped frequency distribution? Consider the class interval 84–86. Because a score of 84 extends down to 83.5 and a score of 86 extends up to 86.5, the interval 84–86 includes everything between 83.5 and 86.5. For this interval, 84 and 86 are only the **apparent limits**. The **real (exact) limits** are 83.5 (the *lower real limit*) and 86.5 (the *upper real limit*). Table 3.6 gives the real limits for the complete distribution of history midterm scores. Notice that the lower real limit of each class interval serves at the same time as the upper real limit of the class interval immediately below. *No score can ever fall right on a real limit because we calculate real limits by taking half the smallest unit of measurement.*

## 3.5  The Relative Frequency Distribution

Suppose that Catherine Candidate received 1,375 votes for mayor in the last election. Is that a large number? In a town where 1,600 people voted, it is; in fact, it is 86% of the vote. In a city of 60,000 voters, the situation is different; it amounts to a little over 2%. For some purposes, an answer to the question "How many?" may give

**TABLE 3.6** *Lower and Upper Real Limits for the Distribution in Table 3.5*

| APPARENT LIMITS | REAL LIMITS | f |
|---|---|---|
| 96–98 | 95.5–98.5 | 1 |
| 93–95 | 92.5–95.5 | 0 |
| 90–92 | 89.5–92.5 | 2 |
| 87–89 | 86.5–89.5 | 7 |
| 84–86 | 83.5–86.5 | 10 |
| 81–83 | 80.5–83.5 | 6 |
| 78–80 | 77.5–80.5 | 8 |
| 75–77 | 74.5–77.5 | 4 |
| 72–74 | 71.5–74.5 | 3 |
| 69–71 | 68.5–71.5 | 4 |
| 66–68 | 65.5–68.5 | 3 |
| 63–65 | 62.5–65.5 | 0 |
| 60–62 | 59.5–62.5 | 2 |
| | | N = 50 |

**TABLE 3.7** *Relative Frequency Distributions of History Midterm Exam Scores*

| APPARENT LIMITS | CLASS A | | | CLASS B | | |
|---|---|---|---|---|---|---|
| | f | rel f (propor.)* | rel f (%)* | f | rel f (propor.)* | rel f (%)* |
| 96–98 | 1 | .02 | 2 | 1 | .01 | 1 |
| 93–95 | 0 | .00 | 0 | 1 | .01 | 1 |
| 90–92 | 2 | .04 | 4 | 3 | .04 | 4 |
| 87–89 | 7 | .14 | 14 | 3 | .04 | 4 |
| 84–86 | 10 | .20 | 20 | 4 | .05 | 5 |
| 81–83 | 6 | .12 | 12 | 7 | .09 | 9 |
| 78–80 | 8 | .16 | 16 | 8 | .10 | 10 |
| 75–77 | 4 | .08 | 8 | 9 | .11 | 11 |
| 72–74 | 3 | .06 | 6 | 12 | .15 | 15 |
| 69–71 | 4 | .08 | 8 | 6 | .08 | 8 |
| 66–68 | 3 | .06 | 6 | 11 | .14 | 14 |
| 63–65 | 0 | .00 | 0 | 7 | .09 | 9 |
| 60–62 | 2 | .04 | 4 | 2 | .02 | 2 |
| 57–59 | | | | 3 | .04 | 4 |
| 54–56 | | | | 3 | .04 | 4 |
| Totals | 50 | 1.00 | 100 | 80 | 1.01 | 101 |

*When actually reporting data, one would show relative frequencies as either proportions or percentages but not both.

us what we want to know. For others, the question "What proportion?" or equivalently "What percentage?" may be more relevant.

We can easily translate obtained frequencies for each class interval of a frequency distribution to relative frequencies by converting each to a proportion or percentage of the total number of cases. This gives us a relative frequency distribution. A **relative frequency distribution** shows the categories or score values and the proportion or percentage of the total number of cases that they represent. Table 3.7 shows the data of Table 3.6 expressed in this form under Class A. To obtain relative frequencies, we divide each frequency by the total number of cases in the distribution ($f/n$ for a sample; $f/N$ for a population). This gives the proportion of cases in the interval expressed as a decimal fraction (as a part relative to one). If you prefer percentages (parts relative to 100), move the decimal two places to the right. Thus we obtain the entry for the interval 60–62 for Class A of Table 3.7 by dividing the frequency of 2 by 50, which results in the decimal fraction .04 or 4%.

*Relative frequencies are particularly helpful when comparing frequency distributions in which the number of cases differs.* Table 3.7 shows the distributions of scores on the same history midterm examination for two classes. Class A lists the distribution for a class of 50; Class B lists the distribution for a class of 80. It isn't easy to compare the two sets of raw frequencies. Conversion to relative frequency puts both distributions on the same basis, and meaningful comparison is easier. (The percentages for the second class add to 101% rather than to 100% exactly because of rounding error.)

Relative frequencies may be inappropriate when there are few cases in the distribution. For example, it can be misleading to say that 50% of a community's auto mechanics are alcoholics when there are only two mechanics in that community.

**relative frequency distribution** shows the proportion or percentage of the total number of observations for the possible categories or score values in a set of data

**relative frequency expressed as a proportion** for a sample, obtained by $f/n$

## 3.6  Stem-and-Leaf Displays

**stem-and-leaf display** the possible values for the first digit of score intervals appear in a column (the stem) and all values in each interval are arranged to the right in order from low to high (the leaves)

We have followed tradition in presenting the frequency distribution as the basic technique for making sense of a jumble of scores. There is, however, an alternative, the **stem–and–leaf display**. The stem-and-leaf display is one of several techniques that constitute an area of statistics called *exploratory data analysis* (Hoaglin, Mosteller, & Tukey, 2000; Tukey, 1977).

Table 3.8 illustrates a simple stem-and-leaf display for the 50 scores on Professor Abelard's history midterm examination (Table 3.1). By convention for a display of

**TABLE 3.8**  *Stem-and-Leaf Display for the Data from Table 3.1*

| STEM | LEAF |
|------|------|
| 6 | 1 2 |
| 6 | 7 8 8 9 |
| 7 | 0 0 0 2 2 3 |
| 7 | 5 6 7 7 8 8 8 8 9 9 |
| 8 | 0 0 1 1 2 2 2 3 4 4 |
| 8 | 5 5 6 6 6 6 6 7 7 8 8 9 9 9 |
| 9 | 0 1 |
| 9 | 6 |

this kind, the lowest scores appear at the top, whereas the usual frequency distribution puts the highest at the top. For this display, we have divided the scores into class intervals with a width of 5 units: 60–64, 65–69, . . . , 95–99. The column of numbers to the left of the vertical line lists the possible values for the first digit (the tens digit) of these two-digit scores. Those values are the *stems* of the display. To the right of the stems are the second digits (the ones digits) of the scores, each a *leaf* of the display. *For each stem, the leaves are arranged in order from low to high.* Although this procedure seems simple, it may not be easy unless the scores have first been arranged in order of magnitude.

Like an ungrouped frequency distribution, a stem-and-leaf display includes all scores in order and shows the highest and lowest at a glance. The particular merit of the stem-and-leaf procedure is that it directly portrays the shape of the distribution, visually showing us where the scores are concentrated and where they are not. It is particularly useful, therefore, in the exploratory stages of analysis.

## 3.7  The Cumulative Frequency Distribution

**cumulative frequency distribution**
shows how many cases lie below the upper real limit of each class interval

Henry earned a score of 52 on an arithmetic achievement test. How many of his class scored lower? How many scored higher? Mary earned a score of 143 on a college entrance test. Among college applicants, what percentage obtains lower scores? On the same test, what score is so low that only 10% of the applicants do worse? What score divides the upper 25% of the distribution from the lower 75%? These are examples of questions that are more easily answered when we organize the distribution in cumulative form.

A **cumulative frequency distribution** shows how many cases lie below the upper real limit of each class interval. As an example of how we construct such a distribution, we begin with the frequency distribution of history exam scores shown in the first three columns of Table 3.9. We start at the bottom and record for each class interval the total frequency of cases falling *below* its upper real limit. (Remember, it is not possible to have a score exactly at the real limit—see Section 3.4.) These figures appear in the fourth column, headed *cum f*. We obtain them by adding the frequency of the given class interval to the cumulative frequency recorded for the next lower class interval. For example, we begin at the bottom by entering 2 for the two cases in the interval 60–62. This tells us that two cases fall below its upper real limit of 62.5. As we move up into the next interval, 63–65, we pick up no new cases, so the total number of cases below 65.5 remains at 2. Moving up one more interval, to 66–68, we pick up an additional three cases, giving a total of 5 (2 + 0 + 3) below its upper real limit of 68.5. We continue to work our way to the top by adding the frequency of each class interval to the cumulative frequency for the interval immediately below. As a check, the cumulative frequency for the uppermost class interval should equal *N*, the total number of cases.

If we desire a **relative cumulative frequency distribution**, we divide each cumulative frequency by *n* (sample) or *N* (population). For example, for the interval 87–89, $cum\ f/N = 47/50 = .94$, with the relative cumulative frequency expressed as a proportion. These values are shown in the fifth column of Table 3.9. We may convert them to percentages by multiplying each by 100, as shown in the last column. We will refer to a relative cumulative frequency distribution that uses percentages as a **cumulative percentage distribution**.

**TABLE 3.9**   *Cumulative Frequency and Relative Cumulative Frequency Distributions*

| APPARENT LIMITS | REAL LIMITS | *f* | cum *f* | cum PROPOR | cum % |
|---|---|---|---|---|---|
| 96–98 | 95.5–98.5 | 1 | 50 | 1.00 | 100.0 |
| 93–95 | 92.5–95.5 | 0 | 49 | .98 | 98.0 |
| 90–92 | 89.5–92.5 | 2 | 49 | .98 | 98.0 |
| 87–89 | 86.5–89.5 | 7 | 47 | .94 | 94.0 |
| 84–86 | 83.5–86.5 | 10 | 40 | .80 | 80.0 |
| 81–83 | 80.5–83.5 | 6 | 30 | .60 | 60.0 |
| 78–80 | 77.5–80.5 | 8 | 24 | .48 | 48.0 |
| 75–77 | 74.5–77.5 | 4 | 16 | .32 | 32.0 |
| 72–74 | 71.5–74.5 | 3 | 12 | .24 | 24.0 |
| 69–71 | 68.5–71.5 | 4 | 9 | .18 | 18.0 |
| 66–68 | 65.5–68.5 | 3 | 5 | .10 | 10.0 |
| 63–65 | 62.5–65.5 | 0 | 2 | .04 | 4.0 |
| 60–62 | 59.5–62.5 | 2 | 2 | .04 | 4.0 |
| | | $N = 50$ | | | |

**cum *f***
symbol for
cumulative
frequency

**cum %**
symbol for
cumulative
percentage

The values in the *cum f* column and the *cum %* column give the frequency and percentage of cases falling below the upper real limits of the various intervals. For instance, 40 cases (80% of the total of 50 cases) in the history class fall below 86.5, and 47 cases (94% of the total) fall below 89.5. What is the score point below which 75% of cases fall? It must be between 83.5 and 86.5 because 60% of scores fall below 83.5 and 80% fall below 86.5, but we cannot pinpoint the value without further work. You will learn how to make a more precise estimate in the next section.

# 3.8 Percentiles and Percentile Ranks

**percentile (point)**
a point on the measurement scale below which a specified percentage of the cases in a distribution falls

**percentile rank**
the percentage of cases in a distribution that falls below a given point on the measurement scale

The percentile system is widely used in educational measurement to report the standing of an individual relative to the performance of a known group. It is based on the cumulative percentage distribution. A **percentile point** is a point on the measurement scale below which a specified percentage of the cases in the distribution falls. It is more commonly called a *percentile* (from the Latin *centrum*, meaning hundred). If, for example, 50% of students in the history course have midterm scores lower than 81, the 50th percentile is 81. A **percentile rank** is the percentage of cases falling below a given point on the measurement scale. In our example, the percentile rank of a score of 81 is 50.

Do not confuse percentiles and percentile ranks: *Percentile ranks may take values only between 0 and 100, whereas a percentile (point) may have any value that scores may have.* It is possible to find that 576 is the value of a percentile, for example. Suppose that Mary earned a score of 143 on a college entrance test and that this score is such that 75% of applicants score below it. The 75th percentile is 143; Mary's percentile rank is 75. Standardized tests, such as the SAT (Scholastic Aptitude Test), GRE (Graduate Record Exam), and NTE (National Teachers Exam), publish their results in terms of either

TABLE 3.10     *General Test Interpretive Data for the GRE® Test*

Based on the performance of all examinees who tested between October 1, 1997, and September 30, 2000.

| SCALED SCORE | PERCENTAGES OF EXAMINEES SCORING LOWER THAN SELECTED SCALED SCORES | | |
| --- | --- | --- | --- |
| | *Verbal ability* | *Quantitative ability* | *Analytical ability* |
| 800 | 99 | 97 | 98 |
| 700 | 97 | 74 | 83 |
| 600 | 85 | 53 | 59 |
| 500 | 60 | 31 | 35 |
| 400 | 29 | 13 | 15 |
| 300 | 5 | 2 | 3 |
| Number of examinees | 1,075,348 | 1,075,053 | 1,073,300 |

Reprinted by permission of Educational Testing Service, the copyright owner. Permission to reprint GRE materials does not constitute review or Endorsement by Educational Testing Service of this publication as a whole or of any other testing information it may contain.

percentiles or percentile ranks. Table 3.10 shows the percentile ranks of some scores for all those who took the GRE® Test in the period October 1997 through September 2000. From this table we see that a score of 600 had a percentile rank of 85 on verbal ability, 53 on quantitative ability, and 59 on analytical ability.

***P***

symbol for a percentile

We shall use the symbol ***P*** to represent a percentile: the 50th percentile is written as $P_{50}$, and the 28th as $P_{28}$. For Mary we may write: $P_{75} = 143$. The subscript indicates the percentile rank for the score of 143. In Table 3.9, we find that $P_{94}$ (the 94th percentile point) is 89.5, the upper limit of the fourth from the top class interval. Similarly, the same table shows that $P_{60} = 83.5$ and $P_{10} = 68.5$. In the next section, you will learn how to compute percentiles from cumulative frequency distributions.

## 3.9 Computing Percentiles from Grouped Data

In Table 3.11, we present the data for Class B of Table 3.7 in cumulative frequency form. This is the starting point for finding percentiles. Suppose that our problem is to find the values of $P_{25}$, $P_{50}$, and $P_{82}$. What is $P_{25}$? By definition, it is the point on the measurement scale below which 25% of the actual scores fall. There are 80 cases; because 25% of 80 is 20, $P_{25}$ is the point below which 20 cases fall. Working up from the bottom of the distribution, we find that the 20th case will fall in the class interval 65.5–68.5. (We must be sure to think in terms of real limits.) At this point, it is not clear what score value we should assign because the point we seek lies somewhere within the interval.

There are 11 scores in this interval. To proceed, *we will make the assumption that the scores are evenly distributed throughout the interval.* This assumption underlies the procedure called **linear interpolation**. (For a detailed explanation, see section 10 of Appendix A.) We show the results of this assumption in Figure 3.2. From this point on,

TABLE 3.11 *Cumulative Percentage Distribution and Percentile Calculations*

| APPARENT LIMITS | REAL LIMITS | $f$ | cum $f$ | cum % | PERCENTILE CALCULATIONS |
|---|---|---|---|---|---|
| 96–98 | 95.5–98.5 | 1 | 80 | 100.0 | |
| 93–95 | 92.5–95.5 | 1 | 79 | 98.8 | |
| 90–92 | 89.5–92.5 | 3 | 78 | 97.5 | |
| 87–89 | 86.5–89.5 | 3 | 75 | 93.8 | |
| 84–86 | 83.5–86.5 | 4 | 72 | 90.0 | |
| 81–83 | 80.5–83.5 | 7 | 68 | 85.0 | $P_{82} = 80.5 + (4.6/7 \times 3)$ $= 82.5$ |
| 78–80 | 77.5–80.5 | 8 | 61 | 76.2 | |
| 75–77 ① | 74.5–77.5 | 9 | 53 | 66.2 | ② ③ |
| 72–74 | 71.5–74.5 | 12 | 44 | 55.0 | $P_{50} = 71.5 + (8/12 \times 3)$ $= 73.5$ |
| 69–71 | 68.5–71.5 | 6 | 32 | 40.0 | |
| 66–68 | 65.5–68.5 | 11 | 26 | 32.5 | $P_{25} = 65.5 + (5/11 \times 3)$ $= 66.9$ |
| 63–65 | 62.5–65.5 | 7 | 15 | 18.8 | |
| 60–62 | 59.5–62.5 | 2 | 8 | 10.0 | |
| 57–59 | 56.5–59.5 | 3 | 6 | 7.5 | |
| 54–56 | 53.5–56.5 | 3 | 3 | 3.8 | |
| | | $N = 80$ | | | |

it will be easier to grasp the procedure by closely studying Figure 3.2. The value of the 25th percentile (point) will be located at a point 20 scores (cases) up from the bottom of the distribution. Because there are 15 cases below the lower limit of the class interval concerned, we must come up 5 more to reach this position. This means that we are to come up 5 out of the 11 equal parts in the interval, or 5/11 of the interval's width. The width of the interval is 3 score points, and the calculation is as follows: (5/11) × 3 = 1.4 points. We therefore add this quantity to the lower *real* limit of the interval.

$$P_{25} = 65.5 + 1.4 = 66.9$$

We provide a formula for this calculation in the mathematical notes at the end of the chapter, but it is more important that you follow the logic of the procedure. Once the logic is grasped, it is much easier to remember than any formula because it makes sense.

We will review and summarize the steps in calculating a percentile by determining $P_{50}$.

**Problem**  Find $P_{50}$.

**Step 1:** First objective: find the class interval in which $P_{50}$ falls.

(a) $P_{50}$ is the score point below which 50% of the cases fall.
(b) 50% of $N = .50 \times 80 = 40$ scores.
(c) The 40th score (from the bottom) falls in the class interval 72–74 (see ① in Table 3.11).

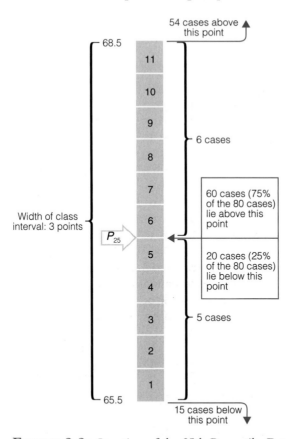

**FIGURE 3.2**   Location of the 25th Percentile. Data from Table 3.11.

**Step 2:**   Determine the number of cases between the bottom of the distribution and the lower real limit of the class interval containing the desired percentile. In this case, the number is 32.

**Step 3:**   Determine the additional number of cases required to make up the number of scores found in 1(b). In this case, 8; $32 + 8 = 40$.

**Step 4:**   Assume the (12) scores in the class interval are evenly distributed throughout the interval.

**Step 5:**   Find the additional distance into the interval needed to arrive at the score point: 8/12 of the interval width, or $(8/12) \times 3 = 2.0$. This is shown at ② in Table 3.11.

**Step 6:**   Add this additional distance to the lower real limit of the class interval to obtain the percentile

$$P_{50} = 71.5 + 2.0 = 73.5$$

See ③ in the same table.

Elements of the calculation of $P_{50}$ and $P_{82}$ are shown in Table 3.11. To be certain of the procedure, you should verify that $P_5 = 57.5$ and that $P_{75} = 80.1$.

A good way to check calculation of percentiles is to count *downward* in the distribution to the appropriate point. Checking the calculation of $P_{25}$ by this method, one must come down 75% of the cases, or 60 scores. This is six cases below the upper real limit of the class interval 65.5–68.5. By the same reasoning applied previously,

$$P_{25} = 68.5 - (6/11 \times 3) = 66.9$$

A special situation arises when a percentile coincides with an empty class interval. In the data of Table 3.9 this occurs for $P_4$. By the definition of a percentile, $P_4$ could be said to be any score value between 62.5 and 65.5, inclusive. The preferred procedure is to split the difference; we therefore take $P_4$ as the midpoint of this interval, 64.0.

## 3.10 Computation of Percentile Rank

For some studies, we may require percentile ranks rather than percentiles. If we make the same assumption we did for the computation of a percentile, the general nature of the procedure is the same. We will work one example.

What is the percentile rank of a score of 86? We must find the percentage of cases that lie below 86.0. First, we find the number of cases below this point. We see from Table 3.11 that the score of 86.0 is located in the class interval 83.5–86.5. The interval width is 3 score points, and to reach 86.0 one must come up 2.5 of these points from the bottom of the interval (83.5 + 2.5 = 86.0). There are four cases in the interval, and we *assume them to be evenly distributed*. We must therefore come up $(2.5/3) \times 4$ or 3.3 cases from the bottom of the interval. Because there are 68 scores below this lower limit, the point in question is 68 + 3.3 = 71.3 cases up from the bottom of the distribution. Finally, 71.3/80 = .89 or 89%. The score of 86 is at a point below which 89% of the cases fall, and therefore its percentile rank is 89. We may summarize the calculation as follows.

$$\text{PERCENTILE RANK OF A SCORE OF 86} = 100\left[\frac{68 + \left(\dfrac{2.5}{3} \times 4\right)}{80}\right] = 89$$

To be certain you understand the procedure, verify the following calculation of the percentile rank of a score of 61.

$$\text{PERCENTILE RANK OF A SCORE OF 61} = 100\left[\frac{6 + \left(\dfrac{1.5}{3} \times 2\right)}{80}\right] = 9$$

For further practice, verify that the percentile rank of a score of 71 is 39, and that the percentile rank of a score of 90 is 94.

## 3.11 Summary

Statistical procedures often deal with large numbers of observations. When observations are ordered and grouped, their meaning is easier to understand. A frequency distribution shows the number of observations for the possible categories or score values in a set of data. Although grouping (putting scores into class intervals) adds convenience, there is a cost—we no longer know exactly where the scores are in a particular class interval. For this reason, class intervals should not be too wide. A good compromise for most purposes is to use between 10 and 20 intervals.

We can construct frequency distributions to show frequency (how many?) or relative frequency (what proportion or percentage of the whole?). Which is preferred depends on the question under consideration. Relative frequency distributions are usually best for comparing two or more distributions containing different numbers of cases. The cumulative percentage distribution is particularly useful in stating the location of a score by describing the percentage of cases that fall below it. It is this distribution that is most closely related to the widely used percentile system.

A percentile rank is the percentage of cases falling below a given point on the measurement scale. Thus, it allows us to see the standing of an individual relative to the performance of the entire group. A percentile is a point along the measurement scale below which a specified percentage of the cases in the distribution falls. Testing services usually use this system when publishing results of standardized tests. To calculate percentiles or percentile ranks from grouped data, we must assume equal distribution of scores within class intervals.

## Mathematical Notes

In this chapter, we begin a series of mathematical notes. They are not intended to provide rigorous derivations of the statistical procedures considered. We offer them to provide additional insight into statistical relationships to the student who wants to know more about the subject. No knowledge of college mathematics is presumed, but a feeling of reasonable comfort in mathematical expression is helpful. *The student whose path of learning does not lead into this area should understand that the text is designed to stand on its own without these notes. They are part of an "enriched curriculum."*

**Note 3.1 Computation of Percentile Points (*Ref.*: Section 3.9)**
To calculate a percentile point, you may use the following general formula.

$$P = LL + (i)\left(\frac{cum\ f\ \text{percentile} - cum\ f\ \text{below}}{f}\right)$$

where:          $LL$ = lower real limit of class interval containing the percentile
$i$ = width of the class interval
$cum\ f$ percentile = number of scores lying below percentile
$cum\ f$ below = number of scores lying below $LL$
$f$ = frequency of scores in the interval containing the percentile

**Note 3.2 Computation of Percentile Rank (*Ref.*: Section 3.10)**

$$\text{Percentile Rank} = 100\left(\frac{cum\ f\ \text{below} + \left(\frac{X - LL}{i}\right)(f)}{N}\right)$$

where:   *cum f* below = number of scores below lower real limit of class interval containing $X$

$X$ = score

$LL$ = lower real limit of class interval containing $X$

$i$ = width of the class interval

$f$ = frequency of scores in the interval containing $X$

$N$ = number of scores in the distribution

## Key Terms, Concepts, and Symbols

frequency distribution   (27)

class intervals   (28)

grouping error   (28)

raw scores   (28)

grouped scores   (28)

range   (29)

$i$   (29)

$f$   (30)

$n$   (30)

$N$   (30)

real limits of a score   (31)

apparent limits   (31)

real (exact) limits   (31)

relative frequency distribution   (33)

relative frequency expressed as a proportion   (33)

stem-and-leaf display   (33)

cumulative frequency distribution   (34)

relative cumulative frequency distribution   (34)

cumulative percentage distribution   (34)

*cum f*   (35)

*cum %*   (35)

percentile (point)   (35)

percentile rank   (35)

$P$   (36)

linear interpolation   (36)

## Problems

**1.** Students in introductory statistics were asked about their academic standings. They gave the following responses:

| | | | |
|---|---|---|---|
| freshman | junior | sophomore | junior |
| sophomore | graduate | sophomore | junior |
| sophomore | junior | sophomore | senior |
| senior | senior | junior | sophomore |
| sophomore | senior | senior | freshman |
| junior | graduate | sophomore | senior |

(a) Organize the results into a frequency distribution. (b) On what measurement scale are these observations? (c) Does it matter in what order we arrange the categories?

**2.** Write the real limits for the following scores: (a) A score of 52; measurement is to the nearest digit. (b) 800 yd.; measurement is to the nearest 100 yd. (c) 460 lb.; measurement is to the nearest 10 lb. (d) .6 in.; measurement

is to the nearest .1 in. (e) .47 sec.; measurement is to the nearest .01 sec.

**3.** For each of the following intervals, give the interval width, the real limits, the apparent limits of the next higher interval, and the real limits of the next higher interval. (a) 5–9, where the scores were rounded to the nearest whole number. (b) 40–49, where the scores were rounded to the nearest whole number. (c) 2.0–2.4, where the scores were rounded to the nearest tenth. (d) 60–70, where scores are accurate to the nearest ten. (e) 1.75–1.99, where scores were rounded to the nearest hundredth.

**4.** In making a frequency distribution, you set the real limits for the lowest two intervals at 29.5–39.5 and 39.5–49.5. A friend objects, saying, "The intervals overlap, because both contain 39.5." (a) Reply to your friend's objection. (b) Give the apparent limits and the interval width for both intervals.

5. In making a frequency distribution to display a sample of scores, there is more than one way to group them. What problems might therefore arise?

6. In making a frequency distribution, what choices magnify grouping error? What can we do to minimize it?

7. For each set of class intervals, identify any shortcomings.

   (a) 50 and up  (b) 20–25  (c) 5–9
       44–49          14–19      10–14
       38–43          8–13       14–19
       26–31          0–7        20–24

8. Given below are the highest and the lowest score for different samples. Each sample is to be grouped into class intervals. For each, give the range, your choice of width for the class intervals, the apparent limits for the lowest interval, and the apparent limits for the highest interval: (a) 75, 36; (b) 117, 54; (c) 171, 27; (d) +21, −22; (e) 3.47, 1.13; (f) 821, 287.

9. Data 3A gives the scores earned by college students on an anthropology test:

## Data 3A

| 44 | 35 | 20 | 40 | 38 | 52 | 29 | 36 | 38 | 38 |
| 38 | 38 | 41 | 35 | 42 | 50 | 31 | 43 | 30 | 41 |
| 32 | 47 | 43 | 41 | 47 | 32 | 38 | 29 | 23 | 48 |
| 41 | 51 | 48 | 49 | 37 | 26 | 34 | 48 | 35 | 41 |
| 38 | 47 | 41 | 33 | 39 | 48 | 38 | 20 | 59 | 37 |
| 29 | 44 | 29 | 33 | 35 | 58 | 41 | 38 | 26 | 29 |
| 32 | 54 | 24 | 38 | 38 | 56 | 56 | 48 | 34 | 35 |
| 26 | 26 | 38 | 37 | 57 | 24 | 44 | 62 | 29 | 41 |

Reorganize these raw scores into an ungrouped frequency distribution.

10. For Data 3A: (a) Construct a grouped frequency distribution with 20–22 as the apparent limits for the lowest class interval. The interval width should thus be 3. (b) Construct another frequency distribution for the same scores, again with a width of 3 for the class intervals, but begin with 18–20 as the lowest interval. (c) List the lower and upper real limits for each interval. (d) Compare the two distributions. Are they generally similar in the impression they give of the raw scores? (e) One place where the two distributions differ is in the class intervals cover-

ing scores of 45 to 52. Why do they differ there?

11. For Data 3A, construct a stem-and-leaf display using the tens digit as the stem.

12. Convert the following proportions to percentages, preserving the accuracy in the proportion: (a) .73; (b) .09; (c) .666; (d) .07; (e) .008.

13. Convert the following percentages to proportions, preserving the accuracy in the percentage: (a) 37%; (b) 56.3%; (c) 4.2%; (d) 9.21%; (e) .4%; (f) .85%; (g) .02%.

14. (a) To the frequency distribution that you constructed for Problem 10a, add a column of relative frequencies expressed as proportions. (b) To the frequency distribution that you, constructed for Problem 10b, add a column of relative frequencies expressed as percentages.

15. Two hundred volunteers from a large section of the introductory psychology course participate in an experiment testing the effect of mood on learning. Some spend 10 minutes thinking of pleasant things to put them into a good mood; the others spend the time thinking of unpleasant things and go into a bad mood. All subjects then devote 30 minutes to studying an unfamiliar, sorrowful folk tale from an African culture, after which they take a test on it. Data 3B gives the frequency distributions of scores on this test. (The higher the number, the better the learning of the folk tale.)

## Data 3B

| SCORE | GOOD MOOD | BAD MOOD |
|---|---|---|
| 155–159 | | 1 |
| 150–154 | 2 | 2 |
| 145–149 | 4 | 7 |
| 140–144 | 7 | 12 |
| 135–139 | 12 | 10 |
| 130–134 | 14 | 7 |
| 125–129 | 25 | 4 |
| 120–124 | 23 | 3 |
| 115–119 | 18 | 0 |
| 110–114 | 20 | 2 |
| 105–109 | 12 | 1 |
| 100–104 | 8 | 0 |
| 95–99 | 3 | 1 |
| 90–94 | 2 | |
| | $n = 150$ | $n = 50$ |

(a) Present the distributions in terms of relative frequency, using percentages. (b) Suppose you wish to compare the two conditions of the experiment with regard to the results for the range 130–139 inclusive. Which provide the more meaningful comparison: the original frequencies or the relative frequencies? Explain.

**16.** All police officers in New York City have been issued a bullet-proof vest. A radio station reported that only one-third of the officers patrolling Times Square were wearing the vest. Later in the report it was revealed that the total number of officers working Times Square at the time of the survey was six. Any comment on the statistics in this report?

**17.** To the tables that you constructed for Questions 10a and 15a, (a) add a column giving cumulative frequency, and then (b) add a column giving cumulative percentage.

**18.** This problem requires no computation. For the data displayed in Table 3.9, find: (a) the 24th percentile; (b) $P_{60}$; (c) the 10th percentile; (d) $P_{94}$; (e) the percentile rank of the value 62.5; (f) the percentage of cases with a score less than 77.5; (g) the percentile rank of the value 95.5; (h) the percentage of cases with a score below 59.5.

**19.** (a) Can a percentile have the value of 517? Explain. (b) Can a percentile have the value −5.8? Explain. (c) Can a percentile rank have the value 517? Explain. (d) Can a percentile rank have the value −5.8? Explain.

**20.** From the cumulative distribution of the Good Mood scores in Data 3B (Problems 15 and 17), find: (a) the percentile rank of 139.5; (b) the percentile rank of 126; (c) the 25th percentile; (d) the 50th percentile.

**21.** Dr. Smart's first exam in introductory statistics was on frequency distributions. The scores are given in Data 3C. (The highest possible score was 100.)

## Data 3C

| | | | | |
|----|----|----|----|----|
| 52 | 84 | 93 | 78 | 75 |
| 71 | 99 | 81 | 86 | 81 |
| 65 | 70 | 72 | 71 | 91 |
| 87 | 82 | 77 | 66 | 63 |
| 90 | 58 | 89 | 60 | 79 |
| 77 | 72 | 83 | 87 | 87 |
| 83 | 79 | 55 | 97 | 74 |
| 71 | 86 | 75 | 83 | 63 |
| 82 | 70 | 90 | 95 | 92 |
| 75 | 85 | 83 | 71 | 88 |

(a) Construct a grouped frequency distribution. (b) Construct a cumulative frequency distribution. (c) Construct a cumulative percentage distribution. (d) Calculate the percentile rank for your score of 88.

# CHAPTER 4

# Graphic Representation of Frequency Distributions

When you have finished studying this chapter, you should be able to:

- Know how to construct and interpret frequency distributions, relative frequency distributions, and cumulative frequency distributions in graph form; more specifically,

- Know how to construct a bar diagram and pie chart for qualitative data;

- Know how to construct a histogram and frequency polygon for quantitative data;

- Know how to construct a cumulative percentage curve;

- Understand the criteria for choosing between a histogram and frequency polygon; and

- Understand the factors that affect the shape of graphs, and identify some shapes that are common in the behavioral sciences.

Should you construct a frequency distribution as a table or a graph? A graph is based entirely on the tabled data and therefore can tell us nothing more than can be learned by inspecting the table. However, graphic representation often makes it easier for us to see pertinent features of the data.

There are many different kinds of graphs. Books are available that describe graphic procedures in variety and at length (Cleveland, 1995; Cleveland & McGill, 1985). We shall consider here only frequency distributions, which can be represented in graphic form in three main ways: the *histogram* and its variant, the *bar diagram*; the *frequency polygon*; and the *cumulative percentage curve*. These graphs are illustrated in Figures 4.1, 4.6, 4.2, and 4.9, respectively. When you first inspect them, the four graphs may appear to be very different from one another, but they have much in common. Therefore, before describing each one in detail, we will discuss some general procedures in graphing frequency distributions.

## 4.1 Basic Procedures

**abscissa**
the horizontal or *X* axis

**ordinate**
the vertical or *Y* axis

**zero point on a graph**
the intersection of the abscissa and ordinate

Graphed frequency distributions generally have two axes: horizontal and vertical. The horizontal axis is called the **abscissa** or *X* **axis**, and the vertical axis the **ordinate**, or *Y* **axis**. *It is customary to represent scores or categories (for qualitative data) along the horizontal axis and frequency (or some function of frequency) along the vertical axis.* According to mathematical practice, the intersection of the two axes represents the **zero point on a graph**. If it does not, the reader should be warned on the graph. In Figure 4.1, for example, a break in the horizontal axis indicates that a portion of the scale is missing.

The appearance of a graph depends on the choice of scale used to represent position along the two axes. Because similar distributions should appear similar when graphed, *it is customary to make the height of the distribution about three-quarters of the width.* We measure width and height from the span of the graphed data rather than from the borders of the graph. Some trial-and-error may be necessary to create a graph suitable in size and convenient in scale. It is also important that a graph be large enough so that values (both along the horizontal and vertical axes and within the graph itself) can be easily read.

Ideally, a graph should not need accompanying explanation. Thus, *the graph of any frequency distribution should have a succinct and informative title as well as labels on both axes.*

By now you can see that some procedures are basically arbitrary and governed by conventions. These conventions are useful because they result in representations that match our expectations. Then we do not have to approach each new graph as a problem-solving exercise before absorbing its meaning. We could read a book just as well if the page order went from back to front, but it would be a nuisance to find out which way a book was printed every time we picked up a new volume. Keep these general procedures in mind as we look at the different types of graphed frequency distributions.

## 4.2 The Histogram

Suppose that after constructing a grouped frequency distribution of your history exam scores (see Table 4.1), Professor Abelard then graphs the distribution. There are two basic ways in which she could do this. One of them is the histogram shown in

**TABLE 4.1** *Results from 50 Students on Professor Abelard's History Class Midterm Examination*

| A: RAW SCORES | | | | |
|---|---|---|---|---|
| 84 | 82 | 72 | 70 | 72 |
| 80 | 62 | 96 | 86 | 68 |
| 68 | 87 | 89 | 85 | 82 |
| 87 | 85 | 84 | 88 | 89 |
| 86 | 86 | 78 | 70 | 81 |
| 70 | 86 | 88 | 79 | 69 |
| 79 | 61 | 78 | 75 | 77 |
| 90 | 86 | 78 | 89 | 81 |
| 67 | 91 | 82 | 73 | 77 |
| 80 | 78 | 76 | 86 | 83 |

**B: FREQUENCY AND CUMULATIVE FREQUENCY DISTRIBUTIONS**

| Apparent limits | Real limits | $f$ | rel f (%) | cum f | cum % |
|---|---|---|---|---|---|
| 96–98 | 95.5–98.5 | 1 | 2 | 50 | 100.0 |
| 93–95 | 92.5–95.5 | 0 | 0 | 49 | 98.0 |
| 90–92 | 89.5–92.5 | 2 | 4 | 49 | 98.0 |
| 87–89 | 86.5–89.5 | 7 | 14 | 47 | 94.0 |
| 84–86 | 83.5–86.5 | 10 | 20 | 40 | 80.0 |
| 81–83 | 80.5–83.5 | 6 | 12 | 30 | 60.0 |
| 78–80 | 77.5–80.5 | 8 | 16 | 24 | 48.0 |
| 75–77 | 74.5–77.5 | 4 | 8 | 16 | 32.0 |
| 72–74 | 71.5–74.5 | 3 | 6 | 12 | 24.0 |
| 69–71 | 68.5–71.5 | 4 | 8 | 9 | 18.0 |
| 66–68 | 65.5–68.5 | 3 | 6 | 5 | 10.0 |
| 63–65 | 62.5–65.5 | 0 | 0 | 2 | 4.0 |
| 60–62 | 59.5–62.5 | 2 | 4 | 2 | 4.0 |
| | Totals = | 50 | 100% | | |

**histogram**

a graph that consists of a series of rectangles, the heights of which represent frequency or relative frequency

Figure 4.1. The **histogram** consists of a series of rectangles, each of which represents the scores in one of the class intervals of the tabulated distribution. *The two vertical boundaries of a rectangle coincide with the real limits of the particular interval whereas its height depends on the frequency of scores for that interval.* We can use either raw frequencies or relative frequencies (proportions or percentages) with a histogram. Changing from raw to relative frequencies requires only that we relabel the vertical axis. The steps in

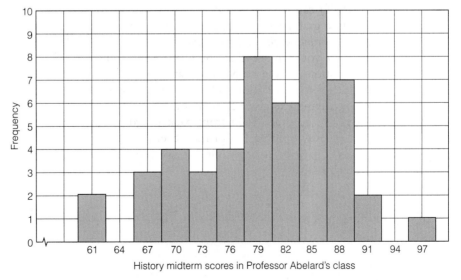

**FIGURE 4.1** Histogram of grouped history exam scores from Table 4.1.

constructing a histogram are summarized as follows (see Table 4.1 and Figure 4.1 for examples):

**Step 1:** Construct a frequency distribution in table form as described in Section 3.3 of the last chapter. A histogram is only a visual display of the tabulated distribution. Alternatively, you may construct a stem-and-leaf display (see Section 3.6). You will best appreciate the resemblance of a stem-and-leaf display to a histogram if you rotate the display 90 degrees counterclockwise (try this with Table 3.8).

**Step 2:** Before drawing your axes (graph paper is advised), decide on a suitable scale for the horizontal axis (scores) and then determine the number of squares (on the graph paper) required for the width of the graph. Multiply this number by .75 to find the approximate number of squares to use for the graph's height (frequency).

**Step 3:** Draw bars of equal width for each class interval. The height of a bar corresponds to the frequency or relative frequency in that particular interval. *There should be no gaps between the bars except for intervals in which there are no scores* (such as 63–65 and 93–95 in Figure 4.1). The edge of a bar represents both the upper real limit for one interval and the lower real limit for the next higher interval.

**Step 4:** Identify your class intervals along the horizontal axis by using either real limits or interval midpoints. Do not use both because it will result in too many numbers along the abscissa and may confuse the reader. *If you use real limits, place them under the edge of each bar* (see Figure 4.10). *If you use interval midpoints, place them under the middle of each bar* (see Figure 4.1). You find the **interval midpoint** by locating the point halfway between the apparent limits (or, alternatively, the real limits) of the interval. In Table 4.1, for example, the midpoint of the first interval (61) is easily obtained by adding half the difference between the apparent limits to the lower apparent limit ($62 - 60 = 2$; $2/2 = 1$; $60 + 1 = 61$). You will obtain the same result if the real limits are used instead ($62.5 - 59.5 = 3$; $3/2 = 1.5$; $59.5 + 1.5 = 61$). Remember, odd-numbered interval widths have midpoints with whole numbers.

**Step 5:** Label your axes and give your histogram a title.

**interval midpoint**
the point halfway between the apparent (or real) limits of an interval

## 4.3 The Frequency Polygon

Another way in which Professor Abelard could construct a graph of the distribution in Table 4.1 is with a frequency polygon (from the Greek meaning "many angles"). As you can see in Figure 4.2, a **frequency polygon** is a series of connected dots above the midpoint of each possible class interval. Each dot is at a height equal to the frequency or relative frequency of scores in that interval. The steps in constructing a frequency polygon are summarized as follows:

**frequency polygon**
a graph that consists of a series of connected dots above the midpoint of each possible class interval (height of the dots corresponds to frequency or relative frequency)

**Step 1:** Construct a frequency distribution in table form.

**Step 2:** Decide on a suitable scale for the horizontal and vertical axes.

**Step 3:** Label your class interval midpoints along the horizontal axis.

**Step 4:** Place a dot above the midpoint of each class interval at a height equal to the frequency or relative frequency of the scores in that interval.

**Step 5:** Connect the dots with straight lines.

**Step 6:** Label your axes and give your polygon a title.

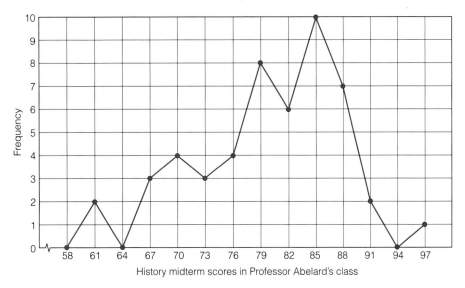

**FIGURE 4.2** Frequency polygon of grouped history exam scores from Table 4.1.

Notice that in Figure 4.2 the polygon touches the horizontal axis at 64 and 94, the midpoints of the intervals 63–65 and 93–95, respectively. This indicates that there were zero scores in those intervals. Ordinarily, we bring the polygon down to the horizontal axis at both ends as well. To do so, identify the two class intervals falling immediately outside those end class intervals containing scores. The midpoints of these intervals, plotted at zero frequency, are then connected to the graph. We did this for the interval 57–59 because scores in this interval were possible, though not obtained. However, what do we do when scores in the next adjacent class interval are not possible? There are problems with any solution, but we suggest the best thing to do in a case like this is to leave the dot "dangling."[1] We have done this in Figure 4.2 for the interval 96–98 because scores greater than 100 were not possible on the history exam and the next adjacent interval is 99–101.

## 4.4 Choosing between a Histogram and a Polygon

Both the histogram and the polygon are used for graphing quantitative data on an interval or ratio scale. Neither graph tells any more nor any less than can be found by an inspection of the same distribution given in table form. You can see the similarities between the two graphs by superimposing a histogram and polygon of the same set of data, as we have done for the history exam scores in Figure 4.3. Nevertheless, there are occasions when one may be preferred over the other.

A histogram is often used when graphing an ungrouped frequency distribution of a discrete variable (or data treated as a discrete variable). For example, Figure 4.4 shows

---

[1]Bringing the polygon down to 0 at the midpoint of the next adjacent midpoint may mislead someone looking at the graph to think that scores in that interval were possible. Bringing the polygon straight down implies there were two frequencies for that interval, including $f = 0$.

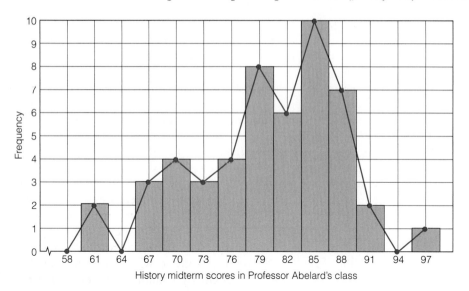

**FIGURE 4.3**   Frequency polygon of grouped history exam scores superimposed on a histogram of the same scores.

a histogram of the results of the mathematics portion of the ACT (American College Testing Program, national profile for 2000–2001 freshman class). The ACT is used by over 1,000 colleges and universities to assess their freshmen's level of knowledge. Scores are given in whole numbers from 1 to 36. In this case, the histogram helps convey to the reader that there are no possible scores other than those reported on the horizontal axis. The general public seems to find a histogram a little easier to understand than a polygon, and hence it may be a good choice for communicating with them.

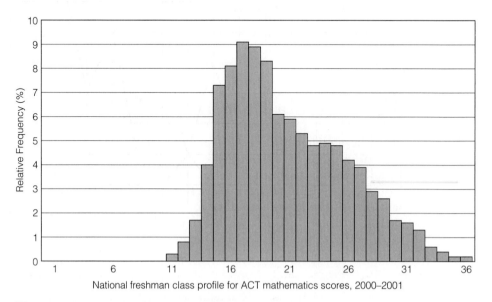

**FIGURE 4.4**   Histograms are often used when graphing ungrouped distributions of a discrete variable. (*Source:* Taken from ACT Class Profile Report, Freshman Class 2000–2001. Copyright by ACT, Inc. Reproduced with permission.)

A histogram also has some merit when displaying relative frequency. The total area in a histogram represents 100% of the scores, and thus the area in the bars of a histogram is directly representative of relative frequency. That is, *the area in any rectangle is the same fraction of the total area of the histogram as the frequency of that class interval is of the total number of cases in the distribution.* If 25% of scores lie below the upper real limit of a particular class interval, then 25% of the area of the histogram will fall to the left of this point. This relationship is approximately (but not exactly) true in the frequency polygon.

A polygon is often preferred for grouped frequency distributions. Representing frequencies by rectangular bars suggests that the scores are evenly distributed within each class interval and that the borders of the intervals are points of decided change. If a definite trend of increasing or decreasing frequency exists over a span of several consecutive class intervals, the frequency polygon will represent this trend more directly. This is because the direction of each straight line in the polygon is determined by the frequencies in two adjacent class intervals, whereas the horizontal top of each rectangle in a histogram is responsive only to what occurs in one class interval.

Frequency polygons are particularly helpful when comparing two or more distributions. Figure 4.5 shows such a comparison, using the two sets of data in Table 3.7. When distributions are based on different numbers of cases, as in this example, we can equalize that difference by using relative frequencies rather than raw frequencies. Figure 4.5 makes it easy to see that the bulk of the scores for Distribution A appear higher on the scale and that the range of performance is a little less than for Distribution B. If we attempted the same comparison using two histograms, there would be considerable confusion created by the overlapping rectangles.

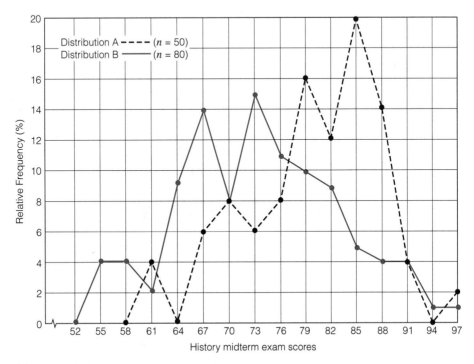

**FIGURE 4.5** Relative frequency polygons used to compare the two score distributions in Table 3.7.

## 4.5 The Bar Diagram and the Pie Chart

**bar diagram**
used for qualitative data, a graph that is similar to a histogram, except that space appears between the rectangles

**pie chart**
used for qualitative data, area in any piece of the pie shows the relative frequency of a category

What should we do when graphing a distribution of qualitative data? In this case, there are two widely used possibilities. Figure 4.6 shows a bar diagram of the distribution of new psychology Ph.D.s in major employment settings. The **bar diagram** is very similar to the histogram and is constructed in the same manner except that *space appears between the rectangles, thus properly suggesting the essential discontinuity of the several categories.* However, within categories, subcategories may be displayed as adjacent bars. For example, in Figure 4.7 the level of education achieved by people in 1968 and 1997 (different categories) is shown for both men and women (subcategories). Because qualitative categories on a nominal scale of measurement have no necessary order, we may arrange them in any order (e.g., in order of their frequencies as in Figure 4.6, if desired). However, for ordinal scales of measurement, the categories should be arranged in order of rank (e.g., freshmen, sophomore, junior, senior).

Another frequently used graph for qualitative data is the **pie chart**. Figure 4.8 shows a pie chart of the same data as in Figure 4.6. Unlike the bar diagram, in which results can be expressed as either raw frequencies or relative frequencies, *pie charts always use relative frequencies.* The area in any piece of the pie is the same fraction of the pie as the frequency of that category is of the total number of cases in the distribution.

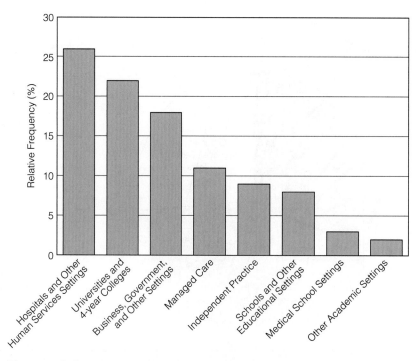

**FIGURE 4.6** Primary employment settings of new American Ph.D.s in psychology. (*Source:* Adapted from the 1999 Doctoral Employment Survey. Copyright © 2000 by the American Psychological Association. Reprinted [or adapted] with permission.)

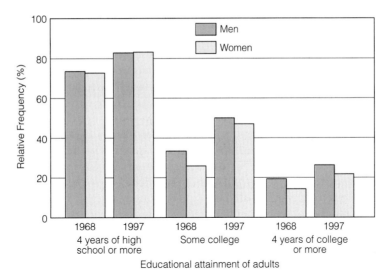

**FIGURE 4.7** Example of a bar diagram for categorical data with subcategories. (*Source:* Census Bureau.)

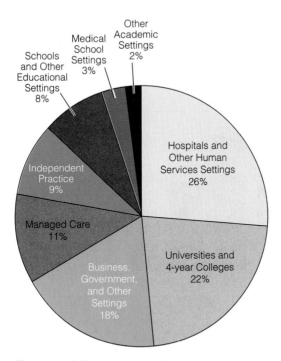

**FIGURE 4.8** Example of a pie chart, showing the primary employment settings of new American Ph.D.s in psychology. (*Source:* Adapted from 1999 Doctoral Employment Survey. Copyright © 2000 by the American Psychological Association. Reprinted [or adapted] with permission.)

# 4.6 The Cumulative Percentage Curve

Both the cumulative frequency distribution and the cumulative percentage distribution can be presented in graphic form. Because their essentials are similar and also because the cumulative percentage curve is widely used in educational and psychological measurement, we will illustrate only this curve.

You will recall that a cumulative percentage indicates the percentage of scores that lies below the upper real limit of the associated class interval (see Section 3.7). Therefore, in constructing a **cumulative percentage curve**, the cumulative percentage is plotted at the upper real limit of the class interval. Note that this procedure differs from that for the frequency polygon, for which we plot class interval frequencies at the midpoint of the interval. The conventions regarding construction that we discussed in Section 4.1 also apply here, including the rule relating height to width.

As an example, let us refer again to the results of Professor Abelard's midterm history exam (see Table 4.1). In Figure 4.9, the upper real limit for each class interval is labeled on the horizontal axis, and cumulative percentage appears on the vertical axis. We then place a point over the upper real limit of each interval corresponding to the cumulative percentage for the interval. For example, the cumulative percentage for the interval 84–86 is 80.0%; therefore, we place a point at the intersection of 86.5 (the upper real limit of the interval) and 80.0%. We then connect the points with straight lines and *bring the curve down to zero at the lower end* at the upper real limit of the next adjacent class interval (in which there were zero scores).

*A cumulative percentage curve never has a negative slope* (that is, it never comes down). For class intervals in which there are zero scores (such as 63–65 and 93–95), the cumulative percentage curve remains horizontal. The curve shows a small rise in intervals with relatively few scores and a sharp rise in intervals with many scores. You can see this by comparing the frequency histogram or polygon of the history exam scores (Figures 4.1 and 4.2) with the cumulative percentage curve in Figure 4.9. Like the

**cumulative percentage curve**

a graph that consists of a series of connected dots above the upper real limits of each possible class interval (height of the dots corresponds to cumulative percentage)

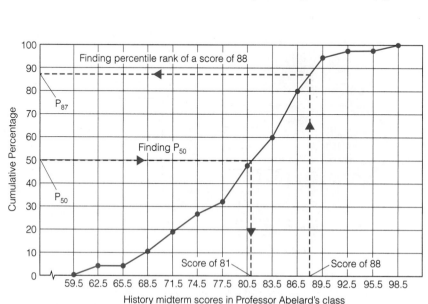

**FIGURE 4.9** Cumulative percentage curve of the grouped history exam scores from Table 4.1.

**ogive curve**

a curve with an
S shape

distribution of history exam scores, many distributions have most of the cases in the middle portion of the distribution. This results in a cumulative percentage curve with an S-shaped figure called an **ogive** (ō′jīv) **curve**.

We may determine percentiles or percentile ranks from the cumulative percentage curve with nearly the same results obtained from the computational procedures outlined in the previous chapter. Connecting the points on the cumulative curve with straight lines is the graphic equivalent of assuming (as we did when computing) that scores are evenly spread throughout the interval. For the history exam scores illustrated in Figure 4.9, for example, we can find the percentile rank of a score of 88 by locating it on the horizontal axis and then moving vertically upward until we intersect the curve. From there we read horizontally to the vertical axis and find the percentile rank to be 87. The process may be reversed as well. To find $P_{50}$, follow the second set of dotted lines from the vertical axis to the intersection with the curve, and then descend to the horizontal axis. Thus, $P_{50} = 81$.

## 4.7  Factors Affecting the Shape of Graphs

There is no such thing as *the* graph of a given set of data. The same set of raw scores may be grouped in different ways, and the grouping will affect the graph of the distribution. For example, the two graphs in Figure 4.10 again show the results of Professor Abelard's history exam scores, but grouped with interval widths of 2 and 4, respectively. Compare the appearance of these two graphs with each other and with Figure 4.1, where $i = 3$. Note how the appearance changes with interval width. All three graphs are properly drawn, and none can be considered to be the "correct" graph for the history exam scores.

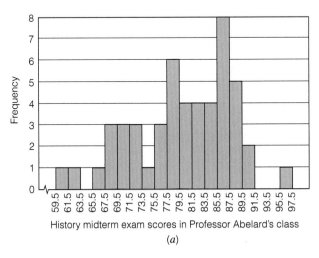

History midterm exam scores in Professor Abelard's class

(a)

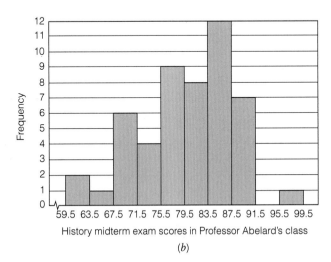

History midterm exam scores in Professor Abelard's class

(b)

**FIGURE 4.10** Histograms of grouped history exam scores from Table 4.1 with (a) $i = 2$ and (b) $i = 4$. Notice that for even-numbered interval widths both the real limits and the midpoints (not shown) are not whole numbers.

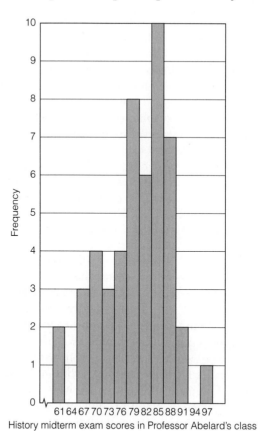

**FIGURE 4.11** Histograms of grouped history exam scores drawn with different relative scales than that shown in Figure 4.1. In all cases the width of the class intervals is 3.

Even more important is the matter of relative scale. Frequencies and scores are like apples and cows; no principle specifies what is an equivalent number of each. Consequently, the decision about relative scale is arbitrary, and the resulting graph can be squat or slender depending on the choice. Figure 4.11 illustrates two different graphs of the data shown in Figure 4.1. The large difference in appearance created by differences in scale is the reason for the convention that the height of the figure should be about three-quarters of the width.

Even if the convention regarding height and width is followed, the same data can appear very different when graphed depending on the scale of measurement used for frequency. Suppose, for example, that two of your classmates are instructed by Professor Abelard to construct a graph of the number of men and women who scored in the top half of the class on the history exam. Both students construct bar diagrams with the same relative scale for height and width (see Figure 4.12), but guess which one wishes to convey that the women were far superior to the men? You will sometimes see graphs with a break in the vertical axis as in Figure 4.12. Never do this! *Frequency on the vertical axis should always be continuous from zero.* When we put a break in the axis, we lose the proportional relationship among class interval frequencies. In Figure 4.12*b*, for example, it incorrectly appears as if women did over twice as well as men. Figure 4.12*a* shows the correct proportional relationship.

If we are interested in learning something about how scores are distributed in a population by examining a sample taken from the population, there is the additional problem of sampling variation or "luck of the draw." *When a limited number of scores is taken from a population, the resulting pattern can be very different from the pattern in the population.* In general, the fewer the cases, the greater the irregular appearance of the distribution. Figure 4.13 shows three samples drawn from a population having a "normal" distribution (which has a regular bell-shaped appearance; see Figure 4.15*f*). Note the closer resemblance to the population distribution as sample size increases. When we have relatively few cases and we wish to see if a pattern exists, we can often reduce irregularity due to chance fluctuation by using fewer class intervals than usual. The greater number of scores in each interval tends to favor a graph of smoother appearance. For example, Figure 4.14 shows three representations of the same raw scores; they differ only in width of interval used in grouping. You can see a pattern in the bottom graph that was not apparent in the top one. We will discuss sampling variation in greater detail in Chapter 12.

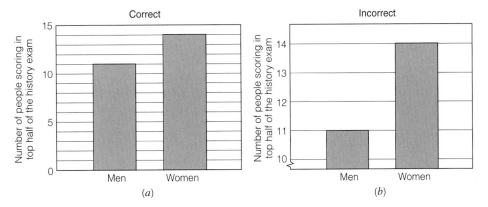

**FIGURE 4.12** Two bar diagrams showing the same results using different scales for frequency. (*a*) The left graph shows the correct proportional relationship between men and women. (*b*) In the right graph, putting a break in the vertical axis results in an incorrect proportional relationship.

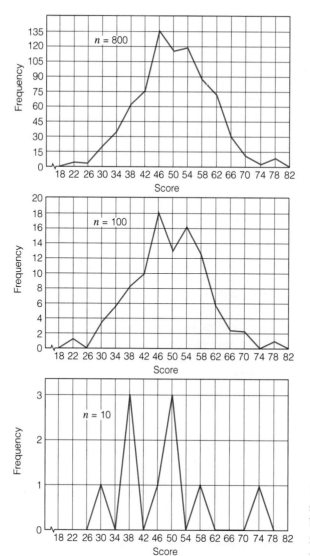

**FIGURE 4.13** Effect of sample size on the regularity of the distribution (samples drawn from a normal bell-shaped distribution such as that shown in Figure 4.15 (*f*).

## 4.8 Characteristics of Frequency Distributions

Three characteristics, taken together, completely describe a distribution of scores. We will introduce them here and examine them in more detail in the next few chapters.

### Shape

What is the pattern of the distribution of scores over the range of possible values? Are most of the scores in the middle, at one end, or clustered in two distinct locations? Certain shapes of frequency distributions occur with enough regularity in statistical work that they have names. The names effectively summarize the general

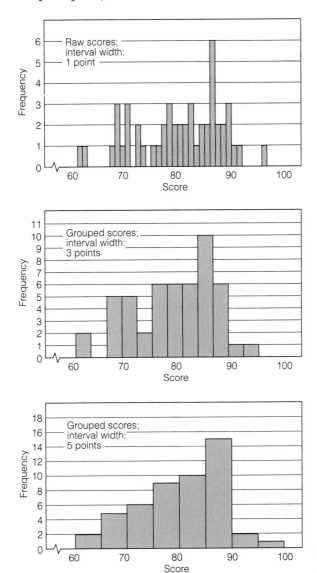

**FIGURE 4.14** Effects of varying width of interval for grouped scores.

characteristics of the distribution. We illustrate several of them in Figure 4.15. The **J-shaped distribution** in Figure 4.15*a* could result from plotting the speeds at which automobiles go through an intersection where a stop sign is present. J-shaped distributions can also have tails that go to the left (from which they take their name). Figures 4.15*b* and 4.15*c* both show **skewed (asymmetrical) distributions.** Figure 4.15*b* is *positively skewed*, or skewed to the right; it might result from a test that is too difficult for most of the group taking it. Figure 4.15*c* is *negatively skewed*, or skewed to the left; it might result from a test that is too easy for most of the group. Figure 4.15*d* is an example of a **rectangular distribution,** where there are an equal number of cases in all class intervals. Figure 4.15*e* shows a **bimodal distribution;** it could result from measuring strength of grip in a group that contained both men and women.

**skewed distribution**

a distribution in which one tail slants to the left (negatively skewed) or to the right (positively skewed)

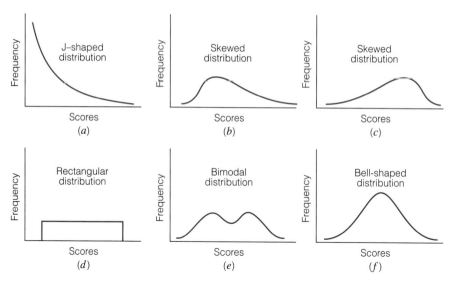

**FIGURE 4.15**   Shapes of some distributions that occur in statistical work.

**kurtosis**

refers to the degree of peakedness of a graphed distribution

Figure 4.15*f* shows a **bell-shaped distribution**. A specific type of bell-shaped distribution, called the *normal curve*, is of great importance in statistical inference. **Kurtosis** refers to the degree of peakedness of a graphed distribution. If a distribution is flatter than the normal curve, we refer to it as *platykurtic*. It is called *leptokurtic* if more peaked, and *mesokurtic* if it has the same peakedness as a normal distribution.

We will say more about the shape of distributions in the next chapter. Most of Chapter 7 will be devoted to the normal distribution.

## Central Tendency

Where, on the scale of possible scores, is a point that best represents the overall level (high, medium, low) of the set of scores? This is a question about central tendency. Two distributions that differ only in central tendency are shown in Figure 4.16*a*. How big is the difference? We could find the averages of the two distributions and compare them. But there are other measures of central tendency that we could use for that comparison as well. You will learn about some of them in the next chapter.

## Variability

Do the scores cluster tightly about their central point or do they spread out around it? How much do they spread out? These are questions of the variability among the scores. Two distributions that differ only in variability are shown in Figure 4.16*b*. Again, a quantitative measure of variability would be helpful. A simple one is the range, the difference between the highest and lowest scores. Other measures of variability are often better, and you will learn about them in Chapter 6.

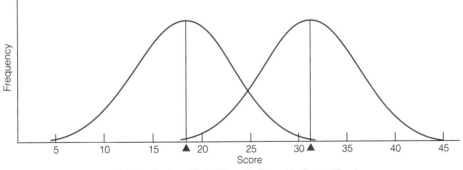

(*a*) Distributions That Differ with Regard to Central Tendency.

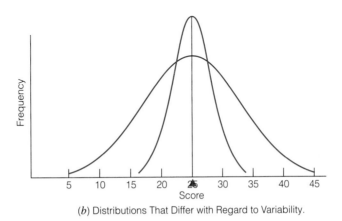

(*b*) Distributions That Differ with Regard to Variability.

**FIGURE 4.16** Differences in central tendency and variability of frequency distributions.

## 4.9 Summary

Graphs often make it easier to see certain characteristics and trends in a set of data. The histogram and the frequency polygon are two important ways of representing a frequency distribution of quantitative data. In the histogram, frequency is represented by the height of adjacent bars erected at the real limits of the class intervals. In the frequency polygon, frequency is indicated by points plotted above the midpoint of each interval. These points are then connected by straight lines. Frequency or relative frequency can be plotted with either graph. A special advantage of the histogram is the exact relationship that exists between area in a bar (or bars) and the frequency of cases in the distribution. It is often preferable for discrete variables, particularly when scores are ungrouped. On the other hand, the frequency polygon better suggests the continuity of a variable and is often preferable for a grouped distribution or for comparing distributions.

Bar diagrams and pie charts are used for qualitative data. The gaps between the bars of a bar diagram emphasize the discontinuity of categorical data.

Cumulative percentage is graphed by plotting points above the upper real limit for each class interval. The straight lines between the points allow us to quickly find percentile ranks and percentiles (when the graph is carefully drawn).

Conventions for constructing graphs help ensure that people working with the same data will construct similar graphs. Nevertheless, different pictures can result from grouping scores in different ways and from using different scales on the horizontal or vertical axes. Thus, there is no such thing as *the* graph of a set of scores.

## Key Terms, Concepts, and Symbols

abscissa   (46)

*X* axis   (46)

ordinate   (46)

*Y* axis   (46)

zero point on a graph   (46)

histogram   (47)

interval midpoint   (48)

frequency polygon   (48)

bar diagram   (52)

pie chart   (52)

cumulative percentage curve   (54)

ogive curve   (55)

J-shaped distribution   (59)

skewed distribution   (59)

rectangular distribution   (59)

bimodal distribution   (59)

bell-shaped distribution   (60)

kurtosis   (60)

## Problems

1. It has been said that a statistically knowledgeable person would rather inspect a frequency distribution than a graph. What supports this position? What is an argument against it?

2. In making a histogram of the data for Class B in Table 3.7, you would draw a series of bars. For each of the following class intervals, state over what point on the abscissa you would place the left side of the bar and over what point you would place the right side of the bar: (a) 57–59, (b) 66–68, (c) 75–77, (d) 84–86, (e) 93–95.

3. (a) Construct a histogram from the data for Class B in Table 3.7. (b) Construct a relative frequency histogram (expressed as percentages) from the same data.

4. In making a frequency polygon of the data for Class B in Table 3.7, you would place dots over various locations on the abscissa. For each of the following class intervals, state over what point the dot would go: (a) 60–62, (b) 69–71, (c) 78–80, (d) 87–89, (e) 96–98.

5. (a) Construct a frequency polygon from the data for Class B in Table 3.7. (b) Construct a relative frequency polygon (using percentages) from the same data.

6. On a 30-point political science exam, scores ranged from 2 to 30. When constructing a frequency polygon with $i = 3$, discuss the problems with bringing the polygon down to the horizontal axis from the midpoint of the intervals 1–3 and 28–30. What should you do in a case like this?

7. (a) Construct a frequency histogram from the data for the Good Mood condition in Data 3B (Problem 15) in Chapter 3. (b) Construct a frequency polygon from the same data.

8. In a university, male psychology majors are distributed as follows: 24 freshmen, 61 sophomores, 109 juniors, 104 seniors, and 92 graduate students. Comparable figures for females are 74, 58, 99, 53, and 67, respectively. Construct a bar diagram suitable for comparing the sexes. What conclusions do the data suggest?

9. From the data in Problem 8, construct a pie chart for males.

10. By the start of 2001, the cumulative number of reported cases of AIDS in the United States was 774,467. Of those diagnosed with AIDS in 2000, 32.2% were homosexual or bisexual males, 20.2% were intravenous drug users, 3.7% were both homosexual and IV

drug users, 0.9% were people who were infected during blood transfusions (hemophiliacs, persons with coagulation disorders, or those who received blood during surgery), 15.5% were people who contracted it by heterosexual intimate contacts, 0.4% were pediatric cases, and 27.1% contracted it from undetermined sources. Construct a relative frequency distribution in graph form for these data in two different ways.

**DATA 4A:**  *Reaction Time in Milliseconds*

| TIME | SIMPLE STIMULUS f | COMPLEX STIMULUS f |
|---|---|---|
| 300–319 | 1 | 3 |
| 280–299 | 1 | 6 |
| 260–279 | 2 | 10 |
| 240–259 | 4 | 18 |
| 220–239 | 3 | 25 |
| 200–219 | 6 | 35 |
| 180–199 | 11 | 28 |
| 160–179 | 12 | 16 |
| 140–159 | 8 | 7 |
| 120–139 | 2 | 2 |
| | $n = 50$ | $n = 150$ |

**11.** Plot relative frequency polygons for the two sets of scores in Data 4A on the same graph. Compare the two distributions and record your conclusions.

**12.** For the reaction times to complex stimuli in Data 4A; (a) Tabulate the cumulative frequencies. (b) Convert the cumulative frequencies to cumulative percentage and tabulate them. (c) Plot the cumulative percentage curve. (d) Find graphically $P_{20}$ and $P_{60}$. Show with dotted lines how you found $P_{20}$. (e) Find graphically the percentile rank of scores of 195 and 245. Show with dotted lines how you found the percentile rank for 195.

**13.** Repeat parts (a) through (d) of Problem 12 for the Good Mood condition in Data 3B in Chapter 3. Find the percentile rank of a score of 137.

**14.** After you have completed Problem 13, find graphically the 20th percentile point.

**15.** Figure 4.5 shows the frequency polygons for the two distributions given in Table 3.7. (a) Construct cumulative percentage curves for these distributions, plotting them on the same graph for comparison. (b) How does the higher level of performance in Distribution A show up in these curves? (c) How does the greater spread of Distribution B show up in these curves? (d) Study your cumulative curves in comparison with the noncumulated ones in Figure 4.5. Which type of representation appears smoother? (e) For what kind of question is each type of curve best suited to provide information?

**16.** Would there be any difference in the shape of a cumulative frequency curve and a cumulative percentage curve if both were constructed from the same basic frequency distribution and if height and width were the same for both types of graph? Explain.

**17.** The cumulative curve tends toward an S-shape when the noncumulated distribution has more scores in the center than elsewhere. Draw an approximation to the cumulative curve that would result if the noncumulated distribution had a shape like that pictured in (a) Figure 4.15*b;* (b) Figure 4.15*c;* (c) Figure 4.15*d;* (d) Figure 4.15*e.*

**18.** For each of the following distributions, describe the shape of a frequency polygon constructed from the data (using the terms in Figure 4.15). If you guess that a distribution is skewed or J-shaped, say whether the tail is on the left or the right. (a) For all Americans who earned wages or a salary last year, their income for that year. (b) For 523 college seniors, the number of correct answers on a 50-item arithmetic test intended for sixth graders. (c) For 523 sixth graders, the number of correct answers on a 50-item spelling test intended for college seniors. (d) For all living people who hold a New Jersey driver's license, the age at which the person first got the license (the minimum age is 17). (e) For all those college professors in North America who have exactly one child in grade school, and for those children, the time required to read the first page of this text. (f) For all female students around the world enrolled in a statistics course this semester, their weight. (g) For all male students enrolled in a statistics course this semester, their height.

# CHAPTER 5

## Central Tendency

When you have finished studying this chapter, you should be able to:

- Understand what is meant by "measure of central tendency";
- Calculate the mode, median, and mean for ungrouped and grouped distributions;
- Appreciate the unique properties of the mode, median, and the mean;
- Understand how each of the three measures of central tendency is influenced by sampling fluctuation;
- Describe where each measure of central tendency falls in symmetrical and skewed distributions; and
- Understand how each of the measures of central tendency is affected by adding a constant to each score, subtracting a constant from each score, or by multiplying or dividing each score by a constant.

The principal of Middlebury High School wishes to know how students in her school compare to students nationally on the California Achievement Test (CAT). This exam tests students' knowledge in a variety of subjects and is one measure often used to see if they are making normal progress. For each subject, she could set the two distributions of scores side by side and compare them, but this will give her only an approximate answer. Instead, she finds the *average* score of each group and compares them.

**measure of central tendency**
a single summary figure that describes the central location of an entire distribution of observations

Measures of this type are called **measures of central tendency**. Their purpose is to provide a single summary figure that best describes the central location of an entire distribution of observations. As we have just seen, a measure of central tendency is helpful in comparing the performance of a group with that of a standard reference group. With one quick comparison of the CAT averages for her school and those nationally, the principal will be able to get an indication of whether her students *as a group* need additional instruction in any subject.

A measure of central tendency also helps simplify comparison of two or more groups tested under different conditions. For example, we may be interested in whether video games can improve mental or physical functioning in the elderly. In one study, psychologists administered an IQ test to 11 volunteers in their 60s and 70s, then gave them 30 minutes of play on a video game twice a week for 2 months, and then tested them again. The average IQ was 101.8 before the 2-month intervention and 108.3 afterward (Drew & Waters, 1985). We would need to know more than this to conclude that video games improve mental functioning in the elderly, but as a first step, a comparison of the group averages suggests that it might.

There are many measures of central tendency. We will consider only the three most commonly used in education and the behavioral sciences: *mode, median,* and *arithmetic mean*. Each of them has unique properties that make them useful in different situations. We will briefly introduce each and then return to discuss their properties in more detail.

## 5.1 The Mode

**mode**
the score that appears with the greatest frequency

**Mo**
symbol for the mode

A common meaning of *mode* is "fashionable," and its meaning in statistics is similar. In ungrouped distributions, the **mode** is the score that occurs with the greatest frequency. For example, in Table 3.2 the mode is 86. In grouped data, it is taken as the midpoint of the class interval that contains the greatest number of scores. Thus, if we did not know the raw scores, we would calculate the mode for the grouped scores in Column A of Table 3.4 as 85. The symbol for the mode is *Mo*.

## 5.2 The Median

**median**
the value that divides the distribution into halves; another name for $P_{50}$.

**Mdn**
symbol for the median

The **median** of a distribution is the point along the scale of possible scores below which 50% of the scores fall. Thus, the median is the value that divides the distribution into halves. Its symbol is *Mdn*. Look again at Section 3.8. You can see that the median is another name for $P_{50}$.

For raw scores, we may think of the median as the middle score of a distribution based on score frequency. To find the median, *we first put the scores in rank order from* lowest to highest. (We must include scores of zero as well.) If $n$ (or $N$) is odd, the median will be the score that has an equal number of scores below and above it. For example, for the following scores:

$$0, 7, 8, 11, 15, 16, 20$$

the median is 11. When there is an even number of scores, there is no middle score, so the median is taken as the point halfway between the two scores that bracket the middle position. For example, for the group of scores:

$$12, 14, 15, 18, 19, 20$$

the median is $15 + (18 - 15)/2 = 16.5$. The only problem occurs when there are repeating scores. For example, what is the median for the following set of scores?

$$5, 7, 8, 8, 8, 8$$

The median is halfway between the first 8 and second 8. In cases like this, some people prefer to simply call the median 8. However, to determine the median precisely requires interpolation. In this example, 8 represents all scores between the lower real limit of 7.5 and the upper real limit of 8.5. Because the median comes after the first of the four 8's, or one-quarter of the way through the interval width of 1.0, we calculate the median by interpolation as $7.5 + (1/4 \times 1.0) = 7.75$.

We gave the procedures for calculating $P_{50}$ for grouped data in Section 3.9 and, you recall, the median may also be determined graphically from the cumulative percentage distribution (see Section 4.6). We provided a formula to find a percentile point in Mathematical Note 3.1. The formula for finding $P_{50}$ would appear as follows:

COMPUTATIONAL
FORMULA FOR
THE MEDIAN

$$Mdn = P_{50} = LL + (i)\left(\frac{.5n - cum\ f\ \text{below}}{f}\right) \tag{5.1}$$

*where:*

$LL$ = lower real limit of class interval containing $P_{50}$
$i$ = width of the class interval
$.5n$ = half the cases (i.e., number of scores lying below the median)
$cum\ f$ below = number of scores lying below $LL$
$f$ = frequency of scores in the interval containing the median

Thus, to calculate the median for the grouped data in Table 3.11,

$$P_{50} = 71.5 + (3)\left(\frac{40 - 32}{12}\right)$$

$$= 71.5 + (3)(8/12)$$

$$= 71.5 + 2$$

$$= 73.5$$

This is the same answer we arrived at in Section 3.9 without an explicit formula. The formula only expresses mathematically the steps we outlined in that section. Review that section and be sure you understand the concepts before using the formula.

# 5.3 The Arithmetic Mean

**arithmetic mean**
the sum of all the scores divided by the total number of scores

The **arithmetic mean** is the sum of all the scores in a distribution divided by the total number of scores. Many people call this measure the average, but we will avoid this term because it is sometimes used indiscriminately for any measure of central tendency. For brevity, the arithmetic mean is usually called the *mean*.

Some symbolism is needed to express the mean mathematically. We will use the capital letter $X$ as a collective term to specify a particular set of scores. (Be sure to use capital letters; lowercase letters are used in a different way.) We identify an individual score in the distribution by a subscript, such as $X_1$ (the first score), $X_8$ (the eighth score), and so forth. You remember that $n$ stands for the number of scores in a sample and $N$ for the number in a population. The last score in a sample can therefore be symbolized $X_n$; in a population it would be $X_N$. Thus a set of scores in a sample may be represented like this:

**$X$**
symbol that serves as a collective term to specify a particular set of scores

$$X: X_1, X_2, X_3, \ldots, X_n$$

**$\Sigma$**
capital Greek letter sigma, read "the sum of"; gives instructions to sum whatever follows

When scores are to be summed, we use the capital Greek letter sigma, $\Sigma$, to indicate this. It should be read "the sum of" whatever follows. It is not called "sigma" because the lowercase sigma ($\sigma$) has a different meaning in statistics (as we shall see in the next chapter), and confusion would result. Use of this symbol is illustrated as follows.

$$\sum X = X_1 + X_2 + X_3 + \cdots + X_n$$

When two groups of scores are involved, we will use the letter $Y$ to symbolize the second set. If you need to review rules about summations, turn to Appendix B.

**$\overline{X}$**
symbol for the mean of a sample of scores (X)

The distinction between the mean of a sample and that of a population is important in inferential statistics, so there are two symbols for the mean. The mean of a sample is represented by $\overline{X}$, read as "X bar." The mean of a population is symbolized by $\mu$ (the Greek letter *mu*, pronounced "mew"). The defining formulas are:

**$\mu_x$**
Greek letter mu with subscript; symbol for the mean of a population of scores (X)

**$\mu_x = \dfrac{\Sigma X}{N}$**
formula for the mean of a population

**$\overline{X} = \dfrac{\Sigma X}{n}$**
formula for the mean of a sample

DEFINITIONAL (RAW SCORE) FORMULAS FOR THE MEAN

$$\mu_X = \frac{\sum X}{N} \quad \text{(mean of a population)} \tag{5.2a}$$

$$\overline{X} = \frac{\sum X}{n} \quad \text{(mean of a sample)} \tag{5.2b}$$

This distinction between sample and population is not crucial at a purely descriptive level, so to avoid unnecessary complication, we will use symbolism appropriate to samples whenever possible in these early chapters.

As an example, let us calculate the mean for the three scores 31.0, 21.0, and 42.0:

$$X: 31.0, 21.0, 42.0$$

$$\sum X = 31.0 + 21.0 + 42.0 = 94.0$$

Therefore the mean for this distribution is:

$$\overline{X} = \frac{\sum X}{n} = \frac{94.0}{3} = 31.3$$

When scores are grouped (and the raw scores are unavailable), we know only that those in a given interval lie somewhere between the lower real limit and the upper real limit. To proceed, *we assume that the midpoint of the interval is the mean of the scores in that interval,* and we use it to represent the scores in the interval. To calculate the sum of scores ($\sum X$), we multiply each midpoint by the number of cases in the corresponding interval and then sum these products over all class intervals.

## 5.4 Properties of the Mode

*The mode is easy to obtain, but it is not very stable* from sample to sample. Further, when quantitative data are grouped, the mode may be strongly affected by the width and location of class intervals. Look, for example, at Table 3.4. In addition, *there may be more than one mode for a particular set of scores.* (This, however, may be very useful information.) In a rectangular distribution the ultimate is reached: Every score shares the honor! For these reasons, the mean or the median is often preferred with numerical data. However, *the mode is the only measure that can be used for data that have the character of a nominal scale.* For example, no other measure of central tendency is appropriate for a distribution of eye color.

Some years ago, a national magazine made use of the mode in a way that capitalized ideally on its virtues. The magazine reported subscribers' ratings of motion pictures as excellent (E), good (G), fair (F), or poor (P). The large number of pictures so rated was arranged alphabetically, coupled with the relative frequency distribution of ratings (expressed as a percentage). A hypothetical illustration is as follows:

|  | E | G | F | P |
|---|---|---|---|---|
| *Purple Passion* | 0 | 10 | 40 | **50** |
| *Puzzle Me Not* | 5 | **55** | 25 | 15 |

As shown in the illustration, the modal relative frequency was printed in boldface type. The prospective theater goer could quickly examine the "excellent" and "good" columns and find the most promising movies.

## 5.5 Properties of the Mean

Unlike the other measures of central tendency, *the mean is responsive to the exact position of each score in the distribution.* Inspect the basic formula $\sum X/n$. It shows that increasing or decreasing the value of any score changes $\sum X$ and thus also changes the value of the mean.

*The mean may be thought of as the balance point of a distribution*, to use a mechanical analogy. If we imagine a seesaw consisting of a fulcrum (balance point), a board, and the scores of a distribution spread along the board like bricks (one brick for each score), the mean corresponds to the position of the fulcrum when the system is in balance. You can see this in Figure 5.1. As with the ordinary seesaw, if one brick (score) is shifted, the balance point will also change.

There is an algebraic way of stating that the mean is the balance point for a distribution: $\Sigma(X - \overline{X}) = 0$.[1] This says that if we express the scores in terms of the amount by which they deviate from their mean, taking into account the negative and positive deviations (scores below the mean deviate negatively from the mean), their sum is zero. To put it another way, *the sum of the negative deviations from the mean exactly equals the sum of the positive deviations*. Figure 5.1 shows that $\Sigma(X - \overline{X}) = 0$ for the data given. We provide a general proof of this proposition in Note 5.1 at the end of the chapter.

*The mean is more sensitive to the presence (or absence) of scores at the extremes of the distribution* than are the median or (ordinarily) the mode. We will discuss this property of the mean further when we examine the properties of the median.

*When a measure of central tendency should reflect the total of the scores, the mean is the best choice* because it is the only measure based on this quantity. If a track coach wants to know whether the four best quarter-milers have improved as a group, the mean will best suit the purpose because the coach has an underlying interest in the total time as an indicator of how the runners would do as a relay team. Similarly, insurance companies express life expectancy as a mean because it is most closely related to their primary concerns, which are total dollars of income from policyholders and total payoffs to survivors.

**$(X - \overline{X})$**
a **deviation score**; shows by how much a score differs from the mean

---

[1] $\Sigma(X - \overline{X})$ means: $(X_1 - \overline{X}) + (X_2 - \overline{X}) + \cdots + (X_n - \overline{X})$. For example, for the three scores 3, 4, 5, $\Sigma(X - \overline{X}) = (3 - 4) + (4 - 4) + (5 - 4) = 0$.

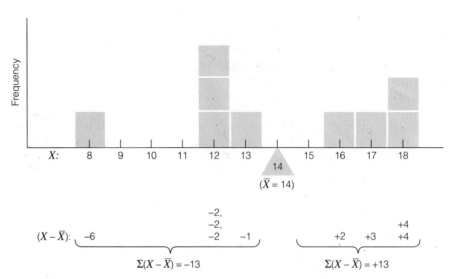

**FIGURE 5.1**   The mean as the balance point of a distribution.

## Point of Controversy

### Is It Permissible to Calculate the Mean for Psychological and Educational Tests?

> Colleges should be free to pay salaries to their athletes.
> Strongly disagree  −3  −2  −1  0  +1  +2  +3  Strongly agree

Questionnaires with items like this are common. To indicate their attitudes, respondents circle numbers.

How shall we summarize a batch of such numbers? Most researchers would do a little arithmetic—addition and division—and find the mean. But critics (e.g., Siegel & Castellan, 1988) would say, "Not so fast. Those operations are permissible only if the scores derive from measurement of the most sophisticated kinds. Are you sure your measurement is good enough to justify calculating a mean?"

The most sophisticated measurements employ a ratio scale. As Section 2.3 reported, a ratio scale is one whose zero point represents an absence of the quantity that the scale measures. But "0" on the scale above certainly does not indicate the absence of an attitude; it merely signifies an attitude that is neither favorable nor unfavorable—perhaps ambivalence or indecision.

Interval-level measurement would still justify calculating means, according to the critics. Does the scale above fall at least at the interval level? It's doubtful. Consider two attitudes, one represented by −3 and the other by −2. The difference between those attitudes in favorability to salaries for college athletes is probably not the same as the difference in favorability between attitudes represented by, say, +1 and +2. So a one-point difference between scores does not necessarily signify an equal difference in attitudes all along the scale.

Does the scale then fall only at the ordinal level of measurement? If so, the seven numbers along the scale would indicate only a rank ordering from the least favorable attitude to the most favorable. But there is probably more information in the numbers than that. A two-point difference between scores probably signifies a greater difference in favorability than a one-point difference.

Measurement on this scale is therefore likely to lie somewhere between the ordinal and the interval levels of sophistication. So it is with many other measuring instruments used in psychology and education—with inventories of moods like anger and elation, with assessments of personality traits like extraversion and conscientiousness, with tests of aptitudes and achievements. They do not yield scores that carry as much intrinsic meaning as, say, temperatures and weights, but they tell us more than ranks do.

So are we or are we not justified in calculating the mean to summarize a batch of such scores? The debate continues (Davison & Sharma, 1988, 1990; Maxwell & Delaney, 1985; Townsend & Ashby, 1984). By a strict interpretation of the theory of measurement presented in Section 2.4, no; we should use the median. (And in doing inferential work on such data, according to the strict interpretation, we should avoid the popular *t* and *F* tests described in later chapters. One defense of the theory of Section 2.4

thunders, "Performing sophisticated analyses that are appropriate for one scale of measurement . . . on data that reflect a less structured scale . . . yields nonsense. The nonsense might be interpreted, but it will be nonsense nonetheless" (Stine, 1989, p. 154). In an extreme example, some researchers have even calculated means and performed advanced statistical tests on data that fall only at the nominal scale of measurement (see Whitley, 1992).

However, most researchers are not so strict, at least for data that lie somewhere between the ordinal and interval scales or higher (e.g., Glass & Hopkins, 1996; Kirk, 1990). They reject the counsel of those who would sharply limit the "permissible statistics" for the scores common in the behavioral sciences.

Some authorities even reject the theory that distinguishes the four levels of measurement (e.g., Adams, 1966; Rozeboom, 1966). In the physical sciences it may make sense to posit some real quantity, such as heat or mass, that researchers hope to capture in numbers, but in the behavioral sciences the phenomena of interest are typically hypothetical. Attitudes, moods, traits, and abilities do not literally exist. Instead of the four levels of measurement, James Terwilliger (1978) of the University of Minnesota argues that we should distinguish three ways to index phenomena: classification systems, ranking techniques, and measurement procedures. Instead of rigidly limiting the algebraic operations on researchers' and teachers' scores, he would welcome any operations that yield lawful relationships and accurate predictions.

*When we need to do further statistical computation, the mean is likely to be the most useful of the measures of central tendency.* One reason for this is that the mean is amenable to arithmetic and algebraic manipulation in ways that the other measures are not. At the moment, it is enough to remark that the mean is often incorporated implicitly or explicitly in other statistical procedures.

One of the most important characteristics of the mean is its stability from sample to sample. Suppose we draw a series of samples from a population of scores. Each sample is the same size, and each is a random selection from the available population of scores. Because chance affects which scores get into the samples, the means of these samples will vary. The medians of the samples will also vary, and so will the modes. However, if a distribution is bell-shaped (resembling the curve shown in Figure 4.15*f*), the means of the successive samples will vary the least among themselves. That is, *under these circumstances, the mean is most resistant to chance sampling variation.* This resistance makes the mean a valuable indicator of what is true about the population with regard to central tendency. We will discuss this virtue further when we get to statistical inference.

## 5.6 Properties of the Median

**outlier**
a very extreme score in a distribution (see Chapter 6)

The median responds to how many scores lie below (or above) it but not to how far away the scores may be. A little below the median or a lot, both count the same in determining its value. Thus, *the median is less sensitive than the mean to the presence of a few extreme scores* (called **outliers**). Consider, for example, the money earned by the

## THE FAR SIDE® BY GARY LARSON

© 1988 FarWorks, Inc. All Rights Reserved/Dist. by Creators Syndicate

"Bob and Ruth! Come on in. ... Have you met
Russell and Bill, our 1.5 children?"

The Far Side® by Gary Larson © 1988
FarWorks, Inc. All Rights Reserved. Used
with permission.

top 200 professionals on the men's PGA (golf) tour (see Table 5.1). The mean earning is $763,448, but the median is $484,166. The money earned by the best player, Tiger Woods, is nearly twice as great as that of the second-ranked player, Phil Mickelson, and Mickelson's earnings were over $1 million greater than the third-ranked player. The earnings of these two players strongly affect the total, and hence the mean, but their values do not affect the median. If Tiger Woods had earned $4 million less, the median would still be the same. In this case, the median is closer than the mean to the aggregate of all the salaries. Therefore in *distributions that are strongly asymmetrical (skewed) or have a few very deviant scores, the median may be the better choice for measuring the central tendency* if we wish to represent the bulk of the scores and not give undue weight to the relatively few deviant ones. We will discuss skewed distributions further in the next section.

In behavioral studies, there are occasions when a researcher cannot record the exact values of scores at the upper end of a distribution. Social psychologists studying behavior in emergencies, for example, may record reaction times. During a 5-minute ride between two stops on a subway line, a confederate of the experimenters pretends to collapse. How long does it take before a bystander comes over to help? On most trials, somebody does come to see what's wrong, and the reaction time ranges from a few seconds to a few minutes. But what about those few trials in which nobody moves until the next stop and the confederate has to get up to avoid being trampled by boarding passengers? (It's happened, as Piliavin, Rodin, and Piliavin, 1969, observed.) The score for such a trial should be greater than the time it took to get

TABLE **5.1**   *Money Earned by the Top 200 Players on the 2000 PGA Tour*

| RANK | PLAYER | MONEY ($) |
|------|--------|-----------|
| 1 | Tiger Woods | 9,188,321 |
| 2 | Phil Mickelson | 4,746,457 |
| 3 | Ernie Els | 3,469,405 |
| 4 | Hal Sutton | 3,061,444 |
| 5 | Vijay Singh | 2,573,835 |
| 6 | Mike Weir | 2,547,829 |
| 7 | David Duval | 2,462,846 |
| 8 | Jesper Parnevik | 2,413,345 |
| 9 | Davis Love III | 2,337,765 |
| 10 | Stewart Cink | 2,169,727 |
| . | . | . |
| . | . | . |
| . | . | . |
| 96 | David Sutherland | 498,749 |
| 97 | Scott McCarron | 495,975 |
| 98 | Olin Browne | 494,307 |
| 99 | Brandel Chamblee | 493,906 |
| 100 | Woody Austin | 485,589 |
| 101 | Glen Hnatluk | 482,744 |
| 102 | Brian Gay | 482,028 |
| 103 | Bradley Hughes | 469,590 |
| 104 | Shaun Micheel | 467,431 |
| 105 | Neal Lancaster | 466,712 |
| . | . | . |
| . | . | . |
| . | . | . |
| 196 | Brian Claar | 90,959 |
| 197 | Curtis Strange | 90,387 |
| 198 | Eric Booker | 88,615 |
| 199 | D. A. Welbring | 87,620 |
| 200 | Jason Caron | 87,110 |

**open-ended distribution**

a distribution for which exact scores cannot be recorded at one end of the distribution

to the next stop, but we do not know how much greater. Distributions like this one are called open-ended. In **open-ended distributions**, we cannot calculate the mean without making assumptions, but we can find the median.

Of the three measures of central tendency we have considered, *the median stands second to the mean in ability to resist the influence of sampling fluctuation in ordinary circumstances.* For large samples taken from a normal distribution, the median varies about one-quarter more from sample to sample than does the mean. For small samples, the difference between the two is smaller, but the median still varies more than the mean.

Although the mean is frequently used in advanced statistical procedures, the median is not. It has some use in inferential statistics, but much less than the mean.

# 5.7 Measures of Central Tendency in Symmetrical and Asymmetrical Distributions

In distributions that are perfectly symmetrical—that is, those in which the left half is a mirror image of the right half—the mean, the median, and (if the distribution is unimodal) the mode all have the same value. It is important to note that the normal distribution (Figure 4.15*f*) falls in this category. Figure 5.2 shows what happens to the mean, median, and mode in **skewed distributions** as compared with the normal distribution. If the mean and median of a distribution have different values, the distribution cannot be symmetrical. Furthermore, the more skewed, or lopsided, the distribution is, the greater the discrepancy between these two measures.

**skewed distribution**
a distribution in which one tail slants to the left (**negatively skewed**) or to the right (**positively skewed**)

We describe the distribution pictured in Figure 5.2*a* as *skewed to the left or* **negatively skewed**, and that in Figure 5.2*b* as *skewed to the right* or **positively skewed**. This nomenclature is easy to remember if you think of a closed fist with the inside of the hand facing you and the thumb sticking out. If the fist represents the bulk of the scores and the thumb represents the tail of the distribution, the thumb points to the direction in which skewness exists (see Figure 5.2).

In a smooth, negatively skewed distribution (Figure 5.2*a*), the mode has the highest value, and the median falls at a point about two-thirds of the distance between the mode and the mean. The mean, as might be expected, has been specially affected by the fewer but relatively extreme scores in the tail and thus has the lowest value. In a positively skewed distribution (Figure 5.2*b*), exactly the opposite situation exists.[2]

---

[2]Remember that the position of the score along the horizontal axis indicates the value of these measures of central tendency and not the height of the ordinate erected at these points. The height is simply an indicator of relative frequency of scores at the particular location.

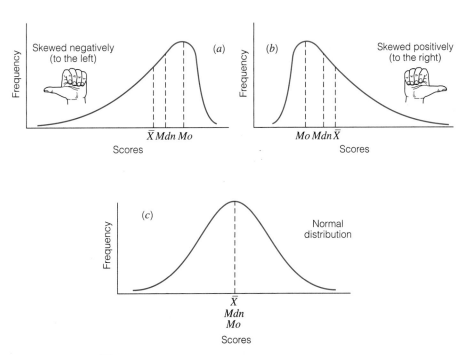

**FIGURE 5.2**    $\overline{X}$, *Mdn,* and *Mo* in skewed distributions and in the normal distribution.

As a consequence, we can use the relative position of the median and the mean to determine the direction of skewness without looking at the entire distribution. The magnitude of the discrepancy between the two measures gives us a general idea about the degree of skewness as well. For example, doctors at Johns Hopkins School of Medicine accumulated records on 10,000 consecutive births. For women giving birth to their first child, the modal duration of labor was 4 hours, the median 10.6 hours, and the mean 13.0 hours (Guttmacher, 1973). This order matches that for a positive skew, and though we don't know for sure that the distribution had that shape, the supposition makes sense. Probably a few women delivered quickly, most mothers took an intermediate length of time, some continued for many hours, and a few had exceptionally long labors.

We can also obtain information about symmetry from an examination of the comparative locations of $P_{25}$, $P_{50}$ (the median), and $P_{75}$. These three percentile points divide the area (and hence the frequency of scores) of the distribution into four equal parts. In the negatively skewed distribution, the distance between $P_{25}$ and $P_{50}$ is greater than that between $P_{50}$ and $P_{75}$. In the positively skewed distribution, the opposite is true. Figure 5.3 shows these characteristics. In manuals accompanying mental tests, these figures are often available, and a quick inspection tells us quite a bit about the distribution of performance of the group on which the test was standardized.

For some data we may wish to calculate more than one measure of central tendency. Why? Because each measure conveys a different kind of information. For example, all three measures are useful for summarizing the distribution of American household incomes. In 1998, the income common to the greatest number of households was about $25,000, half the households earned less than $38,885, and the mean income was $50,600. Reporting only one of these measures of central tendency might be misleading and perhaps reflect a bias.

## 5.8 The Effects of Score Transformations

**score transformation**
a process that changes every score in a distribution to one on a different scale

A **score transformation** is a process that changes every score in a distribution to one on a different scale. In later chapters we will introduce some statistical procedures that require such a change. How will this affect our measures of central tendency?

Consider the following set of scores: 4, 5, 9. Their mean is 6. If we add 10 points to each score, they become 14, 15, 19, and their mean is now 16, 10 points higher.

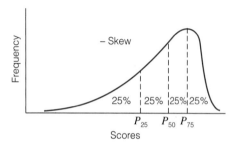
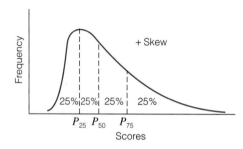

**FIGURE 5.3**  Relative positions of $P_{25}$, $P_{50}$, and $P_{75}$ in negatively and positively skewed distributions.

If some constant amount is added to each score in a distribution, the entire distribution is shifted up by the amount of the constant, and the mean will be increased by that same amount. Similarly, if we subtract a constant from each score, the mean will be reduced by that amount. Other measures of central tendency discussed in this chapter are affected in the same way.

Scores may also be transformed by multiplying or dividing each score by a constant. If we multiply the scores 4, 5, and 9 by 2, they become 8, 10, and 18; if we multiply by 10, they become 40, 50, and 90. Whereas the mean of the original set is 6, the mean of the second set is 12 (twice as large), and the mean of the third set is 60 (10 times as large). Thus, if we multiply each score by a constant, the mean also multiplies by that amount. Similarly, if we divide each score by a constant, it has the effect of dividing the mean by that amount. If we divide each score in the original set by 10, the resultant scores are .4, .5, and .9, and their mean is .6, a value one-tenth of the original mean. The effect of multiplication or division by a constant holds true also for the mode and median.

**linear transformation**

a score transformation that preserves a straight-line relationship between the original scores and their transformations

The transformations described above all fall under the heading of **linear transformations**, so called because they preserve a proportional, or straight-line, relationship between the original scores and their transformations.

## 5.9 Summary

A measure of central tendency provides a single summary figure that describes the central location of a distribution of scores. These measures can be particularly useful when we want to compare the performance of two or more groups on the same variable. Three measures are in common use: mode, median, and arithmetic mean.

The mode is the only measure that can be used for qualitative data. It describes what score or category appears most frequently. The mode sometimes is not a unique point in the distribution, and with grouped data it is more affected by the choice of class interval than are other measures. The mode is also subject to substantial sampling variation and thus is of little use in inferential statistics.

The median shows the point along the scale of possible scores that divides the lower half of scores from the upper half. It is responsive to the number of scores above or below it but not to their magnitude and thus is less affected by extreme scores than the mean.

The mean is the sum of all the scores divided by the total number of scores. It is the balance point of the distribution (i.e., the point about which the sum of the negative deviations equals that of the positive deviations). The mean is responsive to the exact position (magnitude) of each score in the distribution and is therefore more sensitive to extreme scores than are the median and the mode.

The three measures of central tendency are differently affected by the symmetry of a distribution. For a bell-shaped, normal distribution, mean, median, and mode have the same value, but for a lopsided (skewed) distribution, their values will differ. Among the three measures, the mean varies the least from sample to sample, which is why it is the measure of choice in most behavioral science applications. Nevertheless, there are some situations (e.g., open-ended distributions and those that are strongly skewed or have a few very deviant scores) in which the median may have significant advantages.

Finally, we note that changing each score by adding or subtracting a constant amount increases or decreases each of the three measures by that same amount. Similarly, if we multiply or divide each score by a constant, it has the effect of multiplying or dividing these measures of central tendency by the same amount.

## Mathematical Note

### Note 5.1 The Mean as a Balance Point (*Ref.*: Section 5.5)

The algebraic way of saying that the mean is the balance point of the distribution is: $\Sigma(X - \overline{X}) = 0$. The proof is:

$$\sum(X - \overline{X}) = \sum X - n\overline{X}$$

$$= \sum X - n\frac{\sum X}{n}$$

N.B.: $\overline{X}$ is a constant when summing over all values in the sample, so $\Sigma\overline{X} = n\overline{X}$

$$= \sum X - \sum X$$

$$= 0$$

Notice that we made no assumption about the shape of the distribution.

## Key Terms, Concepts, and Symbols

| | | |
|---|---|---|
| measures of central tendency (66) | arithmetic mean (68) | outlier (72) |
| mode (66) | $X$ (68) | open-ended distribution (74) |
| *Mo* (66) | $\Sigma$ (68) | skewed distribution (59, 75) |
| median (66) | $\overline{X}$ (68) | negatively skewed (59, 75) |
| *Mdn* (66) | $\mu_X$ (68) | positively skewed (59, 75) |
| $P_{50}$ (37, 66) | deviation score (70) | score transformation (76) |
| | $X - \overline{X}$ (70) | linear transformation (77) |

## Problems

1. Find the median and the mean for each distribution: (a) 15, 13, 12, 9. (b) 13, 13, 12, 11, 11. (c) 12, 11, 11, 10. (d) 11, 11, 10, 10, 9, 7. (e) 10, 9, 9, 7, 6, 2. (f) 9, 8, 7, 5, 5, 5. (g) 8, 8, 7, 7, 7, 2. (h) 7, 6, 4, 4, 4, 1, 1, 1. (i) 6, 5, 5, 3, 1, 1, 0, 0.

2. Which measure of central tendency is (a) the balance point? (b) best for qualitative data? (c) most sensitive to extreme scores? (d) best for open-ended distributions? (e) sensitive to the value of all scores? (f) responsive to the number of scores below and above it but not to their exact values? (g) lowest in value in

negatively skewed distributions? (h) the most resistant to chance sampling variation?

**3.** Find the mean, median, and mode (a) for Data 5A and (b) for Data 5B.

### DATA 5A

| SCORES | $f$ |
|--------|-----|
| 60–64  | 4   |
| 55–59  | 7   |
| 50–54  | 6   |
| 45–49  | 3   |

### DATA 5B

| SCORES | $f$ |
|--------|-----|
| 60–65  | 4   |
| 54–59  | 9   |
| 48–53  | 7   |

**4.** Look again at Table 3.1. Calculate the mode, median, and mean for these data.

*Problems 5 through 9 concern a distribution of 10 scores. Nine of them are 3, 5, 9, 1, 9, 2, 0, 3, and 9. The tenth score, the mystery score, is greater than 5, but it is not 9.*

**5.** On the basis of the information above, is it possible to determine the mode of the distribution of 10 scores? If yes, what is the mode? Explain.

**6.** On the basis of the information above, is it possible to determine the median of the distribution of 10 scores? If yes, what is the median? Explain.

**7.** On the basis of the information above, is it possible to determine the mean of the distribution of 10 scores? If yes, what is the mean? Explain.

**8.** If the mean of the original distribution of 10 scores is 4.8, what is the value of the mystery score? Explain how you calculated it.

**9.** Assume the mean of the original distribution of 10 scores is 4.8. For each change in the distribution described below, say whether the mean would increase ($+$), remain unchanged (0), or decrease ($-$): (a) A value of 6 becomes the 11th score. (b) A value of 4.8 becomes the 11th score. (c) A value of $-19$ becomes the 11th score. (d) The present value of 2 is removed, leaving nine scores. (e) The mystery value is removed, leaving nine scores. (Remember what was said above about the mystery score.)

**10.** Look again at the cartoon by Gary Larson. Pat says, "The average American family has 1.5 children." Leslie says, "But there's no such thing as an average person, and there's no such thing as ½ of a child." Mediate the dispute between them.

**11.** A distribution can be perfectly symmetrical but have different values for the mode and the median. (a) Explain. (b) Will the mean in this case equal the mode, the median, or something else?

**12.** At a state university, the first-year class numbers about 360. Until recently, few semifinalists (or finalists) in the National Merit Scholarship program attended. Now the state government has begun to offer its own scholarships to state residents who are National Merit semifinalists—but only if they attend a college in the state. In the first semester of the program, 40 National Merit Scholarship students enter the university. How did the distribution of SAT scores for the first-year class change? Which measure of central tendency changed most? Explain.

**13.** A researcher finds that the mean of her distribution of measures is 120 and the median is 130. What can you say about the shape of the distribution?

**14.** A researcher finds that his data form a skewed distribution. He is interested in the bulk of the scores and does not want the few very deviant scores to alter extensively his measure of central tendency. Which measure should he use?

**15.** If $P_{25} = 15$, $P_{50} = 20$, and $P_{75} = 30$, what can you say about the shape of the distribution?

**16.** For which distribution(s) pictured in Figure 5.2 might the following be true: $P_{25} = 25$, $P_{50} = 45$, $P_{75} = 65$? Explain.

**17.** A psychologist conducts a learning experiment in which she records the time it takes rats to run through a maze for food reinforcement. A few rats do not complete the maze within 4 minutes, and because of time constraints, she removes them from the maze. Which measure of central tendency would you use for the following distribution of times to traverse the maze?

| TIME | $f$ |
|---|---|
| 241 sec. and up | 4 |
| 181–240 sec. | 5 |
| 121–180 sec. | 8 2 |
| 61–120 sec. | 5 |
| 1–60 sec. | 3 |

18. In the distribution depicted in Figure 5.1, change the "8" to a "2." Recalculate (a) the mode, (b) the median, and (c) the mean. (d) Which measure was most affected by the change? Why?

19. In the distribution depicted in Figure 5.1, omit the "8." Recalculate (a) the mode, (b) the median, and (c) the mean. (d) Which measure was most affected by the change? Why?

20. The mean of a set of scores is 20. What will the mean become if (a) 5 points are added to each score? (b) 15 points are subtracted from each score? (c) Each score is multiplied by 5? (d) Each score is divided by 4?

(e) Each score is divided by 2, and 10 is then added to each resulting value? (f) Each score is multiplied by 4, and the resulting values are divided by 5?

21. Some years ago, a newspaper editor claimed that more than half of American families earned a below-average income. Is there any sense in which this claim could be correct? Explain.

22. The National Association of Manufacturers and the steel workers union have both stated the "average" wage for workers in the steel industry. The NAM's figure is higher. Can both be correct? Explain.

23. Ten scores have a mean of 50.0. Twenty scores have a mean of 40.0. If we combine the scores so that $n = 30$, what will the mean of the whole distribution be? Write a formula for calculating the mean from these two subgroups. In your symbolism, let subgroup 1 have mean $\overline{X}_1$ and size $n_1$; let subgroup 2 have mean $\overline{X}_2$ and size $n_2$; and so on.

# CHAPTER 6

## Variability and Standard (z) Scores

When you have finished studying this chapter, you should be able to:

- Understand what is meant by "measure of variability";

- Calculate the range, the semi-interquartile range, the variance, and the standard deviation;

- Understand the properties of these four measures of variability and know when it is best to use them;

- Know how each of the measures of variability is affected by adding a constant to each score, subtracting a constant from each score, or by multiplying or dividing each score by a constant;

- Understand that for psychological and educational tests there is no standard unit of measurement for the raw scores; and

- Understand the concept of a standard score ($z$ score) and know what effect changing raw scores to $z$ scores has on the mean, the standard deviation, and the shape of the distribution.

A math instructor is concerned about two of her students. After 12 weekly 20-point tests, both have mean scores of 10. Is there any hope that either one will pass the comprehensive final exam? An inspection of one student's grades reveals a low grade of 7 and a high of 12. The second student has several grades lower than 7, including two zeros, but also several very good grades on the tests, including three perfect scores of 20. Their two distributions of scores look something like those shown in Figure 6.1a. Although the students have the same mean score, the difference in the variability of their scores suggests to our professor that their mean performance is due to different problems. The first student has never had a passing grade and may be in over his head in terms of mathematical ability. However, the perfect scores by the second student demonstrate that she *can* do well. Perhaps there are personal problems affecting the student's studying time on occasions.

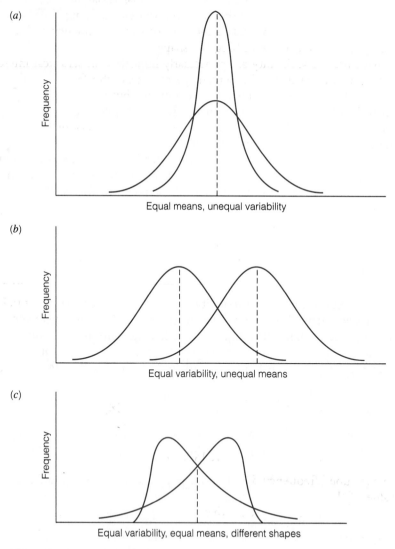

(a)

Equal means, unequal variability

(b)

Equal variability, unequal means

(c)

Equal variability, equal means, different shapes

**FIGURE 6.1**  Differences in central tendency, variability, and shape of frequency distributions (polygons).

**measure of variability**

a single summary figure that describes the spread of observations within a distribution

This example illustrates that we often need to know more about a distribution than just a measure of central tendency. Whereas a measure of central tendency is a summary of the central location of a distribution of observations, a **measure of variability** is a summary of the spread of observations. Information about variability is often as important as that about central tendency. We would not be happy with a weight scale that gives our weight correctly on the average, but on any occasion might read 5 pounds lighter or heavier than it should.

*Measures of variability express quantitatively the extent to which the scores in a distribution scatter about or cluster together.* They describe the spread of an entire set of scores; they do not specify how far a particular score diverges from the center of the group. Nor do measures of variability provide information about the shape of a distribution or the level of performance of a group. Figures 6.1*b* and *c*, for example, show that it is possible to have two distributions with equal variability but unequal means (Figure 6.1*b*) or different shapes (Figure 6.1*c*). To describe a distribution adequately, therefore, we usually must provide a measure of central tendency and a measure of variability in addition to describing the shape.

Measures of variability are particularly important in statistical inference. A pollster must not only estimate the percentage of voters who favor a particular candidate or issue but also the amount of variation attributable to sampling fluctuation, the "margin of error" inherent in such estimates. How much fluctuation will occur in random sampling? This question is fundamental to every problem in statistical inference; it is a question about variability.

We shall consider four measures of variability: the range, semi-interquartile range, variance, and standard deviation. As we did with measures of central tendency, we shall briefly introduce each first and then return to discuss their properties in more detail.

# 6.1 The Range

**range**

the difference between the lowest score and the highest score in a distribution

The simplest measure of variability is the range, which we met earlier in constructing a frequency distribution. The **range** is the difference between the highest and lowest score in the distribution.[1] Like other measures of variability, the range is a distance and not, like measures of central tendency, a location (on the abscissa). For example, all three of the following simple distributions have the same range (20 score points):

$$3, 5, 5, 8, 13, 14, 18, 23$$

$$37, 42, 48, 53, 57$$

$$131, 140, 144, 147, 150, 151$$

In a grouped frequency distribution, calculate the range as the difference between the value of the lowest raw score that *could* be included in the bottom class interval and that of the highest raw score that could be included in the uppermost class interval

---

[1]Some statistics textbooks calculate the range as the difference between the upper real limit of the highest score and the lower real limit of the lowest score. For simplicity sake, we will use raw scores.

(i.e., the upper apparent limit of the highest interval minus the lower apparent limit of the lowest interval).

## 6.2 The Semi-Interquartile Range

**semi-interquartile range**
one-half the distance between the first and third quartile points in a distribution

Because the range depends on only two scores, the highest and the lowest, it is a crude measure of variability unduly influenced by the extremes of a distribution. The **semi-interquartile range**, symbolized by the letter **Q**, is a more sophisticated measure that depends only on the relatively stable central portion of a distribution—specifically, on the middle 50% of the scores. It is defined as one-half the distance between the first and third quartile points, or

**Q**
symbol for the semi-interquartile range

SEMI-INTERQUARTILE RANGE

$$Q = \frac{Q_3 - Q_1}{2} \qquad (6.1a)$$

**quartile points**
the three score points that divide a distribution into four parts each containing an equal number of cases:
$Q_1 (=P_{25})$,
$Q_2 (=P_{50})$,
$Q_3 (=P_{75})$

The **quartile points** are the three score points that divide the distribution into four parts, each containing an equal number of cases. These points, symbolized by $Q_1$, $Q_2$, and $Q_3$, are therefore our old friends, $P_{25}$, $P_{50}$, and $P_{75}$, respectively. We may therefore rephrase Formula 6.1a in familiar terms:

$$Q = \frac{Q_3 - Q_1}{2} = \frac{P_{75} - P_{25}}{2} \qquad (6.1b)$$

For the data in Figure 6.2, the semi-interquartile range is $(80 - 70)/2 = 5$.

One way of understanding $Q$ is to realize that $2Q$ equals the range of the middle 50% of the scores. Because $Q_2$ is, of course, another term for the median, the semi-interquartile range may also be thought of as the mean distance between the median and the two outer quartile points. In Figure 6.2, for example, note that the distance between $Q_1$ and $Q_2$ is 4 points, that the distance between $Q_2$ and $Q_3$ is 6 points, and that the mean of these two distances is 5 points, the value of $Q$.

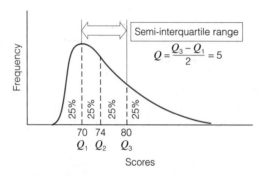

**FIGURE 6.2**  The semi-interquartile range.

## 6.3 Deviation Scores

**(X − X̄)**

a deviation
score; shows by
how much
a score differs
from the mean

You have become acquainted with the concept of a raw score, but for the measures about to be introduced you need to know about another way of expressing a score: the deviation score. You met the deviation score in Section 5.5, but without the benefit of a formal introduction. A **deviation score** expresses the location of a score by indicating how many score points it lies above or below the mean of the distribution. In symbols, the deviation score may be defined as $(X − \overline{X})$. Consider the following raw scores (X) and their corresponding deviation scores $(X − \overline{X})$:

| X | $(X − \overline{X})$ | |
|---|---|---|
| 1 | $(1 − 4) = −3$ | |
| 5 | $(5 − 4) = +1$ | |
| 7 | $(7 − 4) = +3$ | $\overline{X} = \dfrac{16}{4} = 4$ |
| 3 | $(3 − 4) = −1$ | |
| $\sum X = 16$ | | |

When we subtract the mean $(\overline{X} = 4)$ from each of the raw scores, the resulting deviation scores state the position of the scores *relative to the mean*. A plus sign (+) indicates that the original raw score is greater than the mean, whereas a minus sign (−) indicates that it is less than the mean. For example, the raw score of 7 becomes $(7 − 4) = +3$, which says that this score is 3 points above the mean of 4. Similarly, the raw score of 3 becomes $(3 − 4) = −1$, indicating that its location is 1 point below the mean.

Collectively, deviation scores indicate variability. If the scores cluster tightly together, then the deviations from the mean will be small. If the scores scatter widely, then the deviations from the mean will be large. We now turn to two important measures of variability based on the concept of the deviation score.

## 6.4 Deviational Measures: The Variance

Because deviation scores indicate the distances of the raw scores from the mean (the most frequently used measure of central tendency), it might appear that an attractive measure of variability could be obtained by calculating the mean of the deviation scores. This would require finding their sum. Unfortunately, as we learned in Section 5.5, the sum of the deviations about the mean *always* equals zero. Look again at the four deviation scores in the previous section $(−3, +1, +3, −1)$. When we add them together, $\Sigma(X − \overline{X}) = 0$.

We could drop the signs of the deviation scores before taking their mean, but this yields a measure with such awkward mathematical properties that it is useless in inferential statistics. Of course, another way to get rid of the signs is to square the deviation scores. This is what is done in a very useful measure of deviation called the variance.

**variance**

the mean of the
squares of the
deviation scores

The **variance** is defined as the mean of the squares of the deviation scores (or, as many prefer, the "average squared deviation from the mean"). The symbol for the

$\sigma^2$
symbol for the variance of a population

$\sigma_X^2 =$
$$\frac{\Sigma(X - \mu_X)^2}{N}$$
definitional formula for the variance of a population $(X)$

$S^2$
symbol for the variance of a sample

$S_X^2 =$
$$\frac{\Sigma(X - \overline{X})^2}{n}$$
definitional formula for the variance of a sample $(X)$

**sum of squares**
short for sum of the squared deviations from the mean

*SS*
symbol for sum of squares

$SS_X =$
$$\Sigma(X - \overline{X})^2$$
formula for the sum of squares of a sample $(X)$

variance of a population is $\sigma^2$ (the lowercase Greek letter sigma) and that for a sample is $S^2$. The defining formulas for the variance are as follows:

> DEFINITIONAL FORMULA FOR
> VARIANCE OF A POPULATION $(X)$
>
> $$\sigma_X^2 = \frac{\Sigma(X - \mu_X)^2}{N} \quad \text{or} \quad \frac{SS_X}{N} \qquad (6.2a)$$
>
> DEFINITIONAL FORMULA FOR
> VARIANCE OF A SAMPLE $(X)$
>
> $$S_X^2 = \frac{\Sigma(X - \overline{X})^2}{n} \quad \text{or} \quad \frac{SS_X}{n} \qquad (6.2b)$$

The numerator of the variance, $\Sigma(X - \overline{X})^2$, is used so frequently in other statistical formulas that it has its own abbreviated name: the **sum of squares**, which is short for the *sum of the squared deviations from the mean*. It is often symbolized by *SS*. The steps in calculating the variance by formula 6.2*b* are summarized as follows and are illustrated in Table 6.1.

**Step 1:** Record each score.

**Step 2:** Calculate $\overline{X}$.

**Step 3:** Obtain deviation scores by subtracting $\overline{X}$ from each value of $X$ (as a check on your work, remember $\Sigma(X - \overline{X})$ should equal zero).

**Step 4:** Square each deviation score.

**Step 5:** Sum the values of the squared deviation scores to get the sum of squares (*SS*).

**Step 6:** Divide the sum of squares by $n$ as in Formula 6.2*b*.

**TABLE 6.1**    *Calculation of the Variance: Deviation-Score Method*

| ①   $X$ | ③   $(X - \overline{X})$ | ④   $(X - \overline{X})^2$ |
|---|---|---|
| 32 | $32 - 50.6 = -18.6$ | 345.96 |
| 71 | $71 - 50.6 = +20.4$ | 416.16 |
| 64 | $64 - 50.6 = +13.4$ | 179.56 |
| 50 | $50 - 50.6 = -0.6$ | .36 |
| 48 | $48 - 50.6 = -2.6$ | 6.76 |
| 63 | $63 - 50.6 = +12.4$ | 153.76 |
| 38 | $38 - 50.6 = -12.6$ | 158.76 |
| 41 | $41 - 50.6 = -9.6$ | 92.16 |
| 47 | $47 - 50.6 = -3.6$ | 12.96 |
| 52 | $52 - 50.6 = +1.4$ | 1.96 |
| $\sum X = 506$ | $\sum(X - \overline{X}) = 0$ | ⑤ $\sum(X - \overline{X})^2 = 1368.40$ |

$$② \;\; \overline{X} = \frac{506}{10} = 50.6 \qquad\qquad ⑥ \;\; S_X^2 = \frac{\sum(X - \overline{X})^2}{n} = \frac{1368.40}{10} = 136.84$$

## Point of Controversy

### Calculating the Sample Variance: Should We Divide by $n$ or $(n - 1)$?

In Section 6.4, we define the variance as the mean of the squares of the deviation scores. To calculate the variance of a *population* we divided the sum of the squared deviations from the mean ($SS$) by $N$, the number of scores in the population.

To calculate the variance of a *sample* we (like many statisticians) also use this formula (substituting $n$ for $N$). However, some prefer to define the variance of a sample as $\Sigma(X - \overline{X})^2/(n - 1)$. If your calculator has a program for the sample variance, it may also use this latter formula. The use of two different formulas for the sample variance is, of course, confusing to students who have compared textbooks that differ in this respect.

Why do some statisticians divide the sample sum of squares by $n$ and others by $(n - 1)$? The answer has to do with the reason an investigator obtains a sample for study in the first place. Rarely are we interested in the sample itself. Instead, we obtain samples and calculate statistics to make inferences about population parameters. Due to chance factors in drawing a sample, we do not expect our sample statistic (e.g., sample mean, sample variance) to exactly equal the population parameter (e.g., population mean, population variance), but we hope it is close. As we will learn later, the sample mean is an example of what we call an "unbiased" statistic. Although the mean of a particular sample is probably not going to equal the mean of the population from which the sample was drawn, there is no bias in the direction of the error. There is an equal likelihood that it will fall below or above the population mean.

The sample variance, however, is not an unbiased statistic. *It tends to be an underestimate of the population variance.* The reason is that the sum of the squared deviations from the mean of any set of scores is less than the sum of squares calculated from any other point. (We discuss this in Section 6.9 and prove it in Note 6.2.) Because the sample mean is rarely exactly equal to the population mean, the sum of squares calculated from a sample mean is usually less than if it had been calculated from the population mean (which is one of those "any other points"). To correct for this underestimation in the numerator of the formula for the sample variance, statisticians divide $SS$ by $(n - 1)$ instead of $n$. The result is no longer the variance of the *sample*, but what is called the *unbiased estimate of the population variance*. The value of $\Sigma(X - \overline{X})^2/(n - 1)$ will still not be equal to the population variance in most cases, but instead of a biased estimate (tending to be an underestimate), there is an equal likelihood of the value falling below or above the value of the population variance.

So, which formula is correct? Actually, they both are. To obtain the variance for any given set of scores, we always divide by $n$. Thus, the variance of a sample is calculated by dividing by $n$. Ultimately, however, we are interested in estimating the population variance, and to get an unbiased estimate of that we divide by $(n - 1)$ (Cormack & Mantel, 1990). We will discuss this further when we get to inferential statistics.

# 6.5 Deviational Measures: The Standard Deviation

The variance is a most important measure that finds its greatest use in advanced statistical procedures and especially in inferential statistics. However, for basic description, it has a fatal flaw: Its calculated value is expressed in *squared* units of measurement. (If the scores are weights in pounds, the variance will be a certain quantity of squared pounds.) Consequently, it is of little use in descriptive statistics. The defect, however, is easily remedied. By taking the square root of the variance, we return to the original units of measurement and thereby obtain a widely used index of variability called the **standard deviation**. It is a measure of the central tendency of the deviation scores (ignoring their signs). Although it is *not technically correct*, it is easier for beginning students to think of the standard deviation as "the average amount scores deviate from the mean." When there is wider scatter among the raw scores, it appears as bigger deviations from the mean, and thus the "standard" (typical, representative) deviation increases.

The defining formulas for the standard deviation are:

> DEFINITIONAL FORMULA FOR
> STANDARD DEVIATION OF A POPULATION
>
> $$\sigma_X = \sqrt{\frac{\sum (X - \mu_X)^2}{N}} \quad \text{or} \quad \sqrt{\frac{SS_X}{N}} \tag{6.3a}$$
>
> DEFINITIONAL FORMULA FOR
> STANDARD DEVIATION OF A SAMPLE
>
> $$S_X = \sqrt{\frac{\sum (X - \overline{X})^2}{n}} \quad \text{or} \quad \sqrt{\frac{SS_X}{n}} \tag{6.3b}$$

As you can see, the symbols for the standard deviation of a population ($\sigma$) and a sample ($S$) are the same as those used for the variance, but without the square sign. To obtain the standard deviation of the sample of scores in Table 6.1, we simply take the square root of the variance:

$$S_X = \sqrt{\frac{\sum (X - \overline{X})^2}{n}} = \sqrt{\frac{1368.40}{10}} = \sqrt{136.84} = 11.7$$

**Sidebar (margin):**

**standard deviation**

the square root of the variance

$\sigma$

symbol for the standard deviation of a population

$\sigma_X =$

$\sqrt{\dfrac{\Sigma (X - \mu_X)^2}{N}}$

definitional formula for the standard deviation of a population (X)

$S$

symbol for the standard deviation of a sample

$S_X =$

$\sqrt{\dfrac{\Sigma (X - \overline{X})^2}{n}}$

definitional formula for the standard deviation of a sample (X)

# 6.6 Calculation of the Variance and Standard Deviation: Raw-Score Method

When calculating the variance or standard deviation by the deviation-score formula, calculating SS directly from deviation scores is a nuisance. Minium's Second Law of Statistics states: "*For computation, if there is a choice between a deviation-score method and*

**TABLE 6.2** *Calculation of the Standard Deviation: Raw-Score Method*

| ① $X$ | ② $X^2$ |
|---|---|
| 32 | 1,024 |
| 71 | 5,041 |
| 64 | 4,096 |
| 50 | 2,500 |
| 48 | 2,304 |
| 63 | 3,969 |
| 38 | 1,444 |
| 41 | 1,681 |
| 47 | 2,209 |
| 52 | 2,704 |
| ③ $\sum X = 506$ | ③ $\sum X^2 = 26{,}972$ |

Calculation of $SS_X$:

④ $SS_X = \sum (X - \overline{X})^2 = \sum X^2 - \dfrac{\left(\sum X\right)^2}{n}$

$= 26{,}972 - \dfrac{(506)^2}{10}$

$= 26{,}972 - 25{,}603.6$

$= 1368.4$

Calculation of $S_X$:

$S_X^2 = \dfrac{SS_X}{n}$

$S_X = \sqrt{\dfrac{SS_X}{n}}$

⑤ $\quad = \sqrt{\dfrac{1368.4}{10}}$

$= \sqrt{136.84}$

⑥ $\quad = 11.7$

$SS_X = \sum X^2 - \dfrac{(\Sigma X)^2}{n}$
computational formula for the sum of squares

$S_X^2 = \dfrac{SSx}{n}$
another way of expressing the formula for the variance of a sample ($X$)

$S_X = \sqrt{\dfrac{SSx}{n}}$
another way of expressing the formula for the standard deviation of a sample ($X$)

*some other method, choose the other method.*" Without the bother of changing the raw scores to deviation scores, we can find $SS$ by the equation:[2]

COMPUTATIONAL
(RAW SCORE) EQUIVALENT OF $SS$

$$SS_X = \sum (X - \overline{X})^2 = \sum X^2 - \frac{\left(\sum X\right)^2}{n} \qquad (6.4)$$

Remember, $S_X^2 = SS_X/n$ (Formula 6.2*b*), and $S_X = \sqrt{SS_X/n}$ (Formula 6.3*b*). Derivation of Formula 6.4 appears in Note 6.1 at the end of the chapter. The steps in calculating the standard deviation by the raw-score method are summarized as follows and are illustrated for a set of 10 scores in Table 6.2:

[2] For the remainder of the chapter, we will present formulas appropriate to samples for most examples; the modifications necessary for a population should be readily apparent.

**Step 1:** Record each score.

**Step 2:** Record the square of each score.

**Step 3:** Calculate $\Sigma X$ and $\Sigma X^2$.

**Step 4:** Calculate $SS_X$ in accord with Formula 6.4. In doing so, distinguish carefully between $\Sigma X^2$ and $(\Sigma X)^2$. To find the former, we square each score and then sum the squares. To find the latter, we sum the scores and then square the sum. The results are not the same. Keep in mind that the sum of squares *must* be a positive number no matter what the raw score values are.

**Step 5:** Substitute the numerical values for $SS$ and $n$ in the formula for S.

**Step 6:** Complete the calculation of S.

In most instances, particularly when there are decimals or a large number of scores, the raw-score method is a better practical choice for computation.

## 6.7 Properties of the Range

The range is easier to compute than the other measures of variability and its meaning is direct. Therefore, *the range is ideal for preliminary work or in other circumstances where precision is not an important requirement.* Sometimes, of course, it provides precisely the information we need. We have seen this in the course of transforming raw scores into grouped data (see Section 3.3).

The range, however, has some major shortcomings as a measure of variability. Only the two outermost scores of a distribution affect its value; the remainder could lie anywhere between them. In fact, a single outlier (an aberrant score) has a more substantial effect on the range than on the other measures.[3] Thus, *the range is not sensitive to the total condition of the distribution.*

*The range is also of little use beyond the descriptive level.* In most situations, the range varies more with sampling fluctuation than other measures do. In many types of distributions, including the important normal distribution, the range is dependent on sample size, being greater when sample size is greater. This is an important flaw when comparing two distributions that differ substantially in the number of cases on which they are based.

## 6.8 Properties of the Semi-Interquartile Range

The semi-interquartile range is closely related to the median because both are defined in terms of percentile points of the distribution. The median is responsive to the *number* of scores lying below it rather than to their exact position, and $P_{25}$ and $P_{75}$ are points defined in a similar way. We may therefore expect the median and the semi-interquartile range to have properties in common. For example, $Q_3$ is sensitive

---

[3] We introduced the term *outlier* in Chapter 5 and to this point have referred to it as an extreme or aberrant score. Some statisticians state that a score must be at least 2.5 standard deviations from the mean to be called an outlier.

only to the number of scores that lie above it. Consequently, all scores above $Q_3$ are of equal importance in the determination of the semi-interquartile range, and a very extreme score counts no more and no less than a moderately extreme one in its determination. Therefore, *the semi-interquartile range is less sensitive to the presence of a few very extreme scores than is the standard deviation.* If a distribution is badly skewed or if it contains a few very extreme scores, the semi-interquartile range will respond to the presence of such scores, but it will not give them undue weight.

If the distribution is open-ended (see Section 5.6), it is not possible to calculate the standard deviation or the range without making additional (and probably hazardous) assumptions. *With open-ended distributions, the semi-interquartile range may be the only measure that is reasonable to compute.* Unless more than a quarter of the scores lie in the indeterminate end category, we may compute the semi-interquartile range in straightforward fashion.

*The sampling stability of the semi-interquartile range is good, although not up to that of the standard deviation.* However, the usefulness of the semi-interquartile range is essentially limited to the realm of descriptive statistics. We should give it particular consideration when its special properties can be put to good use and when the standard deviation would be adversely affected.

## 6.9 Properties of the Standard Deviation

The range and the semi-interquartile range are intuitively easy to grasp as measures of variability. It is ironic, therefore, that the standard deviation is more important in statistical work than the others, but less easy to understand. Rather than labor over the problem of grasping its nature intuitively, we will develop a picture of its functional properties.

*The standard deviation, like the mean, is responsive to the exact position of every score in the distribution.* Because it is calculated by taking deviations from the mean, if a score is shifted to a position more deviant from the mean, the standard deviation will increase. If the shift is to a position closer to the mean, the standard deviation decreases. Thus, the standard deviation is more sensitive to the exact condition of the distribution than is either the range or semi-interquartile range.

The standard deviation is more sensitive than the semi-interquartile range to the presence or absence of scores that lie at the extremes of the distribution. This should be obvious because the semi-interquartile range is based only on the score points that mark the border of the middle 50% of the scores. Because of this characteristic sensitivity, *the standard deviation may not be the best choice among measures of variability when the distribution contains a few very extreme scores or when the distribution is badly skewed.*

When we calculate deviations from the mean, the sum of squares of these values is *smaller* than if they had been taken about any other point. Putting it another way,

$$\sum (X - A)^2 \text{ is a minimum when } A = \overline{X}$$

(or when $A = \mu_X$ in the case of a population)

We provide proof of this proposition in Note 6.2 at the end of the chapter. This property may seem to be an oddity that only a mathematician could love. In fact, it is an extremely important principle, one that reappears frequently in the further study of statistics (see, for example, Section 9.2). For now, note that this gives us another way to define the mean: *It is the point about which the sum of squares of the deviation scores is a minimum.*

To illustrate this property, consider the scores 2, 3, 5, and 10, which have a mean of 5. Calculate the sum of squares of the deviation scores, taking the deviations from the mean. Then recalculate, this time taking the deviations from 3. Repeat again, taking the deviations from 2. Do it again from 10. What do you find?

*One of the most important points favoring our use of the standard deviation is its resistance to sampling variation.* In repeated random samples drawn from populations of the type most frequently encountered in statistical work, the numerical value of the standard deviation tends to jump about less than would that of other measures computed on the same samples. This is very important if our concern is in any way associated with inferring variation in a population from knowledge of variation in a sample.

When you begin to study additional methods of statistical analysis, you will better understand the importance of the standard deviation. *The standard deviation appears explicitly or lies embedded in many procedures of both descriptive statistics and inferential statistics.*

In many ways, the properties of the standard deviation are related to those of the mean. In its usefulness for further statistical work, its stability in the face of sampling variation, its responsiveness to the location of each score, and its sensitivity to extreme scores, the position of the standard deviation relative to the other measures of variability is much like that of the mean relative to the other measures of central tendency.

As a review, look at Table 6.3. It gives comparisons of the characteristics of the range, the semi-interquartile range, and the standard deviation.

**TABLE 6.3**  *Comparison of Characteristics of Range, Semi-Interquartile Range, and Standard Deviation*

| | MEASURE OF VARIABILITY | | |
| --- | --- | --- | --- |
| **CHARACTERISTIC** | *Range* | *Semi-interquartile range* | *Standard deviation* |
| Frequency of use in behavioral research | Some | Very little | Over 95% of the time |
| Mathematical tractability and application in advanced statistics | Very little | Very little | Great |
| Sampling stability | Worst | Fairly good | Best |
| Use in presence of a few extreme scores or with strongly skewed distributions | Misleading | Okay | Interpret with caution |
| Related measure of central tendency | None | Median | Mean |
| Use with open-ended distributions | No | Generally okay | No |
| Importantly affected by sample size | Yes | No | No |
| Ease of calculation | Easiest | Easy with ordered scores | Fairly easy |

# 6.10 How Big Is a Standard Deviation?

What does it mean to say that a score is 1 standard deviation away from the mean? Two standard deviations? Distributions differ in their shape, so we cannot make generalizations that will apply in all cases. However, as an example, we will examine the normal distribution. We define a normal distribution in Chapter 7—all you need to know for now is that normal curves are bell-shaped (as shown in Figure 4.15*f*). In any normal distribution, the interval:

$\mu \pm 1\sigma$     contains about 68% of the scores

$\mu \pm 2\sigma$     contains about 95% of the scores

$\mu \pm 3\sigma$     contains about 99.7% of the scores

We show these relationships in Figure 6.3.

By now you should be starting to appreciate what we mean when we say that a score is 1 or 2 standard deviations from the mean. Although we usually do not think of 2 as a large number, in terms of standard deviations from the mean it is a rather large distance.

# 6.11 Score Transformations and Measures of Variability

In Section 5.8, we found that certain score transformations had simple and predictable effects on measures of central tendency. What are the effects on measures of variability?

Consider the following set of scores: 12, 13, and 15. The distance between the first and second score is 1 point, and that between the second and third scores, 2 points. If we add 10 points to each score, they become 22, 23, and 25. The interscore

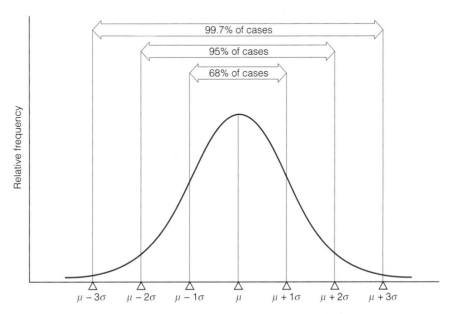

**FIGURE 6.3** Relative frequencies of cases contained within certain limits in the normal distribution.

distances, however, remain the same. If we subtract 5 points from each score, they become 7, 8, and 10. Again, the interscore distances remain the same. Because measures of variability are indices of interscore distance, they are not affected by either of these modifications. *If we add a constant to each score in the distribution or subtract a constant from each score, it does not affect any of the measures of variability described in this chapter.*

Scores may also be transformed by multiplying each score by a constant or by dividing each score by a constant. If, for example, we multiply the scores 12, 13, and 15 by 2, they become 24, 26, and 30. In their original form, the interscore distances are 1 and 2 points, respectively. In their altered form, they are doubled, becoming 2 and 4 points. If we multiply the original scores by 10, the scores become 120, 130, and 150, and the interscore distances are now 10 points and 20 points. If we alter the original set of scores by dividing each score by 10, the scores become 1.2, 1.3, and 1.5. The interscore distances are now .1 and .2, one-tenth of their original values. *When scores are multiplied or divided by a constant, the resultant measure of variability is also multiplied or divided by that same constant.* This applies to all measures of variability discussed in this chapter except the variance.[4]

## 6.12 Standard Scores (z Scores)

A friend has been worried about his performance on a history examination. "How did you do on the history exam?" you ask. "I got a score of 123," he replies. You consider his answer, not knowing whether to be excited or to sympathize. "What was the class mean?" you inquire. "One hundred and five," he responds. You are happy for him, but want to know more: "What was the range?" "The low score was 80, and the high score was 125," he replies.

This example illustrates *the lack of unequivocal meaning that is typical in psychological and educational measurement.* A raw score, by itself, is really uninterpretable. We need a frame of reference to decide whether a given score indicates a good performance or a poor one. In the example, learning the value of the mean of the distribution helped you to understand your friend's level of performance. Additional information was acquired by asking about the range; his answer indicated that his performance was very nearly the best in the class. The raw score, originally without meaning, became interpretable by relating to it a measure of central tendency and a measure of variability.

*The solution to the problem of making scores meaningful involves providing an adequate frame of reference.* If we measure the length of an object in feet, the measurement obtained is meaningful, first because the length obtained is the same whether measured by your yardstick or mine, and second because we have some understanding of how long a foot is. In mental measurement, the situation is different. In measuring achievement in history, or intelligence, or mechanical aptitude, there is no standard unit of measurement for the raw scores, nor should we expect one. On tests of these, the size and spread of the scores depend on the number of test items, the number of points assigned to each item, the difficulty of the items, and other factors. The problem is aggravated by two related matters. First, a test of intelligence, for example, is only a *sample* of questions designed to tap this characteristic. Another test of the same

---

[4]Variance is expressed in terms of squared units of measurement. Consequently, if each score is multiplied or divided by a constant $C$, the variance is multiplied or divided by $C^2$.

characteristic will therefore constitute a somewhat different sample and will have a somewhat different outcome. Second, because we are not in perfect agreement as to what intelligence is, two test constructors may sample different aspects of intelligence. All of these factors indicate that, unlike the measurement of distance, one "yardstick" of intellectual functioning is not necessarily the same as another.

How then can we answer the question? One possibility is to use percentile ranks (Section 3.10). Another, often more useful approach is to convert the raw scores to standard scores. A standard score, or *z* **score**, states the position of a score in relation to the mean of the distribution, using the standard deviation as the unit of measurement. For example, in a distribution that has $\mu = 100$ and $\sigma = 20$, a score of 120 may be expressed as a *z* score of $+1$, indicating that the score is 1 standard deviation above the mean of the distribution. Similarly, a score of 60 in the same distribution is expressed as a *z* score of $-2.0$, because it is 2 standard deviations below the mean. The formula for a *z* score is:

*z* **score**

states how far away a score is from the mean in standard deviation units; one type of standard score

> DEFINITIONAL FORMULA FOR
> *z* SCORE IN A POPULATION
> $$z = \frac{X - \mu_X}{\sigma_X} \tag{6.5$a$}$$
>
> DEFINITIONAL FORMULA FOR
> *z* SCORE IN A SAMPLE
> $$z = \frac{X - \overline{X}}{S_X} \tag{6.5$b$}$$

$$z = \frac{X - \mu_X}{\sigma_X}$$

formula for a *z* score in a population

$$z = \frac{X - \overline{X}}{S_X}$$

formula for a *z* score in a sample

The *z* score makes it possible, under *some* circumstances (see Section 6.14 for further discussion), to compare scores that originally had different units of measurement because after conversion each has a common unit of measurement. For example, how do we compare the performance on a history and a chemistry exam? That is like trying to compare apples to oranges.

Suppose that Helen, a fifth grader, earned an 80 on her American history exam and a 65 on her arithmetic exam in the *same* class. Is she doing better in history or arithmetic? First, we need to know how the rest of Helen's class did on the two exams. Suppose that the mean score on the history exam was 65 and that the mean score on the arithmetic exam was 50. Helen thus scored 15 points higher than the mean for the class on both exams. Can we conclude that she performed equally well in both subjects? We still do not know because we don't know if 15 points on the history exam is the same as 15 points on the arithmetic exam. Suppose also that the standard deviation on Helen's history exam was 15 but that the standard deviation on her arithmetic exam was only 7.5. Now we can determine in which subject she did better. Helen's score of 80 has a *z* value of $+1.0$, because it was $+1.0$ standard deviations greater than the mean for her class [$(80 - 65)/15$]. Her arithmetic score has a *z* value of $+2.0$, because it was $+2.0$ standard deviations greater than the mean [$(65 - 50)/7.5$]. In relation to the rest of her class, Helen did better in arithmetic.

A *z* score is of great importance in statistical work, and it will appear again and again in this book. You will find it a great help to memorize Formulas 6.5*a* and 6.5*b* and the following verbal definition of a *z* score: *the z score states by how many standard deviations the corresponding raw score lies above or below the mean of the distribution.*

There are three important properties of *z* scores (see if you can derive them from the definition):

1. ***The mean of any distribution of scores converted to z scores is always zero:*** $\mu_z = 0$**.** Because the mean of the raw scores is the score that is no standard deviations away from the mean, it is represented by $z = 0$.

2. ***The standard deviation of any distribution expressed in z scores is always one:*** $\sigma_z = 1$**.** In calculating *z* scores, the standard deviation of the raw scores is the unit of measurement, so the standard deviation of the *z* scores is unity.

3. ***Transforming raw scores to z scores changes the mean to 0 and the standard deviation to 1, but it does not change the shape of the distribution.*** (The reason is that for each raw score we first subtract a constant—the mean—and then divide by another constant—the standard deviation.) By shape of the distribution, we really mean the proportional relation that exists among the distances between the scores. For example, consider the following scores and their *z* score equivalents:

Four scores from a distribution where $\mu = 80$ and $\sigma = 10$:

$$70 \quad 75 \quad 85 \quad 100$$

Interscore differences among raw scores:  5   10   15

Equivalent *z* scores:  $-1 \quad -\tfrac{1}{2} \quad +\tfrac{1}{2} \quad +2$

Interscore differences among *z* scores:  $\tfrac{1}{2}$   1   $1\tfrac{1}{2}$

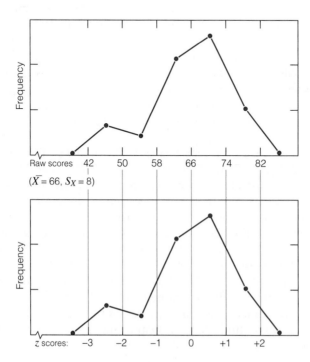

**FIGURE 6.4** Comparison of the shapes of a raw score distribution and the same distribution converted to *z* scores.

**TABLE 6.4** *Some Common Standard Scores and Their Uses*

| TYPE | MEAN | STD DEV | EXAMPLE OF USE |
|------|------|---------|----------------|
| 1 | 50 | 10 | Minnesota Multiphasic Personality Inventory (MMPI) |
|   |    |    | California Psychological Inventory (CPI) |
| 2 | 100 | 16 | Stanford–Binet Intelligence Scale |
| 3 | 100 | 15 | Wechsler Intelligence Scale IQs (WISC-R) |

Note the relation between the interscore distances exhibited for the raw scores and the *z* scores. The proportional magnitude of difference between successive raw scores, 5:10:15, is exactly the same in *z* score terms, $\frac{1}{2}:1:1\frac{1}{2}$. Thus, if a distribution of raw scores is skewed right, with the top score twice as far from the mean as is the bottom score, the *z* scores will still be skewed right, and the absolute value of the top *z* score will be twice as large as that of the bottom *z* score. Figure 6.4 illustrates what happens when a set of raw scores having a mean of 66 and a standard deviation of 8 is expressed as a set of *z* scores (with a mean of zero and a standard deviation of 1).

**standard scores**
all have a fixed mean and fixed standard deviation; a *z* score is one type

The *z* score is only one type of **standard score**. Other varieties have been devised. *Each of them is like the z score in that it has a fixed mean and standard deviation;* this is what is "standard" about them. Table 6.4 gives three common examples.

The fundamental characteristic of all types of standard scores is that they, like the *z* score, locate the raw score by stating by how many standard deviations it lies above or below the mean of the distribution. For example, on the scale having a mean of 50 and a standard deviation of 10, a score of 40 is 10 points below the mean, and because the value of the standard deviation is 10 points, we know that this score is 1 standard deviation below the mean. On the remaining scales in Table 6.4, a score of 84 and 85, respectively, each falls 1 standard deviation below the mean. Despite the inconveniences of the *z* score, it does have the important merit of giving its meaning directly. For example, the meaning of a score of 115 on a standard score scale where the mean is 100 and the standard deviation is 15 is that this score lies 1 standard deviation above the mean. However, that information is given *directly* by its *z*-score equivalent, $z = +1.00$.

## 6.13 A Comparison of *z* Scores and Percentile Ranks

**percentile rank**
the percentage of cases in a distribution that falls below a given point on the measurement scale (see Chapter 3)

Similar to the standard score, the **percentile rank** of a raw score describes its location relative to the other scores in the distribution (see Section 3.8). It has an advantage in terms of directness of meaning, a property always to be desired. The idea that Susan's percentile rank of 85 on a science test means that she performs better than 85% of comparable students is easy to comprehend and is relatively meaningful even to persons without statistical training. If ease of intelligibility were the only criterion, derived scores in the form of percentile ranks would easily win.

Unfortunately, there are some disadvantages. The primary problem is that *changes in raw scores are ordinarily not reflected by proportionate changes in percentile rank.* When one percentile is higher than another, the corresponding raw score of the one is higher than that of the other, but we do not know by how much. Look at Figure 6.5*a*, for

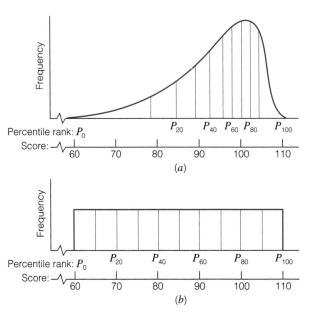

**FIGURE 6.5** Comparative location of percentile ranks in two distributions. The area under the curve in each segment equals 10% of the whole, representing 10% of the scores (see section 4.4).

example. A change of 10 points in percentile rank reflects a change in score that may be larger or smaller than 5 points, depending on the location in the distribution. Changes in raw score are accompanied by proportionate changes in percentile rank only when the distribution of scores is rectangular. The distribution in Figure 6.5*b* illustrates this. Here, a change of 10 points in percentile rank consistently reflects a change of 5 points.

## 6.14 Comparability of Scores

In Section 6.12, we introduced the possibility of comparing scores on different exams. In our example, we compared grades earned by fifth-grader Helen on her history and arithmetic exams. Using $z$ scores, we found that compared to the rest of her class Helen had done better in arithmetic. In that example, the same group of students took both exams. May we use standard scores in the same way to compare raw scores from *different* groups?

Suppose, for example, that Mary, a college freshman, earns a raw score of 37 in her mathematics examination and a score of 82 in history. Suppose further that in her mathematics class the score of 37 falls one-half of a standard deviation above the class mean ($z = +.5$) and that her history score of 82 is one-half of a standard deviation below the class mean ($z = -.5$). It appears that she is doing somewhat better in mathematics than in history, but there are some important qualifications.

If both courses are required of all freshmen, it is possible that the interpretation of Mary's performance as stated is correct. On the other hand, the picture is not so clear

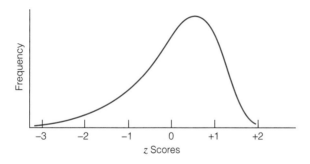

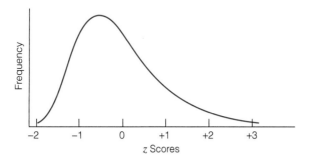

**FIGURE 6.6** Noncomparability of standard scores when distributions differ in shape.

if the mathematics course is a remedial course but the history course is only for honors students. *One element necessary for appropriate comparison is that the reference groups used to generate the standard scores be comparable.* The prerequisite of comparable groups is just as important for the comparison of percentile ranks as it is for standard scores.

Even if two norm groups are similar, the standard scores will not be comparable unless the shapes of the distributions from which they arose are similar. Figure 6.6 shows two distributions that are skewed in opposite directions. (The top distribution would be typical of an easy exam and the bottom one would be typical of a difficult exam.) In the upper distribution, a raw score located at $z = +2$ is the top value in the distribution. In the other, a raw score at $z = +2$ is not the top value; others fall substantially above it. Unless the distributions from which standard scores are computed have the same shape, equal standard scores may not have equal rank in their respective distributions. Thus, *standard scores should be used for comparing scores from two different distributions only if the two distributions have roughly the same shape.*

## 6.15 Summary

To describe a distribution adequately, we must provide a measure of variability as well as information about central tendency and shape. Measures of variability are summary figures that express quantitatively the extent to which the scores in a distribution scatter about or cluster together. We have considered four measures in this chapter: range, semi-interquartile range, variance, and standard deviation.

The range is the distance between the highest and lowest score in the distribution. It is easy to obtain and useful for preliminary work, but as a descriptive measure it has the shortcoming of being unresponsive to the location of intermediate scores. It is also of little use in inferential statistics because the value of the range can vary considerably in different samples taken from the same population.

The semi-interquartile range is one-half the distance between the first ($Q_1$) and the third ($Q_3$) quartile points. Thus, it is related to the median ($P_{50}$) in many respects. It is responsive to the number of scores lying above or below the outer quartile points, but not to their exact location (magnitude). Because of this, the semi-interquartile range is particularly useful with open-ended distributions. However, it is not as resistant to sampling variation as the standard deviation and is of little use in inferential statistics.

The variance is the mean of the squared deviation scores from the mean of the distribution: $S_X^2 = \Sigma(X - \overline{X})^2/n$. It is responsive to the exact position of each score in the distribution, but it is of little use in descriptive statistics because it is a quantity expressed in squared units. However, it has great importance in inferential statistics because of its resistance to sampling variation.

The standard deviation is the square root of the variance and therefore possesses all of its properties. Because it is expressed in original score units, it is the most widely used measure of variability in descriptive statistics. It is widely used in inferential statistics as well. To understand the standard deviation, we began to look at its relationship to the normal curve.

Measurements such as length and weight have a standard reference and thus have the same meaning to everyone. This is not true for most psychological and educational tests. Without a frame of reference, raw scores on these tests are largely uninterpretable. We can compare variables with different measurement units by converting them to standard scores. One type of standard score is the $z$ score. A $z$ score states how far away a raw score is from the mean of the distribution using the standard deviation as the unit of measurement: $z = (X - \overline{X})/S_X$. When we change raw scores in a distribution to $z$ scores, it does not change the shape of the distribution.

# Mathematical Notes

### Note 6.1 The Raw-Score Equivalent of $\Sigma(X - \overline{X})^2$ (*Ref.: Section 6.6*)

$$SS_X = \sum(X - \overline{X})^2$$

$$= \sum(X^2 - 2X\overline{X} + \overline{X}^2)$$

$$= \sum X^2 - 2\overline{X}\sum X + n\overline{X}^2$$

$$= \sum X^2 - 2\left(\frac{\sum X}{n}\right)\left(\sum X\right) + n\left(\frac{\sum X}{n}\right)^2$$

$$= \sum X^2 - 2\frac{\left(\sum X\right)^2}{n} + \frac{\left(\sum X\right)^2}{n}$$

$$= \sum X^2 - \frac{\left(\sum X\right)^2}{n}$$

### Note 6.2 The Standard Deviation as a Minimum Value When Deviations Are Taken from the Mean (*Ref.*: Section 6.9)

Let $A$ be the point about which the deviation of each score is taken, and define it as a point that differs from the mean by an amount $d$: $A = \overline{X} + d$. Then,

$$\sum (X - A)^2 = \sum [X - (\overline{X} + d)]^2$$

$$= \sum [(X - \overline{X}) - d]^2$$

$$= \sum [(X - \overline{X})^2 - 2d(X - \overline{X}) + d^2]$$

$$= \sum (X - \overline{X})^2 - 2d \sum (X - \overline{X}) + nd^2$$

From Note 5.1 at the end of Chapter 5, $\sum (X - \overline{X}) = 0$, so

$$\sum (X - A)^2 = \sum (X - \overline{X})^2 + nd^2$$

The right side of this equation shows that $\sum (X - A)^2$ is smallest when $d = 0$. From the definition of $d$, this occurs when $A = \overline{X}$. Because $S_X = \sqrt{\sum (X - \overline{X})^2 / n}$, it is apparent that $S$ has a minimum value when deviations are taken from $\overline{X}$.

## Key Terms, Concepts, and Symbols

measure of variability   (83)

range   (29, 83)

semi-interquartile range   (84)

$Q$   (84)

quartile points   (84)

$Q_1, Q_2, Q_3$   (84)

deviation score   (70, 85)

$X - \overline{X}$   (70, 85)

variance   (85)

$\sigma^2$   (86)

$S^2$   (86)

sum of squares   (86)

$\Sigma(X - \overline{X})^2$   (86)

$SS$   (86)

standard deviation   (88)

$\sigma$   (88)

$S$   (88)

$z$ score   (95)

standard scores   (95)

mean and standard deviation of
  $z$ scores   (96)

percentile rank   (35, 97)

## Problems

**1.** Which measure of variability—the range, semi-interquartile range, or the standard deviation—is (a) best for open-ended distributions? (b) calculated by using only two scores? (c) calculated by taking sum of squared deviations from the mean? (d) has most use in inferential statistics? (e) not responsive to scores in the middle of the distribution? (f) best for very skewed distributions? (g) responsive to the exact position of every score in the distribution? (h) related to the median in its properties? (i) the most resistant to sampling fluctuation?

**2.** For the history midterm exam scores in Table 3.2, find (a) the range and (b) the semi-interquartile range.

3. We want to compare the variability of the two sets of reaction time scores in Data 4A. (a) Find the range of both distributions. (b) Find Q for both distributions. (c) Which set of scores is more variable?

4. On the midterm exam in their anthropology course, Jan's deviation score was +5, Kim's was −12, and Leslie's was 0. (a) Of these three, who did the best and who did the worst? (b) Exactly where did each fall in the distribution in relation to the mean?

5. On the exam cited in Problem 4, the mean for the class was 80. What was the raw score for (a) Jan, (b) Kim, and (c) Leslie?

6. A distribution consists of five scores. For four of the scores, the deviations from the mean are +5, +2, +1, and −8. What is the deviation of the fifth score?

7. The mean of the distribution cited in Problem 6 is 10. What are the raw scores?

8. For the nine scores shown in Figure 5.1, find (a) the variance, and (b) the standard deviation. Use the deviation-score method.

9. Use the raw-score method to calculate the variance and standard deviation for the same nine scores in Problem 8.

10. Distribution X is 5.1, 8.7, 3.5, 5.4, and 7.9. (a) Find the range. Using the raw-score method and keeping all work to one decimal place, find (b) the variance and (c) the standard deviation. Using the deviation-score method, find (d) the variance and (e) the standard deviation. (f) Which method is easier?

11. If the scores in Figure 5.1 are the lengths in inches of rats' tails, what is the unit of measurement for (a) their variance and (b) their standard deviation?

12. A ninth-grade science teacher gives a standard achievement test to his class and finds that $\overline{X} = 90$ with $S_X = 8$. For a national sample of ninth graders $\overline{X} = 75$ with $S_X = 14$. (a) How do his students compare to the national sample? (b) What do the data suggest for teaching science to this class?

13. Distribution X is: 15, 14, 11, 11, 9, and 6. Using the deviation-score method, find (a) the variance, and (b) the standard deviation. Distribution Y is: 17, 16, 13, 13, 11, and 8. Using the deviation-score method,

find (c) the variance, and (d) the standard deviation. By both measures, X and Y have the same variability. (e) Why does the variance work out to be the same for both distributions? (f) Why does the standard deviation work out to be the same for both?

14. In 88 infants, researchers measure the change in heart rate before and after brightening the room. The distribution of changes ranges from −20 to +5 beats per minute, with a mean of −9.7. (Heart rate usually slows when an organism pays attention to a stimulus.) Upon rechecking, the lowest score turns out to be −24. Which measures of variability are affected by the correction?

15. (a) Can the distribution of heart-rate changes cited in Problem 14 have a variance of −16? Explain. (b) Can the distribution have a standard deviation of −4? Explain.

16. Seven scores are 2, 5, 7, 8, 9, 11, and 14. Find (a) S and (b) Q. Now add the extreme score of 24. For the modified distribution (now with $n = 8$), find (c) S and (d) Q. (e) By what percentage did S increase? (f) By what percentage did Q increase? (g) What generalization is illustrated in comparing answers (e) and (f)?

17. Four scores are 2, 3, 5, and 10. (a) Calculate SS, taking the deviations from the mean. (b) Calculate SS, but this time take the deviations from 4. (c) Again calculate SS, but take the deviations from 6. (d) What generalization is illustrated here?

18. In reporting the frequency distribution of annual household income, the 1999 *Statistical Abstract of the United States* uses these class intervals: under $10,000; $10,000–14,999; $15,000–24,999; $25,000–34,999; $35,000–49,999; $50,000–74,999; and $75,000 and over. Which measures of variability could we compute for the distribution as given in terms of those class intervals?

19. A consumer testing company evaluates eight different brands of tires. The tires are tested individually in a laboratory on an artificial surface to control for differences in driving habits and road conditions. The number of miles elapsed until 2/16 inch of tread remains is recorded. The results are 45,000; 40,000; 80,000; 70,000; 65,000; 60,000; 60,000; and 50,000. Find (a) the range, and (b) the standard deviation.

**20.** The standard deviation of a set of scores is 20. What will the standard deviation become if (a) 15 points are added to each score? (b) Each score is divided by 5? (c) 10 points are subtracted from each score and the resulting values are divided by 2? (d) Each score is multiplied by 5, and 20 is then added to each resulting value?

**21.** When answering Problem 19, did you calculate the standard deviation by using the numbers that were given (e.g., 45,000)? If so, how could you have transformed the scores to make the calculation less cumbersome (if you had to calculate by hand)?

**22.** When the researchers of Problem 14 go to punch the heart-rate change scores into their calculator, they eliminate the negative values by adding 25 points to each value. (a) How does this recoding affect the measures of central tendency? Explain. (b) How does this recoding affect the measures of variability? Explain.

**23.** The Wechsler Intelligence Scale has a mean of 100 and a standard deviation of 15. Find the $z$ score (to two decimal places) of an IQ score of (a) 115, (b) 130, (c) 70, (d) 100, (e) 80, (f) 95, (g) 108, (h) 87, and (i) 122.

**24.** For the same intelligence test, find the actual IQ score for the following $z$ score equivalents (use Formula 6.5): (a) −0.60, (b) +1.40, (c) +2.20, (d) −1.80, (e) 0.00, (f) −2.40, (g) +0.20, and (h) +4.40.

**25.** A student's grade on a very difficult English exam is 85. What can we say about the merits of the student's performance? Explain.

**26.** The mean of a set of $z$ scores is always zero. Does this mean that half of a set of $z$ scores will be negative and half positive? Explain.

**27.** Susan and Robin are arguing about who did better on their final exams. Susan got an 88 on her psychology final exam (mean = 74, standard deviation = 12) whereas Robin earned an 82 on her biology exam (mean = 76, standard deviation = 4). All freshmen are required to take both classes. Who did better? Explain.

**28.** Bob and Bert are also debating about who did better on their exams. Bob got a 65 on the psychology exam, and Bert got a 68 on the biology exam. Who did better? Explain.

**29.** For Problem 19, find the $z$ scores of the eight scores. Has the shape of the distribution of eight scores changed? Explain.

# CHAPTER 7

## Standard Scores and the Normal Curve

When you have finished studying this chapter, you should be able to:

- Summarize the history of the concept of the normal curve;
- Know the defining characteristics of a normal curve;
- Use the normal curve table to find areas under the normal curve that fall above or below a specified score;
- Use the normal curve table to find a score when the area (under the normal curve) above or below the score is known; and
- Understand that although no real variable is exactly normally distributed, the normal curve serves as a useful model for many real variables and also for distributions of sample means.

Suppose we toss 8 coins and record the number of heads. It can vary from 0 to 8. Each coin is as likely to come up heads as tails, and the outcome of the toss of any one of the 8 coins in no way affects the outcome of the toss of any other. Because of chance factors, we cannot say precisely how many heads will appear in any one trial of 8 coins. But suppose we ask other questions: If we repeat the act of tossing the 8 coins an extremely large number of times, how often will we obtain 0 heads? How often will heads come up once? Twice? Early mathematicians developed a theory that provides the answers. We show the relative frequency distribution derived from that theory (called a *binomial distribution*, which we will discuss further in Chapter 11) in Figure 7.1. The figure shows that *on the average* there will be 4 heads and that the more divergent the number of heads and tails in any one trial (e.g., 7 heads and 1 tail), the lower the relative frequency of its occurrence.

If we superimpose a curve on the histogram in Figure 7.1, it approximates the bell-shaped, normal curve shown in Figure 4.15*f*. If we tossed 16 coins, rather than 8, there would be more bars in the histogram, and the normal curve would be an even better fit, as illustrated in Figure 7.2. If the number of coins increases infinitely, the number of bars in the histogram similarly increases, and the histogram grows smoother. It is obvious that in this situation, where the outcome of events is generated by the operation of chance factors, the normal curve gives us a good approximation to the actual relative frequency distribution. Before we proceed, some history of the normal curve may help you understand its widespread use as a model for statistical observations.

## 7.1  Historical Aspects of the Normal Curve

In 1733, the French mathematician **Abraham de Moivre** discovered the formula for the normal curve as the limiting case characterizing an infinite number of independent events (such as coin tosses). His work was initially ignored, and further significant development did not occur until the beginning of the 19th century. Then, it

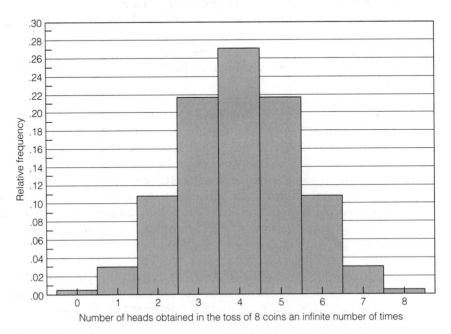

**FIGURE 7.1**  Relative frequencies of heads obtained when 8 coins are tossed an infinite number of times.

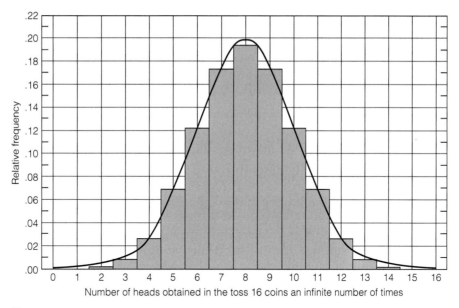

FIGURE 7.2 Relative frequencies of heads obtained when 16 coins are tossed an infinite number of times.

seems that two brilliant mathematicians, the Frenchman **Pierre-Simon** (the Marquis de Laplace) and the German **Carl Friedrich Gauss**, rediscovered the normal curve independently. Gauss was interested in problems in astronomy, such as determining the orbit of a planet. His solutions were based on observations that were subject to error (which he found to be distributed in a bell-shaped fashion), and this led him to a theory of errors of observation. It had such strength that in the 1800s the normal curve came to be known as the "normal law of error." The name is now obsolete, but vestiges of this terminology hang on. Note in Chapter 12, for example, the term *standard error.*

Promotion of the use of the normal curve as a model for other situations is due primarily to the work of **Adolphe Quetelet**, a Belgian, in the middle part of the 19th century. He taught mathematics and astronomy, created the basic methods of physical anthropometrics, and helped found sociology. He believed that the normal curve could be extended to apply to problems in meteorology, anthropology, and human affairs. It was his opinion that "mental and moral traits," when measured, would conform to the "normal law." One of his conceptions was *l'homme moyen* or "the average man." He compared the normal distribution to the notion that Nature, in aiming at a mark (*l'homme moyen*), missed and so produced a distribution of "error" in her effort.

In the late 19th century, the British genius **Sir Francis Galton** began the first serious study of individual differences, an important topic for psychology and education. He found that many mental and physical traits conformed reasonably well to the normal curve, and he was greatly impressed by the applicability of the normal curve to natural phenomena. In 1889 he wrote:

> I know of scarcely anything so apt to impress the imagination as the wonderful form of cosmic order expressed by the "Law of Frequency of Error." The

law would have been personified by the Greeks and deified, if they had known of it. It reigns with serenity and in complete self-effacement amidst the wildest confusion. The huger the mob and the greater the apparent anarchy, the more perfect is its sway. It is the supreme law of Unreason. Whenever a large sample of chaotic elements are taken in hand and marshalled in the order of their magnitude, an unsuspected and most beautiful form of regularity proves to have been latent all along. F. GALTON, *Natural Inheritance*, MacMillan and Co., London, *1889, p. 66.*

His enthusiasm is understandable and worthy of our appreciation. His theory, however, must be tempered in light of current knowledge. We will present a more balanced view in the coming sections.

So the time has come for us to examine the normal curve more closely. We need to know what the normal curve is, what its properties are, the ways in which it is useful as a statistical model, and how to put it to work in answering questions.

## 7.2 The Nature of the Normal Curve

**normal curve**
a mathematical abstraction with a particular defining equation (see Mathematical Note 7.1); the equation describes a family of normal curves

It is important that you learn to distinguish between data that are normally distributed (or approximately so) and the normal curve itself. The **normal curve** is a mathematical abstraction with a particular defining equation (given in Note 7.1 at the end of this chapter). As a mathematical abstraction, it is not associated with (or determined by) any event or events in the real world. It is not, therefore, a "law of nature," contrary to the thought and terminology associated with it a century ago. In the same way, the equation of a circle is a mathematical abstraction and not a law of nature. We may find a boulder that has a circumference approximated by a circle having a particular equation, or observe that the circumference of the earth roughly conforms to the equation of another circle. Nevertheless, the circular objects do not of necessity exist because of the mathematical abstraction called a circle. We shall return to this point in Section 7.6.

Just as the equation of a circle describes a family of circles, some big and some small, so *the equation of the normal curve describes a family of normal curves.* The family differs in their means and standard deviations. We illustrate three possibilities in Figure 7.3: equal means and unequal standard deviations, unequal means and equal standard deviations, and unequal means and unequal standard deviations.[1]

In other respects, members of this family have the same characteristics. All normal curves are **symmetrical distributions**; that is, the left half of the normal curve is a mirror image of the right half. They are **unimodel distributions**, with the mode at the center. Indeed, the mean, median, and mode all have the same value. If we start at the center of the curve and work outward, we see that the height of the curve descends gradually at first, then faster, and finally slower. A curious and important situation exists at the extremes of the curve. Although the curve descends quickly toward the horizontal axis, it never actually touches it, no matter how far out one goes.

---

[1]When the normal curve is an appropriate model for real events, it is most often the population of such events that is so modeled. Consequently, we shall use $\mu$ and $\sigma$ in connection with the normal curve throughout this chapter rather than $\overline{X}$ and $S$.

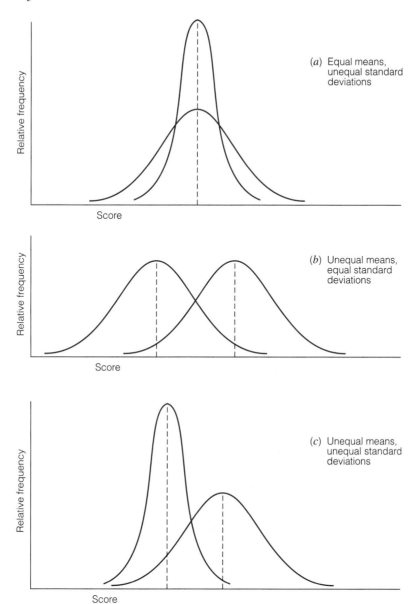

**FIGURE 7.3** Variations of normal curves in means and standard deviations.

**characteristics of normal curves**
symmetrical; unimodal; asymptotic with the horizontal axis; a continuous distribution; the proportion of the area under the curve relative to a particular range of values on the horizontal axis is the same when the values are stated on a comparable basis

It is therefore said to be an **asymptotic curve** with respect to the horizontal axis. You might think that if the curve never touches the $X$ axis, a large proportion of the total area under the curve must lie in the extremes, but this is not so. For example, the area included within the range of $\mu \pm 3\sigma$ comprises approximately 99.7% of the total area, as we learned in Section 6.10 (see Figure 6.3).

The normal curve is a **continuous distribution**. However, remember that the process of measurement always reduces a continuous variable to a discrete variable (see Section 2.5). Thus, when the normal curve is used as a model for events of the real world, it can be only an approximation.

Finally, *for all normal curves, the proportion of the area under the curve relative to a particular range of values on the horizontal axis is the same when the values are stated on a comparable basis.* For example, approximately two-thirds (68.26%) of the area under a normal curve lies within the range of $\mu \pm 1\sigma$ (see Figure 6.3). Thus in a normal curve characterized by $\mu = 100$ and $\sigma = 20$, about two-thirds of the area falls between the values of 80 and 120, and in a normal curve characterized by $\mu = 500$ and $\sigma = 100$, about two-thirds of the area falls between the values of 400 and 600. We will consider problems of this type next.

## 7.3 Standard Scores and the Normal Curve

Recall that the equation defining the normal curve actually describes a whole family of curves. Their means vary, and their standard deviations vary; it is their *shape* that they have in common. To use the normal curve as a model, we need a way to locate a position within a normal distribution that does not depend on the particular mean and the particular standard deviation of the distribution. We can do this by converting raw scores to standard scores.

Look at Figure 7.3. In what sense do the curves there all have the same shape, the shape called normal? *The shapes are the same in that the area under each curve is distributed in the same way.* Thus, we need only a single table of the areas under the normal curve for work with *all* normal distributions, irrespective of their means and standard deviations. All that we need to do is translate the relevant raw score to a $z$ score in order to use the table. Table A in Appendix E gives you the area under the upper half of the normal curve that falls above or below a particular point along the horizontal axis when that point is *expressed as a standard score.*

**standardized normal curve**

a normal distribution in which scores have been transformed to standard ($z$) scores

Why is it important that you learn to calculate area under the normal curve for a specified span along the abscissa? Because *the proportion of area under the curve corresponds to the proportion of scores in the distribution.* Thus, if about 68% of the area under the normal curve falls within 1 standard deviation of the mean (above *and* below), we know that about 68% of the cases in the distribution fall within that range. For example, if we know that scores by college seniors on the Graduate Record Exam (GRE) approximate a normal curve with a mean of 500 and standard deviation of 100, we can quickly determine that about 68% of the seniors score between 400 and 600. Similarly, if IQ as measured by the Wechsler Adult Intelligence Scale (WAIS) is normally distributed with a mean of 100 and standard deviation of 15, we know that about 95% of adults in the United States have an IQ between 70 and 130. The next two sections are concerned only with distributions that follow the normal curve.

## 7.4 The Standard Normal Curve: Finding Areas When the Score Is Known

Given a distribution of scores, we are often interested in knowing what proportion of the scores lie above or below a certain value or between two particular values. If the shape of the curve closely resembles the normal curve, we can use Table A in Appendix E to answer questions like these. In this table, the total area under the curve is defined as unity. To use the table, we need only remember that the normal curve is symmetrical and therefore has 50% of its total area below the mean ($z = 0$) and 50% of its area above the mean.

### Case 1. Finding the Area under the Normal Curve that Falls above a Known Score

You will frequently see questions of the following type in statistical work: Given a normally distributed variable with a mean of 100 and a standard deviation of 20, what proportion of scores will fall above 120? Suppose, for example, that 3,000 entering freshmen at State University are given an entrance examination in mathematics and that the scores prove to be distributed normally with a mean of 100 and a standard deviation of 20. If the university decides to place all students scoring above 120 into honors math, how many students will be placed into the class? We illustrate this problem in Figure 7.4a.

The first step is to translate the score of 120 to a $z$ score: $(120-100)/20 = +1.00$. We may now use Table A in Appendix E. In this table, locate the value $z = 1.00$ in the first column and look across that row for the entry in the column headed "Area beyond $z$." This entry is .1587, which tells us that in *any* batch of scores that is normally distributed, .1587 of the scores fall above $z = +1.0$, regardless of the values of $\mu$ and $\sigma$. Because the total area under the curve is defined as unity in this table, we may interpret the value .1587 as the proportion of the total area falling in the tail. As we noted in the last section, area under the curve is proportional to the frequency of scores. Thus, our question is answered as follows: Because .1587 of the scores fall above the score 120, (.1587 × 3,000) or 476 freshmen will be placed in honors math.

Suppose the problem had been to determine the number of freshmen scoring above 80 on the exam. Figure 7.4b illustrates this problem. The z-score equivalent of 80 is $-1.00$. Negative $z$ scores do not appear in the table. Because the normal curve is symmetrical, as many scores fall below a $z$ score of $-1.00$ as fall above a $z$ score of $+1.00$. The table therefore does not need to show both positive and negative values of the $z$ scores. In this problem, we already know that .5000 of the scores fall above the mean, so all we need to determine is the proportion of scores between the mean and a score that is 1 standard deviation below the mean. You can find this information in Column 2 of Table A. For a score with a $z$ value of $-1.00$, that

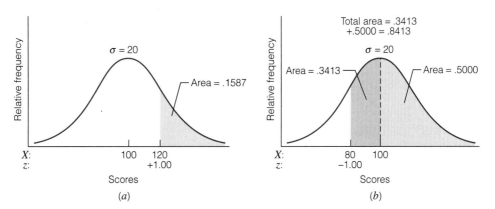

**FIGURE 7.4** Proportion of scores in a normal distribution characterized by $\mu = 100$ and $\sigma = 20$ (a) exceeding a score of 120 and (b) falling above a score of 80.

proportion is .3413. Adding .3413 to .5000, we find the total proportion of students above 80 to be .8413. Thus, about (.8413 × 3,000) or 2,524 students scored above 80 on the entrance exam.

### Case 2. Finding the Area under the Normal Curve that Falls below a Known Score

Suppose that State University has also decided to place all students scoring less than 85 into remedial math. How many must take the remedial course? This problem is illustrated in Figure 7.5*a*. To solve the problem, we must determine the *z*-score equivalent of 85, which is $(85 - 100)/20 = -15/20 = -.75$. We use Column 3 in Table A and see that in any normal distribution .2266 of the area falls below a score that is three-quarters of a standard deviation below the mean. Thus, .2266 × 3,000 = 679.8, or roughly 680 freshmen will have to take remedial math.

As you can see, answers to this type of problem are found very much like those for the first. For example, how many students at State University were not placed into honors math (how many scored below 120)? This is illustrated in Figure 7.5*b*. We know that .5000 of the scores fall below the mean, so we must add this to the proportion of scores falling between the mean and a score 1 standard deviation above the mean: $z = (120 - 100)/20 = +1.00$. Column 2 shows that the proportion is .3413, which when added to .5000 gives .8413. Thus, (.8413 × 3,000) or about 2,524 freshmen did not earn a high enough score on the entrance exam to be placed in honors math. Compare the procedure here with the manner in which we worked the second problem in Case 1.

### Case 3. Finding the Area under the Normal Curve that Falls between Two Known Scores

Given the entrance examination results of Case 1, how many entering freshmen at State University were placed into regular freshmen-level math courses (i.e., were not placed into either remedial or honors courses)? In other words, how many scored between 85 and 120? This problem appears in Figure 7.6*a*. Again, the first step is to obtain the *z*-score equivalents of these two scores. We use Formula 6.5 and find the

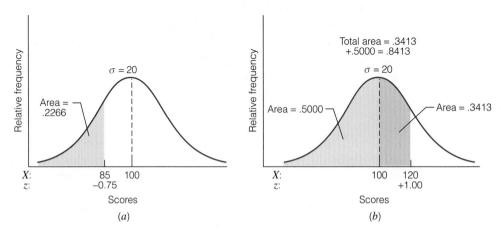

**FIGURE 7.5**  Proportion of scores in a normal distribution characterized by $\mu = 100$ and $\sigma = 20$ (*a*) below a score of 85 and (*b*) below a score of 120.

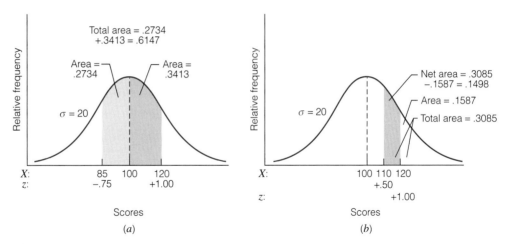

**FIGURE 7.6** Proportion of scores in a normal distribution characterized by $\mu = 100$ and $\sigma = 20$ falling (*a*) between scores of 85 and 120 and (*b*) between scores of 110 and 120.

values to be $z = -.75$ and $z = +1.00$, respectively. If we find the area under the curve between the $z$ score of $-.75$ and the mean and add this to the area between the mean and the $z$ score of $+1.00$, we shall have the proportion of scores that fall within the given range. In Table A, the second column, "Area between mean and $z$," gives the appropriate values:

Area between $z = -.75$ and the mean: .2734

Area between the mean and $z = +1.00$: .3413

Total area: .6147

Multiplying 3,000 by .6147, we find that 1,844.1 or roughly 1,844 students scored between 85 and 120 on the entrance exam.

For the same distribution of entering freshmen, suppose we wanted to know how many scores fall between the values of 110 and 120? We will assume that the mean and standard deviation are the same as before. One way to answer is to determine the proportion of scores falling above 110 and subtract from this value the proportion of scores falling above 120. The problem and its solution appear in Figure 7.6*b*. We begin, as usual, by converting the raw scores to $z$ scores: $X = 110$ becomes $z = +.50$ and $X = 120$ becomes $z = +1.00$. With use of Table A, the solution is

Area above $z = +.50$: .3085

Area above $z = +1.00$: $-.1587$

Difference: .1498

We multiply .1498 × 3,000 and get 449.4 or roughly 449 scores. In solving problems of this kind, beginners are sometimes tempted to subtract one $z$ score from the other and find the area corresponding to that difference. A moment's thought shows that this will not work. It is the difference *between the two areas* that is required. To keep $z$ scores and areas separate in your mind, keep them separate on the page. When you sketch a problem involving the normal curve, show $z$ scores only below the abscissa and areas only above the abscissa, as in our diagrams.

# 7.5 The Standard Normal Curve: Finding Scores When the Area Is Known

Problems of this sort are like those in the previous section, except that their form is inverted. There we knew the score and wanted to find the area under the curve. Here, we know the area and want to find the score. We solve these problems by reading Table A backward, that is, by locating the area in column 2 or 3 and then identifying the $z$-score equivalent of the desired value.

### Case 1. Finding the Score above or below Which a Certain Percentage of the Total Scores Fall

Suppose that neighboring City University also has remedial and honors math courses for entering freshmen, but it determines placement in a slightly different manner. Students take the same entrance exam, but City University places the top 20% into honors math. Let us assume that the mean is again 100 and the standard deviation is again 20. What score separates the upper 20% of the entering freshmen from the lower 80%? If (and only if) the shape of the distribution of scores is well approximated by the normal curve, Table A can help us.

The problem appears in Figure 7.7a. In Table A, we look for a value as close as possible to .2000 in the column headed "Area beyond $z$" and note that the $z$ score associated with it is 0.84. The 0.84 can be positive or negative. Which do we want? Because we wish to separate the top 20% from the remainder, the value of the $z$ score is positive: $z = +0.84$. We then substitute this value into our formula for $z$ and solve for $X$:

$$z = \frac{X - \mu_X}{\sigma_X}$$

$$+0.84 = \frac{X - 100}{20}$$

$$(.84)(20) = X - 100$$

$$16.8 = X - 100$$

$$116.8 = X$$

Thus, to be placed into honors math at City University, a freshman would have to score at least 117 on the entrance exam.

If City University places students who scored in the bottom 20% on the exam in a remedial math course, what score separates these students from the upper 80%? This problem is illustrated in Figure 7.7b and we work it just like before except that, in this case, we must use the negative value for the $z$ score associated with .2000 in Column 3 of Table A. When we substitute this value, $-.84$, in the formula for $z$, we find that $X = 100 - 16.8$, or 83.2. Thus, students who scored 83 or below on the exam would have to take remedial math.

### Case 2. Finding the Limits within Which a Certain Percentage of Scores Fall Equidistant from the Mean

Suppose City University is interested in knowing the values on the mathematics entrance examination within which the central 90% of the scores fall. The problem appears in Figure 7.8. In this case, 45% of the scores within the range of interest fall

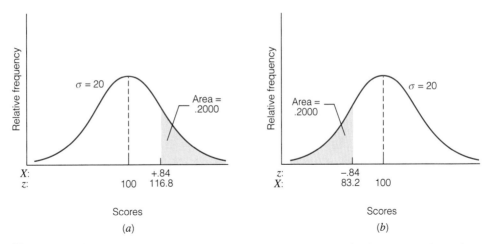

**FIGURE 7.7** The score dividing (*a*) the upper 20% and (*b*) the lower 20% from the remainder of scores in a normal distribution characterized by $\mu = 100$ and $\sigma = 20$.

above the mean and 45% fall below the mean, leaving 5% in each tail of the distribution. What is the score which has 45% of the scores between it and the mean? From Table A, we find that it has a $z$ value of 1.65. The scores are therefore located 1.65 standard deviations above and below the mean. We substitute this value into the formula for $z$ and solve for $X$:

| **LOWER LIMIT** | **UPPER LIMIT** |
|---|---|
| $z = \dfrac{X - \mu_X}{\sigma_X}$ | $z = \dfrac{X - \mu_X}{\sigma_X}$ |
| $-1.65 = \dfrac{X - 100}{20}$ | $+1.65 = \dfrac{X - 100}{20}$ |
| $(-1.65)(20) = X - 100$ | $(+1.65)(20) = X - 100$ |
| $-33 = X - 100$ | $+33 = X - 100$ |
| $67 = X$ | $133 = X$ |

Thus, 90% of the scores on this exam fall between $(100 - 33) = 67$ and $(100 + 33) = 133$.

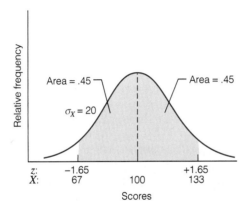

**FIGURE 7.8** The limits that include the central 90% of scores in a normal distribution characterized by $\mu = 100$ and $\sigma = 20$.

In the preceding problems, the transitions from $z$ score to raw score were made by using the formula for a $z$ score. The equivalent formula for making this transition may be obtained by solving Formulas 6.5$a$ and 6.5$b$ for $X$:

| FORMULAS FOR TRANSLATING A $z$ SCORE TO A RAW SCORE | | |
|---|---|---|
| *For populations* | $X = \mu_X + z\sigma_X$ | (7.1$a$) |
| *For samples* | $X = \overline{X} + zS_X$ | (7.1$b$) |

When we use this formula to solve for the upper limit in the preceding problem, we find:

$$X = 100 + (+1.65)(20) = 133.0$$

the same value we obtained previously.

## 7.6 The Normal Curve as a Model for Real Variables

We now know that the normal curve is a rather good fit to a large number of distributions of real data in a wide variety of sciences. The distribution has applications in physics, chemistry, microbiology, meteorology, engineering, and economics, to name only a few. It appears to be a rather good fit to many (but not all) distributions of physical measurements made in biology and anthropology. For example, in reasonably *homogeneous* human populations, the distribution of height follows the normal curve closely. As the mathematical astronomers found, it fits errors of observation in many circumstances.

But is the normal curve a "law of nature," revealing some unifying principle that connects so many disciplines, perhaps even a principle that explains the generation of values? In a few cases it does seem to have an explanatory nature, as in determining the probability of obtaining a given number of heads in the coin-tossing example we described in the beginning of this chapter. However, the hope of the 19th century that it might be a unifying principle of science seems no more justified than the view that the circle is a law of nature that unites the shape of a drop of oil in suspension, the pupil of the eye, and the wave made by dropping a pebble into still water. Nevertheless, it does offer a convenient and reasonably accurate *description* of a great number of distributions.

Several words of caution are in order, however. First, the normal curve as a model best describes an infinity of observations that are on a continuous scale of measurement. As we know, recorded observations are discrete rather than continuous, and among concrete data we do *not* have an infinity of observations. Real populations may be large, but they are not of infinite size. Although the normal curve closely approximates distributions of data of many kinds, it is a fair speculation that *no real variable is exactly normally distributed.*

Second, *many variables are not normally distributed.* This includes the results of many achievement and psychological tests (see Point of Controversy). Some other variables that tend to show at least a degree of skewness are human body weight, size of

# Point of Controversy

## How Normal Is the Normal Curve?

Galton (1889) believed that so many mental and physical traits conformed to the bell-shaped normal curve that it was an expression of cosmic order (the "Law of Frequency of Error"). Though statisticians today do not regard the normal curve as a law, many have continued to assume that real-world variables are frequently distributed in this manner. One textbook even joked that "God loves the normal curve!" (Hopkins, Glass, & Hopkins, 1987, p. 51).

Doubts concerning the utility of the normal curve as a model for the distribution of real-world variables have occasionally surfaced. Nunnally (1978), for example, suggests that because tests of mental ability are usually constructed with items that are positively interrelated, the "test scores are seldom normally distributed." John Tukey and other advocates of exploratory data analysis (see Section 3.6) also express their doubts: "Frequently a few large errors infect the data so that the tails of the underlying distribution are heavier than those of the Gaussian distribution" (Hoaglin, Mosteller, & Tukey, 2000). Geary (1947) earlier voiced even stronger doubts: "Normality is a myth; there never was, and never will be, a normal distribution."

What the naysayers lacked, however, was empirical data to support their claim that large discrepancies from normality occur frequently in psychological and educational measures—until Theodore Micceri, that is. Micceri (1989), a professor of education at the University of South Florida, examined the distributions of 440 measures of achievement and psychological traits obtained in applied settings. Most of the distributions came from recently published research articles, and the remainder from national tests, tests used statewide in Florida, districtwide tests, and college entrance and Graduate Record Examination scores at the University of South Florida. Nearly 70% included samples of 1,000 or more. Only 19 of the 440 distributions were found to approximate the normal curve. Of the remainder, only half of the distributions could be defined as relatively smooth; the others were "lumpy" (29% were bimodal or multimodal). Half of them had at least one extremely heavy tail, and nearly one-third were found to be extremely asymmetric.

The normal curve has been a useful mathematical model for statisticians, particularly because of their faith in the central limit theorem (see Section 12.4). This states that the distribution of an infinite number of sample means (from samples of a fixed size randomly drawn from a population) approaches normality as the sample size increases, irrespective of the shape of the population of scores. The greater the population differs from normality, the greater sample size must be for the central limit theorem to hold. As you will learn in later chapters, we use this theoretical distribution of sample means to make inferences about the mean of the population.

Research regarding the effects of testing samples drawn from nonnormal distributions has generally looked at smooth mathematical models with tails greater than or less than the normal curve's. This research has found that the commonly employed tests used in inferential statistics are good under these nonnormal population conditions. However, until recently no one had yet examined how well these tests hold up using population distributions that vary from the normal curve as much as the "lumpy" and asymmetric real-world distributions found by Micceri. The implications of Micceri's findings for inferential statistics are still being debated, but it is possible that many commonly used statistical tests may not be as good as previously thought when using small samples. (See the Point of Controversy in Chapter 22 for related material.)

family income, reaction time, and frequency of accidents. Even variables that can exhibit a normal distribution in homogeneous populations may fail to do so under other circumstances. The distribution of height of a mixed group of men and women is bimodal, and a mental test that might yield a normal distribution of scores if appropriately constructed may produce distributions skewed to the left or right if the test is too easy or too hard for the group measured.

## 7.7 The Normal Curve as a Model for Sampling Distributions

*The second way in which the normal curve functions as a model is for a distribution of sample statistics.* For instance, if we draw a very great number of random samples from a population, each sample of the same size, and compute the mean of each sample, the distribution of this large number of means will approximate the normal curve. For distributions of this type, the fit of the normal curve is often very good indeed. This is a property of utmost importance in statistical inference because, as you will see in later chapters, we must know the shape of the distribution of sample means to make an inference about the population mean.

We shall see the normal curve in its role as a model from time to time in the next few chapters. Then, beginning with Chapter 12 and throughout most of the remaining chapters, it will be of central importance.

## 7.8 Summary

The normal curve is a mathematical abstraction defined by an equation. The equation describes not just one curve, but a family of them. Although they may differ with respect to means and standard deviations, all normal curves are symmetrical, unimodal, and continuous, with tails that are asymptotic to the horizontal axis.

The area under all normal curves is distributed in the same way. Thus, to use the normal curve as a model, we need a way to locate a position within a normal distribution that does not depend on the particular mean and standard deviation of the distribution. We can compare variables with different measurement units by converting them to standard scores. Changing raw scores in a distribution to $z$ scores does not change the shape of the distribution. Thus, when we convert raw scores in a normal distribution to $z$ scores, the result is the standard normal curve. Table A in Appendix E gives the proportion of the area under the upper half of the curve that falls beyond a stated value of $z$ or between the mean and a particular value of $z$. Because area under the curve is proportional to the frequency of scores in a distribution, we can use this table to calculate the number of scores in a normal distribution that fall above or below any value or between any two score points. Given a proportion of the scores (for example, the upper 20%), we can also determine the value that separates this proportion from the remainder of the distribution.

There is no real variable that is exactly normally distributed, but the resemblance is close enough in some cases that the normal curve serves as a useful model. As we shall see in later chapters, this is especially true for distributions of some sample statistics (such as $\overline{X}$).

## Mathematical Note

### Note 7.1 The Equation of the Normal Curve (*Ref.*: Section 7.2)

The equation of the normal curve is

$$Y = \frac{N}{\sigma\sqrt{2\pi}} \, e^{-(X-\mu)^2/2\sigma^2}$$

As a model for a frequency distribution, it may be interpreted as follows:

where  $Y$ = height of the curve directly above any given value of $X$

      $N$ = number of cases

      $X$ = a raw score

      $\mu$ = mean of the set of scores

      $\sigma$ = standard deviation of the set of scores

      $\left.\begin{array}{l} \pi = 3.1416 \\ e = 2.7183 \end{array}\right\}$ mathematical constants

    The variables that determine what $Y$ will be are $X$, $\mu$, $\sigma$, and $N$. Basically, the area under the curve is determined by $N$, the location of the center of the curve by $\mu$, and the rapidity with which the curve approaches the abscissa by $\sigma$.

    If one chooses to speak of a normal curve of unit area, in which the scores are standard scores, then $N = 1$, $\mu = 0$, and $\sigma = 1$, and the equation becomes

$$Y = \frac{1}{\sqrt{2\pi}} \, e^{-(z^2/2)}$$

In this form, the value of $z$ is the only variable that determines $Y$, the relative frequency.

    Strictly speaking, $Y$ in the normal curve is not interpretable as frequency; it is simply the height of the curve corresponding to a particular (point) value of $X$. Frequency *is* interpretable as the area under the normal curve that falls between two values of $X$ (the frequency of scores within that range). The frequencies of scores between limits of given width differ, depending on where the interval is located on the abscissa. If the distance between the two values of $X$ is decreased to a very small but finite quantity, the area between these limits becomes approximately proportional to the height of the curve at the midpoint of the limits. It is in this sense that we suggest that $Y$ in the normal curve may be taken as an indication of frequency.

## Key Terms, Concepts, and Symbols

Abraham de Moivre  (106)

Carl Friedrich Gauss  (107)

Adolphe Quetelet  (107)

Sir Francis Galton  (107)

normal curve  (108)

symmetrical distribution  (108)

unimodal distribution  (108)

asymptotic curve  (109)

continuous distribution  (109)

standard score  (95, 110)

$z$ score  (95, 110)

standardized normal curve  (110)

# Problems

1. In the population of adult Americans, the variable IQ is found to be normally distributed. Discuss the similarities and differences between a normally distributed variable and the normal curve.

2. For normally distributed scores, what proportion of scores would fall: (a) Above $z = +1.00$? (b) Above $z = +2.00$? (c) Above $z = +3.00$? (d) Below $z = -2.00$? (e) Below $z = -3.00$?

3. For normally distributed scores, what proportion of scores would fall: (a) Above $z = -1.00$? (b) Below $z = 0$? (c) Below $z = +2.00$? (d) Below $z = +0.85$?

4. For normally distributed scores, what proportion of scores would fall (a) Between $z = -1.00$ and $z = +1.00$? (b) Between $z = -2.00$ and $z = +2.00$? (c) Between $z = -3.00$ and $z = +3.00$? (d) Between $z = -0.75$ and $z = +1.25$?

5. For normally distributed scores, what proportion of scores would fall: (a) Between $z = +.25$ and $z = +1.25$? (b) Between $z = -1.00$ and $z = -2.00$? (c) between $z = +2.00$ and $z = +3.00$?

6. For normally distributed scores, what proportion of scores would fall: (a) Outside the limits $z = -2.00$ and $z = +2.00$? (b) Outside the limits $z = -3.00$ and $z = +3.00$? (c) Outside the limits $z = -1.00$ and $z = +2.00$?

7. If scores are normally distributed with a mean of 500 and a standard deviation of 100, what proportion of the scores fall: (a) Above 550? (b) Above 600? (c) Below 420? (d) Above 350? (e) Between 550 and 750? (f) Between 300 and 625? (g) Between 625 and 725? (h) Between 380 and 480?

8. In a normal distribution of 1,000 aptitude test scores, with a mean of 60 and a standard deviation of 8, how many scores fall: (a) Above 76? (b) Below 80? (c) Above 50? (d) Below 46? (e) Between 48 and 52? (f) Between 58 and 70?

9. Among normally distributed scores, what $z$ score (a) Divides the upper 5% of scores from the remainder? (b) Divides the upper 2.5% of scores from the remainder? (c) Divides the upper 1% of scores from the remainder? (d) Divides the upper .5% of scores from the remainder?

10. Among normally distributed scores, what are the $z$ score limits that identify the central (a) 99% of scores? (b) 95% of scores? (c) 50% of scores?

11. You have just learned that you scored 625 on the math portion of the Graduate Record Examination. The GRE has a mean of 500 and a standard deviation of 100. What percentage of students who took the GRE scored lower than you?

12. At Smart University, all new freshmen are given an English proficiency exam during the week of registration. Scores are normally distributed with a mean of 70 and a standard deviation of 10. The university has decided to place the top 25% into honors English and the bottom 20% into remedial English. What scores separate the upper 25% and lower 20% of the students from the rest?

13. General Machines Company is hiring new employees. The positions require some basic arithmetic skills, but the company is worried that the work is not challenging enough to keep highly skilled individuals interested. Therefore, they administer a screening test to all job applicants and decide to eliminate from consideration anyone scoring in the bottom or top 15%. If scores are normally distributed with a mean of 40 and a standard deviation of 8, what are the two outside limits between which applicants must score to be considered for the positions?

14. State University has no honors English course but instead places all freshmen scoring at least 60 on a proficiency exam (mean = 50, standard deviation = 10) into an advanced composition course. If the scores are normally distributed and there are 2,500 entering freshmen, how many will be put into the advanced course?

15. To join the national organization Mensa, you must provide verified evidence that you scored at least 150 on the Wechsler Adult Intelligence Scale (WAIS). WAIS scores are normally distributed in the population with

a mean of 100 and a standard deviation of 15. (a) What proportion of the population are eligible to join? (b) If there are 180 million adult Americans, how many of them could join?

16. Seven thousand runners enter a local marathon in which they can qualify to enter the New York City Marathon if they complete the 26-mile plus distance in under 3 hours and 10 minutes. Only 6,350 runners complete the race. If finishing times are normally distributed with a mean of 3 hours 40 minutes and a standard deviation of 28 minutes, how many runners qualified?

# CHAPTER 8
## Correlation

When you have finished studying this chapter, you should be able to:

- Understand that correlation refers to the degree of relationship between two variables, and the greater the correlation between two variables, the better we are able to predict the value of one from knowledge of the other;

- Construct a scatter diagram to graphically display the relationship between pairs of scores;

- Understand that the greater the degree of linear relationship between two variables, the more closely the points of intersection (for the $X$ and $Y$ variables) on the scatter diagram resemble a straight line;

- Understand that Pearson's product-moment correlation coefficient ($r$) is used to show only the extent of linear relationship between two variables;

- Explain how Pearson's $r$ shows both the degree and direction of correlation between two variables, and know that values of $r$ range from $-1.00$ (a perfect negative correlation) to $+1.00$ (a perfect positive correlation);

- Know how to calculate Pearson's $r$;
- Know when and how to use Spearman's rank-order correlation coefficient ($r_S$) in place of Pearson's $r$;
- Understand that a correlation between two variables does not prove that there is a causal relationship;
- Understand that adding or subtracting a (positive) constant to all scores, or multiplying or dividing all scores by a (positive) constant, does not affect the value of $r$;
- Explain several variables that affect the value of $r$; and
- Know that there are several other methods besides Pearson's $r$ and Spearman's $r_S$ to measure the degree of association between two variables.

Remember the Saturday morning back in high school you spent hunched over the Scholastic Aptitude Test? (Maybe it was the American College Test.) The SAT, like other tests of mental ability, collects only a small sample of a person's knowledge, but that sample is useful to colleges and universities because scores on the SAT (or the ACT) are related to grades earned later in college. Students with higher scores usually go on to do better in college than those with lower scores. However, the relationship is not perfect. Sometimes a person who scored low on the test gets surprisingly good grades in college; sometimes a person who scored high gets low grades.

**correlation**
a measure of the degree of relationship between two variables

How can we best describe the degree of relationship between two variables, such as test scores and college grades? This is an example of a question about **correlation**. Closely related is the problem of **prediction**. If there is a correlation between two variables, then from a person's score on one variable, we can do better than chance in predicting that person's score on the other variable. Many college admissions committees, for example, use SAT or ACT test scores to predict their applicants' freshman-year grade point averages (GPAs). If an applicant's predicted GPA falls below a certain standard, a committee may reject the applicant. As already indicated, the predictive value of the SAT is not perfect. In general, though, *the greater the association between two variables, the more accurately we can predict the standing in one from the standing in the other.*

**prediction**
when two variables are correlated, estimating the value of one variable from the known value of the other; the better the correlation between the variables, the better the prediction

Determining the degree of correlation and prediction is important in many areas of psychology and education. To establish the reliability of a test (i.e., the consistency in scores over repeated administrations), for example, we would want to know to what extent initial performance correlates with performance on the same test at a subsequent time. The test would be useless if it yielded scores that fluctuate widely over time. Correlation and prediction are also important in establishing test validity (i.e., the agreement between a test score and the quality it is supposed to measure). For example, to what extent are scores on a mechanical aptitude test predictive of on-the-job performance as a machinist? A strong correlation between the two would help a vocational counselor do her job. Other examples of problems in association: Is there a relation between reading speed and reading comprehension? If so, how much? Is brain weight related to IQ? Is the number of cigarettes smoked related to the incidence of lung cancer?

Correlation is the topic of this chapter, and prediction is the topic of the next. Chapter 10 will help enrich your understanding of both.

# 8.1 Some History

In 1859, the Englishman Charles Darwin presented his theory of evolution by natural selection. One of the assumptions of the theory is that there is variation among individuals. To verify the theory, it became important to study traits in which organisms of the same species differ and to determine how those traits are influenced by heredity. These problems interested Darwin's cousin **Sir Francis Galton**, a gentleman scholar and genius, and Galton's research on them founded the study of individual differences. From his laboratory, techniques for assessing correlation and making prediction eventually emerged.

To study the inheritance of stature, for example, Galton collected observations on families consisting of parents with grown children. To simplify his data, for each of the offspring he calculated the midparent height as the mean of the mother's and the father's heights. (He first multiplied the mother's height by 1.08 to adjust it for the mean sex difference between the scores.) To organize and summarize the observations, Galton put the midparent height on one axis of a chart and offspring's height on the other axis in the manner displayed in Table 8.1. The data given in the table, in fact, are his (Galton, 1889, p. 208). Each entry in the body of the table is a frequency for that particular row–column intersection, called a *cell*. Look, for example, at the intersection of the row labeled 66–67 (height of offspring) and the column labeled 68–69 (midparent height). The frequency of 25 shown in that cell indicates that there were 25 children whose adult height was between 66 and 67 inches and whose midparent height was between 68 and 69 inches. Distributions like Table 8.1 that show the relation between two variables are called **bivariate distributions**.

**bivariate distribution**
a distribution that shows the relation between two variables

From these data, Galton concluded that taller parents generally—but not inevitably—produced offspring who were also relatively tall. This relationship is apparent if we track the median offspring height column by column. The shaded cells are those in which the medians lie. For children whose midparent height was between 68 and 69 inches, for example, median adult height (found in the cell with 34 observations) was also between 68 and 69 inches. We can see that in the families with taller parents, represented in the columns toward the right of the table, the median offspring height was generally greater than in the families with shorter parents.

Galton perceived that he could summarize such data with a line showing how the children's heights related to the parents' heights, and that a straight line was often appropriate. We have drawn such a line in Table 8.1. Galton also saw that, other things being equal (such as sample variances and scale of measurement), a steeper line indicated a closer relationship between the two variables. In 1896, **Karl Pearson**, a scientist associated with Galton's laboratory, developed a rigorous mathematical treatment of these matters. Pearson's procedures are the ones you will learn about first.

# 8.2 Graphing Bivariate Distributions: The Scatter Diagram

The raw data summarized in Table 8.1 consisted of pairs of scores. For each of the offspring in his sample, Galton knew his or her adult height and the mean height of the parents. Like Galton's study, *any problem in correlation requires pairs of scores*. For each case under observation, we must know the score on a first variable, which we will call $X$, and the score on a second variable, $Y$.

TABLE 8.1   *Galton's Data on Midparent Height and Height of Adult Offspring*

| HEIGHT OF ADULT OFFSPRING* (IN.) | MIDPARENT HEIGHT (IN.) | | | | | | | | | | |
|---|---|---|---|---|---|---|---|---|---|---|---|
| | BELOW 64 | 64–65 | 65–66 | 66–67 | 67–68 | 68–69 | 69–70 | 70–71 | 71–72 | 72–73 | ABOVE 73 |
| Above 74 | | | | | | | | | | | |
| 73–74 | | | | | | | 5 | 3 | 2 | 4 | 3 |
| 72–73 | | | | | | 3 | 4 | 3 | 2 | 2 | |
| 71–72 | | | 1 | | 4 | 4 | 11 | 4 | 9 | 7 | |
| 70–71 | | | 2 | 4 | 11 | 18 | 20 | 7 | 4 | 2 | |
| 69–70 | 1 | 2 | 5 | 13 | 19 | 21 | 25 | 14 | 10 | 1 | |
| 68–69 | 1 | 5 | 7 | 14 | 38 | 48 | 33 | 18 | 5 | 2 | |
| 67–68 | 2 | 5 | 7 | 17 | 28 | 34 | 20 | 12 | 3 | 1 | |
| 66–67 | 2 | 1 | 11 | 17 | 38 | 31 | 27 | 3 | 4 | | |
| 65–66 | 1 | 4 | 11 | 2 | 36 | 25 | 17 | 1 | 3 | | |
| 64–65 | 4 | 4 | 7 | 5 | 15 | 16 | 4 | 1 | 1 | | |
| 63–64 | 2 | 4 | 5 | 3 | 14 | 11 | 16 | 1 | | | |
| 62–63 | 1 | 1 | 9 | 3 | 5 | 7 | 1 | | | | |
| Below 62 | 1 | 1 | 1 | | 3 | 1 | 1 | 1 | | | |

*All female heights multiplied by 1.08 to adjust for sex differences.

**TABLE 8.2** *Bivariate Data: Scores for 10 Male College Students on Two Self-Report Measures*

| STUDENT | STRESS X | EATING DIFFICULTIES Y |
|---------|----------|------------------------|
| A | 17 | 9 |
| B | 8 | 13 |
| C | 8 | 7 |
| D | 20 | 18 |
| E | 14 | 11 |
| F | 7 | 2 |
| G | 21 | 5 |
| H | 22 | 15 |
| I | 19 | 26 |
| J | 30 | 28 |

The initial observations, therefore, can be listed in two columns. Table 8.2 offers an example. The subjects, designated by letters, are 10 male college students who filled out two questionnaires (unpublished data from Bear). One 10-item questionnaire (developed by Cohen & Williamson, 1988) measured the stress currently afflicting the student. Another 14-item questionnaire (developed by Kagan & Squires, 1984) assessed difficulties in eating. We have used $X$ for the total score on the stress questionnaire (higher scores indicate greater perceived stress) and $Y$ for the total score on the eating difficulties questionnaire (higher scores indicate greater perceived difficulty).

To display bivariate data, modern researchers typically use a scatter diagram like Figure 8.1 (sometimes called a *scatterplot*), not a chart like Galton's (Table 8.1). Each

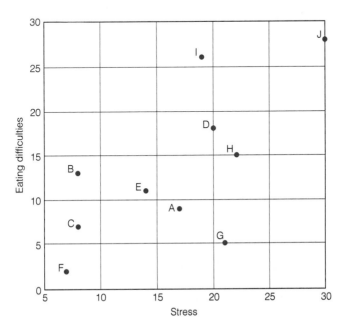

**FIGURE 8.1** Scatter diagram of bivariate distribution of stress scores and eating difficulties scores for 10 male college students. Data from Table 8.2.

**scatter diagram**
a graph of a bivariate distribution consisting of dots at the point of intersection of paired scores

point in a **scatter diagram** represents a single case and shows the scores on the two variables for that case. For example, in Figure 8.1, which plots the $X$ and $Y$ scores from Table 8.2, the dot in the upper right corner represents student J, who scored 30 on the stress test (variable $X$) and 28 on the eating difficulties test (variable $Y$). The steps in constructing a scatter diagram from a set of paired scores are summarized as follows:

**Step 1:** Designate one variable $X$ and the other $Y$. Although it does not matter which is which, in cases where one variable is used to predict the other, we will follow the custom of using $X$ for the "predictor" variable.

**Step 2:** Draw axes of about equal length for your graph. Note that this differs from the convention used for constructing frequency histograms or polygons.

**Step 3:** Place the high values of $X$ to the right on the horizontal axis and the high values of $Y$ toward the top on the vertical axis. Label convenient points along each axis.

**Step 4:** For each pair of scores, find the point of intersection for the $X$ and $Y$ values and indicate it with a dot. Where dots exactly overlap, substitute for them the integer telling how many cases occur in that spot (as Galton did in Table 8.1).

**Step 5:** Name each axis and give the entire graph a name.

**linear relationship**
a relationship that can best be represented by a straight line

The scatter diagram allows us to easily see the nature of the relationship, if any exists, between the two variables. Pearson's mathematical procedures assume an underlying **linear relationship**, that is, a relationship that can be best represented by a straight line. Figure 8.1 shows such a relationship. As a general rule, those students who scored high on the stress questionnaire also had high scores on the eating difficulties questionnaire. The relationship is not perfect. Person G, for example, had a total score of 21 (the third highest) on the stress questionnaire, but had a total score of only 5 (the second lowest) on the eating difficulties questionnaire. Nevertheless, a quick inspection of the graph shows us that Pearson's assumption of linearity is appropriate here.

It must be emphasized that not all relationships are linear. Figure 8.2a, for example, displays the effects of dosage levels of pentobarbital, a barbiturate, on lever-

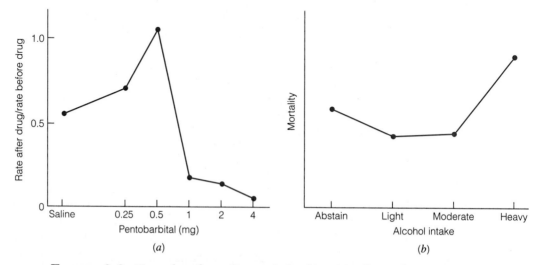

**FIGURE 8.2** Examples of curvilinear relationships. (*a*) Effects of pentobarbital on lever-pressing for food reinforcement in pigeons (modified from Dews, 1955). (*b*) Relationship between weekly alcohol intake and mortality (modified from San José et al., 1999).

pressing for food reinforcement in pigeons. Figure 8.2*b* shows the relationship between weekly alcohol consumption and mortality. Because the relationships here are curvilinear (the points on a scatter diagram cluster about a curved line), Pearson's procedures are not appropriate (and, in fact, will give misleading results). *Except where noted, the techniques of correlation and prediction presented in this text are appropriate only where the underlying relationship between two variables is linear.*

## 8.3 Correlation: A Matter of Direction

**positive correlation**

a linear relationship in which high scores on the first variable are generally paired with high scores on the second, and low scores on the first variable are generally paired with low scores on the second

**negative correlation**

a linear relationship in which high scores on the first variable are generally paired with low scores on the second, and vice versa

The scatter diagram not only shows whether there is a linear relationship between two variables but also shows at a glance the direction of the relationship. If the higher scores on *X* are generally paired with the higher scores on *Y*, and the lower scores on *X* are generally paired with the lower ones on *Y*, then the direction of the correlation between the two variables is positive. In a scatter diagram, a **positive correlation** appears as a cluster of data points that slopes from lower left to upper right. Thus, the correlation shown in Figure 8.1 is positive. It would not matter if we had designated the stress scores as *Y* instead of *X* (and plotted them along the vertical axis instead of the horizontal) and the eating difficulties scores as *X* instead of *Y* (and plotted them along the horizontal axis): the dots in the scatter diagram would still slope from lower left to upper right. Try it. Figure 8.3 offers more examples of positive correlations.

If the higher scores on *X* are generally paired with the lower scores on *Y* and the lower scores on *X* are generally paired with the higher ones on *Y*, then the direction of the correlation is negative. For example, a study conducted by the California Department of Education in 1982 found a negative correlation between hours of TV watched daily by children and their scores on standardized reading and mathematics tests. The results are shown in Table 8.3. Although these are summary figures (means rather than scores for individuals), you can see that as the number of hours spent watching television increased, test scores decreased. In a scatter diagram, a **negative correlation** appears as a cluster of data points that slopes from upper left to lower right, as illustrated in Figure 8.4*b* and 8.4*c*. Again, it does not matter which variable is plotted along the horizontal axis and which along the vertical axis; the direction of the slope will be the same.

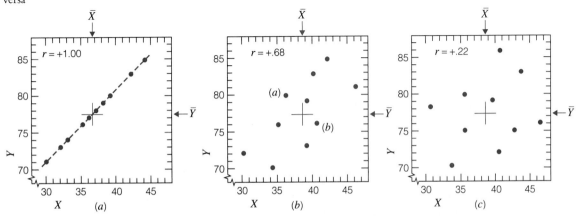

**FIGURE 8.3** Scatter diagrams illustrating various degrees of positive (+) correlation.

**TABLE 8.3** *Negative Correlation Between Time Spent Watching TV and Academic Test Scores*

| MEAN HOURS OF TV WATCHED DAILY | MEAN TEST SCORES | |
|---|---|---|
| | *Reading* | *Math* |
| 0.0–0.5 | 75 | 69 |
| 0.5–1.0 | 74 | 65 |
| 1.0–2.0 | 73 | 65 |
| 2.0–3.0 | 73 | 65 |
| 3.0–4.0 | 72 | 63 |
| 4.0–5.0 | 71 | 63 |
| 5.0–6.0 | 70 | 62 |
| 6.0+ | 66 | 58 |

*Source:* California Department of Education, 1982.

**no correlation**
both high and low values on the first variable are equally paired with both high and low values on the second variable

In cases where there is **no correlation** between two variables (i.e., both high and low values of $X$ are equally paired with both high and low values of $Y$), there is no direction in the pattern of the dots. They are scattered about the diagram in an irregular fashion, as illustrated in Figure 8.4*a*.

## 8.4 Correlation: A Matter of Degree

Look closely again at Figure 8.3. All three scatter diagrams show a positive correlation between $X$ and $Y$. You can tell because the dots tend to go from lower left to upper right. Then how do these correlations differ? They differ in degree. The scatter diagram in Figure 8.3*a* shows a perfect linear correlation, one where all the data points fall on a straight line. The other correlations are less than perfect, but in each case one can still construct (as Galton did) through the cluster of dots a straight line

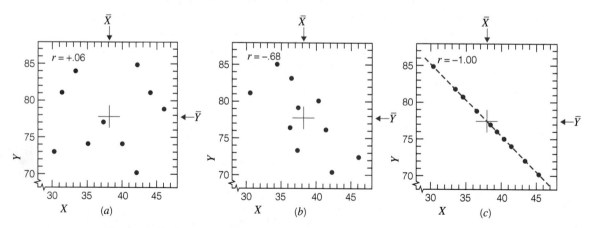

**FIGURE 8.4** Scatter diagrams illustrating (*a*) an essentially zero correlation and (*b* and *c*) two degrees of negative (−) correlation.

that summarizes the relationship between the two variables. With less than perfect correlations, the dots will show some scatter about the straight line. The more scatter, the weaker the correlation.

**coefficient of correlation**

a mathematical expression of the degree of association between two variables

*r*

symbol for Pearson's coefficient of correlation

The degree of association shared by two variables is indicated by the **coefficient of correlation**, invented by Pearson in 1896. Galton was the first to use the symbol *r* for a *sample correlation coefficient*; it is often written with subscripts as $r_{XY}$. It is calculated in a way we will show later, from the *pairs* of scores. When a perfect correlation exists, its value is plus or minus 1.0. When no linear relationship exists, its value is 0. Thus, intermediate degrees of correlation are represented by values between 0 and ±1.0.

*The sign (plus or minus) indicates only the direction of the correlation* (+ for a positive correlation and − for a negative correlation), not its degree. Students sometimes mistakenly believe that a correlation coefficient with a positive value indicates a stronger degree of relationship than does a coefficient with a negative value, but this is not so. Two correlation coefficients having the same absolute value but differing in sign indicate the same degree of relationship. Only the direction of the relationship differs. Thus, a correlation coefficient of −.50 indicates just as strong a relationship between two variables as a coefficient of +.50.

To summarize the relationship between a scatter diagram and the correlation coefficient, *Pearson's correlation coefficient is a number that indicates how well the data points in a scatter diagram "hug" the straight line of best fit.* With perfect correlations, all the data points fall exactly on a straight line as in Figures 8.3*a* and 8.4*c* and the value of the coefficient is ±1.0. When the association between two variables is less than perfect, the data points show some scatter about the straight line that summarizes the relationship, and the *absolute* value of the correlation coefficient is less than 1.0. The weaker the relationship, the more scatter and the lower the absolute value of the correlation coefficient.

**values of *r***

range from −1.00 (a perfect negative correlation) to 0.0 (no correlation) to +1.00 (a perfect positive correlation)

In the real world, perfect correlations occur only in trivial instances; for example, the correlation will be −1.00 between the number of correct answers on a test and the number of errors plus omissions. Table 8.4 lists typical values of *r* for some correlations of interest in psychology and education. We began this chapter by noting that there is a relationship between SAT scores and freshman-year GPAs. In fact, SAT scores typically correlate about +.35 with freshman-year GPAs. The value of the coefficient indicates a modest degree of relationship—not nearly as strong as the correlation between alternate forms of a finely honed instrument like the Wechsler intelligence test (over +.90), but not nearly as weak as the correlation between a wife's weight and her husband's weight (+.10).

# 8.5 Understanding the Meaning of Degree of Correlation

Although the absolute value of *r* does represent the degree of linear correlation between pairs of scores, the representation is complex. A correlation between *X* and *Y* does not mean that variation in *X* causes variation in *Y*, or vice versa (more about this in Section 8.11). Moreover, a correlation coefficient of .50 *does not* even indicate "50% association." *Correlations are not percentages.* Nor does a correlation of .50 indicate twice the strength of association as a correlation of .25. What does it mean, then, to say that there is a +.35 correlation between SAT scores and freshman-year GPAs?

**TABLE 8.4**   *Typical Values of* r

| VARIABLES | r |
|---|---|
| IQ from one form of Wechsler Adult Intelligence Scale (WAIS) and IQ from an alternate form | +.90 |
| Childhood IQ and adult IQ | +.70 to +.85 |
| Age of man and age of woman among married American parents | +.85 |
| Age of man and age of woman among unmarried American parents | +.70 |
| Father's years of education and grown child's years of education | +.60 |
| Verbal score on Scholastic Aptitude Test (SAT) and mathematics score on SAT | +.60 |
| IQ of husband and IQ of wife | +.50 |
| Total score on SAT and freshman-year grade point average (GPA) | +.35 |
| Total score on Graduate Record Exam (GRE) and undergraduate GPA among applicants to a highly selective graduate program in psychology | +.20 |
| Height of man and height of woman among American parents, married or unmarried | +.20 |
| Weight of man and weight of woman among American parents, married or unmarried | +.10 |
| Attitudes about school and cutting school among junior high and high school students | −.29 |
| Authoritarianism and aestheticism among high school seniors | −.42 |
| Latency of visual evoked response and conceptual age at time of birth | −.61 |

*Sources:* Information on WAIS from Matarazzo (1972); on childhood IQ from McCall (1977); on American parents from Plomin, DeFries, and Roberts (1977) and Follman (1984); on SAT and GPA from Slack and Porter (1980); on GRE and GPA from Dawes (1975); on attitudes about school from Epstein and McPartland (1976); on attitudes about authoritarianism and aestheticism from Nolan, Bram, and Tillman (1963); on visual evoked response and conceptual age from Engel and Benson (1968).

Many students with low or mediocre SAT scores who are doing well in school may decide that what they learn in statistics class has little to do with the real world. Whenever there is less than perfect correlation between two variables, there will be exceptions. One way to appreciate the meaning of size differences in correlation co-efficients is to understand how often exceptions are expected with different degrees of correlation. We can do this by comparing the percentage of cases scoring above the median on the first variable with the percentage scoring above the median on the second variable. With perfect correlations, all the cases above the median for the first variable are also above the median for the second. When there is zero correlation (no association), only 50% of the cases above the median on the first variable will also be above the median on the second. This indicates, of course, that half of those above the median on the first variable will be below the median on the second.

Table 8.5 shows us what we can expect with different size correlations. For the correlation of +.35 between SAT scores and freshman-year GPAs, the table tells us that of those who scored above the median on the SAT, we can expect that 61.2% will also be above the median for GPA and that 38.8% will have GPAs lower than the median. This is better than chance (50–50), but far from perfect. The data in the table assume that the variables are continuous, normally distributed, and de-scribe an entire population. However, even with modestly sized samples, the figures provide ballpark estimates. As a first step this table should provide some help in un-derstanding the meaning of degree of correlation. We provide a more technical ex-planation of what correlations measure in Chapter 10 (see Sections 10.4–10.5 and 10.8–10.10).

**TABLE 8.5**   *The Meaning of True Correlations*[a]

| TRUE CORRELATION | CASES EXPECTED ON SECOND VARIABLE (%) | |
|---|---|---|
| | *Above median* | *Below median* |
| 0.00 | 50.0 | 50.0 |
| 0.10 | 53.1 | 46.9 |
| 0.20 | 56.2 | 43.8 |
| 0.30 | 59.5 | 40.5 |
| **0.35** | **61.2** | **38.8** |
| 0.40 | 63.0 | 37.0 |
| 0.50 | 66.5 | 33.5 |
| 0.60 | 70.3 | 29.7 |
| 0.70 | 74.5 | 25.5 |
| 0.80 | 79.3 | 20.7 |
| 0.90 | 85.3 | 14.7 |
| 1.00 | 100.0 | 0.0 |

[a] For cases above the median on variable 1, this table gives the expected percentages of cases falling above and below the median on variable 2 for true correlations. Column entries are reversed for negative correlations.

*Source:* Credit is owed to W. B. Michael, "An Interpretation of the Coefficients of Predictive Validity and of Determination in Terms of the Proportions of Correct Inclusions or Exclusions in Cells of a Fourfold Table," *Educational and Psychological Measurement,* **26**, no. 2 (1966): 419–24.

# 8.6 Formulas for Pearson's Coefficient of Correlation

This section introduces formulas for computing Pearson's coefficient of correlation. There are other indices of association suited for special situations, as we shall see later, but Pearson's is by far the most common. In fact, when researchers speak of a correlation coefficient without being specific about which one they mean, you may safely assume they are referring to Pearson's *r*. Technically, it is a **product-moment correlation coefficient**.[1]

A correlation, you recall, shows the relationship between pairs of scores. In its simplest form, the Pearson correlation coefficient is defined as follows:

$$r = \frac{\Sigma(z_X z_Y)}{n}$$

*z*-score formula for Pearson's *r*

> ### *z*-SCORE FORMULA FOR PEARSON'S CORRELATION COEFFICIENT
>
> $$r = \frac{\sum (z_X z_Y)}{n} \qquad (8.1)$$

where *n* is the number of pairs of scores. To find *r*, we must convert each raw score to a *z* score. Then for each pair of *z* scores we multiply the scores, sum the results,

---

[1] The term *moment* is borrowed from physics and refers to a function of the distance of an object from the center of gravity. With a frequency distribution, the mean is the center of gravity and, thus, deviation scores are the moments. As you will see in Formula 8.2, Pearson's *r* is calculated by taking the *products of the paired moments*.

called the **cross-products**, and divide by the number of pairs of scores. Thus, $r$ is the mean of the cross-products of the paired $z$ scores.

Formula 8.1 is elegantly simple, but it is awkward for computation. We can also define Pearson's coefficient directly in terms of deviation scores:

$$r = \frac{\Sigma(X - \overline{X})(Y - \overline{Y})}{nS_X S_Y}$$

deviation-score formula for Pearson's $r$

DEVIATION-SCORE FORMULA FOR PEARSON'S CORRELATION COEFFICIENT

$$r = \frac{\sum(X - \overline{X})(Y - \overline{Y})}{nS_X S_Y} \qquad (8.2)$$

where $n$ is again the number of pairs of scores and $S_X$ and $S_Y$ are the standard deviations of the two samples. (Note 8.1 shows how Formula 8.2 is derived from Formula 8.1.)

We will calculate Pearson's $r$ using this formula because doing so will help us see what factors make the coefficient positive or negative and what factors result in a high or low value. Many pocket calculators now include programs to calculate $r$. However, for those who must calculate $r$ by hand, the raw-score method described in the next section is much easier. (Remember Minium's Second Law of Statistics?)

Table 8.6 demonstrates the computation of $r$ by the deviation-score formula for the data presented in Table 8.2 on stress and eating difficulties for 10 male college students. The steps in calculating $r$ by Formula 8.2 are summarized as follows:

**TABLE 8.6**  *Calculation of* r *from Deviation Scores (Data from Table 8.2)*

| STUDENT | $X$ | $Y$ | ③ $X - \overline{X}$ | ④ $Y - \overline{Y}$ | ⑤ $(X - \overline{X})^2$ | ⑥ $(Y - \overline{Y})^2$ | ⑪ $(X - \overline{X})(Y - \overline{Y})$ |
|---------|-----|-----|-----------|-----------|-------------|-------------|-----------------------|
| A | 17 | 9 | +0.4 | −4.4 | 0.16 | 19.36 | −1.76 |
| B | 8 | 13 | −8.6 | −0.4 | 73.96 | 0.16 | +3.44 |
| C | 8 | 7 | −8.6 | −6.4 | 73.96 | 40.96 | +55.04 |
| D | 20 | 18 | +3.4 | +4.6 | 11.56 | 21.16 | +15.64 |
| E | 14 | 11 | −2.6 | −2.4 | 6.76 | 5.76 | +6.24 |
| F | 7 | 2 | −9.6 | −11.4 | 92.16 | 129.96 | +109.44 |
| G | 21 | 5 | +4.4 | −8.4 | 19.36 | 70.56 | −36.96 |
| H | 22 | 15 | +5.4 | +1.6 | 29.16 | 2.56 | +8.64 |
| I | 19 | 26 | +2.4 | +12.6 | 5.76 | 158.76 | +30.24 |
| J | 30 | 28 | +13.4 | +14.6 | 179.56 | 213.16 | +195.64 |
| $n = 10$ | Sum: 166 | 134 | 0 | 0 | 492.40 | 662.40 | +385.60 |
| | ① Mean: 16.6 | ② 13.4 | | | ⑦ | ⑧ | ⑫ |

⑨ $S_X = \sqrt{\sum(X - \overline{X})^2/n} = \sqrt{492.40/10} = 7.017$

⑬ $r = \sum(X - \overline{X})(Y - \overline{Y})/nS_X S_Y = 385.60/(10)(7.017)(8.139) = +.675$

⑩ $S_Y = \sqrt{\sum(Y - \overline{Y})^2/n} = \sqrt{662.40/10} = 8.139$

**Step 1:** List the pairs of scores in two columns. The order in which you list the pairs makes no difference in the value of *r*. However, if you shift one raw score you must shift the raw score that is paired with it. To do otherwise would affect the value of the numerator.

**Step 2:** Find the mean for $X$ (indicated by ① in Table 8.6) and the mean for $Y$ ②.

**Step 3:** Convert each raw score to a deviation score, ③ and ④.

**Step 4:** Calculate the standard deviation for $X$ (⑨) and $Y$ (⑩). Because you already have deviation scores, the deviation-score method may be easier. Square the deviation scores, (⑤ and ⑥), and calculate the sums of squares, (⑦ and ⑧). Then divide by *n* (the sample size) and take the square root. You now have all the pieces necessary to calculate *r*.

**Step 5:** To calculate the numerator for Formula 8.2, multiply the two deviation scores for each person (⑪) and then obtain the sum of the cross-products (⑫).

**Step 6:** To obtain the denominator for Formula 8.2, multiply $S_X$ by $S_Y$ by *n* (the number of pairs of scores).

**Step 7:** Complete the final division (⑬) to obtain *r*, which in this example proves to be $+.675$.

*n*
in formulas for a correlation coefficient, the number of pairs of scores

The positive correlation we have obtained tells us that it was at least generally true that those with higher perceived stress also had greater perceived eating difficulties. As a check on your work, always look at the scatter diagram after you have calculated *r*. Remember that with a positive correlation the cluster of dots should go from the lower left to the upper right. If they do not, you have made a mistake in your calculations. In this example, the value $+.675$ indicates that the relationship between the two variables was a fairly close one, but certainly not perfect. So, low perceived stress did not necessarily guarantee a lack of eating difficulties, just as high stress did not guarantee that the student had eating difficulties (witness Student G).

To better understand Formula 8.2 for Pearson's *r*, look at Figure 8.5. This scatter diagram is the same as that in Figure 8.1 except that numbers have been placed beside each dot to indicate the cross-products, and lines have been added to show the means for $X$ and $Y$. The lines divide the scatter diagram into four **quadrants**, which are labeled Quadrant I through Quadrant IV going counter-clockwise from the upper right. Dots to the right of the vertical line (Quadrants I and IV) indicate positive deviations for $X$, and those above the horizontal line (Quadrants I and II) indicate positive deviations for $Y$. Positive cross-products result from multiplying either two positive deviation scores together (Quadrant I) or two negative deviation scores (Quadrant III). Negative cross-products result from multiplying a positive deviation score by a negative deviation score (Quadrants II and IV).

Now look carefully again at the numerator for Formula 8.2. Because the denominator always has a positive value (*n*, $S_X$, and $S_Y$ are always positive numbers), it is apparent that the sum of the cross-products determines whether the coefficient will be negative, zero, or positive. It will be zero when the sum of the negative cross-products from Quadrants II and IV equals the sum of the positive products from Quadrants I and III. The coefficient will be negative when the cross-products from Quadrants II and IV exceed those from Quadrants I and III, and it will be positive when the reverse is true. Typically, the greater the predominance of cross-products bearing one sign over those bearing the other, the greater the magnitude of the coefficient. In our example, the two negative cross-products, for Students A and

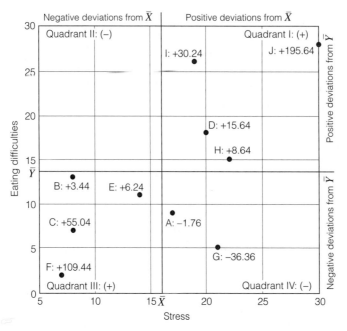

**FIGURE 8.5** Scatter diagram showing cross-products, $(X - \overline{X})(Y - \overline{Y})$. Data from Tables 8.2 and 8.6. Compare with Figure 8.1.

G, are swamped by the eight positive cross-products. As a result, the sum of the cross-products is positive and so is $r$ ($+.675$).

The magnitude of the coefficient really depends on the similarity of the paired $z$ scores. Look again at Formula 8.1. The sum of the cross-products ($\Sigma z_X z_Y$) is maximal (equal to $\Sigma z_X^2$ or $\Sigma z_Y^2$) only when both scores in each pair are at the same relative distance from their means (that is, when the magnitudes of the two $z$ scores are the same). When both scores in each pair do share the same relative position, the result is a straight-line relationship and a maximum value for the correlation coefficient. Thus, the correlation coefficient is really an index of how similar the paired $z$ scores are.

For more insight into how $r$ behaves, inspect Figures 8.3 and 8.4 again. We have shown where $\overline{X}$ and $\overline{Y}$ fall, so you can readily tell which quadrant each data point is in. Look to see how the distribution of the points over the four quadrants determines the value of $r$.

## 8.7 Calculating $r$ from Raw Scores

The $z$-score formula and the deviation-score formula for $r$ are useful for teaching purposes, but they are cumbersome if you have to calculate $r$ by hand. However, it is easy to transform the deviation-score formula to a useful computing formula:

$$r = \frac{\sum(X - \overline{X})(Y - \overline{Y})}{nS_X S_Y} = \frac{\sum(X - \overline{X})(Y - \overline{Y})}{n\sqrt{\dfrac{\sum(X - \overline{X})^2}{n}}\sqrt{\dfrac{\sum(Y - \overline{Y})^2}{n}}}$$

$$= \frac{\sum(X - \overline{X})(Y - \overline{Y})}{\sqrt{\sum(X - \overline{X})^2(Y - \overline{Y})^2}}$$

Thus,

> COMPUTATIONAL FORMULA FOR PEARSON'S
> CORRELATION COEFFICIENT
>
> $$r = \frac{\sum(X - \overline{X})(Y - \overline{Y})}{\sqrt{(SS_X)(SS_Y)}} \qquad (8.3)$$

The two expressions in the denominator are, of course, the sums of squares of the deviation scores for $X$ and $Y$. In Section 6.6 you learned how to compute these quantities from raw scores. Here are the formulas again:

$$SS_X = \sum(X - \overline{X})^2 = \sum X^2 - \frac{\left(\sum X\right)^2}{n}$$

and

$$SS_Y = \sum(Y - \overline{Y})^2 = \sum Y^2 - \frac{\left(\sum Y\right)^2}{n}$$

The numerator of Formula 8.3, $\sum(X - \overline{X})(Y - \overline{Y})$, is the sum of cross-products of deviation scores and can also be expressed in terms of raw scores.

> RAW SCORE EQUIVALENT
> OF $\Sigma(X - \overline{X})(Y - \overline{Y})$
>
> $$\sum(X - \overline{X})(Y - \overline{Y}) = \sum XY - \frac{\left(\sum X\right)\left(\sum Y\right)}{n} \qquad (8.4)$$

Derivation of this formula appears in Note 8.2 at the end of the chapter.

We illustrate the raw-score method of calculating Pearson's $r$ in Table 8.7, using the data from Table 8.2 again. The steps are summarized as follows:

$r =$

$\dfrac{\Sigma XY - (\Sigma X)(\Sigma Y)/n}{\sqrt{(SS_X)(SS_Y)}}$

computational
raw score formula
for Pearson's $r$

**Step 1:** Find the six building blocks from which everything else is generated: $n$, $\Sigma X$, $\Sigma Y$, $\Sigma X^2$, $\Sigma Y^2$, $\Sigma XY$. The outcomes are indicated by ① in Table 8.7.

**Step 2:** Find $SS_X$, $SS_Y$, and $\Sigma(X - \overline{X})(Y - \overline{Y})$. These are shown at ②, ③, and ④.

**Step 3:** Substitute these last three values in Formula 8.3 and do the remaining arithmetic ⑤.

With a calculator that has a memory system, it is not necessary to record each of these values because they are stored internally by the instrument.

## 8.8 Spearman's Rank-Order Correlation Coefficient

Recall from Section 2.4 that in psychology and education there are many measuring instruments that lack equal intervals and an absolute zero point. We can, however, place the observations in rank order (see ordinal scale, Section 2.3). **Spearman's**

TABLE 8.7   *Calculation of r from the Raw Scores of Table 8.2*

| STUDENT | $X$ | $Y$ | $X^2$ | $Y^2$ | $XY$ |
|---|---|---|---|---|---|
| A | 17 | 9 | 289 | 81 | 153 |
| B | 8 | 13 | 64 | 169 | 104 |
| C | 8 | 7 | 64 | 49 | 56 |
| D | 20 | 18 | 400 | 324 | 360 |
| E | 14 | 11 | 196 | 121 | 154 |
| F | 7 | 2 | 49 | 4 | 14 |
| G | 21 | 5 | 441 | 25 | 105 |
| H | 22 | 15 | 484 | 225 | 330 |
| I | 19 | 26 | 361 | 676 | 494 |
| J | 30 | 28 | 900 | 784 | 840 |
| $n = 10$ | Sum: 166 | 134 | 3,248 | 2,458 | 2,610 |

① 

② $SS_X = \sum X^2 - \left(\sum X\right)^2/n = 3{,}248 - 166^2/10 = 492.4$

③ $SS_Y = \sum Y^2 - \left(\sum Y\right)^2/n = 2{,}458 - 134^2/10 = 662.4$

④ $\sum (X - \bar{X})(Y - \bar{Y}) = \sum XY - \dfrac{\left(\sum X\right)\left(\sum Y\right)}{n} = 2{,}610 - \dfrac{(166)(134)}{10} = 385.6$

⑤ $r = \dfrac{\sum(X-\bar{X})(Y-\bar{Y})}{\sqrt{(SS_X)(SS_Y)}} = \dfrac{385.6}{\sqrt{(492.4)(662.4)}} = \dfrac{385.6}{\sqrt{326{,}165.76}} = \dfrac{385.6}{571.11} = +.675$

Usually, we also want the means and standard deviations:

$\bar{X} = \dfrac{\sum X}{n} = \dfrac{166}{10} = 16.6 \qquad \bar{Y} = \dfrac{\sum Y}{n} = \dfrac{134}{10} = 13.4$

$S_X = \sqrt{\dfrac{SS_X}{n}} = \sqrt{\dfrac{492.4}{10}} = 7.017 \quad S_Y = \sqrt{\dfrac{SS_Y}{n}} = \sqrt{\dfrac{662.4}{10}} = 8.139$

$r_S$
symbol for Spearman's rank-order correlation coefficient

**rank-order correlation coefficient,** $r_S$, is closely related to the Pearson correlation coefficient.[2] In fact, if the paired scores are both in the form of ranks (and there are no ties in rank), calculation of $r_S$ and Pearson's $r$ will yield identical outcomes.

When would one want to use the rank-order coefficient? Suppose 10 aspects of a job are identified, such as hours of work, working conditions, quality of supervision, wages, and so forth. Suppose we ask workers to place these job aspects in rank order according to their importance, and suppose we also ask their supervisors to rank the same aspects according to the importance that they believe workers would assign. We may now ask about the extent to which one worker agrees with another and the

[2] The Spearman rank-order correlation coefficient is sometimes called Spearman's rho and symbolized $\rho$. In this book, $\rho$ is reserved for the population value of Pearson's $r$.

extent to which supervisors understand workers' feelings. We can study the degree of agreement between any two persons by calculating the coefficient of correlation between the ranks they assign to the 10 job aspects. Because the data are in the form of ranks, $r$ and $r_S$ will yield the same coefficient. We prefer $r_S$ in this case because it is simpler to calculate.

In another situation, suppose that we show photographic portraits of 12 persons to subjects who are then requested to place the portraits in rank order with respect to estimated IQ. We then evaluate the reliability with which the subjects make such judgments by determining the correlation between the rank order assigned and measured IQ. In this case, one set of measures is in rank form and one is not. It might be convenient to convert measured IQ to rank order and use the Spearman coefficient.

We can also use $r_S$ when both sets of measures are in score form. In this case, we translate each set of measures into rank form, assigning 1 to the lowest score, 2 to the next lowest, and so on. When would we do this? Sometimes the scale properties of the measures appear doubtful (see Section 2.4). If what matters is that one score is higher than another and how much higher is not really important, translating scores to ranks will be suitable. In any event, we typically use $r_S$ only in circumstances in which $n$ is rather small. When $n$ is large, the proportion of tied ranks is apt to increase, and the work of translating scores to ranks becomes progressively more burdensome and error-prone.

The formula for the Spearman rank-order correlation coefficient is:

SPEARMAN RANK-ORDER
CORRELATION COEFFICIENT

$$r_S = 1 - \frac{6 \sum D^2}{n(n^2 - 1)} \tag{8.5}$$

*where:*  $D =$ the difference between a pair of ranks.
$n =$ the number of pairs of ranks.

$r_S =$

$$1 - \frac{6 \sum D^2}{n(n^2 - 1)}$$

formula for Spearman's $r_S$

Before we proceed, you must first learn how to place scores in rank order.

## 8.9 How to Place Scores in Rank Order

Most rank-order procedures in statistics require that the underlying variable be continuous. However, many dependent measures in psychology and education are discrete variables (such as scores on a multiple-choice test), which often results in identical scores. This poses a problem because identical scores lead to ties in rank.

There are various ways to deal with ties in rank. A simple and reasonably satisfactory way is to assign each of the tied scores the mean of the ranks that would be available to them. Consider the following nine scores

| 4 | 5 | 5 | 8 | 11 | 11 | 11 | 15 | 19 |

By this principle, we would assign these ranks:

| 1 | 2.5 | 2.5 | 4 | 6 | 6 | 6 | 8 | 9 |

This procedure usually has little or no effect on the mean, but it tends to reduce the variance. The effect of this on the statistic being calculated is usually slight *unless* a third or more of all scores are involved in ties.

When scores are fairly numerous, and especially when there are ties, it is easy to make a mistake in assigning ranks. We therefore use the following check:

$$sum\ of\ the\ ranks = \frac{n(n+1)}{2}$$

*where:* $n$ = the number of scores being ranked.

This check holds whether or not there are ties.

## 8.10 Calculating Spearman's $r_S$

Suppose an instructor is curious about the relation between the order in which the 15 members of her class completed an examination and the number of points earned on it. After the test, the examination booklets form a pile on her desk; the bottom booklet is the first one turned in and the remainder are in the order in which they were submitted. She assigns a rank of 1 to the first paper turned in and succeeding ranks according to the order of completion. After she has scored the tests, she records the order of turn-in (①) and the score obtained (②) as shown in Table 8.8. She then converts the test scores to ranks, assigning a rank of 1 to the lowest score. Because two scores are tied, the instructor assigns the average of the ranks available for them to each, according to the procedure explained in Section 8.9. The set of paired ranks appears in the columns headed $R_X$ (③) and $R_Y$ (④). Next, she records the differences between the pairs of ranks in the column headed $D$ (⑤). If the algebraic signs are retained, a useful check may be based on the fact that $\Sigma D$ must be zero. The instructor then squares and sums the values of $D$ (⑥) and completes the calculation of $r_S$ as shown in the table (⑦). The value of $r_S$ is $+.38$.

## 8.11 Correlation Does Not Prove Causation

If variation in $X$ causes variation in $Y$, that causal connection will appear in some degree of correlation between $X$ and $Y$ (at least when we remove any obscuring complications). However, we cannot reason backward from a correlation to a causal relationship. The fact that $X$ and $Y$ vary together is a necessary but not a sufficient condition for us to conclude that there is a cause-and-effect connection between them.

To appreciate this point, we will review a study by psychologist Sandra Scarr (1985). Scarr wanted to know whether the technique used by a mother to discipline her children was related to the children's later social adjustment, intelligence, and communication skills. On the basis of interviews with and observations of the mothers, she distinguished several measures of discipline ranging from negative (including things like physical punishment) to very positive (including reasoning and explaining things to the child). Good disciplinary technique was positively correlated with all three of the

**TABLE 8.8**  *Calculation of $r_S$*

| SUBJECT | ① ORDER OF TURN-IN $X$ | ② TEST SCORE $Y$ | ③ RANK OF X $R_X$ | ④ RANK OF Y $R_Y$ | ⑤ D = $R_X - R_Y$ | ⑥ $D^2$ |
|---|---|---|---|---|---|---|
| A | 1 | 28 | 1 | 6.5 | −5.5 | 30.25 |
| B | 2 | 21 | 2 | 2 | 0.0 | 0.00 |
| C | 3 | 22 | 3 | 3.5 | −.5 | .25 |
| D | 4 | 22 | 4 | 3.5 | .5 | .25 |
| E | 5 | 32 | 5 | 10 | −5.0 | 25.00 |
| F | 6 | 36 | 6 | 13 | −7.0 | 49.00 |
| G | 7 | 33 | 7 | 11 | −4.0 | 16.00 |
| H | 8 | 39 | 8 | 15 | −7.0 | 49.00 |
| I | 9 | 25 | 9 | 5 | 4.0 | 16.00 |
| J | 10 | 30 | 10 | 8 | 2.0 | 4.00 |
| K | 11 | 20 | 11 | 1 | 10.0 | 100.00 |
| L | 12 | 28 | 12 | 6.5 | 5.5 | 30.25 |
| M | 13 | 31 | 13 | 9 | 4.0 | 16.00 |
| N | 14 | 38 | 14 | 14 | 0.0 | 0.00 |
| O | 15 | 34 | 15 | 12 | 3.0 | 9.00 |

$n = 15$ $\qquad\qquad\qquad\qquad\qquad\qquad\qquad\qquad\qquad\qquad\qquad\qquad \sum D^2 = 345.00$

Calculation: $\qquad\qquad ⑦\ r_S = 1 - \dfrac{6\sum D^2}{n(n^2 - 1)} = 1 - \dfrac{6(345)}{15(15^2 - 1)} = .38$

tested variables. Children who had been raised by mothers using good discipline techniques were better adjusted, more intelligent, and more communicative. The "obvious" conclusion is that the good discipline techniques caused the children's higher IQs and better social skills.

Do the positive correlations found by Scarr really provide evidence of cause-and-effect relationships? No, for there may have been other variables affecting both the mothers' use of discipline and the children's scores. In fact, when Scarr measured the mothers' IQs, she found that they correlated positively with both. After using other statistical techniques to remove the factor of the mothers' IQs, Scarr no longer found a positive correlation between their discipline technique and their children's later IQs and behavioral skills. Mothers with higher IQs simply tended to prefer positive discipline techniques and to have children with higher IQs and better skills.

Here is another example. A 1992 study of 11,000 adults found a positive correlation between vitamin C intake and life expectancy. Men with a daily intake of 150 mg vitamin C lived 2 years longer than men in the lowest intake group, whereas men with a daily intake of 300 mg lived 6 years longer. The men who took vitamin C had much lower rates of heart disease. Can we conclude from this that vitamin C causes lower rates of heart disease and increased lifespan? Many doctors say probably not, because men who take lots of vitamin C are also likely to take better care of themselves in other ways as well—exercise more, smoke less, eat more vegetables and fruit, and so on.

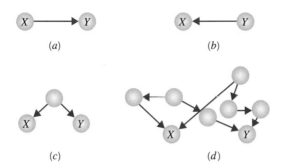

**FIGURE 8.6** Possible relationships between variables $X$ and $Y$ that may underlie a correlation.

Figure 8.6 shows four of the possibilities that may underlie a correlation between two variables: (a) The condition of $X$ determines (in part, at least) the condition of $Y$. (b) The opposite is true—$Y$ is a cause of $X$. (c) Some third variable influences both $X$ and $Y$. (d) A complex of interrelated variables influences $X$ and $Y$. Moreover, two or more of these situations may occur simultaneously. For example, $X$ and $Y$ may influence each other. Thus, an investigator must be alert to the several possible interpretations of a correlation.

Although a correlation by itself does not prove causation, we do not wish to leave you with the impression that correlations are of no importance in research. The finding of a strong correlation between two variables is often the starting point for additional research. In 1955, for example, a researcher found a correlation of $+.70$ between the mean number of cigarettes smoked and the incidence of lung cancer in 11 countries (Doll, 1955). The correlation alone did not prove causation, for the countries also differed in levels of air pollution and other factors that might cause lung cancer, but the results were nevertheless suggestive and stimulated a great deal of additional research. On the basis of this other research, the U.S. surgeon general later ordered that all packages of cigarettes sold in the United States carry the warning that smoking can be hazardous to your health.

"CONTRARY TO THE POPULAR VIEW, OUR STUDIES SHOW THAT IT IS REAL LIFE THAT CONTRIBUTES TO VIOLENCE ON TELEVISION."

## 8.12 The Effects of Score Transformations

SAT scores and GPAs are not the prettiest numbers. SAT scores are big, up in the hundreds. In fact, if we add the verbal and math SAT scores for each student, as college admissions committees commonly do, the sum is often over 1,000. GPAs, on the other hand, are small numbers with decimal points. Calculated on a four-point scale, where A = 4, B = 3, C = 2, D = 1, and F = 0, GPAs are commonly carried to two decimal places, such as 2.34. However, we can avoid these complications in calculating Pearson's *r* for SATs and GPAs if we wish.

Suppose the SAT totals are numbers like 1,010, 1,130, and 1,260, all in the 1,000s (this is an elite college). We could simplify the figures by subtracting 1,000 from each score. What would change? As we learned in Sections 5.8 and 6.11, the mean would go down by 1,000 points, but because the distances among the scores would remain the same, the standard deviation would not change and neither would the coefficient of correlation between the SAT scores and GPA.

To better understand this, imagine the scatter diagram for a bivariate distribution of untransformed SAT sums and GPAs (look ahead to Figure 9.1 for an example). How would the cluster of points change if we subtracted 1,000 from each SAT sum? The cluster would simply slide 1,000 points to the left. It would still slope in the direction it now does, and the extent to which the points hug a straight line would stay the same. So *r* would also remain the same.

Now let's rid the GPAs of their decimal points by multiplying each by 100; 2.34 becomes 234, for example. The distribution of GPAs thus acquires a mean that is 100 times greater and a standard deviation also 100 times greater. (Again, see Sections 5.8 and 6.11 for the principles.) But *r* would not change. You need only picture the scatter diagram again to understand why. To plot the data points for the transformed GPAs, we would need to alter only the labels for the horizontal axis, changing 2.00 to 200, 3.00 to 300, and so on. The cluster of data points would stay the same, so *r* would stay the same.

The general principle is that *r is unaffected by any positive linear transformation of the raw scores.* (Linear transformations, of course, will not change the rankings for Spearman's $r_S$.) The *z* scores used in Formula 8.1 are, in fact, linear transformations of the raw scores. A **linear transformation**, you recall, is one in which each raw score changes only by the addition of a constant, the subtraction of a constant, multiplication by a constant, or division by a constant. We can work such transformations on just the *X* scores, on just the *Y* scores, or on both, and *r* will remain constant. We can even transform the *X*s in one linear way and the *Y*s in another—subtracting 1,000 from each *X*, for example, and multiplying each *Y* by 100—and *r* will still remain constant. It does not matter whether our measurements are in the metric system or English system; *r* remains the same.

Other kinds of transformations—those in which each raw score is squared, for example—would affect *r*. For more insight into the effects of transforming scores, see Problems 12–14.

## 8.13 Cautions Concerning Correlation Coefficients

You might think that interpreting a correlation coefficient would be straightforward, but that is not always true. We have just seen in Section 8.11, for example, that establishing causation between two correlated variables can be complex. Other difficulties may also arise. We discuss many of these in detail in Chapter 10, but we preview a few of these important matters here.

**1.** *Remember that Pearson's and Spearman's correlation coefficients are appropriate only for linear relationships.* A "hugging" principle is involved: The more closely the scores hug the straight line of best fit, the higher the value of *r*. What would happen if we calculated *r* for the curvilinear data graphed in Figure 8.7? It would come out positive, as it ought to, for the data points swarm from lower left to upper right. But *r* would insist on telling us how closely the points hug a straight line, and because it is not very closely, the absolute value of *r* would be low. The relationship between *X* and *Y* here is strong, though, for there is little scatter around the curved line. Techniques exist for estimating relationships when two variables are nonlinearly related, as we shall learn in the next section. In sum, *when the relationship between two variables is curvilinear,* r *will underestimate the degree of association.* The greater the departure from a straight-line relationship, the more Pearson's *r* will underestimate the strength of association.

Fortunately, a great many relationships of interest in psychology and education are linear. This was Galton's discovery, and this is why *r*, the Pearson correlation coefficient, is so useful for measuring association.

**range of talent**

the variability in the distribution of *X* and *Y* scores

**2.** *The correlation coefficient is sensitive to the* **range of talent** *(the variability) characterizing the measurements of the two variables.* The smaller the range of talent in *X* or in *Y*, or in both, the lower the absolute value of the coefficient, other things being equal. For example, at your college the correlation coefficient between SAT and GPA may be only +.30. But remember, only the best students from your and other high schools went on to college. If everyone in high school took the SATs and then attempted college, the correlation would probably be substantially higher. At the same time, if we assessed the same correlation for only the honors students at your college, the coefficient would be even lower. For more about how *r* is affected by the range of talent, see Section 10.1.

**3.** *The correlation coefficient, like other statistics, is subject to sampling variation.* Depending on the particular sample, the coefficient may be higher or lower than it would be in a different sample from the same population. In accord with the principle of random sampling variation (see Section 2.1), it will fluctuate more from sample to sample when the samples are small than when they are large.

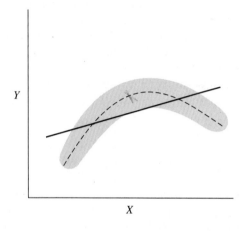

**FIGURE 8.7** A curvilinear relationship between *X* and *Y* to which a straight line has been fitted. Observations of age (*X*) and strength of grip (*Y*) would yield data like those plotted here.

**TABLE 8.9** *Limits within which 95% of Random Sample Values of* r *Will Fall when the Correlation in the Population Is Zero*

| SAMPLE SIZE | LIMITS FOR *r* (95%) |
|---|---|
| 5 | $-.88$ to $+.88$ |
| 15 | $-.51$ to $+.51$ |
| 25 | $-.40$ to $+.40$ |
| 50 | $-.28$ to $+.28$ |
| 100 | $-.20$ to $+.20$ |
| 200 | $-.14$ to $+.14$ |

For very small samples, *r* is quite unstable from sample to sample, so we cannot trust it to come close to the value for the population. Table 8.9 illustrates this point for the situation in which the value of *r* for the population is zero. For samples consisting of 5 pairs of scores, 95% of them will yield a value of *r* between $+.88$ and $-.88$, which means that in 5% of the samples the value will fall even further away from the true value (0.00) than these very broad limits. As you can see in Table 8.9, as sample size increases, these limits decrease substantially. In other words, using a sample to estimate the degree of association between two variables for an entire population is unsatisfactory unless *n* is large enough to produce reasonably stable results.

Once a correlation coefficient is calculated, the next question researchers most frequently ask is whether there is really any correlation at all. That is, can it be that the obtained (sample) coefficient differs from a true (population) coefficient of zero only because of random sampling variation? We commonly demand that for the sample coefficient to be declared "significantly" different from zero, it must differ enough that such a departure would occur by random sampling variation only 5% (or, more rigorously, 1%) of the time if the hypothesis of no correlation in the population were really true. We shall treat this question in detail after laying the groundwork for statistical inference. However, those who must know now should find Section 17.2 reasonably comprehensible.

**4.** *There is no such thing as "the" correlation coefficient for two variables.* The exact value of *r* or $r_S$ depends on several things. One is the particular sample of subjects we happen to get, as just noted. Another is exactly how we measure the variables; swap the SAT for a different aptitude test, and the correlation with GPA will change. A third factor is the specific conditions under which the variables are operating. If your college changes its grading policies—allowing students to take more courses on a pass-fail basis, for example—the correlation between SAT and GPA may also change.

Any report of *r* of $r_S$ values, therefore, should include a careful description of the measures used and the circumstances under which the correlation coefficients were obtained. Similarly, values reported by others may or may not hold up under the conditions with which you are concerned. Take the others' results only as working hypotheses, subject to confirmation under your conditions. If you investigate the relationship between perceived stress and eating difficulties (using the same questionnaires used by Bear), for example, do not be surprised if your value for *r* differs appreciably from the +.675 reported here.

## 8.14 Other Ways to Measure Association

Pearson's correlation coefficient is best suited to measuring the association between two variables that are each continuous and quantitative. For other circumstances there are other measures, many directly or indirectly derived from Pearson's. We shall briefly describe some of them, but for all after the first we leave the details to other texts (for example, Glass & Hopkins, 1996).

1.  *Biserial correlation.* The biserial coefficient is suited to cases in which one variable is continuous and quantitative and the other *would* be, except that it has been reduced to just two categories. (This, of course, discards valuable information and should be done only under special circumstances.) Suppose we wish to assess the correlation between scores on the SAT mathematics section (a continuous variable) and performance in the final exam in a statistics course. The biserial technique is required if each student's exam score has been simplified to "above the median" or "below the median." A special requirement is that the second variable would be normally distributed if the facts were known.

2.  *Tetrachoric correlation.* If both variables are like the second one just described, tetrachoric correlation is in order—if, for example, the SAT math scores are also expressed as simply above or below the median. The biserial and tetrachoric correlations are estimates of what the Pearson correlations would be for the uncollapsed data.

3.  *Point biserial correlation.* If one variable is continuous and quantitative, like the SAT math score, but the other is qualitative and dichotomous (either–or) with no underlying continuum (e.g., male–female, normal–psychotic), then the corresponding correlation coefficient is called point biserial.

4.  *The phi ($\phi$) coefficient.* The $\phi$ coefficient is the Pearson correlation coefficient for two variables that are both qualitative and dichotomous.

5.  *The contingency coefficient.* If both variables have no underlying continuum and if at least one consists of three or more categories, we need the contingency coefficient. It would be appropriate, for example, if we wish to assess the association between parent's eye color and offspring's eye color.

6.  *The correlation ratio $\eta$ (eta).* For a curvilinear relationship between two continuous, quantitative variables, *r* will underestimate the degree of association, as we discussed in Section 8.13. In this case, $\eta$ will be more appropriate. It has certain limitations that are not characteristic of Pearson's *r*, so it should not be used for linearly related variables. Age and motor skill are two variables that are curvilinearly related. We would expect motor skill to be highest during the middle years of life and lower among the very young and the very old.

7.  *Multiple correlation.* Suppose we want to predict the performance of machinist trainees. We find that scores on a test of spatial relations are related to this variable, as are scores on a mechanical aptitude test and a finger dexterity test. We

do not have to choose only one predictor from among the three. The technique of multiple correlation makes it possible to combine the predictor variables and thus to make a better prediction than any one could do alone. In finding the coefficient of multiple correlation, we determine the weights to apply to each predictor variable so that the weighted total of these variables has the highest possible correlation with the variable we are attempting to predict. The coefficient of multiple correlation, symbolized by $R$, gives the Pearson correlation coefficient between the variable to be predicted and the best-weighted composite of the several predictor variables. To calculate $R$, we must know Pearson's $r$ between each pair of variables.

8. *Partial correlation.* Partial correlation shows what Pearson's correlation coefficient between two variables would be in the absence of one or more other variables. For example, across a sample of children ranging in age from 8 to 13, strength of grip might correlate $+.75$ with mathematics ability. (Why? Remember that correlation does not establish causation.) But if we remove the influence of age on these two variables, we would be left with a partial correlation that is essentially zero. In effect, the partial correlation would hold age constant and ask, now what is the correlation between the original two variables?

9. *Part correlation.* If we remove the influence of one or more additional variables from only one of the two that we are correlating, we are calculating a part correlation, also called a *semipartial correlation.* This was the technique used by Scarr (1985) to remove the factor of the mothers' IQs in studying the relationship between mothers' discipline techniques and children's later intellectual and social skills (Section 8.11).

# 8.15 Summary

Determining the degree to which two variables vary together is important in many fields of inquiry. In behavioral science, a measure of association is helpful in theoretical areas, such as the study of individual differences, and in practical problems, such as determining predictors of success for on-the-job performance. The two basic tasks are (1) determining the degree of association between two variables and (2) predicting a person's standing in one variable when we know the standing in an associated variable. In this chapter, we discussed the problem of association; we consider prediction in the next chapter.

The Pearson product-moment correlation coefficient, $r$, is the most commonly used measure of association when two quantitative variables are characterized by a linear (straight-line) relationship. It reflects agreement between relative standing in one variable and relative standing in the other and so is an index of how well bivariate data points hug the straight line of best fit. The sign of the coefficient specifies whether the two variables are positively or negatively (inversely) related. The magnitude of the coefficient varies from zero when no association is present to $\pm1.00$ when the correlation is perfect.

Making a scatter diagram of the data points of a bivariate distribution is an excellent preliminary step to see if there is any association between two variables. It also provides a rough check on the accuracy of the calculated value of $r$, and it lets us examine several conditions (such as the linearity of the relationship) that may influence the correlation coefficient and its interpretation.

We can use Spearman's correlation coefficient, $r_S$, in place of Pearson's $r$ if the paired observations are converted to ranks. In fact, Spearman's correlation is found merely by applying Pearson's procedure to the ranks. However, there should be no ties in ranks, so we typically use $r_S$ only in circumstances in which the sample size is rather small.

A degree of correlation between two variables means that they vary together to some extent, but it does not necessarily mean that a causal relationship exists between them. We must also keep in mind that if Pearson's $r$ is applied to data that show a curvilinear relationship, the index obtained will underestimate the degree of relationship. Other techniques exist for estimating relationships when two variables are nonlinearly related.

There is no such thing as *the* correlation between two variables. Many factors may influence the correlation coefficient's value. It is sensitive to the range of talent (variability) characterizing the measurements of the two variables. Like other statistics, it is also subject to sampling variation. Variation from sample to sample will, as usual, be greater when samples are small than when they are large. The value of $r$ also depends on how the variables were measured and on the conditions under which the measurements were obtained. We shall therefore need careful description of these circumstances to interpret $r$ properly. We discuss these matters further in Chapters 10 and 18.

The coefficient is unaffected by positive linear score transformations, such as adding or subtracting a constant to the scores or multiplying or dividing them by a constant. Consequently, $r$ remains unchanged whether raw scores or standard scores are used and whether measurement is in the metric system or the common English system.

Although the Pearson correlation coefficient is the index most frequently encountered with bivariate data, other indices exist. Many of these are based on Pearson's index but are adapted to special circumstances.

# Mathematical Notes

### Note 8.1 Derivation of Deviation-Score Formula for $r$ from $z$-Score Formula (*Ref.*: Section 8.6)

$$r = \frac{\sum (z_X z_Y)}{n}$$

$$= \frac{\sum \left( \dfrac{X - \overline{X}}{S_X} \right) \left( \dfrac{Y - \overline{Y}}{S_Y} \right)}{n}$$

$$= \left[ \sum \left( \frac{X - \overline{X}}{S_X} \right) \left( \frac{Y - \overline{Y}}{S_Y} \right) \right] \frac{1}{n}$$

$$= \frac{\sum (X - \overline{X})(Y - \overline{Y})}{n S_X S_Y}$$

### Note 8.2 The Raw-Score Equivalent of $\Sigma(X - \overline{X})(Y - \overline{Y})$ (*Ref.*: Section 8.7)

$$\sum(X - \overline{X})(Y - \overline{Y}) = \sum(XY - \overline{X}Y - \overline{Y}X + \overline{X}\,\overline{Y})$$

$$= \sum XY - \overline{X}\sum Y - \overline{Y}\sum X + n\overline{X}\,\overline{Y}$$

$$= \sum XY - \frac{\left(\sum X\right)\left(\sum Y\right)}{n} - \frac{\left(\sum Y\right)\left(\sum X\right)}{n} + \frac{\not{n}\left(\sum X\right)\left(\sum Y\right)}{(\not{n})(n)}$$

$$= \sum XY - \frac{\left(\sum X\right)\left(\sum Y\right)}{n}$$

## Key Terms, Concepts, and Symbols

correlation   (124)

prediction   (124)

Sir Francis Galton   (107, 125)

bivariate data   (125)

Karl Pearson   (125)

scatter diagram   (128)

linear relationship   (128)

curvilinear relationship   (128)

positive correlation   (129)

negative correlation   (129)

no correlation   (130)

coefficient of correlation   (131)

$r$   (131)

product-moment correlation coefficient   (133)

cross-products   (134)

quadrants   (135)

Spearman's rank-order correlation coefficient   (137)

$r_s$   (138)

linear transformation   (143)

range of talent   (144)

## Problems

[c] *2c, 3b, 4, 5a, 7e, 9, 11a, 23a. The symbol* [c] *is used here and in later chapters to indicate problems that can be worked either by calculator or by computer.*

**1.**  For each pair of variables, say whether you would expect the correlation to be positive, negative, or close to zero: (a) Among school children (from grades one to six, say), height and weight. (b) Among adults, height and intelligence. (c) Among motor vehicles, weight and miles per gallon. (d) Among married couples, age of husband and age of wife.

**2.**  Seven students made the following scores on two quizzes, $X$ and $Y$:

| Student: | A | B | C | D | E | F | G |
|---|---|---|---|---|---|---|---|
| Score on $X$: | 3 | 9 | 7 | 8 | 4 | 6 | 7 |
| Score on $Y$: | 2 | 7 | 8 | 6 | 6 | 5 | 7 |

(a) Construct a scatter diagram of the relationship between these two variables. What is the direction of the relationship? (b) Compute $r$ to two decimals using the deviation-score method. (c) Compute $r$ to two decimals using the raw-score method. (d) Did you get exactly the same answer in (b) and (c)? Explain. (e) Which method was easier? Why? (f) If the two quizzes covered the same subject matter, what is it about the students' performance that $r$ measures?

**3.**  Using a 10-point scale, two managers independently rate the performance of the same five salespeople.

| Salesperson: | H | I | J | K | L |
|---|---|---|---|---|---|
| Rating by first manager ($X$): | 9 | 4 | 5 | 3 | 5 |
| Rating by second manager ($Y$): | 4 | 8 | 4 | 8 | 7 |

*Pg. 134

(a) Construct a scatter diagram and determine the direction of the relationship. (b) Compute $r$, using the raw-score method. (c) Compute $S_X$ and $S_Y$, making the best use of quantities already found in computing $r$. (d) What aspect of the managers' judgments does $r$ measure?

4. Four subjects obtained the following scores on two measures:

Subject:       M   N   O   P
Score on $X$:  7   6   5   8
Score on $Y$:  9   6   7   3

(a) Find $r$ by the raw-score method. (b) Find $S_X$ and $S_Y$.

5. In Figure 8.3, one of the scatter diagrams is described by $r = +.68$. The 10 pairs of scores are

$X$: 30 34 35 36 39 39 40 40 42 46
$Y$: 72 70 76 80 73 79 76 83 85 81

(a) Verify, by the raw-score method, that $r = +.68$. (b) Suppose that $X$ is a person's score on a personality test designed to measure sociability and $Y$ is the rating of that person's sociability made by a close friend. What do the results say about the *validity* of the personality test (the degree to which it measures what it's supposed to)?

6. Compare Formula 8.4 for calculating $\Sigma(X - \overline{X})(Y - \overline{Y})$ from the raw scores $X$ and $Y$ to the formula for calculating $\Sigma(X - \overline{X})^2$ or $\Sigma(Y - \overline{Y})^2$ from the corresponding raw scores $X$ or $Y$. (The latter equation appears just above Formula 8.4 in Section 8.7.) Formula 8.4 parallels the other formula. How?

7. In most of the examples in this chapter, the variables (e.g., SAT score, GPA) characterize an individual person. But the "subject" in a correlational study need not be an individual. Data 8A below gives some of the evidence on smoking and lung cancer (U.S. Department of Health and Human Services, 1982):

(a) In Data 8A, the "subjects" of the research are not individuals but rather what? (b) Make a scatter diagram of these data. (c) In words, describe the relationship between the two variables. (d) Estimate the correlation coefficient. (e) Calculate $r$.

8. Rank each of the following sets of scores from lowest to highest and perform the check suggested at the end of Section 8.9. (a) 11, 13, 15, 19, 19; (b) 11, 13, 13, 13, 15, 19, 19, 21.

9. Two judges at an art show are asked to place the six pictures that reached the "finals" in order of merit. Their rankings are

| Picture: | A | B | C | D | E | F |
|---|---|---|---|---|---|---|
| Judge A: | 3 | 2 | 6 | 4 | 1 | 5 |
| Judge B: | 2 | 1 | 5 | 3 | 4 | 6 |

## DATA 8A

| NATION | PER CAPITA CONSUMPTION OF CIGARETTES IN 1930 | MALE DEATH RATE (PER MILLION) FROM LUNG CANCER IN 1950 |
|---|---|---|
| Iceland | 240 | 60 |
| Norway | 250 | 90 |
| Sweden | 310 | 120 |
| Denmark | 370 | 160 |
| Australia | 450 | 160 |
| Holland | 450 | 240 |
| Canada | 500 | 150 |
| Switzerland | 530 | 250 |
| Finland | 1,110 | 350 |
| Great Britain | 1,130 | 460 |
| United States | 1,280 | 190 |

Calculate $r_S$, the Spearman rank–order coefficient of correlation, as an index of agreement between the two judges.

**10.** For Problem 9, if you calculated Pearson's $r$ as the index of agreement between the two judges, would you expect $r$ to be identical with $r_S$? Explain.

**11.** (a) Consider the data for Problem 7 about the relationship between smoking and lung cancer. Translate these scores to ranks and compute $r_S$, the Spearman coefficient. (b) Pearson's $r$ for these data is $+.74$. Does this agree with the $r_S$ you calculated? Explain.

**12.** Assume that the correlation between height in inches and weight in pounds for the students in a statistics course is about .6. How would the correlation for a given class change under the following circumstances? If the change would be unpredictable, say so. Treat each question as independent of the others. (a) Height is measured in feet and tenths of a foot (so that 66 in. becomes 5.5 ft.). (b) Height is measured in centimeters. (c) Weight is measured in terms of the stone (a British unit equal to 14 lb.). (d) Weight is measured in kilograms. (e) Both (a) and (c) are done simultaneously.

**13.** In what sense do linear transformations involve a straight line?

**14.** An $r$ of $+.60$ was obtained between points earned on a spelling test and IQ for all current members of the sixth grade in a particular school. For each of the following, state whether the correlation would be affected, and if so, how. If it would be affected in an unpredictable manner, say so. Treat each question as independent of the others. (a) Score in spelling is changed to number of answers not correct. (h) Each IQ is divided by 10. (c) Ten points are added to each spelling score. (d) Ten points are added to each spelling score *and* each IQ is divided by 10. (e) Spelling scores are converted to $z$ scores. (f) Spelling scores are converted to $z$ scores and IQ to standard scores with a mean of 50 and a standard deviation of 10.

**15.** The more cigarettes a person has smoked over his or her lifetime, the greater the probability that the person has developed lung cancer. (a) What is the direction of the correlation between these two variables? (b) This finding does not, by itself, prove that smoking causes lung cancer. Why not? (c) If smoking does not cause lung cancer, what might explain the correlation between the two variables? (d) Medical authorities believe that a cause-and-effect relationship between smoking and lung cancer has been proven well beyond reasonable doubt. What kind of evidence do you think has persuaded them?

**16.** Across the cities of Europe, the greater the number of storks nesting within the city limits, the greater the number of babies born in a given year. (a) What is the direction of this correlation? (b) Does this correlation prove that storks bring babies? Why or why not? (c) Explain the correlation without assuming that birds affect birth rates. (d) Which part of Figure 8.6 does your explanation illustrate?

**17.** Over the 365 days of any year in any major city, the greater the quantity of ice cream sold, the greater the number of murders. (a) What is the direction of this correlation? (b) Does this correlation prove that eating ice cream drives people to violence? Why or why not? (c) Explain the correlation without assuming a causal connection between the two variables. (d) Which part of Figure 8.6 does your explanation illustrate?

**18.** Does a low value of $r$ between two variables necessarily indicate that there is very little association between them? Explain.

**19.** Among the 10 women in a statistics course, the correlation between mathematical ability and the score on the final exam is .5. Among the 10 men it is .3. A friend suggests that the relationship between the two variables is stronger for women than for men. Any objections?

**20.** The personnel director for the Miniscule Corporation often lunches with her counterpart for the Megasize Corporation. This noon she mentions her difficulty in selecting workers for an assembly line. Her friend says that she's had good results with the Acme Aptitude Test: Among 400 workers, score on the test correlated .77 with performance on the job. Have you any caution to offer the Miniscule director before she rushes out to buy the test?

**21.** The army finds a correlation of .63 between extraversion and leadership ability among noncommissioned officers. The navy finds the two variables to be uncorrelated. Cite some factors that could explain the difference.

**22.** In a statistics class, the instructor gave a test of elementary mathematics skills ($X$) on the first day. At the end of the course, she had the final exam scores ($Y$) for the same students. The data are given in Data 8B below.

## DATA 8B

| STUDENT | X | Y | STUDENT | X | Y |
|---------|-----|-----|---------|-----|-----|
| 1 | 29 | 56 | 16 | 14 | 37 |
| 2 | 9 | 26 | 17 | 21 | 41 |
| 3 | 14 | 43 | 18 | 14 | 25 |
| 4 | 28 | 38 | 19 | 22 | 44 |
| 5 | 21 | 53 | 20 | 16 | 24 |
| 6 | 10 | 36 | 21 | 19 | 42 |
| 7 | 16 | 33 | 22 | 12 | 39 |
| 8 | 11 | 38 | 23 | 9 | 36 |
| 9 | 18 | 48 | 24 | 10 | 33 |
| 10 | 27 | 42 | 25 | 19 | 36 |
| 11 | 23 | 42 | 26 | 34 | 42 |
| 12 | 11 | 37 | 27 | 23 | 34 |
| 13 | 12 | 37 | 28 | 34 | 56 |
| 14 | 16 | 34 | 29 | 19 | 38 |
| 15 | 23 | 49 | 30 | 18 | 44 |

(a) Construct a scatter diagram for the 30 pairs of scores. Rather than plotting points in a space defined by axes that show every possible score, as in Figure 8.3 and 8.4, group the $X$ scores and group the $Y$ scores, using the techniques introduced in Sections 3.2–3.3. Then in a rough draft of the scatter diagram, plot tally marks to represent the individual cases. In a final draft, replace the tally marks with the corresponding numbers, as in Table 8.1. (b) On the basis of your scatter diagram, describe the relationship between the two variables.

**23.** (a) Using a calculator, find $r$ for the 30 pairs of scores in Data 8B. (b) Calculate $S_X$ and $S_Y$.

# CHAPTER 9

## Prediction

When you have finished studying this chapter, you should be able to:

- Understand that the greater the linear correlation between two variables, the better we are able to predict the standing in one variable from knowledge of the standing in the other;
- Understand that to predict $Y$ from $X$, we first determine a line of best fit—the regression line—that estimates the mean of $Y$ for each value of $X$;
- Plot the regression line according to the least-squares principle;
- Predict $Y$ from $X$ by the raw-score form of the regression equation;
- Understand that except in the case of perfect correlations ($\pm 1.00$), the predicted value of $Y$ from $X$ will be in error;
- Calculate the standard error of estimate, $S_{YX}$; and
- Explain the underlying assumptions (linear relationship, homoscedasticity, normal distribution of scores) in predicting $Y$ from $X$.

**prediction**

when two variables are correlated, estimating the value of one variable from the known value of the other; the better the correlation between the variables, the better the prediction

We learned in the last chapter that SAT scores are positively correlated with freshman-year grade point averages (Slack & Porter, 1980). If someone scores well above average on the SATs, there is a good chance that his or her GPA is also above average. In general, if two variables are correlated, it is possible to make a **prediction**, with better than chance accuracy, of the standing in one of the variables from knowledge of the standing in the other. *The closer the relationship between the two variables, the higher the correlation coefficient and the better the prediction.* Still, the value of the coefficient by itself does not tell us how to proceed. How, then, do we make predictions from correlated data?

This chapter considers predictions only for cases in which the relationship between bivariate data can best be described by a straight line. The Pearson correlation coefficient was developed for linear relationships. Here we consider the equation for the straight line of best fit and learn how to make predictions. If the correlation between two variables is less than perfect, as it always is in real-world cases, then our prediction will also be less than perfect. This means that we will make mistakes when making predictions. Thus, we must also consider the error of prediction and how to measure it.

## 9.1 The Problem of Prediction

Given the correlation between the SAT and freshman-year GPA, college admissions committees looking at applicants' SAT scores can predict with some success how well those students would do if admitted. Two possible ways to make that prediction are demonstrated with the scatter diagram in Figure 9.1. In the scatter diagram, we can

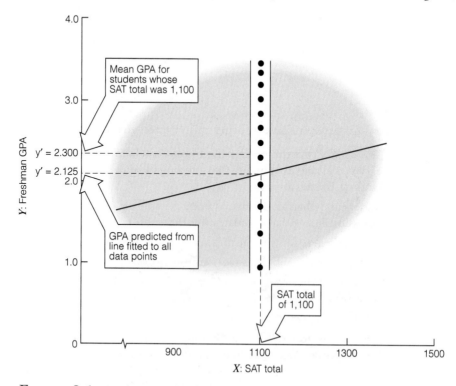

**FIGURE 9.1** Prediction of $Y$ for persons with SAT total scores of 1,100 from column mean and from line of best fit to $Y$ values.

see the positive association between SAT score and freshman-year GPA for a sample of the students admitted to a hypothetical college in the past. Consider a new applicant with an SAT total of 1,100. To take the simplest possible approach to predict his or her GPA, we could look only at the students who had that particular score. Their data points appear in the column erected over the value 1,100 on the abscissa. Suppose the mean GPA for those students was 2.3. Then 2.3 will be our prediction for this applicant.

This method of prediction has a major shortcoming; it ignores cases that have SAT scores other than 1,100. The prediction is based on a relatively small sample and is therefore somewhat unstable; the prediction from another sample of students with scores of 1,100 may differ markedly from this one. However, recall from Section 2.1 that larger samples from a given population vary less among themselves than do smaller samples. Thus, if we can find a way to use the full sample of observations, we can generate predictions that are more resistant to sampling variation.

**regression line**

in prediction of *Y* from *X*, the straight line of best fit to the *Y* values

**regression equation**

the equation that locates the regression line

If it is reasonable to assume that *X* and *Y* are linearly related (our scatter diagram should tell us), we can improve our prediction of *Y* from *X* by finding the straight line of best fit to the *Y* values. This will be a line determined by all the scores in the sample on hand. Statisticians call the line of best fit a **regression line**; the equation that locates the line is the **regression equation**. The regression line is shown in Figure 9.1, and as shown, we can use it to make predictions for new cases. Just start with the SAT score on the abscissa, go up to the line, and then go over to the ordinate. By this method, the best prediction for a student with an SAT total of 1,100 is a GPA of about 2.12.

*"What's even more astonishing is it coincides exactly with the World Series."*

**assumption of linearity**

the assumption that a straight line is the best description of the relationship between $X$ and $Y$

Predictions made by this technique are better in their resistance to sampling variation, but two limitations remain. First, a regression line that has been fitted to a sample of points is probably not the same as the line that would best fit the entire population. (Other things being equal, however, the larger the sample, the closer the approximation.) Second, the technique depends on the assumption that a straight line is a reasonable description of the interrelationship between $X$ and $Y$. Fortunately, the **assumption of linearity** is often satisfactory (see the first caution in Section 8.13). Let us now consider how to define "best fit."

## 9.2 The Criterion of Best Fit

**$Y'$**

symbol for the predicted value of $Y$

**$d_Y$**

symbol for the discrepancy of $Y - Y'$

**criterion for the regression line**

the line of best fit is the one that minimizes the sum of the squares of the discrepancies between the actual value of $Y$ and the predicted value (called the least-squares criterion)

It is all very well to speak of finding the straight line of best fit, but how is one to know when the "best fit" has been achieved? Best fit could be defined in more than one (reasonable) way. Karl Pearson's solution to this problem was to apply the *least-squares criterion*. Figure 9.2 illustrates his thinking for predicting $Y$ from $X$.

The figure shows a bivariate distribution and a possible regression line. How good are the predictions from this line? For the seven cases shown in the scatter diagram, the errors of prediction appear as vertical lines, each connecting the actual value of $Y$ to the predicted value, which we call $Y'$, given by the regression line. The longer the vertical line, the greater the error in prediction.

Let $d_Y$ stand for the discrepancy between the actual value of $Y$ and the predicted value: $d_Y = Y - Y'$. Pearson's **least-squares criterion** for the regression line is this: the **line of best fit** is the one that minimizes the sum of the squares of the discrepancies. Thus $\Sigma d_Y^2$ is to be as small as possible.

Why not just minimize the sum of the absolute magnitudes of the discrepancies rather than the sum of the squares? The answer has two parts: (1) It is difficult to deal mathematically with the absolute discrepancies, whereas the squared discrepancies permit mathematical developments of practical value. (2) The location of the regression line and the value of the correlation coefficient will fluctuate less under the influence of random sampling than would happen if another criterion were used.

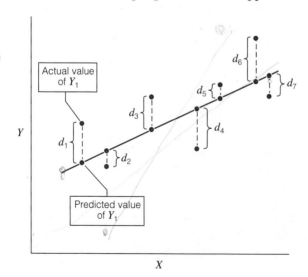

**FIGURE 9.2** Discrepancies between seven $Y$ values and the line of regression of $Y$ on $X$.

---

## Point of Controversy

### Least-Squares Regression versus the Resistant Line

In Chapter 5 we discussed why, in most instances, the mean is the best indicator of central tendency. One of the main reasons, you recall, is that the mean is affected by all the scores in the distribution. However, for the same reason, the mean is *not* the best indicator of central tendency when the distribution is severely skewed or there are a few very aberrant scores ("outliers"). In the latter case, the median is often preferred because its value is not affected by outliers.

The regression line is a running mean, a series of means (Section 9.2). It is located such that it minimizes the sum of the squares of the discrepancies between the actual value of $Y$ and the predicted value, $Y'$. As a score becomes more deviant from the batch, it increases the sum of the squared deviations at an increasing rate. Thus, an outlier has considerable influence on the location of the line. In other words, the regression line tends to reflect the influence of outliers. (It lacks resistance to the substantial influence of atypical scores.)

Because the median is resistant to outliers, John Tukey (1977) and other advocates of exploratory data analysis prefer it for fitting lines to points on a scatter plot (e.g., see Hartwig & Dearing, 1979, and Hoaglin, Mosteller, & Tukey, 2000). The result is called the **resistant line**. The technique for fitting such a line can be found elsewhere (see the cited references).

Which is better, the least-squares regression line or the resistant line? When a distribution contains clear outliers, the resistant line may well be superior. On the other hand, the median, unlike the mean, does not lend itself to further mathematical manipulations. If we use the standard regression equation, further analysis is possible. For example, the standard error of estimate and its applications depend on the fact that we have the least-squares regression line (see Section 9.5). Tests are available for confirming the presence of outliers in a distribution, and some investigators prefer to make the regression line more resistant by trimming them rather than use a technique (the resistant line) that does not allow for further analysis.

Whichever technique you choose to analyze your own data, remember the following: Never compute and interpret correlation coefficients or slopes and intercepts without *first* plotting the $X$ and $Y$ variables, checking for nonlinearity and outliers, and generally inspecting your data.

**resistant line**
uses the median, rather than the mean, to fit lines to points on a scatter diagram

---

This is not the first time we have encountered a sum of squared discrepancies. Recall that the sum of the squared deviations from the mean, $\Sigma(X - \overline{X})^2$, is minimal (see Section 6.9 and Note 6.2 at the end of Chapter 6). Is there some connection between Pearson's regression line and the mean? Yes.

First, just as the mean is a least-squares solution to the problem of finding a measure of central tendency, so the regression line is a least-squares solution to the problem of finding the best-fitting straight line. Both minimize the sum of squared discrepancies; thus they have analogous properties, including resistance to sampling variation.

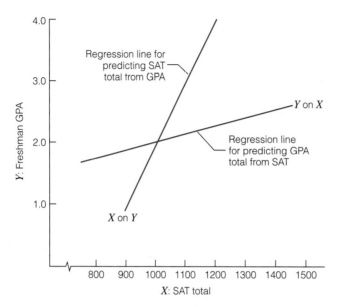

**FIGURE 9.3** Two regression lines for SAT totals and GPAs.

Second, *the regression line is actually a kind of mean. It is a running mean, a series of means.* For each value of $X$, the regression line tells us the mean, or expected, value of $Y$. In other words, whereas $\overline{Y}$ is the mean of all $Y$ values in a set of scores, $Y'$ is an estimate of the mean of $Y$ given the condition that $X$ has a particular value.

Thus far we have been thinking only of predicting $Y$ from $X$. What if we wish to predict $X$ from $Y$? The least-squares criterion would require us to minimize the squared discrepancies in $X$, $\Sigma(X - X')^2$, rather than in $Y$. Unless $r = \pm 1.00$, the two lines will differ. Figure 9.3 shows the two regression lines as they might appear for the SAT scores and GPAs.

In the real world, we are interested in predicting in only one direction, not both directions (because we already know values for one variable). Therefore it is always possible to define the variable to be predicted as $Y$ and the variable used to make the prediction as $X$. Consequently, we will discuss only the prediction of $Y$ from $X$.

## 9.3 The Regression Equation: Standard-Score Form

$Y = bX$, **or**
$Y = bX + a$
general formulas
for a straight
line (compare to
Formulas 9.1
and 9.2)

In practice, we need not experiment with various lines on a scatter diagram to find the one that fits best by Pearson's criterion. And we need not lay a straight edge on a graph to make predictions. To every straight line that we could draw, there corresponds an equation. Recall from your college algebra course that the formula for a straight line is $Y = bX$. Here, $b$ is a constant that multiplies each value of $X$. A straight line may also be expressed as $Y = bX + a$, where both $a$ and $b$ are constants. In this section and the next, it will help to notice the similarity between these two formulas for a straight line and Formulas 9.1 and 9.2. If you need to, refer to Appendix A.9 for a review. We will return to a comparison of the regression equation and that for a straight line in Section 10.4.

The straight line established according to the least-squares principle is the one with this elegantly simple **regression equation**:

REGRESSION OF *Y* ON *X*: STANDARD-SCORE FORMULA

$$z'_Y = rz_X \qquad\qquad (9.1)$$

*where:* $z'_Y =$ the predicted standard-score value of *Y*.
$r =$ the coefficient of correlation between *X* and *Y*.
$z_X =$ the standard-score value of *X* from which $z'_Y$ is predicted.

$z'_Y$
symbol for the predicted standard-score value of *Y*

$z'_Y = rz_X$
regression equation of *Y* on *X*, standard-score formula

Note the title of this equation; it is customary to speak of the **regression of *Y* on *X*** when we predict *Y* from *X*.

The standard-score regression equation is seldom used for actual predictions, because the scores from which a prediction is made are usually in the form of raw scores. However, it reveals some important things about the workings of prediction and so is worth closer study.

First, suppose we wish to predict *Y* from a case at the mean of *X*. Because the mean of a set of scores expressed in standard-score form is always zero (see Section 6.12), the predicted standard score on *Y* is also zero: $z'_Y = (r)(0) = 0$, the mean of *Y*, no matter what the value of *r*. Thus, *for all values of* r, *the regression equation predicts that a case at the mean of* X *will score at the mean of* Y. On a graph, then, the regression line will always pass through the point defined by the mean of *X* and the mean of *Y*, as illustrated in Figure 9.4.

Second, if *r* = 0, then the predicted standard-score value of *Y* will always be zero: $z'_Y = (0)(z_X) = 0$. In raw-score terms, *if the correlation is zero, then the predicted value of* Y *is the mean of* Y *no matter what value of* X *is used to predict* Y. The implications are both interesting and logical. If knowing the value of *X* affords no advantage in predicting *Y*, what value of *Y* shall we predict? Not only is the mean of *Y* an intuitively reasonable prediction, it satisfies the least-squares criterion as well; the sum of the

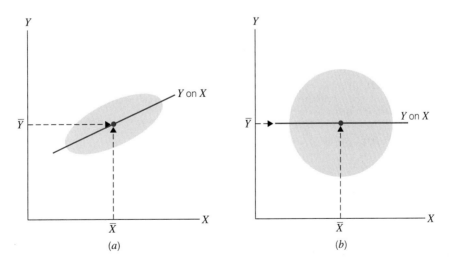

**FIGURE 9.4** Two scatter diagrams showing the lines of regression of *Y* on *X* when (*a*) *r* > 0 and (*b*) *r* = 0. Both regression lines pass through the point $X = \overline{X}, Y = \overline{Y}$.

squares of errors of prediction is minimized. Figure 9.4*b* shows the line of regression of *Y* on *X* when $r = 0$. We will discuss these topics in greater detail in the next chapter (Sections 10.4–10.7).

## 9.4 The Regression Equation: Raw-Score Form

Although the standard-score formula helps us understand the straight line of best fit, most practical problems in prediction are expressed in terms of raw scores. A little algebra transforms the standard-score form of the regression equation into a raw-score form that is more useful for practical work. First, replace the *z* scores with their raw-score equivalents:

$$\frac{Y' - \overline{Y}}{S_Y} = r \frac{X - \overline{X}}{S_X}$$

Then, solving the equation for *Y'*, we obtain the raw-score form of the regression equation:

REGRESSION OF *Y* ON *X*:
RAW-SCORE FORMULA

$Y' = \left( r \frac{S_Y}{S_X} \right) X - \left( r \frac{S_Y}{S_X} \right) \overline{X} + \overline{Y}$

regression equation
of *Y* on *X*, raw-
score formula

$$Y' = \left( r \frac{S_Y}{S_X} \right) X - \left( r \frac{S_Y}{S_X} \right) \overline{X} + \overline{Y} \qquad (9.2)$$

*where:* $Y'$ = the predicted raw score in *Y*.
$S_X$ and $S_Y$ = the two standard deviations.
$\overline{X}$ and $\overline{Y}$ = the two means.
$r$ = the correlation coefficient between *X* and *Y*.

The formula looks more complicated than it really is. To predict *Y'*, we need to know the value of *X* from which the particular prediction is to be made, the two means, the two standard deviations, and the value of the correlation coefficient. For an example of the formula in action, let us predict the freshman-year GPA for an applicant to a college where past experience has yielded the following figures:

**Given**

| | |
|---|---|
| $X$ = SAT total | $Y$ = GPA |
| $\overline{X} = 1000$ | $\overline{Y} = 2.00$ |
| $S_X = 140.0$ | $S_Y = .50$ |
| | $r = +.35$ |

**Problem**

An applicant's SAT scores total 1,100. What is the best prediction of the person's freshman-year GPA if he or she is admitted to the college?

**Solution**     Step 1:   Insert the means, standard deviations, and the correlation coefficient in the raw-score formula and simplify it:

$$Y' = \left( r \frac{S_Y}{S_X} \right) X - \left( r \frac{S_Y}{S_X} \right) \overline{X} + \overline{Y}$$

$$= (+.35)\left( \frac{.50}{140.0} \right) X - (.35)\left( \frac{.50}{140.0} \right) 1{,}000 + 2.00$$

$$= .00125X - 1.250 + 2.00$$

$$= .00125X + .75$$

Step 2:   Insert the value of $X$ from which the prediction is to be made, and find the predicted value $Y'$:

$$Y' = .00125X + .75$$

$$= (.00125)(1{,}100) + .75$$

$$= 1.375 + .75$$

$$= 2.12$$

Note that we did not insert the particular value of $X$ from which $Y'$ is to be predicted until after we simplified the equation. This is particularly desirable if we wish to make more than one prediction, as is usually the case. For example, if we now wish to predict the freshman-year GPA for a person whose SAT total is 1,200, just insert that value in the formula $Y' = .00125X + .75$ to arrive at a prediction of 2.25 for the GPA.

Because the regression equation specifies a straight line, it is easy to graph the equation and then use the line to make predictions from various values of $X$. Figure 9.5

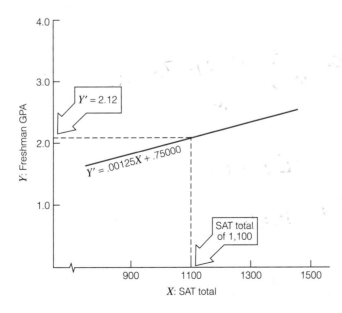

**FIGURE 9.5**  Graph of regression equation for predicting freshman GPA from SAT total. Data from Section 9.4.

shows the regression line for the preceding example. We explain how to graph a straight line in Appendix A.9.

## 9.5 Error of Prediction: The Standard Error of Estimate

**standard error of estimate**

a measure of variability of the actual $Y$ values around the predicted value, $Y'$

$S_{YX}$

symbol for the standard error of estimate

The regression equation states what value of $Y$ is expected ($Y'$) when $X$ takes a particular value. Of course, $Y'$ is not likely to be the actual value of $Y$ that corresponds to the particular value of $X$. If a man is 6 feet tall, the appropriate regression equation may predict his weight to be 175 lbs., but we do not expect a given 6-footer to have exactly that weight. Remember, *the predicted value is only an estimate of the mean value of* Y *for cases with the given score on* X. Thus, 175 lbs. is only a "best estimate" of our 6-footer's weight. If the correlation is low, expect considerable variation of actual values around the predicted value. If the correlation is high, the actual values will cluster more closely about the predicted value. *Only when the correlation is unity ($\pm 1.00$) will the actual values regularly and precisely equal the predicted values.*

What we need is a way to measure the predictive error, the variability of the actual $Y$ values around the predicted value ($Y'$). Such a measure will have desirable properties if it is cast in the form of a standard deviation (see Chapter 6). The **standard error of estimate**, $S_{YX}$, is exactly that kind of measure. Compare its formula with that of the standard deviation:

STANDARD DEVIATION
OF $Y$

$$S_Y = \sqrt{\frac{\sum (Y - \overline{Y})^2}{n}}$$

STANDARD ERROR OF
ESTIMATE OF $Y$ ON $X$

$$S_{YX} = \sqrt{\frac{\sum (Y - Y')^2}{n}} \tag{9.3}$$

$S_{YX} =$

$$\sqrt{\frac{\Sigma(Y - Y')^2}{n}}$$

formula for the standard error of estimate

Figure 9.6 illustrates the discrepancies, $(Y - Y')$, on which Formula 9.3 is based. These are the same values we called $d_Y$ in Section 9.2 and illustrated in Figure 9.2.

When the correlation is perfect, every value of $(Y - Y')$ is zero, and therefore $S_{YX}$ is zero. In short, there is no error of prediction. When the correlation is zero, $Y' = \overline{Y}$ for all values of $X$ (as noted in Section 9.3). We may therefore substitute $\overline{Y}$ for $Y'$ in Formula 9.3 to obtain $\sqrt{\Sigma(Y - \overline{Y})^2/n}$, which is $S_Y$. So, we can see that *the value of* $S_{YX}$ *ranges from zero when the correlation is perfect to* $S_Y$ *when there is no correlation at all.*

We will illustrate some of these characteristics using the 10 pairs of scores from Table 8.2. In practice, 10 cases would be too small a sample to yield reliable results in the application of the regression equation and the standard error of estimate (see Section 9.7). For present purposes, however, it will help keep things simple.

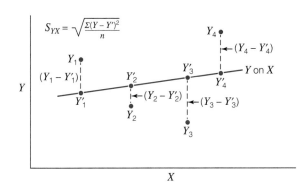

These large values of $(Y - Y')$ are characteristic of a low correlation; they will lead to a large value of $S_{YX}$.

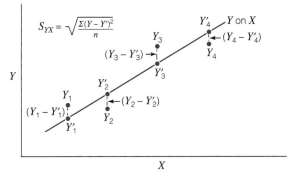

These small values of $(Y - Y')$ are characteristic of a high correlation; they will lead to a small value of $S_{YX}$.

FIGURE 9.6 The standard error of estimate ($S_{YX}$) as a function of the magnitude of the $(Y - Y')$ discrepancies.

Table 9.1 shows the calculation of $S_Y$ and $S_{YX}$ for this small sample. The first two columns list the paired raw scores (indicated by circled numbers). Columns 3 and 4 contain the values needed to calculate $S_Y$. Column 5 presents the value of $Y$ predicted by the regression equation for each value of $X$. Columns 6 and 7 contain the values needed for the calculation of $S_{YX}$. Because the correlation coefficient here (+.675) lies between zero and one, we expect $S_{YX}$ to be less than $S_Y$ (8.139) but greater than zero. In fact, it is 6.00.

Is $S_{YX}$ really a standard deviation? Formula 9.3 looks very much like the formula for the standard deviation, except that $Y'$ rather than $\overline{Y}$ is subtracted from each actual value of $Y$. But as we noted earlier (Section 9.2), $Y'$ is a kind of mean, namely, the estimated mean of $Y$ when $X$ has a particular value. Therefore, $S_{YX}$ is a kind of standard deviation; $S_{YX}$ *is the standard deviation of obtained Y scores about the predicted Y scores.*

Because $S_{YX}$ really is a standard deviation, it should have the properties of one. One such property is that the sum of the squares of the deviations of each score from the mean, $\Sigma(Y - \overline{Y})^2$, is a minimum (Section 6.9). So it is also with the standard error of estimate: The regression line is laid down so as to minimize $\Sigma(Y - Y')^2$, which is the sum of the squares of the discrepancies between each value of $Y$ and the corresponding value of $Y'$.

**TABLE 9.1** *Calculation of $S_Y$ and $S_{YX}$ (Data from Table 8.2)*

| SUBJECT | ① X | ② Y | ③ $(Y - \overline{Y})$ | ④ $(Y - \overline{Y})^2$ | ⑤ $Y'$ | ⑥ $(Y - Y')$ | ⑦ $(Y - Y')^2$ |
|---|---|---|---|---|---|---|---|
| A | 17 | 9 | −4.4 | 19.36 | 13.71 | −4.71 | 22.1841 |
| B | 8 | 13 | −0.4 | 0.16 | 6.67 | 6.33 | 40.0689 |
| C | 8 | 7 | −6.4 | 40.96 | 6.67 | 0.33 | 0.1089 |
| D | 20 | 18 | +4.6 | 21.16 | 16.06 | 1.94 | 3.7636 |
| E | 14 | 11 | −2.4 | 5.76 | 11.36 | −0.36 | 0.1296 |
| F | 7 | 2 | −11.4 | 129.96 | 5.88 | −3.88 | 15.0544 |
| G | 21 | 5 | −8.4 | 70.56 | 16.85 | −11.85 | 140.4225 |
| H | 22 | 15 | +1.6 | 2.56 | 17.63 | −2.63 | 6.9169 |
| I | 19 | 26 | +12.6 | 158.76 | 15.28 | 10.72 | 114.9184 |
| J | 30 | 28 | +14.6 | 213.16 | 23.89 | 4.11 | 16.8921 |
| $\Sigma =$ | 166 | 134 | 0.0 | 662.40 | 134.00 | 0.00 | 360.4594 |
| $\Sigma/n =$ | 16.6 | 13.4 | | 66.24 | 13.40 | | 36.0459 |

Calculation of $S_Y$:

$$S_Y = \sqrt{\Sigma(Y - \overline{Y})^2/n}$$

$$= \sqrt{66.24}$$

$$= 8.139$$

Calculation of $S_{YX}$:

$$S_{YX} = \sqrt{(Y - Y')^2/n}$$

$$= \sqrt{36.0459}$$

$$= 6.00$$

A second property of the standard deviation that $S_{YX}$ shares is that the sum of the deviations of the scores (unsquared) from the mean of the scores must be zero (see Section 5.5). Look at the third and sixth columns in Table 9.1. Just as $\Sigma(Y - \overline{Y})$ is zero at the bottom of Column 3, so $\Sigma(Y - Y')$ is zero at the bottom of Column 6. Note 9.1 at the end of the chapter shows this property to be a general one, not just a coincidence.

## 9.6 An Alternative (and Preferred) Formula for $S_{YX}$

The formula given in the previous section for the standard error of estimate, $S_{YX} = \sqrt{\Sigma(Y - Y')^2/n}$, is convenient for studying the nature of the statistic. For actual prediction, it is better to use Formula 9.4:

STANDARD ERROR OF
ESTIMATE OF $Y$ ON $X$

$$S_{YX} = S_Y\sqrt{1 - r^2} \qquad (9.4)$$

$S_{YX} =$

$S_Y\sqrt{1 - r^2}$

preferred formula for the standard error of estimate

      Formula 9.4 is the exact algebraic equivalent of Formula 9.3. Note, for example, that if $r = 0$, then $S_{YX} = S_Y$, and that if $r = +1.00$, then $S_{YX} = 0$. We can use Formula 9.4 to calculate $S_{YX}$ for the data of Tables 8.2 and 9.1,

$$S_{YX} = 8.139 \sqrt{1 - (.675)^2}$$

$$= 8.139 \sqrt{1 - .456}$$

$$= 8.139 \sqrt{.544}$$

$$= (8.139)(.738)$$

$$= 6.01$$

which differs from the answer obtained by Formula 9.3 (see Table 9.1) only because of rounding error.

## 9.7  Error in Estimating *Y* from *X*

If we can reasonably assume that the actual scores on *Y* are normally distributed about the predicted scores, we can use our knowledge of the normal curve to answer questions about errors of prediction. For example, using principles explained in Chapter 7 and assuming a normal curve, we can determine that:

    68% of the *Y* scores fall within the limits $\overline{Y} \pm 1.00 S_Y$

    95% of the *Y* scores fall within the limits $\overline{Y} \pm 1.96 S_Y$

    99% of the *Y* scores fall within the limits $\overline{Y} \pm 2.58 S_Y$

Because a predicted score, $Y'$, is a kind of mean and the standard error of estimate, $S_{YX}$, is a kind of standard deviation, it is also true, given a normal bivariate distribution, that:

    68% of actual *Y* values fall within the limits $Y' \pm 1.00 S_{YX}$

    95% of actual *Y* values fall within the limits $Y' \pm 1.96 S_{YX}$

    99% of actual *Y* values fall within the limits $Y' \pm 2.58 S_{YX}$

The admissions office at a college may apply this reasoning in predicting grades from SAT scores. From Section 9.4, recall that our prediction for an applicant whose SAT total of 1,100 was 2.12. This prediction is only a best estimate of the mean of the distribution of GPAs for students whose SAT totals are 1,100. Some of those students will obtain higher GPAs, and some lower. To attach a margin of error to the prediction, the admissions office can apply the principle that 95% of the values in a normal distribution fall within 1.96 standard deviations of the mean. Here 2.12 serves as the mean, and the standard error of estimate serves as the standard deviation. The standard error of estimate, from Formula 9.4, is

$$S_{YX} = S_Y\sqrt{1 - r^2} = .50\sqrt{1 - .35^2} = .47$$

Thus 95% of the actual GPAs will lie within these limits:

    LOWER LIMIT:       $Y' - 1.96 S_{YX} = 2.12 - (1.96)(.47) = 1.20$

    UPPER LIMIT:       $Y' + 1.96 S_{YX} = 2.12 + (1.96)(.47) = 3.04$

Figure 9.7 illustrates the situation, showing that for 95% of persons with a test score like our applicant's, freshman GPAs will fall between 1.20 and 3.04. In this sense, one can be 95% confident that this particular applicant's GPA will fall between those limits.

If you are thinking that this margin of error is rather broad, you are not alone. Critics of the SAT argue that it does not sufficiently enhance the prediction of GPA beyond what rank in high school class allows (Slack & Porter, 1980). In practice, it is always desirable to include information about the margin of predictive error, for lacking that information, laypeople often think that performance is "pinpointed" by the predicted value.

The principles of Section 7.4 and 7.5 enable us to answer other types of questions about prediction. For example, what proportion of students whose SAT total is 1,100 may we expect to achieve a GPA of 2.00 or below? To solve a problem of this kind, the first step is to find the predicted value of $Y$ as we did in Section 9.4, where we found $Y'$ to be 2.12.

We take the mean GPA (of students whose SAT total is 1,100) to be 2.12 and the standard deviation to be .47 (the value of $S_{YX}$). The problem now becomes one of the type described in Section 7.4. We must therefore translate the GPA of 2.00 to a $z$ score and find the area that lies below this point in a normal curve. Remembering that a $z$ score is *(score − mean)/standard deviation*, we have:

$$z = \frac{Y - Y'}{S_{YX}}$$

$$= \frac{2.00 - 2.12}{.47}$$

$$= -.26$$

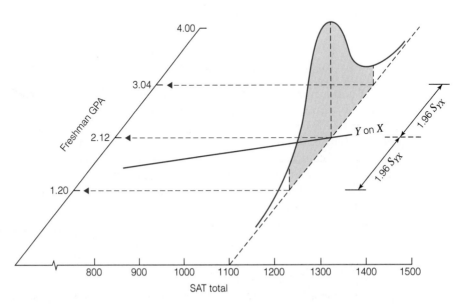

**FIGURE 9.7** The 95% limits for actual GPAs of students scoring 1,100 on the SAT. The shaded area represents 95% of the cases with an SAT total of 1,100.

Consulting Table A in Appendix E, we find that .3974 of the area under the curve falls beyond a $z$ score of $-.26$ in a normal distribution. This is the answer to the problem: For those whose SAT total is 1,100, 39.74% may be expected to achieve a GPA of 2.00 or lower.

# 9.8 Cautions Concerning Estimation of Predictive Error

**homo-scedasticity**

the assumption that the variability of actual $Y$ values around $Y'$ is the same for all values of $X$

Several conditions must be met for the procedures of the preceding section to work well. First, *the relationship between the two variables must be linear.* If it is not, as in Figure 8.7, then for most values of $X$, $Y'$ will underestimate or overestimate the mean of the actual $Y$ scores.

Second, *the variability of actual Y values around Y' must be the same for all values of* $X$. This is the assumption of **homoscedasticity**, the assumption that variability in $Y$ is the same from column to column, as on the left side of Figure 9.8. In the defining formula for the standard error of estimate, $S_{YX} = \sqrt{(Y - Y')^2/n}$, we can see that $S_{YX}$ is a function of the average of magnitude of the squared discrepancies between each $Y$ value and the corresponding $Y'$. If the data are like those of Figure 9.8*b*, $S_{YX}$ will approximate the standard deviation of the $Y$ values only for intermediate values of $X$; it will overestimate predictive error in $Y$ for low values of $X$ and underestimate it for high values. Another problem that sometimes occurs is outliers (very discrepant data points). A field of regression analysis, called regression diagnostics, has developed to identify whether discrepant data points are present (see Chatterjee & Yilmaz, 1992, for a review).

Third, *the actual Y scores must be normally distributed for all values of* $X$. Remember that for problems like those in the previous section we used the table of areas under the normal curve to find the proportion of cases expected to fall above or below a given point.

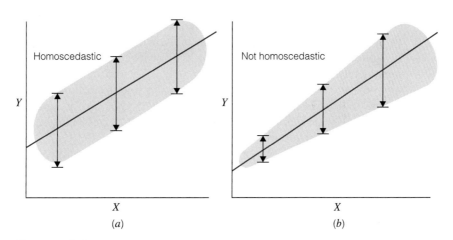

**FIGURE 9.8** (*a*) A homoscedastic bivariate distribution. The variability among the $Y$ values is the same at all values of $X$, as suggested by the three double-headed arrows. (*b*) A bivariate distribution lacking homoscedasticity. The variability among the $Y$ values differs at different values of $X$.

The three conditions just listed must sound formidable. Fortunately, they are well met sufficiently often for the procedures of Section 9.7 to be reasonably accurate. If you inspect the scatter diagram, it will usually reveal any important departures from the three conditions, but there are statistical tests that objectively identify departures. You can find such tests in computer programs designed to calculate correlation and regression statistics.

We must now add one more warning: *The procedures of Section 9.7 do not take into account the influence of random sampling variation*. Because in any realistic prediction situation we are dealing not with the population of paired scores (why predict if we already know?) but with a sample from that population, the "true" correlation coefficient, regression line, and standard error of estimate will probably differ somewhat from those of the sample with which we are confronted. More sophisticated procedures are available that do allow for random sampling variation (see, for example, Hays, 1994).

As we would expect, *taking account of the additional variability due to sampling variation extends the limits within which the actual* Y *values will likely be found*, less so for predictions made from central values of *X* and more so for those made from more distant values of *X*. With the problem used for illustration in Section 9.7, if sample size were 100 and the more accurate procedure were used, the interval expected to contain the central 95% of actual *Y* values would be about 4% wider than what we obtained. With fewer cases, the error would be greater, and with more it would be less. In general, predicting and estimating the error of prediction are best done when the sample size is large enough to reduce the margin of error to a tolerable amount. A larger sample size also makes it easier to determine whether the conditions of linearity, homoscedasticity, and normality are reasonably met. A sample with $n = 100$ is really rather small for these purposes.

## 9.9 Summary

If two variables are correlated, knowledge of the standing in one variable can be used to predict the standing in the other. If the variables are linearly related, we can fit a straight line to the data and use that line (or its equation) to make such a prediction. Fortunately, linear relationships are frequently found in the real world.

The standard procedure is to establish the line according to the least-squares criterion, which specifies the line that minimizes the sum of squares of the predictive errors, $\Sigma(Y - Y')^2$. This line of best fit (called a regression line) estimates the mean value of *Y* for each particular value of *X*.

There are actually two regression equations (and therefore two regression lines). One is for predicting *Y* from *X*, and the other is for predicting *X* from *Y*. We avoid this problem by defining the variable to be predicted as *Y* and the predictor variable as *X*.

The regression equation can be expressed very simply in standard score form: $z'_Y = rz_X$. This equation shows that (1) the regression line always passes through the point defined by the mean of *X* and the mean of Y no matter what the value of *r*; and (2) when the correlation is zero, the predicted value of *Y* is always the mean of *Y*, no matter what the value of *X*—an intuitively reasonable idea. The raw-score form of the regression equation and its corresponding graph are more useful for practical prediction work.

Unless the correlation is $\pm 1$, predicted values are only the expected values of $Y$ corresponding to particular values of $X$, and we must consider the question of predictive error. The standard error of estimate, $S_{YX}$, measures that error. It is a kind of standard deviation, the standard deviation of the distribution of observed scores about the corresponding predicted score. Values of $S_{YX}$ range from zero when the correlation is perfect to $S_Y$ when there is no correlation at all. Our use of $S_{YX}$ as a measure of predictive error in $Y$ requires the assumption that the variability in $Y$ is the same irrespective of the corresponding value of $X$. This is called the assumption of homoscedasticity.

If it is possible to assume that $Y$ scores are normally distributed about their predicted scores, we can use the normal curve to answer questions about errors of prediction. Thus, we can estimate the limits that mark out the central 95% of $Y$ scores that would be expected given a particular value of $X$.

The procedures described in this chapter make no allowance for the influence of random sampling variation, which affects the bivariate distribution and therefore the value of the correlation coefficient and the precise location of the regression line. As usual, the larger the sample, the less the sampling variation.

# Mathematical Note

### Note 9.1 Sum of the Deviations of Scores about Their Predicted Values (*Ref.*: Section 9.5)

Substituting the raw score equivalent of $Y'$ (from Formula 9.2) in the expression $\Sigma(Y - Y')$, we obtain

$$\Sigma(Y - Y') = \Sigma\left[Y - \left(r\frac{S_Y}{S_Y}\right)X + \left(r\frac{S_Y}{S_X}\right)\overline{X} - \overline{Y}\right]$$

$$= \Sigma\left[(Y - \overline{Y}) - \left(r\frac{S_Y}{S_X}\right)(X - \overline{X})\right]$$

$$= \Sigma(Y - \overline{Y}) - r\frac{S_Y}{S_X}\Sigma(X - \overline{X})$$

Because $\Sigma(Y - \overline{Y}) = 0$ and $\Sigma(X - \overline{X}) = 0$ (see Note 5.1, Chapter 5), $\Sigma(Y - Y') = 0$.

# Key Terms, Concepts, and Symbols

prediction (124, 154)

regression line (155)

regression equation (155, 159)

assumption of linearity (156)

least-squares criterion (156)

line of best fit (156)

$Y'$ (156)

$d_Y$ (156)

resistant line (157)

regression line as a running mean (158)

$z'_Y$ (159)

regression of $Y$ on $X$ (159)

standard error of estimate (162)

$S_{YX}$ (162)

homoscedasticity (167)

# Problems

1. Under what two circumstances is the prediction of $Y$ from $X$ better made from the regression equation than from the mean of the $Y$ column corresponding to the particular value of $X$?

2. Identify two advantages of using the least-squares criterion of best fit in comparison to a criterion based on the raw (unsquared) errors of prediction.

3. Would the regression line shown in Figure 9.2 look the same if it showed the prediction of $X$ from $Y$ rather than $Y$ from $X$? Explain.

4. If $r = 1.00$, what is the value of $\Sigma d_Y^2$? Why?

5. If $r = -1.00$, what is the value of $\Sigma d_Y^2$? Why?

6. Suppose the correlation coefficient between the SAT verbal score and IQ is $r = +.50$. What $z$ score on the SAT verbal test do you predict for someone whose $z$ score on IQ is (a) $+3.00$? (b) $-2.00$? (c) $0.00$? (d) $-1.00$? (e) $+1.00$? (f) $-0.50$?

7. Suppose $X = $ IQ with $\overline{X} = 100$ and $S_X = 15$, while $Y = $ SAT verbal score with $\overline{Y} = 500$ and $S_Y = 100$. Use the standard-score formula for the regression of $Y$ on $X$ to predict $Y'$ (the raw score) for the following values of $X$, assuming $r = .50$. (You can do these in your head, but in writing your answer show both the $z$ score and the raw score values.) (a) 100, (b) 115, (c) 130, (d) 85, (e) 70, (f) 145, (g) 55.

8. Suppose $\overline{X} = 50$, $S_X = 10$, $\overline{Y} = 200$, and $S_Y = 30$. What is the value of $r$ for each of the following circumstances? (*Hint:* You can do these mentally if you think in terms of the standard-score formula for the regression of $Y$ on $X$.) (a) For $X = 40$, the regression equation predicts $Y' = 170$. (b) For $X = 40$, the equation predicts $Y' = 230$. (c) For $X = 60$, $Y' = 215$. (d) For $X = 30$, $Y' = 230$. (e) For $X = 70$, $Y' = 215$.

9. Suppose $\overline{X} = 55$, $S_X = 12$, $\overline{Y} = 118$, and $S_Y = 27$. For a case that stands at 55 on $X$, the regression equation predicts that $Y' = 118$. Can you tell the value of $r$? Explain.

10. According to the regression equation for a particular problem in prediction, when $X = 81$, $Y' = 317$; when $X = 84$, $Y' = 317$, and when $X = 92$, $Y' = 317$. (a) What is the value of $r$? How can you tell? (b) What is $\overline{Y}$? How can you tell? (c) Can you infer the value of $\overline{X}$? Explain.

11. If $r = 0$, then $Y' = \overline{Y}$, no matter what the value of $X$. What justification is there for such a prediction, aside from intuition?

12. For the example presented in Section 9.4, use the raw-score regression equation to predict the GPA for applicants with these SAT totals: (a) 900, (b) 800, (c) 1,250, (d) 1,400, (e) 1,600.

13. For the data in Problem 7, repeat parts (a), (c), and (e) using the raw-score regression equation.

14. For the data in Problem 4 of Chapter 8, (a) find the raw-score regression equation, and predict the score on $Y$ for these values of $X$: (b) 2, (c) 3, (d) 8, (e) 9.

15. For the data in Problem 5 of Chapter 8, (a) make a scatter diagram, (b) find the regression equation for raw scores, and (c) plot the regression line on your diagram. Now use the equation to predict the score on $Y$ for these values of $X$: (d) 28, (e) 38, and (f) 47. (g) Verify that your predictions in (d) through (f) lie on the regression line in your diagram (show where they are on your graph).

16. For the 19 students in a statistics course, where $X = $ height in inches and $Y = $ weight in pounds, $\overline{X} = 69.18$, $S_X = 3.01$, $\overline{Y} = 147.42$, $S_Y = 24.61$, and $r = +.83$. (a) Write the raw-score formula for the regression of $Y$ on $X$. Now predict the weight for students of these heights: (b) 60 in., (c) 62 in., (d) 68 in., (e) 72 in., (f) 80 in.

17. Using the data for Problem 16, (a) predict weight for a child who is 36 in. tall. (b) Any comments?

18. Calculate $S_{YX}$ for the example of Section 9.4, using (a) Formula 9.3 and (b) Formula 9.4.

19. Calculate $S_{YX}$ for the data in (a) Problem 7 and (b) Problem 16.

20. For the example of Section 9.4, find (a) the predicted GPA for an applicant whose SAT

total is 1,300, (b) the limits within which 95% of the actual GPAs will probably lie for applicants with SAT totals of 1,300, and (c) the limits within which 68% of the actual GPAs will probably lie for applicants with SAT totals of 1,300.

**21.** The following data are for freshman students at Spartan University:

| APTITUDE SCORE: $X$ | FRESHMAN GPA: $Y$ |
|---|---|
| $\overline{X} = 560$ | $\overline{Y} = 2.65$ |
| $S_X = 75$ | $S_Y = .35$ |
| $r_{XY} = +.50$ | |

(a) Write the raw-score regression equation for predicting $Y$ from $X$. (b) John and Will score 485 and 710, respectively, on the aptitude test. Predict the freshman GPA for each. (c) What assumption is necessary for this prediction to be valid? (d) What is the value of the standard error of estimate of $Y$ on $X$? (e) For students whose aptitude scores are the same as John's: What proportion will be expected to obtain a GPA equal to the freshmen mean or better? (f) What proportion will be expected to obtain a GPA of 2.0 or lower? (g) Within what central GPA limits will 95% of students with aptitude scores equal to John's be likely to be found? For students whose aptitude score is the same as Will's: (h) What proportion will be expected to obtain a GPA equal to 2.5 or better? (i) What proportion will be expected to obtain a GPA of 3.0 or lower? (j) Within what central GPA limits will 50% of students with aptitude scores equal to Will's likely to be found? (k) What assumptions are necessary for the answers to (e)–(j) to be valid?

**22.** Look at Figure 8.7. If we use the formulas for the regression equations given in this chapter, what will be the consequences of predicting $Y$ (a) from an extremely low $X$ score? (b) from an $X$ score near the mean of the $X$ values?

**23.** Look at Figure 9.8*b*. If the data of Problem 21 actually look like that, how (in broad terms) would the results of parts (e)–(j) of Problem 21 be affected? Explain.

# CHAPTER 10

## Interpretive Aspects of Correlation and Regression

When you have finished studying this chapter, you should be able to:

- Describe several factors that affect the value of $r$ (e.g., the degree of variation in each variable, discontinuous distributions, heterogeneity of samples);
- Understand the several different ways of interpreting the degree of correlation between two variables (e.g., the regression coefficient, coefficient of nondetermination, coefficient of determination, proportion of correct placements); and
- Explain what is meant by regression toward the mean.

In the previous two chapters, we presented an introduction to the Pearson correlation coefficient and the regression equation, both based on the assumption of a linear relation between two variables. Along the way, we have warned that interpretation of the correlation coefficient is not always as straightforward as one might be tempted to believe. We know, for example, that a coefficient of .50 does *not* mean that there is 50% association between the two variables (Section 8.5). What, then, is the meaning of the correlation coefficient? We have also warned that a coefficient must be interpreted in the light of the circumstances under which it was obtained (Section 8.13). As we shall see, the regression equation also has some surprising consequences that are important to understand. These and other interpretive matters are the subject of this chapter.

## 10.1 Factors Influencing *r*: Range of Talent

**range of talent**
the variability in the distribution of *X* and *Y* scores

In Chapter 8 we cautioned that the correlation coefficient is sensitive to the **range of talent** (the variability) characterizing the measurements of the two variables. For example, look at Figure 10.1. If a university had only minimal entrance requirements, the relationship between total SAT scores and freshman GPA might look like that shown in Figure 10.1*a*. Here, SAT scores range from 800 to 1,400 and there is a moderate degree of relationship between the two variables (the cluster of dots slope from the lower left to the upper right). However, suppose that a more selective private university admitted students only with SAT scores of 1,200 or higher. These would be the students represented by the dots to the right of the vertical line in Figure 10.1*a*. The scatter diagram for these individuals would look like that represented by Figure 10.1*b*. As you can see, the relationship between SAT totals and freshman GPAs is much weaker when the range of talent has been restricted. Had we looked only at this restricted group of individuals, we would have underestimated the value of the SAT as a screening device for all applicants who apply to college.

We will now demonstrate mathematically that the degree of variability characterizing each variable is an important consideration in understanding what a correlation coefficient means (or does not mean). First, let us lay a little ground work. According to Formula 9.4,

$$S_{YX} = S_Y\sqrt{1 - r^2}$$

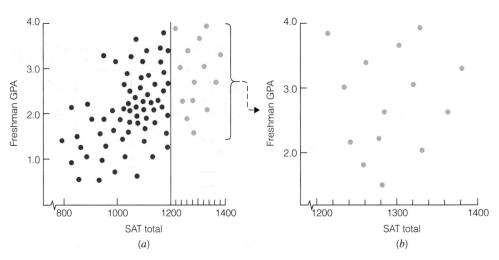

**FIGURE 10.1** Relations between SAT scores and freshman GPA when range is unrestricted (*a*) and when it is restricted (*b*).

$S_{YX} =$
$S_Y\sqrt{1 - r^2}$

the variability of
$Y$ scores around
the regression
line (sometimes
called the error
of prediction)

We can solve this equation for $r$:

---

ALTERNATIVE FORMULA FOR $r$

$$r = \sqrt{1 - \frac{S_{YX}^2}{S_Y^2}}$$ (10.1)

---

**hugging principle**

the degree of
correlation in-
creases the
closer the $Y$
scores "hug" the
regression line

This is not a practical formula for computing the correlation coefficient, but it is helpful for understanding the meaning of $r$. As you will remember, in Section 8.4 it was contended that if the $Y$ scores "hugged" the regression line closely, the correlation would be high, and if not, it would be low. We now give a more precise expression of this **hugging principle**. The magnitude of $r$ is not a function of the size of $S_{YX}$, the absolute measure of the variation of $Y$ about the regression line. Rather, it is a function of the size of $S_{YX}$ relative to $S_Y$. If $S_{YX}$ is zero, there is no error of prediction, and the correlation coefficient, according to Formula 10.1, is $\pm 1$. On the other hand, if $S_{YX}$ has the same value as $S_Y$, the correlation will be zero. Whether $S_{YX}$, the standard error of estimate, by itself is small or large therefore does not matter. What matters is whether it is small in relation to $S_Y$.

**restriction of range**

in relation to
correlation, lim-
iting the calcu-
lation of $r$ (and
the prediction
of $Y$ values) to a
limited range of
values within
the total range
of $X$ values

Figure 10.2 illustrates a bivariate distribution and shows the consequences of the **restriction of range** of the variables. Imagine two situations: In the first, the range of $X$ values is unrestricted, and the bivariate distribution is represented by the entire oval in Figure 10.2. In the second, the scores to the left of the vertical line have been eliminated, and the bivariate distribution is represented only by that part of the oval that lies to the right of the vertical line. It is clear that $Y$ values would vary to a greater extent in the unrestricted situation. In accord with this observation, let us suppose that $S_{Y_U}^2$, the variance of the $Y$ scores in the unrestricted case, is 8, and $S_{Y_R}^2$, the variance of the $Y$ scores in the restricted case, is 6. Now chopping off the left side of the bivariate distribution shrinks the variability of $Y$, but if the assumption of homoscedasticity (see Section 9.8) holds, $S_{YX}^2$, the variance of $Y$ when $X$ is held constant,

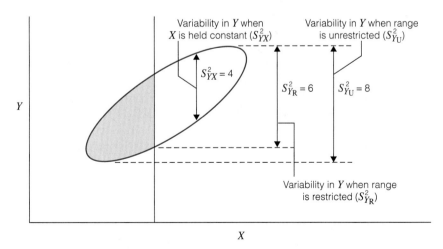

**FIGURE 10.2** Relation between $S_{YX}^2$ and $S_Y^2$ when range of talent differs.

does not change. We shall suppose that $S_{YX}^2$ is 4 for both the restricted and unrestricted situation. Let us calculate $r$ by Formula 10.1 for both cases:

| RANGE OF TALENT UNRESTRICTED | RANGE OF TALENT RESTRICTED |
|:---:|:---:|
| $r = \sqrt{1 - \dfrac{S_{YX}^2}{S_Y^2}}$ | $r = \sqrt{1 - \dfrac{S_{YX}^2}{S_Y^2}}$ |
| $= \sqrt{1 - \dfrac{4}{8}}$ | $= \sqrt{1 - \dfrac{4}{6}}$ |
| $= \sqrt{\dfrac{1}{2}}$ | $= \sqrt{\dfrac{1}{3}}$ |
| $= .71$ | $= .58$ |

To sum up, in moving from an unrestricted situation to a restricted one, $S_Y^2$ shrank, but $S_{YX}^2$ did not, so the ratio $S_{YX}^2/S_Y^2$ became larger and consequently $r$ became smaller.

The immediate consequence of this fact is that *the value of the correlation coefficient depends on the degree of variation characterizing each variable as well as on the relationship present.* It is common to find that the correlation coefficient between score on an academic aptitude test and academic achievement is highest among grade school children, lower among high school seniors, and still lower among college students. These differences may indicate not so much that something different is going on among the three groups as that the range of ability is greatest among the students in the lower grades and is successively smaller as one progresses into the realms of higher education.

In a given situation, restriction of range may take place in $X$, in $Y$, or in both. *Other things being equal, the greater the restriction of range in X and/or Y, the lower the correlation coefficient.* When reporting a correlation coefficient, state the standard deviations of $X$ and $Y$ so that others may judge whether the ranges of talent are similar to those with which they are concerned, or whether some allowance must be made.

## 10.2 The Correlation Coefficient in Discontinuous Distributions

Suppose someone in the admissions office of a university wants to know the relation between SAT score and freshman GPA for last year's entering class. At lunch with a friend from the student personnel office, he learns that a ready-made sample of personnel records awaits him. His friend is sending disqualification notices to those who failed during their first year and is also sending notices of election to the Gold Star Society to those who qualified for that scholastic honor during their first year. His friend offers to pass on the records of these students, thus saving him the effort of pulling records from the file. If the man from the admissions office accepts the offer, pools the two sets of personnel records, and computes the coefficient of correlation between test score and GPA, his data might look like those pictured in Figure 10.3. Note that a distribution that usually would be continuous has been rendered

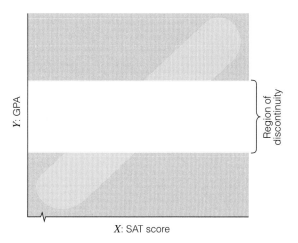

**FIGURE 10.3**   Scatter diagram for discontinuous data.

discontinuous by excluding students with intermediate GPAs. If you take a sample in this manner, it will yield a correlation coefficient different from what you would obtain by sampling *all* elements of the population. *Usually, discontinuity, whether in* X, *in* Y, *or in both, results in a higher correlation coefficient.*

## 10.3 Factors Influencing *r*: Heterogeneity of Samples

In Section 8.13, we cautioned that the correlation coefficient should be interpreted in terms of the circumstances under which it was obtained. In Section 10.1, we made one aspect of this warning explicit. Here is another.

Suppose Professor Haggerty, a physics instructor, obtains the correlation between academic aptitude test score and grade given in one of her courses; let us say that it is +.50. She persuades Professor Eagan, a colleague who teaches the same course, to repeat the study in his class to verify the result. Professor Eagan does so and also finds the correlation to be +.50. In a moment of idle curiosity, Haggerty decides to pool the pairs of scores from the two classes and recalculate the correlation coefficient. She does so, and obtains a value of +.30! How could this be?

The answer lies in something well known to physics students although perhaps inadequately appreciated by the instructors. The fact of the matter is that the first instructor is known as "Hard-Nosed Haggerty" and the second as "Easy-Aces Eagan." Professor Haggerty is a hard grader; once, 8 years ago, she had a student who she thought deserved an A. Professor Eagan, on the other hand, thinks all students are wonderful and rarely gives a grade below C. Consequently, the scatter diagrams obtained from the two samples are like those shown in Figure 10.4*a*. Note that the ability of the students (the X distributions) appears to be about the same in the two classes, but the distributions of grades (the Y distributions) are not. The reason for the different correlation coefficient is that when the data are pooled, the points no longer hug the regression line (which now must be a line lying amidst the two distributions) as closely as they did in each separate distribution. In terms of our more

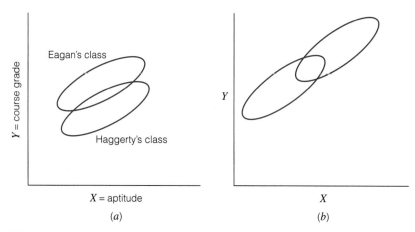

**FIGURE 10.4**   Correlation resulting from the pooling of data from heterogeneous samples.

recent knowledge, the ratio of $S_{YX}^2$ to $S_Y^2$ is smaller in each sample than it is among the pooled data.

In the case illustrated, the distributions differed between samples in the mean of $Y$ but not in the mean of $X$. Other differences are quite possible. Figure 10.4*b* shows a situation in which a second sample differs in that *both* the mean of $X$ and the mean of $Y$ are higher than in the first sample. In this case, the fraction $S_{YX}^2/S_Y^2$ is *smaller* when the data are pooled than it is for either sample alone, and the correlation will therefore be greater among the pooled data than among the separate samples.

In summary, *when samples are pooled, the correlation for the aggregated data depends on where the sample values lie relative to one another in both the* X *and the* Y *dimensions.*

## 10.4 Interpretation of *r*: The Regression Equation I

Earlier (in Section 8.5) we observed that there was no simple way to interpret the meaning of the correlation coefficient. In this section, we consider the first of several ways to interpret *r*.

Recall from Section 9.3 that the equation for any straight line can be put into the following form (reviewed in Section A.9 of Appendix A):

GENERAL EQUATION
OF A STRAIGHT LINE
$$Y = bX + a \qquad\qquad (10.2)$$

**Y intercept**

the point on the $Y$ axis at which a straight line crosses it

In this equation, *a* is a constant that identifies the point on the $Y$ axis at which the line crosses it. It is known as the **Y intercept**. For the two lines in Figure 10.5, the equation of one is $Y = 3X - 4$, and the equation of the other is $Y = .25X + 2$. Note that in each case the value of *a* identifies the point on the $Y$ axis at which the line crosses it.

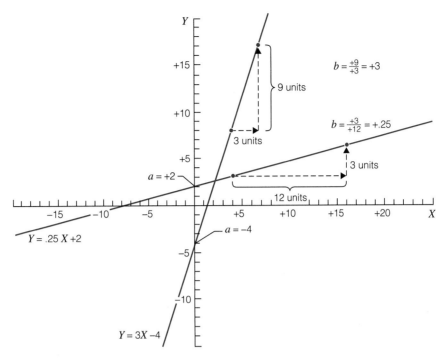

**FIGURE 10.5** Plots of two straight lines showing the slope and *Y* intercept of each.

**slope of a line** specifies the amount of increase in *Y* that accompanies one unit of increase in *X*

The other constant in the equation is *b*, and it is called the slope of the line. It will be positive when the value of *Y* increases with increasing values of *X*, as is the case with the two lines pictured. It will be negative if the line slants the other way—that is, when *Y* decreases as *X* increases. The **slope of a line** specifies the amount of increase in *Y* that accompanies one unit of increase in *X*. Consider the line for which the equation is $Y = 3X - 4$. The dotted lines show that if *X* is increased by 3 units, *Y* increases by nine units. The ratio of the increase in *Y* (the vertical distance) to the increase in *X* (the horizontal distance) is the slope of the line. Thus, the slope is

$$b = \frac{vertical\ change}{horizontal\ change} = \frac{+9}{+3} = +3.0$$

In the second equation, *Y* increases 3 units for every 12 units of increase in *X*, so the slope is $b = 3/12$ or $+.25$. Note that if *Y* decreased 3 units for every 12 units of increase in *X*, we would have a "negative increase" in the numerator of the fraction, and the resultant value of *b* would be $-.25$ rather than $+.25$.

Using this model, let us examine the several forms of the equation for the line of regression of *Y* on *X*:

GENERAL EQUATION OF
A STRAIGHT LINE
$$Y = bX + a$$

**one inter-pretation of r**
the amount of increase in Y that, on average, accompanies a unit increase in X (when both measures are expressed in standard-score units)

**regression coefficient**
the amount of increase in Y that, on the average, accompanies a unit increase in X (when both measures are expressed in raw-score terms)

**$r(S_Y/S_X)$**
symbol for the regression coefficient

REGRESSION OF Y ON X:
STANDARD-SCORE FORMULA

$$z_Y' = \overbrace{rz_X}^{b} + \overbrace{0}^{(a=0)}$$

REGRESSION OF Y ON X:
RAW-SCORE FORMULA

$$Y' = \overbrace{\left( r\frac{S_Y}{S_X}\right)}^{b} X + \overbrace{\left(-r\frac{S_Y}{S_X}\right)\overline{X} + \overline{Y}}^{a}$$

The value $b$ is most interesting when the regression equation is cast in standard score form. In this case, the correlation coefficient *is* the slope of the regression line. There-fore, *one interpretation of the correlation coefficient is that it states the amount of increase in Y that, on the average, accompanies a unit increase in X when both measures are expressed in standard-score units.* It indicates how much of a standard deviation Y will increase for an increase of one standard deviation of X.

When we state the regression equation for predicting Y from X in raw-score form, its slope is $b = r(S_Y/S_X)$ rather than $r$. This expression is known as the regression coefficient. It may also be used to interpret a given correlation. The **regression coefficient**, $r(S_Y/S_X)$, states the amount of increase in Y that, on average, accompanies a unit increase in X when both measures are expressed in raw-score terms.

In his early work in measuring association, Sir Francis Galton apparently thought that the slope of the line of best fit might be an indicator of the degree of associa-tion. From what we have learned in this section, it is clear that this would work if the two standard deviations were equal because in that case $r(S_Y/S_X)$ reduces to $r$. In-deed, much of Galton's work on heredity involved just such variables. Think back, for example, to Table 8.1, which contained the data from his investigation of the re-lationship between parental height and height of adult offspring. But for many vari-ables, the two standard deviations differ substantially (e.g., the association between GPA and SAT scores).

## 10.5 Interpretation of *r*: The Regression Equation II

In the previous section, we presented one way of using the regression equation to in-terpret *r*. Here is a second way. Consider the standard-score formula for the regres-sion of Y on X: $z_Y' = rz_X$. Let us see what this equation says about the consequences of three possible values of *r*: 0, +.50, and +1.00. We show graphic representation of the regression of Y on X in Figure 10.6 for each of these situations together with the regression equation appropriate to each. As the diagram at the top shows, when the correlation is +1, the predicted standard score in Y is the same as the standard score in X from which the prediction is made. When the correlation is zero, the mean of $Y(z = 0)$ is predicted, no matter what value X has, as shown at the bottom. This

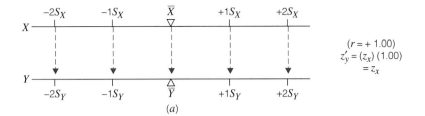

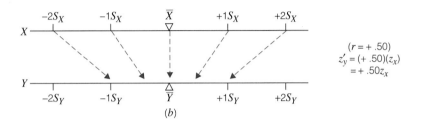

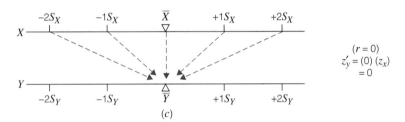

**FIGURE 10.6** Regression toward the mean for three values of r.

is logical because information about $X$ supplies no information that would improve on a sheer guess as to the value of $Y$.

**regression toward the mean**

when the correlation between two variables is less than perfect, the more extreme the score on one variable, the more likely it will be paired with a less extreme score on the other variable

The most interesting of the three situations is where $r$ has an intermediate value. Think, for example, of the correlation between intelligence of parents and of offspring, which indeed has a value close to +.50. If parental intelligence is 2 standard deviations above the mean, the predicted intelligence of their offspring is 1 standard deviation above the mean. On the other hand, if the parents' intelligence is 2 standard deviations below the mean, the predicted intelligence of their offspring is only 1 standard deviation below the mean. To put it in other words, bright parents will tend to have children who are brighter than average but not as bright as they, and dull parents will tend to have children who are dull but not as dull as their parents. Remember that the predicted value is to be thought of as an *average* value; it is quite possible for bright parents to have a child brighter than they or one whose intelligence is below average.

This phenomenon is precisely what Galton observed in his studies of inheritance. He referred to it first as "reversion" and later as "regression." Today we call it **regression toward the mean**. You understand now why the straight line of best fit is termed a regression line and why the symbol $r$ was chosen for the correlation coefficient.

Regression toward the mean is, of course, characteristic of *any* relationship in which the correlation is less than perfect. Consequently, we would expect that a very short person would tend to have short children but children less short than he or she, and that the brightest student in the class would tend to earn a good grade but not necessarily the best in the class.

Both the extremity of the value from which prediction is made and the value of $r$ influence the amount of regression. First, *the more extreme the value from which prediction is made, the greater the amount of regression toward the mean.* In Figure 10.6*b*, the amount of regression is 1 standard deviation when prediction is made from a value 2 standard deviations above the mean, whereas regression is half that amount when prediction is made from a value 1 standard deviation above the mean.

Second, as the $z$-score form of the regression equation ($z'_Y = rz_X$) shows, *the higher the value of* r, *the less the amount of regression.* For $z_X = +1$, $z'_Y = +.9$ when $r = .90$, $+.5$ when $r = +.50$, and $+.2$ when $r = +.20$.

## 10.6  Regression Problems in Research

When designing a study, we must consider how regression might affect our results. For example, suppose we hypothesize that special education at an early age can improve the level of intelligence of children who score low on such tests. We test a group of children and select those with low IQs for the experimental training program. After the training program, we find their mean IQ to be higher than before. This is *not* adequate evidence that the training program improved the children's performance on the intelligence test. The children were selected *because* they had low IQs, and because the correlation between test scores on the two different occasions is less than perfect, we would, according to the regression equation, predict that their scores would be higher on retesting *even if no treatment intervened.* Therefore, it may be that the improvement in performance is simply another example of regression toward the mean. A better research design would be to select two groups of children of comparable initial intelligence, subject only one group to the experimental treatment, retest both, and compare the two samples of scores.

To sum up Sections 10.4 and 10.5, *when subjects are selected because of their extreme position (either high or low) on one variable, their position on a positively correlated variable will probably be in the same direction away from the mean, but less extreme.* The two variables could be test and retest on the same measure, or they could be two different variables. For example, suppose we select students for study because they are doing poorly in history. If we now inquire how they are doing in other courses, we expect to find that they are below average, but not as much below as they are in history. As you learned in the previous section, the amount of regression will depend on the size of the correlation between the two variables.

Regression toward the mean often goes unrecognized by laypeople. When the most promising rookies in a professional sports league return for their second seasons, for example, they will generally do well again, but not as well as in their first year. Sportswriters will offer fancy explanations for why the rookie of the year is now in a sophomore slump: "The pitchers finally learned how to throw to him." However, the reason may simply be regression toward the mean, for performance in the second year of a sport is imperfectly correlated with performance in the first year (Nisbett & Ross, 1980).

## 10.7 An Apparent Paradox in Regression

If parents with extreme characteristics tend to have offspring with characteristics less extreme, how is it that, after a few generations, we do not find everybody at the center of the distribution? Galton's attention was attracted to this apparent paradox. The answer is that *the regression of predicted values toward the mean is accompanied by variation of obtained values about the predicted values, and the greater the degree of regression toward the mean, the greater the amount of variation.* The inward movement of regression is therefore accompanied by the expansive action of variability, which makes it possible for the more extreme values of $Y$ to occur. Specifically, $Y'$, the predicted value of $Y$, is only the predicted mean of $Y$ for those who obtain a particular score in $X$. The obtained $Y$ values corresponding to that value of $X$ will be distributed about $Y'$ with a standard deviation equal to $S_{YX}$. The lower the value of the correlation coefficient, the greater the value of $S_{YX}$. Thus, the greater the degree of regression toward the mean, the greater the variation of obtained $Y$ values about their predicted values.

We illustrate the situation in Figure 10.7. Figure 10.7a shows that when $r = +1$, each obtained $Y$ exactly equals its predicted value. If this were the correlation between the heights of fathers and that of their grown sons, we might presume that the distribution of height of sons would be the same as that of their fathers, unless factors *external* to the phenomenon of regression were operating.

Figure 10.7b illustrates an intermediate degree of correlation. There is partial regression, accompanied by a degree of variability of $Y$ values about $Y'$. Again, unless external factors are involved, we see that the distribution of offspring height would be the same as that of their parents.

Finally, Figure 10.7c shows the situation when regression is complete ($r = 0$). Although the predicted value of $Y$ is $\overline{Y}$ for every value of $X$, the variability of the obtained values of $Y$ about their predicted value is $S_Y$ (because $S_{YX} = S_Y$ when $r = 0$; see Section 9.5). Barring the influence of external factors, the features (mean and standard deviation) of the parental distribution are re-created in that of their children.

## 10.8 Interpretation of *r*: Proportion of Variation in *Y* Not Associated with Variation in *X*

Recall that the variability of $Y$ scores about the regression line, or as we might call it, the error of prediction, is measured by the standard error of estimate, $S_{YX} = S_Y\sqrt{1 - r^2}$. The maximum possible error of prediction occurs when $r = 0$, in which case $S_{YX} = S_Y$. Therefore, one way we can interpret the correlation coefficient is by comparing the magnitude of error in the present predictive circumstances

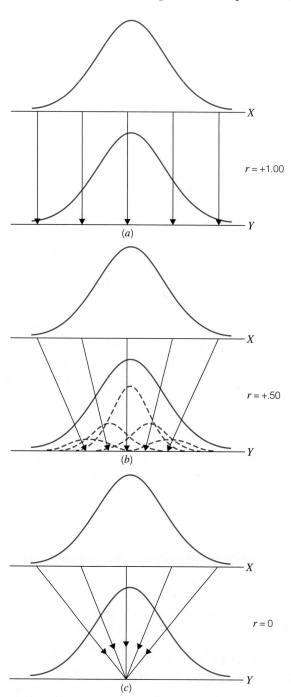

$r = +1.00$

$(a)$

$r = +.50$

$(b)$

$r = 0$

$(c)$

**FIGURE 10.7** Regression toward the mean and variation of obtained values about the regressed values. Compare with Figure 10.6.

with that obtained in the worst possible predictive circumstances, that is, when $r = 0$. We have

$$\frac{\begin{bmatrix} \textit{magnitude of predictive error} \\ \textit{characterizing our predictive} \\ \textit{situation} \end{bmatrix}}{\begin{bmatrix} \textit{magnitude of predictive error} \\ \textit{in the worst possible} \\ \textit{predictive situation } (r = 0) \end{bmatrix}} = \frac{S_{YX}}{S_Y} = \frac{S_Y\sqrt{1 - r^2}}{S_Y} = \sqrt{1 - r^2} \qquad (10.3)$$

When this ratio is close to unity (its maximum value), the predictive error is close to its maximum. On the other hand, when the ratio is close to zero, most of the possible predictive error has been eliminated.

**coefficient of nondetermination**

$S_{YX}^2/S_Y^2 = 1 - r^2$; the proportion of the variance in $Y$ that is *not* associated with differences in $X$

$k^2$

symbol for the coefficient of nondetermination

The ratio $S_{YX}^2/S_Y^2 = 1 - r^2$ shows the proportion of variation in $Y$ that is not associated with differences in $X$ (i.e., cannot be predicted from the regression equation). This is called the **coefficient of nondetermination** (symbolized $k^2$). Older textbooks often referred to the ratio $S_{YX}/S_Y$ (which equals $\sqrt{1 - r^2}$) as the coefficient of alienation (symbolized $k$). Today, it is more common to look at the variance in $Y$ that *is* associated with differences in $X$.

In Table 10.1 (page 188) we present the coefficient of nondetermination for selected values of $r$. The table shows that the coefficient of nondetermination decreases very slowly as the correlation coefficient increases from zero. For instance, when the correlation coefficient has reached .50, the coefficient of nondetermination is still 75% of the size that it would be if the correlation were zero. Note also that a change in $r$ from .20 to .30 results in a reduction in the coefficient of nondetermination of .05, whereas a change in $r$ from .80 to .90 yields a reduction of .17. This shows that *a given change in the magnitude of a correlation coefficient has greater consequences when the correlation is high than when it is low.*

## 10.9 Interpretation of $r$: Proportion of Variance in $Y$ Associated with Variation in $X$

Assemble a number of scores; their values differ. What is the source of this variation? If we apply this question to the $Y$ scores in a bivariate distribution, the answer has two parts. First, some of the variation in $Y$ is associated with variation in $X$. That is, assuming some degree of correlation between $X$ and $Y$, $Y$ will likely take different values depending on whether the associated value of $X$ is high or low. However, if we settle on any single value of $X$, there is still some variability in $Y$ (this second kind of variability is measured by $S_{YX}$). *Total variation in* Y *may therefore be thought of as having two components: variation in* Y *that is associated with or attributable to differences in* X, *and variation in* Y *that is inherent in* Y *and, hence, independent of differences in* X.

We can partition the total $Y$ variation in such a way as to reflect the contributions of these two components. We must make the partition in terms of the *variance of* Y, which can be partitioned into additive components, rather than in terms of the standard deviation of $Y$, which cannot. We begin by dividing the deviation of any $Y$ score from its mean into two components:

$$(Y - \overline{Y}) - (Y - Y') + (Y' \quad \overline{Y})$$

Note that the equation is an algebraic identity because on the right side of the equation the two values of $Y'$ will cancel each other, if we wish, leaving the expression on the right the same as that on the left. Figure 10.8 illustrates the partition. We now have three deviation scores. Each measures variation of a particular kind:

$(Y - \overline{Y})$  This measures the total variation among $Y$ scores. When these deviations are squared, summed, and divided by their number, we have: $S_Y^2 = \Sigma(Y - \overline{Y})^2/n$, the variance of the $Y$ scores defined in the usual manner.

$(Y - Y')$  This measures the variation of obtained $Y$ scores about the values predicted for them ($Y'$); it is the variation in $Y$ that remains when $X$ is held constant. Therefore, $(Y - Y')$ measures the $Y$ variation that is independent of differences in $X$. When these deviations are squared, summed, and divided by their number, we have $S_{YX}^2 = \Sigma(Y - Y')^2/n$, the variance in $Y$ that is independent of differences in $X$. This quantity is the square of the standard error of estimate (see Section 9.5).

$(Y' - \overline{Y})$  This quantity, unlike the other two, is new to us. It measures the variation of the predicted $Y$ values about the mean of $Y$ and, as explained shortly, measures the variation in $Y$ that is associated with differences in $X$. When these deviations are squared, summed, and divided by their number, we have: $S_{Y'}^2 = \Sigma(Y' - \overline{Y})^2/n$, the variance in $Y$ that is associated with differences in $X$.

A few more words about $S_{Y'}^2$ are in order. First, look at Figure 10.8 and find the discrepancy $(Y' - \overline{Y})$ from which this variance is generated. What would happen if $r = 0$? In this case, the predicted value of $Y$ is $\overline{Y}$, irrespective of the value of $X$ from which the prediction is made (see Section 9.3). Then all values of $(Y' - \overline{Y})$ would become $(\overline{Y} - \overline{Y})$, and $S_{Y'}^2$ becomes zero. In other words, when $r = 0$, none of the $Y$

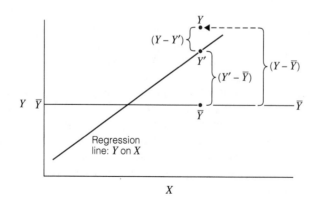

**FIGURE 10.8** Partition of a deviation score $(Y - \overline{Y})$ into component deviations: $(Y - Y')$ and $(Y' - \overline{Y})$.

variance is associated with variation in $X$. On the other hand, if $r = 1.00$, each predicted value of $Y$ is the actual value of $Y$. Then each value of $(Y' - \overline{Y})$ would become $(Y - \overline{Y})$, and $S_{Y'}^2$ becomes $S_Y^2$. This would mean that *all* the variation in $Y$ is associated with variation in $X$. We can express the relationships developed above in the following equation:

PARTITION OF $Y$ VARIANCE
INTO TWO COMPONENTS

$$S_Y^2 \quad = \quad S_{YX}^2 \quad + \quad S_{Y'}^2 \qquad (10.4)$$

$$\begin{bmatrix} total \\ Y \\ variance \end{bmatrix} = \begin{bmatrix} variance\ in\ Y \\ independent\ of \\ variation\ in\ X \end{bmatrix} + \begin{bmatrix} variance\ in\ Y \\ associated\ with \\ variation\ in\ X \end{bmatrix}$$

**partition of Y variance ($S_Y^2$) into two components**
1. variance in $Y$ independent of variation in $X$ ($=S_{YX}^2$), and 2. variance in $Y$ associated with variation in $X$ ($=S_{Y'}^2$)

Another way we can interpret the correlation coefficient is in terms of the *proportion of the total* Y *variance that is associated with differences in* X. This proportion is given by:

$$\frac{[variance\ in\ Y\ associated\ with\ differences\ in\ X]}{[total\ variance\ in\ Y]} = \frac{S_{Y'}^2}{S_Y^2}$$

This expression can be simplified by appropriate substitution. Because

$$S_Y^2 = S_{YX}^2 + S_{Y'}^2$$

then

$$S_{Y'}^2 = S_Y^2 - S_{YX}^2$$

and

$$\frac{S_{Y'}^2}{S_Y^2} = \frac{S_Y^2 - S_{YX}^2}{S_Y^2}$$

$$= \frac{S_Y^2 - (S_Y\sqrt{1 - r^2})^2}{S_Y^2}$$

$$= \frac{S_Y^2 - S_Y^2(1 - r^2)}{S_Y^2}$$

$$= \frac{S_Y^2 - S_Y^2 + S_Y^2 r^2}{S_Y^2}$$

$$= r^2$$

**$r^2$**
symbol for the coefficient of determination

**coefficient of determination**
$S_{Y'}^2 / S_Y^2 = r^2$; the proportion of the Y variance that is associated with differences in X

Thus, $r^2$, called the **coefficient of determination**, gives the proportion of the $Y$ variance that is associated with differences in $X$. If $r = +.50$, for example, $r^2 = .25$. This means that 25% of the $Y$ variance is associated with differences in $X$ (and 75% is not). Values of $r^2$ are given for selected values of $r$ in Table 10.1. Note, once more, that the proportion of $Y$ variance accounted for by variation in $X$ increases more slowly than does the magnitude of the correlation coefficient. Not until $r = +.71$ does $r^2 = .50$.

**TABLE 10.1**  *Several Interpretations of* r *for Different Levels of the Correlation Coefficient*

| $r_{XY}$ | $k^2$ | $r^2$ | $A$ | $B$ |
|------|-------|-------|-----|-----|
| 1.00 | .00 | 1.00 | .50 | 1.00 |
| .95 | .10 | .90 | .40 | .80 |
| .90 | .19 | .81 | .35 | .71 |
| .85 | .28 | .72 | .32 | .65 |
| .80 | .36 | .64 | .30 | .59 |
| .75 | .44 | .56 | .27 | .54 |
| .70 | .51 | .49 | .25 | .49 |
| .65 | .58 | .42 | .23 | .45 |
| .60 | .64 | .36 | .20 | .41 |
| .55 | .70 | .30 | .19 | .37 |
| .50 | .75 | .25 | .17 | .33 |
| .45 | .80 | .20 | .15 | .30 |
| .40 | .84 | .16 | .13 | .26 |
| .35 | .88 | .12 | .11 | .23 |
| .30 | .91 | .09 | .10 | .19 |
| .25 | .94 | .06 | .08 | .16 |
| .20 | .96 | .04 | .06 | .13 |
| .15 | .98 | .02 | .05 | .10 |
| .10 | .99 | .01 | .03 | .06 |
| .05 | 1.00− | .00+ | .02 | .03 |
| .00 | 1.00 | .00 | .00 | .00 |

$k^2$: coefficient of nondetermination (see Section 10.8)
$r^2$: coefficient of determination (see Section 10.9)
$A$: proportion of correct placements in excess of chance (see Section 10.10)
$B$: proportion of improvement in correct placement relative to the chance proportion of .50 (see Section 10.10)
*Note:* $k^2$, $r^2$, $A$, and $B$ are unaffected by the sign (+ or −) of $r$.

The entries for columns A and B of Table 10.1 are owed to W. B. Michael, "An Interpretation of the Coefficients of Predictive Validity and of Determination in Terms of the Proportions of Correct Inclusions or Exclusions in Cells of a Fourfold Table," *Educational and Psychological Measurement*, **26**, no. 2 (1966): 419–24.

Note that the manner of interpreting $r$ in this section is closely related to the manner we presented in the last section ($k^2 = 1 - r^2$). Thus,

$$\frac{S_{\hat{Y}}^2}{S_Y^2} = k^2 + r^2 \tag{10.5}$$

$$\begin{bmatrix} \text{total } Y \text{ variance} \\ \text{expressed as a} \\ \text{proportion} \end{bmatrix} = \begin{bmatrix} \text{proportion of } Y \\ \text{variance independent} \\ \text{of } X \text{ variance} \end{bmatrix} + \begin{bmatrix} \text{proportion of } Y \\ \text{variance associated} \\ \text{with } X \text{ variance} \end{bmatrix}$$

Look again at Table 10.1 to see the relationship between $k^2$ and $r^2$.

## 10.10 Interpretation of $r$: Proportion of Correct Placements

The interpretation of $r$ according to $k^2$ or $r^2$ is certainly not very encouraging as to the use of values of $r$ of moderate magnitude. However, in practical problems of prediction, we are often interested in estimating, from a person's score in $X$, the likelihood that she or he will "succeed" (i.e., score above a given point in $Y$). In these cases, we can often do much better by using the predictor than by not doing so, even when the correlation is modest. We introduced this manner of interpreting $r$ in Section 8.5 and expand on it here.

Assume a normal bivariate distribution of 200 applicants, that success is defined as scoring above the median on the criterion variable ($Y$), and that those who are selected as potentially successful are those who score above the median on the predictor variable ($X$). If $r = 0$, 50% correct placement will be achieved by using score on the predictor for selection. Look at the first picture in Table 10.2. Correct predictions have been made for the 50 individuals who were predicted to succeed and did, plus the 50 who were predicted to fail and did, that is, those individuals who fall in the Quadrants I and III of the diagram. The proportion of correct placements is therefore 100 out of the 200 candidates or 50%.

Now look at the second picture in Table 10.2. In this case, the correlation coefficient is $+.50$, and the number of correct placements is $67 + 67 = 134$. The proportion of correct placements is therefore 134/200 or .67. The proportion of correct placements in excess of chance (.50) is .17. The proportion of improvement in correct placement relative to chance is .17/.50 or .33 (.17/.50 actually equals .34, but .33 is the right value; the discrepancy is due to rounding). Viewed this way, a correlation coefficient of .50 appears to have greater use than the interpretations of Sections 10.8–10.9 suggest.

**TABLE 10.2**   *Proportion of Successful Placements for Two Levels of* r

|  | ($r = .00$) | | ($r = +.50$) | |
|---|---|---|---|---|
|  | BELOW X MEDIAN | ABOVE X MEDIAN | BELOW X MEDIAN | ABOVE X MEDIAN |
| ABOVE Y MEDIAN | II  50 | I  50 | II  33 | I  67 |
| BELOW Y MEDIAN | III  50 | IV  50 | III  67 | IV  33 |
|  | | $n = 200$ | | $n = 200$ |
|  | | X: PREDICTOR | | X: PREDICTOR |

Y: Criterion

The last two columns of Table 10.1 present, for selected values of *r*, the proportion of correct placements in excess of chance and the proportion of improvement in correct placements relative to the chance value of .50. This interpretive approach and the entries for *A* and *B* of Table 10.1 are owed to Michael (1966).

Remember that the interpretation just offered depends on splitting the two variables at the median and on the assumption of a normal bivariate distribution. If these conditions do not hold, a different result will follow. Some years ago, Taylor and Russell (1939) pointed out that the effectiveness of prediction depends not only on the magnitude of the correlation coefficient but also on where the cut is made on the predictor variable. Indeed, their work shows that a rather low coefficient may be quite useful when there are a large number of applicants and a small number to be selected. Their work also shows that a high correlation between predictor and criterion may be of little value if a large proportion of those who apply are accepted.

## 10.11  Summary

The facts that the correlation coefficient is zero when two variables are linearly unrelated and $\pm 1$ when the linear relation is perfect suggest that interpreting the degree of association must be an easy task. Alas, we have found it to be much more complex than we might have supposed. We learned that Pearson's *r* is determined by the degree to which scores hug the straight line of best fit, and so the adequacy of this coefficient to describe the degree of association depends on the appropriateness of the assumption of linearity for the data at hand (Section 8.13). Furthermore, the value of the coefficient can be importantly affected by the circumstances under which it is obtained. Continuity of the distributions (Section 10.2), range of talent (Section 10.1), and heterogeneity of samples (Section 10.3) are some of the factors that can affect it. Others include the kind of persons that constituted the sample, the particular measures taken for each of the two variables, and the specific circumstances under which these variables and persons operated (Section 8.13).

Although the absolute value of the correlation coefficient varies from zero to one, the degree of association is, as stated earlier, not ordinarily interpretable in direct proportion to its magnitude. Nevertheless, we have found several ways of saying what a given coefficient means. The slope of the straight line of best fit gives us one way: it specifies the amount of increase (or decrease) in one variable that accompanies 1 unit of increase in the other variable (Section 10.4). A second interpretation may be made through the ratio $S_{YX}^2/S_Y^2$ (called $k^2$, the coefficient of nondetermination) (Section 10.8). This gives information about the reduction in the magnitude of the predictive error accomplished by using the knowledge of the extent of association rather than by just guessing. A third interpretation is given by examining $r^2$, the coefficient of determination (Section 10.9). It states the proportion of variance of the one variable that is associated with differences in the other. Study of the behavior of both $k^2$ and $r^2$ shows that a change of a given magnitude (.10, for example) in the correlation coefficient has greater consequence when it is applied to coefficients having high values than those having low values. Finally, another way of interpreting correlation (and prediction) is in terms of the proportion of correct placements expected when the regression equation is used in practical problems of prediction (Sections 8.5 and 10.10).

These several ways of interpreting correlation and prediction are quite diverse. It is clear not only that the problem of interpretation is not simple but also that there is no one "best" way. The particular nature of the problem, theoretical or applied, and the context in which it is set must guide the investigator to an appropriate choice.

## Key Terms, Concepts, and Symbols

range of talent   (144, 174)

hugging principle   (175)

restriction of range   (175)

$Y$ intercept   (178)

slope   (179)

regression coefficient   (180)

$r(S_Y/S_X)$   (180)

regression toward the mean (181)

coefficient of nondetermination   (185)

$k^2$   (185)

partition of variance   (186, 187)

total $Y$ variance   (186)

variance in $Y$ independent of variation in $X$   (186)

variance in $Y$ associated with variation in $X$   (186)

$(Y - \overline{Y})$, $(Y - Y')$, $(Y' - \overline{Y})$   (186)

$S_Y^2, S_{YX}^2, S_{Y'}^2$   (186)

$r^2$   (187)

coefficient of determination   (187)

## Problems

**1.** Solve the equation $S_{YX} = S_Y\sqrt{1 - r^2}$ for $r$, thus obtaining Formula 10.1.

**2.** Among a group of retarded 10-year-old children, it is found that the correlation between IQ and reading achievement is $+.25$. However, on a school-wide basis the correlation is $+.50$. Assuming these results to be typical, what explanation do you suggest?

**3.** To study creativity, a number of outstandingly creative persons are assembled and tested. It is found that ratings on creativity and IQ correlate $+.20$. It is concluded that creativity is really quite different from intelligence. Any objections?

**4.** It is common to find that the correlation between airline pilot aptitude test score and pilot proficiency is higher among aviation cadets than among experienced pilots. What could account for this?

**5.** One way to learn whether an aptitude test works is to test applicants for the particular job, hire them all, and subsequently correlate test score with a measure of job proficiency. Another way, usually more practical,

is to test all currently employed workers of the particular type and obtain the same correlation. Is there any reason to think that the coefficient might be different when obtained in these two ways? Explain.

**6.** To assess the "predictive validity" of the Graduate Record Examination (GRE), the professors in a department of psychology collect data on their graduate students. For each student, they find the mean grade earned in his or her graduate courses, and they correlate this GPA with the student's score on the part of the GRE that measures analytic ability. They also correlate GPA with the GRE's measure of quantitative ability and again with its measure of verbal ability. All three correlation coefficients turn out to be low, about $+.2$. Some professors therefore argue that GRE scores are poor predictors of success in graduate school and that the department should not rely on them in choosing among the applicants to their department. Defend the GRE.

**7.** For which group would you expect a higher correlation between height and weight: all students at a 4-year high school, or a sample composed (only) of the ninth graders and the seniors at the same school? Explain.

8. A researcher used a personality test to measure two traits, sociability and impulsiveness. He is impatient to learn the relationship between them, so he decides to estimate the correlation for all 100 subjects by looking at the data on just 20 subjects. Would he get a good estimate if he picked for his subsample of 20 those people with the 10 lowest sociability scores and those with the 10 highest sociability scores? Explain.

9. At certain stages in school, girls tend to be superior to boys in verbal skills. Suppose the correlation between spelling score and IQ is $+.50$ for a sample of girls and the same for a sample of boys. (a) Sketch the scatter diagram for the two sets of subjects. Show IQ on the $X$ axis. (b) If the two sets were pooled and the coefficient computed on the total group, would you expect $r$ to be about $+.50$? Explain.

10. Suppose the correlation is $-.30$ between strength of grip and time in the 100-yard dash for a sample of men and the same for a sample of women. (a) Sketch the scatter diagram for the two sets of subjects. Show strength of grip on the $Y$ axis. (b) If the two samples were combined and $r$ were recomputed, would $r$ still be about $-.30$? Explain.

11. One regression equation reads: $Y' = 2X - 5$. (a) Could the $X$ and $Y$ scores to which this equation refers be in standard score form? Explain. (b) Interpret $r$ in terms of the slope of the regression equation.

12. Another regression equation reads: $Y' = -.25X + 5$. (a) Could the $X$ and $Y$ scores to which this equation refers be in standard score form? Explain. (b) Could $r$ be negative? Explain. (c) Is $r = -.25$? Explain. (d) Interpret $r$ in terms of the slope of the regression equation.

13. Another regression equation reads: $Y' = 3X$. Is that possible? Explain.

14. Another regression equation reads: $Y' = 12$. State all the things that we know from this about $X$, $Y$, and/or $r$.

15. Section 9.4 presented an equation for predicting GPA ($Y$) from SAT total score ($X$): $Y' = .00125X + .75$. (a) What is the re-

gression coefficient for this equation? (b) Interpret the regression coefficient in terms of the slope of the regression line.

16. For the data used as an example in Section 9.4, the equation for predicting SAT total score ($X$) from GPA ($Y$) is $X' = 98Y + 804$. (a) What is the regression coefficient for this equation? (b) Interpret the regression coefficient in terms of the slope of the regression line.

17. For the data from Chapter 9 used in Problem 16, (a) write the raw-score formula for the regression of weight on height. (b) What is the regression coefficient for this equation? (c) Interpret the regression coefficient in terms of the slope of the regression line.

18. A board of education once hired the junior author of this text to investigate a phenomenon that puzzled them. Students in their school district who scored low on aptitude tests at the beginning of the school year generally improved when retested at the end of the year. But the same teachers who apparently did so well in helping students of low ability actually seemed to be reversing the mental growth of the gifted students, for the latter did less well on retesting. What would you have told the board?

19. A teacher praises those students who did well on an examination and rebukes those who did poorly. On the next examination in this subject, most of those who did well the first time have lower scores, and most of those who did poorly the first time have higher scores. Do these observations mean that the praise didn't motivate the best students to keep working, whereas the rebuke did motivate the worst students to improve? Explain.

20. Someone proposes a "hothouse" treatment for gifted children. Four-year-olds are tested, and those whose IQs appear to be above 140 are selected for special treatment. Before treatment, mean IQ of this group is 150. Let us suppose that treatment has no effect on IQ. What mean IQ would you expect when the children are retested 1 year later? Explain.

21. In one company, it is found that the frequency of accidents correlates about $+.40$ from one year to the next. It institutes a safety course for the 10% least safe workers

last year. This year, the accident record of these men is distinctly better. Your comment?

**22.** The correlation between sociability and impulsiveness is about $+.6$ among college students. (a) In a large sample of college students, do you expect those in the top 5% on sociability all to be in the top 5% on impulsiveness? Explain. (b) Do you expect those in the bottom 5% on sociability to be in the bottom 5% on impulsiveness? Explain.

**23.** For the relationship between SAT score and freshman-year GPA (see Section 9.4), (a) what is the coefficient of nondetermination? (b) Explain what this value means. (c) What is the coefficient of determination? (d) Explain what this value means.

**24.** For the data presented in Tables 8.2, 8.6, and 8.7, (a) what is the coefficient of nondetermination? (b) Explain what this value means. (c) What is the coefficient of determination? (d) Explain what this value means.

**25.** When $r = \pm 1.00$, what value would $\Sigma(Y - Y')^2$ have? Explain.

**26.** When $r = 0$, what value would $\Sigma(Y - Y')^2$ have? Explain.

**27.** Under what conditions will $S_Y = S_{Y'}$? Explain.

**28.** Under what conditions will $S_Y = S_{YX}$? Explain.

**29.** Given the data in Section 9.4 on SAT scores and college GPAs, (a) use Table 10.1 to determine how well an admissions office can expect to do in predicting which of their applicants would earn a GPA in the top half of the freshman class. (b) How well would they do if they flipped a coin to make the prediction (heads predicts top half, tails predicts bottom half)? (c) What assumptions underlie the answer to (a)?

**30.** Interpret the correlation coefficients $+.10$, $+.30$, $+.60$, and $+.90$ in terms of (a) the coefficient of nondetermination, (b) the coefficient of determination, and (c) the proportion of correct placements when the split is at the median in $X$ and $Y$.

**31.** We are trying to identify alcoholics from a pencil-and-paper test of personality that makes no reference to alcohol and thus provokes no defensiveness in the subjects. By revising the test, we are able to increase the correlation between the score and the actual extent of alcohol abuse from $+.25$ to $+.50$. Interpret the gain made by the revision according to (a) the coefficient of nondetermination, (b) the coefficient of determination, and (c) the proportion of correct placements when the split is at the median in $X$ and $Y$. (d) Do any of these interpretations suggest that the increase from $+.25$ to $+.50$ doubled the strength of the relationship?

# CHAPTER 11

## Probability

When you have finished studying this chapter, you should be able to:

- Understand that the probability of an event is the relative frequency with which that event occurs over an infinite number of repetitions of the process that generated it;

- Know that as a proportion, the probability of an event lies between 0 (an impossible event) and 1 (a certain event);

- Know that probability does not tell us what will happen in the short run;

- Estimate the probability of event A by assuming equally-likely outcomes and dividing the number of possible outcomes of A by the total number of possible outcomes;

- Explain the addition theorem and the multiplication theorem of probability;

- Understand what is meant by a probability (theoretical relative-frequency) distribution, and explain why the binomial distribution is an example of a probability distribution; and

- Understand that any frequency distribution can be used as a probability distribution when it is expressed in terms of proportions.

Have you ever bought a lottery ticket and dreamed of what you would buy with all that money if you actually won? We all know, of course, that because millions of lottery tickets are usually purchased before each drawing, our chances of winning are very remote. But for a few people—a very few—the dream really does come true. It came true for Evelyn Marie Adams in 1986. She entered and won the New Jersey Lottery, making her an instant millionaire. State officials said that for a person buying a single ticket, the probability of winning was about 1 in 4.123 million. What makes the story interesting is that 4 months later, Ms. Adams purchased another ticket in the New Jersey Lottery and won again. Statisticians quickly calculated that the probability of Ms. Adams winning both times (assuming that she had bought a single ticket each time) was one in 17 trillion!

Is this an amazing, unbelievable coincidence? For Evelyn Marie Adams it was a 1-in-17 trillion coincidence, but statisticians Perci Diaconis and Frederick Mosteller of Harvard University (1989) claimed that the probability of someone somewhere in the United States winning a lottery twice within 4 months was really closer to 1 in 30. According to them, Ms. Adams's accomplishment was not quite that amazing after all.

Which is correct: 1 in 17 trillion or 1 in 30? Actually, both are correct. To fully understand why, let us first develop the concept of probability.

## 11.1 Defining Probability

**event**
an observable outcome

**generating event**
any repeatable process that results in only one outcome at a time

**probability (Pr) of an event**
the relative frequency with which that event would be observed over an *infinite* number of repetitions of the generating event, when each generating event is conducted in the same manner

What is the probability that when:

A coin is tossed, it will come up heads?

A die is rolled, it will result in a 4?

A card is selected blindly from a deck of 52 cards, it will be an ace?

A score is selected blindly from a distribution, its value will exceed $P_{75}$?

To answer questions like these, let us begin with a few definitions. An **event** is an observable outcome. A **generating event** is any repeatable process that results in only *one* outcome at a time. For example, tossing a coin is a generating event, and the outcome (heads or tails) is an event.

In each of the preceding examples, it is possible to think of a generating event (e.g., a toss of a particular coin) as repeating indefinitely. One way of viewing the probability of an event is as the proportion of time that the event occurs in the long run. Here, the "long run" means an infinite number of trials. Thus, the **probability (Pr) of an event** is the relative frequency with which that event would be observed over an infinite number of repetitions of the generating event, when each generating event is conducted in the same manner. By this definition, the probability of observing heads when we toss a particular coin is

$$\text{Pr (heads)} = \frac{number\ of\ observations\ of\ heads}{total\ number\ of\ observations} = \frac{f\ (of\ heads)}{N}$$

when observations are recorded for an infinite number of tosses. As a proportion, probability lies between 0 (an impossible event) and 1 (a certain event).

Because a probability is a proportion characterizing an infinitely long series of occurrences, it does not tell us precisely what will happen over any short run. Even if

"HOW DO YOU WANT IT—THE CRYSTAL BALL MUMBO-JUMBO OR STATISTICAL PROBABILITY?"

it is true that the probability of heads is 1/2 for a toss of a particular coin, that does *not* mean that in the next 2 tosses 1 of the outcomes must be heads, nor that in 100 tosses 50 will be heads. However, if we repeat the generating event over and over, the relative frequency of observations of heads would approach 1/2 (but would probably not be *exactly* equal to 1/2 even after 1 million tosses) and would be exactly 1/2 for an infinite number of tosses.

Now let us return to our initial question: What is the probability that when we toss a coin it will come up heads? The probability does not have to be 1/2 just because there are two possible outcomes. Maybe the coin is bent, resulting in heads coming up only 45% of the time in an infinitely long series of tosses. If tossing a certain coin yields heads on 45% of the tosses in the long run, then the probability of the event heads is .45 for a toss of that coin.

So how do we know the probability of obtaining heads on the toss of a particular coin? To determine the precise probability we would have to toss the coin an infinite number of times. This, of course, is not humanly possible. We might toss a coin several thousand times to obtain an estimate of the true value, called an **empirical probability**, but in inferential statistics we will be more concerned with outcomes of experiments than with outcomes of coin tosses. No researcher would wish to repeat an experiment thousands of times to closely estimate the probability of an outcome. Fortunately, there is a mathematical model we can use to determine long-run probabilities without having to repeat the generating event an infinite number of times. However, using this model requires that we make an important assumption, which we discuss next.

**empirical probability**
an estimate of the probability of an event, obtained by finding the frequency of the event over a large number of repetitions of the generating event

## 11.2 A Mathematical Model of Probability

**equally-likely model of probability**
given a population of possible outcomes, each of which is equally likely to occur, Pr(A) =

$$\frac{\text{number of possible A outcomes}}{\text{total number of possible outcomes}}$$

Because probability is the relative frequency of an event over an infinite number of observations, we can never know a probability through direct observation. However, if we can assume that the primary generating event yields equally-likely outcomes, we can solve for the probabilities of more complex events without actually having to make an infinite number of observations. We will call this way of looking at probability the **equally-likely model of probability**:

> Given a population of possible outcomes, each of which is equally likely to occur, the probability of event A on a single trial is equal to the number of possible outcomes yielding A divided by the total number of possible outcomes.

In a deck of 52 cards, there are four suits of 13 cards each. Spades and clubs are black and diamonds and hearts are red. If we draw cards from a deck (the generating event) in such a manner that each card is equally likely to be selected, what is the probability of drawing a spade?

$$\text{Pr (spade)} = \frac{\textit{number of possible spade outcomes}}{\textit{total number of possible outcomes}} = \frac{13}{52} = \frac{1}{4}$$

Similarly, the probability of drawing an ace is 4/52, the probability of drawing an ace in a red suit is 2/52, and the probability of drawing a card (of any denomination) in a red suit is 26/52 = 1/2.

If we assume that the two outcomes of tossing a coin (heads or tails, no edge landings) are equally likely, then

$$\text{Pr (heads)} = \frac{\textit{number of possible heads outcomes}}{\textit{total number of possible outcomes}} = \frac{1}{2}$$

Compare this ratio for Pr (heads) with that given in the previous section. If the assumption that the generating event yields equally-likely outcomes is true, this ratio gives the same value as that obtained for relative frequency. When the assumption is not true, the probability values provided by the equally-likely model will not be accurate. For example, a bent coin may have a long-run probability of heads of .45, but the equally-likely model will yield a value of .5. Fortunately, many real events are close enough to the assumption of equally-likely outcomes that we can use the equally-likely model to determine probabilities.

Probability is a difficult concept to understand. Logicians and mathematicians have wrestled with it for years and still do. The two approaches we have presented, although widely used, are inadequate logically from a rigorous point of view. (For example, "equally likely" really means equally probable, which results in a circular definition.) However, these approaches are very useful as preliminary guides for considering how to make decisions in the face of uncertainty—an important part of inferential statistics.

## 11.3 Two Theorems in Probability

Let us look again at a problem introduced in the previous section. In a deck of 52 cards, what is the probability of drawing an ace? We observed that there were four

**addition theorem of probability (the "or" rule)**

the probability of occurrence of any one of several particular events is the sum of their individual probabilities (provided that they are mutually exclusive)

**mutually exclusive**

the occurrence of one event precludes the occurrence of any others

ways of drawing an ace out of the 52 ways in which a card might be drawn. According to the principle of relative frequency among equally-likely outcomes, the probability of drawing an ace is 4/52.

The same problem may be viewed another way. The probability of drawing an ace of spades is 1/52, and the same is true for the ace of hearts, the ace of diamonds, and the ace of clubs. The probability of drawing the ace of spades *or* the ace of hearts *or* the ace of diamonds *or* the ace of clubs is the sum of the individual probabilities, that is, 1/52 + 1/52 + 1/52 + 1/52 = 4/52. Similarly, the probability of obtaining a 5 or a 6 on a single toss of a die is 1/6 + 1/6 = 2/6. These examples illustrate the **addition theorem of probability**:

> The probability of occurrence of any one of several particular events is the sum of their individual probabilities, provided that they are mutually exclusive.

One can usually recognize when the rule may apply by the use of the word *or* (some refer to the addition theorem as the *"or" rule*). Notice that the rule is valid only when the outcomes are **mutually exclusive**; that is, when the occurrence of one precludes the occurrence of any of the others. In the examples above, the card drawn may be the ace of spades *or* the ace of hearts, but it cannot be both. Similarly, a die may come up 5 *or* 6, but we cannot have it both ways.

Of the students at a given college, suppose (1) that 60% are men and 40% are women and (2) that 50% of the students are in the lower division, 40% are in the upper division, and 10% are in the graduate division. The addition theorem may be applied to calculate that in selecting a student at random (i.e., the possible outcomes are equally likely), the probability that he or she will be either a lower division or an upper division student is .50 + .40 = .90. However, the same theorem may *not* be applied to obtain the probability that the student will be either a graduate student or a male; these are not mutually exclusive outcomes. Note 11.1 at the end of the chapter presents a modification of the addition theorem that is appropriate when outcomes are not mutually exclusive.

**multiplication theorem of probability (the "and" rule)**

the probability of several particular events occurring successively or jointly is the product of their separate probabilities (provided that the generating events are independent)

**independent events**

the outcome of one event has no influence on and is not related to the other events

Another useful theorem concerns successive and joint events. If we toss the same coin twice, what is the probability of heads coming up on the first toss *and* again on the second toss? Let us view the tossing of the same coin twice as an experiment that is to be repeated indefinitely. In the long run, the first toss will come up heads half the time. The second toss will come up heads in but half of those trials in which the first toss came up heads. Therefore, the proportion of *all* trials in which both tosses will come up heads is (1/2)(1/2) = 1/4. The probability of obtaining two heads in a row is thus 1/4. The same is true of joint (simultaneous) events: The probability of obtaining two heads if we toss two coins at once is 1/4. This illustrates the **multiplication theorem of probability** (which some call the *"and" rule*):

> The probability of several particular events occurring successively or jointly is the product of their separate probabilities, provided that the generating events are independent.

Again, we have a qualification: The generating events must be **independent events**. This means that the outcome of one event must have no influence on and must in no way be related to the outcome of the other event. (Formal consideration of independence in a probability sense is given in Note 11.3, but read Note 11.2 first.) For coin tosses, the way the first toss falls has no influence on the way the second toss will fall. The outcome of the two tosses is therefore the outcome of two independent events.

Note that the rule may be extended to more than two independent events. If we ask the probability of obtaining three heads on three successive tosses of a coin, it is $(1/2)(1/2)(1/2) = (1/2)^3 = 1/8$.

People being what they are, it is not unusual for them to act as though events are not independent when in fact they are. This failure occurs so often that it has been given a name: the *gambler's fallacy*. If we look over the shoulder of a person playing roulette, a game in which one guesses which of 38 numbers a ball will land on, we may find him keeping track of the numbers that have come up, with the idea that he will bet on one that has not appeared recently and so is "due." Such a system is useless. Assuming a fair wheel, fairly spun, there is no way in which the outcome of an earlier trial may affect the outcome of the present trial. The wheel has no memory.

Many events are, of course, *not* independent. What is the probability of rain on Monday *and* rain on Tuesday? If the first happens, the second is more likely to occur. The multiplication theorem does not apply.

Those just getting acquainted with probability sometimes become confused about mutually exclusive outcomes and independent events. Look carefully at the explanations that accompany their introduction; they do not mean the same thing. The concept of independence applies to a pair of generating events (e.g., two coin tosses), not to specific outcomes. For example, the particular outcomes that may result from a *single* trial are always completely dependent if they are mutually exclusive: The occurrence of one predicts with certainty that the other(s) will *not* occur. The multiplication theorem applies only when two or more events are considered together, as in the tossing of two coins or the tossing of one coin twice.

## 11.4 An Example of a Probability Distribution: The Binomial

If we toss a coin two times, what are the possible outcomes? Assuming that heads or tails are the only possible outcomes, we could get two heads in succession, two tails in succession, a head followed by a tail, or a tail followed by a head (HT and TH are two *different* outcomes). We find the probability of any of these successive outcomes by the multiplication theorem: $(1/2)(1/2) = 1/4$. The addition theorem gives the probability of obtaining one head and one tail in either order (HT or TH): $1/4 + 1/4 = 1/2$. The resultant probabilities are shown in Figure 11.1*a*.

Suppose we toss the coin three times. How many possible outcomes are there now? There are eight: three tails in succession, three combinations of two tails and one head (TTH, THT, and HTT), three combinations of two heads and one tail (HHT, HTH, THH), and three heads in succession. Which outcome is more likely, HHH or HTH? Think about it a moment. The probability is the same for each: $(1/2)(1/2)(1/2) = 1/8$. Which outcome is more likely, HHH or two heads and a tail in any order? This is a different question, for the latter includes the three combinations HHT, HTH, and THH, with a total probability of $1/8 + 1/8 + 1/8 = 3/8$. The resultant probabilities are shown in Figure 11.1*b*.

**dichotomous observations**
observations that can be classified in only two categories

When tossing a coin, we can get only a head or a tail on any toss, and the result of one toss does not affect the next. When observations can be classified in just two categories like this, they are called **dichotomous observations**. Other examples include the results of a T-maze experiment in which rats must turn left or right and the results of a survey of voters in which respondents must state their preference for Jones or Smith. For a specified number of independent generating events in which

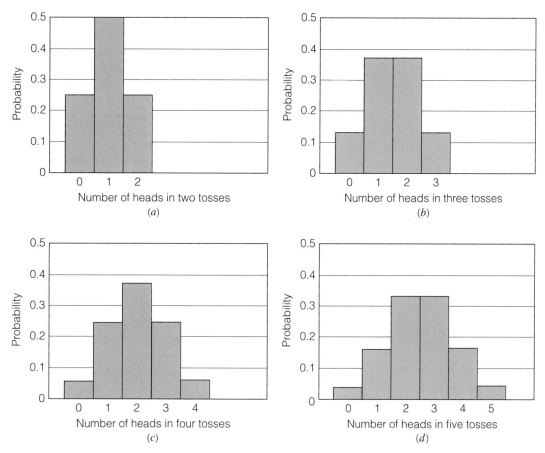

**FIGURE 11.1** The binomial distribution for (*a*) *N* = 2, (*b*) *N* = 3, (*c*) *N* = 4, and (*d*) *N* = 5 when Pr (heads) = .5.

**binomial distribution**

when there are only two possible events, the distribution that shows each possible outcome and the probability of each

**probability distribution**

(a **theoretical relative-frequency distribution**) shows the relative frequency with which certain outcomes occur over an *infinite* number of trials

there are only two possible events, the distribution that shows each possible outcome and the probability of each is called a **binomial distribution**.

A binomial distribution may be interpreted as a **probability distribution** or, alternatively, as a **theoretical relative-frequency distribution** (see Section 3.5). It shows *the relative frequency with which certain outcomes occur in the long run*, that is, over an infinite number of trials. It does not mean that you will get exactly those outcomes in the short run. For example, look at the binomial distribution for tossing a fair coin three times in succession (Figure 11.1*b*). There are eight possible outcomes. The probability is .125 for TTT; .375 for TTH, THT, or HTT; .375 for HHT, HTH, or THH; and .125 for HHH. This does not mean that if we toss a coin three times, record the outcomes, and repeat the triple tossing seven more times, we would get exactly the distribution shown in Figure 11.1*b* (although that could happen). But if we were to keep recording the outcomes of the three tosses over a long series of triple tosses, and if we were to construct a relative frequency distribution of our results, it would look very much like Figure 11.1*b*. For an infinite number of a series of three tosses, our relative frequency distribution would look exactly like Figure 11.1*b* (assuming a fair coin fairly tossed).

Suppose we want to construct the binomial distribution for five tosses in a row. As the number of trials (in this case, successive coin tosses) increases, the number of possible outcomes increases dramatically (in fact, there are $2^5 = 32$ different possible outcomes for five successive coin tosses). Trying to figure out all the possible outcomes when the number of trials is five or greater is very cumbersome without help. Fortunately, help comes in the form of a mathematical equation called the binomial expansion. For independent events, the **binomial expansion** is

$$(P + Q)^N \qquad\qquad (11.1)$$

*where:*   $P$ = the probability of one of the events.
$Q$ = the probability of the other event ($= 1 - P$).
$N$ = the number of trials in the series.

**$(P + Q)^N$** **the binomial expansion;** formula to derive the binomial distribution

The letters $P$ and $Q$ are standard symbols used to represent the probabilities of the two possible events. In our coin tossing example, we could just as easily use $H$ and $T$, but the binomial describes a great number of distributions, not just coin tossing, so it is best to use the same symbols in all cases. Let us see how the binomial expansion can be used to derive the binomial distribution when we toss a coin two times. For this example, let $P$ = probability of heads, $Q$ = probability of tails, and $N = 2$. (Using the equally-likely model of probability, we have $P = Q = .5$.)

$$(P + Q)^2 = P^2 + 2PQ + Q^2$$
$$= (.5)^2 + 2(.5)(.5) + (.5)^2$$
$$= .25 + .50 + .25$$

Each term shows us a possible outcome and the exponent tells us how many heads or tails there are. Thus, $P^2$ represents two heads, $Q^2$ represents two tails, and $2PQ$ represents two possible outcomes of one head and one tail. The final probabilities of each are the same as those shown in Figure 11.1*a*.

For the example of three coin tosses, the binomial expansion gives us:

$$(P + Q)^3 = P^3 + 3P^2Q + 3PQ^2 + Q^3$$
$$= (.5)^3 + 3(.5)^2(.5) + 3(.5)(.5)^2 + (.5)^3$$
$$= .125 + .375 + .375 + .125$$

In this case, $P^3$ represents three heads in succession, $3P^2Q$ represents three possible outcomes of two heads and one tail, $3PQ^2$ represents three possible outcomes of one head and two tails, and $Q^3$ represents three tails in succession.

As you can see, except for a small number of trials, deriving different possible outcomes and the probabilities of each with the binomial expansion is also cumbersome.[1] Fortunately, there are tables based on the binomial expansion. Look at Table B in Appendix E. It gives the binomial distribution for values of $N$ up to 15. For example,

---

[1] The equation to expand $(P + Q)^N$ is

$$(P + Q)^N = P^N = \frac{N}{1} P^{N-1}Q + \frac{N(N - 1)}{1(2)} P^{N-2}Q^2 + \frac{N(N - 1)(N - 2)}{1(2)(3)} P^{N-3} Q^3 + \ldots + Q^N.$$

when $N = 3$ and $P = .5$, the probabilities are the same as those we derived earlier. To determine the probability of getting four heads in five tosses, we only need to look in the table to see that it is .1562.

## 11.5 Applying the Binomial

**Example 1**  Suppose that a psychologist is testing a rat using food reinforcement in a maze with six left–right choice points. At each choice point, one of the tunnels has been blocked (decided by tossing a coin). The psychologist first allows the rat to explore the maze and then tests the animal. If the rat makes five correct choices, what is the probability that it did so by chance (i.e., no learning)?

In the absence of learning, the probability of the rat choosing the correct side ($P$) at any choice point would equal 1/2, the same as the probability of making an incorrect choice ($Q$). Here $P = Q = 1/2$ and $N = 6$. To answer this question, let us expand the binomial:

$$(P + Q)^6 = P^6 + 6P^5Q + 15P^4Q^2 + 20P^3Q^3 + 15P^2Q^4 + 6PQ^5 + Q^6$$

$$= (.5)^6 + 6(.5)^5(.5) + 15(.5)^4(.5)^2 + 20(.5)^3(.5)^3 + 15(.5)^2(.5)^4$$
$$+ 6(.5)(.5)^5 + (.5)^6$$

$$= .0156 + .0938 + .2344 + .3125 + .2344 + .0938 + .0156$$

We could, of course, have used Table B in Appendix E to obtain this same result. We see that the probability of exactly five correct choices is $6P^5Q = .0938$. The probability of six correct choices is $P^6 = .0156$. Thus, if the rat had not yet learned anything, the probability of five *or* six correct choices is .0938 + .0156 = .1094, or roughly 1 in 11.

**Example 2**  An instructor gives a 10-item multiple-choice quiz. Each question has five alternatives. If the student knows nothing about the subject and guesses on each question, what is the probability of him or her passing if the lowest passing score is six correct?

Let us assume that for each question the choices are equally likely. If we let $P =$ the probability of a correct guess on any question, then $P = .20$. Looking in Table B in Appendix E for $N = 10$ and $P = .20$, we see that the probability of the student answering six or more questions correctly is .0055 (6 correct) + .0008 (7 correct) + .0001 (8 correct) + .0000 (9 correct) + .0000 (10 correct) = .0064.

**Example 3**  Suppose that a friend claims to have a homemade remedy for the common cold—a concoction made from chicken broth, vitamins, and some "secret" ingredients. We are skeptical and wish to put the remedy to a test. To do so, we find 16 other friends who are presently suffering with colds and match them in terms of severity of symptoms, forming eight pairs. In some pairs, both individuals have bad colds, and in other pairs both have moderate symptoms, but the two persons of any given pair have nearly equal symptoms. One member of each pair receives the remedy for 24 hours (in addition to his or her usual diet) and the other receives a placebo (water with artificial chicken flavoring). We determine which member of each pair receives the remedy by tossing a coin. We then find two friends in medical school to judge the subsequent severity of symptoms (neither of them know which concoction was administered).

There are only two possible outcomes for each pair if ties are not allowed: the person taking the concoction is more improved or the other person is better. If the concoction does not work, for each pair the probability of the person taking the concoction being better is 1/2 (the same as obtaining heads on a toss of a coin). Let us suppose that at the end of 24 hours seven of the eight persons who consumed the concoction are judged to be better than their partners. If the concoction has no healing powers, what is the probability of this outcome? Looking in Table B in Appendix E, we see that the probability is .0312. What is the probability that *at least* seven of the eight persons taking the concoction will be better than their partners? From the same table, we see that the probability of all eight being better is .0039, thus the probability of seven *or* more being better is .0312 + .0039 = .0351.

Theoretical probability distributions are a crucial part of inferential statistics. It is important that you understand the concept as fully as possible. What does it mean to say that the probability of at least seven of the eight persons who took the homemade remedy being better is .0351? *If the homemade concoction really has no healing powers*, and we were to repeat the test by observing the eight pairs again and again for an infinite number of times, on only 3.51% of the eight-pair tests would seven *or* eight persons taking the concoction be found to be better than the partner not taking the remedy. Thus, such an outcome would occur by chance less than 1 in 20 times if the concoction does not work. If seven of eight persons taking the concoction actually did get better, we would begin to suspect that the concoction really does have healing powers. But we are getting ahead of ourselves here. We will return to this type of problem in Chapter 13.

## 11.6 The Frequency Distribution (and Normal Curve) as a Probability Distribution

Any frequency distribution may be considered a *probability distribution* when it is expressed in terms of proportions. Suppose an instructor has a statistics class of 200 students, and at the end she has assigned course grades as shown in Table 11.1. Considered as a relative frequency distribution, the data in Table 11.1 show that .15 of the students made an A grade. Viewed as a probability distribution, the same table tells us that *if a student were selected at random*, the probability is .15 that his or her course

**TABLE 11.1**   *Statistics Grades as a Frequency Distribution and a Probability Distribution*

| GRADE | *f* | **Pr** |
|-------|------|------|
| A | 30 | .15 |
| B | 60 | .30 |
| C | 80 | .40 |
| D | 20 | .10 |
| F | 10 | .05 |
| | *n* = 200 | 1.00 |

grade would be an A. Similarly, if we ask the probability of drawing a student who earned a B or better, the answer is .15 + .30 = .45.

We obtained the relative frequencies for the statistics instructor's class by actually counting students. Most probability distributions used in statistical inference are not developed in this way. Instead, the relative frequencies are theoretical values derived rationally by applying the laws of probability. The normal curve is a good example of this. The relative frequency, or proportion, of cases falling between any two points in a normal distribution is easily determined by reference to the normal curve table. Such a relative frequency can be viewed as a probability; thus, we can view the normal curve as a *theoretical probability distribution*.

Let us return now to the question posed at the beginning of Section 11.1: What is the probability that when a score is selected blindly from a distribution, its value will exceed $P_{75}$? In a distribution of 100 scores, there are 25 scores above $P_{75}$ and 75 below. In drawing blindly, each score is equally likely to be selected. Therefore, there are 25 ways to select a score above $P_{75}$, out of the 100 ways in which a score can be selected. The probability of selecting a score above $P_{75}$ is therefore 1/4. It is important that you understand the process in this example. The major application of probability in future chapters will be to ask, for a specified distribution, with what probability will a score arise that is as deviant as a certain value.

## 11.7 Are Amazing Coincidences Really That Amazing?

What are the chances that:

Someone will win a state lottery twice within 4 months?

You will meet someone at a party with the same birthday as you?

Surely these are highly unlikely chance events—one-in-a-trillion coincidences. Actually they are not. In fact, they are very probable.

Let us consider again the case of Evelyn Adams, the woman we met at the beginning of the chapter who won the New Jersey Lottery twice in a 4-month time span in 1986. The probability of Ms. Adams doing this was 1 in 17 trillion. This is easily obtained from the multiplication theorem. If there were 4,123,000 lottery tickets sold for each lottery, and Ms. Adams had purchased 1 ticket for each, the probability of her winning both was (1/4,123,000)(1/4,123,000), the same as for any other *specific* person who purchased 1 ticket in each lottery.

But the probability of *someone, somewhere* winning two lotteries in 4 months is a different matter altogether. Professors Diaconis and Mosteller (1989) calculated the chance of this happening to be only 1 in 30. It is an example of what they call the "law of very large numbers": "With a large enough sample, any outrageous thing is apt to happen" (*New York Times*, Feb. 27, 1990, p. C1). Professor Diaconis gives the example of the blade-of-grass paradox: "Suppose I'm standing in a large field and I put my finger on a blade of grass. The chance that I would choose that particular blade may be one in a million. But it is certain that I will choose a blade." With millions of people buying lottery tickets in the United States, it's a pretty sure bet that someone, somewhere will win a lottery twice in his or her lifetime. For example,

Joseph Crowley won a $3 million jackpot in the Ohio Lottery and then moved to Florida, where he won the $20 million Florida Lotto jackpot. For one-in-a-million coincidences, we would expect that in the United States, which has a population of approximately 250 million, there will be 250 such coincidences every day—another example of the law of very large numbers.

What about the probability that any two people at a party will have the same birthday? This really isn't uncommon at all. Professor Diaconis calculates that if you are in a room with 22 other persons, the chances are about even that 2 of you will have a birthday on the same day: $1 - \text{Pr}$ (nobody has the same birthday) $= 1 - (364/365 \times 363/365 \times \ldots)$, and that value approaches .5 as $n = 22$.

Are there implications for this application of probability in science and education? Suppose that a group of researchers has conducted clinical trials of several new drugs with thousands of patients. They discover that in a certain subgroup (e.g., elderly, over-weight men who drink heavily) twice as many who take drug A die compared to those taking drug B. One might immediately conclude that drug A is dangerous for certain people. However, with thousands of people taking dozens of drugs, the law of very large numbers comes into play—the probability is high that just by chance in *some* subgroup, twice the normal number of deaths will occur. The job of statistics is to determine these probabilities in advance so that we can tell if our own results are to be expected or are indeed truly amazing.

## 11.8 Summary

The probability of an event is defined as the relative frequency with which that event would be observed over an infinite number of trials, when each trial is conducted in the same manner. It is thus a proportion (with a value between 0 and 1) characterizing an infinitely long series of occurrences.

We will never be able to determine a probability through direct observation of an infinite number of trials. However, if we can assume that all possible outcomes of a generating event have an equal likelihood of occurrence, we can calculate the probability of an event as the number of possible outcomes characterized by that event divided by the total number of all possible outcomes.

When outcomes are mutually exclusive, the probability of occurrence of any one of several particular outcomes is the sum of their individual probabilities. We call this the addition theorem of probability. When generating events are independent, the probability of successive or joint outcomes is the product of their separate probabilities. We call this the multiplication theorem.

When observations are dichotomous (classified in just two categories), we can construct a distribution that shows each possible outcome and its probability for a specified number of trials. This binomial distribution is a probability distribution that shows the relative frequency with which particular outcomes would occur over an infinite number of trials. Possible outcomes can be calculated from the binomial expansion, $(P + Q)^N$, but for the sake of convenience we provide a table for up to 15 trials.

When expressed in terms of proportions, any frequency distribution may be considered a probability distribution. In future chapters, we will be asking questions about the probability of a score greater than $X$ in a distribution with a given mean and standard deviation.

# Mathematical Notes

### Note 11.1 Probability of Occurrence of A or B When A and B Are Not Mutually Exclusive (*Ref.* Section 11.3)

$$\text{Pr (A or B)} = \text{Pr (A)} + \text{Pr (B)} - \text{Pr (AB)}$$

*where:*   Pr (A) = the probability of A

Pr (B) = the probability of B

Pr (AB) = the probability of A *and* B occurring together

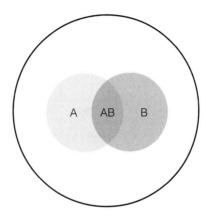

The outcome (A *or* B) is satisfied if A occurs without B, if B occurs without A, or, when A and B are not mutually exclusive, if both A and B occur. Note the accompanying illustration, in which A and B are *not* mutually exclusive. If the number of outcomes characterized by A is added to the number characterized by B, their sum includes *twice* the number characterized by the intersection of A and B. To determine the number of outcomes characterized by A or B, this total must therefore be reduced by the number characterized by A *and* B, so that the latter quantity will be counted only once. Similarly, the probability of A *or* B ought to include the probability of AB only once. When A and B *are* mutually exclusive, Pr (AB) = 0, and the formula for Pr (A or B) reduces to the addition theorem given in Section 11.3:

$$\text{Pr (A or B)} = \text{Pr (A)} + \text{Pr (B)}.$$

### Note 11.2 Conditional Probability (*Ref.* Section 11.3)

**conditional probability**
the probability of occurrence of A given that B has occurred

Pr (A|B) is the symbolic representation for the probability of occurrence of A *given that* B has occurred. (The vertical bar is read "given that.") Probabilities of this type are called **conditional probabilities**. Consider the selection of a card from a 52-card deck from which we have already drawn 1 card. According to the above definition, Pr (second card is an ace|first card is an ace) = 3/51, whereas Pr (second card is an ace|first card is not an ace) = 4/51.

The notion of conditional probability is important in defining the independence of events (see Note 11.3), in finding the probability of joint events (see Note 12.1*c*), and in considering sampling without replacement (see Note 12.1*c*).

### Note 11.3 Independence in a Probability Sense (*Ref.* Section 11.3)

Read Note 11.2 first.

Section 11.3 stated that **independence** of events means that the outcome of one event must in no way alter the probability of occurrence of the other. Symbolically, we may say that A and B are independent if $\Pr(A) = \Pr(A|B)$. For example, in tossing coins, $\Pr(\text{second coin is heads}) = \Pr(\text{second coin is heads}|\text{first coin is heads})$, and the two events are independent. However, in a university, $\Pr(\text{admission of an applicant}) \neq \Pr(\text{admission of an applicant}|\text{applicant's high school record is straight "A"})$; these two events are not independent.

## Key Terms, Concepts, and Symbols

event  (196)

generating event  (196)

relative-frequency definition of probability  (196)

probability of an event  (196)

Pr  (196)

empirical probability  (197)

equally-likely model of probability  (198)

addition theorem of probability  (199)

mutually exclusive  (199)

multiplication theorem of probability  (199)

independent events  (199)

dichotomous observations  (200)

binomial distribution  (201)

probability distribution  (201)

theoretical relative-frequency distribution  (201)

binomial expansion  (202)

conditional probability  (207)

independence in a probability sense  (207)

## Problems

1. An instructor gives a 100-item multiple-choice examination. Each question has four alternatives. If the student knows nothing about the subject and selects answers by chance, (a) what is the probability for a given question that it will be answered correctly? (b) What is the expected number of correct answers for a given student (assume he or she attempts all questions)?

2. An honest die is cast. What is the probability of rolling (a) a 5? (b) A 1 or a 6? (c) A 3 or higher? (d) On two rolls, a 2 followed by a 5? (e) On two rolls, a 2 followed by another 2?

3. Two honest dice are thrown. What is the probability of rolling (a) snake eyes—both 1s? (b) A 6 and a 6? (c) A 3 and a 4?

4. You toss a fair coin and roll an honest die. What is the probability of getting a head in combination with a 4?

5. From a deck of 52 cards, 2 cards are drawn at random. You replace the first card before drawing again. What is the probability that

(a) both cards will be the jack of diamonds? (b) Both cards will be jacks? (c) Both cards will be diamonds? (d) The first card will be an ace and the second a king? (e) One card will be an ace and the other a king?

6. From a deck of 52 cards, 2 cards are drawn at random, but you do not replace the first card before drawing the second. What is the probability that (a) both cards will be the jack of diamonds? (b) Both cards will be jacks? (c) Both cards will be diamonds? (d) The first card will be an ace and the second a king? (If you have problems, look ahead to Note 12.1c.)

7. In sporting events, the probability of an event is often expressed as the *odds* against the occurrence of the event. For example, if the probability of a particular horse winning a race is .25 (1 in 4), the odds against the horse winning are 3 to 1. Given this example, start with the formula for probability in Section 11.2 and see if you can derive a formula for calculating the odds against an event.

**8.** Do you think that weather predictions ("the chance of rain tomorrow is 3 in 10") are better considered as theoretical probabilities or empirical probabilities? Explain.

**9.** Two honest dice are tossed. (a) List the 36 ways the dice may fall (remember to distinguish between the outcome of die #1 and the outcome of die #2). (b) Consider the sum of the points on the two dice; they may be from 2 to 12. With what relative frequency does each possible sum occur? (c) What is the probability of obtaining a 1 with the first die and a 3 with the second die? (d) What is the probability of obtaining a sum of points equal to 4? (e) What is the probability of obtaining a sum of points equal to 7 on one toss? (f) What is the probability of obtaining a sum of points greater than 7? Greater than 4? (g) What is the probability of obtaining a sum of points equal to 7 on two successive throws? Of 2 points on two successive throws?

**10.** You and five of your friends toss six fair coins at the same time. Construct the binomial distribution for all the possible results. What is the probability (a) that all six coins will come up tails? (b) That five of the six coins will come up tails? (c) That four of the six coins will come up tails?

**11.** You toss a fair coin 15 times. What is the probability of getting (a) 2 heads and 13 tails? (b) 5 heads and 10 tails? (c) 12 heads and 3 tails? (d) 10 or more heads?

**12.** A con artist uses a coin with a shaved edge to separate fools from their money. He bets that he can get at least 7 heads in 10 tosses. If altering the coin has made the Pr (heads) = .75, what is the probability of getting (a) 7 heads in 10 tosses? (b) At least 7 heads in 10 tosses?

**13.** A biology instructor gives a quiz consisting of 15 true–false items. She announces that the grades will be assigned as follows: A (14 or 15 correct); B (12 or 13 correct); C (10 or 11 correct); D (9 correct); F (8 or below). If a student has not studied for the quiz and just randomly guesses on each question, what is the probability that he or she will get a grade of: (a) A? (b) B? (c) C? (d) D or F? (e) C or better?

**14.** Fifteen shoppers are asked to participate in a taste test of four soft drinks at the local supermarket. Nine of them choose Brand C. If there were really no difference in taste among the four soft drinks, what would the probability be of 9 or more of 15 people choosing Brand C?

**15.** The Pop-up Toaster Company advertises that their toasters have a probability of .95 of working for 1 year without need of repairs. If you bought eight toasters as wedding gifts, what is the probability that all eight will work for at least 1 year?

**16.** The following are final grades in an English course for 200 students. If a student is selected at random, what is the probability that the student will (a) be male? (b) have earned a B? (c) be female and earned a C? (d) be male and earned a B or better? (e) be female and earned a D or better?

|   | MALES | FEMALES |
|---|-------|---------|
| A | 10 | 20 |
| B | 20 | 22 |
| C | 50 | 40 |
| D | 10 | 8 |
| F | 14 | 6 |

**17.** Your friend reads in the paper about Professor Diaconis's conclusion that the chance of someone winning two state lotteries in 4 months is about 1 in 30. He wants to run out and buy 30 tickets in your state's lottery and another 30 in the neighboring state's lottery. If there are 3 million tickets sold in each lottery, what are his chances of winning both? How do you explain the discrepancy between what you have told him and the conclusion reached by Professors Diaconis and Mosteller?

# CHAPTER 12

## Random Sampling and Sampling Distributions

When you have finished studying this chapter, you should be able to:

- Define and explain random sampling and differentiate between sampling with replacement and sampling without replacement;
- Use a table of random numbers;
- Understand that the random sampling distribution of $\overline{X}$ is a (theoretical) probability distribution that shows the variability in the values of $\overline{X}$ for samples of the same size randomly drawn from a population;
- Determine the mean and standard deviation of the sampling distribution of $\overline{X}$;
- Explain the central limit theorem; and
- Use the sampling distribution of $\overline{X}$ to answer questions about the probability of obtaining $\overline{X}$s within a specified range of values.

**statistical inference**

to draw a conclusion about a population parameter from a sample taken from that population

**statistic**

a descriptive index of a sample

**parameter**

a descriptive index of a population

**hypothesis**

a statement about a population parameter to be subjected to test and, on the outcome of the test, to be retained or rejected

**sampling distribution**

a theoretical relative frequency distribution of the values of a statistic that would be obtained by chance from an infinite number of samples of a particular size drawn from a given population

**probability samples**

samples for which the probability of inclusion in the sample of each element in the population is known

Dr. Brown, the research director of a large school district, wants to know if the sixth-grade students in her district are performing at the same level on a mathematics achievement test as students do nationally. In her district, there are 2,500 sixth-grade students, too many to study conveniently. She therefore selects 100 students from among the 2,500, finds their mean mathematics test score, and compares it with the mean of the nationwide group. If the mean of her group differs from the national mean, what should she conclude?

In the chapters to come, you will learn how to draw conclusions in problems like the one just presented. It is a problem in statistical inference. A basic aim of **statistical inference** is to form a conclusion about a population **parameter** from a sample (**statistic**) taken from that population (see the introduction to Chapter 2).

In inference, we often use a procedure called hypothesis testing. The investigator first poses a research question (see Section 1.5). However, the procedure for answering a statistical question is easier if it is translated into a **hypothesis**, a statement about a population parameter to be subjected to test and, on the outcome of the test, to be retained or rejected. In our example, Dr. Brown will hypothesize that the mean of the mathematics achievement test in her school district (her *population*) is equal to the mean of the national group. *To evaluate her hypothesis, Dr. Brown will ask what type of sample results are likely to occur if the hypothesis were correct. If her sample outcome is unlikely, she will reject the hypothesis.*

In our example problem, the data at hand are not those about which Dr. Brown really wishes to draw her conclusion. She wants to know how all 2,500 sixth-grade students in her school district score on the mathematics achievement test, not just the 100 she selected. In short, Dr. Brown wants to draw a conclusion about the population represented by the sample she studied and not simply about the particular sample itself.

In inference, the fundamental factor that must be taken into account is that the value of the characteristic we are studying will vary from sample to sample. Suppose Dr. Brown replicates her study several times. On each repetition she will employ a different selection of 100 subjects from the 2,500 sixth-grade students in her district. Even if sixth-grade students in her school district score as well on the mathematics achievement test as students do nationally, the mean scores from different samples will differ from the national mean (and from one another) due to chance factors involved in sampling.

*The key to any problem in statistical inference is to discover what sample values will occur by chance in repeated sampling and with what probability.* A sample is drawn and the mean is computed. A second sample of the same size yields a mean of somewhat different value. A third, still another value. What kind of distribution will be formed by the means when the sampling is repeated time after time? A distribution of this type is known as a **sampling distribution**. We must be able to describe it completely if we are to say what would happen when samples are drawn.

To learn what sample values will occur and with what probability, there must be known rules that connect the "behavior" of the samples to the population from which they are drawn. We can know these rules only if a systematic method of drawing samples is adopted and used *consistently*. As it turns out, there is just one basic method of sampling that permits the rules to be known. This is to draw **probability samples**—samples for which the probability of inclusion in the sample of each element of the population is known. One kind of probability sample is the random sample; it is the kind we consider in this book. If we draw a random sample, we can know the necessary facts about the distribution of the statistic under consideration, permitting inference of the type illustrated earlier.

# 12.1 Random Sampling

In Chapter 2 (Section 2.1) you were introduced to the concepts of random sampling and random sampling variation. Recall the story of the *Literary Digest* survey during the 1936 presidential election. The sample was very large (over 2 million) and was drawn from lists of telephone owners, yet it was not a random sample. What, then, is a random sample?

**random sample**
a sample obtained in a way that ensures that all samples of the same size have an equal chance of being selected from the population

A **random sample** of a given population is a sample so drawn that each possible sample of that size has an equal probability of being selected from the population. The method of selection, not the particular sample outcome, defines a random sample. If we were given a population and a sample from that population, it would be impossible to say whether the sample was random without knowing the method by which it was selected. Although characteristics of random samples *tend* to resemble those of the population, those of a particular random sample may not. If we deal 13 cards from a 52-card deck, each of the four suits (clubs, hearts, diamonds, spades) will usually be represented. Somewhat infrequently, a hand of 13 cards will contain cards from only three suits, and even less frequently, from only two suits. It is possible that the hand might consist of cards from just one suit, but this is indeed a rare random sampling result: the probability is approximately .000000000006 (6 chances in 1 trillion).

**sampling with replacement**
a sampling procedure in which an element may appear more than once in a sample

**sampling without replacement**
a sampling procedure in which no element may appear more than once in a sample

Although there is only one way to define a random sample, there are two sampling plans that yield a random sample: **sampling with replacement** (in which an element may appear more than once in a sample) and **sampling without replacement** (in which no element may appear more than once). We discuss and compare these sampling plans in Note 12.1 at the end of the chapter. However, from this point on assume that we are using the *with* replacement plan.

To obtain a random sample, *every element in the population must have an equal chance of being included in the sample.* (Note that this satisfies the basic assumption of the equally-likely model of probability—see Section 11.2.) However, the reverse is *not* true; that is, giving equal probability to the elements does not necessarily result in equal probability for the samples. For example, consider the following population of scores: 10, 11, 12, 13, 14, and 15. Suppose our task is to draw a sample of three different scores at random. It might occur to us to toss a coin, and if it comes up heads, we will take as our sample the first, third, and fifth scores. Otherwise our sample will be the second, fourth, and sixth scores. With this scheme, just two samples are possible—10, 12, and 14 and 11, 13, and 15—as shown in Figure 12.1. Now what is the

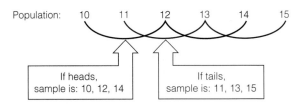

**FIGURE 12.1** The two possible samples resulting from a systematic sampling scheme.

probability under this sampling method that 10 will appear in the sample? Clearly, 1/2. What about 14? Also 1/2 because it will be included if the coin comes up heads. It is also true of 11 and of 13 and, indeed, of each and every element in this population. The sampling method therefore satisfies the equal probability requirement for elements. However, it does *not* satisfy the requirement that each sample of size 3 that could be formed shall have an equal opportunity of selection; only two samples are possible. The sample 10, 11, 12, for example, has no chance of selection. In true random sampling, the sample means will range from 11.0 (for a sample consisting of the three lowest scores) to 14.0. But in our case, the variability of means will be less because only the means 12.0 and 13.0 are possible.

In the real world of data, it is often difficult or costly (and sometimes impossible!) to draw a simple random sample from the population that we would truly like to study. To do it the right way, we would have to identify every element of the population and then arrange to follow the implications of the definition of a random sample.

Sometimes we are tempted to use a shortcut to reduce the amount of work. One popular shortcut is to draw cases by what is known as *systematic sampling* (e.g., selecting every 10th name from an alphabetical list). This may approximate random sampling in many cases, but if there is a cyclical trend in the data that happens to coincide with the periodicity of selection of cases, we are in trouble. For example, if you are sampling every fifth floor in a block of five-story walk-ups, all down the row you will be interviewing people on the same floor. The rents probably vary with the floor (the top floor is probably the cheapest because of the walk-up), so this sampling plan would yield a sample unrepresentative of the tenants in the block.

Another shortcut is to attempt to deliberately choose a sample of people that matches the population in demographic characteristics (for example, age, sex, race) as closely as possible. But if this is done with success, the sample means will vary less than in random sampling. *Any* sample, however deviant from the expected, has *some* chance of occurring. How much less? That's the problem; we can no longer say. We are therefore in no position to make accurate inferential conclusions.

A third method is to select what might be called a *casual sample*. The essence of this method is that the investigator attempts to act as a human randomizer. He or she tries to choose "at random" from the available subjects, but the method will more likely fail than succeed. Suppose a male investigator wants to ascertain the public's view on the adequacy of compensation of women who work. But suppose also that he dearly prefers talking to women than to men and to pretty, young women than to older women. Would you trust the adequacy of his sampling procedure, however earnest he was? What about assigning rats from the new shipment to two conditions of an experiment? Our research assistant reaches into the shipping containers to select those animals to receive Treatment A. Do you think animated and lethargic rats will have an equal chance of being chosen? What about those that bite at fingers versus those that do not? Take it from Minium's Third Law of Statistics: "*Human beings are rotten randomizers.*"

As an alternative, we could write the number of each rat on a ticket, place the tickets in a can, shake the can thoroughly, and make a blindfolded selection of subjects for the two groups. However, a better method is to use a table of random numbers to select the sample (or use a computer program that accomplishes the same thing). We tell how to use a table of random numbers in the next section.

## 12.2 Using a Table of Random Numbers

Because human judgment cannot be depended upon to select at random, how shall we do it? If each element of the population can be identified and assigned a different number, a convenient and reliable procedure is to use a **table of random numbers**, such as Table C in Appendix E. Such tables are usually constructed by computer, according to a program that ensures each digit from 0 to 9 has an equal probability of occurrence.

A table of random numbers may be read as successive single digits, as successive two-digit numbers, as three-digit numbers, and so on. We may also read the numbers vertically (in either direction) or horizontally (in either direction). For example, in Table C, if we begin at the top left on the first page and *read down*, the random order of single-digit numbers would be 1, 9, 0, 7, 3, . . . If we wish to read two-digit numbers, they would be 11, 96, 07, 71, 32, . . . To use the table properly, we must adopt some scheme *in advance*, including how to enter the table and how to proceed when the end of a column or row has been reached.

As an example, let us suppose that 30 scores are to be selected at random from a population of 700. To begin, assign each element of the population an identification number. The order in which you number the elements does not matter because subsequent random sampling will eliminate any bias. Each element may be given a three-digit identification number, from 000 to 699 or from 001 to 700, if preferred. For the sake of simplicity, suppose that our scheme requires that we start at the upper left of the first page of the table and read down. (We could start anywhere else.) The first random number is 113, and the first element to be included in the sample is therefore that bearing the identification number 113. The next random number is 969; we skip it because it identifies no element of the population. The next number is 077, which identifies the second score to be included in the sample. We continue until 30 elements have been selected.

If our sampling is *with replacement* and the same element is selected again, we must include it again. If our sampling is *without replacement* and an identification number appears again, we skip it.

## 12.3 The Random Sampling Distribution of the Mean: An Introduction

Suppose there is a very large population of scores ($X$) with a mean, $\mu_X$, equal to 100. We now draw from this population a random sample of 25 cases; its mean, $\overline{X}_1$, proves to be 97.4. We now replace the 25 cases in the population, "stir well," and select a second sample of 25 cases at random. Its mean, $\overline{X}_2$, is 101.8. Theoretically, we could repeat this sampling procedure indefinitely, and for each sample calculate and record the mean. Figure 12.2 illustrates the situation.

If we continued these sampling trials for an infinite number of trials, and if we then cast all the sample means into a relative frequency distribution, what sample values will occur in repeated sampling, and with what probability (relative frequency)? The distribution of sample means that would be generated is known as a random

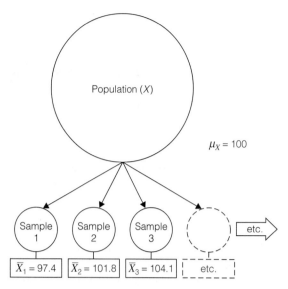

$\mu_X = 100$

**FIGURE 12.2**   Means of successive random samples.

**random sampling distribution of the mean ($\overline{X}$)**
a theoretical relative frequency distribution of all the values of $\overline{X}$ that would be obtained by chance from an infinite number of samples of a particular size drawn from a given population

sampling distribution of the mean. A **random sampling distribution of the mean** is the relative frequency distribution of $\overline{X}$ obtained from all possible random samples of a given size that could be drawn from a given population.

Notice that the sampling distribution of the mean, like the binomial distribution, is a *probability distribution*. Whereas the binomial distribution shows all the possible outcomes for dichotomous observations (such as tossing a coin) and the probability of each, a sampling distribution of the mean shows all the possible values that the sample mean can take on (for samples of a given size) and the probability of each.

If the population is of finite size, the number of possible samples will also be finite. This makes it possible to generate an entire sampling distribution and to explore its properties in a way not open to us when the distribution is defined as the outcome of a never-ending series of sampling trials. But to do this we will have to keep things simple.

Consider a population of four scores—2, 4, 6, and 8—from which we are to select samples of size 2. What are the possible samples? When sampling is done *with replacement* (i.e., each score is drawn, recorded, and then returned to the population before the next score is chosen), there are four ways in which the first score may be chosen and also four ways in which the second may be chosen. Consequently, there are $4 \times 4 = 16$ possible samples. These are shown in the first column of Table 12.1.

What is the probability of drawing the sample (2,2)? When each score is given an equal opportunity of selection, the probability that the first element will be 2 is 1/4, and when the score is replaced before selecting the second element, the probability that the second element will be 2 is also 1/4. Selection of the second element is in no way dependent on the outcome of the first element, so the two events are independent. The probability, therefore, of the sample (2,2) is the product of the two probabilities, $(1/4)(1/4) = 1/16$, according to the multiplication rule for independent

**TABLE 12.1** *Possible Samples and Sample Means for Samples of Size 2 (Sampling with Replacement)*

POPULATION: 2, 4, 6, 8

| Sample | Probability of occurrence | Mean |
|--------|---------------------------|------|
| 2,2 | 1/16 | 2.0 |
| 2,4 | 1/16 | 3.0 |
| 2,6 | 1/16 | 4.0 |
| 2,8 | 1/16 | 5.0 |
| 4,2 | 1/16 | 3.0 |
| 4,4 | 1/16 | 4.0 |
| 4,6 | 1/16 | 5.0 |
| 4,8 | 1/16 | 6.0 |
| 6,2 | 1/16 | 4.0 |
| 6,4 | 1/16 | 5.0 |
| 6,6 | 1/16 | 6.0 |
| 6,8 | 1/16 | 7.0 |
| 8,2 | 1/16 | 5.0 |
| 8,4 | 1/16 | 6.0 |
| 8,6 | 1/16 | 7.0 |
| 8,8 | 1/16 | 8.0 |

**TABLE 12.2** *Sampling Distribution of the Mean (Data from Table 12.1).*

| SAMPLE MEANS | RELATIVE FREQUENCY |
|--------------|--------------------|
| 8.0 | 1/16 |
| 7.0 | 2/16 |
| 6.0 | 3/16 |
| 5.0 | 4/16 |
| 4.0 | 3/16 |
| 3.0 | 2/16 |
| 2.0 | 1/16 |

events (presented in Section 11.3). By similar reasoning, the probability of any one of the other samples is also 1/16. If samples are selected in this manner, each of the 16 possible samples is equally likely to occur, and the basic condition of random sampling is satisfied.

Our fundamental interest is in the means of these samples rather than in the samples themselves. The mean of each sample is given in the third column of Table 12.1. Note that although there are 16 different samples, each equally likely, there are not 16 different means, each equally likely. For example, there is only one sample (2,2) that yields the mean of 2.0, but there are two samples for which the mean is 3.0: (2,4) and (4,2).[1] The probability of obtaining a sample with a mean of 2.0 is therefore 1/16, whereas the probability of obtaining a sample with a mean of 3.0 is 1/8, twice as great. This illustrates an essential point: *Random sampling results in equal probability of all possible samples, not in equal probability of all possible sample means.*

We may cast the 16 means in a relative frequency distribution, as Table 12.2 shows. This relative frequency distribution is, of course, the random sampling distribution of $\overline{X}$ for samples of size 2 drawn with replacement from the particular population of size 4. This distribution is shown graphically in Figure 12.3. For comparative purposes two features have been added. First, the distribution of the population of scores appears in the same figure. Second, a normal curve has been fitted to the sampling distribution of the mean. What features appear in this sampling distribution?

---

[1] The sample (2,4) must be treated as distinct from the sample (4,2). Each is possible, and each yields a sample mean that must be accounted for, just as head-tail is different from tail-head.

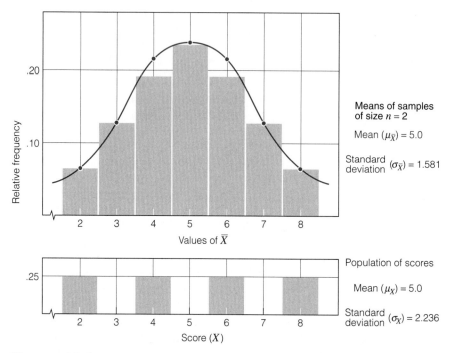

**FIGURE 12.3**   Distribution of means of the 16 possible samples of size 2 obtainable from a population of four scores. Data from Table 12.2. Population: 2, 4, 6, and 8.

# 12.4  Characteristics of the Random Sampling Distribution of the Mean

**expected value (of the sample mean)**
the mean of a random sampling distribution of $\overline{X}$

$\boldsymbol{\mu_{\overline{X}}}$
symbol for the expected value of the sample mean; $\mu_{\overline{X}} = \mu_X$

In most real-world examples, it is impossible to produce the actual relative frequency distribution of $\overline{X}$ from samples randomly drawn from a population because it calls for an *infinitely* long series of samples. However, mathematicians have been able to derive its characteristics and are thus able to tell us what would happen *if* an infinite series of trials were conducted. It is the fact that the samples are selected *at random* that makes this possible.

Recall that a distribution is completely defined by its mean, standard deviation, and shape. Let us consider the mean first. The mean of any random sampling distribution of $\overline{X}$, called the **expected value** of the sample mean, is the same as the mean of the population of scores. This is true regardless of $n$, $\sigma$, and the shape of the population. To put it symbolically:

MEAN OF THE SAMPLING
DISTRIBUTION OF THE MEAN ($\overline{X}$)

$$\mu_{\overline{X}} = \mu_X \qquad (12.1)$$

Using Figure 12.3 as an example, $\mu_{\overline{X}} = \mu_X = 5.0$.

**standard error of the mean**
the standard deviation of the random sampling distribution of $\overline{X}$

The standard deviation of the random sampling distribution of the mean, called the **standard error of the mean**, depends on the standard deviation of the population, $\sigma_X$, and the sample size, $n$. Symbolically:

STANDARD ERROR OF THE MEAN

$$\sigma_{\overline{X}} = \frac{\sigma_X}{\sqrt{n}} \tag{12.2}$$

$\sigma_{\overline{X}}$
symbol for the standard error of the mean, $\sigma_{\overline{X}} = \sigma_X/\sqrt{n}$

For the sampling distribution in Figure 12.3, we see that $\sigma_{\overline{X}} = 2.236/\sqrt{2} = 1.581$, which is *less* than the standard deviation of the population of scores from which the samples were taken (see Note 12.2). The standard error of the mean is the standard deviation of the sampling distribution of $\overline{X}$ based on samples of a specified size. The term *standard error* is a vestige from the time when the normal curve was known as the "normal law of error" (see Section 7.1). Theory leads us to its value, rather than actual calculation from the sample means in the distribution. Nevertheless, its value is the same as if that had been done, and therefore it *is* a standard deviation.

Study Formula 12.2 carefully. It shows (a) that sample means vary less than scores do (when the sample size is at least 2), (b) that sample means vary less when scores in the population vary less, and (c) that sample means vary less when sample size is greater.

**shape of the sampling distribution of $\overline{X}$**
if the population of scores is normally distributed, the sampling distribution of $\overline{X}$ will also be normally distributed, regardless of sample size

Note that Greek letters are used to specify the mean and standard deviation of the sampling distribution ($\mu_{\overline{X}}$, $\sigma_{\overline{X}}$). They remind us that the sampling distribution constitutes a population of values, not a sample of them. This distribution represents *all* the possible means of samples of a specified size and therefore constitutes the population of them—not just *some* of them.

With regard to the shape of the distribution, *if the population of scores is normally distributed, the sampling distribution of the mean will also be normally distributed, regardless of sample size.* If the population of scores is normally distributed, it does not matter whether we take an infinite number of samples of size 2 or an infinite number of samples of size 200. In both cases the sampling distribution of $\overline{X}$ will also be normally distributed. (The normal curve is described in Chapter 7.)

You can see these three properties of the sampling distribution of the mean in Figure 12.4, which shows two different sampling distributions (for samples of sizes 3 and 9) along with the normally distributed population of scores from which the samples were drawn. Note particularly how the sampling distribution changes with a change in sample size. This figure reminds us that there is not just one random sampling distribution of $\overline{X}$ corresponding to a given population, but a *family* of such distributions, one for each possible sample size.

**central limit theorem**
see definition in text; regardless of the shape of the population of scores from which random samples are drawn, the sampling distribution of $\overline{X}$ more and more resembles a normal distribution as sample size increases

Now all is well and good if the population is normally distributed, but what if it is not? Fortunately, a remarkable bit of statistical theory comes to the rescue: the **central limit theorem**. This theorem informs us that

the random sampling distribution of the mean tends toward a normal distribution irrespective of the shape of the population of observations sampled; the approximation to the normal distribution improves as sample size increases.

With some populations, the distribution of scores is sufficiently similar to a normal distribution so that little assistance from the central limit theorem is needed. But even when the distribution of the population of scores differs substantially from a normal

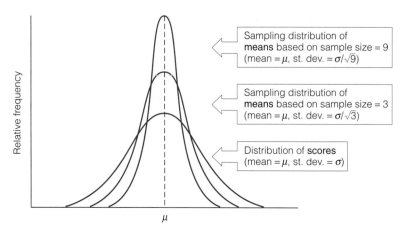

**FIGURE 12.4** A normally distributed population of scores and random sampling distributions of means for *n* = 3 and *n* = 9.

distribution (see Point of Controversy in Chapter 7), the sampling distribution of $\overline{X}$ may be treated as though it were normally distributed when the sample size is reasonably large. How large is reasonably large? Depending on the problem, 25 to 30 cases is usually quite large enough.

Figure 12.5 gives some idea of the tendency of the sampling distribution of $\overline{X}$ to resemble the normal curve as sample size rises. Figure 12.5*a* shows two populations of scores, one rectangular, one skewed. Figure 12.5*b* shows sampling distributions of $\overline{X}$ for samples based on *n* = 2. Note that the shapes of these distributions differ from those of their parent populations of scores and that the difference is in the direction of a normal curve. Figure 12.5*c* shows the sampling distribution of $\overline{X}$ of samples based on *n* = 25. In both cases the degree of resemblance to the normal distribution is remarkable, though the resemblance is closer for means of samples drawn from the rectangular distribution. The truth of the central limit theorem is beautifully illustrated in Figure 12.3. Look at the distribution of population scores at the bottom of the figure. This certainly is no normal distribution; if it had to be given a name, we might call it the "tooth distribution of the Halloween pumpkin." But look at the random sampling distribution of the mean. It comes very close to a normal distribution. Compare the heights of the rectangles with the dots showing the elevation of the normal distribution at similar locations.

## 12.5 Using the Sampling Distribution of $\overline{X}$ to Determine the Probability for Different Ranges of Values of $\overline{X}$

In the same way that a frequency distribution may be considered a probability distribution (see Section 11.6), we may use the random sampling distribution of the mean to determine the probability with which sample means would fall between certain limits. From Chapter 7 you know that many useful questions can be answered when we have a normal distribution of known mean and standard deviation. In this

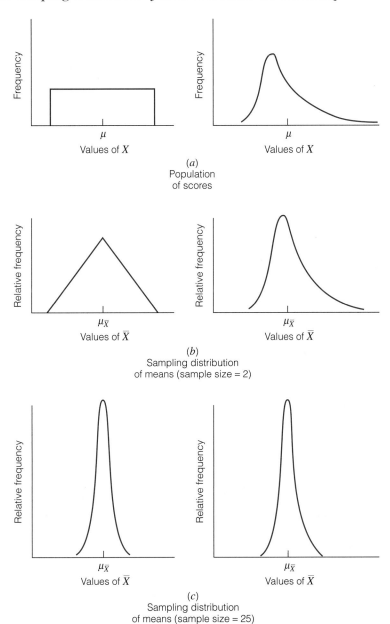

**FIGURE 12.5** Effect of the central limit theorem.

section you will learn to use those procedures to answer four common types of questions about the sampling distribution of $\overline{X}$. Be sure to review the methods of Chapter 7 (Sections 7.3–7.5) before proceeding.

**Given**     A normally distributed population, with $\mu = 70$ and $\sigma = 20$. Assume that your sample size is 25.

**Problem 1**    What is the probability of obtaining a random sample with a mean of 80 or higher?

Figure 12.6 illustrates the sampling distribution of $\overline{X}$ for an infinite number of samples of $n = 25$ drawn from a normally distributed population with $\mu_X = 70$ and $\sigma_X = 20$. Because the population of scores is normally distributed, the sampling distribution of $\overline{X}$ is also normally distributed. We also know that the sampling distribution has a mean (expected value) of 70 (remember, $\mu_{\overline{X}} = \mu_X$).

**Solution**     **Step 1:**    Calculate the standard deviation of the sampling distribution, that is, the standard error of the mean (Formula 12.2).

$$\sigma_{\overline{X}} = \frac{\sigma_X}{\sqrt{n}} = \frac{20}{\sqrt{25}} = 4.00$$

**Step 2:**    Translate your sample mean of 80 to a $z$ score. The general formula for a $z$ score is *(score − mean)/(standard deviation)*. In a sampling distribution of $\overline{X}$, the sample mean is the score, the mean of the sampling distribution (which is equal to the mean of the population) is the mean, and the standard error of the mean is the standard deviation. Therefore,

**z-score formula for a value of $\overline{X}$ (in a sampling distribution of $\overline{X}$)**

$$z = \frac{\overline{X} - \mu_{\overline{X}}}{\sigma_{\overline{X}}}$$

$$z = \frac{\overline{X} - \mu_{\overline{X}}}{\sigma_{\overline{X}}} = \frac{80 - 70}{4} = +2.50$$

**Step 3:**    Take the $z$ score to the table of areas under the normal curve (Table A in Appendix E), and determine the proportionate area beyond $z$. It is .0062. Now

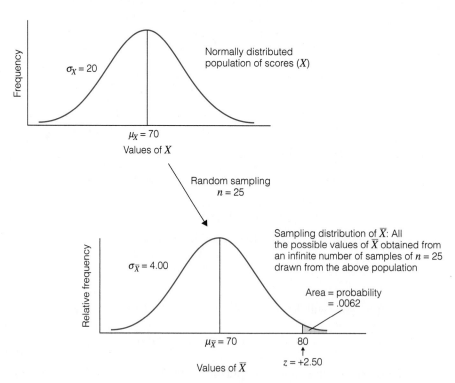

**FIGURE 12.6**    Finding the proportion of sample means exceeding a given value.

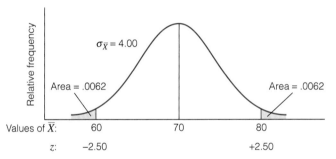

**FIGURE 12.7** Finding the proportion of sample means that differ from the population mean by more than a given amount.

because proportion of area under the curve corresponds to proportion of scores in the distribution (see Section 7.3), you can see that in random sampling means of 80 or higher would occur with a relative frequency of .0062 for samples of size 25. Therefore, the probability of obtaining such a mean or larger in random sampling from the given population is .0062.

**Problem 2** What is the probability of obtaining a sample with a mean that differs from the population mean by 10 points or more?

**Solution** In Problem 1, the mean of 80 fell 10 points above the expected value, which was the mean (70) of the sampling distribution. Because the normal curve is symmetrical, the same area lies below a mean of 60 (10 points below 70) as above one of 80 (10 points above 70). The $z$ scores of both will have the same magnitude; we must double the corresponding area to find the required probability. The probability of obtaining a sample mean differing from the population mean by 10 points or more is therefore $(2)(.0062) = .0124$. The problem is illustrated in Figure 12.7).

**Problem 3** What mean has such a value that the probability is .05 of obtaining one as high or higher in random sampling? This problem is illustrated in Figure 12.8.

**Solution** **Step 1:** From Column 3 in Table A of Appendix E, find the $z$ score above which .05 of the area under the normal curve falls; it is between $z = 1.64$ and $z = 1.65$, or about $+1.645$.

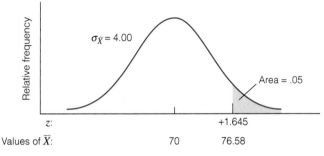

**FIGURE 12.8** Finding the value above which a given proportion of sample means will fall.

**Step 2:**   The value of $z$ informs us that the desired value is 1.645 standard deviations above the mean of the distribution. Therefore (remembering that our concern is with the sampling distribution of $\overline{X}$ and that its standard deviation is $\sigma_{\overline{X}}$, not $\sigma_X$):

$$\overline{X} = \mu_{\overline{X}} + z\sigma_{\overline{X}}$$

$$= 70 + (1.645)(4.00)$$

$$= 70 + 6.58$$

$$= 76.58$$

For this example, 5% of the sample means will have a value of at least 76.58; the probability is .05 of obtaining such a mean.

**Problem 4**   Within what limits would the central 95% of the sample means fall?

**Solution**   If .95 of the values are to fall in the center, the remaining .05 must be divided equally between the two tails of the distribution. Therefore, we must find the value of $z$ beyond which .025 of the sample means are located. The method is the same as that for Problem 3, and the solution is outlined as follows:

| **Lower Limit** | **Upper Limit** |
|---|---|
| $z_{LL} = -1.96$ | $z_{UL} = +1.96$ |
| $\overline{X}_{LL} = \mu_{\overline{X}} + z_{LL}\sigma_{\overline{X}}$ | $\overline{X}_{UL} = \mu_{\overline{X}} + z_{UL}\sigma_{\overline{X}}$ |
| $= 70 + (-1.96)(4.00)$ | $= 70 + (+1.96)(4.00)$ |
| $= 70 - 7.84$ | $= 70 + 7.84$ |
| $= 62.16$ | $= 77.84$ |

For this example, 95% of the sample means fall between 62.16 and 77.84. In random sampling, the probability is .95 of obtaining a mean within these limits and .05 of obtaining one beyond these limits. The problem is illustrated in Figure 12.9.

Problems like the four preceding are more than just mathematical exercises. Starting with the next chapter, we will use procedures like these to answer real research questions.

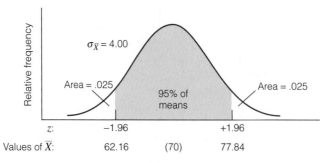

**FIGURE 12.9**   Finding the centrally located score limits between which a given proportion of sample means will fall.

## 12.6 Summary

A sampling distribution of a statistic is a probability distribution. It shows all the values of a statistic for an infinite number of samples of a given size drawn from a particular population. Some values are more probable than others. To construct a sampling distribution, a method of drawing samples must be specified and used consistently. Random sampling is the fundamental method that makes it possible to discover the properties of the sampling distribution. For the random sampling distribution of $\overline{X}$, the mean of the infinite number of $\overline{X}$s, $\mu_{\overline{X}}$, called the expected value, is equal to $\mu_X$, the mean of the population of observations from which the samples were taken. Its standard deviation, $\sigma_{\overline{X}}$, called the standard error of the mean, is equal to $\sigma_X/\sqrt{n}$. Thus, as sample size increases, the standard error of the mean becomes smaller (i.e., the sample means cluster closer to the true population mean). If the population of observations is normally distributed, so will be the sampling distribution of $\overline{X}$. If not, the central limit theorem tells us that the normal distribution will often still be a close and therefore usable approximation if sample size is not too small. If we know these three characteristics, we can determine the probability of obtaining a sample mean (drawn from a specified population) with values as extreme or more extreme than the one we have drawn.

# Mathematical Notes

### Note 12.1*a* Random Sampling with and without Replacement
(*Ref.*: Section 12.1)

If there are 50 tickets in a lottery and we draw one ticket, set it aside, draw another, and continue until five tickets have been selected, we are *sampling without replacement*. Under this sampling plan no element may appear more than once in a sample. On the other hand, if we select a ticket, note its number, and return it before choosing the next ticket, we are *sampling with replacement*. Under this plan it is possible to draw a sample in which the same element appears more than once. For other examples of these two methods, look again at Problems 5 and 6 from the previous chapter.

Both of these plans satisfy the condition of random sampling, but *certain sample outcomes that are possible when sampling with replacement are not possible when sampling without replacement*. This is illustrated in the following example. Suppose a population consists of three scores: 2, 4, and 6. Samples of size 2 are drawn from this population. Table 12.3 shows the possible samples that could result when sampling is done with and without replacement.

When sampling without replacement, the samples are the same as when sampling with replacement, except for those in which the same element appears more than once. Notice that the sample in which 2 was obtained on the first draw and 4 on the second is treated as a different sample from that in which 4 was obtained on the first draw and 2 on the second. *Both* are possible samples, and account must be taken of each. We shall now consider the methods for calculating the probabilities of samples under both sampling methods.

TABLE 12.3 *Possible Samples When Sampling with and without Replacement (Population: 2, 4, 6)*

| SAMPLING WITH REPLACEMENT | | SAMPLING WITHOUT REPLACEMENT | |
|---|---|---|---|
| *First draw* | *Second draw* | *First draw* | *Second draw* |
| 2 | 2 | — | — |
| 2 | 4 | 2 | 4 |
| 2 | 6 | 2 | 6 |
| 4 | 2 | 4 | 2 |
| 4 | 4 | — | — |
| 4 | 6 | 4 | 6 |
| 6 | 2 | 6 | 2 |
| 6 | 4 | 6 | 4 |
| 6 | 6 | — | — |

### Note 12.1*b* Independence and Sampling with Replacement (*Ref.*: Section 12.1)

Read Notes 11.2 and 11.3 again first.

The property of independence is pertinent in sampling *with replacement*. Consider a population of three scores: 2, 4, and 6. What is the probability of selecting the sample (2,6)? The probability that the first element of the sample will be 2 is 1/3. When that element has been replaced before selecting the second element, the probability that the second element will be 6 is also 1/3; selection of the second element is independent of the outcome of the selection of the first element. In terms of the definition of independence, Pr (second element is 6|first element is 2) = Pr (second element is 6) = 1/3. The probability, then, of selecting the sample (2,6) follows the multiplication theorem for independent events (Section 11.3): Pr (2,6) = (1/3)(1/3) = 1/9.

### Note 12.1*c* Probability of Joint Occurrence of Dependent Events and Sampling without Replacement (*Ref.*: Section 12.1)

Read Notes 11.2 and 11.3 again first.

When A *and* B are dependent events, the probability of both A *and* B is given by the product of the two probabilities: Pr (AB) = Pr (A|B) × Pr (B). This concept can be illustrated in application to sampling *without replacement*. Consider a population of three scores: 2, 4, and 6. What is the probability of selecting the sample (2,6)? The probability that the first element of the sample will be 2 is 1/3. Given that 2 has been selected (and removed from further selection), the probability that the second element will be 6 is 1/2. Because the outcome of selection of the first element affects the probability of occurrence of the second element, the two events are not independent. In terms of the definition of the probability of the joint occurrence of dependent events, Pr (2,6) = Pr (second element is 6|first element is 2) × Pr (first element is 2) = (1/2)(1/3) = 1/6. Compare this with the probability of occurrence of the same sample drawn with replacement (Note 12.1*b*).

According to Note 11.3, if Pr $(A|B)$ = Pr $(A)$, A and B are independent. Therefore, when A and B are independent, the expression for probability of joint occurrence of A and B reduces to the multiplication theorem given in Section 11.3: Pr $(AB)$ = Pr $(A)$ × Pr $(B)$.

### Note 12.2 Standard Error of the Mean when Sampling without Replacement (*Ref.*: Section 12.4)

Formula 12.2 assumes sampling with replacement. The standard error of the mean is smaller when sampling without replacement.

STANDARD ERROR OF THE MEAN
WHEN SAMPLING WITHOUT REPLACEMENT

$$\sigma_{\overline{X}} = \frac{\sigma_X}{\sqrt{n}} \sqrt{\frac{N-n}{N-1}}$$

In this formula, $N$ is the size of the population. Note that the formula would be the same as for sampling with replacement (Formula 12.2) except for the "correction factor" appearing at the far right: $\sqrt{(N-n)/(N-1)}$. *The correction will be trivial if the sample is small relative to the population.* For example, if the sample is .05 of the population, $\sigma_{\overline{X}} = .975(\sigma/\sqrt{n})$, approximately. Where the sample is a still smaller fraction of the population, the difference from $\sigma_X/\sqrt{n}$ is even less.

Despite the fact that most sampling in behavioral science is done without replacement, we typically use the other formula (Formula 12.2) for the standard error of the mean because although we do not know $N$, it is reasonable to assume that it is large. No harm is done in the usual case, where the sample is substantially smaller than 5% of the population.

## Key Terms, Concepts, and Symbols

# Problems

1. You are a "person-in-the-street" interviewer for a radio station. Take as your population those who come close enough that you might buttonhole them for an interview. Name four biases that you think might prevent you from obtaining a truly random sample of interviewees.

2. In recent years, shopping malls have become a favorite site for companies to test consumers' responses to new products through interviews. These interviews, called "mall intercepts," have largely replaced door-to-door interviewing because they are relatively quick and inexpensive. Research has shown that 95% of American households shop at malls at least once a year and that two-thirds shop at malls at least once every 2 weeks. (a) Can consumers interviewed in this manner be considered a random sample of the population as a whole? Explain. (b) Is the sample a random sample of people who go to malls? Explain. (c) What about just for people who go to that mall? Explain.

3. Consider the $X$ scores in Data 8B in Chapter 8. Using the table of random numbers (Table C in Appendix E) and the without-replacement sampling plan, select a sample of 10 scores from this set of 30 scores. Describe the steps in your procedure, including how you used the table of random numbers.

4. Consider Table 12.2. In random sampling, what is the probability of obtaining a sample mean (a) of 3.0 or less? (b) Of 4.0 or 5.0 or 6.0? (c) Greater than 5.0?

5. Consider a population of five scores: 1, 2, 4, 7, and 11. (a) Find the mean and standard deviation of this set of scores. (b) List the 25 possible samples of size 2 that may be drawn from this population by sampling with replacement. (c) Calculate the mean of each of the 25 samples found in (b). (d) Cast the 25 means into a frequency distribution. (e) Find the mean and standard deviation of the distribution formed in (d). (f) Calculate the standard error of the mean of samples of size 2: $\sigma_{\overline{X}} = \sigma/\sqrt{2}$. (g) Does $\mu_{\overline{X}} = \mu_X$? (h) Is $\sigma_{\overline{X}}$ as calculated in (f) the same as the standard deviation calculated in (e)? (i) The population of five scores does not form a symmetrical distribution. Does the distribution of means found in (d) appear to follow the normal curve? If not, does it seem closer to a normal distribution than the distribution formed by the population of five scores? What principle is involved?

6. Given: A normally distributed population with $\mu = 150$ and $\sigma = 24$. If samples of size 36 are drawn at random, what is the probability of obtaining (a) a sample mean of 154 or higher? (b) A sample mean that differs from 150 by 6 points or more?

7. Given: A normally distributed population with $\mu = 120$ and $\sigma = 10$. If samples of size 25 are drawn at random, what is the probability of obtaining (a) a sample mean of 118.25 or lower? (b) A mean that differs from 120 by 2 points or more?

8. Given: A normally distributed population with $\mu = 150$ and $\sigma = 25$. If samples of size 100 are drawn at random, what is the probability of obtaining (a) a sample mean of 156 or higher? (b) A mean that differs from 150 by 7 points or more?

9. For the data of Problem 6, (a) what sample mean is so great that it would be exceeded only 1% of the time in random sampling? (b) Within what central limits would 99% of the sample means fall?

10. For the data of Problem 7, (a) what sample value is so small that the probability of one smaller is .02? (b) Within what central limits would 95% of the sample means fall?

11. For the data of Problem 8, (a) what sample mean is so high that 10% of means would be higher? (b) Within what central limits would 90% of the sample means fall?

12. The Wechsler Adult Intelligence Scale is standardized to have a mean of 100 and a standard deviation of 15. If we draw a random sample of 25 people from the population, what is the probability of obtaining (a) a sample with a mean IQ of 95 or less? (b) A sample with a mean IQ of 105 or greater? (c) Within what central limits would 95% of the sample means fall?

13. For Problem 12, suppose instead that we draw a random sample of 100 people. What

is the probability of obtaining (a) a sample with a mean IQ of 95 or less? (b) A sample with a mean IQ of 105 or greater? (c) Within what central limits would 95% of the sample means fall? (d) Compare these answers with those for the last question. What general conclusion can you make?

**14.** Look again at Table 12.3. (a) Calculate the mean for each sample. (b) For each sampling plan, calculate the mean of the sample means. (c) For each sampling plan, calculate the standard deviation of the sample means. (d) What principle is demonstrated by your results? (See Note 12.2.)

**15.** By what percentage would the standard error of the mean for sampling with replacement (Formula 12.2) be reduced if sampling were done *without* replacement and if (a) $N = 1001, n = 50$? (b) $N = 1001, n = 100$? (c) $N = 1001; n = 500$? See Note 12.2.

**16.** Suppose you measured everyone's height $(X)$ in your class to the nearest one-half inch and obtained the following results:

*Recommended*

| | | | | | |
|---|---|---|---|---|---|
| 63.0 | 76.5 | 70.0 | 68.5 | 63.0 | 58.0 |
| 72.5 | 67.0 | 65.5 | 70.0 | 65.5 | 69.5 |
| 64.5 | 66.0 | 63.5 | 67.5 | 69.5 | 68.5 |
| 58.5 | 65.5 | 59.0 | 73.5 | 72.5 | 60.0 |
| 70.0 | 60.5 | 66.0 | 59.0 | 64.5 | 75.0 |

Consider this to be your population and calculate $\mu_X$. Now suppose that you did not really have time to complete this assignment, but that you did have time to select two students at random from the class and obtain the mean of this little sample to make a "best guess" (inference) about the population mean. To do so, assign each subject's height a number and, using your table of random numbers (Table C in Appendix E), draw your sample of 2 and calculate $\overline{X}$. Does $\overline{X} = \mu_X$? Repeat this 19 more times. Do any of your 20 values of $\overline{X}$ equal $\mu_X$? How many different values of $\overline{X}$ did you get? Construct the partial sampling distribution for the 20 values of $\overline{X}$ and calculate $\mu_{\overline{X}}$ (the estimate of $\mu_X$). Does $\mu_{\overline{X}} = \mu_X$? Why not? Is it close?

Now try the same thing again using samples of size 6. Do any of your values of $\overline{X}$ equal $\mu_X$? Construct the partial sampling distribution for the 20 values of $\overline{X}$ and calculate $\mu_{\overline{X}}$ (the estimate of $\mu_X$).

Reflect for a moment on what you have just learned. When we infer the population mean from the sample value, how often will we be correct? Although we may not be correct, we want to be close. Were most of the values of $\overline{X}$ closer to $\mu_X$ when $n = 2$ or when $n = 6$? What can you conclude about the effect of sample size?

# CHAPTER 13

# Introduction to Statistical Inference: Testing Hypotheses about Single Means (z and t)

When you have finished studying this chapter, you should be able to:

- Understand that the aim of statistical inference is to form a conclusion about a population parameter from a sample statistic;

- Understand that the key to hypothesis testing is to discover what sample values will occur in repeated sampling and with what probability;

- Formulate the null and alternative hypotheses;

- Know what is meant by level of significance and how it is used to test hypotheses;

- Know when to use a one-tailed or a two-tailed test;

- Know how to test a hypothesis about the population mean when the population standard deviation is known ($z$) and when it is unknown ($t$);

- Understand the assumptions in testing hypotheses about the mean of a population; and

- Understand the difference between the level of significance and a $p$-value.

Let us now return to the question posed by Dr. Brown at the beginning of Chapter 12. Suppose that Dr. Brown, the research director of a large school district has read in a test manual that the national norm for sixth-grade students on a mathematics achievement test is 85. She wants to know if students in her district are performing at the same level. She selects at random 100 students from all the sixth-grade students in the district and arranges to have the same test administered to them. Dr. Brown will then calculate their mean score and compare it to the national norm. If the mean of her group differs from the national norm, what should she conclude?

**statistical inference**

to draw a conclusion about a population parameter from a sample statistic

This is a problem in statistical inference. Recall from Chapter 12 that the basic aim of **statistical inference** is to form a conclusion about a population parameter from a sample taken from that population. That parameter may be a mean, a median, a proportion, a standard deviation, a correlation coefficient, or any other of a number of statistical parameters. In this chapter we will concern ourselves with the mean.

Look at Figure 13.1. Ideally, if we wanted to know the value of a population parameter (for example, $\mu_X$), we would gather all the observations in the population and, using the techniques we learned in the chapters on descriptive statistics, directly calculate the parameter. This direct approach is represented by the dotted line. But what if the population is too large for us to take the direct approach? That is when statistical inference is of use. Look now at the solid lines. In Step 1, we randomly draw a sample from the population of interest. In Step 2, we use the same descriptive techniques to calculate the sample statistic (in our example, $\overline{X}$). From the obtained value of our sample statistic ($\overline{X}$), we now infer the value of the population parameter ($\mu_X$).

The population of interest to Dr. Brown consists of the test scores of *all* 2,500 currently enrolled sixth-grade students in her district. From study of the sample, she wants to draw an inference as to whether $\mu_X$, the mean of her population, is 85. However, her sample of 100 student scores is just one of numerous random samples she could have drawn from the population. Suppose, for example, that Dr. Brown replicated her study several times. On each replication she would randomly draw a different selection of 100 students from the population. Because of sampling variation, we do not expect the means of all the samples to be the same. The value of $\overline{X}$ would probably be different from sample to sample (look again at Section 12.3 and Figure 12.2). How, then, can Dr. Brown infer the population mean when *her* sample mean is only one of many different possible sample means?

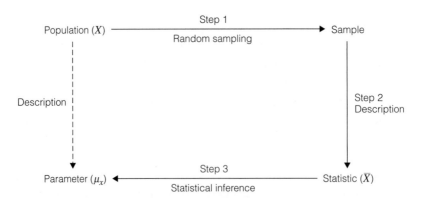

**FIGURE 13.1**    The steps used in statistical inference (modified from Games and Klare, 1967).

# 13.1 Testing a Hypothesis about a Single Mean

To answer her question (do sixth-grade students in her school district perform as well on the mathematics achievement test as students nationally?), Dr. Brown first translates her question into a statistical hypothesis: $\mu_X = 85$ (the mean of the population of sixth-grade mathematics achievement scores in her district is 85). She then subjects her hypothesis to examination, and, at the end, retains or rejects it.

**random sampling distribution of $\overline{X}$**
a theoretical relative frequency distribution of all the values of $\overline{X}$ that would be obtained by chance from an infinite number of samples of a particular size drawn from a given population

To examine the validity of her hypothesis, Dr. Brown asks what sample means would occur if many samples of the same size were drawn at random from her population *if the hypothesis that the population mean is 85 is true.* Dr. Brown can now refer to the **random sampling distribution of $\overline{X}$** that you learned about in the last chapter. She envisions the theoretical random sampling distribution of $\overline{X}$ for an infinite number of samples of size 100 drawn from a population whose mean is 85, and she compares her sample mean with those in this sampling distribution. *The key to any problem in statistical inference is to discover what sample values will occur in repeated sampling and with what probability.*

Suppose the relation between Dr. Brown's sample mean and those of the random sampling distribution of $\overline{X}$ looks like that pictured on the left in Figure 13.2. If so, her sample mean is one that could reasonably occur if the hypothesis is true, and she will retain the hypothesis as a plausible possibility. If the relationship is like that pictured on the right, on the other hand, her sample mean is so deviant that it would be quite unusual to obtain such a value when the hypothesis is true. In this case, she will reject the hypothesis and conclude that it is more likely that the mean of her population is not 85.

# 13.2 The Null and Alternative Hypotheses

**null hypothesis**
a hypothesis about a population parameter (e.g., $\mu_X$) that a researcher puts to test

**$H_0$**
symbol for the null hypothesis

The hypothesis that the researcher puts to test is called the **null hypothesis**, symbolized **$H_0$.** It is the hypothesis that he or she will decide to retain or reject. In Dr. Brown's problem, $H_0$: $\mu_X = 85$. For every null hypothesis, there is also an

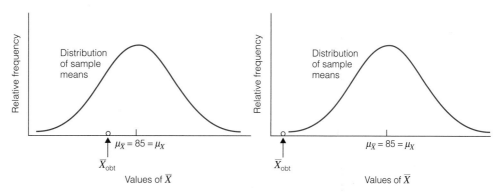

**FIGURE 13.2** Possible locations of the obtained sample mean relative to the distribution of expected sample means when the hypothesis is true.

**alternative**
**hypothesis**
a hypothesis
about a popula-
tion parameter
that contradicts
the null hypoth-
esis; in research,
the hypothesis
the researcher
wishes to prove
is true

$H_A$
symbol for
the alternative
hypothesis

**alternative hypothesis,** symbolized $H_A$. Because Dr. Brown is interested in discovering a difference (if one exists) *irrespective of direction*, her alternative hypothesis is
expressed as $H_A: \mu_X \neq 85$. Notice that *both $H_0$ and $H_A$ are always statements about the
population parameter.* They are never statements about the sample statistic.

Notice also that the alternative hypothesis is true if the mean mathematics achievement score for *all* sixth graders in Dr. Brown's district is *either* greater than *or* less than
85. Had Dr. Brown been interested in knowing *only* if mathematics achievement scores
in her district are *worse* than the national norm, her alternative hypothesis would be
expressed as $H_A: \mu_X < 85$; or, if *better* than the national norm, as $H_A: \mu_X > 85$. (We
will discuss $H_A$ in more detail in Section 13.7.) In either case, if the evidence
Dr. Brown obtains in her sample is contrary to $H_0$ and indicates with sufficient strength
that $H_A$ is true, she will reject $H_0$; otherwise, she will retain it. The decision to reject
or retain the hypothesis always refers to $H_0$ and never to $H_A$. While we reject $H_0$ only
when the evidence substantially favors $H_A$, it is $H_0$ that is the subject of the test.

Although $H_0$ is referred to as the null hypothesis, no special meaning should be
attached to the term *null*. It does not mean "zero" or "no difference." The null hypothesis is simply whatever hypothesis we choose to test.

## 13.3 When Do We Retain and When Do We Reject the Null Hypothesis?

**level of**
**significance**
the probability
value that is used
as a criterion to
decide that an
obtained sample
statistic ($\overline{X}$) has a
low probability
of occurring by
chance if the
null hypothesis is
true (resulting in
rejection of the
null hypothesis)

$\alpha$ **(alpha)**
symbol for
the level of
significance

What criterion should Dr. Brown use to decide when to reject the null hypothesis?
When we draw a random sample from a population, *our obtained value of $\overline{X}$ will almost never exactly equal $\mu_X$.* Thus, the decision to reject or to retain the null hypothesis depends on the selected criterion for distinguishing between those $\overline{X}$s that would
be common and those that would be rare *if $H_0$ is true*.

If the sample mean is so different from what is expected when $H_0$ is true that its
appearance would be unlikely, $H_0$ should be rejected. But what degree of rarity of
occurrence is so great that it seems better to reject the null hypothesis than to retain
it? This decision is somewhat arbitrary, but common research practice is to reject $H_0$
if the sample mean is so deviant that its probability of occurrence in random sampling is .05 or less. Such a criterion is called the **level of significance** and is
symbolized by the Greek letter $\alpha$ **(alpha).** In some cases, the researcher may wish to
be even more stringent and use a level of significance of .01 or less, but it is rarely
greater than .05. We discuss issues governing the choice of level of significance in
Section 14.3.

## 13.4 Generality of the Procedure for Hypothesis Testing

The general logic and procedure for testing *all* statistical hypotheses, whether about
means, frequencies, or other population characteristics, is essentially that described in
the previous sections:

**Step 1:** A specific hypothesis, called the null hypothesis, is formulated about a parameter of the population (e.g., about the population mean) along with an alternative hypothesis.

**Step 2:** A random sample is drawn from the population of observations, and the value of the sample statistic (e.g., the value of the sample mean) is obtained.

**Step 3:** Characteristics of the random sampling distribution of the statistic under consideration are examined to learn what sample outcomes would occur over an infinite number of repetitions and with what relative frequencies) if the null hypothesis is true.

**Step 4:** The null hypothesis is retained if the particular sample outcome is in line with the outcomes expected *if* the hypothesis is true; otherwise, it is rejected and the alternative hypothesis is accepted.

# 13.5 Dr. Brown's Problem: Conclusion

**region of rejection**

the portion of the sampling distribution of $\overline{X}$ (consisting of values of $\overline{X}$ that are unlikely to have occurred by chance if $H_0$ is true) that leads to rejection of $H_0$

In Dr. Brown's problem, $H_0$: $\mu_X = 85$. Let us assume that Dr. Brown wishes to adopt the .05 level of significance. She therefore will reject $H_0$ only if her obtained sample mean is so deviant that it falls in the upper 2.5% or lower 2.5% of all the possible sample means that would occur when $H_0$ is true (.025 + .025 = .05). If her $\overline{X}$ falls in the central 95% of the values of $\overline{X}$ that could occur when $H_0$ is true, she will retain the null hypothesis. The portions of the sampling distribution that include values of $\overline{X}$ that lead to rejection of the null hypothesis (in our example, the two extreme tails) are called the **regions of rejection**. The portion leading to retention of the null hypothesis (in our example, the central 95% of the sampling distribution) is called the **region of retention**.

**region of retention**

the portion of the sampling distribution of $\overline{X}$ that leads to retention of $H_0$

What sample means would occur if $H_0$ is true? If it is true, the random sampling distribution of $\overline{X}$ would center on $\mu_{hyp}$, or 85, as shown in Figure 13.3. If Dr. Brown can reasonably assume that the random sampling distribution of $\overline{X}$ approximates a normal curve (and with $n = 100$ she can, regardless of the shape of the population of scores, according to the central limit theorem), then she can use the normal curve table to calculate the $z$ values that separate the upper 2.5% and lower 2.5% of sample means from the remainder. These are referred to as the **critical values**. From Table A in Appendix E, the values are found to be: $z = \pm 1.96$.

**critical value(s)**

the value(s) that separates the region of rejection from the region of retention

Suppose Dr. Brown's obtained sample mean is 90. Even if the population mean really is 85, because of random sampling variation we do not expect the mean of a sample randomly drawn from that population to be exactly 85 (although it could be). Thus, the important question is, what is the relative position of the obtained sample mean among all those that could have been obtained by chance *if* the hypothesis is true? To determine the position of the obtained $\overline{X}$, it must be expressed as a $z$ score (see Section 12.5 and Table 13.1 for review):

$$z = \frac{\overline{X} - \mu_{hyp}}{\sigma_{\overline{X}}}$$

formula for $z$ required for testing hypotheses about single means

DEFINITIONAL FORMULA FOR $z$
REQUIRED FOR TESTING HYPOTHESES
ABOUT SINGLE MEANS

$$z = \frac{\overline{X} - \mu_{hyp}}{\sigma_{\overline{X}}} = \frac{\overline{X} - \mu_{hyp}}{\sigma_X / \sqrt{n}} \qquad (13.1)$$

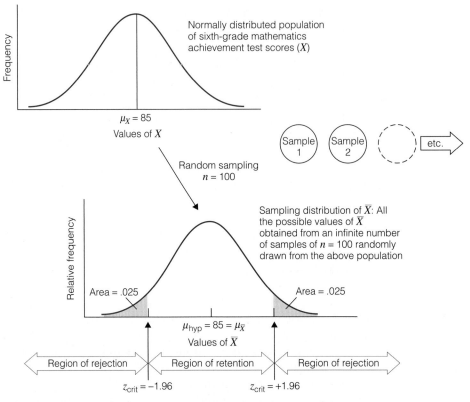

**FIGURE 13.3** Dr. Brown's problem: The random sampling distribution of $\overline{X}$ for samples of $n = 100$ drawn at random from a population with $\mu_X = 85$; $\alpha = .05$.

**TABLE 13.1** *Formula for Calculating z*

| | |
|---|---|
| In general: | $z = \dfrac{score - mean\ of\ scores}{standard\ deviation\ of\ scores}$ |
| To locate a raw score within a sample: | $z = \dfrac{X - \overline{X}}{S_X} = \dfrac{score - sample\ mean}{sample\ standard\ deviation}$ |
| To locate a raw score within a population: | $z = \dfrac{X - \mu_X}{\sigma_X} = \dfrac{score - population\ mean}{population\ standard\ deviation}$ |
| To locate a sample mean within a sampling distribution: | $z = \dfrac{\overline{X} - \mu_{\overline{X}}}{\sigma_{\overline{X}}} = \dfrac{sample\ mean - mean\ of\ the\ sampling\ distribution\ of\ \overline{X}}{standard\ error\ of\ the\ mean}$ |

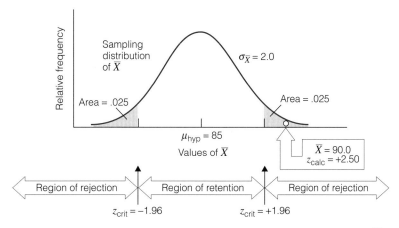

**FIGURE 13.4** Dr. Brown's problem: The sampling distribution of $\overline{X}$ for samples drawn at random from a population with $\mu_X = 85$ and $\sigma_X = 20$; $\alpha = .05$. Dr. Brown's sample mean falls in the region of rejection.

Look at this formula closely. What it says is:

$$z = \frac{\text{obtained sample mean} - \text{hypothesized population mean (when } H_0 \text{ is true)}}{\text{standard error of the mean}}$$

Thus, this $z$ value shows by how many standard errors of the mean the obtained sample mean deviates from the hypothesized population mean stated in $H_0$. To convert her $\overline{X}$ to $z$, Dr. Brown must know $\sigma_X$. Let us assume it to be 20. So,

$$z = \frac{90 - 85}{20/\sqrt{100}} = \frac{+5}{2} = +2.5$$

In our example, Dr. Brown's sample mean is 2.5 standard errors of the mean greater than expected *if* the null hypothesis is true. You can see the location of this obtained $z$ in the sampling distribution shown in Figure 13.4. As you can see, the value falls in the upper region of rejection, so Dr. Brown rejects $H_0$ and accepts $H_A$. In short, she concludes that it is *not* reasonable to believe that the mean of the population from which the sample came is 85. Under the circumstances, it seems reasonable to go a step further and say that the mean of her population is very likely greater than 85. Notice that the conclusion is about the population *represented by the sample under study and not simply about the particular sample itself.*

## 13.6 The Statistical Decision

Has Dr. Brown proven absolutely that the mean of the population is greater than 85? Suppose she had used $\alpha = .01$ as her decision criterion rather than $\alpha = .05$. Her sample mean, as well as its $z$ value would still be the same, but the critical values of $z$ that separate the regions of rejection from the region of retention would be different, $z = \pm 2.58$, as shown in Figure 13.5. When this decision criterion is used, the sample mean falls in the region of retention, and therefore the decision would be to retain $H_0$. Thus our final decision may depend on our decision criterion. We will return to this in Section 14.3.

What does it mean when our sample mean does not fall in the region of rejection and we retain $H_0$? *The decision to "retain" $H_0$ does not mean that it is likely that $H_0$ is true.* Rather, this decision merely reflects the fact that we do not have sufficient evidence to reject the null hypothesis. Certain other hypotheses that might have been stated would also have been retained if tested in the same way. Consider our example where the hypothesis is $H_0$: $\mu_X = 85$. If our sample mean is 86 and is related to the hypothesized sampling distribution of $\overline{X}$ as illustrated at the left in Figure 13.6, our decision will be to retain the null hypothesis. But suppose the hypothesis had been $H_0$: $\mu_X = 87$. If the same sample result had occurred, $\overline{X} = 86$, we would again be led to retain the null hypothesis that $\mu_X = 87$. This is shown at the right in Figure 13.6.

In short, **rejecting the null hypothesis** means that it does not seem reasonable to believe that it is true, but **retaining the null hypothesis** merely means that we believe that the hypothesis *could* be true. It does *not* mean that it must be true, or even that it is probably true, for there are many other null hypotheses that if tested with the same sample would also be retained.

Look at the formula for the $z$ test and consider the effect of changing sample size. Suppose that the actual population mean differs from the hypothesized mean. If Dr. Brown had drawn a random sample of 25 students instead of 100, she would not have rejected the null hypothesis, because $z = (90 - 85)/(20/\sqrt{25}) = +1.25$, and $+1.25$ falls in the region of retention when $\alpha = .05$.

In general, if the sample drawn to test the null hypothesis is small, sampling variation will be large and may mask a difference between $\mu_{\text{hyp}}$ and $\mu_{\text{true}}$. In other words, the null hypothesis may not be rejected when it should be. Large samples increase precision by reducing sampling variation. However, for a given study there is a limit

**rejecting the null hypothesis**
the obtained sample statistic ($\overline{X}$) has a low probability of occurring by chance if the value of the population parameter stated in $H_0$ is true

**retaining the null hypothesis**
we do not have sufficient evidence to reject $H_0$ (it does not mean that $H_0$ must be true, only that it *could* be true)

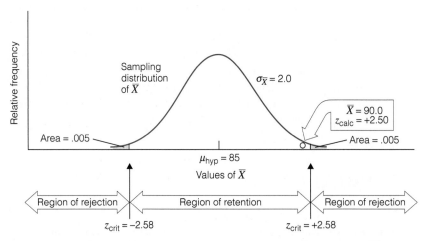

**FIGURE 13.5** Dr. Brown's problem: The sampling distribution of $\overline{X}$ for samples drawn at random from a population with $\mu_X = 85$ and $\sigma_X = 20$; $\alpha = .01$. Dr. Brown's sample mean falls in the region of retention.

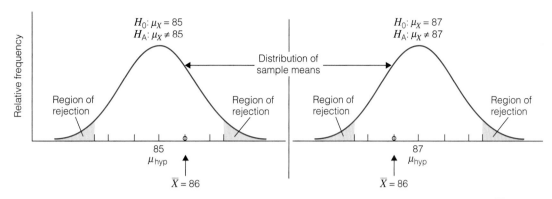

**FIGURE 13.6**    Testing the null hypothesis that $\mu_X = 85$ or that $\mu_X = 87$ when $\overline{X} = 86$.

to the precision needed. In Section 14.11, we will show how to determine optimum size for testing hypotheses about single means.

## 13.7 Choice of $H_A$: One-Tailed and Two-Tailed Tests

**nondirectional (two-tailed) test**
the alternative hypothesis, $H_A$, states that the population parameter may be either less than or greater than the value stated in $H_0$ (and the critical region is divided between both tails of the sampling distribution)

**directional (one-tailed test)**
the alternative hypothesis, $H_A$, states that the population parameter differs from the value stated in $H_0$ in one particular direction (and the critical region is located in only one tail of the sampling distribution)

As you learned in Section 13.2, the alternative hypothesis may be directional or nondirectional, depending on the purpose of the study. When the alternative hypothesis is **nondirectional**, a **two-tailed test** results, and it is possible to detect a discrepancy between the true value and the hypothesized value of the parameter irrespective of the direction of the discrepancy. This capability is often desirable in examining research questions. For example, in most cases in which the performance of a group is compared with a known standard, it would be of interest to discover that the group is superior *or* to discover that the group is substandard.

Sometimes a directional test (a one-tailed test) is more appropriate. Some examples of situations in which a one-tailed test might be suitable are as follows:

1. A manufacturer wishes to know the life span of light bulbs made by a new process. She plans to adopt the new process only if the mean length of life is greater than 1,500 hours.

2. The physical fitness of schoolchildren is tested. If mean performance is substandard, it will be necessary to institute a special physical training program.

3. The claim is made that when Hairy Hormone is ingested, more hair will grow.

4. A new teaching method is proposed, it is decided that the new method should be instituted if it can be demonstrated that learning accomplished under the new method is superior to that under the standard method.

In a **directional (one-tailed) test**, interest is in discovering whether or not there is a difference *in a particular direction*. For instance, in Example 2, the question is whether or not the children are substandard with regard to physical fitness. This may be tested by hypothesizing that the mean physical fitness score of the population of schoolchildren equals the standard value versus the alternative that it is less than this value. Note that if the children's physical fitness equals or exceeds the standard, no action

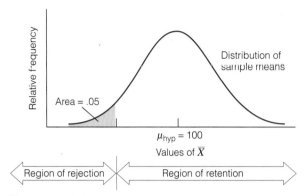

**FIGURE 13.7**   Testing $H_0$: $\mu_X = 100$ against $H_A$: $\mu_X < 100$; $\alpha = .05$.

is necessary. A special training program will be instituted only if their performance is substandard.

The alternative hypothesis states what the researcher has a chance to discover. If $H_A$ says that the population mean is less than $\mu_{hyp}$, then the *only* thing the researcher can discover in this study is that the mean is less than $\mu_{hyp}$. For example, Figure 13.7 illustrates the design for decision when testing $H_0$: $\mu_X = 100$ against the alternative hypothesis $H_A$: $\mu_X < 100$. As we can see, the region of rejection is entirely at the left. A value of $\overline{X}$ that falls above 100 *cannot* lead to rejection of the null hypothesis, *no matter how deviant it may be.*

The major disadvantage of a one-tailed test is that it precludes any chance of discovering that reality is just the opposite of what the alternative hypothesis says. From a marketing perspective, a researcher may only be interested in whether Hairy Hormone causes hair growth (Example 3), but suppose that it actually causes hair loss. This would not be discovered with a one-tailed test where $H_A$ states that hair growth is greater than normal. If such a state of affairs is unacceptable, a directional alternative is inappropriate and a two-tailed test should be used. In general, a *a directional alternative hypothesis is appropriate only when there is no practical difference in meaning between retaining the null hypothesis and concluding that a difference exists in a direction opposite to that stated in the directional alternative hypothesis.*

You may be asking, "Why not wait until you see the results of the statistical test before deciding to use a directional or nondirectional alternative hypothesis?" The decision to use a one-tailed alternative must always flow from the logic of the research question, as just illustrated. Therefore, *the time to decide on the nature of the alternative hypothesis is at the beginning of the study, before the data are collected.* It is not proper to observe the sample outcome and then set the region of rejection in the tail of the sampling distribution toward which the sample outcome tends. For example, if we adopt the 5% level of significance and follow this erroneous procedure systematically, we are really, in the long run, conducting two-tailed tests at the 10% significance level. Likewise, it is not satisfactory to set our one-tailed trap in the direction in which we *think* the outcome might go, only to switch to a two-tailed test if the sample mean appears to fall in the opposite direction. If tests are conducted in this manner, using $\alpha = .05$, they are equivalent to two-tailed tests at $\alpha = .075$, with an area of .05 in one tail and an area of .025 in the other—but with the larger area located by the prejudice of preconception. It is because of misuses like these that most journal editors look askance at one-tailed tests.

## 13.8 Review of Assumptions in Testing Hypotheses about a Single Mean

Whenever we perform a *z* test, we refer to the normal curve table. For the normal-curve model of statistical inference about single means to be precisely correct, several conditions must hold:

1. A random sample has been drawn from the population.
2. The sample has been drawn by the with-replacement sampling plan.
3. The sampling distribution of $\overline{X}$ follows the normal curve.
4. The standard deviation of the population of scores is known.

A truly random sample is often difficult to achieve in practice. Violation of this assumption may affect the mean and standard deviation of the sampling distribution in unpredictable ways (more about that later).

For the model of inference about single means described in this chapter to be strictly correct, it is assumed that sampling is with replacement (see Note 12.1*a*). Nevertheless, it is common practice to sample without replacement. The consequent error in inference is quite small as long as the sample size is a small fraction of the population size, say, .05 or less (see Note 12.2).

The third assumption is that we may treat the sampling distribution of $\overline{X}$ as a normal curve. As indicated in Section 12.4, this assumption is quite reasonably approximated when the scores in the population are reasonably close to a normal distribution. When the scores in the population are *not* normally distributed, the central limit theorem comes to the rescue when sample size is 25 or larger (Section 12.4). In this situation, assuming that the sampling distribution follows the normal curve results in minimal error.

The fourth assumption is that we know $\sigma_X$, the standard deviation of the population from which our sample is drawn. Look again at formula 13.1; $\sigma_X$ appears in the formula for the *z* test (it is the numerator of the standard error of the mean). But in actual practice, we will rarely know the value of $\sigma_X$. Why not? Look at the formula for $\sigma_X$:

$$\sigma_X = \sqrt{\frac{\sum (X - \mu_X)^2}{N}}$$

If we know the value of $\sigma_X$, we probably already know the value of $\mu_X$. If we know the value of $\mu_X$, why would we want to estimate it from $\overline{X}$? Thus, we will have to estimate $\sigma_X$ from the sample data. Let us now examine how this is done.

## 13.9 Estimating the Standard Error of the Mean When σ Is Unknown

To test hypotheses about means using *z*, we must calculate the standard error of the mean ($\sigma_{\overline{X}}$). In Dr. Brown's problem, we gave its value. However, the standard error of the mean requires knowledge of $\sigma$, the standard deviation of the population, which in actual practice we must almost always estimate from the sample:

$$z = \frac{\overline{X} - \mu_{\text{hyp}}}{\sigma_{\overline{X}}} = \frac{\overline{X} - \mu_{\text{hyp}}}{\sigma_X / \sqrt{n}} = \frac{\overline{X} - \mu_{\text{hyp}}}{? / \sqrt{n}}$$

# Point of Controversy

## The Single-Subject Research Design

Hypothesis testing, with its reliance on comparisons of means and variances between samples, has been the traditional way of analyzing data in the behavioral sciences for nearly 100 years. In the chapters to come, you will learn about some recent challenges to hypothesis testing, with some statisticians calling for a ban of significance testing.

In actuality, the controversy is not new. One of the original challenges to statistical hypothesis testing came from scientists and practitioners who championed single-subject designs. Rather than obtain a sample of several observations from a population and then worry about whether or not it is representative of that population, why not just use a single subject and study that subject in depth? Early researchers such as Ebbinghaus (human memory) and Pavlov (conditioned responses) used single-subject designs, and this approach is common today in psychophysics and applied behavioral analysis. Perhaps the two strongest proponents of this approach were Sidman (1960) and the famed B. F. Skinner (1966).

Skinner and his colleagues totally rejected comparison of group means and inferential statistics, and eventually created *The Journal of the Experimental Analysis of Behavior*, which was devoted to publishing the results of studies of single subjects. In single-subject experimentation, the dependent variable is measured at multiple times during the study, and the results are not averaged with results from other subjects. The subjects provide their own baselines. In experimental analysis of behavior, for example, the dependent variable is often the subject's response rate, and results are displayed in a real-time graph in which changes in the independent variable across time are shown on the abscissa and changes in the dependent variable are shown on the ordinate. Conclusions about the effects of manipulating the independent variable are made by inspection of the graph (e.g., for changes in response rate after introduction of the variable).

This approach of assessing behavior change is also used to assess the effects of therapy interventions in individual subjects. Proponents claim that collapsing data across subjects obscures "the orderly and systematic development" of behavior in an individual organism (Hopkins, Cole, & Mason, 1998; Morgan & Morgan, 2001; Perone, 1998). In a recent review, Morgan and Morgan (2001) concluded that

> the single-participant alternative features a design power and flexibility well suited to both basic science and applied research. . . . [Its] features should be especially appealing to practicing clinicians who are delivering services to individual clients and whose professional responsibilities increasingly include documentation of treatment efficacy.

**observer bias**
observations and conclusions that are biased by the observer's own emotions and/or values

Not surprisingly, many researchers oppose the single-subject design. For example, in another review, Jasienski (1996) called it "seriously flawed." There is a risk of **observer bias** (observations and conclusions biased by the observer's own emotions, moods, and values) and there are no control subjects. This is a particular weakness in pharmacological studies, in which one must be alert to the possibility of a *placebo effect* (e.g., the subject feeling better because he or she believes the treatment will work, even if in fact it does not).

The risk of a placebo effect is particularly great in self-experimentation, for which there is a long history in biomedical science (Brown, 1995). According to Jasienski, the major flaw is the lack of individual differences. In a much-publicized case in 1996, baboon bone marrow was used to treat a single AIDS patient (Jasienski, 1996). The treatment failed, but even if it had succeeded, how could the results have been interpreted? The patient had received considerable attention from doctors and a variety of prior drug treatments and radiation. There is also the possibility that the patient was biologically and medically unique in some way. Which aspect of the treatment or subject characteristic, or combination of factors, was responsible for the outcome? In every measurement there is also some degree of error.

Proponents of hypothesis testing say that the only way to deal with these problems is by randomly drawing samples from a population and treating everyone the same except for the independent variable. There will still be individual differences and errors in measurement (however small), but "without statistics, there is no way of knowing if the errors matter. . . . The only way is through 'averaging out' the superficial differences among individuals, to see what meaningful similarities remain" (Jasienski, 1996). Even Morgan and Morgan (2001) admit that "when . . . one is interested in population parameters for the purpose of establishing social policies or regulations affecting educational, political, or social institutions, then group designs may have considerable usefulness."

Although single-subject design research without formal inferential statistics still has its defenders (e.g., Hopkins, Cole, & Mason, 1998; Morgan & Morgan, 2001; Perone, 1999), there is a growing awareness of the use of inferential statistics in such designs (e.g., Franklin, Allison, & Gorman, 1997) and even manuscripts submitted to *The Journal of the Experimental Analysis of Behavior* have increasingly included inferential statistics (Ator, 1999).

---

**unbiased estimator**

the mean of the estimates made from all possible samples equals the value of the parameter estimated ($\overline{X}$ is an unbiased estimator of $\mu_X$; $S_X$ is not an unbiased estimator of $\sigma_X$)

Intuition suggests substituting $S_X$, the sample standard deviation, as an estimate of $\sigma_X$, but as it turns out, this creates an additional problem.

The basic problem is that the sample variance, $S_X^2$, is a *biased estimator* of the population variance, $\sigma_X^2$. What we need is an unbiased estimator. With an **unbiased estimator,** the mean of the estimates made from all possible samples equals the value of the parameter estimated. For example, the sample mean is an unbiased estimator of the population mean because the average of the values of $\overline{X}$ computed from all possible samples exactly equals $\mu_X$. The same relationship does not hold between $S_X^2$ and $\sigma_X^2$; the mean value of $S_X^2$ calculated from all possible samples is a little smaller than $\sigma_X^2$. We introduced this problem, as well as the following correction, in the Point of Controversy in Chapter 6.

Recall that the formula for the sample variance (Formula 6.2*b*) is:

$$S_X^2 = \frac{\sum (X - \overline{X})^2}{n}$$

It has been shown that the tendency toward underestimation will be corrected if $\Sigma(X - \overline{X})^2$ is divided by $n - 1$ rather than by $n$. The following formula incorporates this correction:

$SS_X$
symbol for the sum of the squared deviations from the mean

$s_X^2 = \dfrac{SS_X}{n-1}$
unbiased estimate of the population variance

$s_X = \sqrt{\dfrac{SS_X}{n-1}}$
a better estimate (than $S_X$) of $\sigma_X$

## UNBIASED ESTIMATE OF THE POPULATION VARIANCE

$$s_X^2 = \frac{\sum (X - \overline{X})^2}{n-1} = \frac{SS_X}{n-1} \tag{13.2}$$

The use of the lowercase letter in $s_X^2$ distinguishes this formula from that for $S_X^2$. Taking the square root of the formula, we obtain a better estimate of the standard deviation of the population:

$$s_X = \sqrt{\frac{\sum (X - \overline{X})^2}{n-1}}$$

We give a mathematical explanation of why $S_X^2$ is a biased estimator of $\sigma_X^2$ in Note 13.1 at the end of the chapter. We offer a demonstration in Table 13.2. This table presents the 16 possible samples arising when we draw samples of size two from a population of four observations. Calculation of the variance of the four scores by Formula 6.2a yields $\sigma_X^2 = 5.0$. Now let us calculate $s_X^2$ using Formula 13.2 from each of

**TABLE 13.2** *Possible Samples, Together with Estimates of the Population Variance Computed for Each (Data from Table 12.1)*

**POPULATION: 2, 4, 6, 8**

**POPULATION VARIANCE:** $\sigma_X^2 = \dfrac{\sum (X - \mu_X)^2}{N} = 5.0$

| Sample | $\overline{X}$ | $\sum (X - \overline{X})^2$ | Estimate of population variance $s_X^2 = \dfrac{\sum (X - \overline{X})^2}{n-1}$ |
|---|---|---|---|
| 2,2 | 2 | 0 | 0 |
| 2,4 | 3 | 2 | 2 |
| 2,6 | 4 | 8 | 8 |
| 2,8 | 5 | 18 | 18 |
| 4,2 | 3 | 2 | 2 |
| 4,4 | 4 | 0 | 0 |
| 4,6 | 5 | 2 | 2 |
| 4,8 | 6 | 8 | 8 |
| 6,2 | 4 | 8 | 8 |
| 6,4 | 5 | 2 | 2 |
| 6,6 | 6 | 0 | 0 |
| 6,8 | 7 | 2 | 2 |
| 8,2 | 5 | 18 | 18 |
| 8,4 | 6 | 8 | 8 |
| 8,6 | 7 | 2 | 2 |
| 8,8 | 8 | 0 | 0 |

Mean value of $s_X^2$: 5.0

the 16 possible samples. The 16 samples and the 16 variance estimates are shown, respectively, in the first and last columns of the table.

We observe that the mean of these estimates is 5.0, which is also the true value of $\sigma_X^2$, the quantity estimated. This demonstrates that $s^2$ is an unbiased estimator of $\sigma^2$ because the mean of all the estimates equals the quantity estimated. Obviously, if we had made the 16 estimates by dividing by $n = 2$ rather than $n - 1 = 1$, the mean of *these* estimates would have been less than 5.0. Although the correction introduced for estimating the standard error of the mean makes for a better estimate *on the average*, recognize that any particular sample will probably yield an estimate that is either too large or too small.

**estimated standard error of the mean**
an estimate of the standard deviation of the random sampling distribution of $\overline{X}$

$s_{\overline{X}} = s_X/\sqrt{n}$
symbol and formula for the estimated standard error of the mean ($\overline{X}$)

When we substitute $s_X$ for $\sigma_X$ the result is called the **estimated standard error of the mean**, symbolized $s_{\overline{X}}$:

> ESTIMATED STANDARD
> ERROR OF THE MEAN
> $$s_{\overline{X}} = s_X/\sqrt{n} \qquad (13.3)$$

Note that the lowercase $s$ signifies an estimate of a standard deviation in both symbols. When we substitute $s_{\overline{X}}$ for $\sigma_{\overline{X}}$ in the formula for $z$, the result is a new statistic (an approximation of $z$) called $t$. Unlike $z$, however, $t$ is not normally distributed.

## 13.10 The *t* Distribution

If the assumptions of Section 13.8 are satisfied, the true $z$ corresponding to the sample mean is a normally distributed variable. Why? The values of $\overline{X}$ will vary as we move from random sample to random sample, but the values of $\mu_X$ and $\sigma_{\overline{X}}$ are constants and will remain fixed. Consequently, the values of $z$ are formed as follows:

$$z = \frac{(normally\ distributed\ variable) - (constant)}{(constant)}$$

*where:* $\overline{X}$ = the normally distributed variable

$\mu_X$ = a constant

$\sigma_{\overline{X}}$ = a constant

Subtracting a constant from each score in a normal distribution does not change the shape of the distribution, nor does dividing by a constant (see Section 6.12). Consequently, $z$ will be normally distributed when $\overline{X}$ is normally distributed, and the normal distribution is therefore the correct distribution to which to refer $z$ for evaluation.

Consider the same problem, but this time assume $\sigma$ is not known and must be estimated from the sample. To evaluate the position of the sample mean, we calculate the statistic $t$:

> DEFINITIONAL FORMULA FOR *t* REQUIRED FOR
> TESTING HYPOTHESES ABOUT SINGLE MEANS
> $$t = \frac{\overline{X} - \mu_X}{s_{\overline{X}}} \qquad (13.4a)$$

The value $\mu_X$ is the value stated in the null hypothesis ($\mu_{hyp}$). So,

$$t = \frac{\overline{X} - \mu_{hyp}}{s_{\overline{X}}} \tag{13.4b}$$

Now look again at Formula 13.1, the Formula for $z$ required for testing hypotheses about single means. We may summarize the formula for $t$ as

$$t = \frac{obtained\ sample\ mean - hypothesized\ population\ mean\ (when\ H_0\ is\ true)}{estimated\ standard\ error\ of\ the\ mean}$$

$t = \dfrac{\overline{X} - \mu_X}{s_{\overline{X}}}$

formula for the $t$ statistic; used when the population standard deviation ($\sigma_X$) is not known

Recall from formula 13.3 that $s_{\overline{X}} = s_X/\sqrt{n}$. The $t$ statistic differs from $z$ in that *the denominator of the expression is a variable.* As we move from random sample to random sample, not only will values of $\overline{X}$ vary but *each sample will probably yield a different estimate ($s_{\overline{X}}$) of $\sigma_{\overline{X}}$*.[1] The resulting statistic is formed as follows:

$$t = \frac{(normally\ distributed\ variable) - (constant)}{(variable)}$$

**student's distribution of *t***

a theoretical relative frequency distribution of all the values of $\overline{X}$ converted to $t$ that would be obtained by chance from an infinite number of samples of a particular size drawn from a given population

If we were to draw an infinite number of samples of the same size $n$ from a population, calculate $\overline{X}$, $s_X$, and $s_{\overline{X}}$ for each sample, and then find $t$ for each sample, we would have the sampling distribution of $t$. Because of the presence of the variable in the denominator, this statistic does *not* follow the normal distribution. Just what distribution does it follow? Shortly after the turn of the century, British mathematician William S. Gosset, writing under the name of "Student," solved this problem and presented the proper distribution for it. Since that time, the statistic has been called $t$, and its distribution has been referred to as *Student's distribution* or **Student's distribution of *t***.

A common error is to think that it is the sampling distribution of $\overline{X}$ that becomes nonnormal when $\sigma_X$ must be estimated from the sample. But if the assumptions of Section 13.8 are met, $\overline{X}$ will be normally distributed regardless of the sample size. However, the position of $\overline{X}$ is not evaluated directly; rather, it is the value of the statistic $t = (\overline{X} - \mu_X)/s_{\overline{X}}$. Although $\overline{X}$ is *normally distributed, the resulting value of* t *is not,* for the reason cited previously. Indeed, $\overline{X}$ *must* be normally distributed for Student's distribution to be exactly applicable.

## 13.11 Characteristics of Student's Distribution of *t*

What are the characteristics of Student's sampling distribution of $t$? When samples are large, the values of $s_{\overline{X}}$ will be close to that of $\sigma_{\overline{X}}$, and $t$ will be much like $z$. Consequently, its distribution will be very nearly normal. In fact, if the samples are large enough and we persist in using the normal-curve model, no great harm is done (with an infinitely large sample, $t = z$). On the other hand, when the sample size is small,

---

[1]The sampling distribution of $s_{\overline{X}}$ tends to be positively skewed.

the values of $s_{\bar{X}}$ will vary substantially about $\sigma_{\bar{X}}$. The distribution of $t$ will then depart considerably from that of the normally distributed $z$.

It is becoming clear that *Student's distribution of t is not a single distribution but rather a family of distributions.* The members of the family differ in their degree of approximation to the normal curve. The exact shape of a particular member of the family depends on the sample size or, more accurately, on the number of **degrees of freedom (df)**, a quantity closely related to sample size. For problems of inference about single means, $df = n - 1$. We will explain the concept of degrees of freedom in greater detail in the next section.

When the number of degrees of freedom is less than infinite, the theoretical distribution of $t$ and the normal distribution $z$ are alike in some ways and different in others. They are alike in that both distributions

**degrees of freedom (df)** the number of observations that are completely free to vary; for the variance or standard deviation, $df = n - 1$ (see Section 13.12)

1. Have a mean of zero.
2. Are symmetrical.
3. Are unimodal.

The two distributions differ in that the distribution of $t$

1. Is *platykurtic* compared to the normal distribution (i.e., it is narrower at the peak and has a greater concentration in the tails than does a normal curve).
2. Has a larger standard deviation (remember that $\sigma_Z = 1$).
3. Depends on the number of degrees of freedom.

Figure 13.8 illustrates this last point. It shows the normalized $z$ distribution, and, in contrast, Student's distribution of $t$ for $df = 4$, $df = 12$, and $df = \infty$.

The ways in which Student's $t$ differ from the normal $z$ have an important consequence in statistical inference. For example, if we test a null hypothesis at $\alpha = .05$, the critical value of $z$ is $\pm 1.96$. The tails of the $t$ distribution descend less rapidly to the horizontal axis than do those of the normal distribution. Therefore, in the $t$ distribution, it will be necessary to go to a more extreme location to find the point beyond which .025 of the area (in one tail) falls, as Figure 13.8 shows.

How much larger $t$ must be than $z$ to correspond to the same rarity of occurrence depends on the sample size (or, more accurately, on the number of degrees of freedom). Look at Table 13.3. It shows, for selected values of $df$, the critical magnitude

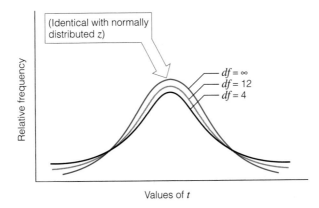

**FIGURE 13.8** The distribution of Student's $t$ for three levels of degrees of freedom.

**TABLE 13.3** *Critical Values for Student's Distribution of* t *for* $\alpha = .05$ *and Selected Degrees of Freedom*

| df | 5 | 10 | 25 | 50 | 100 | 500 | $\infty$ |
|-----|------|------|------|------|------|------|------|
| $t_{.05}$ | $\pm 2.571$ | $\pm 2.228$ | $\pm 2.060$ | $\pm 2.008$ | $\pm 1.984$ | $\pm 1.965$ | $\pm 1.960$ |

of *t* corresponding to a two-tailed test conducted according to the decision criterion $\alpha = .05$. Note that

1. For an infinite number of degrees of freedom, the critical magnitude of *t* is the same as the critical magnitude of *z*: $+1.96$.

2. The smaller the number of degrees of freedom, the larger the critical magnitude of *t*.

3. The behavior of *t* is very similar to that of *z* until the number of degrees of freedom drops below 100.

4. As the number of degrees of freedom decreases, the change in Student's distribution of *t*, slight at first, progresses at an increasingly rapid rate.

Be sure to distinguish between values of *t* calculated from sets of data and the theoretical distribution of *t*. Just as calculated values of *z* follow the normal distribution only under certain conditions, so calculated values of *t* follow Student's distribution of *t* only when certain assumptions are met. The necessary conditions are exactly the same as for the normal-curve model, except that we do not need to know the population standard deviation.

## 13.12 Degrees of Freedom and Student's Distribution of *t*

In general, the degrees of freedom associated with a quantity like *s*, the estimated standard deviation of a population, corresponds to the number of observations that are completely free to vary. One might at first suppose that this would be the same as the number of scores in the sample, but often conditions exist that impose restrictions such that the number of degrees of freedom is smaller. We will illustrate the concept of degrees of freedom in connection with the calculation of *s*.

Suppose a sample consists of three scores: $X_1$, $X_2$, and $X_3$. If we calculate $s_X$ by the deviation-score formula, $s_X = \sqrt{\Sigma(X - \overline{X})^2/(n - 1)}$, the value of $s_X$ will be determined by the values of the three deviation scores: $(X_1 - \overline{X})$, $(X_2 - \overline{X})$, and $(X_3 - \overline{X})$. Now only two (any two) of the deviation scores are free to vary. We could, if we wish, arbitrarily assign $(X_1 - \overline{X})$ the value $+3$ and $(X_2 - \overline{X})$ the value $-7$. But as soon as two of the three have been given numerical values, the third is no longer free to vary. Do you remember from Chapter 5 that *the sum of deviations taken about the mean is always zero*? (See Section 5.5 and Note 5.1.) In other words, $\Sigma(X - \overline{X}) = 0$. So as soon as the first two deviations are assigned, the third must be a value such that the three deviations sum to zero. In our numerical example, the value of $(X_3 - \overline{X})$ must be $+4$.

For a variance estimate made from a single sample, there will be *n* deviations. All but one of them will be free to vary; the last will be determined by the constraint that $\Sigma(X - \overline{X}) = 0$. The number of degrees of freedom in a problem involving the calculation of $s$ is therefore $n - 1$. (For other kinds of problems, $df$ may be different.)

## 13.13 Using Student's Distribution of *t*

$$t = \frac{\overline{X} - \mu_{hyp}}{s_{\overline{X}}}$$

formula for $t$ required for testing a null hypothesis about a single population mean

The theoretical distribution of $t$ appears in Table D in Appendix E. When using this table, remember that the area under a given distribution of $t$ is taken to be 1.00, just as in the normal-curve table. The table makes no distinction between negative and positive values of $t$ because the area falling above a given positive value of $t$ is the same as the area falling below the same negative value.

When testing hypotheses about the mean, you find the critical value of $t$ in Table D at the intersection of the row corresponding to the appropriate degrees of freedom (given at the left of the table) and the column corresponding to the appropriate level of significance for each tail (given at the top of the table). Here are two examples:

**Problem 1**   When $df = 20$ and $\alpha = .05$, what values of $t$ differentiate the regions of rejection from the region of retention? Assume that we wish to discover a difference (if one exists) irrespective of direction.

**Solution**   We must identify the values of $t$ such that the central 95% of the obtained $t$s will be included within these limits. These are (1) the value of $t$ below which 2.5% of the $t$s will be located and (2) the value of $t$ above which 2.5% of the $t$s will be located. The requisite magnitude of $t$ is found under the heading *Area in one tail* = .025. For $df = 20$ the value is $t = \pm 2.086$. The problem is illustrated in Figure 13.9.

It should be clear that the distribution of $t$ may be interpreted as a probability distribution, just as may be done with the normal distribution. For example, when $df = 20$ and sampling is random, the probability of obtaining a value of $t$ exceeding the limits $\pm 2.086$ is .05.

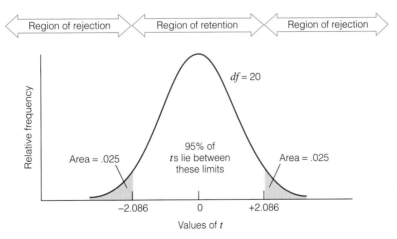

**FIGURE 13.9**   Student's distribution: Values of $t$ for $df = 20$ between which the central 95% of $t$s will fall.

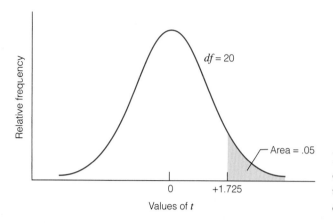

**FIGURE 13.10** The value of $t$ for $df = 20$ that corresponds to area in the upper tail of Student's distribution $= .05$.

**Problem 2**   Assuming random sampling, when $df = 20$, what value of $t$ is so high that the probability of obtaining one as high or higher is .05?

**Solution**   Consult Table D and identify the row corresponding to $df = 20$. Then find the column corresponding to *Area in one tail* = .05. At the intersection of this row and column, read the entry of $t = 1.725$. In effect, we are looking for the 95th percentile point of the $t$ distribution, so its value is positive: $t = +1.725$. This is illustrated in Figure 13.10.

## 13.14 An Example: Professor Dyett's Question

Professor Dyett, director of Health at the local university, believes that students at her campus are very health-conscious and as a result consume less sugar than do most people living in the United States. She knows that the average person in the United States eats 100 lbs. of sugar a year, mostly in the form of soft drinks, candy, and pastries (Whitney & Nunnelley, 1987).

To test her belief, Professor Dyett decides to draw a random sample of 25 students presently enrolled at the university and determine the quantity of sugar consumed by each during a 2-week period. Yearly sugar consumption will be calculated by multiplying the 2-week total by 26. Her research question leads to a statistical hypothesis to be tested, she decides, at the .05 level of significance:

$$H_0: \mu_X = 100$$

Although Professor Dyett believes that students at her campus consume less sugar than normal, she would also want to know if they are consuming more sugar. Thus, her alternative hypothesis is expressed as

$$H_A: \mu_X \neq 100$$

The mean yearly consumption of sugar by her sample of 25 students turns out to be 80 lbs. Would drawing a sample with this or a more extreme mean be likely if the null hypothesis is true?

To answer this question, she must estimate the standard error of the mean from her sample data and convert $\overline{X}$ to a $t$ value. Let us assume that $s_X$ proves to be 35.5. Thus,

$$s_{\overline{X}} = \frac{s_X}{\sqrt{n}} = \frac{35.5}{\sqrt{25}} = 7.1$$

and

$$t = \frac{\overline{X} - \mu_{\text{hyp}}}{s_{\overline{X}}} = \frac{80 - 100}{7.1} = -2.82$$

What does a $t$ value of $-2.82$ indicate? It means that Professor Dyett's sample mean was 2.82 estimated standard error of the mean units less than the value stated in $H_0$. The number of degrees of freedom is $n - 1 = 24$. For $\alpha = .05$, the critical value of $t$ is the one that in each tail of the distribution divides the outer 2.5% of the area from the remainder. From Table D in Appendix E, we see that the critical value is $\pm 2.064$. In other words, if the null hypothesis is true (that $\mu_X = 100$), only 5% of all possible sample means would differ by as much as 2.064 estimated standard errors of the mean. Figure 13.11 shows the sampling distribution of $\overline{X}$ (for when $H_0$ is true), the region of rejection, and the location of the calculated value of $t$.

Professor Dyett's sample data lead her to reject the null hypothesis and accept the alternative. However, this is just the statistical decision (see Section 1.5). Based on this, Professor Dyett can now reach a research conclusion. For example, she may conclude that the increased attention given to health-related issues has led to a decrease in sugar consumption at her campus.

Professor Dyett cannot be certain that students at her campus consume less sugar than other Americans. She would have to survey the entire student population at her campus to be 100% certain. Inferential statistics, you recall, only deals with probabilities. What inferential statistics says here is that a sample mean of 80 was *unlikely* to occur in random sampling from a population with a mean of 100.

However, even if Professor Dyett's statistical conclusion is correct (let us assume that mean sugar consumption at her school really is less than the national mean), it

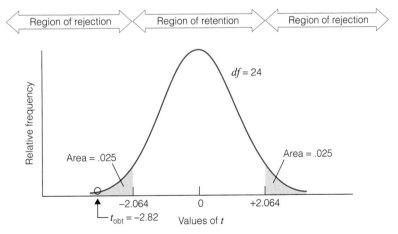

**FIGURE 13.11**   Testing a hypothesis about $\mu_X$ against a nondirectional alternative; $\alpha = .05$.

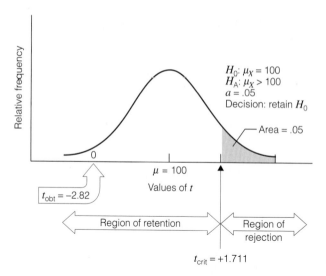

**FIGURE 13.12** Location of regions of retention and rejection when $H_A$ is $\mu_X > 100$; $\alpha = .05$.

**statistical conclusion**

a conclusion about the numerical property of the data (reject or retain $H_0$)

**research conclusion**

a conclusion about the subject matter

does not mean that her research conclusion is correct. Rather than being very health-conscious, students at her campus may consume less sugar because they are less able to afford soft drinks, candy, and pastries than are most other Americans. Be sure to review Section 1.5 to appreciate the difference between a **statistical conclusion** and a **research conclusion**.

Recall from Section 13.7 that sometimes a directional alternative hypothesis is better suited to the problem at hand. If Professor Dyett had been concerned *only* with the possibility that students at her campus consume *more* sugar than most people and that she might therefore have to overhaul her campus health programs, she might have adopted the alternative hypothesis $H_A$: $\mu_X > 100$ and used a one-tailed test. She would have placed the entire region of rejection in the *right* tail of the sampling distribution rather than dividing it between the two tails. Then, she would have rejected $H_0$: $\mu_X = 100$ only in the face of evidence that $\mu_X$ is greater than 100. Figure 13.12 shows how the test would have been conducted. If $\alpha = .05$, the critical

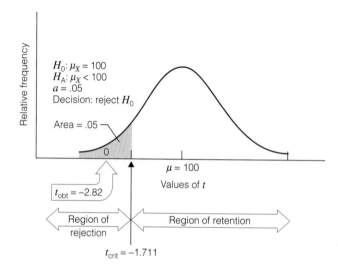

**FIGURE 13.13** Location of regions of retention and rejection when $H_A$ is $\mu_X < 100$; $\alpha = .05$.

value of $t$ is $+1.711$. Professor Dyett's calculated value of $t$ $(-2.82)$ does not fall in the region of rejection, so her decision must be to retain $H_0$.

Suppose, however, that Professor Dyett had only been interested in knowing if the students at her school consumed less sugar than most people. In that case, she would have adopted the alternative hypothesis $H_A: \mu_X < 100$, and the region of rejection would have been placed entirely in the *left* tail of the distribution. This is illustrated in Figure 13.13. In this event, her sample mean falls in the region of rejection. Remember, *the choice between a nondirectional or directional alternative hypothesis should be determined by the rationale that gives rise to the study and should be made before the data are gathered.*

## 13.15 Computing *t* from Raw Scores

In the real world, we are not given $s_X$; we must calculate it from our sample data. Of course, computers can perform all of these operations for you, but there may be occasions when you do not have access to a computer and you have to calculate $t$ by hand. A computational formula for computing $t$ from raw sample data can easily be derived from Formula 13.4 as follows. From Section 13.10, Formula 13.4,

$$t = \frac{\overline{X} - \mu_{hyp}}{s_{\overline{X}}}$$

From Section 13.9,

$$t = \frac{\overline{X} - \mu_{hyp}}{s_X/\sqrt{n}}$$

Therefore,

$$t = \frac{\overline{X} - \mu_{hyp}}{\sqrt{\dfrac{SS_X}{n-1}}\Big/\sqrt{n}} = \frac{\overline{X} - \mu_{hyp}}{\sqrt{\dfrac{\sum(X - \overline{X})^2}{n-1}}\Big/\sqrt{n}}$$

In Section 6.6, we learned that the raw-score method (Formula 6.4) is generally easier to use when calculating the sum of squares (SS). Thus,

$$t = \frac{\overline{X} - \mu_{hyp}}{\sqrt{\dfrac{SS_X}{n-1}}\Big/\sqrt{n}} = \frac{\overline{X} - \mu_{hyp}}{\sqrt{\dfrac{\sum X^2 - \dfrac{\left(\sum X\right)^2}{n}}{n-1}}\Big/\sqrt{n}}$$

Because both parts of the denominator are under a square root sign, we can express all of it as one square root:

$$t = \frac{\overline{X} - \mu_{hyp}}{\sqrt{\dfrac{SS_X}{n(n-1)}}}$$

computational formula for $t$ for testing a null hypothesis about a single mean

COMPUTATIONAL FORMULA FOR *t* FOR TESTING
HYPOTHESES ABOUT SINGLE MEANS

$$t = \frac{\overline{X} - \mu_{hyp}}{\sqrt{\dfrac{SS_X}{n(n-1)}}} \tag{13.5}$$

Do not lose sight of the fact that the denominator in Formula 13.5 is the same as that in Formula 13.4, both are the estimated standard error of the mean.

We will now illustrate the use of Formula 13.5 with an example. Suppose the claim has been made that the height of adult males is different from what it used to be and we wish to test this hypothesis. A campus–wide survey made 20 years ago found that the mean height of freshman males was 69.5 in. (The data are hypothetical.) The research question is then translated into a statistical hypothesis to be tested at $\alpha = .05$:

$$H_0: \mu_X = 69.5$$

$$H_A: \mu_X \neq 69.5$$

$$\alpha = .05$$

To study the question, we select at random 15 males of the same age from the current freshman class and measure their height to the nearest one-half inch. The data appear in Table 13.4 (①). The mean of the 15 measurements proves to be 70.4 (②). Because the population standard deviation is not available, we must estimate the standard error of the mean according to Formula 13.3 (③). It proves to be 0.71. Our calculated value of $t$ is $+1.27$ (④). Thus, our sample mean of 70.4 is 1.27 estimated standard error of the mean units greater than 69.5.

TABLE 13.4   *Calculation of* t *from the Computational Formula*

| ①<br>HEIGHT $(X)$ | $X^2$ | |
|---|---|---|
| 65.0 | 4225.00 | ③ Calculation of $s_{\bar{X}}$: |
| 67.5 | 4556.25 | |
| 68.0 | 4624.00 | |
| 68.5 | 4692.25 | |
| 69.0 | 4761.00 | $s_{\bar{X}} = \sqrt{\dfrac{\sum X^2 - \dfrac{(\sum X)^2}{n}}{n(n-1)}}$ |
| 69.5 | 4830.25 | |
| 69.5 | 4830.25 | |
| 70.0 | 4900.00 | |
| 71.0 | 5041.00 | |
| 71.5 | 5112.25 | $= \sqrt{\dfrac{74{,}447.5 - \dfrac{(1056)^2}{15}}{15(14)}}$ |
| 71.5 | 5112.25 | |
| 72.5 | 5256.25 | |
| 72.5 | 5256.25 | $= \sqrt{\dfrac{74{,}447.5 - 74{,}342.4}{210}}$ |
| 74.5 | 5550.25 | |
| 75.5 | 5700.25 | $= \sqrt{0.50}$ |
| $\sum X = 1056$ | $\sum X^2 = 74{,}447.5$ | $= .71$ |

② $\bar{X} = 70.4$

Calculation of $t$:

④ $t = \dfrac{\bar{X} - \mu_{\text{hyp}}}{s_{\bar{X}}} = \dfrac{70.4 - 69.5}{.71} = +1.27$

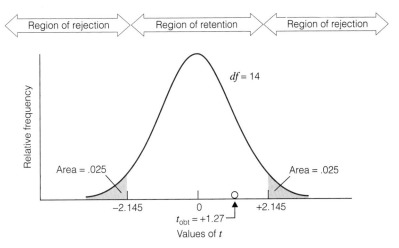

**FIGURE 13.14**   Testing a hypothesis about $\mu_X$ against a nondirectional alternative; $\alpha = .05$.

Our estimate of the standard error of the mean, $s_{\overline{X}}$, was based on 15 observations, so $df = n - 1 = 14$. For $\alpha = .05$ (2.5% in each tail), the critical value of $t$ (from Table D in Appendix E) is $t = \pm 2.145$. Figure 13.14 shows the critical value of $t$, the region of rejection thereby established, and the location of the calculated value of $t$. Because the sample mean of 70.4 is not sufficiently discrepant to lead to a $t$ of 2.145 or larger, our decision will be to retain $H_0$.

Remember, retaining $H_0$ does not mean that we necessarily believe it to be true. Therefore, we cannot conclude that the heights of freshman males on our campus have not changed in the past 20 years. However, it is proper to say that our sample data do not support the claim that freshman male heights have changed.

## 13.16 Levels of Significance versus *p*-Values

**p-value**

the probability, when $H_0$ is true, of observing a sample mean as deviant or more deviant (in the direction specified in $H_A$) than the obtained value of $\overline{X}$

Alpha ($\alpha$) is the probability of rejecting $H_0$ when $H_0$ is true. We reject $H_0$ if $\overline{X}$ falls in the region of rejection based on that level of significance. Although experimenters *should* choose the decision criterion *in advance* of conducting the test (by considering the risk they are willing to take of committing such an error when the sample is drawn), most do not explicitly report the level of significance they chose to use. In fact, some investigators do not always have a precise level of significance in mind prior to examining their results. However, in these cases it can be assumed that the level of significance was no higher than .05, the least stringent criterion allowed by most psychology and educational journals.

Although many investigators do not report their selected level of significance, they do report *p*-values. A **p-value** is the probability, when $H_0$ is true, of observing a sample result as deviant or more deviant (in the direction specified in $H_A$) than the result actually obtained. It is not established in advance and is not a statement of risk; it simply describes the rarity of the sample outcome if $H_0$ is true.

Look, for example, at Dr. Brown's results for a sample of 100 sixth-grade mathematics achievement scores (Section 13.5). Dr. Brown's obtained sample mean of 90.0

is 2.50 standard errors of the mean greater than the expected value (85.0) if the null hypothesis is true. Only .62% of all the scores in a normal distribution fall at or beyond a score that is 2.50 standard errors above the mean. Thus, for a two-tailed test the probability of obtaining a sample mean that far beyond the hypothesized mean if $H_0$ is true is $p = 0.62 + 0.62 = 1.24\%$. Because this was less than Dr. Brown's selected level of significance, she rejected $H_0$ and accepted $H_A$. *If the p-value is less than or equal to the level of significance, the sample result is considered sufficiently rare to call for rejecting* $H_0$.

Investigators seldom report their sample *p*-values as exact figures. Instead, they commonly report them relative to the landmarks of .05 and .01—and sometimes .001. If an investigator considers his or her result to be a **significant result** (i.e., $H_0$ is to be rejected), the *p*-value is commonly reported as falling below the landmark, whereas if the result is considered nonsignificant, it will be reported as falling above the landmark. Here are some examples:

**significant result**

an obtained sample statistic ($\overline{X}$) that has a low probability of occurring by chance if $H_0$ is true

|  | REPORTED $p$-VALUE | |
| --- | --- | --- |
|  | *Investigator considers the results to be* | |
| **EXACT $p$-VALUE** | *Significant* | *Nonsignificant* |
| .003 | $p < .01$ | — |
| .03 | $p < .05$ | $p > .01$ |
| .08 | — | $p > .05$ |

In actual research reports, where it is customary to state the obtained statistic (e.g., $t_{calc}$) and the associated *p*-value, look closely to see if one-tailed or two-tailed probabilities are intended.

The terminology used by some investigators in describing their results can be quite confusing and can blur the distinction between the *p*-value and the level of significance. An investigator may, for example, report that one set of results was "significant at the .01 level," a second set was "significant at the .001 level," and a third "did not reach significance at the .05 level." Does this mean that $\alpha = .01$, $\alpha = .001$, and $\alpha = .05$, respectively, were used for evaluating the three sets of results? Almost assuredly not. This is just a way of reporting three *p*-values: $p < .01$, $p < .001$, and $p > .05$. Chances are that the level of significance the investigator had in mind, although not explicitly stated, would be the same for evaluating all three sets of results, say, .05.

## 13.17 Summary

To test a hypothesis about a single population mean using the normal curve model:

**Step 1:** Define the target population.

**Step 2:** Specify the null hypothesis, the statistical hypothesis to be tested ($H_0$). It is always a hypothesis about the population (e.g., $H_0$: $\mu_X = 100$) and is chosen according to the research question to be studied. The researcher usually hopes to reject $H_0$.

**Step 3:** Specify the alternative hypothesis ($H_A$). We must choose between a directional and a nondirectional alternative, depending on the rationale of the research inquiry.

**Step 4:** Specify the level of significance ($\alpha$) to be used as the criterion for decision and determine the $z$-score value or values that differentiate the region(s) of rejection from the region of retention in the sampling distribution of $\overline{X}$.

**Step 5:** Decide on $n$ and draw a random sample of that size from the specified population.

**Step 6:** Calculate $\overline{X}$ and $\sigma_{\overline{X}}$.

**Step 7:** Calculate in $z$-score terms the position of $\overline{X}$ in the sampling distribution of the mean that would result when sampling from a population about which $H_0$ is true:

$$z = \frac{\overline{X} - \mu_{\text{hyp}}}{\sigma_{\overline{X}}} = \frac{\text{obtained sample mean} - \text{hypothesized population mean}}{\text{standard error of the mean}} \text{ (when } H_0 \text{ is true)}$$

**Step 8:** Reject $H_0$ if $\overline{X}$ is located in the region of rejection; otherwise retain $H_0$.

The discrepancy between $\overline{X}$ and $\mu_{\text{hyp}}$ depends on random variation and, when the null hypothesis is false, on the additional discrepancy between $\mu_{\text{hyp}}$ and $\mu_{\text{true}}$. Random variation (due to random sampling) is reduced by increasing the sample size.

Although the level of significance should be decided on before any data are collected, many investigators fail to report their $\alpha$ level and instead report only the $p$-values—the probability of the sample outcome if $H_0$ is true. In these cases, it is usually safe to assume that the level of significance was no higher than .05.

To test hypotheses about the population mean using $z$, we must know the population standard deviation, $\sigma_X$, to calculate the standard error of the mean, $\sigma_{\overline{X}}$. In actuality, we seldom know the value of $\sigma_X$. Without $\sigma_X$, we do the next best thing and estimate it from our sample data. However, the sample standard deviation is biased; it tends to underestimate the population parameter. We can obtain a better estimate of $\sigma_X$ by dividing the sample sum of squares, $\Sigma(X - \overline{X})^2$, by $n - 1$ instead of $n$. This gives us $s_X$. When $s_X$ is then divided by $\sqrt{n}$, the result is the estimated standard error of the mean, $s_{\overline{X}}$.

When we substitute $s_{\overline{X}}$ for $\sigma_{\overline{X}}$ in the formula for $z$, the result is no longer $z$ but a new variable called $t$:

$$t = \frac{\overline{X} - \mu_{\text{hyp}}}{s_{\overline{X}}} = \frac{\text{obtained sample mean} - \text{hypothesized population mean}}{\text{estimated standard error of the mean}} \text{ (when } H_0 \text{ is true)}$$

Although $\overline{X}$ is normally distributed when certain conditions are met (mainly random sampling), $t$ is not. There is a whole family of $t$ distributions, with the shape of each one depending on the number of degrees of freedom. For hypotheses about single means, $df = n - 1$. The most important difference between $z$ and $t$ is that there is a greater concentration of area in the tails of $t$ distributions. Thus, it takes a larger deviation from expectation ($\overline{X} - \mu_{\text{hyp}}$) to reject $H_0$ using $t$. However, as sample size increases, the $t$ distributions more closely resemble the $z$ distribution.

# Mathematical Notes

### Note 13.1 Further Comments on Unbiased Estimates of $\sigma^2$
(*Ref.*: Section 13.9)

The variance of a population of scores is given by Formula 6.2*a*

$$\frac{\sum_{}^{N}(X - \mu_X)^2}{N}$$

where $N$ is the number of scores in the population. The best unbiased estimate of this quantity (made from a sample) is:

$$\sigma^2_{X(\text{est})} = \frac{\sum_{}^{n}(X - \mu_X)^2}{n}$$

Note that the deviation of each score in the sample is taken from $\mu_X$. You can demonstrate for yourself that this estimate is unbiased by calculating variance estimates according to this formula for each of the 16 samples shown in Table 13.2. You will find that the mean of the 16 estimates is 5.0, precisely the value of $\sigma^2_X$.

When $\mu_X$ is unknown, it becomes necessary to take the deviation of each score from its own sample mean: $\sum_{}^{n}(X - \overline{X})^2$. Recall (Section 6.9) that the sum of the squares of deviation scores is a minimum when the deviations are taken from the mean of *that set of scores,* that is, $\overline{X}$. But we should, if we could, compute $\sum_{}^{n}(X - \mu_X)^2$. Because $\overline{X}$ and $\mu_X$ will not ordinarily be identical, $\sum_{}^{n}(X - \overline{X})^2 < \sum_{}^{n}(X - \mu_X)^2$, and therefore $S^2_X < \sigma^2_{X(\text{est})}$. To obtain an unbiased estimate of $\sigma^2_X$, $\sum_{}^{n}(X - \overline{X})^2$ must be divided by $n - 1$ rather than by $n$. This adjustment is incorporated in Formula 13.2:

$$s^2_X = \frac{\sum_{}^{n}(X - \overline{X})^2}{n - 1}$$

It is tempting to think that $S^2$ tends to underestimate $\sigma^2$ because, when sampling from a normal distribution, very deviant scores are less likely to be present in any particular small sample than in a large one. Like most temptations, this one should be resisted. Although the *number* of rare scores is expected to be less in small samples, their *proportional frequency* of occurrence is unaltered if sampling is random. Also, the shape of the population sampled is fundamentally irrelevant. Underestimation stems from use of $\overline{X}$ rather than $\mu_X$ as the point about which deviations are taken.

One interesting point remains. Although $s^2$ is an unbiased estimator of $\sigma^2$, $s$ still tends to underestimate $\sigma$ (because a square root is not a linear transformation); however, $s$ is an improved estimate. This does not cause important trouble in testing hypotheses about means. First, the degree of underestimation is quite small for samples in which $n > 10$. Second, when the sample size is small, the procedures of this chapter take *exact* account of the substitution of $s$ for $\sigma$, so no error is involved.

# Key Terms, Concepts, and Symbols

statistical inference   (212, 232)

random sampling distribution
   of $\overline{X}$   (216, 233)

null hypothesis   (233)

$H_0$   (233)

alternative hypothesis   (234)

$H_A$   (234)

level of significance   (234)

$\alpha$   (234)

region(s) of rejection   (235)

region of retention   (235)

critical value(s)   (235)

rejecting the null hypothesis
   (238)

retaining the null hypothesis
   (238)

nondirectional (two-tailed)
   test   (239)

directional (one-tailed)
   test   (239)

observer bias   (242)

unbiased estimator   (243)

$s_{\overline{X}}^2, s_X$   (244)

estimated standard error of the
   mean   (245)

$s_{\overline{X}}$   (245)

$t$   (245)

Student's distribution of $t$
   (246)

degrees of freedom   (247)

$df$   (247)

statistical conclusion   (6, 252)

research conclusion   (6, 252)

p-value   (255)

significant result   (256)

# Problems

$\boxed{c}$ *26, 28, 30*

1. State whether each of the following could be a null hypothesis: (a) $\mu_X \neq 12$; (b) $\overline{X} > 345$; (c) $\overline{X} = 67$; (d) $\mu_X < 89$; (e) $\overline{X} < 123$; (f) $\mu_X = 45$; (g) $\mu_X > 678$; (h) $\overline{X} \neq 910$.

2. State whether each of the items in Problem 1 could be an alternative hypothesis, and if so, whether it would indicate a one-tailed or a two-tailed test.

3. For each of the following situations, state the appropriate null and alternative hypotheses. (a) On a placement test of verbal skills, the freshman class at a certain college typically attains a mean of 82% correct. Because of new admissions policies, we suspect that the incoming class will differ, and we want to give ourselves a chance to discover whether their verbal skills are, on average, better or worse. (b) We wish to know whether an experimental drug lowers the cholesterol level in a population of elderly men whose mean level is normally 210. If the drug has no effect or if it backfires and raises the level, we would cease testing the drug. (c) A restaurant has kept records of the "liquor mix," which is the percentage of a party's bill that comes from the alcoholic drinks the party purchased. Over the past 2 years, the average has been 24%. Now the profit margin on drinks has increased and management has instituted a new policy: waiters and waitresses whose liquor mix is at or below 24% will be fired. To assess an employee's performance, management will inspect a random sample of the checks from his or her tables over the next month.

4. Why should the choice of a one- or two-tailed test be made before the data are gathered?

5. Why is it inadequate to choose a one-tailed test on the basis that we expect the outcome to be in that direction?

6. In a two-tailed test conducted at the .01 level of significance, we have rejected the null hypothesis. Say whether each of the following is true or false. (a) The probability that the null hypothesis is false is .99. (b) The probability that the null hypothesis is true is .99. (c) The probability that we made the wrong decision on the null is .01. (d) The probability that we made the wrong decision on the null is .99. (e) If we always use the .01 level of significance in our hypothesis testing, over the long run, we will make a wrong decision on the null hypothesis 1% of the time. (f) If we always use the .01 level of significance, over the long run, we will make

the wrong decision on the null hypothesis on 1% of those occasions when we reject the null. (g) If we always use the .01 level of significance, over the long run, we will make a wrong decision on the null hypothesis on 1% of those occasions when we retain the null. (h) If we always use the .01 level of significance, over the long run, we will make a wrong decision on the null hypothesis on 1% of those occasions when the null is true. (i) If we always use the .01 level of significance, over the long run, we will make a wrong decision on the null hypothesis on 1% of those occasions when the null is false.

**7.** The meaning of "retaining $H_0$" is not exactly the opposite of "rejecting $H_0$." Explain.

**8.** An experimenter used $\alpha = .05$ for a statistical test and retained the null hypothesis. Would it be correct to say that the experimenter can be 95% sure that $H_0$ is true? Explain.

**9.** A researcher used $\alpha = .05$ for a statistical test and rejected the null hypothesis. Would it be correct to say that the researcher can be 95% confident that $H_0$ is false? Explain.

**10.** Some investigators have praised the use of small samples in hypothesis testing, saying that such usage is better for the development of their science. (a) Explain the merit of this position. (b) Explain the limitations and/or defects of this position.

**11.** Translate each of the following statements into symbolic form involving a $p$-value: (a) "The results did not reach significance at the .05 level." (b) "The sample mean fell significantly below 50 at the .01 level." (c) "The results were significant at the .001 level." (d) "The difference between the sample mean and the hypothesized value of 100 barely missed significance at the .05 level."

**12.** The symbolic expression "$p < .001$" occurs in the results section of a research report. Does this indicate that the investigator used the very conservative level of significance $\alpha = .001$ to evaluate the outcome of that particular test? Explain.

**13.** For the question posed by Dr. Brown, if the population standard deviation on the mathematics achievement test for sixth-grade students is 10, what will Dr. Brown conclude if she uses a two-tailed test at the .05 significance level and obtains a mean of 87.1 for her sample of 100 students?

**14.** For Problem 13, calculate the critical values of $\overline{X}$ in raw-score form.

**15.** You are given the following data: $\overline{X} = 63$, $\sigma_X = 12$, $n = 100$, $H_0$: $\mu_X = 60$, and $H_A$: $\mu_X \neq 60$. (a) Test the null hypothesis at the .05 significance level and state your conclusions. (b) Test the null hypothesis at the .01 significance level and state your conclusions. (c) What is the probability, in random sampling, of obtaining a mean of 63 or higher when samples of this size are drawn from a population in which $\mu = 60$? (d) Of obtaining a sample mean which differs by three points or more (in either direction) from $\mu_X = 60$?

**16.** Repeat parts (a) and (b) of Problem 15, but assume that the alternative hypothesis reads $H_A$: $\mu_X > 60$.

**17.** Assume the same data as are given in Problem 15. Suppose that the alternative hypothesis reads $H_A$: $\mu_X < 60$. Test the null hypothesis at the .05 significance level and state your conclusions.

**18.** The eighth-grade national norm for a social science test is a score of 123. The research director of a school district wants to know how the scores of pupils in his district compare with this standard. He selects a random sample of 81 students and finds that $\overline{X} = 117$. Assume $\sigma_X = 10$. (a) State the null hypothesis and alternative hypothesis best suited to the nature of his inquiry. Test the null hypothesis (b) at the .05 level of significance and state your conclusions and (c) at the .01 level of significance and state your conclusions. (d) What is the probability of obtaining through random sampling a sample mean as deviant (in either direction) from $\mu_X$ as his sample mean is?

**19.** From Table D in Appendix E, identify the value of $t$ that for 15 degrees of freedom is (a) so high that only 1% of $t$s would be higher and (b) so low that only 10% of $t$s would be lower.

**20.** From Table D, identify the centrally located limits for 8 degrees of freedom that would include (a) 50% of $t$s, (b) 90% of $t$s, (c) 95% of $t$s, and (d) 99% of $t$s.

**21.** From Table D, for 25 degrees of freedom what proportion of $t$s would be (a) less than $t = -1.316$? (b) Less than $t = +1.316$? (c) Greater than $t = +1.708$? (d) Greater than $t = -.684$? (e) Between $t = -2.060$

and $t = +2.060$? (f) Between $t = -1.708$ and $t = +2.060$?

**22.** From Table D, for 20 degrees of freedom what is the probability in random sampling of obtaining (a) $t \geq +2.6$; (b) $t \geq +1.8$; (c) $t \leq -1.9$; (d) $t = \pm 1.4$ or of greater magnitude; and (e) $t = \pm 2.2$ or of greater magnitude?

**23.** We adopt $\alpha = .05$ and test the hypothesis $H_0: \mu_X = 50$. What conclusion should we draw if (a) $n = 10$, $t_{calc} = +2.10$, and $H_A: \mu_X \neq 50$? (b) $n = 20$, $t_{calc} = +2.10$, and $H_A: \mu_X \neq 50$? (c) $n = 10$, $t_{calc} = +2.10$, and $H_A: \mu_X > 50$? Show the critical value of $t$ for each part.

**24.** Given the following scores: 2, 4, 4, 7, 8. (a) Calculate $s_X$ by the raw-score formula. (b) Calculate $t$ required to test $H_0: \mu_X = 8.0$ versus $H_A: \mu_X \neq 8.0$. (c) Evaluate $t$ for $\alpha = .05$ and state your conclusions. (d) Evaluate $t$ for $\alpha = .01$ and state your conclusions.

**25.** The national mean for the English component of the ACT test is 18.9. You wish to compare how students at your school perform on this test. You randomly select a sample of 25 students and obtain the following results: $\overline{X} = 16.1$, $s_X = 5.2$. (a) State formally the hypotheses necessary to conduct a nondirectional test. (b) Determine the critical value of $t(\alpha = .05)$. (c) Calculate $t$. (d) What do you conclude?

**26.** The PTA at Central High School is concerned that students who graduate from the school do not score as well on mathematics achievement tests, on average, as do students from other schools in the district. To address their concerns, the school principal randomly selects 15 students from the graduating class and administers the standardized mathematics achievement test used in that school district. The mean score for graduating students in the school district is 98. The scores of the 15 students from Central High are as follows:

105  98    101  110  96    103  104  101
98    105  112  95    105  100  108

(a) State formally the hypotheses necessary to conduct a nondirectional test. (b) Complete the test at the .05 level of significance and state your conclusion.

**27.** (a) For the data in Problem 26, state $H_A$ if a one-tailed test had been used to address

the concerns of the PTA. (b) What would you have concluded with this one-tailed test? Explain.

**28.** A new brand of automobile tire is advertised to outlast the leading brand, which has a mean lifetime of 80,000 miles. A consumer agency randomly selects six tires from the manufacturer's first production run and tests the tires on a machine that guarantees even tread wear. The results are as follows:

78,000  87,000  85,000  79,000  80,000  86,000

(a) State formally the hypotheses necessary to conduct a nondirectional test. (b) Determine the critical value of $t$ ($\alpha = .05$). (c) Calculate $t$. (d) State your conclusion. (Do these results cast doubt on the advertised claim?)

**29.** Another consumer agency tests (in exactly the same manner) tires from the same batch of tires tested by the agency in Problem 28. It randomly selects 25 tires and obtains $\overline{X} = 82,200$ and $s_X = 900$. (a) Calculate $t$. (b) What does the second consumer agency conclude ($\alpha = .05$)? (c) The mean mileage in the second test was less than in the first. How do you account for the different conclusions?

**30.** A training director for a large company has been told that, on completion of the training course, the average score of her trainees on the final evaluation should be 100. Her only concern is whether she will have to begin remedial steps to ensure that the population of trainees is not below standard. She draws a random sample of 10 scores of recent trainees: 94, 98, 101, 90, 86, 102, 95, 100, 98, and 92. (a) State the null and alternative hypotheses best suited to the nature of her inquiry. Test the null hypothesis (b) at the .05 level of significance and state your conclusions and (c) at the .01 level of significance and state your conclusions. (d) What is the probability of obtaining through random sampling a sample mean as low or lower if $\mu_X$ is as stated in the null hypothesis?

**31.** Look again at Table 13.2, which demonstrates that $s_X^2$ is an unbiased estimate of $\sigma_X^2$. (a) Calculate $\sigma_X$. (b) Calculate $s_X$ for each sample. (c) Calculate the mean of the 16 values of $s_X$. (d) Does the mean value of $s_X$ equal $\sigma_X$? Why is $s_X$ not an unbiased estimator of $\sigma_X$? (See Note 13.1).

# CHAPTER 14

## Interpreting the Results of Hypothesis Testing: Effect Size, Type I and Type II Errors, and Power

When you have finished studying this chapter, you should be able to:

- Understand that to say a result is statistically significant does not mean it is important;
- Calculate effect size and understand how it differs from a *p*-value;
- Discuss the two types of errors in hypothesis testing;
- Explain what is meant by the power of a test;
- List and discuss five factors that influence the power of a test;
- Estimate the sample size necessary to discover the smallest discrepancy (between $\mu_{\text{hyp}}$ and $\mu_{\text{true}}$), if it exists, that we are interested in; and
- Understand the limitations in drawing conclusions about a population if one does not use a random sample drawn from that population.

In Section 13.16 you learned that when the outcome of a statistical test is reported in research literature, it is common to see statements such as "the difference was not significant," "none of the tests were statistically significant," and "the outcome was significant at the .05 level." What does it mean, for example, to say that "the outcome was significant at the .05 level"? In the more exact language that you have recently learned, this usually means that a null hypothesis and an alternative hypothesis were formulated, the decision criterion was $\alpha = .05$, and the evidence from the sample led to rejection of the null hypothesis. Similarly, the phrase "not significant" implies that the null hypothesis could not be rejected.

**significant result**
an obtained sample statistic ($\overline{X}$) that has a low probability of occurring by chance if $H_0$ is true (and thus $H_0$ is rejected)

The use of the word *significant* in connection with statistical outcomes is unfortunate. In common English it implies "important." However, in statistics, a **significant result** means only that an obtained result had a low probability of occurring by chance (that is, the sample value was not within the limits of sampling variation expected under the null hypothesis). Whether the difference between what is hypothesized and what is true is large enough to be important is another matter.

# 14.1 A Statistically Significant Difference versus a Practically Important Difference

To test the hypothesis $H_0$: $\mu_X = 100$, we calculate $t$ as

$$t = \frac{\overline{X} - \mu_{\text{hyp}}}{s_X/\sqrt{n}}$$

If $t$ is large enough, the result will be statistically significant and we will reject the null hypothesis. Remember, as applied to the results of a statistical analysis, *significant* is a technical term with a precise meaning: It means that $H_0$ has been tested and rejected according to a given decision criterion—nothing more, nothing less.

Look again at the formula for $t$. You can see that the magnitude of $t$ depends both on the quantity in the numerator *and* on the quantity in the denominator. In the numerator, the difference between $\overline{X}$ and $\mu_{\text{hyp}}$ depends on random variation and, when the null hypothesis is false, on the difference between $\mu_{\text{hyp}}$ and $\mu_{\text{true}}$. Other things being equal, the larger the discrepancy between $\mu_{\text{hyp}}$ and $\mu_{\text{true}}$, the larger the value of $t$.

The denominator is a measurement only of random variation (due to random sampling). Ordinarily, if the sample size is very large, the denominator $s_X/\sqrt{n}$ will be quite small. In this event, a relatively small difference between $\overline{X}$ and $\mu_{\text{hyp}}$ may produce a value of $t$ large enough to lead us to reject the null hypothesis. In cases of this kind, we may have a result that is "statistically significant" but in which the difference between $\mu_{\text{true}}$ and $\mu_{\text{hyp}}$ is so small as to be unimportant.

Keep in mind that the end product of statistical inference is a conclusion about descriptors, such as $\mu$. Therefore, the simplest remedy is to examine them to evaluate the importance of a "significant" outcome. Look at how much difference exists between $\mu_{\text{hyp}}$ and the obtained sample mean. Is the size of the difference large enough that it matters?

Recall, for example, Dr. Brown's problem (Chapter 13). She asked if the mean mathematics achievement score of sixth-graders in her school district could be 85. To study this question, she drew a sample of 100 students. Suppose someone in the

U.S. Department of Education asked the same question about sixth-graders in general and drew a random sample of 10,000 students. If we assume that the estimated standard deviation of test scores is the same as the standard deviation in Dr. Brown's case (20), the estimated standard error of the mean is $s_{\overline{X}} = 20.0/\sqrt{10,000} = .20$. Adopting $\alpha = .05$ (as before), the Department of Education's researcher will reject the hypothesis that the mean is 85 if his or her calculated $t$ is 1.961 or larger. This value will be reached when the sample mean differs from $\mu_{\text{hyp}}$ by only about 0.39 points (i.e., an $\overline{X}$ of 85.39 or greater or 84.61 or smaller). Although a value this discrepant indicates that the mean of the population of sixth-graders is not 85, a difference of this order is probably not worth bothering about. We say "probably" because *the question of whether the size of the difference is important or not depends on the research question, not the statistical question.* For some research questions, a very small obtained difference between $\overline{X}$ and $\mu_{\text{hyp}}$ could have important consequences. On the other hand, if the research question is a trivial one, even a very large obtained difference between $\overline{X}$ and $\mu_{\text{hyp}}$ is of no practical importance.

**statistically significant result**
does not mean that the result is important

What about the statistical test when samples are quite small? In this case, the standard error of the mean will be relatively large, and it will be difficult to discover that the null hypothesis is false, if indeed it is, unless the difference between $\mu_{\text{true}}$ and $\mu_{\text{hyp}}$ is quite large. This suggests that an important consideration in experimental design is the size of the sample that should be drawn. We explore the question of importance and optimum sample size for tests of hypotheses about means in Section 14.11.

## 14.2 Effect Size

In 1986, *The New York Times* reported a study that found a "definite" link between children's height (adjusted for age and sex) and IQ. The study was conducted with 14,000 children and the results were "highly significant."

Do these results mean that you should run out and get growth hormone injections for yourself and your children? Before you do, consider the following. If you assume that "highly significant" means $p < .001$, with 14,000 subjects you need a correlation of only .0278 to reach this level of significance. (We discuss inference about correlation in Chapter 17.) If you further assume a causative relationship, with this low degree of relationship, raising your child's IQ from 100 to 130 would require that you inject enough growth hormone so that his or her height would increase by 14 feet (example and calculations from Cohen, 1990).

**p-value**
the probability, when $H_0$ is true, of observing a sample mean as deviant or more deviant (in the direction specified in $H_A$) than the obtained value of $\overline{X}$

This example demonstrates how foolish it is to rely exclusively on **p-values** when evaluating statistical results. With a large enough sample size, we can detect even a very small difference between the value of the population mean stated in the null hypothesis and the true value, but the difference may be of no practical importance. Conversely, with too small a sample size, a researcher may have little chance to detect an important difference.

How much of a difference between $\mu_{\text{hyp}}$ and $\mu_{\text{true}}$ is so great that we want to be reasonably certain of discovering it if one of this size or larger exists? To put it another way, some differences between $\mu_{\text{hyp}}$ and $\mu_{\text{true}}$ are so small that if the null hypothesis is falsely retained, the error is one that we would be willing to overlook. For example, suppose a school principal tests the null hypothesis that $\mu_{\text{IQ}} = 100$ for her population of school children. If she retains that hypothesis when the mean IQ of the

# Point of Controversy

## The Failure to Publish "Nonsignificant" Results

Because they are limited to a yes or no decision (null hypothesis rejected or null hypothesis retained), some researchers regard results with $p > .05$ as unimportant and those with $p < .05$ as important (and regard highly significant results, i.e., those with very low $p$-values, such as $p < .001$, as very important). Although textbooks strive to convince the novice that significance $\neq$ importance (rejecting the null hypothesis says nothing about the magnitude of the effect—the real difference between $\mu_{hyp}$ and $\mu_{true}$), journal editors have translated the yes–no statistical decision into publishable–nonpublishable, thereby bestowing a significant result with an even greater kind of importance. Doctoral degrees are delayed, academic positions and promotions are lost, and grant proposals remain unfunded all because researchers have obtained nonsignificant and, consequently, nonpublishable results.

The consequences to research of journals refusing to publish nonsignificant results are many. For one, this policy encourages the publication of "false positives." For example, if a null hypothesis is true and 20 researchers are independently testing it using $\alpha = .05$, by chance we would expect 1 of the 20 to obtain a significant difference. Though he or she has made an error, this result will probably end up in print while the remaining 19 remain buried in file drawers. The reader of scientific literature will know only of the former. How often this occurs is unknown, but it does happen. Recall from Chapter 1, for example, the studies with cannibal planaria (see Section 1.6).

You might think that the replication of results would serve as a safeguard against incorporating false positives into scientific theory. It would indeed, but journals also tend to emphasize original studies at the expense of replications (Rosnow & Rosenthal, 1989). In most journals, replications are rarely published (Mahoney, 1976; Sterling, 1959). This bias against replication was echoed by the director of the Federal Trade Commission's Bureau of Consumer Protection in 1982: "If additional substantiation will probably just confirm what the evidence already suggests, then added evidence will not be useful" (*Science*, December 24, 1982, p. 1292).

Another negative consequence of journals refusing to publish nonsignificant results is cheating. If a researcher's results fall just short of statistical significance (say, $p = .06$), because the rewards of publishing are high, there is a temptation to throw out or alter a few observations so that $p < .05$. This is commonly referred to as "fudging." There have been cases of researchers grossly altering data as well (see Section 1.6). While in graduate school, the second author witnessed a fellow student throw out half his control group because they were "not responding like normal control animals." The study was published.

Perhaps the biggest price humanity pays for this journal policy is that scientific theory is evolving through inductive inference achieved primarily by rejecting null hypotheses at the .05 level (Cohen, 1990). To counter this, the editor of the journal *Applied Psychological Measurement* offered a modest proposal (Weiss, 1989). Rather than submit finished manuscripts to journals, scientists and educators will submit detailed research designs in advance of collecting any data. Journal editors will then accept or reject the design. If they accept it, they will agree to publish the results even if they prove to be statistically nonsignificant.

266

From *How to Lie with Statistics,* by Darrell Huff, illustrated by Irving Geis. Copyright © 1954 and renewed © 1982 by Darrell Huff and Irving Geis. Used by permission of W. W. Norton & Company, Inc.

**effect size**
an estimate of the degree to which the treatment effect is present in the population, expressed as a "number . . . free of the original measurement unit" (Cohen, 1988)

**(Cohen's) *d***
a measure of effect size; expresses the difference between $\overline{X}$ and $\mu_{\text{hyp}}$ relative to the standard deviation of the population: $(\overline{X} - \mu_{\text{hyp}})/\sigma_X$

**(Hedges') *g***
a measure of effect size; expresses the difference between $\overline{X}$ and $\mu_{\text{hyp}}$ relative to $s_X$, the estimated population standard deviation: $(\overline{X} - \mu_{\text{hyp}})/s_X$

population is really 103, she might feel that the error is of no practical consequence. On the other hand, she would probably be quite unwilling to retain that hypothesis if the mean of the population is really 110.

Now it is fair to say that very likely all null hypotheses are false. The null hypothesis is stated as a point value, and it is most unlikely that any real population has, for example, a mean IQ of *exactly* 100. *The value of hypothesis testing is that it can be used to reveal discrepancies that are large enough that we care about them.*

The decision as to just how big a difference between $\mu_X$'s hypothesized value and its true value must be to be considered important is fundamentally a research question and not a statistical one. It can be made only by a person who knows the meaning of a given difference in the context of the question that gave rise to the study. For general use, it is convenient to express the magnitude of the difference between $\mu_{\text{hyp}}$ and $\mu_{\text{true}}$ in terms of the number of standard deviations of the measure under consideration (Cohen, 1965, 1988). We refer to such a measure as the **effect size**, symbolized as *d*. For tests of hypotheses about single means,

$$d = \frac{\mu_{\text{true}} - \mu_{\text{hyp}}}{\sigma} \tag{14.1}$$

For practical purposes the formula becomes $(\overline{X} - \mu_{\text{hyp}})/\sigma_X$.

Note that Cohen's *d* expresses the discrepancy relative to the standard deviation of the set of measures, not the standard error. If we do not know $\sigma$, which is almost always the case, we can estimate it by *s*, giving an estimated *d* called *g* (Hedges, 1981; Hedges & Olkin, 1985):

$$\text{estimated } d = g = \frac{\overline{X} - \mu_{\text{hyp}}}{s_X} \tag{14.2}$$

$$= \frac{\overline{X} - \mu_{\text{hyp}}}{\sqrt{\dfrac{SS_x}{n - 1}}}$$

As an example, look again at Professor Dyett's question (Section 13.14). Recall that $\mu_{hyp} = 100$, $\overline{X}_{obtained} = 80$, and $s_X = 35.5$. Thus, $g = (80 - 100)/35.5 = -.56$. If $g = -.56$, this means that the discrepancy between the true value and that hypothesized is estimated to be 0.56 of the standard deviation of the variable measured. The negative sign means that the true value is less than the hypothesized value.

These two measures (Cohen's *d* and Hedges' *g*) are members of what is called the *d* family of effect sizes. Today, many leading statisticians advocate the use of *r* for measuring effect size. We will introduce this family of effect sizes in Chapter 15.

Effect size does not tell us the same thing as a *p*-value. Highly significant *p*-values do not indicate that there is a large effect; the study of children's height and IQ with which this section opened is a good example of this. In that study, you recall, *p* was <.001, but because of the very large sample size, this level of significance could have been achieved with a correlation of only .0278. Conversely, in other studies a non-significant result may still be important as judged by the effect size.

> Convenient as it is to note that a hypothesis is contradicted at some familiar level of significance such as 5% or 2% or 1%, we do not . . . ever need to lose sight of the exact strength which the evidence has in fact reached. Ronald A. Fisher, 1960 (p. 25)

**effect size (*d* and *g*)**
useful convention: small = .2
medium = .5
large = .8

Jacob Cohen (1988, 1992) has suggested that *small, medium, and large effects may be defined as corresponding to values of* d *of .2, .5, and .8, respectively.* This view has been adopted by others as a useful convention for evaluating studies. However, it is best considered as a general rule of thumb; *importance can properly be judged only relative to the circumstances of the particular setting.*

Here is an example. In 1988, the steering committee of the Physicians' Health Study Research Group reported that one aspirin taken every day reduced the rate of heart attack in one group of doctors compared to another group that did not take aspirin. There were approximately 11,000 subjects in each group, and the obtained *r* of −.034 between taking aspirin and heart attacks was highly significant ($p < .00001$). The correlation is quite low and can account for only 0.1% of the variability in the results (Section 10.9). However, the effect size for this type of study (calculated differently from the single-group design in this chapter) was described as "far from unimpressive" (Rosnow & Rosenthal, 1989). The group that took aspirin had 72 fewer heart attacks and 13 fewer deaths. Generalized to the entire population, that means that the low-cost practice of taking an aspirin daily might result in thousands of fewer heart attacks each year.

In 1999, the American Psychological Association's Task Force on Statistical Inference (Wilkinson et al., 1999) stated that authors should "always present effect sizes for primary outcomes":

> We must stress again that reporting and interpreting effect sizes in the context of previously reported effects is essential to good research. It enables readers to evaluate the stability of results across samples, designs, and analyses. Reporting effect sizes also informs power analyses and meta-analyses needed in future research. (p. 599)

The fifth edition of the *Publication Manual of the American Psychological Association* (2001) also emphasizes the need for reporting effect size. The APA already required that authors provide the symbol of the statistic (such as *t*), the degrees of freedom, the alpha level selected, the obtained value of the statistic, and the *p*-value. It is probably only a matter of time before most journal editors require that persons submitting manuscripts include some estimated measure of the effect size (some editors already do require it). In the meantime, we urge you to include such measures in your reports. After all, the most important product of a statistical test is not whether or not one rejects the null hypothesis, which we all know is probably false anyway, but the magnitude of the difference between $\mu_{\text{hyp}}$ and $\mu_{\text{true}}$.

### I. The Problem

Oh, $t$ is large and $p$ is small
That's why we are walking tall.

What it means we need not mull
Just so we reject the null.

Or chi-square large and $p$ near nil
Results like that, they fill the bill.

What if meaning requires a poll?
Never mind, we're on a roll!

The message we have learned too well?
Significance! That rings the bell!

### II. The Implications

The moral of our little tale?
That we mortals may be frail
When we feel a $p$ near zero
Makes us out to be a hero.

But tell us then is it too late?
Can we perhaps avoid our fate?
Replace that wish to null-reject
Report the *size* of the effect.

That may not insure our glory
But at least it tells a story
That is just the kind of yield
Needed to advance our field.

ROBERT ROSENTHAL (1991)

From R. Rosenthal, "Cumulating psychology: An appreciation of Donald T. Campbell," *Psychological Science*, 2 (no. 2), 1991:213, 217–221. Copyright © 1991 by the American Psychological Society. Reprinted with permission of Cambridge University Press and the author.

## 14.3 Errors in Hypothesis Testing

There are, so to speak, two "states of nature": Either the null hypothesis, $H_0$, is true or it is false. Similarly, there are two possible decisions: we can reject the null hypothesis or we can retain it. Taken in combination, there are four possibilities. They are diagramed in Table 14.1. If the null hypothesis is true and we retain it, or if it is false and

**TABLE 14.1** *Two Types of Error in Hypothesis Testing*

| | | State of Nature | |
|---|---|---|---|
| | | $H_0$ false | $H_0$ true |
| *Decision* | *Retain* $H_0$ | **Type II Error** | *Correct decision* |
| | *Reject* $H_0$ | *Correct decision* | **Type I Error** |

we reject it, we have made a correct decision. Otherwise, we have made an error. Note that there are two kinds of error. They are called *Type I error* and *Type II error.*

**Type I error**
rejection of a true null hypothesis

A **Type I error** is committed when we reject $H_0$ and in fact it is true. Consider the picture of the sampling distribution shown in Figure 14.1 (for simplicity sake, we will consider the sampling distribution of $\overline{X}$ rather than $t$). It illustrates a situation that might arise if we were testing the hypothesis $H_0: \mu_X = 150$ (against the alternative that it is not) and using the 5% significance level. Suppose our sample mean is 146, which, when the test has been conducted in the usual way, leads us to reject $H_0$. The logic in rejecting $H_0$ is that if the hypothesis is true, a sample mean this deviant would occur less than 5% of the time. Therefore, it seems more reasonable for us to believe that this sample mean arose through random sampling from a population with a mean different from that specified in $H_0$. By definition, however, the region of rejection identifies a degree of deviance such that even when the null hypothesis is true, 5% of sample means will reach or exceed it. Our sample mean *could* be one of those deviant values obtained through random sampling. Therefore, when conducting tests using the 5% significance level, and *when the null hypothesis is true*, 5% of sample means will lead us to an erroneous conclusion: rejection of the null hypothesis.

**$\alpha$ (alpha)**
probability of a Type I error

The probability of a Type I error is indicated by the Greek letter **$\alpha$ (alpha)**. More formally:

$$\alpha = \text{Pr (Type I error)} = \text{Pr (rejecting } H_0 \text{ when } H_0 \text{ is true)}$$

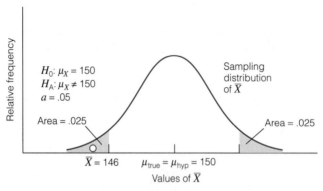

$H_0: \mu_X = 150$
$H_A: \mu_X \neq 150$
$a = .05$

**FIGURE 14.1** Testing $H_0$: $H_0$ is true, but $\overline{X}$ leads to a Type I error.

Note that the possibility of our committing a Type I error exists *only* in situations where the null hypothesis is true. If the null hypothesis is false, it is impossible to commit this error.

**Type II error**
retention of
a false null
hypothesis

A **Type II error** is committed when we retain $H_0$ and in fact it is false. As in the previous example, suppose that we test the hypothesis that $\mu_X = 150$ against the alternative that it is not. Again, we adopt the 5% level of significance. We draw a sample and find its mean to be 152. Now it may be that, unknown to us, the mean of the population is really 154. This situation is pictured in Figure 14.2. In this figure, two sampling distributions are shown. The true distribution is shown with a dotted line and centers on 154, the true population mean. The other is the sampling distribution of $\overline{X}$ that would occur if $H_0$ is true; it centers on 150, the hypothesized mean. The sample mean actually belongs to the true sampling distribution. But to test the hypothesis that $\mu_X = 150$, we evaluate the mean according to its position in the sampling distribution shown with a solid line. Relative to *that* distribution, it is not deviant enough (from the mean of 150) for us to reject $H_0$. Our decision will therefore be to retain the null hypothesis that $\mu_X = 150$. It is, of course, an incorrect decision; we have committed a Type II error. To put it another way, we have failed to claim that a real difference existed when in fact it did.

The probability of committing a Type II error is indicated by the Greek letter $\beta$ (beta):

**$\beta$ (beta)**
probability of a
Type II error

$$\beta = \text{Pr (Type II error)} = \text{Pr (retaining } H_0 \text{ when } H_0 \text{ is false)}$$

Note that the possibility of committing a Type II error exists *only* in situations where the null hypothesis is false. If the null hypothesis is true, it is impossible to commit this kind of error.

It is common for research workers to evaluate the outcome of tests according to the .05 or .01 level of significance. In one sense these values are arbitrary, but in another they are not. It is both possible and permissible to use values such as .02 or .04, for example. But consider the larger question: How shall we choose the level of significance? Should $\alpha$ be .05 or should it be .01, or perhaps some other value? Suppose we were to choose $\alpha = .25$. If the null hypothesis is true, now 25% of sample

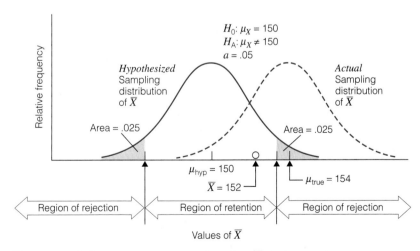

**FIGURE 14.2** Testing $H_0$: $H_0$ is false, but $\overline{X}$ leads to a Type II error.

means will fall in the region of rejection we have established, so one test in four will lead to the incorrect conclusion that the null hypothesis is false. The risk of committing this error seems uncomfortably high.

To reduce the risk, we may set $\alpha$ at a lower level. Suppose we set it very low, say .001. Now suppose we conduct a test and obtain a sample mean that is so deviant that its probability of occurrence under the null hypothesis is .002. According to the new criterion adopted, we have insufficient evidence to reject the null hypothesis and therefore must retain it. In this case, we run a substantial risk of retaining the null hypothesis when it is false.

How, then, should we choose the level of significance ($\alpha$)? Think about the practical consequences of rejecting the null hypothesis when it is true. In Dr. Brown's case (Chapter 13), it would mean concluding that the mean mathematics achievement score of sixth-graders in her school district is better than the national norm or that it is worse than the norm when, in fact, it really is the same. If the conclusion is that the mean score is better, Dr. Brown will "point to the score with pride" when the facts don't justify it; if the conclusion is that it is worse, she will begin revising the mathematics program when it is not necessary. What risk should be accepted for the two taken together? In general, one should translate the error into concrete terms and then decide what level of risk is tolerable.

In the same manner, it is useful to translate the abstract conception of a Type II error into practical consequences. Consider Dr. Brown's problem again. A Type II error would occur if she had retained the null hypothesis that the mean of the population of sixth-grade test scores was 85 when in fact they were really above standard or below standard. How important would it be to avoid this error? Once that judgment is made, it can be taken into account in designing the study. We shall learn how to do that in Section 14.11.

For general use, $\alpha = .05$ and $\alpha = .01$ make quite good sense. They tend to give reasonable assurance that the null hypothesis will not be rejected unless it really should be. At the same time, they are not so stringent as to raise unnecessarily the likelihood of retaining false hypotheses. *Whatever the level of significance adopted, the decision should be made in advance of collecting the data.* If, so to speak, we "peek" at the outcome of the sample data before arriving at this decision, there is a temptation to set the level of significance at a point that permits the conclusion to be in line with whatever preconception we may have. Setting the level of significance should flow from the substantive logic of the study and not from the specific outcome obtained in the sample.

## 14.4 The Power of a Test

**power of the test**

the probability of rejecting a false null hypothesis; $1 - \beta$

In Dr. Brown's problem (Chapter 13), she would be making a correct decision (i.e., rejecting a false null hypothesis) if she claimed that the mean mathematics achievement score of sixth-graders in her school district was superior to the national norm and in fact it really *was* superior. Because the probability of retaining a false null hypothesis is $\beta$, the probability of correctly rejecting a false null hypothesis is $(1 - \beta)$:

$$(1 - \beta) = \mathrm{Pr} \text{ (rejecting } H_0 \text{ when } H_0 \text{ is false)}$$

In other words, $(1 - \beta)$ is the probability of claiming a significant difference when a true difference really exists. The value of $(1 - \beta)$ is called the **power of the test**.

Among several ways of conducting a test, the most powerful one is that offering the greatest probability of rejecting $H_0$ when it should be rejected. Because $\beta$ and the power of a test are complementary, *any condition that decreases $\beta$ increases the power of the test, and vice versa.*

Once an investigator decides on a desired level of power, he or she can arrange certain aspects of the experimental design to achieve the specified level. In the next several sections, we will examine the factors affecting the power of a test (and $\beta$). We will consider which factors the experimenter might profitably manipulate to obtain the desired level. In Section 14.11, we will show how to use the most important of the methods available—selection of sample size—to achieve this end.

## 14.5 Factors Affecting Power: Discrepancy between the True Population Mean and the Hypothesized Mean (Size of Effect)

Suppose that we are testing the null hypothesis to find whether a new learning method is superior to a standard method. Suppose we conduct a two-tailed test of the hypothesis that $\mu = 100$, the known national mean for the standard method. If the null hypothesis is true, the sampling distribution of $\overline{X}$ (for samples using the new method) will center on $\mu_{hyp}$, as shown by the distribution drawn in dotted outline in Figure 14.3a. This is the distribution from which we determine the region of retention, as

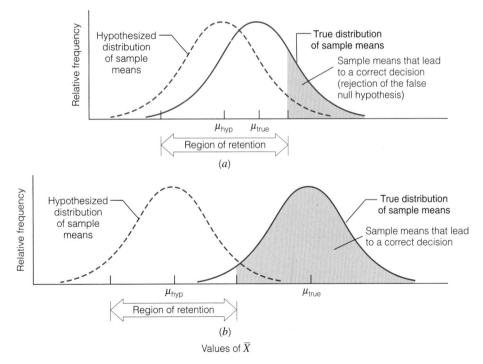

**FIGURE 14.3** Probability of rejecting a false null hypothesis as a function of the size of the difference between $\mu_{hyp}$ and $\mu_{true}$.

shown in the figure. Now, if the null hypothesis is false, the true sampling distribution of $\overline{X}$ will center on some other value, $\mu_{\text{true}}$, rather than on $\mu_{\text{hyp}}$. In practice, we would not know the value of $\mu_{\text{true}}$. However, for purposes of discussion, we will assume possible values for it.

Let us assume, for example, that $\mu_{\text{true}} = 103$ and that the true sampling distribution of $\overline{X}$ is that shown in solid outline in Figure 14.3*a*. These are the values of $\overline{X}$ we shall actually get in random sampling. What will lead to rejection of the false null hypothesis in this situation? Clearly, getting a sample mean that falls outside the region of retention will lead us to reject the null hypothesis. Because our sample means will actually be drawn from the true distribution, those means in the shaded area (under the solid outline) are the ones that will lead us to reject the null hypothesis. Power, the probability of rejecting a false null hypothesis, is therefore the probability of obtaining such a mean in random sampling: judging by eye, it appears that this probability is about .2. (In Section 14.10, we will show how to calculate power.)

Now let us assume that the true population mean and the hypothesized mean are substantially different, say, $\mu_{\text{true}} = 112$. This is illustrated in Figure 14.3*b*. Here, there is little overlap of the two sampling distributions of $\overline{X}$, and most samples have means that will lead to the rejection of $H_0$. *In general, the greater the discrepancy between $\mu_{\text{true}}$ and $\mu_{\text{hyp}}$, the more powerful is the test.*

## 14.6 Factors Affecting Power: Sample Size

The probability of rejecting a false null hypothesis is also related to sample size. Suppose, for example, that in our test of the new learning method we consider a sample size of 25. The estimated standard error of the mean is $s_{\overline{X}} = s_X/\sqrt{25} = .2s_X$. If, instead, the sample size were 100, the estimated standard error of the mean would be $s_{\overline{X}} = s_X/\sqrt{100} = .1s_X$, which is only half as large (assuming that the two values of $s_X$ are about equal). In general, the larger the size of the samples, the smaller the standard deviation ($s_{\overline{X}}$) of the sampling distribution of $\overline{X}$. Figure 14.4 shows how the sampling distribution might appear when all factors are the same except for sample size.

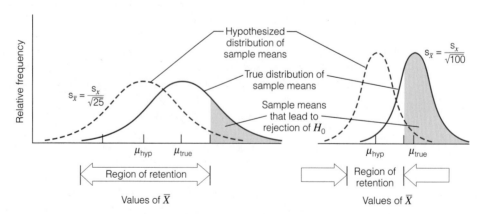

**FIGURE 14.4**   Probability of rejecting a false null hypothesis as a function of sample size.

When sample size is larger, there is less overlap between the true and the hypothetical sampling distributions of $\overline{X}$. Consequently, the probability is greater of drawing a sample that leads to rejection of the false null hypothesis. *Other things being equal, the larger the size of the sample, the smaller the standard error of the mean and the greater the power of the test.* The selection of sample size is the simplest method of increasing power (see Section 14.11).

## 14.7 Factors Affecting Power: Variability of the Measure

In the previous section, we showed that an increase in sample size increases power by reducing the standard error of the mean. Because the estimated standard error of the mean is $s/\sqrt{n}$, *another way to increase power is to reduce the size of* s. At first glance, one might think that this is beyond the control of the investigator. Actually, this opportunity is often open, but advance planning is necessary.

The standard deviation reflects variation attributable to the factors we wish to study, but it also reflects variation attributable to extraneous and irrelevant sources. *Any source of extraneous variation tends to increase* s *over what it would be otherwise*, so an effective effort to eliminate such sources of variation will tend to decrease s and thus increase power. For example, measures in the behavioral sciences (e.g., tests, ratings) suffer from inconsistency (unreliability) to some degree. Some are really rather poor in this regard. Improving the consistency of the measuring instrument will have the effect of reducing s, other things being equal.

## 14.8 Factors Affecting Power: Level of Significance ($\alpha$)

**factors affecting power**
(1) difference between $\mu_{hyp}$ and $\mu_{true}$;
(2) $n$; (3) $s$;
(4) choice of a one-tailed or two-tailed test;
and (5) level of significance

Power is also related to the choice of $\alpha$. Figure 14.5$a$ shows the probability of rejecting $H_0$ when it is false and $\alpha = .05$. Figure 14.5$b$ shows the identical situation except that $\alpha = .01$. In both diagrams, the sample means represented by the shaded areas in the distributions shown in solid outline are those that fall in the region of rejection. The proportionate frequency of such means is greater when $\alpha = .05$ than when $\alpha = .01$. There is therefore a greater chance of obtaining a sample mean that will lead to the rejection of a false $H_0$ when $\alpha$ is larger. *In general, reducing the risk of Type I error increases the risk of committing a Type II error and thus reduces the power of the test.*

Recognition of the relationship between $\alpha$ and $\beta$ is reflected in a change in research practice from that of 70 years ago. In the "old days" (before the $t$ test was widely accepted), it was common to require that $z \geq \pm 3$ before rejecting the null hypothesis. This $z$ is so discrepant that it would occur less than 3 times in 1,000 in a normal distribution. In current practice, it is common to reject the null hypothesis when the discrepancy is so great that it would occur 5% (or sometimes 1%) of the time or less. The modern view is more satisfactory; it takes better account of the necessity of rejecting a false null hypothesis and still maintains an adequate watch over Type I error. Sometimes the older view is thought to be more "conservative," but it is now understood that conservatism in setting $\alpha$ is costly with regard to power.

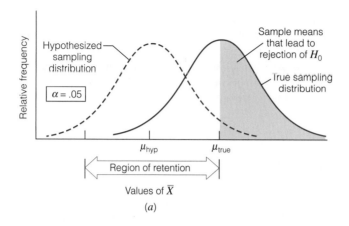

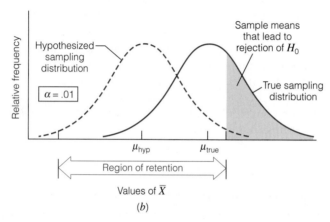

**FIGURE 14.5**   Probability of rejecting a false null hypothesis as a function of $\alpha$.

## 14.9 Factors Affecting Power: One-Tailed versus Two-Tailed Tests

The power of a test is additionally affected by the choice of the alternative hypothesis. Consider again our study of the new learning method. In conducting a one-tailed test of the hypothesis $H_0: \mu_{hyp} = 100$ against the alternative $H_A: \mu_{hyp} > 100$, we consider $H_0$ to be false (and therefore rejected) if and only if $\mu_{true} > \mu_{hyp}$. Figure 14.6 shows the test of $H_0$ when $\alpha$ is .05 and $\mu_{true} > \mu_{hyp}$. The two diagrams represent identical test conditions except for the alternative hypothesis. In a $z$ test, for example, $z_{crit} = \pm 1.96$ when $H_A$ is nondirectional and $+1.645$ when $H_A$ is directional. Compare the proportion of the sample means leading to rejection of $H_0$ (the shaded area) in the two diagrams. It is greater for the one-tailed test. *Other things being equal, the probability of rejecting a false null hypothesis is greater for a one-tailed test than for a two-tailed test (but only when the direction specified by $H_A$ is correct).*

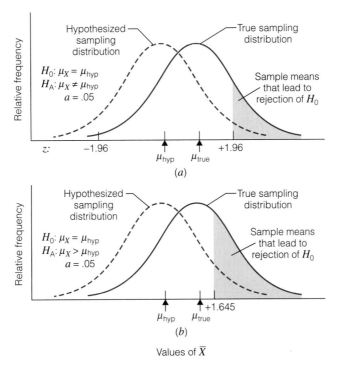

**FIGURE 14.6**   Probability of rejecting a false null hypothesis in (*a*) a two-tailed test and (*b*) a one-tailed test when $\alpha = .05$.

## 14.10  Calculating the Power of a Test

In this section you will learn how to calculate power. *Power can be calculated only when the true value of $\mu$ can be specified.* Although we do not know this value, we can calculate power for different *possible* values of $\mu_{\text{true}}$. The result is a table or graph that allows us to see the consequences of testing hypotheses under various circumstances and from which we can determine the sample size required to keep power at the level we desire.

Suppose that we wish to test the following hypothesis:

$$H_0: \mu_X = 100$$

$$H_A: \mu_X > 100$$

$$\alpha = .05$$

For the sake of simplicity, we shall work with $z$ rather than $t$. If the sample size is 25 and we know that $\sigma_X = 20$, then $\sigma_{\overline{X}} = \sigma_X/\sqrt{n} = 4.00$. To test the null hypothesis, we construct the sampling distribution of $\overline{X}$ that occurs when the hypothesis is true. We show this sampling distribution in dotted outline in Figure 14.7. If, relative to this distribution, we obtain a sample mean that falls above the limit $z = +1.645$, we reject $H_0$.

Suppose that the null hypothesis is false because $\mu_{\text{true}} = 104$. In random sampling, the values of $\overline{X}$ actually obtained will follow the true sampling distribution, shown

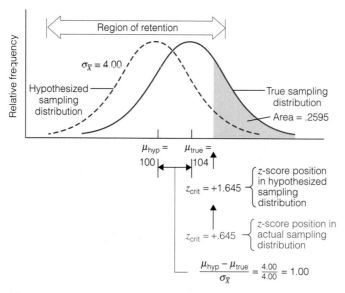

**FIGURE 14.7**  Probability of rejecting a false null hypothesis when testing the hypothesis that $\mu_X = 100$.

in solid outline in Figure 14.7. If our obtained sample mean is one of those shown in the shaded portion of this distribution, the decision will be to reject $H_0$, and we will have made a correct decision. What is the probability of making this correct decision? It is the probability of getting one of the means that falls in the shaded region of the true sampling distribution.

To find the area in the shaded portion of the curve, we must express its boundary in $z$-score terms. We already know what the boundary is in $z$-score terms *relative to the hypothesized population mean:* $z = +1.645$. But we must know what this $z$-score position is in the true distribution. Note the magnitude, taken without regard for direction, of the difference between $\mu_{hyp}$ and $\mu_{true}$; it is $|\mu_{hyp} - \mu_{true}| = 4.00$. We convert it to $z$-score units by dividing by $\sigma_{\overline{X}}$:

$$\frac{|\mu_{hyp} - \mu_{true}|}{\sigma_{\overline{X}}} = \frac{4.00}{4.00} = 1.00$$

We see that the boundary, which was 1.645 $z$-score units above $\mu_{hyp}$, is $(1.645 - 1.00)$ units above $\mu_{true}$. *Relative to the true distribution,* then, $z_{crit} = +.645$. We can now find the area above this boundary using the methods discussed in Section 7.4, assuming the normality of the sampling distribution. The area between $z_{crit}$ and $\mu_{true}$ is approximately .2405 according to the table of areas under the normal curve. Thus, the probability of obtaining a sample mean that falls outside the boundary is $.5000 - .2405 = .2595$, the power of this test. Although the null hypothesis is false (remember, $\mu_{true} = 104$), our chances of rejecting it are not very good under these circumstances.

In the calculations just shown, we assumed that we knew $\sigma_X$. When we estimate it from the sample, the normal curve is only an approximate model, with the approximation growing worse as sample size is reduced. Other models are available for these circumstances, but space limitations do not allow us to consider them here. Also, keep in mind that in our example we used a one-tailed test (because it is easier to show graphically), but computing power in a two-tailed test requires that we consider both tails of the distribution.

# 14.11　Estimating Power and Sample Size for Tests of Hypotheses about Means

[Authors of papers submitted for publication should] provide information on sample size and the process that led to sample size decisions. Document the effect sizes, sampling and measurement assumptions, as well as analytic procedures used in power calculations. (Wilkinson & the Task Force on Statistical Inference, 1999)

One of the greatest problems in the scientific literature today is that many studies are conducted with low power. Surveys of some leading psychology journals, for example, have found that the median power to detect a medium effect size is only about .45 or less (Cohen, 1962; Rossi, 1990; Sedlmeier & Gigerenzer, 1989). The same is true of studies published in medical journals (Moher, Dulberg, & Wells, 1994). Jacob Cohen, one of the leading advocates of power analysis (Cohen, 1988), recommends that *the desirable level of power be .8* (Cohen, 1965, 1992). With the low levels of power actually used in most studies, researchers often fail to reject the null hypothesis in situations in which $H_0$ is false and there is a medium or even a large effect size (Hunter, 1997).

**desirable level of power**
recommended to be .8

The easiest way to increase power is to increase sample size. We can determine the amount of power for a particular sample size or, conversely, the sample size required to achieve a desired level of power if we can specify the following:

1.　The risk ($\alpha$ level) we are willing to take of rejecting a true null hypothesis.

2.　The magnitude of the *smallest* discrepancy that, if it exists, we wish to be reasonably sure of discovering.

Any one of these four variables we have discussed is a function of the other three.

To show the relationship among these variables, let us adopt $\alpha = .05$ and test $H_0: \mu_X =$ some specified value using a two-tailed test. The relationships are shown in Figure 14.8. Effect size is on the horizontal axis and power is on the vertical axis. The **power curves** (as Cohen calls them) show the relationship between effect size and power for a variety of sample sizes.

**power curves**
"used to plan studies by ensuring that the power of statistical tests used will be adequate for the smallest effect size deemed to be of practical significance in a given context" (Hedges & Pigott, 2001)

Recall Dr. Dyett's question (Section 13.14). We estimated $d$ to be $-.56$ (Section 14.2). With 25 subjects, what was the power of her test? To determine this, we locate a point between .5 and .6 on the horizontal axis (effect size) and move vertically as shown by the dotted line to the curve for $n = 25$ and then horizontally to the vertical axis (power), where we find that power is about .78. This means that if the difference between $\mu_{hyp}$ and $\mu_{true}$ really is $d = -.56$, Professor Dyett could expect to reject the null hypothesis and conclude that there is a difference in only 78 out of 100 identical replications of her study; in the remaining 22 replications, chance would lead her to retain $H_0$. Notice that for a smaller effect size, 25 subjects provide even less certainty of detecting a difference.

All too frequently, studies are performed by setting the level of significance and then deciding intuitively (or out of convenience) on sample size. Power-curve charts

# Point of Controversy

## Meta-Analysis

In this book, we focus on how to summarize and analyze a batch of scores obtained in a single study. It is rare, however, that a single study ever completely answers a research question. For any given topic, there are typically a large number (sometimes hundreds) of studies. Although each may address the same general question, they often differ with regard to type of subjects, size of samples, variables, procedures, and definitions. Eventually, the results of these separate studies must be compared and integrated, and conclusions must be drawn to advance knowledge in a particular area.

The traditional approach has been the "authoritative" review article, in which an "expert" (i.e., someone who has published several papers in the particular area) forms a judgment based on a selection of the available data. But how do these experts weigh the results of different studies? The assessments are qualitative, not quantitative, and often very subjective (generally giving more weight to the reviewer's own research findings and others with similar results). According to one analysis of review articles, experts' opinions are "always dependent on how they are trained, not on the body of evidence" (Chalmers, cited in Mann, 1990). As a result, it is not uncommon for two or more reviews of the same research question to differ in their conclusions.

Attempts to find a quantitative means to compare the results of different studies can be traced back to Ronald A. Fisher in the 1920s. One of the biggest problems is dichotomous hypothesis testing with its emphasis on $p$-values. What does it mean when one study reports results with $p < .001$, another (investigating the same research question with slightly different methodology) reports $p < .05$, and still a third (with slightly different methodology again) reports a failure to reach significance? Even when two studies employ the same methodology, the $p$-values may differ substantially if sample sizes are not the same. In other words, when significance tests are the only tool that researchers use, the results can obscure underlying regularities (Schmidt, 1992). Sections 14.1 and 14.2 pointed out the weakness of comparing $p$-values from different studies and also showed the advantage of using effect size for such comparisons. In fact, effect size measures, particularly the standardized mean difference $d$, have led to a new method of comparing results from different studies. The new methodology, named **meta-analysis** by Glass in 1976, uses formal statistical procedures to combine results from many similar studies.

The basic logic of meta-analysis is easy to understand. *The observational unit is a study.* For each study, the technique compares what was found with the "null" hypothesis—the hypothesis that there is no effect. The effect sizes in the many studies will differ only randomly from zero effect if the null hypothesis is true. In other words, the final result should be near zero if we add all the effect sizes together. But, if there is an effect, the results of most of the studies should be in the same qualitative direction (regardless of differences in subjects, procedures, etc.), and the cumulative result should differ sharply from the null hypothesis (see Mann, 1990, or Garfield, 1991). The goal of meta-analysis is to provide an estimate of the level and variability of the effect size for a particular area of research.

**meta-analysis**

a quantitative procedure that allows us to combine the numerical results from multiple studies

As an example, consider the question of whether a full moon affects behavior. Does a full moon result in an increase in mental and emotional disorders, suicides, crimes, and so forth? Many people apparently believe so, for there were over 40 studies conducted on the subject between 1961 and 1984. Rotton and Kelly (1985) combined these 40+ studies in a meta-analysis. Although some studies had found significant results, when they were quantitatively combined, the effect size was found to be negligibly small.

Meta-analysis is *not* done by reading abstracts or the conclusion sections of research papers but by extracting and cumulating data. Therein lies one of the biggest problems; effect size is rarely reported in research articles (see Section 14.2) and must be estimated, often from inadequately reported significance levels. Meta-analysts are among the leaders pushing for stricter standards for publication (see Wachter, 1988). Further problems arise from the fact that journals tend to publish only significant results and few replications (see the first Point of Controversy in this chapter), raising the possibility that the procedure may summarize an unrepresentative batch of studies (Hedges & Vevca, 1996; Moher & Pham, 1999). Ideally, a summarizing process should include the results of all the studies in a particular area, including those for which $p > .05$. One of the biggest criticisms of meta-analysis is that in dealing with bulk, particularly in an area in which there are a large number of poorly designed or nonexperimental (observational) studies, bad science wins by sheer weight of numbers ("garbage in and garbage out") (Moher & Pham, 1999; Shapiro, 1994).

We must not lose sight of the fact that all of these criticisms of meta-analysis are equally true of the traditional, nonquantitative, "expert" review (Rosenthal & DiMatteo, 2001). With meta-analysis, poor studies are more easily exposed *by comparing effect size* than by informally reading the authors' own summaries of their work. Meta-analysis is not vote-counting, and proponents say that good studies should stand up against a larger number of bad studies.

Like any other technique, meta-analysis should be done properly and with caution. "If the meta-analysis is based on randomized experiments, strong causal inferences are often warranted. If the meta-analysis is based on observational studies, causal inferences are as risky as they are in the case of individual observational studies" (Rosenthal & DiMatteo, 2001). Despite some misuses, meta-analysis has already helped focus attention on effect size and the advancement of science as a cumulative process (instead of as a function of reaching some magical *p*-value). We must not forget "that with further trial it (a hypothesis) might come to be stronger or weaker" (Ronald A. Fisher, 1960, p. 25).

(such as Figure 14.8) make a more rational approach possible. Using the charts, one decides on a desired level of power and then selects sample size *according to the minimum effect size one wishes to discover* (if it exists). For example, if Professor Dyett had wanted a probability of .9 of finding a medium-sized effect ($d = .5$) to be significant, a sample size of about 44 would have been required.

Charts like Figure 14.8 are also useful for evaluating the adequacy of published studies. We obtain from the study information about $\alpha$ and the sample size and then select whatever value of power seems appropriate. We may then use the power curve for the particular values of $\alpha$ and $n$ to learn what value of $d$ corresponds to these parameters. (Conversely, we may select an effect size and determine with what level of power the test was conducted.) This will tell us what effect size had a good chance of being discovered if it had existed. Suppose, for example, that a two-tailed test had

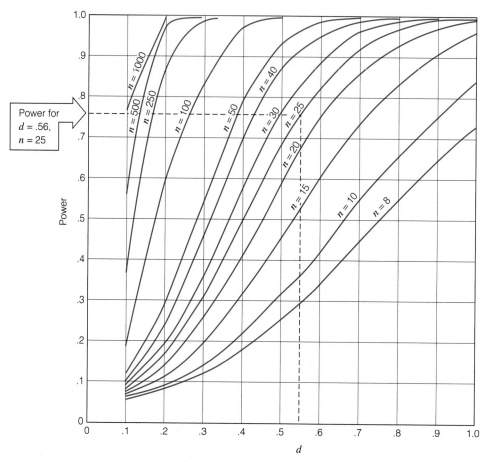

**FIGURE 14.8** Power curves for the *t* test of $H_0$: $\mu_X$ = some specified value; $\alpha$ = .05 against a two-tailed alternative. (*Source:* Data for this figure were obtained from J. Cohen, *Statistical Power Analysis for the Behavioral Sciences,* 2nd ed., Lawrence Erlbaum Associates, New York, 1988. Used with permission.)

been conducted with $\alpha$ = .05 and *n* = 20. If we assume power = .8, we find .8 on the vertical axis, move horizontally to the curve for *n* = 20, and then move vertically to the horizontal axis to find the effect size. We find that *d* is about .65. Under the conditions of the test, then, a difference between $\mu_{hyp}$ and $\mu_{true}$ of about .65 of a standard deviation had a probability of .80 of being detected.

Cohen (1988) provides extensive tables for obtaining precise power values under a variety of circumstances—different $\alpha$ levels and one- and two-tailed tests—as well as other statistical indices (such as correlation coefficients and proportions).

# 14.12 Problems in Selecting a Random Sample and in Drawing Conclusions

The ideal way to conduct statistical inference is to define carefully the target population, identify each element of the population and assign it an identification number, and draw a random sample using a computer or a table of random numbers. In behavioral science, only occasionally do real problems permit these specifications to be met. For example, the theoretical scientist who is studying the learning behavior of "laboratory rats in general" cannot draw a truly random sample and must limit his or her observations to the learning behavior of rats in the latest shipment from Superba Breeding Laboratories. One problem that arises is that there are important differences among strains of laboratory rats. On statistical grounds, it is possible to generalize the inferential outcome of a test *only* to the population from which the observations may be considered to be a random sample.

Another aspect of the problem often occurs with human subjects. If a scientist about to study a problem in learning, motivation, attitude change, perception, or whatever, attempts to define the population about which she would really like to draw conclusions, she will usually be overwhelmed with the difficulties that would lie ahead.

**generalizing results of a statistical test**

we may properly make conclusions only about the specific population from which we drew our sample

The learning scores of all elementary school children in the United States? All women? All members of a minority group? And if she could find the subjects and identify them, how many could come to her laboratory? For that matter, how many would be willing to participate under any conditions? She pushes these thoughts to the back of her mind and reaches for a convenient group of subjects to begin her exploration. This often turns out to be students currently enrolled in a general psychology class. She does not really wish to draw conclusions about the learning scores of such students, but that is, at best, the population for which it is appropriate to generalize the outcome. In situations of this kind, it is common to refer to sampling from a *hypothetical population*, a polite term for a group that you didn't really want to study.

Many research reports sound as though a general conclusion had been reached, but because generalization can be made with total assurance only to the population sampled, a little probing may reveal that the conclusion applies to subjects of a particular sex, a particular age, a particular educational background, or a particular cultural and ethnic origin who happen to be attending a particular institution of higher education at a particular moment in time.

Why do reports sound the way they do? One reason may be that the sampling problem is so overwhelming and so universal that there is a tendency to "forget" about it. A second reason may be that once the data are fed into the statistical testing hopper and the crank is turned, out comes a statement that says "the null hypothesis is probably false." This is a definite statement, derived "scientifically." So it must be true, right? What is often forgotten is that it applies only to the population sampled. If wider generalization is considered, it is incumbent on the researcher to repeat the study in the wider population or to make a reasonable showing that there is no relevant difference between the population sampled and the wider population about which it is desired to draw conclusions. The latter is a very difficult thing to do with confidence and requires the most profound knowledge on the part of the researcher. This is a far cry from the automation of turning the statistical crank. It should be clear that teaching a person statistics provides a tool but does not make him or her a researcher.

**statistical conclusion**

a conclusion about the numerical property of the data (reject or retain $H_0$)

We now see that there are two very important and frustrating problems: the *problem of sampling* and the *problem of generalizing of results.* Yet in many ways, they are two aspects of the same thing. It is often very difficult if not impossible to get a true random sample of the population of observations we would really like to study. If we do limit the population to what we can sample with reasonable adequacy, the outcome may, on statistical grounds, be generalizable only to a trivial population.

What we have been discussing is closely related to a matter developed in Chapter 1. In Section 1.5, the distinction was made between a statistical conclusion and a

**research
conclusion**

a conclusion
about the sub-
ject matter

research conclusion (one about the subject matter). A **statistical conclusion** says something about a parameter of the population, such as $\mu$. But a **research conclusion** says something about the meaning of the study for psychology, or education, or some other discipline. The former can be done as an "automatic" process once statistics is learned. However, moving from the research question to an appropriate statistical question, and finally from a statistical conclusion to a research conclusion, requires the highest qualities of knowledge and judgment on the part of the investigator.

## 14.13 Summary

The difference between $\overline{X}$ and $\mu_{hyp}$ depends on random variation and, when the null hypothesis is false, on the additional difference between $\mu_{hyp}$ and $\mu_{true}$. With a large enough sample, it is possible to detect even a very small difference between $\mu_{hyp}$ and $\mu_{true}$. In statistics, calling a result significant means only that it led the researcher to reject the null hypothesis because it had a low probability of occurring by chance. However, statistical procedures cannot tell us if the result is important.

The dichotomous nature of hypothesis testing has resulted in undue importance being given to *p*-values. Unfortunately, *p*-values tell us nothing about the effect size. This chapter emphasized the importance of determining *how big* rather than how significant an observed difference is. This is measured by finding effect size, *d* or *g*. Many researchers consider small, medium, and large effects to correspond to values of *d* of .2, .5, and .8, respectively.

At the beginning of a study, *before* any data are collected, the researcher must decide on the level of significance to be used. Setting the level of significance high increases $\alpha$, the probability of rejecting a true null hypothesis (a Type I error). Setting the level of significance low increases $\beta$, the probability of retaining a false null hypothesis (a Type II error).

The power of a test is $(1 - \beta)$, where $\beta$ is the probability of retaining $H_0$ when $H_0$ is false (a Type II error). Thus, $\beta$ and power are complementary, so any condition that decreases $\beta$ increases the power of the test, and vice versa.

Power analysis necessitates that researchers consider the size of effect they consider to be important. Among several ways of conducting a statistical test, the most powerful one is that offering the greatest probability of rejecting $H_0$ when $H_0$ is false. The probability of committing a Type I error ($\alpha$) is set by the investigator in advance of collecting the data, but power is affected by a number of factors, including: (1) the magnitude of the discrepancy between what is hypothesized and what is true; (2) the sample size (the larger the sample size, the greater the power); (3) the standard deviation of the variable (the smaller $\sigma$ is, the greater the power is); (4) the choice of a one-tailed or a two-tailed test (power is greater for a one-tailed test if the direction of $H_A$ is correct); and (5) the choice of level of significance (reducing $\alpha$ increases $\beta$ and reduces power).

Effect size, sample size, $\alpha$ level, and power are all related; any one is a function of the other three. Thus, if investigators specify the magnitude of the smallest discrepancy that is important for them to discover (if it exists), then they can calculate (based on the selected level of $\alpha$) the size of the sample(s) necessary to ensure a given level of power for discovering a discrepancy of that size. From knowledge of sample size and significance level, one can also evaluate published studies in terms of their power to discover a particular effect size. Unfortunately, most published studies are conducted with low power.

When moving from the statistical conclusion to the research conclusion, on statistical (mathematical) grounds we can really only make conclusions about the specific population from which we drew our random sample. If wider generalization is desired, we must repeat the study in the wider population or reasonably show that there is no relevant difference between the population sampled and the wider population about which we wish to draw conclusions.

## Key Terms, Concepts, and Symbols

significant result   (256, 264)

practically important difference   (264)

*p*-value   (255, 265)

effect size   (267)

*d*   (267)

*g*   (267)

Type I error   (270)

$\alpha$   (234, 270)

Type II error   (271)

$\beta$   (271)

power of the test   (272)

$1 - \beta$   (272)

power curves   (279)

meta-analysis   (280)

generalizing results   (283)

statistical conclusion   (6, 283)

research conclusion   (6, 284)

## Problems

**1.** In a 1977 study (Smith & Glass), a correlation of .32 was found between whether or not an individual had psychotherapy and whether or not his or her condition improved. For this study, $r^2 = .10$, meaning that psychotherapy could account for only 10% of the variability in results. Are you impressed with the results? Why or why not?

**2.** A researcher drew a sample of 400 people, measured their IQs, and tested the hypothesis that $\mu_{IQ} = 100$. The researcher obtained $z = +3.00$, which led her to reject the hypothesis ($\sigma$ was 15.0). (a) What was the standard error of the mean? (b) What was the mean of the sample? (c) The test yielded a statistically significant outcome. Does it appear to be an important one? Explain. (d) How much of a standard deviation did the discrepancy between $\overline{X}$ and $\mu_{hyp}$ amount to?

*explain intuitively*

*compute effect size*

**3.** Calculate the effect size for the example in Section 14.10.

**4.** Calculate *g* for Problem 26 in Chapter 13.

**5.** Calculate *g* for (a) Problem 28 in Chapter 13 and (b) Problem 29 in Chapter 13.

**6.** Calculate *g* for Problem 30 in Chapter 13.

### DATA 14A

| | |
|---|---|
| $H_0$: $\mu_X = 80.0$ | $\sigma_X = 20.0$ |
| $H_A$: $\mu_X \neq 80.0$ | $n = 100$ |

**7.** With regard to Data 14A, (a) if $\alpha = .05$ and $\mu_{true} = 81.0$, what is $\beta$? What is the power of the test? (b) if $\alpha = .05$ and $\mu_{true} = 82.0$, what is $\beta$? What is the power of the test?

**8.** With regard to Data 14A, (a) if $\alpha = .05$ and $\mu_{true} = 83.0$, what is $\beta$? What is the power of the test? (b) If $\alpha = .01$ and $\mu_{true} = 83.0$, what is $\beta$? What is the power of the test?

**9.** With regard to Data 14A, (a) if $\alpha = .05$ and $\mu_{true} = 82.0$, what is $\beta$? What is the power of the test? (b) If $\alpha = .05$ and $\mu_{true} = 82.0$, but $\sigma_X = 10.0$, what is $\beta$? What is the power of the test?

**10.** With regard to Data 14A, (a) if $\alpha = .05$ and $\mu_{true} = 84.0$, what is $\beta$? What is the power of the test? (b) If $\alpha = .05$ and $\mu_{true} = 84.0$, but $H_A$: $\mu_X > 80.0$, what is $\beta$? What is the power of the test?

*Revised*

*don't compute beta power.*

*Draw diagram for each scenarios showing alpha, beta and power*

*EC: Calculate beta + power*

**11.** A psychologist wonders whether performance by students in her class has fallen this semester. Among students in past semesters, mean GPA = 3.1 and $\sigma_{GPA}$ = .30. She decides to adopt $\alpha$ = .05 and power = .8. If the difference between present students and those in past semesters is as great as .09 grade points, she would want to know it. (a) State the null hypothesis and alternative hypothesis for a two-tailed test. (b) What should the size of the sample be to test this null hypothesis? Use the power curve chart.

**12.** In reference to Problem 11, what should sample size be if the psychologist feels that she should choose power = .90 and it is important to know it if the difference is .15 grade point (or more) and power = .95?

**13.** If you conduct the same experiment 100 times under identical circumstances and the power of your test is .7, how many times would you expect to obtain significant results?

**14.** Given that $\mu_X$ = 97 and $\sigma_X$ = 4, if you conduct a two-tailed test of $H_0$: $\mu_X$ = 100 with $\alpha$ = .05, how many times in 50 replications would you expect to obtain significant results for samples of size (a) 10? (b) 20? (c) 50?

**15.** For a two-tailed test of $H_0$: $\mu_X$ = 100 with $\alpha$ = .05 and $n$ = 10, what is the probability of detecting a $d$ of (a) .2? (b) .5? (c) .8? (d) What does this tell you about using samples of this size?

**16.** For a two-tailed test of $H_0$: $\mu_X$ = 50 with $\alpha$ = .05 and $n$ = 100, what is the probability of detecting a $d$ of (a) .2? (b) .5? (c) .8? (d) What does this tell you about using samples of this size (compare with Problem 15)?

**17.** To see if Public Health Service attempts to educate the public about the dangers of having multiple sexual partners have been effective, a survey was conducted of the sexual behaviors of women at Brown University in Providence, RI (DeBueno et al., 1990). The researchers found that about the same number of college women were having multiple partners as was found in a 1975 survey. The researchers concluded, "Public health campaigns have not had a substantial influence on the habits and behavior of these well-educated young adults." *The Washington Post* reported, "A study published today found that college women are just as sexually active with multiple partners as they were in the mid-1970s." Comment on the similarities and differences of these two conclusions.

# CHAPTER 15

## Testing Hypotheses about the Difference between Two Independent Groups

When you have finished studying this chapter, you should be able to:

- Understand the nature of the random sampling distribution of $(\overline{X} - \overline{Y})$;
- Calculate $s_{\overline{X}-\overline{Y}}$ (the estimated standard error of the difference between two means) and $t$ for testing hypotheses about the difference between two independent means;
- Calculate effect size and estimate power;
- Understand the assumptions underlying the testing of hypotheses about the difference between two independent means;
- Understand the difference between random sampling and random assignment; and
- Appreciate how random sampling and random assignment serve as experimental controls.

In many fields of inquiry, including psychology and education, one of the most important ways of increasing knowledge is to ask whether it makes a difference when some variable is measured under two different conditions. Is the reading comprehension of dyslexic children the same under conditions of normal and reduced visual contrast? Do AIDS patients who are given the drug AZT show higher CD4+ blood cell counts than patients who are not given the drug? Is speed of reaction to a light the same as that to a sound? Is the ability to spell equal for male and female high school seniors? Is the error rate of typists the same when work is done in a noisy environment as in a quiet one?

**independent samples**
samples drawn so that the selection of elements in one sample is in no way influenced by the selection of elements in the other, and vice versa

Let us designate scores obtained under one condition as $X$ and scores obtained under the second condition as $Y$. Now suppose one sample is drawn at random from the population of $X$ scores and another sample is drawn at random from the population of $Y$ scores. The two random samples are selected *independently* from their respective populations. **Independent samples** exist when the selection of elements comprising the sample of $Y$ scores is in no way influenced by the selection of elements making up the sample of $X$ scores, and vice versa. Sometimes samples are selected that do not meet this criterion. We will consider the dependent samples case in Chapter 16.

## 15.1 The Null and Alternative Hypotheses

Each of the questions posed in the introduction is an example of a problem for which hypothesis testing may be helpful in finding the answer. However, the hypotheses you will test in this chapter are different from those you tested in Chapter 13. Here we are concerned with the hypothesis that *two* means are equal.

Consider the first question. Dyslexia refers to a specific reading disability that affects 10% to 15% of the general population. A dyslexic child is defined as a child of normal or above-normal intelligence with no known organic or gross behavioral disorders, who, despite normal schooling, shows a reading lag of at least 2 years. Most intervention programs have focused on remediation of language skills, but with little success. Psychologist Mary Williams proposed that dyslexia was the result of a complex visual deficit that could be immediately corrected by simply putting a blue plastic overlay on the reading material. (The following procedure and results are modified, with permission, from Williams, LeCluyse, and Rock-Faucheux, 1992.) To test this, 24 dyslexic children were randomly assigned to one of two groups, one of which read from pages with a clear plastic overlay and the other of which read from pages with a blue plastic overlay. The dependent variable was percentage correct on a multiple-choice reading comprehension test. The mean of the group using clear overlays was 56.7%, whereas the mean of the group using the blue overlay was 75.0%. Is this a meaningful difference? *Because of the variability introduced by random assignment, we would expect two samples to yield different means even if the two groups had been treated alike.*

The important question is not about the samples but about the populations from which the samples came. Is it possible that the mean of the population of reading comprehension scores obtained with blue overlays is the same as the mean of the population of observations obtained with clear overlays? The two *population* means would be the same if the blue overlay had no effect. We may express this question as a statistical hypothesis to be subjected to test. If scores obtained under the blue overlay condition are designated by $X$ and those obtained under the clear overlay condition by $Y$, we have:

$$H_0: \mu_X - \mu_Y = 0$$

The test of the difference between two means always involves the difference between measures of the *same* dependent variable taken under two conditions. In the dyslexic-children example, $X$ stands for the reading comprehension scores of subjects treated one way, and $Y$ stands for the reading comprehension scores of subjects treated another way.

The alternative hypothesis, $H_A$, may be directional or nondirectional, depending on the logic of the study. If our only interest is in discovering whether the blue overlay *improved* reading ability in dyslexic children, $H_A: \mu_X - \mu_Y > 0$ would be the appropriate alternative. In the usual case, investigators want to know if an effect exists in *either* direction and therefore choose a nondirectional alternative hypothesis, as Williams and her colleagues did here:

$$H_0: \mu_X - \mu_Y = 0$$

$$H_A: \mu_X - \mu_Y \neq 0$$

From this point on, the procedure for testing the null hypothesis follows the same basic principles outlined in Chapter 13. We must choose $\alpha$, the criterion for decision, and select a sample size that will give us a good chance of discovering a difference (if one exists). Next, we must examine the characteristics of the pertinent sampling distribution so that the present sample outcome can be compared with those outcomes expected when the null hypothesis is true. In the sampling distribution, we establish a region of rejection according to the nature of $H_A$ and the value of $\alpha$. In the present problem, if the difference between the two sample means is so great in either direction that it could not reasonably be accounted for by chance variation when the population means are the same, Williams and her colleagues will reject the null hypothesis. In short, the logic and general procedure for testing a null hypothesis about the difference between two means are the same as for testing a null hypothesis about a single mean.

## 15.2 The Random Sampling Distribution of the Difference between Two Sample Means

Recall from Chapter 13 that the random sampling distribution of *single* means described all the sample means that can possibly occur when sampling at random from a population having the mean specified in $H_0$. Here we are concerned with the *difference* between two population means, and the distribution that we will refer to is the random sampling distribution of the *difference* between two sample means. Just what is this distribution?

We began this chapter by drawing one sample at random from the population of $X$ scores and another from the population of $Y$ scores. Now we compute the mean of each sample and obtain the difference between these two means. Suppose then that we return the samples to their respective populations and select a second pair of samples of the same size in the same way. We again calculate the two means and compute and record the difference between them. If we repeat this experiment indefinitely, the differences—the values of $(\overline{X} - \overline{Y})$ thus generated—form the **random sampling distribution of the difference between two sample means**.

**random sampling distribution of $(\overline{X} - \overline{Y})$**
a theoretical relative frequency distribution of all the values of $(\overline{X} - \overline{Y})$ that would be obtained by chance from an infinite number of samples of a particular size drawn from two populations, $\mu_X$ and $\mu_Y$

$\boldsymbol{\mu_{\overline{X}-\overline{Y}}}$
symbol for the mean of the sampling distribution of $(\overline{X} - \overline{Y})$

The usefulness of this sampling distribution is that it describes all the differences that would occur by chance between $\overline{X}$ and $\overline{Y}$ *when* $H_0$ *is true.* When asking about the difference between two means, $H_0$, the hypothesis to be tested, is almost always that $\mu_X$ and $\mu_Y$ do not differ. (The null hypothesis could state that $\mu_X - \mu_Y = +5$, for example, but the nature of inquiry seldom leads us to ask such a question.) Now if pairs of samples are drawn at random from two populations, *and if the means of the two populations are the same*, because of chance factors we will find that sometimes $\overline{X}$ is larger than $\overline{Y}$—leading to a positive value for $(\overline{X} - \overline{Y})$—and sometimes it is the other way around—leading to a negative value for $(\overline{X} - \overline{Y})$. When all the possible differences are considered, their mean will be zero. Thus, *the mean of the sampling distribution of differences* $(\overline{X} - \overline{Y})$ *is zero when the difference between the two population means is zero.* We will use $\mu_{\overline{X}-\overline{Y}}$ as the symbol for the mean of the sampling distribution of $(\overline{X} - \overline{Y})$. To summarize, then,

$$\mu_{\overline{X}-\overline{Y}} = 0$$

when $\mu_X - \mu_Y = 0$.

More generally, the mean of the sampling distribution of the difference between two means is equal to the difference between the means of the two populations:

$$\mu_{\overline{X}-\overline{Y}} = \mu_X - \mu_Y$$

In Section 12.3, we found that another way of looking at the random sampling distribution of $\overline{X}$ is to consider it as the distribution of the means of all possible samples. The same is true for the random sampling distribution of the difference between $\overline{X}$ and $\overline{Y}$. If we specify sample sizes for $X$ and $Y$ (they need not be the same), enumerate each possible sample that can be formed from the two populations, calculate the mean of each, couple each sample mean of $X$ with all of the possible sample means of $Y$, and obtain the difference between each resulting pair, we shall have the complete set of possible differences between pairs of sample means. The distribution of $(\overline{X} - \overline{Y})$ thus formed is equivalent to that formed by repeated sampling over an infinity of trials in that both lead to the same conclusions when interpreted as relative frequency or probability distributions.

## 15.3 An Illustration of the Sampling Distribution of the Difference between Means

It will be helpful to use real numbers to explore the nature of the distribution of $(\overline{X} - \overline{Y})$, but to do so, we shall have to confine our attention to miniature populations. Suppose that the population of $X$ scores consists of three scores: 3, 5, and 7. Because the question we usually ask in statistics is what would happen if the "treatment" had no effect, we shall also suppose that the population of $Y$ scores consists of the same three scores: 3, 5, and 7. If samples of two cases are drawn with replacement from either population, there are nine possible samples and therefore nine possible means that may occur. These are shown in Table 15.1. Note that we say that there

**TABLE 15.1**  *Possible Samples and Sample Means for Samples of Size 2 (Sampling with Replacement)*

| POPULATION OF X SCORES: 3, 5, 7 | | POPULATION OF Y SCORES 3, 5, 7 | |
|---|---|---|---|
| | $\mu_X = \mu_Y = 5$ $\sigma_X = \sigma_Y = 1.633$ | | |
| Sample from X population | $\overline{X}$ | Sample from Y population | $\overline{Y}$ |
| 3, 3 | 3 | 3, 3 | 3 |
| 3, 5 | 4 | 3, 5 | 4 |
| 3, 7 | 5 | 3, 7 | 5 |
| 5, 3 | 4 | 5, 3 | 4 |
| 5, 5 | 5 | 5, 5 | 5 |
| 5, 7 | 6 | 5, 7 | 6 |
| 7, 3 | 5 | 7, 3 | 5 |
| 7, 5 | 6 | 7, 5 | 6 |
| 7, 7 | 7 | 7, 7 | 7 |

are nine possible means, even though some of them have the same value. We must take all of them into account.

When we ask what differences may occur between sample means in X and sample means in Y, we must consider that there are nine sample means in X, and that each may be coupled with any one of the nine sample means in Y. Thus, there are 81 possible pairings of the means of X with the means of Y. The possible sample means are shown at the top and in the left column of Table 15.2, and the 81 differences between pairs $(\overline{X} - \overline{Y})$ are shown in the body of the table. *If the samples are drawn independently and at random, each of the listed differences is equally likely to appear.* If we collect these differences in a frequency distribution, the result is as given in Table 15.3 and is graphically illustrated in Figure 15.1.

**TABLE 15.2**  *Differences between Pairs of Sample Means $(\overline{X} - \overline{Y})$ for All Possible Paired Samples of X and Y (Data from Table 15.1)★*

| $\overline{X}$ | $\overline{Y}$ | | | | | | | | |
|---|---|---|---|---|---|---|---|---|---|
| | 3 | 4 | 4 | 5 | 5 | 5 | 6 | 6 | 7 |
| 7 | 4 | 3 | 3 | 2 | 2 | 2 | 1 | 1 | 0 |
| 6 | 3 | 2 | 2 | 1 | 1 | 1 | 0 | 0 | −1 |
| 6 | 3 | 2 | 2 | 1 | 1 | 1 | 0 | 0 | −1 |
| 5 | 2 | 1 | 1 | 0 | 0 | 0 | −1 | −1 | −2 |
| 5 | 2 | 1 | 1 | 0 | 0 | 0 | −1 | −1 | −2 |
| 5 | 2 | 1 | 1 | 0 | 0 | 0 | −1 | −1 | −2 |
| 4 | 1 | 0 | 0 | −1 | −1 | −1 | −2 | −2 | −3 |
| 4 | 1 | 0 | 0 | −1 | −1 | −1 | −2 | −2 | −3 |
| 3 | 0 | −1 | −1 | −2 | −2 | −2 | −3 | −3 | −4 |

★The body of the table contains values of $(\overline{X} - \overline{Y})$.

**TABLE 15.3**  *Distribution of Differences between All Possible Pairs of Sample Means (Data from Table 15.2)*

| $(\overline{X} - \overline{Y})$ | $f$ | |
|:---:|:---:|:---|
| 4 | 1 | |
| 3 | 4 | |
| 2 | 10 | $\mu_{\overline{X}-\overline{Y}} = 0$ |
| 1 | 16 | $\sigma_{\overline{X}-\overline{Y}} = 1.633$ |
| 0 | 19 | |
| −1 | 16 | |
| −2 | 10 | |
| −3 | 4 | |
| −4 | 1 | |
| | $n = 81$ | |

Several features of the resulting frequency distribution are notable. First, the mean of the distribution (the expected value) is zero, the difference between $\mu_X$ and $\mu_Y$. Second, the distribution is very reasonably approximated by the normal curve. In Figure 15.1, a normal curve has been fitted to the distribution, and it is apparent that the expected frequencies of the normal curve (shown by points on the curve) are close to the actual frequencies of particular means (shown by the height of the bars in the histogram). *If the sampling distributions of the mean for* X *and* Y *are approximately normal, the distribution of the difference between pairs of means selected at random will also be approximately normal.* In the present situation, the distribution of the population of scores in $X$ and $Y$ resembles a rectangular distribution more than it does a normal distribution. Yet the distribution of the difference between pairs of sample means resembles the normal curve. Thus, *the effect predicted for single means by the central limit theorem (see Section 12.4) also applies to the distribution of the difference between sample means.* The normal curve is therefore an important model for the sampling distribution of $(\overline{X} - \overline{Y})$ even when the population distributions depart to some extent from normality.

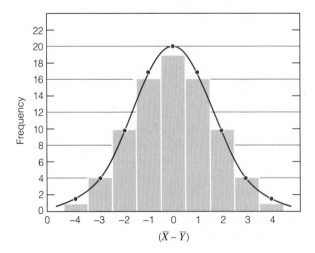

**FIGURE 15.1**  Distribution of differences between all possible pairs of sample means; data from Table 15.3.

# 15.4 Properties of the Sampling Distribution of the Difference between Means

As we know, three characteristics completely define any distribution: mean, standard deviation, and shape. We now know that the mean of the random sampling distribution of the difference between pairs of sample means, $\mu_{\bar{X}-\bar{Y}}$, is the same as the difference between the two population means, $\mu_X - \mu_Y$. We also know that the sampling distribution of $(\bar{X} - \bar{Y})$ will be normally distributed when the two populations are normally distributed and that the sampling distribution tends toward normal even when the two populations are not normal. But what about its standard deviation?

**standard error of the difference between two means**
the standard deviation of the sampling distribution of $(\bar{X} - \bar{Y})$

The standard deviation of the sampling distribution of $(\bar{X} - \bar{Y})$ is called the **standard error of the difference between two means**, and its symbol is $\sigma_{\bar{X}-\bar{Y}}$. If the sampling distribution is composed of differences between means of *independent* samples, its standard deviation is:

> STANDARD ERROR OF THE DIFFERENCE
> BETWEEN TWO INDEPENDENT MEANS
>
> $$\sigma_{\bar{X}-\bar{Y}} = \sqrt{\sigma_{\bar{X}}^2 + \sigma_{\bar{Y}}^2} \qquad (15.1)$$

$\boldsymbol{\sigma_{\bar{X}-\bar{Y}}}$
symbol for the standard error of the sampling distribution of $(\bar{X} - \bar{Y})$

Like the formula for the standard error of the mean, Formula 15.1 has been derived through theoretical considerations and based on the assumption of random sampling with replacement. (See Note 12.2 for a discussion of the influence, ordinarily negligible, of sampling without replacement.)

In the example of Section 15.3, the distribution of possible differences was constructed on the assumption of independence of sample means. According to Formula 15.1, its standard deviation should be

$$\sigma_{\bar{X}-\bar{Y}} = \sqrt{\left(\frac{1.633}{\sqrt{2}}\right)^2 + \left(\frac{1.633}{\sqrt{2}}\right)^2} = 1.633$$

Note that actual calculation of the standard deviation (see Table 15.3) yields the same value, 1.633. It is just a coincidence that in this problem $\sigma_X = \sigma_Y = \sigma_{\bar{X}-\bar{Y}}$.

# 15.5 Determining a Formula for *t*

In this section we will develop a formula for *t* for testing the difference between the means of two independent groups. For those of you who are strong in mathematics, you will find the progression to be very logical. If you are not, we do not want this section to discourage you. If you want, read the next paragraph of this section (through Formula 15.2*a*) and then skip ahead to Formula 15.4.

Formula 15.1 requires that we know the standard error of the mean of $X$ and of $Y$, and these, in turn, require that we know $\sigma_X$ and $\sigma_Y$. As usual, in practice we usually do not know the population standard deviations and so must estimate them from

**estimated standard error of the difference between two means**

an estimate of the standard deviation of the sampling distribution of $(\overline{X} - \overline{Y})$

the samples. The symbol for the **estimated standard error of the difference be-tween two means** is $s_{\overline{X}-\overline{Y}}$. The formula for estimating $\sigma_{\overline{X}-\overline{Y}}$ is:

ESTIMATE OF $\sigma_{\overline{X}-\overline{Y}}$ FOR INDEPENDENT SAMPLES

$$s_{\overline{X}-\overline{Y}} = \sqrt{s_{\overline{X}}^2 + s_{\overline{Y}}^2} \qquad (15.2a)$$

To test the difference between two independent means, we could calculate an "ap-proximate $z$" where $z = (score - mean)/standard\ deviation$. In the sampling distribution of differences, our difference—$(\overline{X} - \overline{Y})$—is the score, the hypothesized difference is the mean, and $s_{\overline{X}-\overline{Y}}$ is the estimated standard deviation:

**assumption of homo-geneity of variance**

the assumption that $\sigma_X^2 = \sigma_Y^2$, that the vari-ances in the two populations from which the samples are drawn are the same

$$\text{"}z\text{"} = \frac{(\overline{X} - \overline{Y}) - (\mu_X - \mu_Y)_{\text{hyp}}}{s_{\overline{X}-\overline{Y}}}$$

When the sample size is relatively large, "$z$" is very nearly normally distributed. As sample size decreases, its distribution departs from the normal, but, unfortunately, *except in the special case when* $n_X = n_Y$, neither is it distributed exactly as Student's $t$.

The eminent British statistician Sir Ronald A. Fisher showed that a slightly differ-ent approach results in a statistic that *is* distributed as Student's $t$. The change that Fisher introduced was, in effect, to assume that $\sigma_X^2 = \sigma_Y^2$. This is often called the **assumption of homogeneity of variance**. To understand the consequences of this assumption, it will be helpful to rewrite Formula 15.1 for $\sigma_{\overline{X}-\overline{Y}}$. According to Formula 12.2, we may substitute $\sigma_X^2/n_X$ for $\sigma_{\overline{X}}^2$ and $\sigma_Y^2/n_Y$ for $\sigma_{\overline{Y}}^2$. The result is

$$\sigma_{\overline{X}-\overline{Y}} = \sqrt{\frac{\sigma_X^2}{n_X} + \frac{\sigma_Y^2}{n_Y}}$$

This formula clearly allows for the possibility that $\sigma_X^2$ might be different from $\sigma_Y^2$ and so does the following formula, which is used when *estimates* of the two variances must be made from the *samples*:

$$s_{\overline{X}-\overline{Y}} = \sqrt{\frac{s_X^2}{n_X} + \frac{s_Y^2}{n_Y}} \qquad (15.2b)$$

**pooled estimate of the population variance ($s_p^2$)**

a single estimate of the popula-tion variance based on com-bining the data from both samples

If $\sigma_X^2$ and $\sigma_Y^2$ differ, then each sample estimates its corresponding population value. Under the assumption of homogeneity of variance, however, both $s_X^2$ and $s_Y^2$ are esti-mates of the same population variance. If this is so, then rather than make two sepa-rate estimates, each based on a small sample, it is preferable to combine the informa-tion from both samples and make a single **pooled estimate of the population variance** (symbolized $s_p^2$). In general, the "best estimate" of a population variance is made as follows:

$$\sigma_{\text{est}}^2 = \frac{sum\ of\ squares\ of\ deviation\ scores}{degrees\ of\ freedom} = \frac{SS}{df}$$

This is exactly what we do when we calculate

$$s_X^2 = \frac{\sum (X - \overline{X})^2}{n - 1}$$

We can make a pooled estimate from the two samples by pooling the sums of squares of the deviation scores from each sample and dividing by the total number of degrees of freedom associated with the pooled sum of squares. Thus, $s_p^2$ is:

**ESTIMATE OF $\sigma^2$ MADE BY POOLING
INFORMATION FROM TWO SAMPLES**

**$(n_X - 1) + (n_Y - 1)$**
degrees of freedom for the pooled estimate of the population variance obtained from two independent samples

$$s_p^2 = \frac{SS_X + SS_Y}{(n_X - 1) + (n_Y - 1)}$$ (15.3)

We may substitute this quantity for $s_X^2$ and for $s_Y^2$ in the formula for $s_{\overline{X}-\overline{Y}}$:

$$s_{\overline{X}-\overline{Y}} = \sqrt{\frac{s_p^2}{n_X} + \frac{s_p^2}{n_Y}}$$

**$s_{\overline{X}-\overline{Y}}$**
symbol for the estimated standard error of $(\overline{X} - \overline{Y})$

Factoring out $s_p^2$, the formula may be rewritten as

$$s_{\overline{X}-\overline{Y}} = \sqrt{s_p^2 \left( \frac{1}{n_X} + \frac{1}{n_Y} \right)}$$

If the expression for $s_p^2$ given by Formula 15.3 is substituted in this formula, we have:

**ESTIMATE OF STANDARD ERROR
OF THE DIFFERENCE BETWEEN TWO
INDEPENDENT MEANS WHEN $\sigma_X^2 = \sigma_Y^2$**

$$\sqrt{\frac{SS_X + SS_Y}{(n_X - 1) + (n_Y - 1)} \left( \frac{1}{n_X} + \frac{1}{n_Y} \right)}$$

$$s_{\overline{X}-\overline{Y}} = \sqrt{\frac{SS_X + SS_Y}{(n_X - 1) + (n_Y - 1)} \left( \frac{1}{n_X} + \frac{1}{n_Y} \right)}$$ (15.4)

general formula for the estimated standard error of $(\overline{X} - \overline{Y})$ in the independent-samples design

When the two *n*s are equal, we can calculate $s_{\overline{X}-\overline{Y}}$ by a simpler formula than Formula 15.4. It is:

**ESTIMATE OF STANDARD ERROR OF THE DIFFERENCE
BETWEEN TWO INDEPENDENT MEANS WHEN
$\sigma_X^2 = \sigma_Y^2$ AND $n_X = n_Y = n$**

$$s_{\overline{X}-\overline{Y}} = \sqrt{\frac{SS_X + SS_Y}{n(n - 1)}}$$ (15.5)

When we calculate *t* according to the following formula and calculate $s_{\overline{X}-\overline{Y}}$ according to Formula 15.4 or 15.5, *t* will be distributed according to Student's distribution with $(n_X - 1) + (n_Y - 1)$ degrees of freedom:

$$t = \frac{(\overline{X} - \overline{Y}) - (\mu_X - \mu_Y)_{\text{hyp}}}{s_{\overline{X}-\overline{Y}}} \tag{15.6}$$

*t* FOR TESTING HYPOTHESES ABOUT
THE DIFFERENCE BETWEEN TWO MEANS

## 15.6 Testing the Hypothesis of No Difference between Two Independent Means: The Dyslexic Children Experiment

$t =$

$\dfrac{(\overline{X} - \overline{Y}) - (\mu_X - \mu_Y)_{\text{hyp}}}{s_{\overline{X}-\overline{Y}}}$

formula for the *t* statistic for testing a null hypothesis about the difference between two population means

Let us return to the study we introduced at the beginning of the chapter. Is the reading ability of dyslexic children improved by placing a blue plastic overlay on reading material? Williams and her colleagues (1992) tested the statistical hypothesis that

$$H_0: \mu_X - \mu_Y = 0$$

$$H_A: \mu_X - \mu_Y \neq 0$$

using the 5% level of significance ($\alpha = .05$). Twenty-four dyslexic children were randomly assigned to one of the two groups. The data for this problem and the calculations are shown in Table 15.4.

We begin our calculations by finding $n_X$, $\Sigma X$, $\Sigma X^2$, $n_Y$, $\Sigma Y$, and $\Sigma Y^2$. In this example, there were 12 scores under each condition, but we nevertheless used Formula 15.4 to calculate *t*. Because $n_X = n_Y$, we could have used Formula 15.5, but it seemed best to demonstrate the more general procedure, which is appropriate when $n_X \neq n_Y$ as well as when both are the same.

© 2002 by Sidney Harris

"WE PLAN TO DETERMINE, ONCE AND FOR ALL, IF THERE REALLY ARE ANY CULTURAL DIFFERENCES BETWEEN THEM."

**TABLE 15.4** *Calculations for Testing a Hypothesis about the Difference between Two Independent Means for the Dyslexic-Children Experiment*

| BLUE OVERLAY $X$ | CLEAR OVERLAY $Y$ | $X^2$ | $Y^2$ |
|---|---|---|---|
| 70 | 50 | 4,900 | 2,500 |
| 80 | 40 | 6,400 | 1,600 |
| 90 | 50 | 8,100 | 2,500 |
| 80 | 50 | 6,400 | 2,500 |
| 50 | 60 | 2,500 | 3,600 |
| 80 | 60 | 6,400 | 3,600 |
| 70 | 60 | 4,900 | 3,600 |
| 80 | 40 | 6,400 | 1,600 |
| 70 | 60 | 4,900 | 3,600 |
| 80 | 70 | 6,400 | 4,900 |
| 80 | 60 | 6,400 | 3,600 |
| 70 | 80 | 4,900 | 6,400 |
| $\sum X = 900$ | $\sum Y = 680$ | $\sum X^2 = 68,600$ | $\sum Y^2 = 40,000$ |

① $\bar{X} = \dfrac{\sum X}{n_X} = \dfrac{900}{12} = 75.0 \qquad \bar{Y} = \dfrac{\sum Y}{n_Y} = \dfrac{680}{12} = 56.7$

② $SS_X = \sum X^2 - \dfrac{\left(\sum X\right)^2}{n_X} = 68,600 - \dfrac{900^2}{12} = 1,100$

$s_X = \sqrt{\dfrac{SS_X}{n_X - 1}} = \sqrt{\dfrac{1100}{12 - 1}} = \sqrt{100} = 10$

② $SS_Y = \sum Y^2 - \dfrac{\left(\sum Y\right)^2}{n_Y} = 40,000 - \dfrac{680^2}{12} = 1466.7$

$s_Y = \sqrt{\dfrac{SS_Y}{n_Y - 1}} = \sqrt{\dfrac{1466.7}{12 - 1}} = \sqrt{133.3} = 11.5$

③ $t = \dfrac{(\bar{X} - \bar{Y}) - (\mu_X - \mu_Y)_{\text{hyp}}}{\sqrt{\left(\dfrac{SS_X + SS_Y}{(n_X - 1) + (n_Y - 1)}\right)\left(\dfrac{1}{n_X} + \dfrac{1}{n_Y}\right)}}$

$= \dfrac{(75.0 - 56.7) - 0}{\sqrt{\left(\dfrac{1,100 + 1466.7}{(12 - 1) + (12 - 1)}\right)\left(\dfrac{1}{12} + \dfrac{1}{12}\right)}}$

$= +4.15$

④ $df = (n_X - 1) + (n_Y - 1) = (12 - 1) + (12 - 1) = 22$

⑤ $t_{\text{crit}} = \pm 2.074$

**Decision:** Reject $H_0$

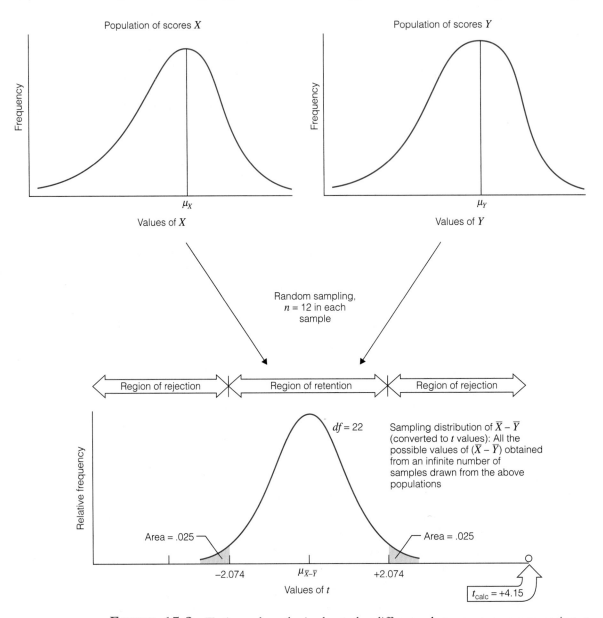

**FIGURE 15.2**   Testing a hypothesis about the difference between two means against a nondirectional alternative; $\alpha = .05$.

Next, we calculate the two means in step ① and the two sums of squares of the deviation scores in steps ②a and ②b. Although the two estimated standard deviations are not required for the subsequent calculations, good practice requires reporting them, and the necessary calculations are shown.[1] Step ③ shows the calculation of $t$, and step

---

[1] If $s_X$ and $s_Y$ are already available, the sums of squares of the deviation scores may be found using $SS_X = (n_X - 1)s_X^2$, and $SS_Y = (n_Y - 1)s_Y^2$. Similarly, if $S_X$ and $S_Y$ are known, $SS_X = n_X S_X^2$, and $SS_Y = n_Y S_Y^2$.

④ shows the determination of the degrees of freedom. Notice that when we test null hypotheses of no difference between two independent means, the number of degrees of freedom is $(n_X - 1) + (n_Y - 1)$. In step ⑤, the critical value of $t$ is obtained from Table D in Appendix E.

The outcome of the test is shown in Figure 15.2. The value of $t$ obtained by Williams and her colleagues falls in the region of rejection. It is so different from the value stated in $H_0$ that they concluded that it had a low probability of occurring by chance if $H_0$ is true. Thus, they rejected $H_0$. Their research conclusion was that blue plastic overlays on reading material improves visual processing and thereby provides immediate improvement in the reading ability of dyslexic children.

## 15.7 The Conduct of a One-Tailed Test

**directional (one-tailed) test**
the alternative hypothesis, $H_A$, states that $\mu_X$ differs from $\mu_Y$ in one particular direction (and the critical region is located in only one tail of the sampling distribution)

Suppose it had been important in the dyslexic–children study only to discover whether the blue overlay *improved* reading. In this case, a one-tailed test would have been in order. The null hypothesis and the alternative hypothesis would then have been

$$H_0: \mu_X - \mu_X = 0$$

$$H_A = \mu_X - \mu_Y > 0$$

We must now place the region of rejection entirely in the upper tail of the sampling distribution of $(\overline{X} - \overline{Y})$. In the $t$ distribution with degrees of freedom = 22, $t = +1.717$ identifies the point above which 5% of the values will be found. Figure 15.3 illustrates the situation. Our calculation of $t$ is exactly the same as for a two-tailed test, and the obtained value remains $t = +4.15$. Our obtained $t$ again falls in the region of rejection.

## 15.8 Sample Size in Inference about Two Means

When we test a hypothesis about two independent sample means, the samples may be of different size. However, if $\sigma_X$ and $\sigma_Y$ are equal, the *total* of the sample sizes $(n_X + n_Y)$ is used most efficiently when $n_X = n_Y$. This will result in a smaller value of

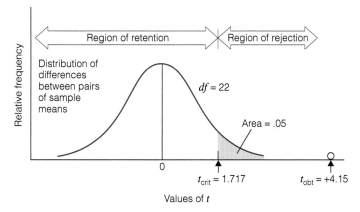

**FIGURE 15.3** Testing the hypothesis that $\mu_X - \mu_Y = 0$ against the alternative that $\mu_X - \mu_Y > 0$; data from Table 15.4.

# Point of Controversy

## Testing for Equivalence between Two Experimental Groups

At this point we have emphasized several times that probably all null hypotheses are wrong, and that with a large enough sample size even a very small (or trivial) difference from that stated in the null hypothesis can be detected (e.g., Sections 14.1 and 14.2). Therefore, all introductory statistics textbooks also emphasize that when we retain the null hypothesis, it does not mean that the null is true. However, since the early 1980s some statisticians have been extending traditional hypothesis testing methods to test whether or not two groups can be considered to be equivalent (Rogers, Howard, & Vessey, 1993; Westlake, 1981).

Equivalency testing has been used most often to compare the effect of two drugs (e.g., Havek & Anderson, 1986; Westlake, 1988). Suppose, for example, that a team of researchers wanted to know whether a new inexpensive experimental drug is as effective in treating depression as an often-used costly drug. The question the researchers are interested in is not whether there is a zero difference (the question that is traditionally asked in hypothesis testing) but whether or not the two drugs are equivalent.

The first step is to define equivalence—what is the smallest nonzero difference ($\delta$, delta) between the two drugs that the researchers would regard to be large enough so that the drugs would not be regarded as equivalent? Mathematically, this means establishing an *equivalence interval* around a value of zero difference. If the researchers regard a difference of 10% or less to be clinically trivial, then their equivalence interval would be $0 \pm 10\%$. A difference larger than this would be regarded as large (important) enough so that the two groups would not be considered to be equivalent.

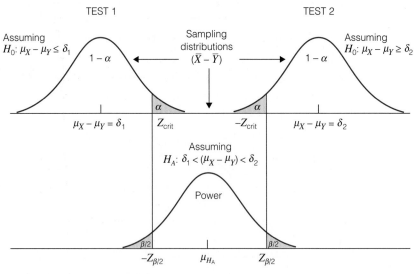

**FIGURE 15.4**   Testing for equivalence between two independent groups with the use of two one-tailed tests (from Rogers, Howard, & Vessey, 1993).

Once equivalence has been defined, the next step is to perform two one-tailed hypothesis tests. Look at Figure 15.4, which shows three different sampling distributions for $\overline{X} - \overline{Y}$. The null hypothesis for the first test is $\mu_X - \mu_Y \leq \delta_1$, and for the second test it is $\mu_X - \mu_Y \geq \delta_2$; the alternative hypothesis is $\delta_1 < (\mu_X - \mu_Y) < \delta_2$. Notice that in test 1 the values of $\overline{X} - \overline{Y}$ come from a distribution with a mean $\delta$ less than $\mu_{H_A}$, and in test 2 the values come from a distribution with a mean $\delta$ greater than $\mu_{H_A}$. To demonstrate equivalence, the researchers must simultaneously show that $\overline{X} - \overline{Y}$ is too great to have come from the sampling distribution in the upper left and yet too small to have come from the sampling distribution in the upper right. If so, then $\overline{X} - \overline{Y}$ must have come from a distribution somewhere in between (e.g., lower middle distribution).

Note that to conclude that the two drugs are equivalent, the researchers must reject both one-tailed null hypotheses. However, in practice, it is necessary to reject only the null hypothesis for the single test with the shortest observed distance between $\overline{X} - \overline{Y}$ and the value stated in the null hypothesis (because the second test will result in an even smaller $p$-value). The probability of a Type I error is the Type I error for the single test that is conducted. The formulas to perform an equivalency test are:

$$z_1 = \frac{(\overline{X} - \overline{Y}) - \delta_1}{s_{\overline{X} - \overline{Y}}} \quad \text{and} \quad z_2 = \frac{(\overline{X} - \overline{Y}) - \delta_2}{s_{\overline{X} - \overline{Y}}}$$

The criteria for rejection of $p(z_1) \leq \alpha$ and $p(z_2) \leq \alpha$.

For details on equivalency testing, as well as some excellent examples, see Rogers, Howard, and Vessey (1993).

$\sigma_{\overline{X} - \overline{Y}}$ than otherwise. For example, when one sample is twice as large as the other, $\sigma_{\overline{X} - \overline{Y}}$ is about 6% larger than it would be if the same total sample size were distributed equally between the two samples (assuming $\sigma_{\overline{X}} = \sigma_{\overline{Y}}$). The inflation of $\sigma_{\overline{X} - \overline{Y}}$ continues at an accelerated pace as the relative sample sizes become increasingly more discrepant. The advantage of a smaller $\sigma_{\overline{X} - \overline{Y}}$ is that, if there *is* a difference between $\mu_X$ and $\mu_Y$, the probability of rejecting $H_0$ is increased.

The preceding discussion relates to the *relative* sizes of the two samples. But what about the *absolute* magnitudes of the sample sizes? Other things being equal, large samples increase the probability of detecting a difference when a difference exists. We discuss the question of the optimum sample size for testing hypotheses about two means in Section 15.10.

## 15.9 Effect Size

**effect size**
an estimate of the degree to which the treatment effect is present in the population, expressed as a "number . . . free of the original measurement unit" (Cohen, 1988)

Recall from Chapter 14 that it is often convenient to express the magnitude of the difference between $\mu_{hyp}$ and $\mu_{true}$ in terms of the number of standard deviations of the measure under consideration. We referred to such a measure as the effect size, $d$ (Cohen, 1965, 1988). For tests of hypotheses about the difference between two independent means, *and assuming that* $\sigma_X = \sigma_Y = \sigma$:

$$d = \frac{(\mu_X - \mu_Y)_{true} - (\mu_X - \mu_Y)_{hyp}}{\sigma} \tag{15.7}$$

**(Cohen's) *d***
a measure of effect size; expresses the difference between $(\mu_X - \mu_Y)_{true}$ and $(\mu_X - \mu_Y)_{hyp}$ relative to the population standard deviation

**(Hedges') *g***
a measure of effect size; expresses the difference between $\overline{X}$ and $\overline{Y}$ relative to $s_p$, the pooled estimate of the population standard deviation

Note that *d* expresses the discrepancy *relative to the population standard deviation of the set of measures*, not to the standard error.

To get a feel for effect sizes of different magnitudes, look at Figure 15.5. It shows the amount of overlap between two populations with means that differ by .25, .50, .75, and 1.0 standard deviations.

Ordinarily, $\sigma$ is not known, so we must estimate it. In the case of two independent samples, we use the pooled estimate. Recall also that ordinarily $(\mu_X - \mu_Y)_{hyp} = 0$. Therefore, once we have completed our study, we may estimate effect size by *g* (Hedges & Olkin, 1985):

FORMULA FOR EFFECT SIZE, *g*

$$\text{estimated } d = g = \frac{\overline{X} - \overline{Y}}{\sqrt{\dfrac{SS_X + SS_Y}{(n_X - 1) + (n_Y - 1)}}} \tag{15.8}$$

where, similar to Cohen's *d* (1988; 1992), 0.2 = small effect, 0.5 = medium effect, and 0.8 = large effect.

Remember, effect size does not tell us the same thing as a *p*-value (Section 14.2). Highly significant *p*-values do not indicate that there is a large effect. Conversely, a nonsignificant result may still be important as judged by the effect size. As an example, consider the following two studies described by Rosnow and Rosenthal (1989a). (The studies are real, but the names have been changed.) Professor Smith uses 80 subjects to compare two styles of leadership and discovers that style A is significantly better than style B at fostering productivity ($t = 2.21$, $df = 78$, $p < .05$). Professor Jones, who invented style B, is not pleased with this result and replicates the study using only 20 subjects; he reports nonsignificant results ($t = 1.06$, $df = 18$, $p > .30$). Although the *p*-values differ substantially, the estimated effect size is the same for both studies ($d = .50$). Thus, the second study did not really contradict the first. Professor Jones's power to reject the null hypothesis was much lower than Professor Smith's because of the smaller sample size. Professor Jones's *p*-value is not impressive, but his effect size indicates a difference that may have practical importance.

The two measures of effect size, *d* and *g*, are members of what is known as the *d* family of effect sizes. Many statisticians prefer to express effect size as a correlation coefficient (see Rosenthal & DiMatteo, 2001; Rosnow, Rosenthal, & Rubin, 2000). For testing a hypothesis about the difference between two independent means:

FORMULA FOR EFFECT SIZE, *r*

$$r = \sqrt{\frac{t^2}{t^2 + df}} \tag{15.9}$$

***r***
point-biserial between groups *r*; a correlational measure of effect size = $\sqrt{\dfrac{t^2}{t^2 + df}}$

where, $df$ = degrees of freedom for *t* ($n_X - 1 + n_Y - 1$) for the two-group design. Here, *r* is a point-biserial correlation between groups (*X* and *Y*; experimental and control) and scores on a continuous variable (see Section 8.14).

Compared to *d* or *g*, *r* more directly "represents the relationship between two levels of the independent variable and scores on the dependent variable" (Rosenthal &

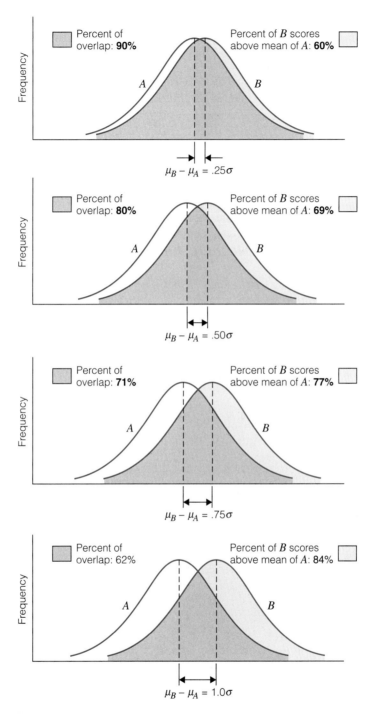

**FIGURE 15.5** Amount of overlap of two normally distributed populations with means that differ by .25 $\sigma$ (top), .50 $\sigma$, .75 $\sigma$, or 1.0 $\sigma$ (bottom).

DiMatteo, 2001). Recall from Section 10.9 that $r^2$, the coefficient of determination, gives the proportion of the $Y$ variance that is associated with differences in $X$.

As examples, let's return to the dyslexic children experiment (Table 15.4). By formula 15.8,

$$g = \cfrac{75.0 - 56.7}{\sqrt{\cfrac{1{,}000 + 1466.7}{(12 - 1) + (12 - 1)}}} = \frac{18.3}{10.8} = 1.69$$

By formula 15.9,

$$r = \sqrt{\frac{(4.15)^2}{(4.15)^2 + 22}} = \sqrt{.439} = .66$$

The two measures of effect size, $g$ and $r$, can be transformed from one to the other (Rosnow, Rosenthal, & Rubin, 2000). For the two-sample, equal-$n$ study:

---

### FORMULA FOR CONVERTING
### $g$ TO $r$ ($n_X = n_Y$)

$$r = \frac{g}{\sqrt{g^2 + 4\left(\dfrac{df}{n_{\text{total}}}\right)}} \tag{15.10}$$

---

Take the value we just calculated for $g$ in the dyslexic children experiment and convert it to $r$. It works! For unequal sample sizes, use the following formula:

---

### FORMULA FOR CONVERTING
### $g$ TO $r$ ($n_X \neq n_Y$)

$$r = \frac{g}{\sqrt{g^2 + 4\left(\dfrac{\bar{n}}{n_h}\right)\left(\dfrac{df}{n_{\text{total}}}\right)}} \tag{15.11}$$

*where*   $\bar{n}$ = arithmetic mean sample size
   $n_h$ = harmonic mean sample size
   $= \dfrac{2n_X n_Y}{n_X + n_Y}$

---

What about the sign of the effect-size correlation coefficient? It has become a convention to report it as positive "when the effect is in the predicted direction and as negative when the effect is in the unpredicted direction" (Rosnow, Rosenthal, & Rubin, 2000).

There is a whole family of $r$ effect size measures. In the chapters to come, we will introduce you to some other members of this family.

# 15.10 Estimating Power and Sample Size for Tests of Hypotheses about the Difference between Two Independent Means

Recall that we can determine the amount of power for a particular sample size or, conversely, the sample size required to achieve a desired level of power if we can specify the following:

1. The risk ($\alpha$ level) we are willing to take of rejecting a true null hypothesis.

2. The magnitude of the *smallest* discrepancy that, if it exists, we wish to be reasonably sure of discovering.

Let us adopt $\alpha = .05$ and test $H_0: \mu_1 - \mu_2 = 0$ using a two-tailed test with independent samples. (We assume that $\sigma_1 = \sigma_2$, or nearly so.) The relationships are shown in Figure 15.6. Effect size is on the horizontal axis and power is on the vertical axis. The power curves (as Cohen calls them) show the relationship between effect size

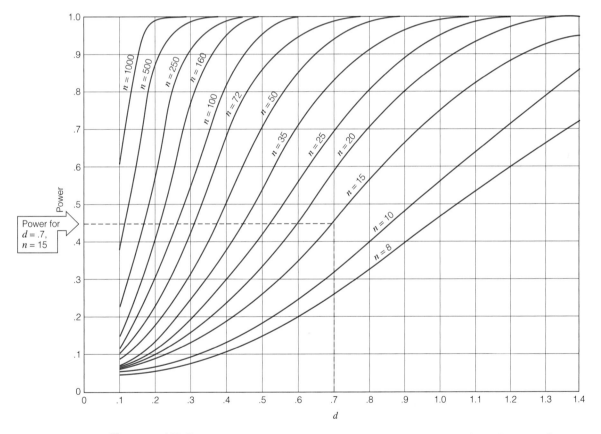

**FIGURE 15.6** Power curves for the *t* test of $H_0: \mu_1 - \mu_2 = 0$ (independent samples; $\alpha = .05$) against a two-tailed alternative. (*Source*: Data for this figure were obtained from J. Cohen, *Statistical Power Analysis for the Behavioral Sciences,* 2nd ed., Lawrence Erlbaum Associates, New York, 1988. Used with permission.) Here, *n* is the number of cases in each group.

**power
of a test**
the probability
of rejecting a
false null
hypothesis

and power for a variety of sample sizes. (The value for $n$ is the number of cases in *each* group. If the samples differ in size but neither is more than twice the size of the other, we may use the average of the two sample sizes for $n$, and the power values will be sufficiently accurate for most purposes.) The power curves shown in Figure 15.6 apply only to the independent samples case.

Recall the experiment conducted by the Centers for Disease Control that compared CD4+ cell counts in AIDS patients given the drug AZT or a placebo (Fischl et al., 1987; see the introduction to Chapter 1). Suppose that AZT actually does result in higher CD4+ cell counts and that the difference between the means of the AZT and placebo populations is $d = .7$ (a rather large difference). If the research team had used 15 subjects per group, what would the power of their test have been? To determine this, we locate .7 on the horizontal axis (the effect size) and move vertically up as shown by the dotted line to the curve for $n = 15$ and then horizontally to the vertical axis (power), where we find that power is about .45. This means that if the difference between $\mu_{AZT}$ and $\mu_{placebo}$ really is $d = .7$, the team could expect to reject the null hypothesis and conclude that there is a difference in only 45 out of 100 identical replications of the experiment; in the remaining 55 replications, chance would lead them to retain $H_0$. The sample size of 15 subjects per group does not give them a very good chance of detecting this large (and in this case, important) difference. Notice that for a smaller effect size, 15 subjects per group affords even less certainty of detecting a difference.

What if $d$ is negative? This would happen if AZT proved to be harmful and accelerated the decline in CD4+ cell counts (if $\mu_{AZT} - \mu_{placebo}$ resulted in a negative value). For a two-tailed test, we can disregard the minus sign and use the same chart because the curves are symmetric about $d = 0$. We have included only the right half of each (where $d$ is positive), to avoid duplication.

All too frequently, studies are performed by setting the level of significance and then deciding intuitively (or out of convenience) on sample size. Power curve charts such as Figure 15.6 make a more rational approach possible. Using the charts, one decides on a desired level of power and then selects sample size *according to the minimum effect size one wishes to discover* (if it exists). For example, if the CDC had wanted a probability of .9 of finding a medium-sized effect ($d = .5$) to be significant, a sample size of about 86 would have been required. In actuality, they used an $n$ of about 140.

## 15.11 Assumptions Associated with Inference about the Difference between Two Independent Means

When we test a hypothesis about the difference between two means, the statistical conditions must be fundamentally the same as those previously described for the normal-curve model (see Section 14.8). The major points are summarized as follows:

1. Each sample is drawn at random from its respective population.
2. The two random samples must be independently selected.
3. Samples are drawn with replacement.
4. The sampling distribution of $(\overline{X} - \overline{Y})$ follows the normal curve.

Under the normal-curve model, the ideal condition requires that we know $\sigma_X$ and $\sigma_Y$. Use of the $t$ statistic and evaluation of the outcome in terms of Student's distribution of $t$ evades this assumption. The $t$ distribution makes allowance for the estimation of $\sigma_X$ and $\sigma_Y$ from the samples.

A second exception applies only to inference about the difference between two *independent* means. For the $t$ distribution to be exactly applicable, homogeneity of variance is assumed. At first, this assumption sounds formidable. In practical application, there is help from several quarters.

First, experience suggests that the assumption of homogeneity of variance appears to be reasonably satisfied in many cases. It is relatively rare that a striking difference in variance occurs. Second, violation of the assumption causes less disturbance when samples are large than when they are small. As a rule of thumb, a moderate departure from the homogeneity of variance will have little effect when each sample consists of 20 or more observations.

Finally, the problem created by heterogeneity of variance is minimized when the two samples are of equal size. There are other benefits from using equal sample sizes; look back at Section 15.8. If the sample size is small and we suspect that the assumption of homogeneity of variance may not be satisfied, it is possible to test the significance of the difference between the two variance estimates ($s_X^2$ and $s_Y^2$). However, tests of homogeneity of variance are not very satisfactory in small-sample situations. To combat the influence of nonhomogeneity of variance, *the best bet is to select samples of equal (or approximately equal) size and the larger the better.*

Another point deserves special mention. A requirement, as you will remember, is that the sampling distribution of $(\overline{X} - \overline{Y})$ follows the normal distribution. (Remember that it is the distribution of $t$ which is platykurtic, *not* the sampling distribution of the mean or the difference between means—see Section 15.3.) Strictly speaking, the sampling distribution will be normal only when the distribution of the population of scores is also normal. However, according to the **central limit theorem**, the sampling distribution of the mean tends toward normality even when the population of scores is not normally distributed (see Section 12.4). *The strength of this tendency toward normality is pronounced when samples are large but is less so when samples are small.*

**central limit theorem**
regardless of the shape of the population(s) of scores from which random samples are drawn, the sampling distribution of $\overline{X}$ (or $\overline{X} - \overline{Y}$) more and more resembles a normal distribution as sample size increases

Now *only* the central limit theorem offers aid for the potential nonnormality of the sampling distribution. The use of $t$ and the $t$ distribution has no remedial effect; they make no allowance for nonnormality in the population of scores. *Because the effect of the central limit theorem is weakest when samples are small, it is particularly important to inquire as to the shape of the population (or populations) of scores when working with small samples.* (See Point of Controversy in Chapter 7.)

Fortunately, the effect of the central limit theorem is rather pronounced unless sample size is quite small. For example, a moderate degree of skewness in the population can probably be tolerated if sample size is, say, 25 or more. When we have a serious question about the normality of the parent populations, a "nonparametric" statistical test will be better (see Chapter 22). These techniques are, in some circumstances, less responsive to the totality of information conveyed by the data, but they are free of assumptions about the specific shape of the distribution of the population of scores.

## 15.12 The Random-Sampling Model versus the Random-Assignment Model

The goal of inferential statistics is to infer the nature of a population parameter from study of a sample. One of the basic assumptions that allows us to do so is that of

**random-sampling model**

a procedure that ensures that a sample is obtained in a way so that all samples of the same size have an equal chance of being selected from the population

random sampling from the population of interest. The **random-sampling model** makes it possible for us to know the characteristics of sampling distributions, which show the influence of chance sampling variation. We can then make *statistical conclusions* based directly on the laws of probability and properly generalize those conclusions to the entire population.

We discussed problems in selecting random samples and drawing proper conclusions in Section 14.12. (A random sample refers to a set of observations, but for convenience we will sometimes refer to a sample of subjects in this and the next two sections—see the introduction to Chapter 2.) Recall that in the real world it is usually impossible for investigators to work with samples that are randomly drawn from the population of interest. Most work with convenient samples. For example, biomedical researchers rely on volunteers for subjects. Faculty members who do research with humans often use students who are currently enrolled in courses they teach. In the dyslexic children experiment, Williams and her colleagues did not randomly sample all dyslexic children but instead took an available group of subjects and randomly assigned them to the two different conditions.

**random assignment**

any procedure that allows chance to divide an available group of subjects or observations into two or more subgroups

In the case of testing hypotheses about the difference between *two* means, the random assignment of available subjects is generally used as a substitute for random sampling. **Random assignment** is a method for dividing an available group of subjects or observations into two or more subgroups. It refers to any set of procedures that allows chance to determine who is included in what subgroup. For example, a researcher might assign available subjects to one of two groups by tossing a coin. The random-assignment model differs from the random-sampling model in that there is no well-defined population from which the samples are selected.

A problem arises because the procedures for inference for the two models are different. Those required for the random-assignment model are more burdensome and require the use of a computer to produce an exact solution. (We discuss these procedures in Section 22.2.) Now for the good news: *For most situations in which groups are formed by random assignment, application of the random-sampling model will lead to the same statistical conclusion as would result from application of the proper model* (Boik, 1987; McHugh, 1963). For this reason, you will find that in the research literature the simpler random-sampling model is almost always applied, even when random assignment has been used to form treatment groups. In the latter situation, for example, the *t* test can be and is used to account for chance sampling variation in the sample results.

There is, however, a difference between the two models that is of great importance. *With random assignment of available subjects, statistical conclusions do not go beyond the exact subjects studied and the exact set of conditions at the time.* This does not mean that broader generalizations (research conclusions) cannot properly be made. It only means that *statistics* does not provide a sufficient basis for making them. Research conclusions must be made on the basis of knowledge and understanding of the research area.

## 15.13 Random Sampling and Random Assignment as Experimental Controls

We have grown well acquainted with the role of random sampling in making it possible to know the characteristics of sampling distributions. When two or more groups are compared, random sampling serves a second function not always fully appreciated: experimental control.

Consider a study in which an investigator wishes to study the accuracy of perception under two different conditions. The two samples will consist of the two sets of perception scores. How will the investigator obtain these two samples? If the subjects are assigned by casual methods to one group or the other, there may well be factors associated with the assignment that are related to the performance being tested. If subjects first to volunteer are placed in one group, the two groups may differ in level of motivation and so subsequently in performance. If subjects are inspected as they report for the experimental chore and assigned by whim, the experimenter may unconsciously tend to assign those without glasses to the condition where better performance is expected.

The primary experimental (as opposed to statistical) benefit of random sampling lies in the chance (and therefore impartial) assignment of extraneous influence between the groups to be compared. Those who are likely to do well have just as much chance of being in one treatment group as in another, and the same is true of those who are likely to do poorly. The beauty of random sampling is that it affords this type of experimental control over extraneous influences whether or not they are known to exist by the experimenter. Similarly, random assignment of available subjects provides experimental control over extraneous factors that might bias the results. It provides an impartial manner of assigning extraneous influences between the groups to be compared. How important is this? In a review of outcome studies of marital and family therapy, Shadish and Ragsdale (1996) found that studies that used random assignment of subjects resulted in consistently higher and less variable posttest effects than studies that used nonrandom assignment.

Now random sampling or random assignment for each treatment group does not guarantee equality, any more than 50 heads are guaranteed every time we toss 100 coins. But random sampling or random assignment tends to produce equality, and that tendency increases in strength as sample size increases. In any event, if these procedures are practiced consistently, equality will result in the long run. Thus, random sampling or random assignment ensures a lack of bias whereas other methods may not.

One caution is in order. Inspection of the outcome of random sampling or random assignment sometimes tempts the experimenter to exchange a few subjects from group to group before proceeding with the treatment to obtain groups more nearly alike. Such a move leads to disaster. The standard error formulas, for example, are based on the assumption of random sampling, and casual adjustment of this kind makes them inappropriate.

The specific advantage of experimental control, such as can be achieved through random sampling or random assignment is that the outcome of the study is more readily interpretable. In a two-group comparison, we want to know if it is the difference in treatment that is responsible for a difference in outcome. If the two groups are balanced in all respects except the treatment imposed, conclusions are relatively straightforward. But if they differ in other respects, it will be harder (if not impossible) to say what is responsible for a difference if one is found.

The importance of *adequate* control cannot be overstressed. Only through such control is it possible to move from a statistical conclusion to a research conclusion without ambiguity. Statements of causal relationship, in the sense of asserting that certain antecedents lead to certain consequences, can be made with confidence only in such circumstances.

## 15.14 The Experiment versus the *In Situ* Study

Two primary characteristics of an experiment are (1) the manipulation of a variable of interest to the investigator (the independent variable) and (2) control of extraneous factors. We might, for example, vary the type of motivation and observe its effect on the speed of learning (the dependent variable). We would select the type of motivation and arrange the conditions of the test such that if motivation does make a difference, its effect will not be clouded by group differences in kinds of subjects, learning task employed, circumstances of learning (other than motivation), and so forth.

Many independent variables of potential interest are not subject to manipulation by experimenters. In some cases, it is because we are unwilling to do so. For example, the effect of varying brain damage among human subjects must be studied by examining individuals to whom damage has occurred through injury or disease. Other variables are unmanipulable because they are inherent characteristics of the organism. Among such variables are ethnic origin, sex, and age. If we wish to study the effect of differences in such a variable, we must identify subpopulations possessing the desired differences. For example, if we wish to study the effect of differences in age on a particular learning task, we might obtain the correlation between age and task performance. Alternatively, we might identify subpopulations described as young, middle-aged, and elderly, draw samples from each, and compare their mean performance on the learning task.

*Studies in which manipulation of the independent variable is absent cannot be called experiments.* There is no universal name for this type of investigation; we will refer to them as *in situ* **studies** (pronounced sy-too, where "sy" rhymes with "try") in reference to the fact that the characteristic must be taken as we find it in the intact individual. The important difference between an experiment and an *in situ* study is that in the latter, a significant degree of control is lost. This loss of control makes it more difficult to interpret the outcome of such studies. For example, suppose we learn that only 50% of chemistry majors marry by age 30, whereas 80% of music majors do so. Statistical procedures that assume random sampling, such as *t*, can often provide useful information in circumstances like this if we are careful in our interpretations. Although our *t* test might indicate that the difference is not due to chance, it is completely unjustified to conclude that marital practice is owed to differential educational experience. What about the factors of personality, interest, and intellect that led these individuals to these educational paths? Had it been possible to assign subjects at random to the two majors, interpretation of the outcome of the study would be clearer.

When individuals are selected according to differences that they possess in the variable we wish to investigate, such as difference in college major in the example just cited, they inevitably bring with them associated differences in other dimensions. If differences in these extraneous dimensions are related to the dependent variable, we may well find that the different "treatment" groups are significantly different with regard to the dependent variable, but the origins of these differences may be so entangled that it is extremely difficult or even hopeless to sort them out. In short, it is most difficult to develop statements of causal relationship in studies of this type.

This is not to say that *in situ* studies are worthless. Some of the most important empirical questions are not approachable in any other way, and there are many instances in which such studies have made important contributions to knowledge. Advancement of knowledge through *in situ* studies often calls on the highest degree of knowledge of the research area and the most skillful devising of investigatorial tactics.

*in situ*
**studies**

studies in which manipulation of the independent variable is absent

## 15.15 Summary

Many questions asked in education and psychology require measuring a dependent variable under two different conditions. The techniques that you learned about in this chapter apply only to samples that are obtained independently and at random. Samples are drawn from two populations and the difference between the sample means, $(\overline{X} - \overline{Y})$, is determined. If the experimental manipulation of the variable under study has no effect, then there should be no difference between the two population means; that is, $\mu_X - \mu_Y = 0$. However, even when this is true, we do not expect $\overline{X} = \mu_X$ or $\overline{Y} = \mu_Y$ because of random sampling variation, and thus we do not expect $\overline{X} - \overline{Y} = \mu_X - \mu_Y$. But if $H_0: \mu_X - \mu_Y = 0$ is true, the mean of an infinite number of $(\overline{X} - \overline{Y})$s will be equal to zero (the value stated in the null hypothesis) and so we expect our value of $(\overline{X} - \overline{Y})$ to be close to zero.

If the sampling distributions of $\overline{X}$ and $\overline{Y}$ are normal, the distribution of an infinite number of $(\overline{X} - \overline{Y})$'s selected at random will also be normal. As predicted by the central limit theorem, the distribution of $(\overline{X} - \overline{Y})$ approximates a normal curve as sample size increases even when $X$ and $Y$ are not normally distributed. We could convert an actual $(\overline{X} - \overline{Y})$ obtained from sampling to a $z$-value and use the normal-curve table if we knew the standard error of the difference, $\sigma_{\overline{X}-\overline{Y}}$, but this requires that we know $\sigma_X$ and $\sigma_Y$. As in tests of a single mean, we must estimate the two population standard deviations from the sample data. The result is $s_{\overline{X}-\overline{Y}}$, the estimated standard error of the difference between sample means. To test differences between means, we assume homogeneity of variance and obtain a pooled estimate of $\sigma_{\overline{X}-\overline{Y}}$ with $(n_X - 1) + (n_Y - 1)$ degrees of freedom. Protection from unfortunate consequences of violating the assumption of homogeneity of variance is best assured by using large samples of equal size.

We obtain a $t$ value by dividing the deviation of $(\overline{X} - \overline{Y})$ from $(\mu_X - \mu_Y)_{\text{hyp}}$ by the estimate of $\sigma_{\overline{X}-\overline{Y}}$:

$$t = \frac{(\overline{X} - \overline{Y}) - (\mu_X - \mu_Y)_{\text{hyp}}}{s_{\overline{X}-\overline{Y}}} = \frac{\begin{array}{c}\text{obtained difference}\\\text{between sample}\\\text{means}\end{array} - \begin{array}{c}\text{hypothesized difference}\\\text{between population means}\end{array}}{\begin{array}{c}\text{estimated standard error of the difference}\\\text{between two means}\end{array}}$$

If the resultant $t$ value falls in the region of rejection (which is determined by the nature of $H_A$, the chosen value of $\alpha$, and the particular distribution of $t$ related to $df$), we reject $H_0$ and conclude that the two samples were not drawn from two populations having the same mean.

One of the basic assumptions that allow us to make inferences about population parameters from sample statistics is that of random sampling. In comparisons of two (or more) conditions, the random assignment of available subjects is often used as a substitute for random sampling. In some studies, manipulation of the independent variable is not possible at all; the characteristic of interest must be taken as we find it in the intact individual. Although the $t$ test can be used in all three situations (random sampling, random assignment, or neither), in the latter two cases statistics does not provide the basis for making generalizations beyond the exact subjects studied and the exact set of conditions at the time.

# Key Terms, Concepts, and Symbols

independent samples   (288)

random sampling distribution of $(\overline{X} - \overline{Y})$   (290)

$\mu_{\overline{X}-\overline{Y}}$   (290)

standard error of $(\overline{X} - \overline{Y})$   (293)

$\sigma_{\overline{X}-\overline{Y}}$   (293)

estimated standard error of $(\overline{X} - \overline{Y})$   (294)

$s_{\overline{X}-\overline{Y}}$   (294)

assumption of homogeneity of variance   (294)

pooled estimate of the population variance   (294)

$s_p^2$   (294)

formula for $t$, unequal $n$   (295)

formula for $t$, equal $n$   (295)

degrees of freedom   (295)

effect size   (301)

$d$   (267, 302)

$g$   (267, 302)

$r$   (302)

power   (272, 306)

central limit theorem   (219, 307)

random-sampling model   (308)

random assignment   (308)

*in situ* studies   (310)

# Problems

⊡ *4, 7, 9, 10, 11*

1. Forty subjects are randomly assigned to receive either a new memory pill or a placebo. After treatment, they are all given a difficult recall test. The mean for the memory-pill group is 82%, whereas that for the placebo group is 64%. Can we conclude that the memory pill worked? Explain.

2. Given: independent samples with $s_X = s_Y = 10$. (a) Calculate $s_{\overline{X}-\overline{Y}}$ from Formula 15.2b, assuming $n_X = n_Y = 30$. (b) Recalculate $s_{\overline{X}-\overline{Y}}$, assuming $n_X = 15$ and $n_Y = 45$. (c) Compare the two values of $s_{\overline{X}-\overline{Y}}$. What principle does this outcome illustrate?

3. Given: $\overline{X} = 165.0$, $SS_X = 840$, $n_X = 36$, $\overline{Y} = 175.0$, $SS_Y = 1008$, and $n_Y = 49$; assume the samples are independent. (a) State formally the hypotheses necessary to conduct a nondirectional test of no difference between the two population means. (b) Calculate $s_{\overline{X}-\overline{Y}}$. (c) Calculate $t$. (d) Evaluate $t$ for $\alpha = .05$ and $\alpha = .01$, and state your conclusions.

4. You are given the following scores from two randomly drawn independent samples:

    X: 6, 7, 8, 8, 11     Y: 3, 4, 4, 7, 7

    (a) State formally the hypotheses necessary to conduct a nondirectional test of no difference between the two population means. (b) Calculate $s_X$ and $s_Y$. (c) Complete the test

at the .05 and .01 levels of significance, and state your conclusions.

5. Given: $\mu_X = 100$, $\sigma_X = 16$, $\mu_Y = 104$, $\sigma_Y = 16$. Compute $d$ and make a rough sketch of the populations to show the degree of separation (or overlap).

6. Professor Jones conducts a study to compare two different dosages of AZT and obtains $\sigma_1 = \sigma_2 = 5.2$ and $d = .68$ for the response measure. How far apart are $\mu_1$ and $\mu_2$?

7. Many studies have found a negative correlation between amount of exercise and level of depression. People who exercise tend to be less depressed than people who do not exercise. Recall from Chapter 8, however, that correlation does not *prove* causation. (Does exercising regularly lower depression, or are less depressed individuals more likely to exercise?) Suppose we wished to investigate the effects of exercise on depression. We randomly assign 20 subjects who tests show suffer from depression to one of two groups of 10: those that will participate in an aerobic exercise program 4 days a week for 2 months, and those that are not prescribed an exercise program. A study similar to this was, in fact, conducted by McCann and Holmes (1984).

    Let us assume that one of the subjects in the exercise group and two of those in the control group drop out before completing the study. At the end of the study, the hypothetical depression scores for the remaining subjects are as follows (higher scores indicate higher levels of depression):

| EXERCISE | NO EXERCISE |
|---|---|
| 19 | 25 |
| 8 | 32 |
| 25 | 27 |
| 17 | 35 |
| 15 | 38 |
| 17 | 26 |
| 27 | 35 |
| 13 | 42 |
| 21 | |

(a) State formally the hypotheses necessary to conduct a nondirectional test of no difference between the two population means. (b) Complete the test at the .05 level of significance, and state your conclusion. (c) Does it matter which group we designate as $X$ and which as $Y$? (d) Compute the estimated effect size, $g$, and $r$.

**8.** (a) Did the experiment described in Problem 7 employ random sampling or random assignment? (b) What technique of introducing randomness into research does the $t$ test assume? (c) How do you resolve the discrepancy?

**9.** At the start of Chapter 1 we cited the study by Fischl et al. (1987) about the effects of the drug AZT in patients with AIDS. Suppose you were assigned to investigate the effects of a new experimental AIDS drug called ABZ on CD4+ cell counts in blood (the virus that causes AIDS kills the CD4+ cells). You randomly assign 20 AIDS patients that have CD4+ cell counts of fewer than 200 to one of two groups: those receiving ABZ for 90 days and those receiving a placebo (an inert substance) for the same period. Imagine that the CD4+ cell counts at the end of 90 days are as follows:

| ABZ GROUP | PLACEBO GROUP |
|---|---|
| 240 | 160 |
| 300 | 195 |
| 195 | 180 |
| 230 | 150 |
| 250 | 170 |
| 310 | 175 |
| 270 | 180 |
| 290 | 165 |
| 180 | 175 |
| 210 | 190 |

(a) State formally the hypotheses necessary to conduct a nondirectional test of no difference between the two population means. (b) The 10 individuals given ABZ are the only 10 people ever to have received ABZ; are they the entire population or a sample? (c) Complete the test at the .01 level of significance, and state your conclusion. (d) Compute the estimated effect size, $g$, and $r$. (e) Is it really possible to randomly select 20 AIDS patients from all those individuals who have AIDS? How might this affect the conclusions?

**10.** Albert Bandura has conducted a number of studies on aggression in children. In one study (Bandura, Ross, & Ross, 1963), one group of nursery school children were shown a film of adults punching, hitting (with a hammer), kicking, and throwing a large rubber Bobo doll. Another group was not shown the film. Afterward, both groups were allowed to play with Bobo dolls in a playroom, and the number of violent contacts were measured in each child. Let us imagine that we replicated this study and obtained the following data (scores are the number of violent contacts with the Bobo doll):

| FILM GROUP | NO FILM GROUP |
|---|---|
| 20 | 5 |
| 65 | 20 |
| 41 | 0 |
| 80 | 0 |
| 52 | 10 |
| 35 | 8 |
| 15 | 30 |
| 75 | 13 |
| 60 | 0 |
| 50 | 25 |
| 47 | |
| 33 | |

(a) State formally the hypotheses necessary to conduct a directional test of no difference between the two population means. (b) Complete the test at the .01 level of significance, and state your conclusion. (c) Compute the estimated effect size, $g$, and $r$.

11. We wish to know if supplementing the diet with extra quantities of vitamin A makes a difference in ability to see under conditions of dim illumination. We randomly assign 20 subjects to one of two groups, and feed one group a normal diet and the other a normal diet plus supplementary vitamin A. After 1 week under this regimen, each individual is tested for visual acuity in conditions of dim illumination. The following visual acuity scores are obtained:

| SUPPLEMENTARY VITAMIN A $(X)$ | NORMAL DIET $(Y)$ |
|---|---|
| 38 | 37 |
| 41 | 34 |
| 42 | 45 |
| 47 | 40 |
| 42 | 43 |
| 45 | 40 |
| 48 | 42 |
| 31 | 22 |
| 38 | 28 |
| 30 | 31 |

(a) State formally the hypotheses necessary to conduct a nondirectional test of no difference between the two population means. (b) Complete the test at the .05 level of significance, and state your conclusions. (c) Does the result mean that $H_0$ is true? Explain. (d) Compute the estimated effect size, $g$, and $r$.

12. A psychologist wishes to compare mean reaction time on a frequently used reaction task with that on a new task. He or she assumes that the standard deviation will be 15 msec on both tasks and wants to estimate at the 95% level of confidence the difference between the two population means. The psychologist wants this difference to be within 5 msec of the difference between the sample means. If the psychologist selects two random samples, what should be the size of each?

13. A psychologist wonders whether midsemester warning notices affect performance. She decides to select a sample of delinquent students and, at random, to send such notices to half of them and no notices to the other half. Experience suggests that among such delinquent students, $\sigma_{GPA} = .30$. She decides to adopt $\alpha = .05$ and power $= .95$. If the difference between the warned and unwarned students is as great as .075 grade points, she would want to know it. (a) State the null hypothesis and the alternative hypothesis for a two-tailed test. (b) What should the size of the sample be to test this null hypothesis? Use Cohen's power curves.

14. In reference to Problem 13, what should sample size be if the psychologist feels that: (a) She should choose power $= .80$? (b) Is it important to know it if the difference between the means is .15 grade point (or more) and power $= .95$?

15. Given that $\mu_X = 30$, $\sigma_X = 4$, $\mu_Y = 33$, and $\sigma_Y = 4$, if you conduct a two-tailed test of $H_0: \mu_X - \mu_Y = 0$ with $\alpha = .05$, how many times in 50 replications would you expect to obtain significant results for samples of size (a) 10? (b) 20? (c) 50? (d) 100?

16. For a two-tailed test of $H_0: \mu_X - \mu_Y = 0$ with $\alpha = .05$ and $n = 10$, what is the probability of detecting a $d$ of (a) .2? (b) .5? (c) .8? (d) What does this tell you about using samples of this size?

17. For a two-tailed test of $H_0: \mu_X - \mu_Y = 0$ with $\alpha = .05$ and $n = 100$, what is the probability of detecting a $d$ of (a) .2? (b) .5? (c) .8? (d) What does this tell you about using samples of this size? (Compare with Problem 16.)

18. Professor Smith wishes to compare the performance of students in her class on multiple-choice and fill-in-the-blank exams. She randomly chooses half the class for each test. If each test has a standard deviation of 10, what is the probability of detecting a true difference $(\mu_X - \mu_Y)$ of 5 points with a two-tailed test, $\alpha = .05$, when the sample size is (a) 10? (b) 25? (c) 50? (d) 100?

19. For Problem 18, if Professor Smith wishes power $= .8$, what size sample would she need to detect a true difference of (a) 2 points? (b) 5 points? (c) 8 points? (d) 12 points?

# CHAPTER 16

## Testing for a Difference between Two Dependent (Correlated) Groups

When you have finished studying this chapter, you should be able to:

- Describe the different ways in which dependent samples may be generated;
- Understand the nature of the random sampling distribution of $(\overline{X} - \overline{Y})$ and $\overline{D}$ for dependent samples;
- Calculate $s_{\overline{X}-\overline{Y}}$ for dependent samples and explain how it differs from the estimated standard error of the difference for independent samples;
- Calculate effect size for the difference between two dependent means;
- Understand the underlying assumptions necessary for testing hypotheses about the difference between two dependent means; and
- Recognize some potential hazards of the dependent-groups design.

**dependent-samples design**
a study in which measurements in one sample are related to measurements in the other sample(s)

**repeated-measures design**
a study in which observations are measured on the same subject under two (or more) conditions

**matched-subjects design**
a study in which subjects from two (or more) samples are paired (matched) by the experimenter on an extraneous variable

**matched-pairs investigations**
a study in which subjects from two groups are naturally paired

In Chapter 15, we considered differences obtained from two independent random samples, where measurements in the two samples are unrelated to each other. Under the proper conditions, it is also possible to conduct a study in which measurements are related. This is called a **dependent-samples design**.

In what circumstances would samples be dependent? Consider our hypothetical vitamin A experiment in Problem 11 of the previous chapter. In that problem, we wished to know if supplementing the diet with extra quantities of vitamin A makes a difference in the ability to see under conditions of dim illumination. Instead of selecting two sets of 10 subjects at random and feeding one a normal diet and the other a diet supplemented with vitamin A, we could have selected one group of 10 subjects at random, fed half of them a normal diet and fed the other half a normal diet supplemented with vitamin A, tested their vision, and then retested them under the condition of the other diet. This is a **repeated-measures design**. In this case, we would have 10 *pairs* of observations, with each pair measured on the *same* subject. The potential advantage of this design is that it can reduce differences between the two groups of scores due to random sampling. Each subject serves as his or her own control. Presumably, a subject who was relatively good under one condition would tend to be relatively good under the other, aside from possible difference due to vitamin A. A person whose vision is 20–20, for example, might be expected to perform better (relatively) under both conditions than one whose visual acuity is 20–40. Thus, for a given pair of observations, the value of Y is in part determined by (or related to) the particular value of X, and the samples cannot be said to be independent.

Samples may be dependent even when different subjects have been used. In designing the vitamin A experiment, for example, we probably would consider that an extraneous source of variation is contributed by differences in basic visual acuity among individuals selected at random. We could eliminate this source of variation by pairing individuals matched on pretest performance in basic visual acuity. This is called a **matched-subjects design**. Thus, the two members of the first pair of subjects may each have 20–40 vision, the members of the second pair may each have 20–20 vision, and so forth. When observations are paired in this way, the value of any particular Y score will be in part related to the value of its paired X score, and so the values of X and Y cannot be said to be completely independent.

In a matched-subjects design, it is not always necessary that the experimenter match subjects on some variable to form pairs. Some pairs of observations occur naturally in the population. For example, investigators may choose to study identical twins, fathers and sons, mothers and daughters, or husbands and wives. Many people prefer to call such studies **matched-pairs investigations** (rather than matched-pairs experiments).

There are, then, three basic ways in which dependent samples may be generated: (1) the same subjects are used for both conditions of the study; (2) different subjects are used, but they are matched by the experimenter on some variable related to performance on the variable being observed; and (3) natural pairings.

# 16.1 Determining a Formula for *t*

For dependent means, the ideal model supposes that there exists a population of paired observations (through matching or repeated measures) and that a sample is selected at random from this population. It also presupposes that we know $\rho$ (rho), the correlation between pairs of observations in the population. The standard error of the difference between dependent means takes account of the correlation induced by the existing relationship between the samples. It is:

STANDARD ERROR OF THE DIFFERENCE
BETWEEN TWO DEPENDENT MEANS

$$\sigma_{\overline{X}-\overline{Y}} = \sqrt{\sigma_{\overline{X}}^2 + \sigma_{\overline{Y}}^2 - 2\rho_{XY}\sigma_{\overline{X}}\sigma_{\overline{Y}}} \tag{16.1}$$

*where:* $\sigma_{\overline{X}}$ = standard error of the mean of $X$
$\sigma_{\overline{Y}}$ = standard error of the mean of $Y$
$\rho_{XY}$ = correlation coefficient for the population of pairs of $X$ and $Y$ measures

$s_{\overline{X}-\overline{Y}}$
symbol for the estimated standard error of $(\overline{X} - \overline{Y})$

Notice that formula 16.1 is identical to formula 15.1 (the standard-error formula for independent samples) except for the last term, $(-2\rho_{XY}\sigma_{\overline{X}}\sigma_{\overline{Y}})$. If $\rho = 0$, the last term drops out completely. When the parameters are unknown, as usually is the case, the formula that estimates $\sigma_{\overline{X}-\overline{Y}}$ is:

$\sqrt{s_{\overline{X}}^2 + s_{\overline{Y}}^2 - 2rs_{\overline{X}}s_{\overline{Y}}}$
formula for the estimated standard error of $(\overline{X} - \overline{Y})$ in the dependent-samples design

ESTIMATED STANDARD ERROR
OF THE DIFFERENCE BETWEEN
TWO DEPENDENT MEANS

$$s_{\overline{X}-\overline{Y}} = \sqrt{s_{\overline{X}}^2 + s_{\overline{Y}}^2 - 2rs_{\overline{X}}s_{\overline{Y}}} \tag{16.2}$$

$t = \dfrac{(\overline{X} - \overline{Y}) - (\mu_X - \mu_Y)_{hyp}}{s_{\overline{X}-\overline{Y}}}$
formula for the $t$ statistic for testing a null hypothesis about the difference between two population means

As with independent samples, the **estimated standard error for dependent samples** varies from sample to sample. Therefore, we must convert the difference between two means to a $t$ value rather than a $z$ value. The calculation of $t$ for a test of the difference between two dependent means is:

$$t = \frac{(\overline{X} - \overline{Y}) - (\mu_X - \mu_Y)_{hyp}}{\sqrt{s_{\overline{X}}^2 + s_{\overline{Y}}^2 - 2rs_{\overline{X}}s_{\overline{Y}}}} \tag{16.3}$$

## 16.2 Degrees of Freedom for Tests of No Difference between Dependent Means

**$n - 1$**
degrees of freedom for $t$ in the dependent-samples design, where $n$ equals the number of pairs of scores

After we have calculated $t$, we evaluate $t$ with

$$df = n - 1$$

where $n$ is the number of *pairs* of scores. Note that $df = (n - 1)$ is but half of the $(n_X - 1) + (n_Y - 1)$ degrees of freedom that we would use if the same study were conducted using independent samples. Why are there fewer degrees of freedom for dependent samples?

When samples are independent, the score recorded for the first subject in the first group and that recorded for the first subject in the second group are completely unrelated. But when the same subjects are used under both treatment conditions, or when subjects are matched, this is not so. In the repeated-measures design, subjects who do well under one condition tend to do well under the second condition, and those who do poorly under one condition tend to do so under the other also. In the matched-subjects design, if a subject does very well as compared with the others under one condition, his or her matched counterpart will tend to do well as compared with the others under the other condition if the matching has been on a relevant variable. For example, suppose the study compares two methods of learning and pairs of subjects have been formed on the basis of level of learning aptitude. We may expect that a pair of apt subjects will tend to perform relatively well, each in his or her own group. In short, performance of one member of the pair is *not* independent of that of the other member. Thus, *when the score of one member of the pair is specified, that of the other is not completely free to vary.* Consequently, only one degree of freedom can be ascribed to each pair of scores. Because there are $n$ pairs of scores, there will be $n - 1$ degrees of freedom.

## 16.3 Testing a Hypothesis about Two Dependent Means

Imagine that we are assistant principals of the local elementary school. As conscientious assistant principals, we are, of course, interested in seeing that students at our school receive the best instruction possible. We have just learned of a new method of teaching arithmetic to second graders. However, we do not want to commit all 12 second-grade classes to this as yet unproven technique. We could choose one class in which to use the method and compare the arithmetic scores of the students in that class with the scores of the students in the other classes at the end of the year. However, we are concerned that students in the class chosen might, by chance, differ in their initial arithmetic ability from the other students. We are also concerned that the ability to teach arithmetic may vary among the teachers.

We finally decide to select 30 students *at random* and assign them to Ms. Mathis, whom we know to be a good arithmetic teacher. Based on their standardized test scores, we *match* the students in terms of intellectual ability, forming 15 pairs. In some pairs, both students score high; in other pairs, both score low; but for any given pair, the two aptitude scores are close or equal. Ms. Mathis will teach arithmetic by the traditional method to one member of each pair and will use the new method with the other 15 students. Both groups will receive equal amounts of instruction. *Which member of each pair receives which instructional method is determined at random,* by flipping a coin. We decide to use the students' math scores on the California Achievement Test (CAT), which is administered near the end of the school year, as our measure of performance in mathematics.

We will test $H_0: \mu_X - \mu_Y = 0$ (where $X$ represents the scores of those students given the traditional instruction and $Y$ the scores of those given the new instruction) against $H_A: \mu_X - \mu_Y \neq 0$, using the 5% significance level.

We illustrate use of Formula 16.3 in Table 16.1. This table contains hypothetical CAT scores and the calculations necessary for the $t$ test. The process of computation is divided into two parts. First, we find the basic quantities from which the rest of

**TABLE 16.1** *Test of the Difference between Two Dependent Means by Formula 16.3*

| PAIR | CAT SCORES TRADITIONAL METHOD $X$ | CAT SCORES NEW METHOD $Y$ | $X^2$ | $Y^2$ | $XY$ |
|---|---|---|---|---|---|
| 1 | 78 | 74 | 6,084 | 5,476 | 5,772 |
| 2 | 55 | 45 | 3,025 | 2,025 | 2,475 |
| 3 | 95 | 88 | 9,025 | 7,744 | 8,360 |
| 4 | 57 | 65 | 3,249 | 4,225 | 3,705 |
| 5 | 60 | 64 | 3,600 | 4,096 | 3,840 |
| 6 | 80 | 75 | 6,400 | 5,625 | 6,000 |
| 7 | 50 | 41 | 2,500 | 1,681 | 2,050 |
| 8 | 83 | 68 | 6,889 | 4,624 | 5,644 |
| 9 | 90 | 80 | 8,100 | 6,400 | 7,200 |
| 10 | 70 | 64 | 4,900 | 4,096 | 4,480 |
| 11 | 50 | 43 | 2,500 | 1,849 | 2,150 |
| 12 | 80 | 82 | 6,400 | 6,724 | 6,560 |
| 13 | 48 | 55 | 2,304 | 3,025 | 2,640 |
| 14 | 65 | 57 | 4,225 | 3,249 | 3,705 |
| 15 | 85 | 75 | 7,225 | 5,625 | 6,375 |
| | $\sum X = 1046$ | $\sum Y = 976$ | $\sum X^2 = 76,426$ | $\sum Y^2 = 66,464$ | $\sum XY = 70,956$ |

Calculations:

① $\overline{X} = \dfrac{\sum X}{n} = \dfrac{1046}{15} = 69.73 \quad \overline{Y} = \dfrac{\sum Y}{n} = \dfrac{976}{15} = 65.07$

②ⓐ $SS_X = \sum X^2 - \dfrac{\left(\sum X\right)^2}{n} = 76,426 - \dfrac{(1046)^2}{15} = 3484.93$

②ⓑ $s_X = \sqrt{\dfrac{SS_X}{n-1}} = \sqrt{\dfrac{3484.93}{14}} = 15.78$

③ⓐ $SS_Y = \sum Y^2 - \dfrac{\left(\sum Y\right)^2}{n} = 66,464 - \dfrac{(976)^2}{15} = 2958.93$

③ⓑ $s_Y = \sqrt{\dfrac{SS_Y}{n-1}} = \sqrt{\dfrac{2958.93}{14}} = 14.54$

④ⓐ $\sum(X - \overline{X})(Y - \overline{Y}) = \sum XY - \dfrac{\left(\sum X\right)\left(\sum Y\right)}{n} = 70,956 - \dfrac{(1046)(976)}{15} = 2896.27$

④ⓑ $r = \dfrac{\sum(X - \overline{X})(Y - \overline{Y})}{\sqrt{(SS_X)(SS_Y)}} = \dfrac{2896.27}{\sqrt{(3484.93)(2958.93)}} = +.902$

⑤ⓐ $s_{\overline{X}} = s_X/\sqrt{n} = 15.78/\sqrt{15} = 4.08$

⑤ⓑ $s_{\overline{Y}} = s_Y/\sqrt{n} = 14.54/\sqrt{15} = 3.76$

*(continued)*

**TABLE 16.1**     *Test of the Difference between Two Dependent Means by Formula 16.3 (Continued)*

Calculations:

⑥ $s_{\overline{X}-\overline{Y}} = \sqrt{s_{\overline{X}}^2 + s_{\overline{Y}}^2 - 2rs_{\overline{X}}s_{\overline{Y}}}$

$= \sqrt{4.08^2 + 3.76^2 - 2(+.902)(4.08)(3.76)} = 1.76$

⑦ $t = \dfrac{(\overline{X} - \overline{Y}) - (\mu_X - \mu_Y)_{hyp}}{s_{\overline{X}-\overline{Y}}}$

$= \dfrac{69.73 - 65.07}{1.76} = +2.65$

the calculations flow: $\Sigma X$, $\Sigma X^2$, $\Sigma Y$, $\Sigma Y^2$, $\Sigma XY$, and $n$. Next, we calculate the means in step ①, the estimated population standard deviations in steps ② and ③, the correlation coefficient in step ④, the estimated standard error of the means in step ⑤, the estimated standard error of the difference between the means in step ⑥, and finally $t$ in step ⑦.

Our obtained value of $t$ is 2.65. The sampling distribution of $t$ when $H_0$ is true is shown in Figure 16.1. The expected value is 0; the critical value of $t$ for a two-tailed test with $\alpha = .05$ and $df = 14$ is $\pm 2.145$ (from Table D in Appendix E). The probability of drawing samples this deviant from the value stated in $H_0$ is less than 1 in 20 when $H_0$ is true. Our obtained $t$ falls in the region of rejection, and therefore we reject $H_0$. We have reached the statistical conclusion.

**Dunagin's People**

"The placebo proved more effective than our product ... let's market the placebo!"

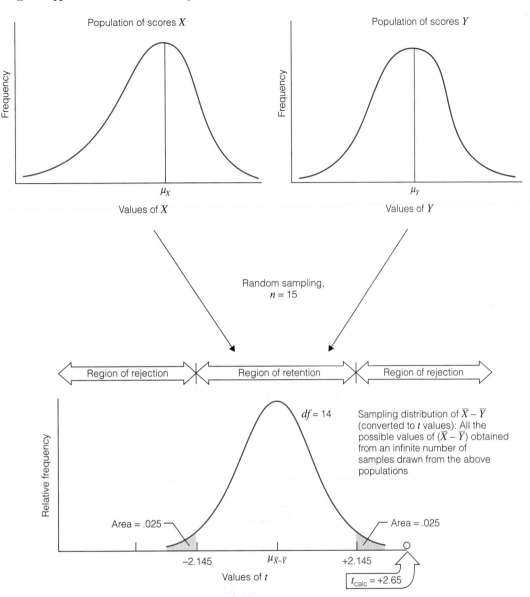

**FIGURE 16.1**    Testing a hypothesis about the difference between two dependent means against a nondirectional alternative; $\alpha = .05$.

Our *research conclusion* is that students' learning of arithmetic is worse under the new method. This is opposite to our hopes. This example illustrates why it is often preferable to use a two-tailed test. If we had elected to use a one-tailed test, $H_A$: $\mu_X - \mu_Y < 0$, we would have been unable to conclude that the new method was worse than the traditional method. Although we were hoping that the new method would prove to be beneficial, we would also want to know if the new method of instruction proved to be worse than the traditional method. Remember, a one-tailed test is appropriate only when a finding in the direction opposite to that stated in $H_A$ is of no practical or theoretical importance.

**D**

symbol for a
difference score,
$X - Y$

**$\overline{D}$**

symbol for
the mean of
a sample of
difference scores

There is an important factor to be considered before using the *matched-subjects* design. Note that the reduction of $\sigma_{\overline{X}-\overline{Y}}$ induced by pairing the observations depends on the value of $r$, the correlation coefficient induced by pairing. In general, when pairing is on the basis of a variable importantly related to the performance of the subjects, the correlation will be higher than otherwise, and the reduction in $\sigma_{\overline{X}-\overline{Y}}$ will consequently be greater. A reduction in $\sigma_{\overline{X}-\overline{Y}}$ reduces the probability of committing a Type II error. For example, matching subjects on the basis of their intelligence test scores for an experiment on rate of learning will probably be beneficial. However, when the correlation must be estimated from the sample, it is rare that the sample coefficient exactly equals the population coefficient. For example, the correlation in the population might actually be zero and yet the sample coefficient might be, say, $+.20$. In practice, this means that we should not match subjects on a variable that "might help" but only on one that we are sure will have a reasonably substantial influence.

## 16.4 An Alternative Approach to the Problem of Two Dependent Means

**sampling
distribution
of $\overline{D}$**

a theoretical relative frequency
distribution of
all the possible
values of $\overline{D}$
that would be
obtained by
chance from an
infinite number
of samples of a
particular size
drawn from two
populations
($X$ and $Y$)

**$s_D$**
symbol for
the estimated
population standard deviation
of $D$

Formula 16.3 requires that we compute the correlation between the paired values of $X$ and $Y$. There is an alternative method for calculating $t$ for the test of two dependent means that provides an identical outcome with less computation. This method focuses on the characteristics of the **sampling distribution of differences** between the paired $X$ and $Y$ scores.

Consider the null hypothesis that $\mu_X - \mu_Y = 0$. If the hypothesis is true, then it is also true that the mean of the population of differences between the paired values of $X$ and $Y$ is zero. If the difference between paired $X$ and $Y$ scores is designated by $D$, the initial hypothesis may be restated as: $H_0: \mu_D = 0$. With this method, we find $\overline{D}$, the mean of the sample set of different scores, and inquire whether it differs significantly from the hypothesized mean of the population of difference scores, $\mu_D$. Note that *this transforms the test from a two-sample test (of X and Y scores) to a one-sample test (of difference scores)*.

Instead of a sample of scores, $X$, we have a sample of difference scores, $D$. The **estimated standard deviation of the difference scores,** $s_D$, is:

$$s_D = \sqrt{\frac{SS_D}{n-1}} = \sqrt{\frac{\sum(D-\overline{D})^2}{n-1}} = \sqrt{\frac{\sum D^2 - \dfrac{\left(\sum D\right)^2}{n}}{n-1}}$$

The **estimated standard error of the mean of the difference scores,** $s_{\overline{D}}$, is thus:

$$s_{\overline{D}} = \frac{s_D}{\sqrt{n}}$$

$$\sqrt{\frac{\sum D^2 - \dfrac{(\sum D)^2}{n}}{n-1}}$$

formula for the estimated population
standard deviation
of $D$

and our formula for $t$ becomes:

---

FORMULA FOR $t$ FOR TESTING HYPOTHESES
ABOUT DEPENDENT MEANS

$$t = \frac{\overline{D} - \mu_{D(hyp)}}{s_{\overline{D}}} \qquad (16.4)$$

$s_{\overline{D}}$
symbol for the estimated standard error of $\overline{D}$

A computational formula for $t$ for dependent means is easily derived from the preceding formulas:

$t =$

$\dfrac{\overline{D} - \mu_{D(hyp)}}{s_{\overline{D}}}$

alternative formula for the $t$ statistic for testing a null hypothesis about the difference between two dependent means

---

**COMPUTATIONAL FORMULA FOR $t$ FOR DEPENDENT MEANS**

$$t = \frac{\overline{D} - \mu_{D(hyp)}}{\sqrt{\dfrac{\sum D^2 - \dfrac{\left(\sum D\right)^2}{n}}{n(n-1)}}} \qquad (16.5)$$

---

Compare Formula 16.5 with Formula 13.5 in Section 13.15, the computational formula for $t$ for testing hypotheses about single means.

We illustrate the use of Formula 16.5 in Table 16.2 with the same data used in the previous section. To conduct the $t$ test, we subtract each value of $Y$ from its paired value of $X$ and record the difference in a new column, $D$ (step ①). The only

**TABLE 16.2**　*Test of the Difference between Two Dependent Means by Formula 16.5*

| PAIR | CAT SCORES UNDER TRADITIONAL METHOD $X$ | CAT SCORES UNDER NEW METHOD $Y$ | ① $D = X - Y$ | $D^2$ | |
|---|---|---|---|---|---|
| 1 | 78 | 74 | 4 | 16 | Calculations: |
| 2 | 55 | 45 | 10 | 100 | ④ $\overline{D} = \dfrac{\sum D}{n} = \dfrac{70}{15} = 4.67$ |
| 3 | 95 | 88 | 7 | 49 | |
| 4 | 57 | 65 | −8 | 64 | |
| 5 | 60 | 64 | −4 | 16 | |
| 6 | 80 | 75 | 5 | 25 | ⑤ $t = \dfrac{\overline{D} - \mu_{D(hyp)}}{\sqrt{\dfrac{\sum D^2 - \dfrac{\left(\sum D\right)^2}{n}}{n(n-1)}}}$ |
| 7 | 50 | 41 | 9 | 81 | |
| 8 | 83 | 68 | 15 | 225 | |
| 9 | 90 | 80 | 10 | 100 | |
| 10 | 70 | 64 | 6 | 36 | |
| 11 | 50 | 43 | 7 | 49 | |
| 12 | 80 | 82 | −2 | 4 | |
| 13 | 48 | 55 | −7 | 49 | $= \dfrac{4.67 - 0}{\sqrt{\dfrac{978 - \dfrac{4900}{15}}{15(14)}}}$ |
| 14 | 65 | 57 | 8 | 64 | |
| 15 | 85 | 75 | 10 | 100 | |
| | | | $\sum D = 70$ ② | $\sum D^2 = 978$ ③ | |
| | | | | | $= \dfrac{4.67}{\sqrt{3.10}}$ |
| | | | | | $= 2.65$ |

*Note:* In Table 16.1 $\overline{X} - \overline{Y} = 4.66$, but here $\overline{D} = 4.67$. The difference is due to rounding.

quantities needed for the calculation of $t$ (step ⑤) are $\Sigma D$, $\Sigma D^2$, and $\overline{D}$ (steps ②, ③, and ④, respectively).

Although the simpler method described in this section reduces the computational burden substantially, it also yields less information. When we are done, we know the size of the difference between the two sample means $(\overline{D})$ and whether the difference was or was not significant according to the decision criterion adopted. In most research, we will want to know (and will be obliged to report) the two means and the two standard deviations. If we are curious how much correlation was induced by pairing, we will also want to know $r$. The short method yields none of this information. If these quantities are desired, we shall have to return to the data and compute them, and so may find that the total amount of work is about the same as with the longer method described in the previous section.

## 16.5 Effect Size

Look again at Section 15.9. Recall that for tests of hypotheses about the difference between two means, effect size $d$, is

$$d = \frac{(\mu_X - \mu_Y)_{\text{true}} - (\mu_X - \mu_Y)_{\text{hyp}}}{\sigma}$$

where $\sigma$ is the population standard deviation, not the standard error $(\sigma_{\overline{X}-\overline{Y}})$. Because we do not know $\sigma$, we must estimate it with $s$. Remember also that ordinarily $(\mu_X - \mu_Y)_{\text{hyp}} = 0$. Therefore,

$$\text{estimated } d = g = \frac{\overline{X} - \overline{Y}}{s}$$

For dependent samples, $s$, the estimated population standard deviation, is $s_{X-Y} = \sqrt{s_X^2 + s_Y^2 - 2r_{XY}\, s_X\, s_Y}$. Therefore,

**(Hedges') $g$**
a measure of effect size; expresses the difference between $\overline{X}$ and $\overline{Y}$ relative to $s_{X-Y}$ (or $s_D$), the estimated population standard deviations

$$\text{estimated } d = g = \frac{\overline{X} - \overline{Y}}{\sqrt{s_X^2 + s_Y^2 - 2r_{XY}\, s_X\, s_Y}} \tag{16.6}$$

As usual, it is much easier to estimate $d$ if we use difference scores, $D$ (remember, $\overline{X} - \overline{Y} = \overline{D}$):

$$\text{estimated } d = g = \frac{\overline{D}}{\sqrt{\dfrac{SS_D}{n-1}}} \tag{16.7}$$

After you have finished your calculations, use Cohen's (1988, 1992) conventions: $0.2 = $ small effect, $0.5 = $ medium effect, and $0.8 = $ large effect.

For our example about comparing methods of teaching arithmetic,

$$g = \frac{4.67}{\sqrt{\dfrac{978 - \dfrac{(70)^2}{15}}{15 - 1}}} = .68$$

Some sources advise using Formula 15.8 to calculate $g$ for dependent groups. Formula 15.8 is for independent groups and will give an overestimate of $g$.

What about $r$ as a measure of effect size? Recall from Formula 15.9 that

$$r = \sqrt{\frac{t^2}{t^2 + df}}$$

*r*
a correlational
measure of
effect size

and that for the independent-samples design, $r$ is a point-biserial correlation between groups ($X$ and $Y$) and scores on a continuous variable. For the dependent-samples design, $r$ "is no longer the simple point-biserial correlation, but is instead the correlation between group membership and scores on the dependent variable with indicator variables for the paired individuals partialed out" (Rosnow, Rosenthal, & Rubin, 2000).

## 16.6 Power

**power
of a test**
the probability
of rejecting
a false null
hypothesis

In Section 14.6, we showed that an increase in sample size increases power by reducing the standard error of the mean. Because the estimated standard error of the mean is $s/\sqrt{n}$, *another way to increase power is to reduce the size of* s. In comparing the means of two groups, *the dependent-samples design makes it possible to reduce the standard error of the difference between the means by controlling the influence of extraneous variables.* We accomplish this effect by pairing observations. If you compare the formula for the standard error of the difference between two correlated means, $s_{\bar{X}-\bar{Y}} = \sqrt{s_{\bar{X}}^2 + s_{\bar{Y}}^2 - 2rs_{\bar{X}}s_{\bar{Y}}}$, with that for the difference between two independent means, $s_{\bar{X}-\bar{Y}} = \sqrt{s_{\bar{X}}^2 + s_{\bar{Y}}^2}$, you can see the statistical improvement that can be achieved by this method.

## 16.7 Assumptions When Testing a Hypothesis about the Difference between Two Dependent Means

Unlike the test of the difference between two independent means, the assumption of homogeneity of variance is *not* required for the test between two dependent means. However, hypothesis testing still assumes that our sample has been drawn randomly with replacement and that the sampling distribution of $\bar{X} - \bar{Y}$ (or $\bar{D}$) is normally distributed. Therefore, our choice of sample size is an important design consideration. Remember, in the behavioral sciences most dependent variables are not distributed normally (see Point of Controversy in Chapter 7). When sample size is large ($>25$), the central limit theorem tells us that the sampling distribution of $\bar{D}$ should approximate the normal curve regardless of what the original population of scores looks like. But what if our sample size is smaller than 25? If samples are small and we have grounds to believe that the parent population is not normal in shape, a "non-parametric" statistical test may be a better alternative than *t* (see Chapter 22).

# 16.8 Hazards of the Dependent-Samples Design

In Section 15.13 we discussed the role of random sampling from an experimental point of view. We saw that we can obtain control over the influence of extraneous variables by drawing subjects at random for each treatment condition. We also saw that when random sampling cannot be followed, it is much more difficult to interpret the outcome. Those comments apply to studies using dependent samples as well as to those using independent samples. To follow the random sampling model precisely in the *matched-subjects* design, we must first draw a random sample from a single population, form matched pairs of subjects, and then randomly assign the treatment condition to the two members of each pair, taking care to do so independently for each pair of subjects. For the *repeated-measures* design, strict adherence would mean deciding randomly which treatment the subject will receive first and which will be given second. However, problems can arise, especially when the design of the study departs from these conditions (as in the second and third of the following examples). We shall discuss common problems associated with three study designs.

## Study Design 1

Pairs of observations are formed by repeated observations on the *same* subjects. The assignment of the treatment condition is *random* with regard to the two trials for a given subject.

When we make repeated measurements on the same subjects, exposure to the treatment condition assigned *first* may change the subject in some way that will affect his or her performance on the treatment condition assigned *second*. An influence of this sort is called an **order effect**. Practice, fatigue, and change in mental set or attitude are examples of such influences.

**order effect**
when making repeated measurements on the same subjects, exposure to the treatment condition assigned first changes performance on the treatment condition assigned second

When an order effect is present *and* it can be assumed that the influence of one treatment on the other is the same as that of the other on the one, the outcome of the experiment may be interpretable, if the order of the treatment condition has been assigned at random. However, the order effect will introduce an additional source of variation in each set of scores, according to the magnitude of its influence. This tends to increase the standard error and, consequently, to decrease the chance of detecting a difference when one exists. The purpose of choosing a dependent-samples design is ordinarily to *reduce* extraneous sources of variation, but the effect may be quite the opposite.

If the influence of one treatment on the other is not the same as that of the other on the one, bias will be introduced as well as unwanted variation. The outcome then becomes difficult or impossible to interpret. For example, if the two treatment conditions are mild and heavy shocks, a subject receiving the heavy shock first may have a different outlook toward the second trial than one who receives the mild shock first.

## Study Design 2

Pairs of observations are formed by repeated observations on the same subjects. The assignment of the treatment condition to the two trials for a given subject is *nonrandom*. (This design is typical of "growth" studies of the same subjects.)

If a design utilizes repeated observations on the same subjects but the assignment of the order of the treatment condition is not random, we are in grave difficulty. Any order effect will bias the comparison. In many investigations, it is not possible to avoid this problem. For example, it occurs in studies where the object is to determine what change has taken place in the subjects over a period of time. Is a particular type of psychotherapy effective? The subjects' condition may be evaluated before and after therapy, and the results compared. "Before" and "after" cannot be randomly assigned to a subject. The results of comparison will therefore be ambiguous. If there is improvement, is it the result of therapy, the person's belief that he or she is *supposed* to feel better, the mere fact that someone paid attention to him or her, or simply a natural recovery that would have taken place without therapy? To be meaningful, the study must include a comparison group, chosen in the same way and treated alike except for receiving the therapy to be evaluated (Bowers & Clum, 1988).

> **regression effect**
>
> when subjects are selected because of their extreme scores on some measure, and remeasurement on the same variable yields scores closer to the mean

Studies of this type may also be subject to another source of bias: the **regression effect**. If subjects are selected *because* of their extreme scores on some measure, we expect remeasurement on the same variable to yield scores closer to the mean. We discussed this effect and gave an illustration of it in Sections 10.6 and 10.7.

## Study Design 3

The two groups consist of *different* subjects matched on an extraneous but related variable. The assignment of the treatment condition to members of a matched pair is *nonrandom*.

These conditions arise when studying the effect of a nonmanipulable variable in intact groups. For example, one may wish to compare the personality characteristics of delinquent and nondelinquent children matched on parents' socioeconomic level. Such investigations fall in the category of *in situ* studies, described in Section 15.14. They are subject to all of the difficulties described there.

# 16.9 Summary

In this chapter, we introduced procedures for testing for a difference between two dependent groups, where measurements in the two samples are related to each other. There are three ways in which dependent samples may be generated: (1) use of a repeated-measures design, in which the same subjects are used for both conditions of the study; (2) use of a matched-subjects design, in which different subjects are used but are matched by the experimenter on some variable related to performance on the variable being observed; and (3) natural pairings.

The major advantage of the dependent-samples design over the independent-samples design is that an extraneous source of variation (i.e., variation due to subject differences) can be eliminated by pairing observations. For the *t* test, the effect is reflected in the standard error (the denominator in the formula for $t$), which is smaller for dependent samples whenever $r$, the correlation between the set of paired observations, is greater than zero. The greater the correlation, the smaller the standard error, and thus the more likely the experimenter is to notice a true difference between the means of two populations. An alternative formula transforms the $t$ test from a two-sample to a one-sample test by focusing on the distribution of differences, $D$, between paired $X$ and $Y$ scores. In both cases, the degrees of freedom used to evaluate $t$ for dependent means is $n - 1$, where $n$ is the number of pairs of scores.

Although the dependent-samples design has some advantages, consideration must also be given to some possible problems. In the repeated-measures design, exposure to the treatment condition assigned first may change a subject in some way that will affect his or her performance on the second treatment condition. The repeated-measures design assumes counterbalancing of conditions, but in some types of studies it is not possible to reverse the order of conditions. Interpretation of the outcome in these circumstances can be difficult.

## Key Terms, Concepts, and Symbols

dependent-samples design (316)

repeated-measures design (316)

matched-subjects design (316)

matched-pairs investigations (316)

standard error of the difference between dependent means (317)

$\sigma_{\bar{X}-\bar{Y}}$ (317)

estimated standard error (317)

$s_{\bar{X}-\bar{Y}}$ (317)

$t$ for dependent means (317, 323)

$df$ for $t$ test for dependent samples (317)

difference scores (322)

sampling distribution of differences (322)

$D$ (322)

$\overline{D}$ (322)

estimated standard deviation of the difference scores (322)

$s_D$ (322)

estimated standard error of the mean of the difference scores (322)

$s_{\overline{D}}$ (322)

effect size (324)

order effect (326)

regression effect (181, 327)

## Problems

$\boxed{c}$ *4, 6, 7, 8*

1. In our hypothetical example in Section 16.3, suppose we had used $X$ for the new method and $Y$ for the traditional method. (a) Would it have changed the outcome of the test? (b) Would it have changed the research conclusion? Explain. (c) Why was this a dependent-samples design? Is it because both groups of students were taught by the same teacher?

2. Suppose that the scores for the problem in Section 16.3 (Table 16.1) were from two sam-

ples drawn independently. Calculate $t$ using Formula 15.6 for two independent means. Compare your answer with that obtained in Table 16.1. Why do the two results differ? If $r = 0$, what effect would it have for the dependent-samples $t$ test?

3. Given the following data from two dependent samples: $\overline{X} = 88.0$, $s_X = 16.0$, $\overline{Y} = 85.0$, $s_Y = 12.0$, $n = 64$, and $r = +.50$. (a) State formally the hypotheses necessary to conduct a nondirectional test of no difference between the two population means. (b) Calculate $s_{\bar{X}-\bar{Y}}$ using Formula 16.2. (c) Complete the test at the

.05 and .01 levels of significance and state your conclusions.

4. Given the following pairs of scores from dependent samples:

| Pair: | 1 | 2 | 3 | 4 | 5 |
|-------|---|---|---|---|---|
| X: | 4 | 4 | 6 | 5 | 9 |
| Y: | 5 | 2 | 3 | 1 | 6 |

(a) State formally the hypotheses necessary to conduct a nondirectional test of no difference between the two population means. (b) Calculate $\overline{X}$, $\overline{Y}$, $s_X$, $s_Y$. (c) Calculate $r_{XY}$. (d) Calculate $s_{\overline{X}-\overline{Y}}$. (e) Complete the test at the .05 and .01 levels of significance and state your conclusion. (f) Calculate effect size, $g$.

5. Using the data of Problem 4, test the hypothesis of no difference between population means by the difference method described in Section 16.4: (a) Calculate $\overline{D}$ and $s_{\overline{D}}$. (b) Calculate $t$ and compare it with the value of $t$ obtained in Problem 4. (c) Evaluate $t$ for $\alpha = .05$ and $\alpha = .01$ and state your conclusions. (d) Calculate effect size, $g$.

6. Is reaction time to a red light different from that to a green light? Suppose 20 subjects have been selected at random and given a preliminary test to determine the reaction time of each individual to a white light stimulus. From among this group, 10 pairs of subjects are formed such that the two members of any given pair are equal or nearly equal in speed of reaction to white light. Taking each pair in turn, one member is first tested with a green light as the stimulus and the other with a red light. Which member of each pair receives which stimulus first is determined at random. Reaction times are recorded in milliseconds. The results are given in Data 16A.

### Data 16A

| PAIR | GREEN LIGHT (X) | RED LIGHT (Y) |
|------|-----------------|---------------|
| 1 | 208 | 205 |
| 2 | 206 | 207 |
| 3 | 213 | 208 |
| 4 | 210 | 211 |
| 5 | 212 | 209 |
| 6 | 210 | 210 |
| 7 | 211 | 212 |
| 8 | 198 | 201 |
| 9 | 202 | 205 |
| 10 | 204 | 200 |

(a) State formally the null and alternative hypotheses necessary to conduct a nondirectional test. (b) Complete the test at the .05 level of significance, and state your conclusion. (c) Does it matter which group was designated as $X$ and which as $Y$? (d) Calculate effect size, $g$.

7. Dr. Fredericks believes that environment is more important than genetics in influencing intelligence. He locates 12 pairs of identical twins that have been reared apart, one twin in each pair in an enriched environment and the other in an impoverished environment. He administers a standardized IQ test and obtains the results given in Data 16B.

### Data 16B

| PAIR | ENRICHED | IMPOVERISHED |
|------|----------|--------------|
| 1 | 100 | 102 |
| 2 | 95 | 93 |
| 3 | 122 | 116 |
| 4 | 107 | 110 |
| 5 | 85 | 75 |
| 6 | 96 | 100 |
| 7 | 135 | 124 |
| 8 | 110 | 110 |
| 9 | 108 | 100 |
| 10 | 90 | 88 |
| 11 | 100 | 90 |
| 12 | 113 | 108 |

(a) State formally the null and alternative hypotheses necessary to conduct a nondirectional test. (b) Complete the test at the .05 level of significance, and state your conclusion. (c) Why is this a dependent-samples design? (d) Can Dr. Fredericks conclude that environment is more important than genetics from the results of this test? Explain. (e) Calculate effect size, $g$. (f) Could Dr. Fredericks really have obtained the 12 pairs of twins at random? What effect might this violation of one of the assumptions have on the outcome?

8. A psychologist is interested in the effect of social pressure. She selects a group of 10 male subjects at random from her introductory psychology course. Each subject is asked to estimate by eye the length of a stick under two conditions. In one condition, the subject is placed in the presence of four other persons who, unknown to him, have been instructed

to give estimates that are too large. Each of these persons gives his estimate orally to the experimenter before the subject is asked for his estimate. In the other condition, the same procedure is employed, except that the other four persons present are told to give honest estimates. For each subject, the order of the two conditions is determined randomly. Estimates (in inches) made by each subject under both conditions are given in Data 16C.

## DATA 16C

| SUBJECT | ESTIMATES MADE IN UNBIASED ENVIRONMENT | ESTIMATES MADE IN BIASED ENVIRONMENT |
|---------|----------------------------------------|--------------------------------------|
| 1 | 38 | 47 |
| 2 | 35 | 45 |
| 3 | 37 | 42 |

## DATA 16C (*Continued*)

| SUBJECT | ESTIMATES MADE IN UNBIASED ENVIRONMENT | ESTIMATES MADE IN BIASED ENVIRONMENT |
|---------|----------------------------------------|--------------------------------------|
| 4 | 40 | 45 |
| 5 | 45 | 47 |
| 6 | 34 | 40 |
| 7 | 40 | 43 |
| 8 | 36 | 45 |
| 9 | 43 | 40 |
| 10 | 41 | 48 |

(a) State formally the null and alternative hypotheses necessary to conduct a nondirectional test. (b) Complete the test using $\alpha = .05$, and state your conclusion. (c) Calculate effect size, $g$.

# CHAPTER 17

## Inference about Correlation Coefficients

When you have finished studying this chapter, you should be able to:

- Understand that Pearson's $r$ varies from sample to sample because of random sampling variation;
- Understand that a correlation coefficient calculated from a sample of scores is statistically significant only if it has a small probability of occurring by chance;
- Test the null hypothesis that there is no relationship between $X$ and $Y$ in the population; and
- Recognize that the same procedures are used for Spearman's $r_s$ when $n \geq 10$.

The Pearson correlation coefficient (see Chapter 8), like other statistics, varies from sample to sample because of chance factors resulting from random sampling variation. In most cases, we only know the sample coefficient, but we would like to know the "true" correlation in the population. To determine the accuracy of our sample correlation coefficient, we can again use hypothesis testing. Before you begin reading this chapter, you should already be familiar with the basics of inference and Student's distribution of $t$ (Chapter 13).

## 17.1 The Random Sampling Distribution of $r$

**$\rho_{XY}$**
symbol for Pearson's correlation coefficient calculated from a population of paired scores

**$r_{XY}$**
symbol for Pearson's correlation coefficient calculated from a sample of paired scores

**random sampling distribution of $r$**
a theoretical relative frequency distribution of all the values of $r$ that would be obtained by chance from an infinite number of samples of a particular size drawn from a given population

The Pearson correlation coefficient, calculated from a population of paired scores, is $\rho_{XY}$ (Greek letter rho). When the coefficient is calculated from a sample, it is $r_{XY}$. If we drew a sample of given size at random from the population, calculated $r$, returned the sample to the population, and repeated this operation many times, we would see many different values of $r$ due to random sampling variation. If we repeated this procedure an *infinite* number of times, the multitude of sample $r$'s would form the **random sampling distribution of $r$** for samples of that particular size. The mean of this sampling distribution is approximately $\rho$, and the standard deviation is $\sigma_r$:

$$\sigma_r = \frac{1 - \rho^2}{\sqrt{n - 1}}$$

As you can see from the denominator of this formula, $\sigma_r$ becomes smaller as $n$ increases. Thus, *the values of* r *will vary less from sample to sample when the sample size is large.* Now look carefully at the numerator. The standard deviation becomes smaller as $\rho$ increases. Thus, *the values of* r *will also vary less from sample to sample when the true correlation, $\rho$, is strong than when it is weak.* Note that because $\rho$ is squared, it is the absolute value that is important, not its sign (positive or negative).

If the sample values of $r$ formed a normal distribution, we could solve problems of inference by methods learned in earlier chapters. Unfortunately, *the sampling distribution of* r *is not normally distributed.* When $\rho = 0$, the sampling distribution of $r$ is symmetrical and nearly normal. But when $\rho$ has a value other than zero, the sampling distribution is skewed because values cannot exceed $\pm 1.00$. In fact, the larger the absolute value of $\rho$, the greater the skewness. Figure 17.1 shows random sampling distributions for $\rho = -.8$, 0, and $+.8$ when $n = 8$. This graph helps explain why the distribution is skewed when the absolute value of $r$ is high. When $\rho = +.8$, for example, it would not be possible for us to obtain a sample coefficient more than .2

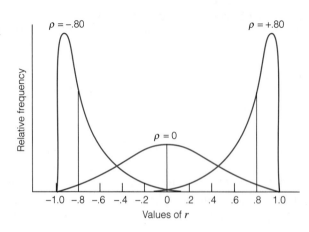

**FIGURE 17.1** Random sampling distributions of $r$ for three values of $\rho$; $n = 8$.

points higher ($r = +1.0$), but random sampling could produce a coefficient substantially lower than .2 points below $r = +.8$ (to a lower limit of $-1.0$).

The degree of skewness of the sampling distribution of $r$ is also a function of sample size. When $\rho \neq 0$, the smaller the size of the sample, the greater the skewness of the sampling distribution.

Because the distribution of sample $r$'s is not normal, we must seek alternative solutions for making inferences about population correlation coefficients. For some problems, the $t$ distribution will give us an appropriate model. For others, transformation of $r$ to a variable that is (approximately) normally distributed offers the best solution.

## 17.2 Testing the Hypothesis that $\rho = 0$

**$\rho = 0$**
the usual null
hypothesis in
inference about
correlation

Without doubt, the most frequent question of inference about correlation is whether there is *any* relationship at all between two variables. Suppose, for example, that we are developing a test with the hope of predicting success in the job of insurance salesperson. We want to know, of course, whether the test has *any* relationship to actual job success. To determine this, we draw a random sample of 25 salespersons and find $r = +.30$ between test performance and job performance rating. It may be that the true correlation ($\rho$) is zero and that we obtained this value of $r$ simply as a matter of chance (random sampling variation). To check on this possibility, we will test the null hypothesis that $\rho = 0$ against the alternative that it is not. (Before doing this, however, we should always examine the scatter diagram to see if the cluster of dots is in agreement with our calculated value of $r$—see Chapter 8.)

Sir Ronald Fisher showed that when $\rho = 0$, the value obtained by the following formula is distributed as Student's $t$ test with $n - 2$ degrees of freedom:

**$t$ REQUIRED FOR TESTING THE
NULL HYPOTHESIS THAT $\rho = 0$**

$t = \dfrac{r}{\sqrt{(1 - r^2)/(n - 2)}}$
formula for $t$ for
testing the null
hypothesis $\rho = 0$

$$t = \frac{r}{\sqrt{(1 - r^2)/(n - 2)}} \tag{17.1}$$

*where:* $r$ = the sample coefficient.
$n$ = the number of *pairs* of scores in the sample.

To test the null hypothesis that $\rho = 0$, we could use Formula 17.1 and refer to the values of $t$ found in Table D in Appendix E.

This method is quite general. We can use it for a variety of levels of significance and for one- or two-tailed tests. (A two-tailed test tests for either a positive or negative correlation; a one-tailed test tests for one or the other, but not both.) However, if we wish to conduct tests at the usual 5% or 1% significance level, Table G in Appendix E eliminates the chore of computing $t$. This table gives the critical value of $r$ required to reach significance. (The $r$'s are expressed as absolute values; for tests of negative correlations insert a minus sign.) To use this table, find the appropriate value of $df$ and read the critical value of $r$ for the desired significance level. If $r_{calc}$ exceeds the tabulated value, we reject the null hypothesis of no correlation; otherwise, we do not. For our example, if we conduct a two-tailed test at $\alpha = .05$, and if $r_{calc} = .30$ based on $n = 25$, we first determine the degrees of freedom:

$$df = n - 2 = 25 - 2 = 23$$

We then enter Table G and look down the left column until we locate this number of degrees of freedom. We then look across to find the entry in the column for a two-tailed test at $\alpha = .05$. This is the critical value of $r$:

$$r_{crit} = .396$$

Because our obtained value of $r = +.30$ is less than this critical value, we cannot reject the null hypothesis of no correlation. Our $r_{calc}$ is one of many that could have occurred by chance when the null hypothesis of no correlation is true. Figure 17.2 illustrates this situation.

What if our $r_{calc}$ proves to be significant? Be careful, a significant $r$ does not mean that the association is important. The expression "significant correlation" means only that $H_0: \rho = 0$ has been tested and rejected, and "nonsignificant correlation" means only that $H_0: \rho = 0$ has been tested and retained—nothing more, nothing less. With large samples, a very small (and perhaps unimportant) $r$ may prove to be "statistically significant."

## 17.3 Fisher's $z'$ Transformation

**Fisher's $z'$**
a logarithmic
function of $r$,
used because
the sampling
distribution of $r$
is not normally
distributed
when $\rho \neq 0$

Although we can use the technique described in the previous section to test the hypothesis that $\rho = 0$, we cannot use it to answer other questions about correlation. The fundamental problem is that the sampling distribution of $r$ is not normally distributed when $\rho$ is not equal to zero. Moreover, the degree of skewness varies with the magnitude of $\rho$. Fisher derived a logarithmic function of $r$, which we shall call **Fisher's $z'$** ($z$ prime), that has certain desirable properties:

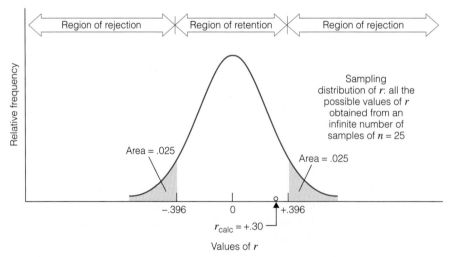

**FIGURE 17.2**   Testing the hypothesis that $\rho = 0$ when $r = +.30$ and $df = 23$.

1. The sampling distribution of $z'$ is approximately normal, irrespective of the value of $\rho$.

2. The standard error of $z'$, unlike the standard error of $r$, is essentially independent of the value of $\rho$.

Thus, we can translate $r$ to $z'$ and then use the familiar properties of the normal curve to conduct the evaluation. The outcome is the same as though inference were conducted directly in terms of $r$.

The formula for $z'$ is

---

### FORMULA FOR TRANSLATING $r$ TO FISHER'S $z'$

$$z' = \tfrac{1}{2}[\log_e(1 + r) - \log_e(1 - r)] \qquad (17.2)$$

---

Note that the value of $z'$ depends *wholly* on the value of $r$. The $z'$ transformation is simply a nonlinear mathematical reformulation that changes the scale of $r$. Note, also, that *Fisher's $z'$ is not a z score, nor is it related to the z score in any way.* The similarity in symbolism is unfortunate; another symbol would be better. Fisher originally called his statistic $z$, which is completely unacceptable because of the wide use of that symbol for a standard score. Usage has perpetuated Fisher's symbolism as closely as possible without creating utter confusion. We will shortly be using the symbols $z$ and $z'$ in close proximity; watch for the difference.

You can best appreciate the improvement in scale the use of $z'$ provides through an illustration. In Figure 17.3, we show the sampling distributions of $z'$ that correspond to $\rho = -.8, \rho = 0$, and $\rho = +.8$ when $n = 8$. Compare these distributions with those of $r$ for the same values of $\rho$ (Figure 17.1). Note that the sampling distributions of $z'$ are essentially similar in shape and variability under these three conditions, whereas those of $r$ are not.

It would be awkward to use Formula 17.2 to translate an $r$ to $z'$, or vice versa. Fortunately, Table H in Appendix E makes the conversion easy. In this table, if $r$ is positive, read the value of $z'$ as positive, and if $r$ is negative, read $z'$ as negative.

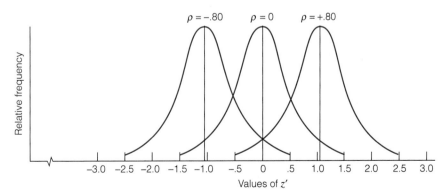

**FIGURE 17.3** Random sampling distributions of $z'$ corresponding to three values of $\rho$; $n = 8$.

Give this table a few moments of study; it reveals what is accomplished by Fisher's transformation. As $r$ increases from zero to one, a discrepancy between $r$ and $z'$ begins to appear, with $z'$ being larger than its parent, $r$. Note, however, that when $r$ is zero, $z'$ is also zero, and that the two values are essentially equivalent up to, say, $r = .25$. The discrepancy between $r$ and $z'$ increases more rapidly as the value of $r$ gets higher. What is accomplished is that the scale of $r$ (which ranges from $-1.00$ through 0 to $+1.00$) is stretched, very little at the center but increasingly more so at the extremes. Note that the original scale of $r$ becomes, in terms of $z'$, a scale ranging from approximately $-3$ to $+3$ (or even farther, if $r$ is allowed to exceed $\pm.995$).

In the suggested uses of the $z'$ transformation that follow, keep in mind that we can obtain reasonable results unless the sample size ($n$) is very small (because of considerable random sampling variation) or $\rho$ is very high (for the reasons discussed in the preceding paragraph). Actually, we have no justification for finding Pearson's $r$ among very small samples, nor do we ordinarily encounter correlation coefficients much above .9. Thus, the limitations are more academic than practical.

## 17.4 Testing the Hypothesis of No Difference between $\rho_1$ and $\rho_2$: Independent Samples

An investigator at Spartan University wonders whether aptitude test score is related to freshman grade point average to the same degree for male and female students. She draws a sample of 100 male students and finds the correlation between these two variables to be $r_1 = +.50$. For a sample of 100 female students, the correlation between the same two variables is $r_2 = +.35$.

The investigator is faced with the facts that the two sampling distributions of $r$ corresponding to $\rho_1$ and $\rho_2$ are unknown and are probably skewed. Hence the sampling distribution of the *differences* between pairs of coefficients will tend to be nonnormal. She gets around this problem by converting $r$ to $z'$ (thus normalizing the sampling distributions) and conducting the test in terms of $z'$.

She first states the null and alternative hypotheses and the desired significance level:

$$H_0: \rho_1 - \rho_2 = 0$$

$$H_A: \rho_1 - \rho_2 \neq 0$$

$$\alpha = .01$$

As for a test of the difference between two means, the investigator could have chosen to use either a nondirectional or directional alternative hypothesis. (As before, a nondirectional test is appropriate if we are interested in discovering a difference, if one exists, in *either* direction.)

From Table H in Appendix E, the investigator finds the $z'$ equivalents of $r_1$ ($z' = +.55$) and $r_2$ ($z' = +.37$). Then she calculates $z$ (not $z'$) according to the following formula:

> $z$ REQUIRED TO TEST THE HYPOTHESIS THAT $\rho_1 = \rho_2$
> WHEN SAMPLES ARE INDEPENDENT
>
> $$z = \frac{(z'_1 - z'_2) - 0}{\sigma_{z'_1 - z'_2}}$$
> (17.3)

To use this formula, we need the following formula for the standard error of the difference between two values of $z'$, $\sigma_{z_1'-z_2'}$:

> **STANDARD ERROR OF THE DIFFERENCE**
> **BETWEEN TWO INDEPENDENT $z$s**
>
> $$\sigma_{z_1'-z_2'} \sqrt{\frac{1}{n_1 - 3} + \frac{1}{n_2 - 3}} \tag{17.4}$$

The investigator can now conclude the test:

$$\sigma_{z_1'-z_2'} \sqrt{\frac{1}{100 - 3} + \frac{1}{100 - 3}} = .14$$

and

$$z = \frac{(.55 - .37) - 0}{.14} = +1.29$$

She treats the obtained value of $z$, $z_{obt} = +1.29$, as a normal deviate and finds that it falls short of the critical value of $z$, $z_{crit} = +2.58$, required to declare significance at the 1% level. The grounds are insufficient to reject the hypothesis so she retains $H_0$.

The procedures we just described are suited *only* to situations involving two *independent* random samples. They are not appropriate, for example, when the two correlation coefficients have been obtained on the same set of subjects or when subjects have been matched. Because solutions to these problems are somewhat special, we will omit their development here (see instead, Glass & Hopkins, 1996).

## 17.5 Strength of Relationship

**coefficient of determination ($r^2$)**

the proportion of the $Y$ variance that is associated with differences in $X$

Suppose your obtained value of $r$ proves to be statistically significant; what about the strength of the relationship? We have already introduced ways of interpreting $r$ in Chapter 10. Be sure to look at Section 10.4 (the slope of the regression line) and Section 10.9 (the coefficient of determination). Recall that $r^2$, the coefficient of determination, gives the proportion of the $Y$ variance that is associated with differences in $X$.

## 17.6 A Note about Assumptions

From earlier chapters, you may recall that no assumption about the shape of the bivariate distribution is required when the correlation coefficient is used purely as a descriptive index. However, *all the procedures for inference about coefficients described in this chapter are based on the assumptions that there is independence among the pairs of scores and that the population of the pairs of scores has a normal bivariate distribution.* The latter assumption implies that $X$ is normally distributed, that $Y$ is normally distributed, and that the relation between $X$ and $Y$ is linear. If we are not dealing with a normal bivariate population, then the procedures for inference we have discussed here will yield only approximate results. If there is reason to believe that the population of the pairs of scores varies considerably from a normal bivariate distribution, you might consider nonlinear transformations (to a normal distribution) before conducting formal hypothesis testing.

## 17.7 Inference When Using Spearman's $r_S$

$r_S$
symbol for
Spearman's
rank-order
correlation
coefficient

In Chapter 8 (Sections 8.8–8.10) we introduced an alternative to Pearson's $r$ when the paired scores are both in the form of ranks and $n$ is rather small. If we choose to use Spearman's $r_S$, how do we test the hypothesis that the population value is zero?

Look again at the example problem in Chapter 8 (Section 8.8). The calculated value of $r_S$ was $+.38$. Can the instructor conclude that those who turn their papers in earlier tend to earn poorer scores? Exact procedures have been developed for testing the hypothesis of no correlation for very small samples. We can obtain good results for $n \geq 10$ by finding the critical values required for significance for $df = n - 2$ in Table G in Appendix E. This is the same table we use to determine the significance of Pearson's $r$. For the present problem, Table G shows that for $df = n - 2 = 13$, the instructor would need a coefficient of $+.514$ or larger to reject the hypothesis of no correlation for a two-tailed test at $\alpha = .05$. The obtained coefficient of $.38$ fails to meet this criterion, so the instructor retains the null hypothesis of no correlation in the population.

## 17.8 Summary

Like other statistics, the sample correlation coefficient, $r$, is subject to sampling error. In this chapter, we introduced statistical inference techniques to test the hypothesis that there is no linear association between two variables ($H_0$: $\rho = 0$). The test is a $t$ test with $n - 2$ degrees of freedom, where $n$ is the number of pairs of observations. For Spearman's $r_S$, we use the same procedure when $n \geq 10$.

Whether or not significance is reached depends importantly on the size of the sample. There is generally a considerable amount of sampling variation with small samples, making it difficult to obtain statistical significance. For large samples, the value of $r$ will be fairly accurate, and statistical significance may be achieved even with a very low degree of association between two variables. We must be careful, therefore, to distinguish between statistical significance and practical significance when dealing with correlations.

## Key Terms, Concepts, and Symbols

$\rho_{XY}$   (332)

$r_{XY}$   (332)

random sampling distribution
of $r$   (332)

$\rho = 0$   (333)

significant correlation   (334)

Fisher's $z'$   (334)

$r^2$   (337)

coefficient of determination
(337)

Spearman's $r_S$   (338)

# Problems

1. What sample value of $r$ would we need for statistical significance if (a) $n = 5$ and $\alpha = .05$ for a two-tailed test? (b) $n = 10$ and $\alpha = .05$ for a two-tailed test? (c) $n = 25$ and $\alpha = .05$ for a two-tailed test? (d) $n = 25$ and $\alpha = .01$ for a two-tailed test? (e) $n = 25$ and $\alpha = .05$ for a one-tailed test? (f) $n = 100$ and $\alpha = .05$ for a two-tailed test? (g) $n = 1000$ and $\alpha = .05$ for a two-tailed test?

2. Given: $H_0$: $\rho = 0$; $H_A$: $\rho \neq 0$; $r = +.35$; $n = 24$. Test the null hypothesis at $\alpha = .10$, .05, and .01.

3. Using Table G in Appendix E, test the null hypothesis that $\rho = 0$ when (a) $r = +.40$, $n = 28$, $H_A$: $\rho \neq 0$, and $\alpha = .05$. (b) $r = -.55$, $n = 18$, $H_A$: $\rho \neq 0$, and $\alpha = .01$. (c) $r = -.40$, $n = 22$, $H_A$: $\rho < 0$, and $\alpha = .05$. (d) $r = +.45$, $n = 25$, $H_A$: $\rho < 0$, and $\alpha = .05$. Show the critical value(s) of $r$ for each problem.

4. The director of personnel at an automobile assembly plant is not satisfied with the performance of recently hired employees. To improve matters, he decides to use an employment test to screen applicants. A group of 14 new applicants is given the test and hired. Three months later they receive their first on-the-job ratings by supervisors. The correlation between test scores and job ratings is found to be $+.41$. Can the director of personnel claim that the test successfully predicts job performance? Use $\alpha = .05$ and a two-tailed test.

5. In a particular study, it is reported that $r = +.75$ between predictor and criterion. You find that this value was obtained on a sample of six cases. Comment.

6. In another study, it is reported that $r = +.12$ between predictor and criterion. This correlation is based on 500 cases. Is it significantly different from zero? Comment.

7. (a) If all we know about a study is that the correlation between two variables was "not significant" for a sample of 1000 cases, can we adequately evaluate the results without knowing $r$? Explain. (b) If the result had been "significant," can we adequately evaluate the results without knowing $r$? Explain.

8. Professor Smith wants to know whether academic test score is related to freshman grade point average to the same extent for male college students as it is for female students. She obtains the following data from samples obtained at her institution: males: $r = +.45$, $n = 103$; females: $r = +.30$, $n = 103$. (a) State the null and alternative hypotheses appropriate to her question. (b) Test the null hypothesis using $\alpha = .05$, and state your conclusions.

9. Look again at Problem 9 in Chapter 8. The calculated value of $r_S$ was $+.60$. (a) Is $r_S$ significantly different from zero according to a two-tailed test at the 5% significance level? Show the basis for your answer. (b) Do you have any qualifications for your answer to Problem 5? Explain.

10. Look again at Problem 11 in Chapter 8. The calculated value of $r_S$ was $+.83$. Is $r_S$ significantly different from zero according to a two-tailed test at the 5% significance level?

# CHAPTER 18

## An Alternative to Hypothesis Testing: Confidence Intervals

When you have finished studying this chapter, you should be able to:

- Understand the merits of confidence intervals compared to dichotomous hypothesis testing;

- Understand what is meant by the terms "95% confidence interval" and "99% confidence interval";

- Calculate a confidence interval for $\mu_X$ or $\mu_X - \mu_Y$ with use of original scores and in terms of standard deviations of the variable;

- Calculate sample size required for estimates of $\mu_X$ or $\mu_X - \mu_Y$; and

- Calculate a confidence interval for the population correlation coefficient, $\rho$.

Interval estimates should be given [when presenting results] for any effect sizes involving principal outcomes. . . . Comparing confidence intervals from a current study to intervals from previous, related studies helps focus attention on stability across studies. (Wilkinson and the Task Force on Statistical Inference. APA Board of Scientific Affairs, 1999)

The inferential technique of testing the null hypothesis is credited to Ronald A. Fisher, "the father of modern statistics." It is a mechanical methodology, not dependent on content, resulting in one of only two possible decisions: Either we can reject the null hypothesis or we can retain it.

But in the real world, the null hypothesis is almost always false; it is almost certain that the population parameter under test is not exactly equal to the value stated in the null hypothesis. The question researchers should ask themselves, according to some critics (Cohen, 1990; Rosnow & Rosenthal, 1989), is by how much is the null hypothesis incorrect, not whether a result is "statistically significant" or not. Interestingly, Fisher opposed the idea of an alternative hypothesis. This was the creation of Jerzy Neyman and Egon Pearson (1928*a,b*), whose views Fisher vehemently opposed (Gigerenzer, 1987). Nevertheless, it became standard practice that when rejecting the null hypothesis, one accepts the alternative. It must be emphasized, however, that a *p*-value does not give the probability of either the null or the alternative hypothesis being true; it gives the probability of the data in the case that the null hypothesis is true (Cohen, 1990). But with **dichotomous decision making**, if one fails to reject the null hypothesis, one cannot conclude anything about it at all. Only a "significant result" allows a definite conclusion, and it thus takes on great importance (to the researcher).

This methodology developed from agricultural experiments, where research required making decisions (for example, whether a particular fertilizer was effective) (Gigerenzer, 1987). Decision-oriented research may be appropriate in some fields, but the research questions asked in psychology (or any other field interested in the development of scientific theories) are often quite different (Rosnow & Rosenthal, 1989). Nevertheless, most research in psychology and education is conducted within the Fisherian dichotomous decision-making scheme.

Compounding the problem is the sanctity that psychology and education have bestowed on the .05 level of significance. Although statistics textbooks teach that if a result is found to be statistically significant it does not mean the result is important, the attainment of doctoral degrees, academic positions, and promotion and tenure have come to depend on producing research that is significant at the .05 level. Thus achieving statistical significance has taken on a different kind of importance.

Is there a basis for the tradition of using .05 as the sharp line of division between a significant and non-significant result? In other fields, $\alpha$ levels other than .05 are traditional. The acclaimed physicist Enrico Fermi, for example, believed the operational definition of a "miracle" to be $p = .10$ (Polanyi, 1961).

The problem is not whether psychology and education should use .05 or some other value as the traditional $\alpha$ level, but dichotomous decision making itself. There is, in fact, no ontological basis for it:

Surely, God loves the .06 nearly as much as the .05. Can there be any doubt that God views the strength of evidence for or against the null as a fairly continuous function of the magnitude of *p?* (Rosnow and Rosenthal, 1989)

**dichotomous decision making**

null hypothesis significance tests can result in one of only two possible decisions: either we reject $H_0$ or we retain it

**p-value**

the probability, when $H_0$ is true, of observing a sample mean as deviant or more deviant (in the direction specified in $H_A$) than the obtained value of $\overline{X}$

The controversy about dichotomous hypothesis testing has never been greater than it is today. In fact, some statisticians and psychologists have called for a ban of significance tests altogether (e.g., Cohen, 1994; Hunter, 1997; Loftus, 1996; Schmidt, 1996; see comment section in *American Psychologist,* 53 (7), 1998). For example, in the 1980s, the editor of the *American Journal of Public Health,* one of the leading journals in the world, sent prospective authors the following instructions:

> All references to statistical hypothesis testing and statistical significance should be removed from the paper. I ask that you delete *p* values as well as comments about statistical significance. If you do not agree with my standards (concerning the inappropriateness of significance tests), you should feel free to argue the point, or simply ignore what you may consider to be my misguided view, by publishing elsewhere. As editor, however, I can hardly be expected to accept papers that violate the scientific principle that I espouse. (Kenneth Rothman)

The ban was lifted 2 years later when the editor resigned from his position.

Although some statisticians applaud attempts to ban the *t* test (and other significance tests), others continue to defend its use (e.g., Abelson, 1997; Chow, 1998; Hagen, 1997; Wainer, 1999). Still others argue for a balanced approach, finding merit (and fault) with both arguments (e.g., Krueger, 2001).

In 1996, the American Psychological Association's Task Force on Statistical Inference stated:

> We endorse a policy of inclusiveness that allows any procedure that appropriately sheds light on the phenomenon of interest to be included in the arsenal of the research scientist. In this spirit, the task force does not support any action that could be interpreted as banning the use of null hypothesis significance testing or *p* values in psychological research and publication. . . . We recommend . . . enhanced characterization of the results of analyses (beyond simple *p* value statements) to include both direction and size of effect . . . and their confidence intervals should be provided routinely as part of the presentation. (p. 2)

This was followed in the final report (1999) by the more strongly worded support of confidence intervals that begins this chapter. In this chapter you will learn about this increasingly popular alternative to dichotomous hypothesis testing.

## 18.1  Examples of Estimation

A Harris poll of nearly 2,000 registered voters conducted over the last 3 days of the 1992 presidential election found that 44% preferred Bill Clinton, 38% preferred George Bush, and 17% preferred Ross Perot, with only 1% still undecided. In five other major media polls, Mr. Clinton's support was identical in four of them—44%—and in a fifth it was 43%. Mr. Bush's support ranged from 35% to 38% and Mr. Perot's from 14% to 17% (*New York Times,* November 3, p. A9). In all surveys, the margin of error was reported as 3%. According to *The New York Times,* which participated in a poll with CBS News, this meant that "in 19 cases out of 20 the results based on such samples will differ by no more than three percentage points in either direction from what would have been obtained by seeking out all American adults." On November 3, over 100 million people cast their votes. The final results were 43%

for Clinton, 38% for Bush, and 19% for Perot (most of the undecided voters apparently voted for Perot). The political surveys, which questioned only a small fraction of the registered voters, had been accurate in their projections. (We will consider the results of the 2000 presidential election later in the chapter.)

The Harris and major media surveys are examples of estimation. In estimation, unlike hypothesis testing, no value is specified in advance. The question is, "What *is* the value of the population parameter?" For some kinds of research questions, such as ascertaining what percentage of voters prefer a particular candidate, hypothesis testing is useless; no specific hypothesis presents itself. On the other hand, estimation procedures are exactly suited to such problems. Although there are some research questions that cannot be answered by hypothesis testing but can be approached through estimation, the reverse is not true. *Any problem for which hypothesis testing might be useful can alternatively be approached through estimation.* In this chapter, we will concentrate on the estimation of means. (The previous example was about percentages; no means were involved.)

**point estimates**

estimations of a single value of a population parameter

An estimation may take two forms. Sometimes we desire a single value as an estimate of the population value. We call such estimates **point estimates**. What percentage of voters will vote for candidate X? What is the mean aptitude test score of applicants for admission to Spartan University? If it is impractical to find the percentage in the entire population (in the first example) or the mean of the entire population (in the second example), we can make an estimate of the population characteristic from a random sample.

**interval estimates**

estimations of a range of values of a population parameter

Point estimates are rarely stated by themselves. Because of the chance factors involved in random sampling, any point estimate is likely to be in error. But by how much will it differ from the population parameter? For **interval estimates**, we calculate a range of values (an interval) within which it appears reasonable that the population parameter lies. In the question about candidate X, a point estimate might state that 49% of the population of voters favor him or her. If we made an interval estimate, the outcome might state that we are 95% confident that no less than 46% and no more than 52% of the voters (in the population) favor him or her.

Of course, we may be wrong in supposing that the stated limits contain the population value. Therefore, any statement of limits must be accompanied by indication of the probability that the limits contain the population parameter. The limits themselves are usually referred to as a *confidence interval* and the statement of degree of confidence as a *confidence coefficient*.

## 18.2 Confidence Intervals for $\mu_X$

Remember from Chapter 7 that in a normal distribution, 95% of the scores are no farther away from the mean than 1.96 standard deviations. Similarly, if the sampling distribution of $\overline{X}$ is normally distributed, 95% of the sample means are no farther away from $\mu_X$ than 1.96 standard errors of the mean ($\sigma_{\overline{X}}$). Now *if 95% of the sample means are no farther away from $\mu_X$ than $1.96\sigma_{\overline{X}}$, it is equally true that for 95% of the sample means, $\mu_X$ is no farther away than $1.96\sigma_{\overline{X}}$.* This fact makes it possible for us to construct an interval estimate of $\mu_X$. Suppose for each sample mean the statement is made that $\mu_X$ lies somewhere within the range $\overline{X} \pm 1.96\sigma_{\overline{X}}$. For 95% of the sample means, this statement would be correct, and for 5% it would not. In drawing samples at random, the probability is therefore .95 that an interval estimate constructed according to the rule

$$\overline{X} \pm 1.96\sigma_{\overline{X}}$$

will include $\mu_X$ within the interval.

We illustrate the application of this rule in Figure 18.1. Suppose we draw random samples of size 100 from a normally distributed population of IQ scores in which $\mu_X = 100$ and $\sigma_X = 20$. In this example, $\sigma_{\overline{X}}$ is $20/\sqrt{100} = 2.00$. If we draw a sample whose mean is 103, we would claim that $\mu_X$ lies somewhere within the interval $103 \pm (1.96)(2.00)$ or between 99.08 and 106.92. This interval is shown at (b) in Figure 18.1, and we see that the claim is correct. On the other hand, if $\overline{X}$ had been 95, we would claim that $\mu_X$ lies within the interval $95 \pm (1.96)(2.00)$ or between 91.08 and 98.92. This interval is shown at (a); the claim is wrong because 95 is one of the 5% of sample means that lie farther from $\mu_X$ than $1.96\sigma_{\overline{X}}$.

A 95% *confidence interval* for $\mu_X$ is an interval so constructed that 95% of such intervals include $\mu_X$. We may wish to be even more sure that our estimate includes $\mu_X$. Suppose that we prefer a probability of .99 to one of .95. Because 99% of sample means fall between $\mu_X \pm 2.58\sigma_{\overline{X}}$, we may make an estimate for which the probability is .99 that the interval will cover $\mu_X$ by the rule

$$\overline{X} \pm 2.58\sigma_{\overline{X}}$$

Note that the result is a wider interval than when a probability of .95 was used. Although the two levels of probability, .95 and .99, are the ones commonly used in interval estimation, it is possible to construct an interval estimate according to any desired level of probability. *Other things being equal, if we set wide limits, the likelihood that the limits will include the population value is high, and if we set narrow limits, there is greater risk of being wrong.*

The procedures that we have described require knowledge of $\sigma_{\overline{X}}$, which in turn requires that we know $\sigma_X$. This normally will not be the case. Thus, as usual, we must

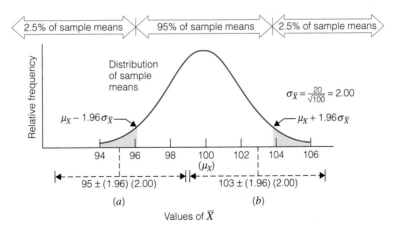

**FIGURE 18.1** Distribution of sample means based on $n = 100$, drawn from a population characterized by $\mu_X = 100$ and $\sigma_X = 20$. (*a*) Confidence interval of $\mu_X$ constructed about $\overline{X} = 95$; estimate does not cover $\mu_X$. (*b*) Confidence interval of $\mu_X$ constructed about $\overline{X} = 103$; estimate covers $\mu_X$.

substitute $s_{\overline{X}} = s_X/\sqrt{n}$ as an estimate of $\sigma_{\overline{X}}$ (see Section 13.9). The manner in which we construct a confidence interval is identical except that we substitute the appropriate value of $t$ for $z$:

$s_{\overline{X}}$
symbol for
the estimated
standard error
of the mean

$t_p$
symbol for the
magnitude of $t$
for which the
probability is $p$
of obtaining a
value of $\overline{X}$ so
deviant or
more so

> RULE FOR CONSTRUCTING A CONFIDENCE
> INTERVAL FOR $\mu_X$ WHEN $\sigma_X$ IS UNKNOWN
>
> $$\overline{X} \pm t_p s_{\overline{X}} \qquad (18.1)$$
>
> *where:* $\overline{X}$ = the sample mean, obtained by random sampling
> $s_{\overline{X}}$ = the estimate of the standard error of the mean
> $t_p$ = the magnitude of $t$ for which the probability is $p$ of obtaining a value
> so deviant or more so (in either direction); $df = n - 1$, the number
> of degrees of freedom associated with $s_X$

**Problem**

Suppose that the following results on a mathematics proficiency exam are obtained for a random sample of 25 college freshmen at Spartan University: $\overline{X} = 85.0$ and $s_X = 15.0$. Construct the 95% confidence interval for $\mu_X$.

**Solution**

We first calculate the estimated standard error of the mean:

$$s_{\overline{X}} = \frac{s_X}{\sqrt{n}} = \frac{15.0}{\sqrt{25}} = 3.00$$

The number of degrees of freedom associated with $s_X$ is $n - 1$, or 24. From Table D in Appendix E, the appropriate value of $t$ is 2.064. The limits are therefore

$\overline{X} \pm t_p s_{\overline{X}}$
formula for
constructing a
confidence
interval for $\mu_X$

$$\overline{X} \pm t_{.05} s_{\overline{X}}$$

| LOWER LIMIT | UPPER LIMIT |
|---|---|
| $= 85.0 - (2.064)(3.00)$ | $= 85.0 + (2.064)(3.00)$ |
| $= 78.8$ | $= 91.2$ |

When we construct intervals according to the rule used in the preceding problem, it is proper to say that the probability is .95 that an interval so constructed will include $\mu_X$. However, *once we establish the specific limits for a given set of data, the interval thus obtained either does or does not cover $\mu_X$.* It is *not* proper to say that the probability is .95 that $\mu_X$ lies within the interval. The probability at this stage is either 1.00 or 0 that the interval covers $\mu_X$; we do not know which. Consequently, it is usual to substitute the term *confidence* for probability in speaking of a *specific* interval. The limits of the interval are referred to as a **confidence interval** and the statement of degree of confidence is called the **confidence coefficient**, **C**. In our example,

**confidence interval**
the limits of the
interval estimate

**confidence coefficient**
the degree of
confidence

**C**
symbol for
the confidence
coefficient

$$C(78.8 \leq \mu_X \leq 91.2) = .95$$

We translate the statement as follows: We are 95% confident that $\mu_X$ falls between 78.8 and 91.2.

But what does it mean to say that we are "95% confident"? We do not know whether the *particular* interval covers $\mu_X$, but when intervals are constructed according to the rule, 95 of every 100 of them (on the average) will include $\mu_X$. Remember that *it is*

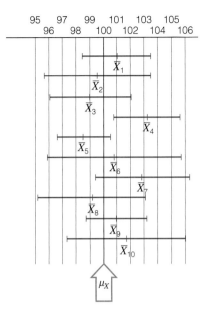

**FIGURE 18.2** Interval estimates of $\mu_X$ constructed from means of several random samples; $\sigma_X$ unknown.

*the interval that varies from estimate to estimate and not the value of* $\mu_X$. Because $\mu_X$ is a fixed value it does not vary. Figure 18.2 shows some of the intervals that might result if we selected samples at random and constructed intervals about the sample means by the procedures just described. We may expect that 95% of such estimates will include $\mu_X$ within their range when $t_P$ is selected to agree with $C = .95$.

In Figure 18.2, note that as we move from sample 1 to sample 10, the *locations* of the intervals vary because the sample means vary. Note also that the *widths* of the intervals differ, too. This is because interval width depends in part on the varying estimates of the population standard deviation obtained from the several samples.

Recall that $s_X$ (and consequently, $s_{\overline{X}}$) is affected by sample size. Thus, *for a given confidence coefficient, a small sample results in a wide confidence interval and a large sample in a narrower one.* We explain how to choose sample size so that the resulting interval is of a desired width in Section 18.8.

## 18.3 The Relation between Confidence Intervals and Hypothesis Testing

Confidence intervals and hypothesis testing are two sides of the same coin. For most population parameters, *the confidence interval contains all values of* $H_0$ *that would be retained had they been tested using* $\alpha = 1 - C$ (for a *nondirectional* alternative hypothesis). If the value specified in $H_0$ falls within the interval, $H_0$ would be retained in hypothesis testing, whereas if that value falls outside the interval it would be rejected.

Consider, for example, a problem in which $\overline{X} = 112$, $s_{\overline{X}} = 5$, and $n = 25$. When the null hypothesis $H_0$: $\mu_X = 100$ is tested, $t = 12/5 = +2.4$; the difference is significant at the .05 level ($t_{\text{crit}} = \pm 2.064$ for 24 $df$). Calculating a confidence interval from exactly the same data produces $C[+1.68 \le \mu_X \le +22.32] = .95$. This interval estimate says that the value of $\mu_X$ exceeds 100 by 1.68 to 22.32 points. Note that the interval does *not* include the possibility that $\mu_X = 100$, the same message conveyed by the null hypothesis. In addition, the confidence interval informs us what the true difference *could* be.

Consider a second example: If a confidence interval reads $C[-16.70 \leq \mu_X \leq +6.70] = .99$, zero is among the possible values that the difference might take. If instead of constructing a confidence interval, we had tested the null hypothesis of no difference at $\alpha = .01$, it would have produced a $t$ smaller than the value needed to reject the hypothesis.

A note of caution needs to be addressed before we proceed. Some statisticians have suggested that we use confidence intervals to test hypotheses (in the manner introduced in the two previous paragraphs). Keep in mind, however, that when used in that way, confidence intervals have the same Type I and Type II error rates as does null hypothesis significance testing (Harris, 1997).

We are beginning to see that estimation may have some advantages over hypothesis testing in some instances. Let's consider the advantages.

## 18.4 The Merits of Confidence Intervals

The behavioral sciences employ hypothesis testing much more often than confidence intervals, but in many studies confidence intervals are superior (Cohen, 1994; Hunter, 1997; Schmidt, 1996). Let us compare the two approaches with particular attention to inference about means.

1.  The final quantitative output of a confidence interval is a statement about the parameter or parameters of interest. In hypothesis testing, the statement is about a derived score, such as $z$ or $t$, or about a probability, $p$. In both forms of inference, the question is about the parameter(s). In hypothesis testing we have to be reminded to look at the values of the descriptors when inference is done; in estimation that view lies before our eyes.

2.  A confidence interval straightforwardly shows the influence of random sampling variation and, in particular, sample size. Remember that for a given level of confidence, a small sample results in a wide confidence interval and a large sample results in a narrower one. The width of the interval gives the investigator a direct indication of whether the estimate is precise enough for the purpose at hand. For hypothesis testing, significance is subject to *two* influences that cannot be untangled without further study: (1) the difference between what was hypothesized and what is true and (2) the amount of sampling variation present. For example, a large value of $t$ could occur in a study where the true difference was small but the sample was large, or where the true difference was large and the sample was small. Unless we look at the descriptors and $n$, we shall not know which.

3.  In hypothesis testing, it is easy to confuse a statistically significant difference with an important one (Section 14.1). Essentially, this problem disappears when we use a confidence interval. Suppose that for a sample of IQ scores, $\overline{X} = 103$, $s_X = 20$, and $n = 1600$. If we test the hypothesis that $\mu_X = 100$, we obtain a $t$ of approximately $+6$ with a corresponding probability $<.000000001$. Impressive! However, the 95% confidence interval of $\mu_X$ is $C(102 \leq \mu_X \leq 104) = .95$, which brings us back to reality. It is up to us to decide whether this result is important.

4. The outcome of testing a hypothesis is to declare that the *one* specific condition stated in the null hypothesis could be true ($H_0$ is retained) or is unlikely to be true ($H_0$ is rejected). A confidence interval, on the other hand, emphasizes the existence of a range of values that might characterize the parameter in question. Where we can, it seems desirable to recognize the variety of possible outcomes rather than develop a "yes–no" mindset toward one particular possibility.

We can divide the problems for which hypothesis testing has typically been used into two categories. In the first, a decision must be made and a course of action followed. Once that action is taken, it is difficult or impossible to turn back. To cite an example in education, suppose that one must decide whether or not to spend $300,000 on a learning laboratory, depending on the estimate of benefit to be derived. Once the money is spent, it cannot be recalled. Problems of this type might be called "either–or" or "decision" problems. It is with this sort of problem that the strongest case can be made for considering hypothesis testing because of the dichotomous "go/no-go" character of the statistical conclusion. Even here, however, a confidence interval can be considered as a workable alternative because it will indicate what parameter values are possible rather than reporting whether a particular value could be true or not true.

In the second type of problem, the "go/no-go" character of decision making is less applicable, and the advantages of confidence interval over hypothesis testing become particularly apparent. Take the polling of registered voters prior to an election, for example. The Harris and major media polls taken the last 3 days of the 1992 presidential election stated that among registered voters, the percentage favoring Bill Clinton over George Bush was

$$C(41 \leq P \leq 47) = .95$$

(where $P$ is the percentage of registered voters favoring Clinton). This meant that even if the actual number of voters in the population favoring Clinton had been at the low end of the "margin of error," nearly all of the undecided voters would have had to vote for Bush for Clinton to lose. As a result of this interval estimate, the Clinton supporters felt very confident going into election day.

## 18.5 Random Sampling and Generalizing Results

A word of caution is necessary before we proceed. There have been some noted mistakes when people have used estimation techniques. In the 1948 presidential election the *Chicago Daily Tribune* published a paper with the headline "Dewey Defeats Truman" (Figure 18.3), when in fact Truman won. They based the story (rather, a prediction) on opinion polls taken before the election. In the 2000 presidential election, the last *New York Times*/CBS News poll (taken 3–5 days before the election) indicated that 46% of registered voters would vote for George W. Bush and 41% for Al Gore, with 6% for other candidates and 7% undecided. On election day, 48.1% voted for Bush and 48.2% for Gore. (Bush was elected president by the electoral college, even though he technically lost the popular vote.)

Do such results condemn the use of estimation techniques? The answer is no. In Sections 14.12 and 15.12 you learned that *we may generalize results only to the population from which the observations may be considered to be a random sample.* Just as with

**FIGURE 18.3**   In 1948, the *Chicago Daily Tribune* declared that Dewey had defeated Truman. This was actually a prediction based on surveys taken before the election. This is a good example of why we cannot properly generalize sample results beyond the exact set of conditions at the time. © Bettmann/CORBIS

hypothesis testing, the techniques you learn about in this chapter assume random sampling. Otherwise, you run into the same problem as the *Literary Digest* did when they attempted to predict the outcome of the 1936 presidential election (Section 2.1). Even with random sampling, *we cannot properly generalize beyond the exact set of conditions at the time* (Sections 14.12 and 15.12). The last polls taken before a presidential election are usually taken a few days *before* the election. With random sampling, the results may be quite accurate for that time period, but over the last few days the undecided voters make a decision, and some of the others might change their decision. Thus, caution about generalizing results holds true for confidence intervals established around sample means as well.

## 18.6  Evaluating a Confidence Interval

In the example we used to demonstrate Formula 18.1, $\overline{X} = 85.0$, $s_X = 15.0$, and $n = 25$. The 95% confidence interval of $\mu_X$ was: $C(78.8 \leq \mu_X \leq 91.2) = .95$. According to this estimate, $\mu_X$ is somewhere between 78.8 and 91.2. A statement of this kind is most meaningful when one is well enough acquainted with the variable to have a reasonably good understanding of the meaning of different scores. For instance, in measuring men's heights, we understand that 5 ft., 1 in. characterizes an unusually short fellow and that a person 6 ft., 4 in. is unusually tall. Psychologists and educators understand reasonably well what a College Entrance Examination Board score of 400 or 750 means. But many times we are not that familiar with the variable under study. For example, are you familiar with measuring change in the electrical resistance of the skin under various kinds of emotional stimulation? The magnitude of this measure may depend on many factors, such as kind of measuring equipment used or the points on the skin between which the resistance is measured. In cases like this, a confidence interval expressed in terms of the variable measured may not be very meaningful.

*One way to add meaning to a confidence interval is to interpret the interval limits in terms of number of standard deviations of the variable rather than in terms of raw-score points.* The

## Point of Controversy

### Objectivity and Subjectivity in Inferential Statistics: Bayesian Statistics

Suppose you wake up in the middle of the night with a headache. In the dark, you find three bottles in the medicine cabinet and by touch decide that you have the correct tablet. You take it and go back to bed. Later you awake with chills, sweats, and nausea. When you turn on the lights, you discover that two of the bottles you got out are aspirin but the third is poison. What is the probability that you took poison?

We introduced probability in Chapter 11. By the model given there, the probability of your having taken poison is 1/3 or .333. But suppose you had additional information. Suppose, for example, that you believe (based on reading medical news) the probability of having these symptoms to be .80 after taking poison but only .05 after taking aspirin. In the 18th century, English clergyman and mathematician Thomas Bayes introduced a theorem to deal with conditional probabilities like these (Bayes, 1763). (Note 11.2 briefly discusses conditional probability.) According to Bayes's theorem, the probability of your having taken poison is actually .89. We will not concern ourselves here with the mathematical formula for Bayes's theorem, but the essence is that *what we know after the event* (e.g., experiencing symptoms likely to be caused by poison) *can alter initial probabilities.*

Today, there is a school of thought that is known as **Bayesian statistics**, whose followers disagree with the "classical" approach to inferential statistics (taught in this textbook). The classical approach attempts to treat statistical decisions with great objectivity.

> Science earns its reputation for objectivity by treating the perils of subjectivity with the greatest of respect. (K. C. Cole, 1985)

Bayesian statistics "support inferences without reference to either significance tests or confidence intervals" (Pruzek, 1997), and offer yet another alternative to null hypothesis significance testing (e.g., Krueger, 2001).

To compare these two approaches, consider the following research question (a hypothetical example by Berger and Berry, 1988): Is vitamin C effective in treating the common cold? Standard statistical practice is to test the null hypothesis that vitamin C has no effect (in the population). Suppose, for example, that we match 17 pairs of subjects, all suffering from cold symptoms, and randomly select one subject in each pair (person C) to receive vitamin C and the other (person P) to receive a placebo. After 24 hours, a group of physicians judge C or P to be healthier, with no ties allowed. If the null hypothesis is true, one would expect the number of pairs in which C is better to be about equal to the number of pairs in which P is better. If vitamin C works, there should be more pairs in which C is better.

How many more? Because there are only two possible outcomes (each with a probability of 1/2), the binomial distribution gives us the probabilities of outcomes of C being healthier than P. For a two-tailed test with $\alpha = .05$, we will reject the null hypothesis if C is judged to be better in fewer than 5 or more than 12 of the pairs. (The sum of the probabilities of these outcomes is .049.) Suppose that the outcome of the vitamin C experiment is 13 pairs in which C is judged to be better than P. We would reject the null hypothesis and, following standard statistical practice, express the outcome as a *p*-value ($p < .05$). Classical statisticians believe this to be an objective way in which to evaluate hypotheses. Bayesians contend that not only do dichotomous tests of significance limit us to a single choice—true or false—but also that the idea of rejecting a hypothesis at some percentage level is not a logical disproof (Howson & Urbach, 1991).

Bayesians prefer to acknowledge subjectivity in statistical analysis. For them, probability is not defined in terms of relative frequency but rather in degree of belief. In addition, there is no alternative hypothesis. The goal of Bayesian statistics is to state a "final" (or "posterior") probability for the hypothesis under test. The "initial" (or "prior") probability of the hypothesis being true, as well as the upper limits of this probability, are subjectively chosen *by the person interpreting the data*. In the vitamin C experiment, for example, we might believe the probability that vitamin C is effective to be 0.9, whereas someone else might believe it to be only 0.1. Some might argue that to be objective we should start with a value of 0.5. Bayesian analysis treats all initial hypotheses (designated *H*) equally and lets the data determine the final probability. This is accomplished by using the Bayes factor—the odds against the hypothesis being true provided by the data. (If you wish to read a good introduction to Bayesian analysis, see Gelman, 1998, or Pruzek, 1997). If one assumes an initial probability of 0.5 for *H* (which says that vitamin C has no effect) and chooses an upper limit of 0.6 (that vitamin C is effective), a final outcome of 13 pairs (out of 17) in which C is judged to be better results in a final probability of 0.41 for *H*. If one initially chooses an upward limit of 0.9 (a much stronger belief that vitamin C is effective), the final probability of *H* is 0.21. Essentially, Bayesian methods entail "use of prior information and empirical data to generate posterior distributions that in turn serve as the basis for statistical inferences" (Pruzek, 1997). Note that even in the case where the initial upward probability is 0.9, the final probability of *H* is still much higher than the *p*-values reported in the standard approach (for significant results). Thus, Bayesians contend that it is wrong to interpret small *p*-values as strong evidence against $H_0$.

The techniques discussed here (as well as throughout the text) emphasize the analysis of single studies, but, in the long run, science is concerned with series of studies. Replication of results is of foremost importance in science. Statisticians who employ the classical approach say that replication results in objective data and that there is no need for prior probabilities (e.g., Nelder, 1988). Bayesians counter that corroborating a hypothesis does not strengthen it, but only strengthens our subjective belief in it (Howson & Urbach, 1991).

**Bayesian statistics**
entails "use of prior information and empirical data to generate posterior distributions that in turn serve as the basis for statistical inferences" (Pruzek, 1997)

interval estimate cited at the opening of this section was constructed by calculating $85.0 \pm (2.064)(3.0)$ or $85.0 \pm 6.19$. In effect, then, the confidence interval as constructed states that $\mu_X$ is no farther away from $\overline{X}$ than 6.19 raw-score points. Let us reexpress this difference in terms of the number of standard deviations of the variable. The estimated standard deviation is 15.0, so the difference becomes $6.19/15.0 = .41$. Reinterpreted, the interval estimate now states that $\mu_X$ is no farther away from $\overline{X}$ than .41 of a standard deviation, which for many purposes would be considered fairly close.

One advantage of expressing a confidence interval in this way is that it compensates for the fact that the importance of a given interscore distance depends on the size of the standard deviation of the variable. For example, a difference of .3 points is minuscule for GRE (Graduate Record Examination) scores, which have a mean of 500 and a standard deviation of 100, but it is quite substantial for grade point averages. By comparing the difference obtained to the standard deviation of the variable, confidence intervals in both these dimensions are placed on common ground.

To summarize the calculation for a single mean, we find

**d**

the difference between $\overline{X}$ and the outer limits of the interval estimate, expressed in terms of the number of standard deviations of the variable

$$\mathbf{d} = \frac{t_p s_{\overline{X}}}{s_X} \qquad (18.2)$$

where $\mathbf{d}$ is the difference between $\overline{X}$ and the outer limits of the interval estimate expressed in terms of the number of standard deviations of the variable. This formula is most convenient if we calculate the ordinary confidence interval first. If you prefer to go directly to this interpretation, it is a little faster to use an alternative formula:

$$\mathbf{d} = \frac{t_p s_{\overline{X}}}{s_X} = \frac{t_p}{\sqrt{n}}$$

formulas for *d*

$$\mathbf{d} = \frac{t_p}{\sqrt{n}} \qquad (18.3)$$

## 18.7 Confidence Intervals for $\mu_X - \mu_Y$

In Section 18.2 you learned how to construct a confidence interval for $\mu_X$. Just as we can make a confidence interval of $\mu_X$, we can also estimate the true difference between $\mu_X$ and $\mu_Y$. The logic and general nature of the procedure are the same as for the single mean.

RULE FOR CONSTRUCTING A CONFIDENCE INTERVAL
FOR $\mu_X - \mu_Y$ WHEN $\sigma_X$ AND $\sigma_Y$ ARE UNKNOWN

$(\overline{X} - \overline{Y}) \pm t_p s_{\overline{X}-\overline{Y}}$

formula for constructing a confidence interval for $\mu_X - \mu_Y$

$$(\overline{X} - \overline{Y}) \pm t_p s_{\overline{X}-\overline{Y}} \qquad (18.4)$$

*where:* $(\overline{X} - \overline{Y})$ = the difference between the means of two random samples
$s_{\overline{X}-\overline{Y}}$ = the estimate of the standard error of the difference between two means
$t_p$ = the magnitude of $t$ for which the probability is $p$ of obtaining a value so deviant or more so (in either direction)
$p = 1 - C$

If the difference $(\overline{X} - \overline{Y})$ is not farther away from $(\mu_X - \mu_Y)$ than $t_p s_{\overline{X}-\overline{Y}}$, the claim will be correct. Otherwise, it will not. Because 95% of the obtained differences (under random sampling) between the two sample means will be within this range, 95% of the claims made by following this procedure will be correct. Accordingly, if we draw a pair of samples at random, the probability is .95 that an interval estimate constructed by this procedure, $(\overline{X} - \overline{Y}) \pm t_p s_{\overline{X}-\overline{Y}}$, will include the true value of $\mu_X - \mu_Y$.

**Problem**

A clinician claims to have a new and better therapy to treat paranoid schizophrenia. We randomly divide 30 institutionalized patients into two samples of 15 each; one will receive the new therapy and the other the standard therapy. Because of physical illness, 2 patients in the new therapy group do not complete the study. We will refer to the new therapy group as group $X$ and the standard therapy group as group $Y$. We wish to calculate the 99% confidence interval for the following data (high scores indicate greater paranoia):

| NEW THERAPY | STANDARD THERAPY |
|---|---|
| $\overline{X} = 87.0$ | $\overline{Y} = 92.0$ |
| $SS_X = 1200$ | $SS_Y = 2016$ |
| $n_X = 13$ | $n_Y = 15$ |

**Solution**

For independent samples, $df = (n_X - 1) + (n_Y - 1)$, and we must determine $t_p$ accordingly. In the present problem, $df = 26$, and the critical value of $t$ is $t_{.01} = 2.779$. The standard error of the difference between the means is given by Formula 15.4 (or Formula 15.5 if $n_X = n_Y$):

$$s_{\overline{X}-\overline{Y}} = \sqrt{\frac{SS_X + SS_Y}{(n_X - 1) + (n_Y - 1)}\left(\frac{1}{n_X} + \frac{1}{n_Y}\right)}$$

We find that $s_{\overline{X}-\overline{Y}} = 4.21$. The 99% confidence interval is therefore constructed as follows:

$$(\overline{X} - \overline{Y}) \pm t_{.01} s_{\overline{X}-\overline{Y}}$$

| LOWER LIMIT | UPPER LIMIT |
|---|---|
| $= (87.0 - 92.0) - (2.779)(4.21)$ | $= (87.0 - 92.0) + (2.779)(4.21)$ |
| $= -5.0 - 11.70$ | $= -5.0 + 11.70$ |
| $= -16.70$ | $= +6.70$ |

Formally, this is expressed as

$$C[-16.70 \leq (\mu_X - \mu_Y) \leq +6.70] = .99$$

A negative value for $\mu_X - \mu_Y$ indicates $\mu_Y$ is larger than $\mu_X$, whereas a positive value indicates $\mu_X$ is larger than $\mu_Y$. Consequently, we can be 99% confident that the true difference between the mean paranoia ratings will fall anywhere between 16.70 points in favor of the new therapy (low scores are favorable here) to 6.70 points in favor of the standard therapy. This is shown in Figure 18.4. Note that a difference of 0, or no difference at all, falls within the interval.

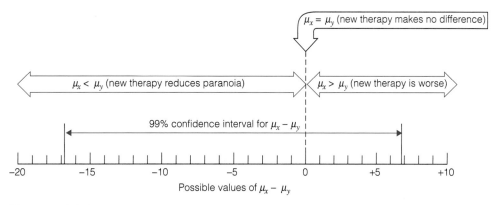

FIGURE 18.4   The 99% confidence interval for the true difference in paranoia ratings in the therapy study.

Recall from Section 18.6 that we can express confidence intervals in terms of number of standard deviations of the variable rather than in terms of raw-score units. To reexpress the difference in standard deviations, we calculate

**d**
the difference between $(\overline{X} - \overline{Y})$ and the outer limits of the interval estimate, expressed in terms of the number of standard deviations of the variable

$$d = \frac{t_p s_{\overline{X} - \overline{Y}}}{s_{av}} \qquad (18.5)$$

where **d** is the difference between $(\overline{X} - \overline{Y})$ and the outer limits of the interval estimate, expressed in terms of the number of standard deviations of the variable, and $s_{av}$ is the average of $s_X$ and $s_Y$ (which is reasonably satisfactory if $n_X$ and $n_Y$ are approximately the same size). Applying Formula 18.5 to the confidence interval in our example, we obtain

$$d = \frac{t_p s_{\overline{X} - \overline{Y}}}{s_{av}}$$

formula for **d**

$$s_X = \sqrt{\frac{SS_X}{n_X - 1}} = \sqrt{\frac{1200}{12}} = 10$$

$$s_Y = \sqrt{\frac{SS_Y}{n_Y - 1}} = \sqrt{\frac{2016}{14}} = 12$$

$s_{AV}$
symbol for the average of $s_X$ and $s_Y$

$$d = \frac{(2.779)(4.21)}{(10.0 + 12.0)/2} = 1.06$$

This informs us that the true difference between the two means is within 1.06 standard deviations of the obtained difference according to our 99% confidence interval.

If we desire, we can restate the difference relative to a difference of zero rather than to the obtained difference between the two sample means. To do this, we simply divide the upper and lower raw-score limits of the confidence interval by $s_{av}$. In the present example, the lower limit becomes $-16.70/11.0 = -1.52$, and the upper limit becomes $+6.70/11.0 = .61$. This states, with 99% confidence, that the difference between the two populations means is such that $\mu_X$ could be lower than $\mu_Y$ by 1.52 standard deviations, that $\mu_X$ could be higher than $\mu_Y$ by .61 standard deviation, or that the difference falls between these limits. When confidence limits are expressed this way, we need to keep in mind that the width of the limits must be considered in the light of the value of the confidence coefficient employed, just as when the limits are expressed in score points.

When our samples are *dependent,* the procedures are the same except for the calculation of $s_{\bar{X}-\bar{Y}}$. For dependent samples, it is given by Formula 16.2:

$$s_{\bar{X}-\bar{Y}} = \sqrt{s_{\bar{X}}^2 + s_{\bar{Y}}^2 - 2r_{XY}s_{\bar{X}-\bar{Y}}}$$

For our example about comparing methods of teaching arithmetic, we calculated $s_{\bar{X}-\bar{Y}}$ to be 1.76 (Table 16.1), $\bar{X} = 69.73$, $\bar{Y} = 65.07$, and $t_{.05} = \pm 2.145$ when $df = 14$. Therefore, to construct the 95% confidence interval:

$$(\bar{X} - \bar{Y}) \pm t_{.05}\, s_{\bar{X}-\bar{Y}}$$

| LOWER LIMIT | UPPER LIMIT |
|---|---|
| $= (69.73 - 65.07) - (2.145)(1.76)$ | $= (69.73 - 65.07) + (2.145)(1.76)$ |
| $= 4.66 - 3.78$ | $= 4.66 + 3.78$ |
| $= .88$ | $= 8.44$ |

$$C[0.88 \leq (\mu_X - \mu_Y) \leq 8.44] = .95$$

If we want, we may also construct confidence intervals from difference scores:

$$\bar{D} + t_p\, s_{\bar{D}}$$

**$\bar{D} \pm t_p s_{\bar{D}}$**
formula for constructing a confidence interval for $\mu_D$

From Table 16.2 we calculate $s_{\bar{D}}$ to be $\sqrt{3.10} = 1.76$. Therefore,

$$4.67 \pm (2.145)(1.76)$$

and we arrive at the same answer. (Note: in Table 16.1, $\bar{X} - \bar{Y} = 4.66$ and in Table 16.2 $\bar{D} = 4.67$; the difference is due to rounding.)

Remember, *the confidence interval contains all values of* $H_0$ *that would be retained had they been tested using* $\alpha = 1 - C$ (for a *nondirectional* alternative hypothesis). Consider, for example, a problem in which $\bar{X} - \bar{Y} = +12$, $s_{\bar{X}-\bar{Y}} = 5$, and $n = 25$ for both groups. When the null hypothesis of zero difference is tested, $t = 12/5 = +2.4$; the difference is significant at the .05 level ($t_{crit} = \pm 2.02$ for 48 $df$). Calculating a confidence interval from exactly the same data produces $C[+1.9 \leq (\mu_X - \mu_Y) \leq +22.1] = .95$. This confidence interval says that the value of $\mu_X$ exceeds that of $\mu_Y$ by 1.9 to 22.1 points. Note that the interval does *not* include the possibility that the difference could be zero, the same message conveyed by the test of the hypothesis. In addition, the confidence interval informs us what the true difference *could* be.

Consider a second example: If a confidence interval reads $C[-16.70 \leq (\mu_X - \mu_Y) \leq +6.70] = .99$, such as we found for the example at the start of this section, zero is among the possible values that the difference might take. Had we tested the null hypothesis of no difference at $\alpha = .01$, it would have produced a $t$ smaller than the value needed to reject the hypothesis.

Here is a third confidence interval: $C[+1 \leq (\mu_X - \mu_Y) \leq +4] = .95$. It shows that the true difference is not likely to be zero; instead, $\mu_X$ is probably higher than $\mu_Y$ by 1 to 4 points. The difference is large enough that chance variation cannot account for it, but if the standard deviations of $X$ and $Y$ are about 15, it is nevertheless a small difference.

# 18.8 Sample Size Required for Confidence Intervals of $\mu_X$ and $\mu_X - \mu_Y$

Suppose we wish to estimate $\mu_X$ such that it will not be farther away from $\overline{X}$ than a given amount, with confidence coefficient equal to .95. If we can estimate $\sigma_X$ before we begin, it is possible to estimate the size of the sample that will be required to produce this result. Required sample size is given by

### SAMPLE SIZE REQUIRED FOR A CONFIDENCE INTERVAL OF $\mu_X$ OF GIVEN WIDTH

$$n = \left( \frac{\sigma_X z_p}{w} \right)^2 \tag{18.6}$$

**$n = \left( \dfrac{\sigma_X z_p}{w} \right)^2$**

formula for calculating sample size required for a confidence interval of $\mu_X$ of given width

**$w$**

symbol for the maximum distance (in score points) desired between $\overline{X}$ and the limits of the estimate of $\mu_X$

where $w$ is the maximum distance (in score points) desired between $\overline{X}$ and the limits of the estimate of $\mu_X$. If $\sigma_X$ is estimated to be 16 and we aim to estimate $\mu_X$ with 95% confidence that it will not be farther away from $\overline{X}$ than 4 points, the calculation will be

$$n = \left[ \frac{(16)(1.96)}{4} \right]^2 = 61$$

We can often make an approximate estimate of $\sigma_X$ by referring to previous studies that used the same variable. Even if we are using a new variable, it may be possible to make some kind of guess.

When construction of the interval depends on estimating $\sigma_X$ from a sample, the estimated sample size tends to be an underestimate, especially if the required sample size is small. In this case, it is best to use a slightly larger sample than that given by Formula 18.6. In fact, whenever it is important to be conservative, take more cases than Formula 18.6 suggests.

We can also estimate $\mu_X - \mu_Y$ with a given degree of confidence that it will not be farther away from $(\overline{X} - \overline{Y})$ than a given amount. For independent samples, when samples are of (nearly) equal size and it is reasonable to believe that $\sigma_X = \sigma_Y$ (or at least approximately so), we find the required size of *each* of the two samples by calculating sample size according to Formula 18.6 *and multiplying that result by 2:*

### SAMPLE SIZE REQUIRED FOR A CONFIDENCE INTERVAL OF $(\mu_X - \mu_Y)$ OF GIVEN WIDTH

$$n = \left( \frac{\sigma z_p}{w} \right)^2 (2) \tag{18.7}$$

**$n = \left( \dfrac{\sigma z_p}{w} \right)^2 (2)$**

formula for calculating sample size required for a confidence interval of $(\mu_X - \mu_Y)$ of given width

*where:*   $w$ = maximum desired discrepancy (in score points) between $(\overline{X} - \overline{Y})$ and the limits of the estimate of $\mu_X - \mu_Y$

Again, in practical applications it is usually possible to make at least an approximate estimate of $\sigma$.

**TABLE 18.1**    *Approximate Maximum Distance (w) Measured in $\sigma$ Units, Expected According to Selected Values of Sample Size between (1) $\overline{X}$ and the Limits of the 95% Confidence Interval for Single Means and (2) $\overline{X} - \overline{Y}$ and the Limits of the 95% Confidence Interval for Two Independent Means*★*

| | SAMPLE SIZE | | | | | | | | |
|---|---|---|---|---|---|---|---|---|---|
| | 10 | 15 | 25 | 50 | 75 | 100 | 200 | 500 | 1,000 |
| Single means: $\|\overline{X} - \mu_X\|/s_X$ | .72 | .55 | .41 | .28 | .23 | .20 | .14 | .09 | .06 |
| Difference between two independent means: $\|(\overline{X} - \overline{Y}) - (\mu_X - \mu_Y)\|/s_{av}$ | .94 | .75 | .57 | .40 | .32 | .28 | .20 | .12 | .09 |

★For two independent samples, $n$ is the size of *each* of the two samples. It is assumed that $n_X = n_Y = n$ and that $\sigma_X = \sigma_Y$.

Suppose we hope to estimate $\mu_X - \mu_Y$ with 95% confidence that it will not be farther away from $(\overline{X} - \overline{Y})$ than 4 score points and that we can safely assume $\sigma_X = \sigma_Y = 16$. What sample size will be required? The calculation is

$$n = 2\left[\frac{(16)(1.96)}{4}\right]^2 = 123$$

Note that (within rounding error) *twice* as many cases are required for *each* sample to maintain the same distance, $w$, for the two-sample estimate as were required for the one-sample estimate.

If samples are dependent, we find the number of *pairs* of elements by the same procedure, except that we multiply the resulting value of $n$ by $(1 - \rho)$. Once again, we will have to estimate $\rho$ (the value of Pearson's correlation coefficient for the population).

Table 18.1 gives an idea of the degree of accuracy that we may achieve in interval estimation from samples of selected sizes. The entries represent $w$, expressed as a fraction of the standard deviation of the variable, for 95% confidence intervals. For example, the table says that if we use 100 cases in estimating $(\mu_X - \mu_Y)$, the 95% confidence interval will be $(\overline{X} - \overline{Y}) \pm .28s_{AV}$. Treat the values in the tables as approximations, particularly for the lowest three values of $n$.

## 18.9 Confidence Intervals for $\rho$

If we want to know within what limits the population coefficient is found (rather than testing the hypothesis that $\rho$ is some specific value), we can construct a confidence interval by translating the sample $r$ to $z'$ and using the following rule:

RULE FOR CONSTRUCTING A CONFIDENCE INTERVAL FOR $\rho$

$z' \pm z_p\sigma_{z'}$
formula for
constructing a
confidence
interval for $\rho$

$$z' = z_p\sigma_{z'} \tag{18.8}$$

*where:*   $z'$ = the value of Fisher's $z'$ corresponding to the sample $r$
$z_p$ = sthe magnitude of normally distributed $z$ for which the probability is $p$ of obtaining a value so deviant or more so (in either direction)
$p = (1 - C)$, where $C$ is the confidence coefficient
$\sigma_{z'}$ = the standard error of Fisher's $z'$

The formula for the standard error of $z'$ is

$\boldsymbol{\sigma}_{z'}$
symbol for the
standard error
of Fisher's $z'$;
$=1/\sqrt{n-3}$

STANDARD ERROR OF FISHER'S $z'$

$$\sigma_{z'} = \frac{1}{\sqrt{n-3}} \qquad (18.9)$$

Formula 18.8 results in a lower limit and an upper limit, both expressed in terms of $z'$. We must then convert these to $r$'s using Table H in Appendix E.

We illustrate the procedure with the same data we used in Section 17.2. Recall that the sample $r$ was $+.30$, based on 25 pairs of observations. What are the limits that we can be 95% confident include $\rho$, the population value of the correlation coefficient? From Table H, we find that $z' = +.31$ corresponds to $r = +.30$. The standard error is $\sigma_{z'} = 1/\sqrt{25-3} = .21$, and 95% of the values in a normal distribution are within $\pm 1.96$ standard errors $(z)$ of the mean. Thus, according to Formula 18.8, the limits of the 95% confidence interval are

LOWER   UPPER
LIMIT   LIMIT

$$+.31 \pm (1.96)(.21) = -.10 \text{ to } +.72$$

Using Table H, we translate these values of $z'$ back to values of $r$. The resulting limits are

$$r_{LL} = -.10 \qquad r_{UL} = +.62$$

Formally, we express the confidence interval as

$$C(-.10 \leq \rho \leq +.62) = .95$$

Note that these limits are not equidistant from $r = +.30$. The upper limit is closer to $r = +.30$ because the sampling distribution of $r$ is skewed (see Section 17.1).

If we were preparing a research report, we would use Formula 18.8 to calculate accurate confidence intervals. However, if we are only concerned with interpreting a sample $r$, Figure 18.5 will give us reasonably accurate limits for estimating 95% confidence intervals. Consider again our example of $r = +.30$ with 25 pairs of observations. We move along the horizontal axis to $r = +.30$ and then move vertically to the lower and upper curves for $n = 25$. (These will have to be estimated between $n = 20$ and $n = 30$.) We now move horizontally from these points of intersection to the vertical axis on the left. This will give you the limits of the 95% confidence interval for $\rho$ (which should be very close to the values we calculated). For negative values of $r$, just reverse the signs of the obtained limits (e.g., $-.62$ to $+.10$ for $r = -.30$ with a sample of 25).

Look carefully at Figure 18.5. Close inspection reveals why correlation coefficients based on small samples are usually not worth much. Note, for instance, that when $n$ is 10 $(df = 8)$ and $r = 0$, the 95% confidence limits for $r$ are $\pm .63$. Suppose that, unknown to us, $\rho = +.60$ and that our sample $r$ happens to have exactly the same value. Nevertheless, if we are testing the hypothesis that $\rho = 0$, we would find no cause to reject it. Even when $n = 32$, the 95% limits are $\pm .35$. It should be obvious that we need a good-sized sample to determine the extent of relationship with any degree of accuracy. At the other extreme, if samples are very large, a relatively small coefficient may lead to the mistaken conclusion that there is a strong relationship ("highly

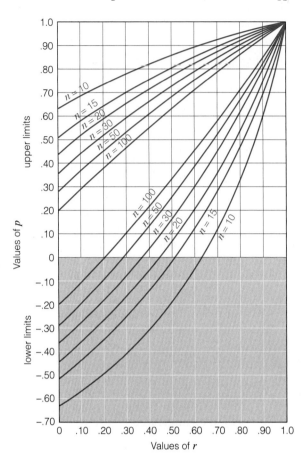

**FIGURE 18.5** Curves for locating the 95% confidence intervals for $\rho$. (*Source:* Reprinted from *Elements of Statistical Reasoning* by Minium, Clarke, and Coladarci. Copyright © 1999 by John Wiley & Sons, Inc. Reprinted by permission.)

significant") between two variables when the hypothesis of no correlation is tested. Recall, for example, the study that found a "definite" link between children's height and IQ (see Section 14.2). Interval estimation can help researchers avoid the traps inherent in using either small or large samples. *It would be good practice to use confidence intervals of $\rho$ much more often than is commonly done in research.*

## 18.10 Summary

Prior to this chapter, we developed models for testing hypotheses about a specific value of the population mean (Chapter 13), the difference between two population means (Chapters 15 and 16), and the population correlation coefficient (Chapter 17). In establishing confidence intervals, no value is specified in advance. Instead, we draw a sample and calculate an interval of values within which it appears reasonable that the population parameter lies (interval estimation). Any problem for which hypothesis testing is useful can also be worked by confidence intervals, but the reverse is not true.

In a normal distribution, 95% of the scores are within 1.96 standard deviations of the mean. When we draw random samples of a particular size from such a distribution,

95% of the sample means are within $\pm 1.96\sigma_{\overline{X}}$ of $\mu_X$. Therefore, it is also the case that for 95% of sample means, $\mu_X$ is no farther away than $1.96\sigma_{\overline{X}}$. In making estimates from sample data, we must, as usual, use $s_{\overline{X}}$ in place of $\sigma_{\overline{X}}$ and the $t$ distribution in place of the normal curve. The interval in which we are reasonably confident of finding $\mu_X$ is thus found by the formula $\overline{X} \pm t_p s_{\overline{X}}$, where $t_p$ is the magnitude of $t$ for which the probability is $p$ of obtaining a value so deviant or more so in either direction. The limits of the confidence interval will vary from sample to sample, but when $p = .05$, 95% of the interval estimates will contain $\mu_X$. To construct a confidence interval for the difference between the means of two populations, the formula is $(\overline{X} - \overline{Y}) \pm t_p s_{\overline{X} - \overline{Y}}$.

If we are not familiar enough with the variable under study to understand whether the estimated interval is large or small, we may express the interval limits in terms of the standard deviation of the variable. If we want to estimate $\mu_X$ such that it will not be farther away from $\overline{X}$ than a given amount, we can calculate the sample size necessary if we can estimate $\sigma_X$ in advance of collecting our data.

Confidence intervals of $\rho$ are a better method of presenting correlational data because they directly show the influence of sampling variation. To compute confidence intervals, we must first convert $r$ to another statistics, $z'$, because the sampling distribution of $r$ is not normally distributed. For quick estimates of sample correlation coefficients, you can obtain approximate confidence limits directly from the curves in Figure 18.5.

Although confidence intervals are used infrequently in education and the behavioral sciences, they have several advantages over hypothesis testing. With either hypothesis testing or confidence intervals, the question is about a parameter, but only confidence intervals give a direct answer. They also show the influence of random sampling variation, and allow the investigator to see directly whether a difference is large enough to be important or not.

## Key Terms, Concepts, and Symbols

dichotomous decision
   making  (342)
$p$-value  (265, 342)
point estimates  (344)
interval estimates  (344)

$t_p$  (346)
confidence interval  (346)
confidence coefficient  (346)
$C$  (346)

Bayesian statistics  (351)
$d$  (353, 355)
$w$  (357)
$\sigma_{z'}$  (359)

## Problems

1. Given: $\overline{X} = 63$, $s_X = 12$, $n = 100$. Construct a confidence interval of $\mu_X$ according to: (a) $C = .95$ and (b) $C = .99$.

2. Repeat parts (a) and (b) of Problem 1, but with the condition that $n$ is four times as large. Compare the size of the intervals obtained in the two problems. State your conclusion.

3. Given: $\overline{X} = 117$, $s_X = 36$, $n = 81$. Construct a confidence interval of $\mu_X$ according to (a) $C = .95$ and (b) $C = .99$.

4. Using the data of Problem 1, interpret a confidence interval estimate of $\mu_X$ in terms of **d**, using $C = .95$. Does it appear that the estimate has considerable precision or not? Explain.

5. Repeat Problem 4, but use $n = 25$.

6. Given: $\overline{X} = 2.90$, $s_X = .30$, $n = 16$. (a) Construct a confidence interval of $\mu_X$ using $C = .95$. (b) What is your feeling about the precision of this estimate? (c) Calculate **d**. (d) What is your feeling now about the precision of this estimate? (e) Comment on the appropriateness of applying the techniques of this chapter to this problem.

7. Given: $\overline{X} = 165$, $s_X = 24$, $n_X = 36$, $\overline{Y} = 175$, $s_Y = 21$, $n_Y = 49$; assume the samples are independent. Construct a confidence interval of $\mu_X - \mu_Y$ according to (a) $C = .95$ and (b) $C = .99$.

8. Given: $\overline{X} = 97$, $s_X = 16$, $n_X = 64$, $\overline{Y} = 90$, $s_Y = 18$, $n_Y = 81$; assume the samples are independent. Construct a confidence interval of $\mu_X - \mu_Y$ according to (a) $C = .95$ and (b) $C = .99$.

9. Using the data of Problem 7, interpret a confidence interval of $\mu_X - \mu_Y$ in terms of **d**, using $C = .95$. Does it appear that the estimate has considerable precision? Explain.

10. Construct the 95% confidence interval for the data of Problem 7 expressing the upper and lower limits in terms of the number of standard deviations relative to a difference of zero between $\mu_X$ and $\mu_Y$.

11. Repeat Problem 9 using the data of Problem 8.

12. Two dependent samples yield the following: $\overline{X} = 88$, $s_X = 16$, $n_X = 64$, $\overline{Y} = 85$, $s_Y = 12$, $n_Y = 64$, $r_{XY} = +.50$. Construct a confidence interval of $\mu_X - \mu_Y$ according to (a) $C = .95$ and (b) $C = .99$.

13. Given: $C(122 \leq \mu_X \leq 128) = .95$. (a) If $H_0$: $\mu_X = 127$ is tested at $\alpha = .05$ using a nondirectional alternative, what is the outcome? (b) If $H_0$: $\mu_X = 118$ is tested at $\alpha = .05$, what is the outcome? (c) Explain your answers to (a) and (b).

14. Given: $C[-8 \leq (\mu_X - \mu_Y) \leq -2] = .95$. (a) What is $\overline{X} - \overline{Y}$? (b) If $H_0$: $\mu_X - \mu_Y = 0$ is tested at $\alpha = .05$ using a nondirectional alternative, what is the outcome?

15. Given: $C[-2 \leq (\mu_X - \mu_Y) \leq +12] = .95$. (a) What is $\overline{X} - \overline{Y}$? (b) If $H_0$: $\mu_X - \mu_Y = 0$ is tested at $\alpha = .05$ using a nondirectional alternative, what is the outcome?

16. Given: $\overline{X} = 83$, $s_X = 15$, $n = 625$. (a) Obtain $z$ corresponding to a test that $\mu_X = 80$. (b) What, in "loose English," does this value for $z$ tell us? (c) Construct the 95% confidence interval of $\mu_X$. (d) What does it tell us? (e) Compare the information obtained by the two approaches.

17. Construct the 95% confidence interval for the data in Problem 7, Chapter 15.

18. Construct the 99% confidence interval for the data in Problem 9, Chapter 15.

19. Construct the 99% confidence interval for the data in Problem 10, Chapter 15.

20. Construct the 95% confidence interval for the data in Problem 11, Chapter 15.

21. Construct the 95% confidence interval for the data in Problem 4, Chapter 16.

22. Construct the 95% confidence interval for the data in Problem 6, Chapter 16.

23. Construct the 99% confidence interval for the data in Problem 7, Chapter 16.

24. Construct the 99% confidence interval for the data in Problem 8, Chapter 16.

25. A psychologist wishes to estimate mean reaction time such that he or she can be 95% confident that $\mu_X$ is not farther than 3 milliseconds (msec.) away from his or her sample mean. The psychologist estimates that the standard deviation of reaction times is 15 msec. What size sample should he or she draw?

26. Repeat Problem 25, but with the condition that the confidence coefficient should be .99.

27. With reference to Problem 25, our psychologist now wishes to change the nature of the reaction task and to compare mean reaction time on the original task with that on the altered task. He or she assumes that the standard deviation will be the same on both tasks and wants to estimate at the 95% level of confidence the difference between the two population means. The psychologist wants this difference to be within 5 msec. of the difference between the sample

means. (a) If the psychologist selects two random samples, what should be the size of each? (b) If he or she uses subjects matched on a pretest of reaction time and $\rho$ is estimated to be $+.40$ between pairs of measurements, what should be the size of each sample?

**28.** For $r = +.25$, construct the 95% confidence intervals using Formula 18.8 when (a) $n = 10$, (b) $n = 20$, (c) $n = 40$, and (d) $n = 80$.

**29.** Repeat Problem 28 for $r = +.65$.

**30.** As accurately as possible, use Figure 18.5 to determine the 95% confidence intervals for (a) $r = +.52$, $n = 50$; (b) $r = -.31$, $n = 20$; and (c) $r = -.70$, $n = 100$.

# CHAPTER 19

## Chi-Square and Inference about Frequencies

When you have finished studying this chapter, you should be able to:

- Understand that the chi-square test is used to test hypotheses about the number of cases falling into the categories of a frequency distribution;
- Understand that $\chi^2$ provides a measure of discrepancy between observed frequencies and the frequencies that would be expected if the null hypothesis were true;
- Explain why the chi-square test is best viewed as a test about proportions;
- Compute $\chi^2$ for one-variable goodness-of-fit problems;
- Compute $\chi^2$ to test for independence between two variables; and
- Compute effect size for the chi-square test.

In previous chapters, we have been concerned with numerical scores and testing hypotheses about summary characteristics of those scores, such as the mean or the correlation coefficient. In this chapter, you will learn to make inferences about frequencies—the number of cases falling into the categories of a frequency distribution. For example, among four brands of cola, is there a difference in the proportion of consumers who prefer the taste of each? Is there a difference among registered voters in their preference for three candidates running for local office? To approach questions like these, a researcher compares the observed (sample) frequencies characterizing the several categories of the distribution with those frequencies expected according to his or her hypothesis. The discrepancy between observed and expected frequencies is expressed in terms of a statistic named *chi-square* ($\chi^2$), introduced by Karl Pearson in 1900.

## 19.1 The Chi-Square Test for Goodness of Fit

**categorical data**
data comprising qualitative categories

**P**
symbol for proportion

**$H_0$ for chi-square test for goodness of fit**
states the *proportion* of cases in each category of a population of qualitative data

**goodness-of-fit problem**
asks whether the relative frequencies observed in the categories of a sample frequency distribution are in agreement with the relative frequencies expected to be true in the population (as stated in $H_0$)

The chi-square (pronounced ki) test was developed for **categorical data**; that is, for data comprising qualitative categories, such as eye color, sex, or political affiliation. Although the chi-square test is conducted in terms of frequencies, it is best viewed conceptually as a test about proportions. For example, let us return to the question of whether four brands of cola are equally preferred by consumers. Here, we explore the possibility that in the population of consumers, the proportion of individuals preferring each brand is 1/4:

$$H_0: P_A = P_B = P_C = P_D = .25$$

The alternative hypothesis is simply that the null hypothesis is untrue in some (any) way. It could be that a preference exists for the first of the colas and the remainder are equally less attractive, or that the first two are preferred more than the second two, and so on.

Our hypothetical cola problem is an example of a class of problems commonly referred to as **goodness-of-fit problems**. The use of chi-square tells us whether the relative frequencies observed in the several categories of our sample frequency distribution are in accord with the set of frequencies hypothesized (expected) to be true of the population distribution. For this type of problem, chi-square is a *one-variable* test with **k** number of categories.

To test the null hypothesis in our cola study, we might allow subjects to taste each of the four brands and then declare their preference. We would, of course, control for possible extraneous influences, such as knowledge of brand name or order of presentation. Suppose we randomly select 100 subjects and that our **observed frequencies ($f_o$'s)** of preference are as shown in Table 19.1.

An **expected frequency ($f_e$)** is the mean of the observed frequencies that would occur on infinite repetitions of an experiment when sampling is random and the null hypothesis is true. (In our example, the null hypothesis is true when there is no differential preference among consumers for the four colas.) We calculate the expected frequency for each category by multiplying the proportion hypothesized to characterize that category in the population by the sample size. According to the null hypothesis, in our example, the expected proportionate preference for each cola is 1/4, and the expected frequency of preference for each is therefore $(1/4)(100) = 25$.

**k**
symbol for number of categories

**observed frequencies ($f_o$)**
numbers of observations within a particular category of a sample of qualitative data

**expected frequency ($f_e$)**
numbers of observations within a particular category that is predicted under the condition that the null hypothesis is true

**TABLE 19.1** *Expected and Observed Frequency of Preference for Four Brands of Cola (100 Subjects)*

|  | Brand A | Brand B | Brand C | Brand D |  |
|---|---|---|---|---|---|
| *Observed frequency* | $f_o = 15$ | $f_o = 36$ | $f_o = 28$ | $f_o = 21$ | $\sum f_o = 100$ |
| *Expected frequency* | $f_e = 25$ | $f_e = 25$ | $f_e = 25$ | $f_e = 25$ | $\sum f_e = 100$ |

In any one experiment, we anticipate that the observed frequency of choices will vary from the expected frequencies in accord with random sampling variation. In our example, even if the null hypothesis is correct and there is no preference among consumers in the population (and thus the expected frequencies for the four colas are 25, 25, 25, and 25), would you be surprised if in a sample of 100 persons randomly drawn from the population the observed frequencies were A = 27, B = 23, C = 24, and D = 26? Or A = 24, B = 28, C = 22, and D = 26? Probably not, because you expect some variation due to chance factors. But how much variation is reasonable to expect? Some measure of discrepancy is needed as well as a method of testing whether the observed discrepancy is within the bounds of random sampling variation.

*"How would you like me to answer that question? As a member of my ethnic group, educational class, income group, or religious category?"*

# 19.2 Chi-Square ($\chi^2$) as a Measure of Discrepancy between Expected and Observed Frequencies

**chi-square statistic**
provides a measure of the discrepancy between expected and observed frequencies

$\chi^2$
symbol for chi-square

$$\sum\left(\frac{(f_o - f_e)^2}{f_e}\right)$$
formula for the chi-square statistic

The **chi-square statistic**, $\chi^2$, provides a measure of the discrepancy between expected and observed frequencies. Its basic formula is:

> FORMULA FOR CHI-SQUARE
>
> $$\chi^2 = \sum\left(\frac{(f_o - f_e)^2}{f_e}\right) \tag{19.1}$$
>
> *where:* $f_e$ = the expected frequency.
> $f_o$ = the observed frequency. Summation is over the number of categories characterizing a given problem.

For the data of Table 19.1 there are four categories (brands), and we calculate chi-square as follows:

$$\chi^2 = \frac{(15 - 25)^2}{25} + \frac{(36 - 25)^2}{25} + \frac{(28 - 25)^2}{25} + \frac{(21 - 25)^2}{25}$$

$$= \frac{(-10)^2}{25} + \frac{11^2}{25} + \frac{3^2}{25} + \frac{(-4)^2}{25}$$

$$= 4.0 + 4.84 + .36 + .64 = 9.84$$

Examine the formula and the calculation; they reveal several points of interest about $\chi^2$:

1. $\chi^2$ cannot be negative because all discrepancies are squared; both positive and negative discrepancies make a positive contribution to the value of $\chi^2$.

2. $\chi^2$ will be zero only in the unusual event that each observed frequency exactly equals the corresponding expected frequency.

3. Other things being equal, the larger the discrepancy between the $f_e$'s and their corresponding $f_o$'s, the larger $\chi^2$.

4. It is not the size of the discrepancy alone that accounts for a contribution to the value of $\chi^2$; rather, it is the size of the discrepancy *relative to the magnitude of the expected frequency.*

   This is intuitively reasonable. For example, if we toss a number of coins and inquire as to the number of "heads," $f_e$ is 6 when we toss 12 coins and 500 when we toss 1000 coins. If we obtain 11 heads in 12 tosses, the discrepancy is 5—most unusual. However, if we obtain 505 heads in 1000 tosses, the discrepancy is also 5—but hardly a rarity.

**$k - 1$**
degrees of freedom in a goodness-of-fit problem

5. The value of $\chi^2$ depends on the *number* of discrepancies involved in its calculation.

   For example, if we use three brands of cola instead of four, there would be one less discrepancy to contribute to the total of $\chi^2$. We take this factor into account by considering the number of **degrees of freedom** (*df*) associated with the particular $\chi^2$. For this type of problem, the degrees of freedom will be

$k - 1$ (because only the values of $k - 1$ categories are free to vary for a fixed value of $\chi^2$). In our cola problem, then, $df = 4 - 1 = 3$.

## 19.3 The Logic of the Chi-Square Test

In the chi-square test, the null hypothesis is that in the population distribution the proportional frequency of cases in each category equals a specified value. The proportions hypothesized are derived from a research question of interest to the researcher, and, as usual, the hypothesis concerns the *population proportions,* not the sample proportions. Our concern with the sample is simply to see whether it is in reasonable accord with what is hypothesized to be true of the population.

When the hypothesis to be tested is true *and* certain conditions hold (see Section 19.8), the sampling distribution formed by the values of $\chi^2$ calculated from repeated random samples closely follows a known theoretical distribution. Actually, there is a *family* of sampling distributions of $\chi^2$, each member corresponding to a given number of degrees of freedom. Figure 19.1 shows the sampling distributions for several difference values of *df.*

Suppose that the null hypothesis is true. Then the observed frequencies will differ from their corresponding expected frequencies only because of random sampling variation. The calculated value of $\chi^2$ will be small when agreement between $f_o$'s and $f_e$'s is good and large when it is not.

When the hypothesized $f_e$'s are *not* the true ones, the set of discrepancies between $f_o$ and $f_e$ will tend to be larger than otherwise and, consequently, so will the calculated

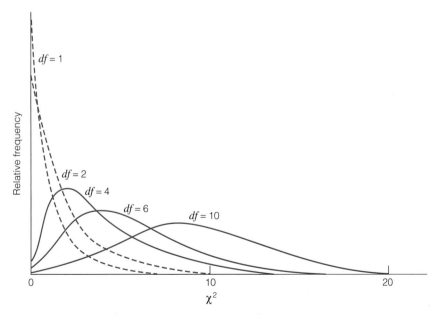

**FIGURE 19.1** Approximate forms of the $\chi^2$ distribution for various degrees of freedom. (*Source:* E. F. Lindquist, *Design and Analysis of Experiments in Psychology and Education.* Copyright © 1953 by Houghton Mifflin Company. Used with permission.)

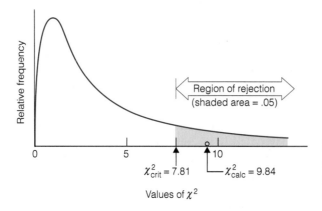

**FIGURE 19.2**  Location of the calculated value of $\chi^2$ relative to the expected distribution of $\chi^2$ when $df = 3$.

value of $\chi^2$. To test the null hypothesis, we must learn what calculated values of $\chi^2$ would occur under random sampling when the hypothesis is true. Then we will compare the $\chi^2$ calculated from our particular sample with this distribution of values. If it is so large that such a value would rarely occur when the null hypothesis is true, we will reject the hypothesis.

*The region of rejection always appears in the upper tail of the sampling distribution of $\chi^2$.* This is because we square discrepancies between observed and expected frequencies; thus larger discrepancies always result in a numerically higher value of $\chi^2_{calc}$.

To conduct the test, we must determine the critical value of $\chi^2$. At the 5% significance level, this is the value of $\chi^2$ so large that it will be equaled or exceeded only 5% of the time in random sampling when the null hypothesis is true. We use Table I in Appendix E to determine the critical value for the desired level of significance and degrees of freedom. As usual, we reject the null hypothesis if $\chi^2_{calc} \geq \chi^2_{crit}$.

In our cola problem, $df = 3$. Entering Table I with this value, we find that the critical value is 7.81 when $\alpha = .05$. We illustrate this test situation in Figure 19.2. Our calculated value of $\chi^2$ is 9.84, which exceeds the critical value. The $(f_o - f_e)$ discrepancies are therefore of a magnitude large enough not to be reasonably expected if the null hypothesis is true, so we reject the null hypothesis.

What of the other tail of the chi-square distribution? A very low obtained value of $\chi^2$ means that, *if the necessary assumptions have been met and the calculations are correct,* the observed frequencies are closer to the expected frequencies than chance would ordinarily allow. A very small value of $\chi^2$ has no significance other than to alert us to check on the adequacy of our procedures.

## 19.4 Interpretation of the Outcome of a Chi-Square Test

For any problem, the observed frequencies will vary with sample size. The simplest way to study what is happening is to convert the observed frequencies to proportions and then compare them with the expected proportions. However, if we find that $\chi^2$ is significant, we have only opened the door to explanatory analysis. In our cola experiment we obtained a sample $\chi^2$ larger than the critical value of 7.81, so we rejected $H_0$ and conclude that some colas are preferred over others. Which ones? We are tempted to say that people prefer brand B. Strictly speaking, however, we cannot tell from our $\chi^2$ value alone because $H_A$, the alternative hypothesis, is simply that $H_0$ is untrue in some (any) way, and there are many ways in which that could occur. It may be that people equally prefer brands B and C, and that both are preferred over brands A and D. Note that the distinction between a directional test and a nondirectional test is not pertinent here; a directional test is possible only in situations where there are only two ways (directions) in which $H_0$ can be wrong.

# 19.5 Different Hypothesized Proportions in the Test for Goodness of Fit

In any goodness-of-fit problem, the hypothesized proportion in each category is dictated by the research question of interest. In our cola problem, the hypothesized proportions reflected the possibility that the four brands are equally attractive. However, the hypothesized (expected) proportions need not be equal, as we will now show.

Chi-square is frequently used in the field of population genetics. Suppose, for example, that a geneticist believes that plants bred in a particular way will show one of four characteristics according to the ratio 9:3:3:1. In an experiment designed to test this hypothesis, the geneticist converts these ratios into expected proportions: $P_1 = 9/16$, $P_2 = 3/16$, $P_3 = 3/16$, and $P_4 = 1/16$. If the geneticist breeds plants in the specified manner and obtains a sample of 256 seedlings, the expected frequencies are 144, 48, 48, and 16, respectively (obtained by multiplying each of the expected proportions by 256). Suppose the geneticist obtained the hypothetical results shown in Table 19.2. By Formula 19.1, the calculated value of $\chi^2$ is:

$$\chi^2 = \frac{(130 - 144)^2}{144} + \frac{(55 - 48)^2}{48} + \frac{(50 - 48)^2}{48} + \frac{(21 - 16)^2}{16} = 4.03$$

Is the discrepancy between expected and observed frequencies so great as to be beyond the realm of chance? Here, $df = k - 1 = 3$. We turn to Table I and find that when $df = 3$, a $\chi^2$ of 7.81 or greater would occur by chance 5% of the time when the hypothesis is true. The geneticist's $\chi^2$ is not so rare an event (when $\alpha = .05$) to give him or her a reason to reject the statistical hypothesis. The sample outcome is one of many that could have easily occurred by chance when the null hypothesis is true.

TABLE 19.2   *Expected and Observed Frequency of Occurrence of Four Inherited Plant Characteristics*

|  | Type 1 | Type 2 | Type 3 | Type 4 |  |
|---|---|---|---|---|---|
| Observed frequency | $f_o = 130$ | $f_o = 55$ | $f_o = 50$ | $f_o = 21$ | $\sum f_o = 256$ |
| Expected frequency | $f_e = 144$ | $f_e = 48$ | $f_e = 48$ | $f_e = 16$ | $\sum f_e = 256$ |

## 19.6 Hypothesis Testing When *df* = 1

When *df* = 1 (i.e., when there are only two categories), we can view the chi-square test as a *test about a single proportion*. Suppose, for example, that we want to know if rats prefer light or dark given two alternative routes at a choice point in a maze. We design a study with controls to guard against extraneous factors (such as a tendency for the animal always to turn left or right) and allow 50 rats the opportunity of choosing two routes, one light and the other dark. We identify *P* as the proportion of choices of dark routes in the population of possible choices and $(1 - P)$ as the proportion of choices of light routes (or vice versa). Thus, we could write the following null and alternative hypotheses:

$$H_0: P = .50$$
$$H_A: P \neq .50$$

*where:*   *P* = the population value of the proportion.

Suppose the observed frequencies are as follows:

Light: $f_0 = 15$       Dark: $f_0 = 35$

Here, the sample value of the proportion of dark choices is $p = 35/50$. The test of a single proportion is therefore conceptually analogous to the test of a single mean. The difference is simply in the statistic involved; that is $\overline{X}$ or *p*.

Let us calculate $\chi^2$ for this problem. By Formula 19.1:

$$\chi^2 = \frac{(15 - 25)^2}{25} + \frac{(35 - 25)^2}{25} = \frac{(-10)^2}{25} + \frac{(10)^2}{25} = 8.00$$

In the special case when chi-square has one degree of freedom, it is possible to perform a one-tailed test if the logic of the study calls for it. When *df* = 1 (only), $\chi^2 = z^2$. We may therefore calculate $z = \sqrt{\chi^2_{calc}}$ and compare our result with the critical one-tailed value of the normally distributed *z* ($z_{crit} = 1.645$ for $\alpha = .05$ and $z_{crit} = 2.33$ for $\alpha = .01$). We reject the null hypothesis only for differences in the direction specified in the alternative hypothesis. In the rat study, for example, suppose the logic of the study calls for rejection of the null hypothesis only if the evidence points toward a significant preference for the dark route. First, note that the evidence from the sample shows a greater proportion of choices of the dark route. (If it did not, there would be no point in pursuing the matter further.) Next, calculate $z = \sqrt{\chi^2_{calc}} = \sqrt{8.00} = 2.83$. For the one-tailed test at $\alpha = .05$, $z_{crit} = 1.645$, so we reject the null hypothesis.

## 19.7 Effect Size for Goodness-of-Fit Problems

**ŵ**

omega; a measure of effect size for the chi-square goodness-of-fit test

$$\sqrt{\sum \left[ \frac{(p_o - p_e)^2}{p_e} \right]}$$

formula for ŵ

Cohen (1988) proposes that the appropriate measure of effect size for the chi-square goodness-of-fit test is **ŵ** (omega):

FORMULA FOR EFFECT SIZE, **ŵ**

$$\hat{\omega} = \sqrt{\sum \left[ \frac{(p_o - p_e)^2}{p_e} \right]} \tag{19.2}$$

*where:*   $p_o$ = observed proportion
$p_e$ = expected proportion

Omega is a member of the *d* family of effect sizes (see Section 14.2). Notice that to calculate $\hat{\omega}$ you must first translate frequencies to proportions. For the data in Table 19.1:

| BRAND | $p_o$ | $p_e$ | $p_o - p_e$ | $\dfrac{(p_o - p_e)^2}{p_e}$ |
|-------|-------|-------|-------------|------------------------------|
| A | 15/100 = .15 | .25 | −.10 | .0400 |
| B | 36/100 = .36 | .25 | .11 | .0484 |
| C | 28/100 = .28 | .25 | .03 | .0036 |
| D | 21/100 = .21 | .25 | −.04 | .0064 |
| | | | 0 | .0984 |

$$\hat{\omega} = \sqrt{.0984} = .31$$

Cohen (1992) suggests that we may interpret effect size, $\hat{\omega}$, as follows: .1 = small effect, .3 = medium effect, and .5 = large effect. Thus, in our cola problem, our outcome has a medium effect size.

## 19.8 Assumptions in the Use of the Theoretical Distribution of Chi-Square

Many people refer to chi-square as a nonparametric test, but it does, in fact, assume the central limit theorem and is therefore neither a "distribution-free" nor an "assumption-free" procedure (Bradley, 1968). The distribution of $\chi^2$ follows from certain theoretical considerations, and thus we may expect obtained values of $\chi^2$ to follow this distribution exactly only when the assumptions appropriate to this model are satisfied. What are these assumptions?

1. It is assumed that the sample drawn is a random sample from the population about which inference is to be made. In practice, this requirement is seldom fully met (see Section 14.12).

2. It is assumed that observations are independent. For example, in the cola experiment utilizing 100 randomly selected subjects, the preference of one individual is not predictable from that of any other. But suppose each subject had been given three trials. The three responses of each subject are not independent of each other. In general, *the set of observations will not be completely independent when their number exceeds the number of subjects.*

3. It is assumed that, in repeated experiments, the observed frequencies will be normally distributed about the expected frequencies. With random sampling, this tends to be true.

## 19.9 Chi-Square as a Test for Independence between Two Variables

**bivariate distribution**
a distribution that shows the relation between two variables

So far, we have considered the application of chi-square only to the one-variable case. However, we can also use it to analyze **bivariate frequency distributions**. For example, suppose we poll 400 students on a college campus and ask what role they feel

**TABLE 19.3**  *Classification of Responses of 400 College Students to the Question: "How Should Students Participate in Determining the Curriculum?"*

| | | Desired Role of Students | | | |
| --- | --- | --- | --- | --- | --- |
| | | Recommendation through student association | Nonvoting membership on curriculum committee | Voting membership on curriculum committee | $f_{row}$ |
| *Major of respondents* | *Humanities and arts* | 46 | 82 | 72 | 200 |
| | *Science* | 42 | 38 | 20 | 100 |
| | *Business* | 52 | 40 | 8 | 100 |
| | $f_{col}$ | 140 | 160 | 100 | $n = 400$ |

students should have in determining the curriculum. We wish to analyze their responses in relation to their majors. Do students with different majors see their role in the same way?

To study this question, we classify the data (observed frequencies) in a bivariate distribution, as shown in Table 19.3. For each variable, the categories are mutually exclusive. As an example of the information conveyed by the table, note that of the 400 students, 200 were majors in humanities and arts (total frequency for the first row). We also see that 100 of the students wanted voting membership on the curriculum committee (total frequency for the third column). These row and column totals are often referred to as **marginal totals** because they are found at the margins of the table. The table also gives more specific information. For example, of the 200 humanities and arts majors, 72 thought that students should be voting members of the college curriculum committee. The frequencies in each cell (box) are called **cell frequencies**.

In many ways, this table is similar to the bivariate frequency distributions you encountered in the study of correlation (see Chapter 8). Indeed, the major difference is that the two variables (student's major and student's role) are both qualitative variables rather than quantitative variables. As with a correlation table, we may ask whether there is a relationship between the two variables in the population sampled. That is, is classification of response independent of classification of the respondent's major, or is one contingent on the other in some way?

Bivariate frequency distributions of the type illustrated in Table 19.3 are known as **contingency tables**. From such a table we can determine what cell frequencies would be expected if the two variables are independent of each other *in the population*. Then, we may use *chi-square to compare the observed cell frequencies with those expected under the null hypothesis of independence*. If the $(f_o - f_e)$ discrepancies are small, $\chi^2$ will be small, suggesting that the two variables could be independent. Conversely, a large $\chi^2$ points toward a contingency relationship.

In general, the **null hypothesis of independence** for a contingency table is equivalent to hypothesizing that in the population the relative frequencies for any row (across the categories of the column variable) are the same for all rows, or that in the population the relative frequencies for any column (across the categories of the row variable) are the same for all columns. So again we can think of the hypothesis to be

**marginal totals**

row totals and column totals in a bivariate distribution

**cell frequency**

the frequency of observations in a cell of a bivariate distribution

**contingency tables**

a bivariate distributions of two qualitative variables

**$H_0$ for chi-square test for independence between two variables**

states that in the population, there is no relationship between the two variables; in practice, a test about proportions

tested by $\chi^2$ as one concerning proportions. For example, look at the data of Table 19.3. There are twice as many humanities and arts majors as there are science or business majors, but if the role students assign to themselves is unrelated to their major, then *on a proportional basis* the role assigned should be the same for students from each of the three majors. To calculate $\chi^2$, we will begin by calculating the sample marginal proportions for columns—the proportion of cases appearing in each column when the three student majors are combined. We do this by dividing each column total by the grand total $(n)$:

$$p_1 = \frac{\begin{bmatrix} \text{number of students} \\ \text{for recommendation} \\ \text{through student} \\ \text{association} \end{bmatrix}}{\text{total number of students}} = \frac{f_{\text{col1}}}{n} = \frac{140}{400} = .35$$

$$p_2 = \frac{\begin{bmatrix} \text{number of students} \\ \text{for nonvoting membership} \\ \text{on college curriculum} \\ \text{committee} \end{bmatrix}}{\text{total number of students}} = \frac{f_{\text{col 2}}}{n} = \frac{160}{400} = .40$$

$$p_3 = \frac{\begin{bmatrix} \text{number of students} \\ \text{for voting membership} \\ \text{on college curriculum} \\ \text{committee} \end{bmatrix}}{\text{total number of students}} = \frac{f_{\text{col 3}}}{n} = \frac{100}{400} = .25$$

In the absence of a dependent relationship, we should expect the distribution of proportions *in each row* to approximate these figures. They are therefore the *expected* cell proportions, as shown in Table 19.4.

**TABLE 19.4** *Expected Cell Proportions for Each Row in a Contingency Table (Data from Table 19.3)*

| | Desired Role of Student | | |
|---|---|---|---|
| | *Recommendation through student association* | *Nonvoting membership on curriculum committee* | *Voting membership on curriculum committee* |
| *Humanities and arts* | $p_e = .35$ | $p_e = .40$ | $p_e = .25$ |
| *Science* | $p_e = .35$ | $p_e = .40$ | $p_e = .25$ |
| *Business* | $p_e = .35$ | $p_e = .40$ | $p_e = .25$ |
| Total | $p = \dfrac{140}{400} = .35$ | $p = \dfrac{160}{400} = .40$ | $p = \dfrac{100}{400} = .25$ |

*Major of respondents* (row label)

# 19.10 Finding Expected Frequencies in a Contingency Table

Under the null hypothesis of independence of classification of the two variables in the population we can easily calculate the expected cell frequencies from the expected cell proportions: In each row, simply *multiply the expected proportion for each cell by the total number of subjects in that row.* For example, for the cell representing humanities and arts majors who thought that students should be voting members on the college curriculum committee, the expected frequency is:

$$f_e = \left[ \begin{array}{c} expected\ proportion \\ for\ voting\ membership \end{array} \right] \times \left[ \begin{array}{c} total\ number\ of \\ humanities\ and\ arts\ majors \end{array} \right]$$

$$= (.25)(f_{row1})$$

$$= (.25)(200) = 50$$

We show the complete results for our student example in Table 19.5. The observed frequencies (from Table 19.3) also appear in this table.

To sum up, we may calculate frequencies expected under the hypothesis of independence in a contingency table as follows:

**Step 1:** Find the column proportions by dividing each column total ($f_{col}$) by the grand total ($n$). In our example, they are .35, .40, and .25, respectively. The sum of these proportions should always be unity.

**Step 2:** Multiply each row total by these column proportions; the result in each instance is the expected cell frequency ($f_e$) for the cells in that row. This is shown in the cells of Table 19.5. Thus, we calculate the expected frequency for any cell by

$$f_e = \left( \frac{f_{col}}{n} \right)(f_{row})$$

**TABLE 19.5** *Expected and Observed Frequencies for Each Cell in a Contingency Table (Data from Table 19.3)*

| | | Desired Role of Student | | | |
|---|---|---|---|---|---|
| | | Recommendation through student association | Nonvoting membership on curriculum committee | Voting membership on curriculum committee | $f_{row}$ |
| *Major of respondents* | Humanities and arts | $f_e = e = .35 \times 200 = 70$<br>$f_o = 46$ | $f_e = .40 \times 200 = 80$<br>$f_o = 82$ | $f_e = .25 \times 200 = 50$<br>$f_o = 72$ | 200 |
| | Science | $f_e = .35 \times 100 = 35$<br>$f_o = 42$ | $f_e = .40 \times 100 = 40$<br>$f_o = 38$ | $f_e = .25 \times 100 = 25$<br>$f_o = 20$ | 100 |
| | Business | $f_e = .35 \times 100 = 35$<br>$f_o = 52$ | $f_e = .40 \times 100 = 40$<br>$f_o = 40$ | $f_e = .25 \times 100 = 25$<br>$f_o = 8$ | 100 |
| | | $f_{col} = 140$ | $f_{col} = 160$ | $f_{col} = 100$ | $n = 400$ |
| | | $p_{col} = \dfrac{140}{400} = .35$ | $p_{col} = \dfrac{160}{400} = .40$ | $p_{col} = \dfrac{100}{400} = .25$ | |

We could also have obtained the same results by finding the row proportions and multiplying them by the column totals:

$$f_e = \left(\frac{f_{\text{row}}}{n}\right)(f_{\text{col}})$$

For understanding purposes, it is best to learn to calculate expected frequencies by column proportions or row proportions, as we have done. However, there is a short-cut. Look at the previous two formulas. Either one may easily be transformed to

$$f_e = \frac{(f_{\text{row}})(f_{\text{col}})}{n} \qquad\qquad f_e = \frac{(f_{\text{row}})(f_{\text{col}})}{n}$$

shortcut formula for calculating expected cell frequencies

As an example, for the cell representing humanities and arts majors who thought that students should be voting members on the college curriculum committee,

$$f_e = \frac{(200)(100)}{400} = 50$$

**Step 3:**   Check to see that the total of the expected frequencies in any row or in any column equals that of the observed frequencies. If they do not, we have made an error in calculation.

# 19.11  Calculation of $\chi^2$ and Determination of Significance in a Contingency Table

Now that we have the expected and observed frequencies for each cell (Table 19.5), we calculate $\chi^2$ according to Formula 19.1. As usual, each $(f_o - f_e)$ discrepancy is squared and divided by $f_e$. The sum of these nine components is the calculated value of $\chi^2$:

$$\chi^2 = \frac{(46-70)^2}{70} + \frac{(42-35)^2}{35} + \frac{(52-35)^2}{35} + \frac{(82-80)^2}{80} + \frac{(38-40)^2}{40}$$

$$+ \frac{(40-40)^2}{40} + \frac{(72-50)^2}{50} + \frac{(20-25)^2}{25} + \frac{(8-25)^2}{25}$$

$$= 40.28$$

**R**
symbol for number of rows

**C**
symbol for number of columns

**(C − 1)(R − 1)**
degrees of freedom in a contingency table

How many degrees of freedom are associated with this $\chi^2$? To figure *degrees of freedom in a contingency table,* we consider that the column totals and the row totals are fixed and ask how many cell frequencies are free to vary. In general, if **R** is the number of rows and **C** is the number of columns, the number of cell frequencies that can vary (and therefore the number of degrees of freedom) for an $R \times C$ contingency table is $(C - 1)(R - 1)$. For our problem, $df = (3 - 1)(3 - 1) = 4$.

If the null hypothesis of independence is true at the population level, we should expect that random sampling will produce obtained values of $\chi^2$ that are close to the tabulated distribution of that statistic. If the hypothesis is false in any way, the obtained values of $\chi^2$ will tend to be larger than when the hypothesis is true. As

## Point of Controversy

### Yates' Correction for Continuity

Theoretical chi-square distributions are smooth and continuous. Calculated chi-square statistics, on the other hand, have only discrete values and are discontinuous (with irregular, stepwise distributions). Thus, discrepancies may exist between calculated and theoretical values of $\chi^2$. To compensate for this, Yates (1934) introduced a **correction for continuity**, which consists of reducing the discrepancies between $f_o$ and $f_e$ by .5 before squaring:

$$\chi^2 = \frac{(|f_o - f_e| - .5)^2}{f_e}$$

Yates' procedure reduces the calculated value of $\chi^2$, thereby making a significant result less likely.

Older statistics textbooks, including previous editions of this text, almost always recommended use of Yates' correction in cases where $df = 1$ (including $2 \times 2$ contingency tables), particularly if the expected frequency in one of the cells is less than 5. Statisticians have now shown, however, that *the uncorrected chi-square statistic is reasonably accurate when the average expected frequency is as low as 2* (e.g., Camilli & Hopkins, 1978; Conover, 1974; Delucchi, 1983; Roscoe & Byers, 1971). Consequently, the correction has been abandoned for the one-variable (goodness-of-fit) case. With regard to $2 \times 2$ tables, old habits linger on, and many investigators continue to use Yates' correction.

There are, in fact, some statisticians who still favor the use of Yates' correction in a $2 \times 2$ table (Fleiss, 1981; Mantel & Greenhouse, 1968, Mantel, 1990; Greenhouse, 1990). Most statisticians disagree. *One* of the problems is that Yates developed his procedure for situations in which the experimenter controls both sets of marginal frequencies in the $2 \times 2$ table, but this is rarely encountered in practice. When applied to most studies (where marginal frequencies are free to vary), Yates' correction makes an already very conservative test even more conservative, "causing the actual proportion of Type I errors to be substantially lower than the nominal alpha levels" (Haviland, 1990). The result is greatly reduced power. Computer simulation studies have shown the uncorrected chi-square test to work quite well for tests of independence (Camilli & Hopkins, 1978).

A word of caution: The use of small expected frequencies increases the chance of making a Type II error (failure to reject a false null hypothesis). Thus, you would still be wise to use a large sample size. For an excellent review of this subject, including comments from both those who favor and those who disfavor Yates' correction, see Haviland (1990).

---

before, then, the region of rejection is placed in the upper tail of the tabulated distribution. For $df = 4$, Table I in Appendix E shows that when the test is conducted at $\alpha = .05$, $\chi^2_{crit} = 9.49$, and when $\alpha = .01$, $\chi^2_{crit} = 13.28$. The calculated $\chi^2$ is 40.28, which exceeds both critical points. Accordingly, we reject the null hypothesis of independence.

It is often easiest to visualize the outcome of the test by converting the observed cell frequencies to proportions ($p_o$'s) and comparing these with the expected cell proportions ($p_e$'s). To calculate the observed proportions, we divide each observed cell frequency by the total number of cases in the row in which that cell falls:

$$p_o = \frac{f_o}{f_{row}}$$

Table 19.6 shows these calculations.

When we examine Table 19.6, it appears that humanities and arts majors differ from business majors in more strongly favoring the fullest student participation, and that science majors fall somewhere in between. You should consider this conclusion as a tentative hypothesis rather than as a confirmed fact. Remember that a significant outcome of the chi-square test is directly applicable *only to the data taken as a whole.* The $\chi^2$ that we obtained is inseparably a function of the nine contributions (one from each cell) composing it. We cannot say for sure whether one group is responsible for the finding of significance or whether all are involved.

In the case of a 2 × 2 contingency table, we can test for a difference between two proportions from independent samples (just as with the 1 × 2 table, where we can test a hypothesis about a single proportion; see Section 19.6). Suppose, for example, that before a big election we asked a random sample of men and women about their preference for candidates Smith and Jones. We could write

$$H_0: P_{men} - P_{women} = 0$$

$$H_A: P_{men} - P_{women} \neq 0$$

*where:*     $P_{men}$ = the population value of the proportion of men who prefer Smith.

$P_{women}$ = the same figure for women.

**TABLE 19.6**   *Observed Frequencies Expressed as Proportions of the Row Totals (Data from Table 19.3)*

| | | Desired Role of Student | | | |
|---|---|---|---|---|---|
| | | *Recommendation through student association* | *Nonvoting membership on curriculum committee* | *Voting membership on curriculum committee* | $f_{row}$ |
| | Humanities and arts | $p_o = \frac{46}{200} = .23$ | $p_o = \frac{82}{200} = .41$ | $p_o = \frac{72}{200} = .36$ | 200 |
| *Major of respondents* | Science | $p_o = \frac{42}{100} = .42$ | $p_o = \frac{38}{100} = .38$ | $p_o = \frac{20}{100} = .20$ | 100 |
| | Business | $p_o = \frac{52}{100} = .52$ | $p_o = \frac{40}{100} = .40$ | $p_o = \frac{8}{100} = .08$ | 100 |
| | | $p_{col} = .35$ | $p_{col} = .40$ | $p_{col} = .25$ | $n = 400$ |

# 19.12 Measures of Effect Size (Strength of Association) for Tests of Independence

**$\phi$**
symbol for the phi coefficient and for Cramer's phi, two measures of the strength of association

Because the contingency table is analogous to the correlation table, you might think that $\chi^2$, like $r$, provides a measure of strength of association. However, $\chi^2$ does not by itself serve this function. The only purpose of the chi-square test as applied to a contingency table is to test a null hypothesis of independence between two variables. But what if the outcome of our $\chi^2$ test leads us to reject the null hypothesis? That means there is some degree of correlation between the variables, but how strong is it? Two measures of association are commonly used *after* the null hypothesis of independence has been rejected. Both are members of the $r$ family of effect sizes (see Section 15.9).

In the case of a 2 × 2 contingency table, a measure of strength of association is provided by the **phi coefficient ($\phi$)** (see Section 8.14):

$$\sqrt{\frac{\chi^2}{n}}$$

FORMULA FOR THE PHI COEFFICIENT

$$\phi = \sqrt{\frac{\chi^2}{n}} \tag{19.3}$$

*where:*  $\chi^2$ = the calculated $\chi^2$ value.
        $n$ = sample size.

formula for the phi coefficient, for a 2 × 2 contingency table

The value of $\phi$ ranges from 0 (no association) to 1 (perfect association).[1] Cohen (1988) suggests that we may interpret $\phi$ in the same manner as we did $\hat{\omega}$: .1 = small effect, .3 = medium effect, and .5 = large effect. As an example, look at Table 19.7. The calculated value of $\chi^2$ is 9.57, which exceeds the critical value of 3.84 for 1 *df* and $\alpha = .05$. Phi is then calculated to be $\sqrt{9.57/190} = .22$. We may then conclude that the level of association between voters' sex and preference for Smith or Jones is small to medium.

---

[1] In a 2 × 2 table where we have two dichotomous variables, if we order the categories for each variable and assign a score of 0 to the lower category and 1 to the higher category, $\phi$ is equivalent to Pearson's $r$.

TABLE **19.7**   *Voter Preference for Candidates Smith and Jones*

|  |  | Candidates | | |
|---|---|---|---|---|
|  |  | *Smith* | *Jones* | $f_{\text{row}}$ |
| *Voters* | *Male* | 42 | 58 | 100 |
|  | *Female* | 58 | 32 | 90 |
|  | $f_{\text{col}}$ | 100 | 90 | $n = 190$ |

We may use phi only with a $2 \times 2$ table. For larger contingency tables, the appropriate measure of association is **Cramer's phi** (also $\phi$, although sometimes symbolized as **V**):

$$\sqrt{\frac{\chi^2}{n(df_{smaller})}}$$

formula for Cramer's phi, for use with any contingency table

---

**FORMULA FOR CRAMER'S PHI**

$$\phi = \sqrt{\frac{\chi^2}{n(df_{smaller})}} \tag{19.4}$$

*where:* $\chi^2 = $ the calculated $\chi^2$ value.

$n = $ sample size.

$df_{smaller} = df$ for the *smaller* of the number of rows and columns.

---

Notice that Cramer's phi is really just an extension of the phi coefficient for a $2 \times 2$ table. In the case of a $2 \times 2$ table, $df_{smaller}$ in Formula 19.4 is 1, and phi = Cramer's phi. Thus, we may use Cramer's phi for any contingency table.

As an example, look again at Table 19.3. Recall that our obtained $\chi^2$ was 40.28 and we rejected the null hypothesis of independence. There were three rows and three columns, so $df_{smaller} = 2$. We calculate Cramer's phi as

$$\phi = \sqrt{\frac{40.28}{(400)(2)}} = \sqrt{.05035} = .22$$

The phi coefficient is equivalent to $\hat{\omega}$, a measure of effect size that we introduced in Section 19.7. However, Cramer's phi is not equivalent to $\hat{\omega}$. To convert Cramer's phi to $\hat{\omega}$, multiply it by the square root of $df_{smaller}$:

---

**FORMULA FOR CONVERSION
OF CRAMER'S PHI TO $\hat{\omega}$**

$$\hat{\omega} = \text{Cramer's } \phi \sqrt{df_{smaller}} \tag{19.5}$$

---

As before, Cohen (1988) states that .1 = small effect, .3 = medium effect, and .5 = large effect.

## 19.13 Power and the Chi-Square Test of Independence

What about power? Cohen (1988) has computed tables based on the effect size $\hat{\omega}$. We reproduced a small part of Cohen's tables in Table 19.8. As an example, suppose you planned a study with a $2 \times 3$ contingency table using 100 subjects. If you anticipate a medium effect size, what would be the power of your test when $\alpha = .05$? For $df = 2$ and $n = 100$, Table 19.8 shows us that power would be approximately .77. Therefore, if the null hypothesis is false (the two variables are really not independent), you have about a 77% chance of rejecting the hypothesis. For more complete tables, see Cohen's text.

TABLE **19.8**    *Power for the Chi-Square Test of Independence,* $\alpha = .05$

| df | n | SMALL EFFECT | MEDIUM EFFECT | LARGE EFFECT |
|----|-----|------|------|------|
| 1 | 50 | .11 | .56 | .94 |
|   | 100 | .17 | .85 | .99+ |
|   | 200 | .29 | .99 | .99+ |
| 2 | 50 | .09 | .46 | .90 |
|   | 100 | .13 | .77 | .99+ |
|   | 200 | .23 | .97 | .99+ |
| 3 | 50 | .08 | .40 | .86 |
|   | 100 | .12 | .71 | .99 |
|   | 200 | .19 | .96 | .99+ |
| 4 | 50 | .08 | .36 | .82 |
|   | 100 | .11 | .66 | .99 |
|   | 200 | .17 | .94 | .99+ |

Source: Data for this figure were obtained from J. Cohen, *Statistical Power Analysis for the Behavioral Sciences,* 2nd ed., Lawrence Erlbaum Associates, Inc., New York, 1988, and are used with permission.

## 19.14 Summary

In previous chapters, we introduced inferential techniques that deal with quantitative variables and are used for testing hypotheses about summary characteristics of the data. Our concern in this chapter has been inferences about frequency—the number of cases falling into the several categories of a population distribution. The statistical test we used to make inferences about frequencies is called chi-square $(\chi^2)$.

In tests of frequency in categories of a single variable (often called tests for goodness of fit), the chi-square test tells us whether the relative frequencies observed in the two or more categories of our sample frequency distribution are in accord with the set of such values hypothesized to be true in the population. The test determines whether the discrepancies between the observed frequencies and the frequencies expected under $H_0$ are greater than would be anticipated on the basis of random sampling variation. When $H_0$ is true, the sample $\chi^2$'s follow a theoretical distribution with $k - 1$ degrees of freedom, where $k$ is the number of categories. Larger discrepancies between $f_o$ and $f_e$ result in larger calculated values of $\chi^2$, so the region of rejection is always in the upper tail of the sampling distribution. With just two categories, we can test a hypothesis about a single proportion, but with more than two categories the alternative hypothesis is very broad ($H_0$ can be untrue in many ways) and any conclusion must be taken as a tentative hypothesis. A measure of effect size is provided by $\hat{\omega}$.

The chi-square test may also be used in the analysis of bivariate frequency distributions to test whether the two variables are independent. To conduct the test, we cross-tabulate the data in a contingency table and calculate the $(f_o - f_e)$ discrepancy for each cell. If our calculated $\chi^2$ is larger than the critical value for $(R - 1)(C - 1)$ degrees of freedom, we reject the null hypothesis and conclude that the two variables are related in *some* way. For a $2 \times 2$ contingency table, we can state the null hypothesis as a test of the difference between two proportions. When the null hypothesis of independence is rejected, that means there is some degree of association between the two variables. The strength of association is provided by the phi coefficient ($\phi$) for $2 \times 2$ tables and Cramer's phi ($\phi$) for larger tables.

## Key Terms, Concepts, and Symbols

categorical data (366)

$P$ (366)

goodness-of-fit problems (366)

null and alternative hypotheses in the one-variable case (366)

$k$ (367)

observed frequencies (367)

$f_o$ (367)

expected frequencies (367)

$f_e$ (367)

chi-square statistic (368)

$\chi^2$ (368)

degrees of freedom (368)

$k - 1$ (368)

chi-square sampling distributions (369)

$\hat{\omega}$ (372)

bivariate distribution (125, 373)

marginal totals (374)

cell frequency (374)

contingency tables (374)

null hypothesis of independence (375)

expected frequencies in a contingency table (376)

$(C - 1)(R - 1)$ (377)

Yates' correction for continuity (378)

phi coefficient (380)

$\phi$ (380)

Cramer's phi (381)

## Problems

$\boxed{c}$ *4, 5, 8, 11, 12, 13, 15, 17*

**1.** In the $\chi^2$ test, why is only the area in the upper tail of the $\chi^2$ distribution of interest?

**2.** An investigator wishes to study the frequency of accidents among four divisions of an industry ($H_0$: $P_1 = P_2 = P_3 = P_4$). Is $\chi^2$ appropriate for this study? Explain. Suppose the investigator wishes to study the frequency of accidents for all workers in the months of January, February, March, and April. Is $\chi^2$ appropriate for this study? Explain.

**3.** The example in Section 19.6 concerned the preference for light or dark of 50 rats. Suppose the question had concerned the preference of one particular rat. Would it be permissible to give it 50 trials and use the $\chi^2$ test in the same way? Explain.

**4.** We wish to determine whether a gambler's die is loaded. We roll the die 60 times and obtain the following results:

| Side coming up: | 1 | 2 | 3 | 4 | 5 | 6 |
|---|---|---|---|---|---|---|
| Number observed: | 8 | 8 | 5 | 10 | 14 | 15 |

(a) In Problem 3, one rat was given 50 trials; in this problem one die is given 60 trials. Why was it not appropriate to use the $\chi^2$ test in Problem 3, whereas it is appropriate here? (See the second assumption in Section 19.8.) (b) State in symbolic form, two equivalent statements of $H_0$ for this situation. (c) Can $H_A$ be written in a single symbolic statement? Explain. (d) Compute the expected frequencies under $H_0$. (e) Compute $\chi^2$ and complete the test ($\alpha = .05$). Draw final conclusions. (f) Do these results prove the die is not loaded? (See Section 13.6.)

**5.** In a grocery store, customers who pass by are asked to sample three cheese spreads and to declare their preference for one. Their frequencies of choice are as follows:

| Spread: | A | B | C |
|---|---|---|---|
| Frequency of choice: | 20 | 39 | 25 |

(a) Test the null hypothesis of equal preference using $\alpha = .05$ and $.01$. What conclusions are allowable when $\chi^2$ proves to be significant? (b) What is the effect size, $\hat{\omega}$, for this result? (c) Is this a small, medium, or large effect?

6. For the data in Problem 5, test the null hypothesis that spread B is as popular as the other two combined, using $\alpha = .05$. Statisticians say that it is proper to examine this question if it is hypothesized in advance of collecting the data. However, if the hypothesis is generated by the finding that spread B is more popular than the rest, the question is improper. Explain.

7. For Problem 5, how does the method of sampling affect the researcher's ability to make inferences about the population? (See Section 14.12.)

8. One hundred students take a multiple-choice test. We wish to test the hypothesis that the students guessed at random on question 36. The frequencies of responses for that question were as follows:

Alternative:  A  B  C  D  E
Frequency of response:  15  40  5  12  28

(a) State $H_0$ in symbolic form. (b) Compute $\chi^2$ and test $H_0$ at $\alpha = .01$. (c) Draw final conclusions. (d) Calculate $\hat{\omega}$ for this result and state whether this is a small, medium, or large effect size.

9. Refer to Problem 8. Suppose alternative B is the correct answer. (a) For this alternative, state the observed frequencies of correct and incorrect answers. (b) What are the expected frequencies if the students are just guessing? (c) Suppose we wish to test the null hypothesis that the frequencies of correct and incorrect answers to alternative B are in accord with random guessing. State $H_0$ in terms of the proportion guessing correctly. (d) Compute $\chi^2$ and perform a nondirectional test of $H_0$ at $\alpha = .05$. Draw final conclusions. (e) Suppose we wish to test $H_0$ against the alternative that at least some students know the correct answer. State $H_A$. (f) Why can we perform a directional test here but not in Problem 8?

10. You may have heard the old adage, "Stay with your first answer on a multiple-choice

test." Is changing answers more likely to be helpful or harmful? To examine this, Best (1979) studied the responses of 261 students in an introductory psychology course. He recorded the number of right-to-wrong, wrong-to-right, and wrong-to-wrong answer changes for each student. More wrong-to-right changes than right-to-wrong changes were made by 195 of the students, who were thus "helped" by changing answers; 27 students made more right-to-wrong changes than wrong-to-right changes and thus "hurt" themselves. (a) For these 222 students, conduct a $\chi^2$ test of the hypothesis that the population proportions of right-to-wrong and wrong-to-right changes are equal. Your conclusions? (b) What is the effect size?

11. A botanist plants a group of hybrid flower seeds she has developed. On the basis of a certain genetic theory, she predicts that, on the average, $1/4$ of the resulting flowers will be red, $1/4$ will be blue, and $1/2$ will be purple. The following are the results for the seeds she has planted:

| COLOR OF FLOWER | | |
| --- | --- | --- |
| *Red* | *Blue* | *Purple* |
| 19 | 38 | 63 |

(a) State $H_0$. (b) Compute $\chi^2$ and test $H_0$ at $\alpha = .05$. Do the results tend to support or disprove the theory as applied to this type of seed? (c) Calculate $\hat{\omega}$.

12. When polled about a proposition on a ballot, the responses of men and women were as follows:

| | AGREE | UNDECIDED | DISAGREE |
| --- | --- | --- | --- |
| **MALES** | 70 | 25 | 40 |
| **FEMALES** | 30 | 20 | 25 |

(a) State in words the null hypothesis of independence for this situation. (b) Complete the $\chi^2$ test ($\alpha = .05$) and draw a conclusion. (c) Convert each observed frequency into a proportion based on its row frequency. What interpretation seems likely?

13. The mechanical aptitude scores of different classifications of workers were as follows:

| | 30–49 | 50–69 | 70 AND ABOVE |
|---|---|---|---|
| **UNSKILLED** | 20 | 30 | 10 |
| **SEMISKILLED** | 10 | 40 | 30 |
| **SKILLED** | 5 | 10 | 20 |

(a) Test the null hypothesis that test score is independent of job classification. Use $\alpha = .05$ and $\alpha = .01$. (b) Translate each observed frequency into a proportion relative to its row frequency. Do the same for the expected frequencies. Comparing the two, and in view of your answer to (a), what interpretation appears likely? (c) Calculate the strength of association, $\phi$. (d) Calculate effect size, $\hat{\omega}$.

14. In one large factory, 100 employees were judged to be highly successful and another 100 marginally successful. All workers were asked, "Which do you find more important to you personally, the money you are able to take home or the satisfaction you feel from doing the job?" In the first group 45% found the money more important, but in the second group 65% responded that way. Test the null hypothesis of no difference in response using $\chi^2$. Use $\alpha = .05$.

15. Recent studies have found that most teens are knowledgeable about AIDS, yet many continue to practice high-risk sexual behaviors. King and Anderson (1993) asked young people the following question: "If you could have sexual relations with any and all partners of your choosing, as often as you wished for the next 2 (or 10) years, but at the end of that time period you would die of AIDS, would you make this choice?" A five-point Likert scale was used to assess subjects' responses. For the following data, the responses "Probably no," "Unsure," "Probably yes," and "Definitely yes" were pooled into the category "Other."

| | DEFINITELY NO | OTHER |
|---|---|---|
| *Males* | 451 | 165 |
| *Females* | 509 | 118 |

(a) State the null hypothesis. (b) Compute $\chi^2$ at $\alpha = .05$, and state your conclusion. (c) Calculate the strength of association, $\phi$. (d) Calculate effect size, $\hat{\omega}$.

16. Forty subjects volunteer for an experiment on attitude change. An attitude item is administered to the subjects before seeing a particular TV movie and then again after seeing the movie, with the following results:

| | RESPONSE TO ATTITUDE STATEMENT | | |
|---|---|---|---|
| | *Agree* | *Undecided* | *Disagree* |
| *Before* | 8 | 20 | 12 |
| *After* | 18 | 12 | 10 |

Can we use the $\chi^2$ test described in this chapter to test the hypothesis that time of administration (before or after) is independent of statement response? Explain.

17. A survey was taken to see if there is a relationship between political affiliation and attitudes toward a bond issue that will be on an upcoming ballot. The following results were obtained:

| | RESPONSE TO BOND ISSUE | | |
|---|---|---|---|
| | *Approve* | *Disapprove* | *Undecided* |
| *Republican* | 20 | 80 | 20 |
| *Democratic* | 90 | 20 | 30 |
| *Independent* | 20 | 5 | 15 |

(a) State the null hypothesis. (b) Compute $\chi^2$; use $\alpha = .05$ (c) State the conclusion. (d) Calculate the strength of association and effect size. (e) Why is it appropriate to use $\chi^2$ for this problem, but not for Problem 16?

# CHAPTER 20

## Testing for Differences among Three or More Groups: One-Way Analysis of Variance (and Some Alternatives)

When you have finished studying this chapter, you should be able to:

- Understand that using multiple $t$ tests to make comparisons among three or more groups increases the likelihood of making a Type I error;

- Explain how analysis of variance uses estimates of the variance to test hypotheses about differences among population means;

- Calculate $SS_{total}$, $SS_w$, and $SS_{bet}$ as well as their respective degrees of freedom;

- Understand that $s_w^2$ is always a measure of inherent variation, whereas $s_{bet}^2$ is a measure of inherent variation plus any treatment effect;

- Construct a summary table and calculate the $F$ ratio;

- Understand the assumptions underlying ANOVA;

- Calculate effect size;

- Make *post hoc* comparisons, when $F$ is statistically significant, to determine which groups differ;

- Know when and how to use planned comparisons as an alternative to ANOVA; and

- Calculate analysis of variance for repeated measures.

In Chapters 15 and 16 you learned how to use the *t* distribution to test the hypothesis of no difference between *two* population means. Suppose, however, that we wish to know about the relative effect of three or more different "treatments." Are there differences in effectiveness among three methods of conducting psychotherapy? Do four types of incentives differentially affect classroom performance among elementary schoolchildren? Among seven experimental drugs being tested for use with Alzheimer's patients, are there differences in their effects on mental ability?

In each of these examples, we could use the *t* test to make comparisons among each possible combination of two means. However, this method is inadequate in several ways. Consider the example involving seven experimental drugs to treat Alzheimer's patients. First, we would have to conduct 21 *t* tests if each drug is to be compared with each of the others. Second, with so many tests, there is an increased likelihood of committing at least one Type I error—that is, of obtaining a "significant difference" when no true difference exists. Suppose, for example, that none of the drugs are effective. If we set the level of significance at .05 for each individual test, the probability of a Type I error is .05 for each. However, taken as a group, the probability that at least one from among the several will prove to be a false positive is greater than .05, and it increases with additional tests. In fact, if all 21 tests are *independent,* the probability of at least one false positive is .64 [calculated by $p = 1 - (.95)^{21}$]. When tests are not independent, as in our example, it is impossible to calculate the exact probability of committing at least one Type I error but it is quite high. Thus if we find one outcome to be "significant at the .05 level" among 21 tests, we should not consider that this result is mined gold.

Third, in any one comparison, we use only the information provided by those two groups. When the 21 tests are completed, there are 21 bits of information, but not a single direct answer as to whether, taken as a whole, there is evidence of differences in effect among the seven drugs.

In the 1920s, Sir Ronald Fisher developed a better answer to such problems. The technique is called **analysis of variance**, abbreviated **ANOVA**. The technique allows us to compare simultaneously several means with the level of significance specified by the investigator. Analysis of variance is actually a class of techniques designed to aid in hypothesis testing; entire volumes have been written about the subject. In this chapter, we shall develop the details of only the simplest form, called *one-way analysis of variance.* We introduce some more complex forms in the following chapter.

Before you continue reading this chapter, you should review some topics covered in previous chapters. Particularly important topics include:

1. The concept of variance (Section 6.4).
2. Calculation of the sum of squares, $\Sigma(X - \overline{X})^2$ (Section 6.4).
3. $s^2$ as an estimate of $\sigma^2$ (Section 13.9).
4. Degrees of freedom in a variance estimate (Section 13.12).
5. Homogeneity of variance (Section 15.5).
6. Type I error (Section 14.3).
7. Assumptions associated with inference about the difference between two means (Section 15.11).

---

**Type I error**
rejection of a true null hypothesis

**analysis of variance**
a statistical procedure used to compare simultaneously the means of two or more populations

**ANOVA**
abbreviation for analysis of variance

## 20.1 The Null Hypothesis

**one-way analysis of variance**

an analysis of variance study with only one independent variable; a single-factor design

**factor**

an independent variable

**treatment conditions**

different values (levels) of the independent variable

**k**

symbol for the number of treatment conditions

**null hypothesis for ANOVA**

$H_0$: $\mu_A = \mu_B = \mu_C \ldots = \mu_k$

In the *t* test, there are two treatment conditions, and we compare the difference between their means. **One-way analysis of variance** allows us to compare the means of two or more groups simultaneously. It is closely related to the *t* test and, for the special case of two groups, leads to exactly the same conclusions as the *t* test. The *t* test therefore may be thought of as a special case of one-way analysis of variance. Conversely, one-way ANOVA may be considered an extension of the *t* test to problems involving more than two groups. We show this in Section 20.8.

In one-way ANOVA, there may be two or more **treatment conditions**, often referred to as different **levels** of the independent variable or **factor**. We will use *k* to represent the number of treatment conditions. The *k* treatments may be identified by letters, such as *A*, *B*, and *C*, and the population means as $\mu_A$, $\mu_B$, and $\mu_C$. If the different treatments have no differential effect on the variable under observation, then we expect these population means to be equal. To inquire whether variation in treatment condition makes a difference, we test the null hypothesis:

$$H_0:\ \mu_A = \mu_B = \mu_C = \ldots = \mu_k$$

The null hypothesis in ANOVA is often referred to as an *omnibus hypothesis* (i.e., covering many situations at once), and ANOVA itself as an *omnibus test*. The alternative hypothesis, often stated simply as "not $H_0$," is that the population means are different in *some* way; that is, at least one of the samples was drawn from a population with a mean ($\mu$) different from the others.

In testing the hypothesis of no difference between *two* means, a distinction was made between directional and nondirectional alternative hypotheses. Such a distinction no longer makes sense when the number of means exceed two. In the multigroup analysis of variance, $H_0$ may be false in any of a number of ways. For example, two or more group means may be alike and the remainder differ, all may be different, and so on.

## 20.2 The Logic of One-Way Analysis of Variance: Variation within and between Groups

We will first develop one-way analysis of variance for independent groups. ANOVA for repeated measures is introduced in Section 20.17.

Suppose that we have selected three samples of 10 cases each at random and have given them three different treatments. If there is *no* differential treatment effect, the null hypothesis that $\mu_A = \mu_B = \mu_C$ is true, and the distribution of scores in the three samples might appear as shown in Figure 20.1. If there *is* a differential treatment effect, $H_0$ is false, and the three samples might appear as shown in Figure 20.2, where $\mu_A$, $\mu_B$, and $\mu_C$ have different values. Let's compare Figures 20.1 and 20.2. For the scores in either figure, we may take the total variation among all the scores and divide it (statisticians say "partition" it) into two parts (see Figure 20.3) (we use the word *variation* here and throughout the chapter in a general sense to mean only that scores vary):

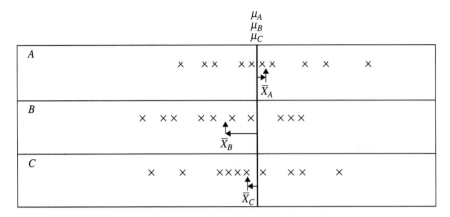

**FIGURE 20.1**  Distribution of 10 scores in three groups with no treatment effect—$H_0$: $\mu_A = \mu_B = \mu_C$ is true.

**within-groups variation**

variation of scores around the mean in a single treatment condition (here, scores can vary only because of inherent variation—chance)

**1.** *Within-groups variation.* Within each sample, the individual scores vary around the sample mean. We will call this **within-groups variation**. Remember what you have learned about the influence of random sampling variation. Within-groups variation is a direct reflection of the *inherent variation* (variation due to chance) among individuals given the same treatment. We can present exactly the same stimulus to everyone in a group and still observe variation in reaction times, or we can use a single strain of rats and still observe individual differences in speed of learning. It's a fact of life that even under identical conditions, individuals vary in performance.

Note that the scores of Groups *A, B,* and *C* in Figure 20.1 (and also in Figure 20.2) vary around their sample means to *about,* though not exactly, the same extent. Note particularly that the amount of within-groups variation is about the same whether the three population means are identical (Figure 20.1) or different (Figure 20.2). *Within-groups variation reflects only inherent variation. It does not reflect differences caused by differential treatment.* The reason is that within a particular treatment group, each subject gets the *same* treatment, so differences among scores in that group cannot be attributed to

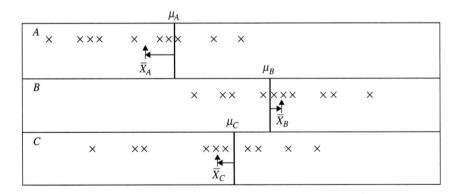

**FIGURE 20.2**  Distribution of 10 scores in three groups with treatment effect present—$H_0$: $\mu_A = \mu_B = \mu_C$ is false.

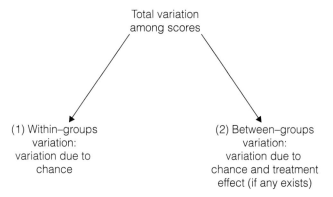

**FIGURE 20.3** The total variation among scores (see Figures 20.1 and 20.2) may be divided into two parts: (1) variation due to chance factors (within-groups variation), and (2) variation due to chance factors plus treatment effect (between-groups variation).

differential treatment. Although we have referred to within-groups variation as inherent variation, you should be aware that some statisticians call it *error*.

**between-groups variation**

variation among the means of the different treatment conditions (here, means can vary because of inherent variation and treatment effect, if any exists)

2. *Between-groups variation.*[1] Look again at Figure 20.1. The means of the samples vary among themselves. Of course, we do not expect $\overline{X}_A$, $\overline{X}_B$, and $\overline{X}_C$ all to have the same value even when $\mu_A = \mu_B = \mu_C$; this, too, is in accord with what you have learned about random sampling. It is important to realize that **between-groups variation** is also a reflection of the inherent (chance) variation among individuals. Consider for a moment what would happen if $\mu_A = \mu_B = \mu_C$ and there were no inherent variation. All individuals in the three populations would obtain the same score, so the means of the three samples could not vary from each other. On the other hand, the greater the inherent variation among individuals, the greater the opportunity for "chance" to produce sample means that vary from one another. But what if there is a treatment effect? In that case, the sample means will also differ from one another. Thus, between-groups variation is due to both inherent variation plus treatment effect (if any exists), as is the case in Figure 20.2. Let us now develop this further.

## The Logic of ANOVA

By now you are probably asking what the variation in scores within and among groups has to do with testing hypotheses about means. The answer is that these two kinds of variation provide the basis for testing $H_0$: $\mu_A = \mu_B = \mu_C$.

Consider first the within-groups variation of individual scores about their sample means. If we assume homogeneity of variance and calculate $s^2$ for each sample, each result is an estimate of the population variance. To obtain an even better estimate, we can pool the several ($k$) sample estimates and take their mean (let us assume that $n_A = n_B = n_C = n_k$):

$$\frac{\sum s^2}{k} \xrightarrow{\text{estimates}} \sigma^2$$

[1]With more than two groups, proper English is "among groups," but "between groups" is the standard terminology in statistics.

We now have one estimate of the population variance (some statisticians refer to it as the **error variance**). Note that it *does not depend on whether or not* $H_0$ *is true.*

Now let us consider between-groups variation of the sample means. Suppose that $H_0$ is true. If it is, the $k$ samples come from identical populations, which is equivalent to saying that they come from the same population. Recall that in the sampling distribution of $\overline{X}$, the variance of the $\overline{X}$'s equals the population variance divided by the sample size:

$$\sigma_{\overline{X}}^2 = \frac{\sigma^2}{n}$$

Our best estimate of $\sigma_{\overline{X}}^2$ is $s_{\overline{X}}^2$. From this we can obtain another estimate of $\sigma^2$, if $H_0$ *is true*:

$$ns_{\overline{X}}^2 \xrightarrow{\text{estimates}} \sigma^2$$

This gives us two estimates of the population variance. If the null hypothesis is true, both reflect only inherent variation, and we expect them to be of similar size. However, if $H_0$ is false in any way (i.e., at least one of the $\overline{X}$'s was drawn from a different population), the between-groups estimate will tend to be larger because it will reflect the differential **treatment effect** in addition to inherent variation. If the between-groups estimate is so much larger than the within-groups estimate that sampling variation cannot reasonably account for it, we will reject $H_0$.

**treatment effect**

differences among groups caused by the difference in treatment conditions

True to its name, analysis of variance is concerned with the variance as the basic measure of variation. Recall from Section 6.4 that the numerator of the variance is the sum of the squared deviations from the mean, commonly called the *sum of squares* and abbreviated *SS*. ANOVA thus involves calculation of sums of squares. We will now develop that procedure in more detail. As we do, keep in mind that although we use variances to make decisions, ANOVA is nonetheless a test about a null hypothesis of differences among means.

## 20.3 Partition of the Sums of Squares

**grand mean**

the mean of all scores in all the treatment conditions

When comparing two or more populations, the mean of all the scores is called the **grand mean**. We obtain it by adding all the scores in all the populations and dividing by the total number of scores. Any single score ($X$) in any of the populations may be thought of as the sum of three components:

$$X = \textit{grand mean} + \textit{treatment effect} + \textit{inherent variation}$$

$\overline{\overline{X}}$

symbol for the grand mean

**inherent variation**

variation due to chance factors

Treatment effect is the amount by which a population mean deviates from the grand mean. Inherent variation (the "error effect") is everything that is left over ($X - \textit{grand mean} - \textit{treatment effect}$). Because all the subjects in a particular group are treated the same, **inherent variation** is the variation due to chance factors. For a score in any one group, it is ($X - \mu_X$). When we draw samples from the populations, our sample estimates for the grand mean ($\overline{\overline{X}}$), treatment effect ($\overline{X} - \overline{\overline{X}}$), and inherent variation may be shown as:

PARTITION OF A SINGLE SCORE $X$

$$X = \overline{\overline{X}} + (\overline{X} - \overline{\overline{X}}) + (X - \overline{X}) \tag{20.1}$$

Any score in any group may be expressed as a deviation from the grand mean: $(X - \overline{\overline{X}})$. In Formula 20.1, simply move the grand mean to the left of the equals sign. The resulting formula shows that how much a score deviates from the grand mean can be broken into two parts: (1) how much the score deviates from the mean of its own sample group, $(X - \overline{X})$, and (2) how much the mean of its sample group deviates from the grand mean, $(\overline{X} - \overline{\overline{X}})$. We can represent this as follows:

PARTITION OF $X - \overline{\overline{X}}$

$$X - \overline{\overline{X}} = (X - \overline{X}) + (\overline{X} - \overline{\overline{X}}) \qquad (20.2)$$

Consider, for example, three sets of scores: 1, 2, 3 ($\overline{X}_A = 2$); 4, 5, 6 ($\overline{X}_B = 5$); and 7, 8, 9 ($\overline{X}_C = 8$), where $\overline{\overline{X}} = 5$. For the score of 7:

$$7 - 5 = (7 - 8) + (8 - 5)$$
$$+2 = -1 + 3$$
$$+2 = +2$$

We can use Formula 20.2 to develop (1) a measure of variation that reflects only inherent variation (within-groups variation) and (2) a measure that reflects inherent variation plus treatment effect, if present (between-groups variation).

**$SS_{total}$**
sum of the squared deviations from the grand mean,
$\sum\limits_{\substack{\text{all} \\ \text{scores}}}^{} (X - \overline{\overline{X}})^2$

To calculate $SS_{total}$, the sum of the squared deviations from the grand mean, we must first square each of the deviations from the grand mean and then sum these squares. Symbolically, this is

$$SS_{total} = \sum_{\substack{\text{all} \\ \text{scores}}} (X - \overline{\overline{X}})^2$$

From Formula 20.2 we can derive another index of $SS_{total}$ by squaring everything to the right of the equals sign in that formula. The result is:

$$\sum_{\substack{\text{all} \\ \text{scores}}} (X - \overline{\overline{X}})^2 = \sum_{\substack{\text{all} \\ \text{scores}}} (X - \overline{X})^2 + \sum^{k} n_i(\overline{X}_i - \overline{\overline{X}})^2 \qquad (20.3a)$$

**$SS_{within}$**
within-groups (treatments) sum of squares
$\sum\limits_{\substack{\text{all} \\ \text{scores}}}^{} (X - \overline{X})^2$

where $n_i$ is the number of scores in the $i$th group, $\overline{X}_i$ is the mean of the $i$th group, and $k$ is the number of groups. Proof of this equality is given in Note 20.1 at the end of the chapter.

From the total sample, we thus obtain three different sums of squares:

1. $\sum\limits_{\substack{\text{all} \\ \text{scores}}} (X - \overline{\overline{X}})^2$, the total sum of squares, called $SS_{total}$.

**$SS_{between}$**
between-groups (treatments) sum of squares
$\sum\limits^{k} n_i(\overline{X} - \overline{\overline{X}})^2$

2. $\sum\limits_{\substack{\text{all} \\ \text{scores}}} (X - \overline{X})^2$, the within-groups sum of squares, called $SS_{within}$ (sometimes called $SS_{error}$).

3. $\sum\limits^{k} n_i(\overline{X}_i - \overline{\overline{X}})^2$, the between-groups sum of squares, called $SS_{between}$.

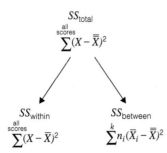

$SS_{\text{total}}$
all scores
$\sum (X - \bar{\bar{X}})^2$

$SS_{\text{within}}$
all scores
$\sum (X - \bar{X})^2$

$SS_{\text{between}}$
$\sum^k n_i(\bar{X}_i - \bar{\bar{X}})^2$

**FIGURE 20.4** Partitioning of the sums of squares for a one-way analysis of variance for independent samples.

Thus, Formula 20.3*a* can also be expressed as follows:

---

PARTITION OF TOTAL SUM OF SQUARES

$$SS_{\text{total}} = SS_{\text{within}} + SS_{\text{between}} \qquad (20.3b)$$

---

**$SS_{\text{total}} =$**
**$SS_{\text{within}} +$**
**$SS_{\text{between}}$**
partition of the
sums of squares

This splitting of $SS_{\text{total}}$ into two parts is referred to as the **partition of the sums of squares**. Let us now examine each part of Formula 20.3b more closely (see Figure 20.4):

1. *Total sum of squares.* This is a measure of the total variation present in the data without regard to group.

2. *Within-groups sum of squares.*

$$SS_{\text{within}} = \sum^{\text{all scores}} (X - \bar{X})^2 = \sum (X_A - \bar{X}_A)^2 + \sum (X_B - \bar{X}_B)^2 + \cdots \qquad (20.4)$$

From now on, we will abbreviate $SS_{\text{within}}$ as $SS_{\text{w}}$. This is a measure of the within-groups variation of individual scores, independent of any differences among group means. It is a direct reflection of *inherent variation, free from the influence of differential treatment effect.* An estimate could be made by taking the sum of squares for any one group. However, on the assumption that the population variances are the same for all groups ($\sigma_A^2 = \sigma_B^2 = \sigma_C^2 = \ldots$, the **assumption of homogeneity of variance**), we may obtain a better estimate by combining information from the several groups. The variance that is assumed to be common to all the populations is $\sigma^2$ (with no subscript).

**assumption of homogeneity of variance**
the assumption that the population variances are the same for all treatment conditions

3. *Between-groups sum of squares.*

$$SS_{\text{between}} = \sum^k n_i(\bar{X}_i - \bar{\bar{X}})^2 = n_A(\bar{X}_A - \bar{\bar{X}})^2 + n_B(\bar{X}_B - \bar{\bar{X}})^2 + \cdots \qquad (20.5)$$

From now on, we will abbreviate $SS_{\text{between}}$ as $SS_{\text{bet}}$. This is a measure of the variation of the sample means among groups. It reflects inherent variation (free from the influence of treatment effect) *plus* any differential treatment effect (variation attributable to differences among population means).

## 20.4  Degrees of Freedom

The test of $H_0$ in one-way ANOVA involves comparing two separate estimates of the variance for the population: one based on the within-groups variation among individual scores about their group means, and the other on the variation among the sample means. We introduced the subject of estimating population variances in Section 13.9. Recall that to calculate the unbiased estimate of a population variance, we divide the sum of squares by the degrees of freedom associated with that sum of squares. This general relationship is summarized by the equation

$$s^2 = \frac{SS}{df}$$

Recall also that the degrees of freedom for the variance estimate based on a single sample is $n - 1$, and that the degrees of freedom for the pooled estimate of the variance used in the $t$ test for two independent means is $(n_1 - 1) + (n_2 - 1)$.

**$df_{total}$**
$n_{total} - 1$

The degrees of freedom associated with $SS_{total}$ is, as you might expect, $n_{total} - 1$. Because there are $n - 1$ degrees of freedom associated with the deviations about a single mean, the degrees of freedom for $SS_w$ is $(n_A - 1) + (n_B - 1) + \ldots = n_A + n_B + \ldots + n_k - k$, or

**$df_{within}$**
$n_{total} - k$

$$df_w = n_{total} - k$$

where $n_{total}$ is the total number of cases and $k$ is the number of groups. For $SS_{bet}$, there are only as many deviations from the grand mean as there are sample means (or number of groups). Thus,

**$df_{between}$**
$k - 1$

$$df_{bet} = k - 1$$

For *any* analysis of variance, the number of degrees of freedom associated with $SS_w$ plus the number of degrees of freedom associated with $SS_{bet}$ equals the number of degrees of freedom associated with $SS_{total}$:

**$df_{total} =$**
**$df_w + df_{bet}$**
partition of degrees of freedom

$$df_{total} = df_w + df_{bet}$$

Proof of this equality is given in Note 20.1 at the end of the chapter.

## 20.5  Variance Estimates and the *F* Ratio

**within-groups variance estimate**
an estimate of inherent variance only

If we now divide $SS_w$ and $SS_{bet}$ by their respective degrees of freedom, we obtain the two variance estimates required to test $H_0$: $\mu_A = \mu_B = \mu_C$, the **within-groups variance estimate**, $s_w^2$, and the **between-groups variance estimate**, $s_{bet}^2$. These variance estimates, as well as what they estimate, are

WITHIN-GROUPS VARIANCE ESTIMATE

$$s_w^2 = \frac{SS_w}{df_w} \xrightarrow{\text{estimates}} \sigma^2 \text{ (inherent variance, also called the error variance)} \qquad (20.6)$$

$s_w^2$
the symbol for within-groups variance estimate; $\dfrac{SS_w}{df_w}$

**between-groups variance estimate**
an estimate of inherent variance plus treatment effect (if any exists)

$s_{bet}^2$
the symbol for between-groups (treatments) variance estimate; $\dfrac{SS_{bet}}{df_{bet}}$

**BETWEEN-GROUPS VARIANCE ESTIMATE**

$$s_{bet}^2 = \frac{SS_{bet}}{df_{bet}} \xrightarrow{\text{estimates}} \sigma^2 + \textit{treatment effect} \tag{20.7}$$

Statisticians often refer to $s_w^2$ as the *mean square within* (or sometimes the *mean square error*) and $s_{bet}^2$ as the *mean square between*, symbolized $MS_w$ and $MS_{bet}$, respectively. Although we will continue to use the former designations, you should be familiar with these alternative terms because they are often used in other books and articles.

If $H_0$ is true (i.e., if there is no differential treatment effect), the sample means will tend to cluster closely about $\overline{X}$, and $s_{bet}^2$ will be an unbiased estimate of the inherent variation, $\sigma^2$. It will, therefore, estimate the same quantity as that estimated by $s_w^2$, and the two should be equal within the limits of sampling variation. On the other hand, if $H_0$ is false (if there is a treatment effect), the sum of squares of the deviations of the $\overline{X}$'s about $\overline{\overline{X}}$ will tend to be larger, and $s_{bet}^2$ will tend to be larger than $s_w^2$. The test of $H_0$ determines whether $s_{bet}^2$ is so much larger than $s_w^2$ that it exceeds the limits of sampling variation.

To complete the analysis of variance, we require a method of comparing $s_{bet}^2$ with $s_w^2$. This is the *F* **ratio**, a statistic named in honor of Ronald Fisher. The *F* ratio is formed by the ratio of the two independent variance estimates:

**F ratio**
a ratio of within- and between-groups variance estimates. $\dfrac{s_{bet}^2}{s_w^2} = $
$\dfrac{\text{inherent} + \text{treatment} \atop \text{variance} \quad \text{effect}}{\text{inherent variance}}$
when there is no treatment effect, the ratio should approximate 1.0

**F distribution**
a theoretical relative frequency distribution of all the values of *F* that would be obtained by chance from an infinite number of samples of a particular size drawn from given populations

**F RATIO FOR ONE-WAY ANALYSIS OF VARIANCE**

$$F = \frac{s_{bet}^2}{s_w^2} \tag{20.8}$$

In constructing this ratio, $s_{bet}^2$ is *always* placed in the numerator and $s_w^2$ is always placed in the denominator. If $H_0$ is true and there is no treatment effect, $s_{bet}^2$ and $s_w^2$ will both be estimates of the inherent variance only, and the ratio should be *about* 1.0:

$$F = \frac{\textit{inherent variance} + \textit{treatment effect}}{\textit{inherent variance}}$$

If $H_0$ is false, $s_{bet}^2$ will estimate the inherent variance plus the differential treatment effect and the ratio should exceed 1.0. The greater the differential treatment effect, the more *F* tends to exceed unity.

When $H_0$ is true and certain assumptions hold (see Section 20.10), *F* ratios follow the theoretical *F* distribution presented in Table E of Appendix E. Like the *t* distribution, the *F* **distribution** is actually a family of curves depending on the degrees of freedom. Figure 20.5 shows the distribution of *F* for 4 degrees of freedom in the numerator and 20 degrees of freedom in the denominator. Note that this distribution is positively skewed. This is intuitively reasonable. If the estimate of $\sigma^2$ in the numerator is smaller than that in the denominator, *F* will be less than 1.00 but not less than zero (because variance estimates are never negative). But if the estimate in the numerator is larger than that in the denominator, the *F* ratio may be much larger than 1.00. *The null hypothesis of equality of population means will be rejected only if the calculated value of* F *is larger than that expected through random sampling if the hypothesis is true.* Consequently, the region of rejection is entirely in the upper tail of the

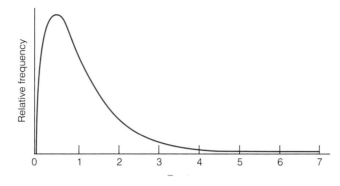

**FIGURE 20.5** Distribution of $F$ for 4 degrees of freedom in the numerator and 20 degrees of freedom in the denominator.

$F$ distribution. (Recall, however, that the $F$ test is nondirectional—see Section 20.1.) An $F$ value less than 1.00 usually signifies that one of the assumptions has not been met (see Section 20.10) and/or that there is sampling error (for example, perhaps the treatment has differentially affected the variance of the groups).

## 20.6 The Summary Table

In analysis of variance, it is convenient (and customary) to present a summary table indicating the source of variation, the corresponding sum of squares, the associated degrees of freedom, the variance estimate, and the calculated value of $F$. Table 20.1 gives the general form of a summary table for one-way analysis of variance. One advantage of such a table is that it shows the basic result of the analysis very clearly.

The first column lists the sources of variation. Note that the between-groups variation is listed above within-groups variation, thus setting up the $F$ ratio. The sums of squares are listed in the second column, and their respective degrees of freedom in the third. As a check on your work, $SS_{bet} + SS_w$ should equal $SS_{total}$, and $df_{bet} + df_w$ should equal $df_{total}$. The numerator ($s^2_{bet}$) and denominator ($s^2_w$) of the $F$ ratio, obtained by dividing $SS$ by $df$, are shown in the fourth column. Notice that $s^2_{bet} + s^2_w$ does *not* equal $s^2_{total}$.

Table 20.1 does not show $s^2_{total}$. This quantity cannot be used in ANOVA because the test of $H_0$ requires the two variance estimates being compared to be independent of one another. Because $SS_{total}$ contains $SS_w$ and $SS_{bet}$ ($SS_w + SS_{bet} = SS_{total}$), a variance estimate based on $SS_{total}$ would obviously not be independent of either $s^2_w$ or $s^2_{bet}$.

**TABLE 20.1** *Summary Table of One-Way ANOVA, Showing the Partition of Sums of Squares, the Degrees of Freedom, the Variance Estimates, and* F

| SOURCE | SS | df | $s^2$ | F |
|--------|----|----|-------|---|
| Between groups | Formula 20.5 | $k - 1$ | $\dfrac{SS_{bet}}{df_{bet}}$ | $\dfrac{s^2_{bet}}{s^2_w}$ |
| Within groups | Formula 20.4 | $n_{total} - k$ | $\dfrac{SS_w}{df_w}$ | |
| Total | Formula 20.3a | $n_{total} - 1$ | | |

## 20.7 Example

To illustrate the calculations required for one-way ANOVA, we will use a hypothetical example with only a few scores. Suppose that the head of the curriculum committee, who happens to be a reading specialist, wishes to compare how first-grade students in her school district respond to three new reading programs. At the start of the school year, she randomly selects 15 first-grade students from the district's schools and randomly assigns them to three groups. Each of the three groups will receive one of the reading programs for 9 weeks, and then each student will be tested and given a reading score. The reading specialist's hypothesis is

$$H_0: \mu_A = \mu_B = \mu_C$$

If any one group differs from the other two or if all three are different, she will reject $H_0$ and accept $H_A$.

Due to illness, one of the subjects in Group B fails to complete the program, resulting in two groups with five subjects each and a third group with four subjects. At the end of the 9 weeks, the reading scores for the 14 subjects are as follows:

**Reading Program**

| GROUP A | GROUP B | GROUP C |
|---------|---------|---------|
| 7 | 12 | 3 |
| 10 | 10 | 3 |
| 8 | 14 | 4 |
| 8 | 11 | 2 |
| 7 | 13 | |

The reading specialist first calculates each sample mean and the grand mean:

$$\overline{X}_A = \frac{40}{5} = 8 \qquad \overline{X}_B = \frac{60}{5} = 12 \qquad \overline{X}_C = \frac{12}{4} = 3$$

$$\overline{\overline{X}} = \frac{112}{14} = 8$$

Next, she calculates $SS_w$ and $SS_{bet}$:

$$SS_w = \overset{\overset{\text{all}}{\text{scores}}}{\sum} (X - \overline{\overline{X}})^2$$

$$= \sum (X_A - \overline{X}_A)^2 + \sum (X_B - \overline{X}_B)^2 + \sum (X_C - \overline{X}_C)^2$$

$$= \begin{bmatrix} (7-8)^2 \\ (10-8)^2 \\ (8-8)^2 \\ (8-8)^2 \\ (7-8)^2 \end{bmatrix} + \begin{bmatrix} (12-12)^2 \\ (10-12)^2 \\ (14-12)^2 \\ (11-12)^2 \\ (13-12)^2 \end{bmatrix} + \begin{bmatrix} (3-3)^2 \\ (3-3)^2 \\ (4-3)^2 \\ (2-3)^2 \end{bmatrix}$$

$$= \quad 6 \quad + \quad 10 \quad + \quad 2$$

$$= 18$$

$$SS_{bet} = \sum_{}^{k} n_i (\overline{X}_i - \overline{\overline{X}})^2$$

$$= 5(8 - 8)^2 + 5(12 - 8)^2 + 4(3 - 8)^2$$

$$= 0 + 80 + 100$$

$$= 180$$

Although it is not required for the *F* ratio, as a check on her work she also calculates $SS_{total}$:

$$SS_{total} = \sum (X - \overline{\overline{X}})^2$$

$$= (7 - 8)^2 + (10 - 8)^2 + (8 - 8)^2 + (8 - 8)^2 + (7 - 8)^2$$
$$+ (12 - 8)^2 + (10 - 8)^2 + (14 - 8)^2 + (11 - 8)^2$$
$$+ (13 - 8)^2 + (3 - 8)^2 + (3 - 8)^2 + (4 - 8)^2 + (2 - 8)^2$$

$$= 198$$

Because $SS_{total} = SS_w + SS_{bet}$, she can be confident that her calculations are correct. With each calculation, the reading specialist enters the result in a summary table, shown in Table 20.2.

The reading specialist then calculates the degrees of freedom:

$$df_{bet} = k - 1 = 3 - 1 = 2$$

$$df_w = n_{total} - k = 14 - 3 = 11$$

$$df_{total} = n_{total} - 1 = 14 - 1 = 13$$

As a check on her work, she sees that $df_{total} = df_{bet} + df_w$. With the sums of squares and their respective degrees of freedom, our specialist may now calculate $s_{bet}^2$ and $s_w^2$:

$$s_{bet}^2 = \frac{SS_{bet}}{df_{bet}} = \frac{180}{2} = 90.0$$

$$s_w^2 = \frac{SS_w}{df_w} = \frac{18}{11} = 1.64$$

The *F* ratio is already set up in the summary table:

$$F = \frac{s_{bet}^2}{s_w^2} = \frac{90.0}{1.64} = 54.88$$

**TABLE 20.2** *Summary Table of Analysis of Variance for the Test of the Hypothesis* $H_0\text{: } \mu_A = \mu_B = \mu_C$ *for Reading Scores*

| SOURCE | SS | df | $s^2$ | F |
|---|---|---|---|---|
| Between groups | 180 | 2 | 90.00 | 54.88 |
| Within groups | 18 | 11 | 1.64 | |
| Total | 198 | 13 | | |

© 2002 by Sidney Harris

"FIND OUT WHO SET UP THIS EXPERIMENT. IT SEEMS THAT HALF OF THE PATIENTS WERE GIVEN A PLACEBO, AND THE OTHER HALF WERE GIVEN A DIFFERENT PLACEBO."

In this example, $df_{bet} = 2$ and $df_{w} = 11$. To obtain the critical value of $F$, turn to Table E in Appendix E and locate the entries at the intersection of 2 $df$ for the numerator and 11 $df$ for the denominator. (Be careful not to look for the value corresponding to 11 $df$ for the numerator and 2 $df$ for the denominator; the critical value of $F$ is not the same!) If our reading specialist has adopted the .05 level of significance, the critical value of $F$ is 3.98 (or 7.20 for the .01 level). If $H_0$ is true, she would obtain a sample $F$ ratio greater than 3.98 only 5% of the time through random sampling. It is clear that the obtained $F = 54.88$ falls beyond the critical value, so she rejects $H_0$. The $F$ distribution for 2 and 11 degrees of freedom and the region of rejection are shown in Figure 20.6.

Because the obtained value of $F$ exceeds the critical value, the reading specialist concludes that the population means differ and, therefore, that there is a real difference among the three reading programs for first-grade students in her school district. It is tempting at this point to scan the sample data and say that reading program $B$ is better than program $A$, which is better than program $C$. However, when the obtained $F$ exceeds the critical value of $F$, *we can conclude only that there is a difference among groups.* To determine the manner in which the groups differ, we must conduct additional tests. We will discuss some of these tests in Section 20.13.

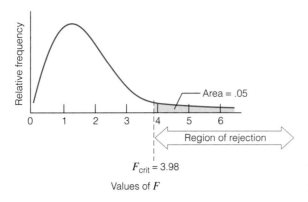

**FIGURE 20.6** Sampling distribution of $F$ for 2 and 11 degrees of freedom; $\alpha = .05$.

## 20.8 Comparison of *t* and *F*

You may use analysis of variance to test the hypothesis $H_0: \mu_1 = \mu_2 = \ldots = \mu_k$ with *two or more* groups. Thus, you can use ANOVA instead of $t$ in the two-sample, independent-groups design. Recall from Chapter 15 that we summarized the $t$ test for a difference between two independent means as

$$t = \frac{\begin{array}{c}\textit{obtained difference} \\ \textit{between sample means}\end{array} - \begin{array}{c}\textit{hypothesized difference between} \\ \textit{population means (when } H_0 \textit{ is true)}\end{array}}{\textit{estimated standard error of the difference between two means}}$$

In this formula, the estimated standard error of the mean ($s_{\overline{X}-\overline{Y}}$) is the difference among scores due to chance (no treatment effect).

Now let us look at the formula for *F.* For two samples,

$$F = \frac{\textit{variance estimate based on the difference between sample means}}{\textit{variance estimate within samples}}$$

The denominator is again the difference among scores due to chance (no treatment effect), except that it is an estimate of the variance whereas the denominator for the $t$ formula is an estimate of a standard deviation. If we square a standard deviation, we get back to the variance. In fact, *with two samples*:

**$F = t^2$**
relationship
between $F$ and
$t$ for a two-
sample, inde-
pendent-groups
design

RELATIONSHIP BETWEEN $F$ AND $t$

$$F = t^2 \tag{20.9}$$

Try using ANOVA with the sample problem in Section 15.6, for which $t$ was calculated to be 2.074. You will find that $F = 2.074^2 = 4.30$.

## 20.9 Raw-Score Formulas for Analysis of Variance

In Sections 20.3 through 20.6, we developed analysis of variance using the sums of squares, obtained by computing each deviation score and squaring it and then summing the results. This approach is best for understanding ANOVA. However, it is doubtful that you would ever use this method to analyze data in the real world. Today, most people use computers to do this work (statistical software packages are readily available). If you have to compute $F$ by hand, and the goal is ease of computation rather than understanding, sums of squares are more easily computed from raw scores. We give the raw score formulas for $SS_w$, $SS_{bet}$, and $SS_{total}$ in this section and illustrate their use with the data from Section 20.7. We start by obtaining the values of $\Sigma X$ and $\Sigma X^2$ for each group separately. All other computations flow from these basic quantities and the sample sizes.

$$\text{Group } A: n_A = 5$$

$$\sum X_A = 7 + 10 + 8 + 8 + 7 = 40$$

$$\sum X_A^2 = 49 + 100 + 64 + 64 + 49 = 326$$

$$\text{Group } B: n_B = 5$$

$$\sum X_B = 12 + 10 + 14 + 11 + 13 = 60$$

$$\sum X_B^2 = 144 + 100 + 196 + 121 + 169 = 730$$

$$\text{Group } C: n_C = 4$$

$$\sum X_C = 3 + 3 + 4 + 2 = 12$$

$$\sum X_C^2 = 9 + 9 + 16 + 4 = 38$$

Next we sum the values of $\Sigma X$, $\Sigma X^2$, and $n$ across the groups to obtain

$$\sum^{\substack{\text{all}\\\text{scores}}} X = \sum X_A + \sum X_B + \sum X_C = 40 + 60 + 12 = 112$$

$$\sum^{\substack{\text{all}\\\text{scores}}} X^2 = \sum X_A^2 + \sum X_B^2 + \sum X_C^2 = 326 + 730 + 38 = 1094$$

$$n_{total} = n_A + n_B + n_C = 5 + 5 + 4 = 14$$

Now we have everything needed to obtain $SS_w$, $SS_{bet}$, and $SS_{total}$:

> **WITHIN-GROUPS SUM OF SQUARES:**
> **RAW-SCORE FORMULA**
>
> $$SS_w = \sum^{\substack{\text{all}\\\text{scores}}} X^2 - \left[ \frac{\left(\sum X_A\right)^2}{n_A} + \frac{\left(\sum X_B\right)^2}{n_B} + \cdots \right] \qquad (20.10)$$

For our example,

$$SS_w = 1094 - \left[ \frac{(40)^2}{5} + \frac{(60)^2}{5} + \frac{(12)^2}{4} \right]$$

$$= 1094 - [320 + 720 + 36]$$

$$= 1094 - 1076$$

$$= 18$$

BETWEEN-GROUPS SUM OF SQUARES:
RAW-SCORE FORMULA

$$SS_{bet} = \left[ \frac{\left(\sum X_A\right)^2}{n_A} + \frac{\left(\sum X_B\right)^2}{n_B} + \cdots \right] - \frac{\left(\overset{\text{all scores}}{\sum X}\right)^2}{n_{total}} \tag{20.11}$$

$$SS_{bet} = \left[ \frac{(40)^2}{5} + \frac{(60)^2}{5} + \frac{(12)^2}{4} \right] - \frac{(112)^2}{14}$$

$$= 1076 - 896$$

$$= 180$$

TOTAL SUM OF SQUARES: RAW-SCORES FORMULA

$$SS_{total} = \overset{\text{all scores}}{\sum X^2} - \frac{\left(\overset{\text{all scores}}{\sum X}\right)^2}{n_{total}} \tag{20.12}$$

$$SS_{total} = 1094 - \frac{(112)^2}{14}$$

$$= 1094 - 896$$

$$= 198$$

Note that the values for $SS_w$, $SS_{bet}$, and $SS_{total}$ are exactly the same as those we obtained using the deviation-score formulas in Section 20.7. The completion of ANOVA from this point on is done just as in that section.

## 20.10 Assumptions Associated with ANOVA

Because $F = t^2$, you should not be surprised to learn that the assumptions underlying the $F$ test for one-way ANOVA are the same as those for the $t$ test for independent samples (see Section 15.11). We present them again:

1. The populations are normally distributed.
2. The variances of the several populations are the same (homogeneity of variance).
3. Selection of elements comprising any particular sample is independent of selection of elements of any other sample.
4. Samples are drawn at random with replacement.

As with the $t$ test for independent means, *moderate* departure from the normal distribution specified in the first assumption does not unduly disturb the outcome of the test (see Glass, Peckham, & Sanders, 1972). This is especially true as sample size increases. However, with highly skewed populations, ANOVA results in less accurate probability statements (Tomarken & Serlin, 1986). (Again, see the Point of Contro-versy in Chapter 7.) When samples are quite small and there is serious question about the assumption of normality, one possible alternative is the Kruskal–Wallis nonpara-metric one-way ANOVA (see Section 22.8).

Violations of the second assumption, homogeneity of variance, are also negligible *when sample sizes are equal.* Heterogeneity of variance ordinarily becomes a problem only when $\sigma^2_{largest} = 4\sigma^2_{smallest}$ or, with more moderate differences, when sample sizes differ considerably (Milligan, Wong, & Thompson, 1987; Tomarken & Serlin, 1986). If there is a choice, you should try to select samples of equal size for each treatment condition. This minimizes the effect of failing to satisfy the condition of homogene-ity of variance.

The third assumption, independence of samples, reminds us that the ANOVA pro-cedure described to this point is not appropriate for repeated measures on the same subjects nor when matched subjects have been assigned to treatment groups. We will introduce ANOVA for repeated measures in Section 20.17.

The most troublesome problem is probably that of obtaining random samples. In our hypothetical problem in Section 20.7 we used random sampling, but in the real world most researchers use random assignment of available subjects. Random sam-pling is more of a premise than a requirement—it allows us to extend conclusions to the population. We call your attention to earlier discussions of this problem in Sec-tions 15.12 and 15.13.

## 20.11 Effect Size

In Section 15.9 you learned about measures of effect size that may be used for tests of a hypothesis about the difference between two independent sample means. Recall that there are two families of effect size: the *d* family (expressing the difference be-tween the two means relative to the standard deviation of the variable) and the *r* fam-ily (expressing effect size as a correlation coefficient).

In this section you will learn about two commonly used measures of effect size for use with ANOVA for independent groups. Both are members of the *r* family. The first is **eta-squared ($\eta^2$)**, which is also known as the correlation ratio:

**eta-squared ($\eta^2$)**

an *r* family measure of effect size for independent-groups ANOVA

$$\frac{SS_{bet}}{SS_{total}}$$

> FORMULA FOR ETA-SQUARED
>
> $$\eta^2 = \frac{SS_{bet}}{SS_{total}} \qquad (20.13)$$

In brief, $\eta^2$ provides a measure of the strength of association between the indepen-dent and dependent variables. More specifically, it gives us the proportion of the to-tal variance due to the independent variable (Section 10.9). Cohen (1988) has sug-gested that for ANOVA, .01 = small effect, .06 = medium effect, and .14 = large effect (but recall from Section 14.2 that importance can be judged only relative to the circumstances of the particular study). In our example in Section 20.7, $\eta^2$ = 180/198 = .909, an unusually high effect size (remember, our example was hypo-thetical). This means that about 91% of the variability in reading scores is associated with reading programs.

Eta-squared is simple, but it is also biased in an upward direction. A newer, and perhaps better measure of effect size for ANOVA is **omega-squared** ($\hat{\omega}^2$) (Fleiss, 1969; Vaughn & Corballis, 1969). Omega-squared provides a relatively unbiased estimate of the strength of association—it estimates the proportion of the variance in the dependent variable (in the population) that is due to the $k$ levels of treatment. The formula is:

$$\hat{\omega}^2_{bet} = \frac{\sigma^2_{bet}}{\sigma^2_{bet} + \sigma^2_{within}}$$

Of course, we do not have the actual population variances, so we have to estimate omega-squared:

> **FORMULA FOR OMEGA-SQUARED**
>
> $$\hat{\omega}^2_{bet} = \frac{SS_{bet} - (k-1)(s^2_w)}{SS_{total} + s^2_w} \qquad (20.14)$$

or, calculating $\hat{\omega}^2_{bet}$ directly from the $F$ ratio:

**omega-squared ($\hat{\omega}^2_{bet}$)**
an *r* family measure of effect size for independent-groups ANOVA

$$\frac{SS_{bet} - (k-1)(s^2_w)}{SS_{total} + s^2_w}$$

$$\hat{\omega}^2_{bet} = \frac{(k-1)(F-1)}{(k-1)(F-1) + (k)(n_{cell})}$$

As with $\eta^2$, Cohen (1988) suggests that we interpret $\hat{\omega}^2$ as follows: .01 = small effect, .06 = medium effect, and .14 = large effect. As an example, we will again use the data in Section 20.7:

$$\hat{\omega}^2_{bet} = \frac{180 - (2)(1.64)}{198 + 1.64}$$

$$= .885$$

Notice that this outcome is slightly lower than that obtained with $\eta^2$. This is due to $\eta^2$ being an overestimate of effect size.

In ANOVA with more than two groups, there are actually several correlation indices that may be used to measure effect size. For a discussion of each, see Rosnow, Rosenthal, and Rubin (2000).

# 20.12 ANOVA and Power

The factors affecting the power (the probability of rejecting a false null hypothesis) of the one-way analysis of variance are very similar to those affecting the *t* test (see Sections 14.4–14.10 and 15.10). The major influences are the following:

1. The actual discrepancy among the population means.
2. The variance that is not attributable to treatment effect.
3. The degrees of freedom in the numerator.
4. The degrees of freedom in the denominator.
5. The level of significance (the probability of a Type I error).

As with hypotheses about two means, we can estimate power and sample sizes for tests of hypotheses about three or more means. If you wish to learn how to do this, a good reference is Cohen (1988).

# 20.13 *Post Hoc* Comparisons

Suppose that in our example concerning three new reading programs (Section 20.7) the obtained $F$ ratio turned out to be *smaller* than the critical value of 3.98. We would conclude that our data do not support the presence of differential treatment effects, and that would be that. There would be no justification for further statistical work.

Such, however, was not the case. Our obtained $F$ of 54.88 led us to reject $H_0$: $\mu_A = \mu_B = \mu_C$ in favor of the very broad alternative hypothesis that the three population means differed in *some* way. But where is the real difference (or differences)? All three might differ from one another, or two of them might be equal and differ from the third. To answer this question we may, on obtaining a significant overall $F$, proceed with further statistical comparisons involving the group means.

**post hoc**
**comparisons**
statistical tests performed after obtaining a significant value of $F$ that indicate which means are significantly different

The tests we use to make these specific comparisons are called *post hoc* comparisons or *a posteriori* (Latin, meaning "what comes later") comparisons. They keep us from taking undue advantage of chance. If we are comparing many means, we would expect some of the differences to be fairly substantial as a result of random sampling variation alone, even if the null hypothesis is true. To apply the conventional $t$ test just to the largest or to all of the possible differences between sample means would substantially increase the probability of making a Type I error—that is, rejecting $H_0$ when it is true. Instead of using a sampling distribution that compares the means of only two samples (as is done with $t$), *post hoc* tests generally employ sampling distributions that compare the means of many samples. In short, *post hoc* tests protect us from making too many Type I errors by requiring a bigger difference (between sample means) before we can declare that difference to be statistically significant.

There are several commonly used *post hoc* tests. The only real difference among them is that some are more conservative than others. In ascending level of conservativeness with regard to Type I errors (but descending power), we could choose from among such tests as Duncan's multiple-range test, the Newman-Keuls test, Tukey's HSD test, or the Scheffé test. *To use any one of these tests, our F ratio must first be significant.*

**Tukey's**
**HSD test**
honestly significant difference; a commonly used *post hoc* test; critical HSD value =
$$q\sqrt{\frac{s_w^2}{n}}$$

We will illustrate only one *post hoc* test, **Tukey's HSD test**. It does not inflate the probability of Type I error as much as many other tests, yet it is not nearly as conservative as the Scheffé test. HSD stands for "honestly significant difference." The test involves determining a critical HSD value for the data. Although the test can be used to make specific comparisons, most investigators make all possible pairwise comparisons. The hypothesis of equal population means is rejected for any pair of samples for which the difference between $\overline{X}$'s is as large as or larger than the critical HSD value.

We determine the critical HSD value using the following formula:

**Studentized**
**range**
**statistic ($q$)**
used with Tukey's HSD test; based on sampling distributions comparing many means

---

CRITICAL HSD VALUE FOR TUKEY'S HSD TEST

$$HSD = q\sqrt{\frac{s_w^2}{n}} \qquad (20.15)$$

*where:* $s_w^2$ = the within-groups variance estimate.
$n$ = the number of cases in each group.
$q$ = the value of a new statistic called the **Studentized range statistic** (based on sampling distributions comparing many means rather than two).

---

The value of $q$ depends on the significance level (.05 or .01), the number of samples to be compared, and $df_w$. To find $q$, look in Table F in Appendix E. If the number

*ñ*

symbol for the
harmonic mean

of cases is not the same for all samples, you may use the harmonic mean, $\tilde{n}$, in place of $n$ (Winer, Brown, & Michels, 1991). The harmonic mean is calculated as follows:

HARMONIC MEAN FOR TUKEY'S HSD TEST

$$\tilde{n} = \frac{k}{(1/n_A) + (1/n_B) + \cdots + (1/n_k)} \tag{20.16}$$

*where:* $k$ = the number of groups.
$n_k$ = the number of cases in the $k$th group.

To illustrate the use of Tukey's HSD test, let us return to our example from Section 20.7, in which we obtained a significant difference among the three new reading programs. We now wish to examine the pattern of differences among group means.

In our example, $df_w = 11$, $k = 3$, and $\alpha = .05$. Entering Table F with these three values, we find that $q = 3.82$. Because the sample sizes were unequal, we must calculate the harmonic mean:

$$\tilde{n} = \frac{3}{(1/5) + (1/5) + (1/4)} = \frac{3}{.65} = 4.62$$

We already have $s_w^2 = 1.64$. The critical HSD value is thus

$$HSD = 3.82 \sqrt{\frac{1.64}{4.62}} = 2.28$$

Now we can compute the differences for all the possible pairs of sample means and display them. In the following table, each entry is the difference between the mean listed on the left and that listed at the top.

| | $\overline{X}_A = 8$ | $\overline{X}_B = 12$ | $\overline{X}_C = 3$ |
|---|---|---|---|
| $\overline{X}_A = 8$ | 0 | $-4$ | 5 |
| $\overline{X}_B = 12$ | | 0 | 9 |
| $\overline{X}_C = 3$ | | | 0 |

In this example, the differences between all the pairs of sample means exceed 2.28 and thus are significant at the .05 level. We can conclude that reading program B was better than program A and that both were better than program C.

For an excellent review of the logic of *post hoc* (multiple) comparisons, as well as an update of the strengths and weaknesses of several different tests, see Curran-Everett (2000).

## 20.14 Some Concerns about *Post Hoc* Comparisons

Although most researchers still follow an ANOVA with *post hoc* tests (either tests of all possible pairs or all possible combinations), many leading statisticians caution about their use (see Wilkinson et al., 1999). Why? First, most researchers do not need to see the results of comparing all possible pairs to answer the question(s) they are interested in, and tests for *all* possible pairs are very conservative, thus sacrificing power. Second, the use of tests of all possible pairs often resemble a fishing expedition:

> Reviewers should require writers to articulate their expectations well enough to reduce the likelihood of *post hoc* rationalizations. Fishing expeditions are often recognizable by the promiscuity of their explanations. (Wilkinson and the Task Force on Statistical Inference, 1999)

In place of *post hoc* tests, these statisticians urge that researchers examine trends or clusters of effects (see Rosnow, Rosenthal, & Rubin, 2000, for these more advanced techniques). Most important, they advise, "If a specific contrast interests you, examine it" (Wilkinson et al., 1999). We will now look at how we might do this.

## 20.15  An Alternative to the *F* Test: Planned Comparisons

**planned comparisons**
tests used in place of ANOVA when the researcher knows in advance which comparisons are of interest; also called *a priori* comparisons

In our example of three new teaching methods, we had no well-developed rationale for focusing on a particular comparison prior to beginning the study. Our study, like many of those in the real world, was a "fishing expedition": We wanted to know whether teaching method makes a difference in first graders' learning to read and, if so, where did the difference lie? Only after finding (through the overall *F* test) that there was a difference did we reexamine the various possible comparisons. However, the price we pay for this approach, you recall, is loss of power; the differences among sample means must be larger (to be significant with *post hoc* tests) than with *t* tests to protect us from making Type I errors.

There is an alternative if we know *in advance* what comparisons will interest us. If theory or the logic of the study (rather than the obtained results) suggests the comparisons to be made, we can use what are known as **planned comparisons** or *a priori comparisons*. Suppose, for example, that we want to compare the effectiveness of these three methods of instruction: lecture, lecture plus movie, and lecture plus audio tape. It might make sense to construct two comparisons: (1) lecture versus the average of the two methods that use supplementary material and (2) lecture plus movie versus lecture plus audio tape. The advantage of planning comparisons in advance is that a *significant overall* F *ratio is not required* and, in fact, we can avoid the omnibus *F* test altogether if these are the only comparisons we are interested in.

To make planned comparisons, we use the *t* test for independent groups. But instead of calculating the standard error by pooling the variance of just two groups, we use $s_w^2$, which pools the data from all the groups and is thus a better estimate:

**$s_k$**
symbol for standard error of a comparison

### STANDARD ERROR OF A COMPARISON

$$s_k = \sqrt{s_w^2 \left( \frac{a_A^2}{n_A} + \frac{a_B^2}{n_B} + \cdots + \frac{a_k^2}{n_k} \right)} \qquad (20.17)$$

*where:*  $s_w^2$ = the variance estimate that constitutes the denominator of the overall *F* test.

$a_A$ = is the coefficient of the mean of group *A,* and so forth. (We will explain this shortly.)

$n_A$ = the number of cases in group *A,* and so forth.

The number of degrees of freedom associated with this standard error is the number associated with $s_w^2$: $\sum\limits^{k}(n-1)$.

At this point you should be saying to yourself, "Now wait a minute—you told us that the major reason for using ANOVA is to avoid multiple $t$ tests." That remains true. If there were no constraints and we did all the possible comparisons, we would substantially increase the likelihood of a Type I error. However, there are *three constraints when using planned comparisons*:

**orthogonal comparisons**

comparisons that are unique and do not overlap

1. All questions are decided in advance so that they are not influenced by the data (as with the decision of whether to use a one-tailed test).

2. All comparisons are **orthogonal comparisons**, which means that each is unique and none overlaps another.

3. All questions can be answered by $k-1$ or fewer comparisons.

## 20.16 How to Construct Planned Comparisons

Suppose a study consists of a control condition ($A$) and three experimental conditions ($B$, $C$, and $D$), with an equal number of subjects in each group. If we wish to compare the control condition with the average of the experimental conditions, we can express the desired comparison as:

$$\overline{X}_A \; v. \; \frac{\overline{X}_B + \overline{X}_C + \overline{X}_D}{3}$$

or

$$1\overline{X}_A \; v. \; (\tfrac{1}{3}\overline{X}_B + \tfrac{1}{3}\overline{X}_C + \tfrac{1}{3}\overline{X}_D)$$

The hypothesis we propose to test is, of course, about the difference at the population level:

$$H_0: 1\mu_A - \tfrac{1}{3}\mu_B - \tfrac{1}{3}\mu_C - \tfrac{1}{3}\mu_D = 0$$

Note the following:

1. In a comparison, two quantities are contrasted with each other. In our example, the mean of $A$ is contrasted with the average of the means of the remaining conditions, $B$, $C$, and $D$.

2. Each term in the null hypothesis of the comparison is multiplied by a coefficient. In our example, $+1$ is the coefficient for $\mu_A$ and $-\tfrac{1}{3}$ is the coefficient for $\mu_B$, $\mu_C$, and $\mu_D$.

3. The total of the positive coefficients equals the total of the negative coefficients.

Other contrasts are, of course, possible. If we wish to compare the average of $A$ and $B$ with the average of $C$ and $D$, the contrast would be

$$\frac{\overline{X}_A + \overline{X}_B}{2} \; v. \; \frac{\overline{X}_C + \overline{X}_D}{2}$$

or more formally

$$\tfrac{1}{2}\overline{X}_A + \tfrac{1}{2}\overline{X}_B - \tfrac{1}{2}\overline{X}_C - \tfrac{1}{2}\overline{X}_D$$

Similarly, for $\overline{X}_A$ *v.* $\overline{X}_B$, we have

$$1\overline{X}_A - 1\overline{X}_B$$

and for a comparison of the average of $A$ and $B$ with $D$, we have

$$\tfrac{1}{2}\overline{X}_A + \tfrac{1}{2}\overline{X}_B - 1\overline{X}_D$$

In general, a comparison, $K$, may be expressed as

---

### A COMPARISON

$$K = a_A\overline{X}_A + a_B\overline{X}_B + \ldots a_k\overline{X}_k \qquad (20.18)$$

*where:* $a_A$, $a_B$, etc. = the coefficients for the several levels of treatment.
$k$ = the number of levels of the particular treatment.

---

If some levels are not included in the comparison, the coefficients of the means of these groups are assigned the value zero.

To sum up, a comparison is constructed as follows:

**Step 1:** Decide what conditions (levels of treatment) are to be compared.

**Step 2:** Select coefficients for the means of the treatment levels to be used in the comparison, assigning a coefficient of zero to means not involved in the comparison, and making certain that the algebraic sum of all the coefficients is zero.

With $k$ groups, there are $k - 1$ possible orthogonal comparisons. Remember, each comparison must be unique and none can overlap another. *When there are an equal number of subjects in each group, two comparisons are orthogonal if the sum of the products of the corresponding coefficients is zero.* Look at Table 20.3, which shows some comparisons possible with five groups. Comparisons 1 and 2 are orthogonal [(+1)(0) + (0)(+1) + (0)(0) + (0)(−1) + (−1)(0) = 0], as are comparisons 2 and 3 [(0)(+1) + (+1)(0) + (0)(−1) + (−1)(0) + (0)(0) = 0], but comparisons 1 and 3 are not [(+1)(+1) + (0)(0) + (0)(−1) + (0)(0) + (−1)(0) = 1]. To meet the requirement of orthogonality, *each comparison must be orthogonal to every other comparison.* If we eliminate comparison 3 in our example, each of the remaining $k - 1$ comparisons is orthogonal with the remaining three.

TABLE **20.3** *Five Comparisons that Are Possible with Five Groups. Only Comparisons 1, 2, 4, and 5 Are Orthogonal*

| | GROUP MEANS | | | | |
| --- | --- | --- | --- | --- | --- |
| | $\overline{X}_A$ | $\overline{X}_B$ | $\overline{X}_C$ | $\overline{X}_D$ | $\overline{X}_E$ |
| *Comparison* | *Coefficients* | | | | |
| 1: $\mu_A - \mu_E$ | +1 | 0 | 0 | 0 | −1 |
| 2: $\mu_B - \mu_D$ | 0 | +1 | 0 | −1 | 0 |
| 3: $\mu_A - \mu_C$ | +1 | 0 | −1 | 0 | 0 |
| 4: $\frac{1}{2}\mu_B + \frac{1}{2}\mu_D - \frac{1}{2}\mu_A - \frac{1}{2}\mu_E$ | $-\frac{1}{2}$ | $+\frac{1}{2}$ | 0 | $+\frac{1}{2}$ | $-\frac{1}{2}$ |
| 5: $\frac{1}{4}\mu_A + \frac{1}{4}\mu_B + \frac{1}{4}\mu_D + \frac{1}{4}\mu_E - \mu_C$ | $+\frac{1}{4}$ | $+\frac{1}{4}$ | −1 | $+\frac{1}{4}$ | $+\frac{1}{4}$ |

When group sample sizes are equal, we can construct a set of $k - 1$ orthogonal comparisons in the following manner:

**Step 1:** Construct the first comparison using all the levels of the treatment. For example, if there are four groups, the first comparison might be

$$1\overline{X}_A \ v. \ (\tfrac{1}{3}\overline{X}_B + \tfrac{1}{3}\overline{X}_C + \tfrac{1}{3}\overline{X}_D)$$

**Step 2:** The second comparison must be constructed wholly from groups that fall on *one* side of the first comparison. In our example, only a comparison involving $B$, $C$, and $D$ will meet this criterion. Again, we must use *all* the available groups. We might, for example, choose

$$1\overline{X}_C \ v. \ (\tfrac{1}{2}\overline{X}_B + \tfrac{1}{2}\overline{X}_D)$$

**Step 3:** Construct the third comparison by applying the procedure of step 2 to the comparison just obtained. In our example, only one comparison is now possible:

$$1\overline{X}_B \ v. \ 1\overline{X}_D$$

Note that we now have a set of $k - 1 = 3$ comparisons constructed from the $k = 4$ treatment means.

You can construct alternative sets of comparisons in this way. For our example, one possible alternative set is

$$(\tfrac{1}{2}\overline{X}_A + \tfrac{1}{2}\overline{X}_B) \ v. \ (\tfrac{1}{2}\overline{X}_C + \tfrac{1}{2}\overline{X}_D)$$
$$1\overline{X}_A \ v. \ 1\overline{X}_B$$
$$1\overline{X}_C \ v. \ 1\overline{X}_D$$

Although comparisons within a particular set approach mutual independence, this cannot be said for comparisons selected from more than one set. Consequently, in consideration of the reasons for doing the study, we decide in advance which set would be most appropriate and choose comparisons from that set only.

Let us return to our example of the three methods of instruction: lecture plus movie and lecture plus audio tape. We suggested that it might make sense to construct two comparisons: (1) lecture versus the average of the two methods that use supplementary material and (2) lecture plus movie versus lecture plus audio tape. Are these two comparisons orthogonal? To answer this, we must determine the appropriate coefficients:

| | 1<br>LECTURE | 2<br>LECTURE + MOVIE | 3<br>LECTURE + AUDIO TAPE |
|---|---|---|---|
| $\mu_1 - \tfrac{1}{2}\mu_2 - \tfrac{1}{2}\mu_3$ | $+1$ | $-\tfrac{1}{2}$ | $-\tfrac{1}{2}$ |
| $\mu_2 - \mu_3$ | $0$ | $+1$ | $-1$ |

We now determine the sum of the products of the corresponding coefficients: $(+1)(0) + (-\tfrac{1}{2})(1) + (-\tfrac{1}{2})(-1) = 0$. The two comparisons are indeed orthogonal.

If we compute $t$ for all $k - 1$ orthogonal comparisons, the mean of the squared $t$ values will equal the omnibus $F$ ratio. *The use of planned comparisons is the most powerful method of discovering a difference between population means, if one exists.* The requirement

# Point of Controversy

## Analysis of Variance versus *A Priori* Comparisons

Professor Jones wishes to compare how four different kinds of incentives affect job satisfaction among assembly line workers. She has no reason to expect in advance that one will be better than any other. Her research is truly exploratory, a "fishing expedition." In research like this, most statisticians believe that ANOVA is the proper test to use to test the hypothesis of equality among means (Denenberg, 1984). The $F$ test is very conservative (a large difference between means is needed to achieve significance) to protect the researcher from making Type I errors. It does so by maintaining the *overall* level of significance at a specified level (e.g., .05 or .01).

There is a price to be paid, however, for conservativeness. For example, consider a hypothetical experiment in which four new drugs are to be compared with a placebo. Suppose only one of the drugs is truly effective. If we compare it alone with the placebo the end result might be $p < .01$. If we include two other groups tested with ineffective drugs, the overall end result might drop to $p < .05$. With all the ineffective drugs included, we might fail to reach a significant result at all (Sinclair, 1988). Thus, the failure to reject the null hypothesis is often due to the insensitivity of the $F$ test.

Some researchers believe that journal editors and reviewers have come to require the use of ANOVA and *post hoc* tests whenever there are three or more groups in a study (Kitchen, 1987; Zivin & Bartko, 1976; Sinclair, 1988). (In fact, many introductory statistics textbooks teach only the ANOVA procedure for analyzing the means of three or more groups.) This belief, and the conservativeness of the $F$ test, has made ANOVA the target of heated criticism. One researcher calls for less use of ANOVA and more use of common sense, or the "bloody obvious test" (Kitchen, 1987). Another advocates the use of multiple $t$ tests whenever there are more than two groups to be compared, reasoning (incorrectly, we believe) that researchers really do not test hypotheses but instead use statistical tests (like the $t$ test) only to generate $p$-values, which are then used as a descriptive statistic (Sinclair, 1988).

Rosnow and Rosenthal (1989) state that one of the major problems is the overreliance on $F$ tests "of diffuse hypotheses that although providing protection for some investigators from the dangers of 'data mining' with multiple tests performed as if each were the only one considered, do not usually tell us anything we really want to know." However, the problem identified here is not really with the $F$ test but rather with researchers who fail to be more precise about their scientific hypotheses.

Many studies are exploratory, in which case ANOVA is a very good test. But when researchers can be specific about which pairs of groups they really wish to compare, *a priori* comparisons are preferred to an omnibus $F$ test because of the increased power and the clarity of interpretation they provide. If journal editors have come to require ANOVA for tests of multiple groups, it is an unfortunate historical accident, for even Fisher (1949) believed that *a priori* comparisons are justified:

> When the $(F)$ test does not demonstrate significant differentiation, much caution should be used before claiming significance for special comparisons. Comparisons,

which the experiment was designed to make, may, of course, be made without hesitation. (R. A. Fisher, 1949, p. 57)

Today, many noted statisticians and methodologists concur (Denenberg, 1984; Rosnow & Rosenthal, 1989; Winer, Brown, & Michel, 1991).

Our conclusion: If possible, develop your scientific hypotheses to the extent that you can design experiments that will utilize the power and clarity of *a priori* tests. Save omnibus *F* tests for truly exploratory studies.

---

of orthogonality minimizes the chances of making a Type 1 error. In fact, *orthogonality allows us to calculate the exact probability of a Type I error.* Today, there are some statisticians who argue that planned comparisons need not be orthogonal. However, with nonorthogonal comparisons it is no longer possible to calculate the probability of committing a Type I error. Therefore, when you start to conduct a study, if you choose to use planned comparisons but ignore the requirement of orthogonality, be sure to limit yourself to only a few comparisons (certainly not to exceed $k - 1$). If you ignore both constraints, you will have the same problem we discussed in the beginning of the chapter.

## 20.17 Analysis of Variance for Repeated Measures

**ANOVA for repeated measures**
an analysis of variance procedure used when one sample is tested under two or more treatment conditions

To this point in the chapter, we have considered only the comparison of independently drawn random samples. Suppose, however, that we wish to test different dosages of a new experimental drug for hyperactive children, and that to control for individual differences among subjects, we prefer to test three dosages in the same subjects. We introduced the *t* test for testing hypotheses about two dependent means (and also discussed the advantages of the dependent-groups design) in Chapter 16. However, just as is the case with independent groups, we should not use multiple *t* tests when comparing three or more dependent means because of the increased probability of a Type I error. Instead, we use **analysis of variance for repeated measures**.

The logic of one-way ANOVA for repeated measures is the same as that for independent measures: We partition the total variability in the data into two parts, within groups and between groups. In the ANOVA for repeated measures, $SS_w$ is also partitioned into two parts: (1) $SS_{subjects}$, a measure of the variability due to individual differences and (2) $SS_{residual}$, a measure of the variability due to random error or chance. Figure 20.7 shows the partitioning for ANOVA for repeated measures.

**partition of the sums of squares with ANOVA for repeated measures**
$SS_{total} = SS_{within} + SS_{between}$
$SS_{within} = SS_{subjects} + SS_{residual}$

We can measure the variability due to individual differences because, unlike in the ANOVA for independent measures, each subject is tested under all conditions. This allows us to record a subject's overall score (by adding together all his or her scores), which we then compare with other subjects' overall scores. If two subjects' overall scores differ, we attribute it to individual differences. In the case where two subjects' overall scores are the same but their scores differ across conditions, we attribute it to random error.

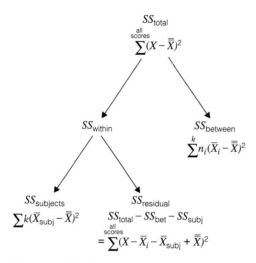

**FIGURE 20.7**  Partitioning of the sums of squares for ANOVA for repeated measures.

**$SS_{subjects}$**
a measure of
the variability
due to individ-
ual differences

**$SS_{residual}$**
a measure of
the variability
due to chance
(excluding the
individual dif-
ferences)

The formula for $SS_{total}$ is the same as for one-way ANOVA with independent groups (Formula 20.3*a*):

$SS_{total}$: DEVIATION-SCORES METHOD

$$SS_{total} = \sum^{\substack{all \\ scores}} (\overline{X} - \overline{\overline{X}})^2$$

The formula for $SS_{bet}$ is also the same. Because each group has the same number of subjects in the repeated-measures design, we can modify the raw-scores formula for $SS_{bet}$ (Formula 20.11).

$SS_{bet}$: DEVIATION-SCORES METHOD

$$SS_{bet} = \sum^{k} n_i(\overline{X}_i - \overline{\overline{X}})^2 \tag{20.19a}$$

$SS_{bet}$: RAW-SCORES METHOD
FOR REPEATED MEASURES

$$SS_{bet} = \frac{\left(\sum X_A\right)^2 + \left(\sum X_B\right)^2 + \cdots}{n_k} - \frac{\left(\sum^{\substack{all \\ scores}} X\right)^2}{n_{total}} \tag{20.19b}$$

To calculate $SS_{subjects}$, use either of the following formulas:

$SS_{subjects}$: DEVIATION-SCORES METHOD

$$SS_{subj} = \sum k(\overline{X}_{subj} - \overline{\overline{X}})^2 \qquad (20.20a)$$

*where:* $\overline{X}_{subj}$ = a subject's mean score across all conditions.
$k$ = the number of conditions.

$SS_{subjects}$: RAW-SCORES METHOD

$$SS_{subj} = \frac{\sum X_{subj}^2}{k} - \frac{\left(\sum\limits^{\substack{all \\ scores}} X\right)^2}{n_{total}} \qquad (20.20b)$$

*where:* $k$ = the number of conditions.

We find $SS_{residual}$ by subtraction:

$$SS_{resid} = SS_{total} - SS_{bet} - SS_{subj} \qquad (20.21)$$

The degrees of freedom for $SS_{subj}$ is the number of subjects minus one. For $SS_{resid}$, the degrees of freedom is $(df_{subj})(df_{bet})$.

To determine if there is a treatment effect, we calculate the $F$ ratio by dividing $s_{bet}^2$ by $s_{resid}^2$:

$$F = \frac{s_{bet}^2}{s_{resid}^2} = \frac{random\ error + treatment\ effect}{random\ error} \qquad (20.22)$$

**F ratio for repeated-measures ANOVA**

$\dfrac{s_{bet}^2}{s_{resid}^2} =$

$\dfrac{\substack{\text{inherent} \\ \text{variance}} + \substack{\text{treatment} \\ \text{effect}}}{\text{inherent variance}}$

when there is no treatment effect, the ratio should approximate 1.0

Table 20.4 gives the general form of the summary table for ANOVA for repeated measures. Notice that only the $F$ ratio for the independent variable is calculated. Rarely is anyone interested in knowing whether there is a significant difference among individuals.

The one-way ANOVA for repeated measures is a more powerful design than the one-way ANOVA for independent groups because it removes the variability due to individual differences ($s_{bet}^2$ is divided by $s_{resid}^2$, which is smaller than $s_w^2$). The dependent-samples design also has some shortcomings, however (see Section 16.8).

To demonstrate ANOVA for repeated measures, let us return to our hypothetical example. We wish to test three levels of the independent variable: zero (Z), moderate (M), and high (H) dosages of a new experimental drug for hyperactive children. As the dependent variable, we choose scores on a reading test that requires sustained attention for 30 minutes. The null and alternative hypotheses are

$$H_0: \mu_Z = \mu_M = \mu_H$$

$$H_A: not\ H_0$$

TABLE 20.4    *Summary Table of One-Way ANOVA for Repeated Measures*

| SOURCE | SS | df | $s^2$ | F |
|---|---|---|---|---|
| Subjects | Formula 20.20a or 20.20b | $n - 1$ | $\dfrac{SS_{subj}}{df_{subj}}$ | — |
| Between groups | Formula 20.19a or 20.19b | $k - 1$ | $\dfrac{SS_{bet}}{df_{bet}}$ | $\dfrac{s^2_{bet}}{s^2_{resid}}$ |
| Residual | Formula 20.21 | $(df_{subj})(df_{bet})$ | $\dfrac{SS_{resid}}{df_{resid}}$ | |
| Total | Formula 20.3a | $(k)(n) - 1$ | | |

We randomly select 12 third-graders from our school district and test them. Four of the children receive the zero dose first, followed by the moderate, and then the high dosage, with 1 week between tests. Four other children receive the drug in the order M, H, Z, and the remaining four are administered the drug in the order H, Z, M. Table 20.5 gives hypothetical results for our experiment, as well as the initial calculations. The sums of squares are calculated as follows:

$$SS_{total} = \overset{\underset{\mathrm{scores}}{\mathrm{all}}}{\sum} (X - \overline{\overline{X}})^2$$

$$= (35 - 43.33)^2 + (23 - 43.33)^2 + \cdots + (33 - 43.33)^2$$

$$= 11{,}550$$

$$SS_{bet} = \sum^{k} n_i(\overline{X}_i - \overline{\overline{X}})^2$$

$$= 12(33 - 43.33)^2 + 12(63 - 43.33)^2 + 12(34 - 43.33)^2$$

$$= 6{,}968.0$$

$$SS_{subj} = \sum k(\overline{X}_{subj} - \overline{\overline{X}})^2$$

$$= 3(41.67 - 43.33)^2 + 3(32.67 - 43.33)^2 \cdots + 3(41.00 - 43.33)^2$$

$$= 3{,}056.03$$

$$SS_{resid} = SS_{total} - SS_{bet} - SS_{subj}$$

$$= 11{,}550 - 6{,}968 - 3{,}056.03$$

$$= 1{,}525.97$$

Table 20.5 also gives the summary table for this example. Note that $F = 50.23$. From Table E in Appendix E, we find that the critical value of $F$ with 2 and 22 degrees of freedom at $\alpha = .05$ is 3.44. If the null hypothesis is true, only 5% of the time would we obtain a value of $F$ that equals or exceeds this value. Therefore, we reject $H_0$ and conclude that different dosages of the new drug have different effects on hyperactive

**TABLE 20.5** *Data, Initial Calculations, and ANOVA Summary Table for the Test of the Hypothesis* $H_0$: $\mu_z = \mu_M = \mu_H$, *Using Repeated Measures*

| SUBJECT | READING SCORE FOR DOSAGE OF DRUG | | | TOTAL $(X_{subj})$ | $X^2_{subj}$ | $\overline{X}_{subj}$ |
|---|---|---|---|---|---|---|
| | Zero | Moderate | High | | | |
| 1 | 35 | 60 | 30 | 125 | 15,625 | 41.67 |
| 2 | 23 | 55 | 20 | 98 | 9,604 | 32.67 |
| 3 | 30 | 65 | 25 | 120 | 11,400 | 40.00 |
| 4 | 40 | 45 | 45 | 130 | 16,900 | 43.33 |
| 5 | 50 | 80 | 40 | 170 | 28,900 | 56.67 |
| 6 | 35 | 75 | 40 | 150 | 22,500 | 50.00 |
| 7 | 30 | 63 | 25 | 118 | 13,924 | 39.33 |
| 8 | 25 | 35 | 30 | 90 | 8,100 | 30.00 |
| 9 | 43 | 75 | 60 | 178 | 31,684 | 59.33 |
| 10 | 15 | 58 | 25 | 98 | 9,604 | 32.67 |
| 11 | 45 | 80 | 35 | 160 | 25,600 | 53.33 |
| 12 | 25 | 65 | 33 | 123 | 15,129 | 41.00 |
| | $\sum X = 396$ | 756 | 408 | $\sum X_{subj} = 1,560$ | $\sum X^2_{subj} = 211,970$ | |
| | $\sum X^2 = 14,228$ | 49,708 | 15,214 | $\sum X^2_{total} = 79,150$ | | |
| | $n = 12$ | 12 | 12 | | | |
| | $\overline{X} = 33$ | 63 | 34 | | | $\overline{\overline{X}} = 43.33$ |

| SOURCE | SS | df | $s^2$ | F |
|---|---|---|---|---|
| Subjects | 3,056.03 | 11 | 277.82 | — |
| Between groups | 6,968.0 | 2 | 3,484.0 | 50.23 |
| Residual | 1,525.97 | 22 | 69.36 | |
| Total | 11,550 | 35 | | |

children. As with one-way ANOVA using independently drawn samples, we must now conduct *post hoc* tests to determine which groups differed from the others.

Tukey's HSD test may also be used with ANOVA for repeated measures. (As before, our overall obtained *F* ratio must first be significant.) However, instead of using $s^2_w$, we use $s^2_{resid}$ to calculate *HSD*:

**Tukey's HSD test**
critical *HSD* value for repeated-measures ANOVA =

$q\sqrt{\dfrac{s^2_{resid}}{n}}$

CRITICAL HSD VALUE FOR TUKEY'S
HSD TEST WITH REPEATED MEASURES

$$HSD = q\sqrt{\frac{s^2_{resid}}{n}} \qquad (20.23)$$

In our example, $s^2_{resid} = 69.36$ and $n = 12$. To calculate the Studentized range statistic, look in Table F in Appendix E and find the value of *q* for $df_{resid} = 11$ and $k = 3$.

For $\alpha = .05$, the value of $q$ is 3.82. The critical HSD value is thus

$$HSD = 3.82 \sqrt{\frac{69.36}{12}} = 9.18$$

This is the minimum difference needed between the means of any two groups to conclude that they are significantly different from one another. As you can see from Table 20.5, the moderate dosage of the drug resulted in significantly higher reading scores ($\overline{X} = 63$) for the hyperactive children than were found with either the zero dosage ($\overline{X} = 33$) or high dosage ($\overline{X} = 34$), which did not significantly differ.

What about effect size? There are several problems with using omega-squared as an estimate of effect size in the repeated-measures design (Keppel, 1991). One measure of effect size that is appropriate for the one-way repeated-measures design is eta-squared:

**eta-squared ($\eta^2$)**
an $r$ family measure of effect size for repeated-measures ANOVA
$$\frac{SS_{subj}}{SS_{subj} + SS_{resid}}$$

> **FORMULA FOR ETA-SQUARED**
>
> $$\eta^2 = \frac{SS_{subj}}{SS_{subj} + SS_{resid}} \qquad (20.24)$$

Eta-squared shows the proportion of variability due to the independent variable after we have removed the variability due to individual differences. In our example (Table 20.5),

$$\eta^2 = \frac{6,968}{6,968 + 1,525.97} = .82$$

**assumption of sphericity**
the assumption that across any two treatment conditions, the variance of the difference scores in the population are the same

Our calculated value of $\eta^2$ indicates that 82% of the variability in scores on the reading tests are due to the dosage of the drug. This is a very strong effect.

The assumptions of the one-way ANOVA for repeated measures are that the sample has been independently and randomly drawn, and that for each condition the scores are normally distributed and have an equal variance (see Section 20.10). However, the repeated measures design has an additional assumption—the **assumption of sphericity**. This is the assumption that across any two conditions, the variance of the difference scores in the population are the same. Substantial departure from these assumptions will affect the accuracy of the ANOVA test.

## 20.18 Summary

Despite its name, analysis of variance is really a test about means (at least in its simplest forms). One way ANOVA may be considered an extension of the $t$ test to problems involving more than two groups, or conversely, the $t$ test may be thought of as a special use of one-way ANOVA.

ANOVA employs the sum of squares ($SS$) as the basic unit of measurement. In one-way ANOVA for independently drawn groups, the total sum of squares ($SS_{total}$) for all scores (across all groups) is partitioned into two parts: $SS_{within}$, a measure of the within-group variation of individual scores, and $SS_{between}$, a measure of the variation of sample means among groups. To derive variance estimates, we divide $SS$'s by their degrees of freedom. When $H_0$ is true ($\mu_A = \mu_B = \mu_C \ldots$), both types of variance estimate inherent variation, which reflects the variation in behavior of individuals tested under identical condition. Thus, when $H_0$ is true, $s_w^2$ and $s_{bet}^2$ should be equal within the limits of sampling error. When $H_0$ is false, the within-groups variance is unaffected (because all subjects within a group are still tested identically), but the between-groups variance now reflects the inherent variance *plus* differential treatment effect. The greater the treatment effect, the greater the value of $s_{bet}^2$.

ANOVA examines the ratio (called the $F$ ratio in honor of Fisher) of these two independent variance estimates. If $H_0$ is true, $F = s_{bet}^2 / s_w^2$ will approximate unity; if $H_0$ is false, $F$ will be greater than unity (a result of the differential treatment effect reflected in $s_{bet}^2$). There is a family of theoretical $F$ distributions that depend on the degrees of freedom for both $s_{bet}^2$ and $s_w^2$. As was the case with the $t$ test, ANOVA is based on the assumptions of random sampling, normally distributed populations of scores, and homogeneity of variance.

The alternative hypothesis ($H_A$) states only that the group means are unequal in some (any) way. When a significant $F$ is obtained, additional *post hoc* tests are employed to determine whether differences exist between specific groups. These tests compensate for the increasing probability, as we make numerous tests, of claiming one or more significant differences when in fact none exist. Among the many possibilities, Tukey's HSD test is a useful *post hoc* test that examines all pairwise comparisons between treatment group means.

As an alternative to ANOVA, we may use planned comparisons. These comparisons, which must be planned in advance of collecting any data, are the most powerful tool available to investigators. Planned comparisons employ a variation of the $t$ test but must be limited to $k - 1$ orthogonal (independent) comparisons.

In analysis of variance for repeated measures, $s_w^2$ is further divided into two parts: $s_{subjects}^2$, a measure of the variability in scores due to individual differences, and $s_{residual}^2$, a measure of the variability due to random error or chance. The $F$ ratio used for this ANOVA is $s_{bet}^2 / s_{resid}^2$.

## Mathematical Notes

**Note 20.1 Partition of the Sum of Squares and Degrees of Freedom in One-Way Analysis of Variance (*Ref.:* Section 20.3)**

$$(X - \overline{\overline{X}}) = (X - \overline{X}) + (\overline{X} - \overline{\overline{X}})$$

Squaring both sides, we obtain

$$(X - \overline{\overline{X}})^2 = (X - \overline{X})^2 + 2(X - \overline{X})(\overline{X} - \overline{\overline{X}}) + (\overline{X} - \overline{\overline{X}})^2$$

Summing within each sample, we obtain

$$\sum^{n_i} (X - \overline{\overline{X}})^2 = \sum^{n_i} (X - \overline{X})^2 + 2(\overline{X} - \overline{\overline{X}}) \sum^{n_i} (X - \overline{X}) + n_i(\overline{X} - \overline{\overline{X}})^2$$

Because $\Sigma(X - \overline{X}) = 0$ (see Note 5.1), the middle term drops out. Then summing over the $k$ subgroups, we obtain

$$\sum^{k}\left[\sum^{n}(X - \overline{\overline{X}})^2\right] = \sum^{k}\left[\sum^{n_i}(X - \overline{X})^2\right] + \sum^{k}n(\overline{X} - \overline{\overline{X}})^2$$

or $\qquad SS_{total} \quad = \quad SS_w \quad + \quad SS_{bet}$

Counting degrees of freedom for each term, we obtain

$$\sum^{k}n - 1 = \sum^{k}[n - 1] + [k - 1]$$

or $\qquad df_{total} \quad = \quad df_w \quad + \quad df_{bet}$

Proof of the proposition follows from

$$\sum^{k}n - 1 = \sum^{k}n - k + k - 1 = \sum^{k}n - 1$$

## Key Terms, Concepts, and Symbols

analysis of variance (388)

ANOVA (388)

one-way analysis of variance (389)

treatment conditions (389)

levels (389)

factor (389)

$k$ (389)

within-groups variation (390)

between-groups variation (391)

treatment effect (392)

grand mean (392)

inherent variation (392)

$\overline{\overline{X}}$ (392)

$SS_{total}$ (393)

$SS_{within}$ (393)

$SS_{bet}$ (393

partition of the sums of squares (394)

assumption of homogeneity of variance (294, 394)

$df_w$, $df_{bet}$, $df_{total}$ (395)

within-groups variance estimate (395)

$s_w^2$ (395)

between-groups variance estimate (396)

$s_{bet}^2$ (396)

$F$ ratio (396)

$F$ distribution (396)

$t^2$ (401)

eta-squared (404, 418)

$\eta^2$ (404, 418)

omega-squared (405)

$\hat{\omega}^2$ (405)

*post hoc* comparisons (406)

Tukey's HSD test (406)

Studentized range statistic (406)

$q$ (406)

$\tilde{n}$ (407)

planned comparison (408)

orthogonal comparison (409)

ANOVA for repeated measures (413)

$SS_{subjects}$ (413)

$SS_{resid}$ (413)

assumption of sphericity (418)

# Problems

□ 10, *12, 15, 17*

1. In the introduction to the chapter, we used the example of seven experimental drugs being tested for use with Alzheimer's patients. If we use the *t* test for independent groups to make all pairwise comparisons, we would need to make 21 comparisons. List them. Suppose one of them proved to be significant at the .05 level. Why might the National Institute of Mental Health not have much faith in our finding?

2. For the example in Problem 1, we decide to use one-way ANOVA to compare the seven group means. (a) Express $H_0$ in symbolic form. (b) Why can't $H_A$ be expressed in simple symbolic form? (c) Why can't we express $H_A$ as $\mu_1 \neq \mu_2 \neq \mu_3 \neq \mu_4 \neq \mu_5 \neq \mu_6 \neq \mu_7$? (d) List several possible ways in which $H_0$ can be false.

3. In the analysis of variance *F* test, why is it that only the area in the upper tail of the *F* distribution is of interest?

4. With reference to Table E in Appendix E, what tabulated value of *F* is so great that it would be exceeded in random sampling only 5% of the time when there are (a) 5 degrees of freedom in the numerator and 20 in the denominator? (b) 20 degrees of freedom in the numerator and 5 in the denominator? (c) 3 degrees of freedom in the numerator and 40 in the denominator? (d) 6 degrees of freedom in the numerator and 100 in the denominator?

5. In a one-way ANOVA, equal numbers of subjects were distributed among the several groups. (a) If $df_{bet} = 3$ and $df_w = 84$, how many groups were there? How many subjects were assigned to each group? What is the numerical value of $df_{total}$? (b) If $s^2_{bet} = 170$ and $s^2_w = 50$, was there a significant treatment effect if $\alpha = .05$? If $\alpha = .01$? Justify your answers. (Use the nearest values in Table E to answer this question.)

## DATA 20A

There are three subjects in each of three treatment groups.

| | SCORES | | |
|---|---|---|---|
| Group *L*: | 2 | 7 | 3 |
| Group *M*: | 6 | 8 | 4 |
| Group *N*: | 9 | 11 | 10 |

6. Explain, using the scores in Data 20A as examples, what is meant by (a) inherent variation and (b) differential treatment effects.

7. Use the deviation-score formulas for this problem. For Data 20A, (a) find $SS_w$, $SS_{bet}$, and $SS_{total}$. Does $SS_{total} = SS_{bet} + SS_w$? (b) What are the values of $df_w$, $df_{bet}$, and $df_{total}$? (c) Find $s^2_w$ and $s^2_{bet}$. (d) Present the outcome developed so far in an ANOVA summary table. (e) Test the hypothesis that $\mu_L = \mu_M = \mu_N$ at $\alpha = .05$, and state your conclusions.

8. Repeat Problem 7 using the raw-score formulas.

9. A one-way ANOVA reveals a significant treatment effect. The sample means are: $\overline{X}_A = 63.7$, $\overline{X}_B = 68.9$, $\overline{X}_C = 61.8$, and $\overline{X}_D = 62.2$. (a) What interpretation seems plausible? (b) What is the only interpretation that we can make with a significant *F*? (c) What must we do at this point to justify a more specific conclusion?

10. Refer to Problem 9 in Chapter 15 (*t* tests for independent groups). Rework this two-sample problem using one-way ANOVA. Does $F = t^2$?

11. We employ one-way ANOVA to compare the performance scores from five groups of nine cases each and obtain a significant *F*. For this analysis, $s^2_w = 18.2$, and the treatment means are as follows: $\overline{X}_1 = 14.5$, $\overline{X}_2 = 11.5$, $\overline{X}_3 = 19.0$, $\overline{X}_4 = 18.1$, and $\overline{X}_5 = 12.0$. (a) Display the difference between the means for all possible pairs of samples as shown

in Section 20.13. (b) Apply Tukey's HSD test with $\alpha = .05$. What do you conclude? (c) Apply Tukey's HSD test, but use $\alpha = .01$.

**12.** The Always Run Company advertises that its flashlight battery lasts longer than batteries made by other companies. We randomly select five batteries from the latest production run of this company and five batteries each from three of its competitors. We then test their lives in a standard flashlight. The results are given in Data 20B (scores are times in minutes). (a) Give $H_0$. (b) Complete an $F$ test ($\alpha = .05$) and show your results in a summary table. (c) If you obtain a significant $F$, apply Tukey's HSD test. (d) Your conclusions? (e) Calculate effect size (eta-squared and omega-squared).

## DATA 20B

| ALWAYS RUN | COMPETITOR A | COMPETITOR B | COMPETITOR C |
|---|---|---|---|
| 98 | 94 | 90 | 92 |
| 92 | 90 | 93 | 86 |
| 98 | 88 | 92 | 87 |
| 97 | 88 | 87 | 93 |
| 94 | 92 | 89 | 92 |

**13.** Suppose that you are the president of Always Run Company (Problem 12). You really do not care about all the comparisons. What more powerful test is more appropriate here than one-way ANOVA?

**14.** (a) If you have four groups, how many comparisons are there in a complete set of independent comparisons? (b) Identify one such set. (c) Identify a different set. (d) Identify another.

**15.** You wish to compare how a low-fat diet, low-fat diet and a brisk four-mile walk each day, and a low-fat diet and a four-mile jog each day affect cholesterol levels. You randomly assign six subjects to each group. The scores in Data 20C show the reduction in cholesterol count after 2 months. (a) Give

$H_0$. (b) Complete an $F$ test ($\alpha = .05$) and show your results in a summary table. (c) Apply Tukey's HSD test. (d) State your conclusions. (e) Calculate effect size.

## DATA 20C

| LOW-FAT DIET | DIET AND WALK | DIET AND RUN |
|---|---|---|
| 10 | 14 | 19 |
| 8 | 12 | 15 |
| 15 | 18 | 14 |
| 12 | 16 | 16 |
| 9 | 13 | 18 |
| 6 | 17 | 20 |

**16.** Prior research suggests to you that exercise is the most effective way to reduce cholesterol levels. In place of ANOVA, conduct planned comparisons (that best address your expectation) for the three groups in Problem 15.

**17.** You wish to compare the short-term effects of three new sleep-aid drugs. You try all three in a sample of eight subjects, with 5 days between each test. Data 20D gives the number of hours slept during the night under each drug. (a) Give $H_0$. (b) Conduct the $F$ test ($\alpha = .05$). (c) Apply Tukey's HSD test. (d) State your conclusion. (e) Calculate effect size.

## DATA 20D

| SUBJECT | DRUG A | DRUG B | DRUG C |
|---|---|---|---|
| 1 | 6 | 5 | 8 |
| 2 | 5 | 6 | 7 |
| 3 | 6 | 6 | 9 |
| 4 | 7 | 7 | 6 |
| 5 | 8 | 6 | 8 |
| 6 | 4 | 5 | 8 |
| 7 | 5 | 7 | 8 |
| 8 | 6 | 6 | 7 |

# CHAPTER 21

## Factorial Analysis of Variance: The Two-Factor Design for Independent Groups

When you have finished studying this chapter, you should be able to:

- Explain how analysis of variance can be used to simultaneously study the effects of two variables;
- Understand what is meant by main effects and interaction, and that main effects must be interpreted cautiously when there is a significant interaction;
- Calculate the three $F$ values in a two-factor ANOVA;
- Make *post hoc* comparisons and calculate effect size; and
- Understand the assumptions for use of the two-factor ANOVA.

Analysis of variance is a broad set of techniques used, for the most part, in studies in which the investigator wishes to compare the means of more than two groups. In the previous chapter, we examined the procedures to use when different groups receive variations of a single treatment variable, such as type of incentive, type of reading program, or different drugs. In this chapter, we move up a step in complexity and examine an analysis of variance design that permits the simultaneous study of the effects of *two* treatment variables or **factors**.

**factor**

an independent (treatment) variable

Suppose, for example, that an experimental psychologist wants to know (1) whether the physiological effects of alcohol influence aggression in male social drinkers and (2) whether psychological expectations about alcohol consumption can affect aggression in males. Most of us have witnessed someone's personality change as the result of drinking alcohol. But are these changes due entirely to physiological effects (alcohol is a central nervous system depressant), or can one's expectation of change contribute to his or her becoming less inhibited? The effect on aggression is a particularly important question because alcohol is involved in over half of all violent crimes in the United States.

A psychologist interested in these questions could carry out two separate one-factor experiments, one dealing entirely with the effects of alcohol and the other

**TABLE 21.1**  *Hypothetical Scores in a 2 × 2 Factorial Experiment of the Effects of Alcohol and Expectation of Alcohol on Aggression*

|  |  | Expectation | | |
|---|---|---|---|---|
|  |  | Expect alcohol | Do not expect alcohol |  |
| *Alcohol* | Received alcohol | 6<br>8<br>5<br>6<br>7<br>8<br>4<br>9<br>6<br>5<br>$\sum X = 64$<br>$\overline{X} = 6.4$ | 6<br>3<br>4<br>2<br>4<br>6<br>4<br>3<br>5<br>3<br>$\sum X = 40$<br>$\overline{X} = 4.0$ | $\overline{X}_{alc} = 5.2$ |
|  | Did not receive alcohol | 5<br>7<br>6<br>5<br>7<br>8<br>4<br>4<br>8<br>6<br>$\sum X = 60$<br>$\overline{X} = 6.0$ | 5<br>3<br>2<br>4<br>4<br>3<br>3<br>1<br>5<br>4<br>$\sum X = 34$<br>$\overline{X} = 3.4$ | $\overline{X}_{no\ alc} = 4.7$ |
|  |  | $\overline{X}_{expect} = 6.2$ | $\overline{X}_{do\ not\ expect} = 3.7$ | $\overline{\overline{X}} = 4.95$ |

**factorial design**

an ANOVA design in which two or more factors are studied simultaneously

**levels**

different values of an independent variable (factor)

**2 × 2 design**

a design with two factors and two levels for each factor; one of many factorial designs (others include 2 × 3, 2 × 4, 3 × 3, etc.)

dealing entirely with expectations about alcohol consumption. If, however, the psychologist were to use the **two-factor analysis of variance design** described in this chapter, he or she would be able to draw conclusions concerning the effects of *both* factors on the completion of a *single* study.

Lang, Goeckner, Adesso, and Marlatt (1975) pursued these research questions with a clever experimental design that used four groups: (1) expect alcohol–receive alcohol, (2) expect tonic water–receive alcohol, (3) expect alcohol–receive tonic water, and (4) expect tonic water–receive tonic water. (The fourth group served as a control group.) Thus, there were two factors, Alcohol and Expectation, and two conditions for each factor, referred to as **levels** of that factor (alcohol–no alcohol; expect alcohol–do not expect alcohol). This design is called a 2 × 2 (read: 2 by 2) design because there are two levels for each factor and because each level of a factor appears in combination with each level of the other factor. Table 21.1 shows these relationships.

Lang's team randomly assigned subjects to each of the four groups and misled them into thinking that they were participating in a taste test of different brands of vodka or tonic water. In fact, the experimenters served only two types of drinks, one with alcohol and one without, which pretesting had shown could not be distinguished from one another. Those given alcohol were allowed to drink until they were legally intoxicated (blood-alcohol levels of .10%). After the taste test, the subjects then participated in a "learning study" in which they were the "teacher" and another person (actually an actor) served as the "student." The subjects were told to administer any of 10 intensities of electric shock whenever the student made a mistake. No current was actually delivered, and the actor pretended to be shocked. The experimenters measured a subject's aggression as the mean chosen level of shock. We present some hypothetical results for this study in Table 21.1.

You will find that what you learned in the last chapter has great relevance here. We will partition, or analyze, the total variation into sums of squares associated with different sources of variation, convert them to variance estimates, and form $F$ ratios for the tests of null hypotheses. We will begin our analysis of these results by explaining how the two-factor ANOVA can simultaneously answer the two questions (in our example, one about the effects of alcohol and the other about the expectation of alcohol) that would otherwise require two separate studies.

## 21.1 Main Effects

**cell**

the combination of a row (level of one factor) and a column (level of the other factor)

In Table 21.1, the two levels of the factor Alcohol are presented in rows and the two levels of the factor Expectation are presented in columns. Each combination of a row level and a column level is referred to as a **cell**. In a 2 × 2 design there are, of course, four cells.

At the conclusion of the study, we can calculate from the levels of shock administered by each subject during the learning study the cell means, the row means, and the column means. Note in Table 21.1 that the row and column means, shown to the right and at the bottom of the cells, respectively, are equal to the means of the two cell means in the particular row or column. This will always be the case *when there are equal numbers of cases per cell*. Also, because there are equal $n$'s, the grand mean ($\overline{\overline{X}}$), the mean of *all* the scores, is also the mean of the four cell means, the mean of the two row means, and the mean of the two column means.

In this study, we want to know about the *overall* influence of alcohol (in both subjects who expect it and in those who don't) and also about the *overall* influence of

**main effect (for a factor)** the mean differences among the levels of one factor averaged across the levels of the other factor

the expectation of alcohol (in both subjects who receive alcohol and in those who don't). These are called questions about main effects. The **main effect** for a factor is an "average" effect. It is the differences among the levels of that factor averaged across the levels of the other factor. We can write null hypotheses for each factor as follows:

NULL HYPOTHESIS FOR ROW FACTOR (ALCOHOL)

$$H_0: \mu_{alc} = \mu_{no\ alc}$$

NULL HYPOTHESIS FOR COLUMN FACTOR (EXPECTATION)

$$H_0: \mu_{expect} = \mu_{do\ not\ expect}$$

When there are only two levels of a factor, as in this case, our alternative hypothesis ($H_A$) can be either directional (e.g., $\mu_{alc} > \mu_{no\ alc}$) or nondirectional (e.g., $\mu_{alc} \neq \mu_{no\ alc}$). When there are more than two levels, the alternative hypothesis is that $H_0$ is untrue in *some* (any) way and is therefore always nondirectional.

The $F$ test of $H_0: \mu_{alc} = \mu_{no\ alc}$ will tell us whether the overall means for the two alcohol levels ($\overline{X}_{alc} = 5.2$ and $\overline{X}_{no\ alc} = 4.7$) are different enough to justify rejecting the null hypothesis. In essence, we divide our 40 subjects into alcohol and no-alcohol groups of 20 each and perform a variation of one-way ANOVA to compare the overall (row) means of the two groups. Similarly, the $F$ test of $H_0: \mu_{expect} = \mu_{do\ no\ expect}$ is analogous to a one-way ANOVA to determine whether the overall means of the two levels of expectation ($\overline{X}_{expect} = 6.2$ and $\overline{X}_{do\ not\ expect} = 3.7$) are significantly different. We use the same 40 subjects, except that we now divide them into two different groups of 20 each according to their expectations.

Consequently, main effects refer exclusively to differences among the overall row means and differences among the overall column means of tables like 21.1. Notice in Table 21.1, for example, that there is a 0.5-point overall difference in aggressiveness between subjects who received alcohol and those who did not ($\overline{X}_{alc} - \overline{X}_{no\ alc} = 0.5$). This is the average of the 0.4-point difference for the subjects who expected alcohol ($6.4 - 6.0$) and the 0.6-point difference for the subjects who did not expect alcohol ($4.0 - 3.4$). When interpreting main effects, it is important to keep in mind their "average" nature.

One advantage of using two-way ANOVA over performing a separate experiment for each factor is that conclusions can be broader. For instance, in a separate one-factor experiment to compare the two levels of alcohol consumption, we would hold everything but the Alcohol factor constant, so all the subjects would have to have the same expectations (either of getting alcohol or of getting tonic). Thus, the conclusions regarding alcohol consumption and aggression would apply only to situations characterized by *that* set of expectations. Here we can draw conclusions concerning the effect of alcohol on aggression under two different sets of expectations.

There is another advantage to the factorial design; you will learn about it in the next section.

## 21.2 Interaction

With the factorial design, we are able to examine a new and important question that we cannot examine using the simple $t$ test or the one-way ANOVA: *Whatever the differences among the several levels of one factor, are they the same for each level of the other*

**interaction (between factors)**

the joint effect of the two independent variables that cannot be predicted from the main effects

*factor*? In analysis of variance, this kind of question is known as one of interaction effect. **Interaction** refers to the joint effect of the two independent variables (factors) on the dependent variable. We can calculate an *F* ratio to test for interaction. If the test for interaction is significant, it means that the effect of one factor depends on the level of the other factor.

You can appreciate main effects and interaction effects more readily by looking at graphs. We present some different hypothetical outcomes of our $2 \times 2$ factorial experiment in Figures 21.1*a* through 21.1*f.* In graphing the results of a two-factor experiment, it is customary to display the dependent variable on the vertical axis and the independent variable with the greater number of levels on the horizontal axis. (Thus, in a $2 \times 3$ design, the factor with three levels would ordinarily be placed on the horizontal axis, as in Figures 21.1*g* and 21.1*h.*) If, however, one of the independent variables is on a nominal or ordinal scale of measurement and the second is on an interval or ratio scale, it is customary to put the variable on the nominal or ordinal scale along the horizontal axis. In either case, we represent the other independent variable (factor) by lines on the graph that are connected to dots representing the cell means. These are not rigid rules, and each researcher must decide how best to portray his or her data. In our $2 \times 2$ example, we have chosen to represent the level of alcohol on the horizontal axis and the expectation of alcohol consumption with lines.

Figure 21.1*a* shows the results of our experiment as they would appear if there were no main effects and no interaction effect. The mean intensity of shock chosen by the subjects is the same regardless of their expectation of alcohol or their consumption of alcohol.

Figure 21.1*b* shows a main effect for Expectation but none for Alcohol. The subjects who expected alcohol chose higher-intensity shocks than those who did not expect alcohol, and it did not matter whether or not they were consuming alcohol. Figure 21.1*c,* on the other hand, shows a main effect for Alcohol (the subjects who consumed alcohol chose higher levels of shock than those who did not consume alcohol) but none for Expectation. Figure 21.1*d* displays main effects for both Alcohol and Expectation. In each of the examples so far, the lines are parallel, which indicates that there was no interaction—the differences (if any) between the two levels of one factor were the same for each level of the other factor.

**ordinal interaction**

an interaction for which the relative ranks for the levels of one factor are the same at all levels of the other factor

**disordinal interaction**

an interaction for which the relative ranks for the levels of one factor differ across levels of the other factor

We display two possible examples of interaction effects in Figures 21.1*e* and 21.1*f.* When interaction is displayed graphically, it shows a nonchance departure from a parallel relation among the lines connecting the group means. In these results, the difference between the expect-alcohol and do-not-expect-alcohol groups depends on whether or not alcohol was actually consumed. Note that the lines in the graphs are no longer parallel. In Figure 21.1*e,* there is a negligible difference between the two expectation groups when no alcohol is consumed, but the group that expected alcohol shows considerably more aggression during intoxication. Thus, the effect of expectation depends on whether or not alcohol is actually consumed. This is an example of what is known as an **ordinal interaction**—the relative ranks for the levels of one factor are the same at all level of the other factor (i.e., the lines do not cross).

Figure 21.1*f* shows an even more dramatic interaction, called a **disordinal interaction** because the ranks for the levels of one factor differ across levels of the second factor (i.e., the lines cross). There are no main effects (because the *average* effect of expected alcohol is not different from the *average* effect of do not expect alcohol), only an interaction effect.

To this point, we have used a $2 \times 2$ example of a factorial design. Suppose, however, that in addition to the completely sober and intoxicated states, our researchers

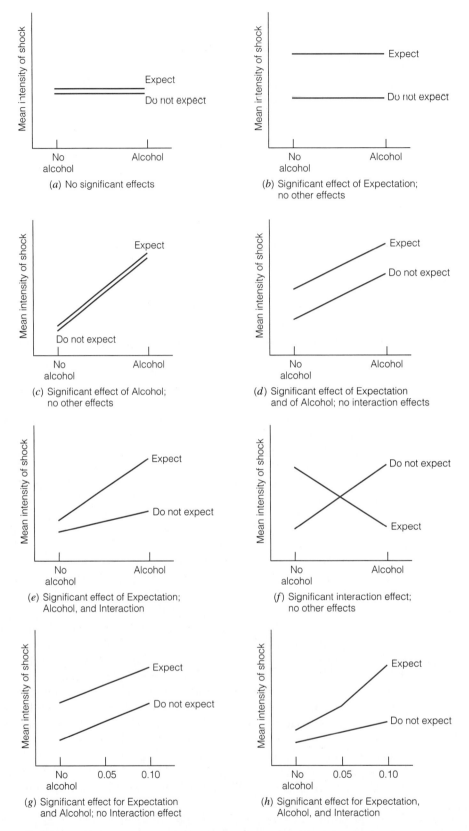

**FIGURE 21.1** Possible outcomes of a hypothetical 2 × 2 design (*a–f*) and a hypothetical 2 × 3 design (*g* and *h*) investigating the effects of alcohol consumption and the expectation of alcohol on aggression measured by the intensity of the shock administered.

had included another group with an intermediate level of alcohol consumption (e.g., a 0.05% blood-alcohol level). We show two possible outcomes in Figures 21.1*g* and 21.1*h*. Figure 21.1*g* again shows main effects for both Alcohol and Expectation but no interaction effect. Figure 21.1*h* shows an ordinal interaction effect. The difference between the expect-alcohol and do-not-expect-alcohol groups is not the same for all three levels of alcohol consumption, but the relative ranks are the same. The effect of expectancy on aggression is greater at higher levels of alcohol consumption.

The third null hypothesis to be tested, then, in a two-factor ANOVA variance is that of *no interaction*. It can be stated in general terms as follows: *When there is no interaction, the population differences in performance among the several levels of one factor are the same regardless of the level of the other factor.* If in the samples the differences among the levels of one factor fluctuate more from level to level of the other factor than would be expected on the basis of sampling variation, we reject the null hypothesis and conclude that the effects of one factor do in fact depend on the particular level of the other factor in the population.

# 21.3 The Importance of Interaction

Because a main effect is an *average effect* (i.e., it reflects the *average* difference across the levels of the other treatment variable), it can be misleading when an interaction is present. Remember Minium's First Law of Statistics: "The eyeball is the statistician's most powerful instrument." Look again at Figure 21.1*g*. In this case, we would make the general conclusion that the expect-alcohol subjects are more aggressive than the do-not-expect-alcohol subjects—it applies equally well at all levels of the second factor. However, if the results were those of Figure 21.1*h* (in which there is an ordinal interaction), the same conclusion about the main effect would be misleading. It fails to take note of the fact that the difference between expect-alcohol and do-not-expect-alcohol subjects is negligible for the no-alcohol condition, whereas the difference is large when considerable alcohol has been consumed. We should be very careful when reporting main effects if there is a disordinal interaction. In this case, we cannot interpret the main effect without referring to the interaction.

The presence of a significant interaction should therefore be a red flag to us when it comes to interpretation. *When interaction is present we should examine the effects of any factor of interest at each level of the interacting factor before making interpretations.* Certainly the best way to begin is to consult the table of cell means and a graph of these values. Remember that a two-factor design is really made up of several one-factor experiments. In addition to main effects, the factorial design also allows us to test for what are called *simple effects*. Consider, for example, a $3 \times 3$ design. If we refer to one factor as *A* and the other as *B,* then the three levels of each are $A_1$, $A_2$, and $A_3$ and $B_1$, $B_2$, and $B_3$, respectively. Main effects compare differences among the levels of one factor *averaged* across all levels of the other. However, this particular design consists of six one-way experiments, and if we wish, we may analyze each of them separately. Perhaps we are interested in the effects of *A* (all three levels) specifically for condition $B_2$. **Simple effects** refer to the results of these one-factor analyses. To make such comparisons, the interaction must first be significant and if so, we may use procedures such as Tukey's HSD test (Section 20.13).

**simple effects**
results of single-factor analyses (differences within a row or a column)

Sometimes the question of interaction is substantially more important than that of a main effect. Consider, for example, a study involving two methods of teaching and learners of low or high aptitude. Researchers long ago established that individuals with low aptitude learn more slowly than individuals with high aptitude; we really are not interested in confirming that effect. The real point of the study is to explore whether the relative difference in effectiveness of the two teaching methods is the same for slow learners as for fast ones, a question about the interaction between method and learning ability. It could well be, for instance, that method and learning ability interact to such a degree that one method is more effective with slow learners and the other is more effective with fast learners. A graphic display of this result would look like Figure 21.1*f.* We will explain how to interpret interaction in greater detail in Section 21.7.

## 21.4 Partition of the Sums of Squares for Two-Way ANOVA

Now let us begin the step-by-step development of two-way ANOVA for independent groups. We designate one factor the column factor (Expectation in our example, Table 21.1) and designate the other factor the row factor (Alcohol in our example). The two levels of each factor are referred to as $C_1$ and $C_2$ and as $R_1$ and $R_2$, respectively.

Recall that in one-way ANOVA we partition the total sum of squares into two parts: $SS_{total} = SS_w + SS_{bet}$. *In the two-way design, $SS_{bet}$ is further partitioned into the three parts shown in Figure 21.2:* $SS_{bet} = SS_{rows} + SS_{columns} + SS_{rows \times columns}$ (read: rows by columns). This is because in the factorial design we consider the rows and columns as groups. Of the five sums of squares to be considered, you should be able to understand the definitional (deviation-score) formulas for the first four from our earlier development of one-way ANOVA. In two-way ANOVA, $SS_{rows}$ reflects the variability due to one factor, $SS_{columns}$ reflects the variability due to the second factor, and $SS_{rows \times columns}$ reflects the interaction variability.

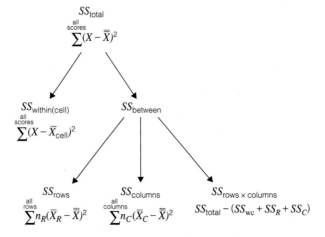

**FIGURE 21.2** Partitioning of the sums of squares for a two-way ANOVA for independent groups.

Although computer packages for factorial ANOVA designs are widely available, we will present the raw-scores formulas as well. The numbers of cases are distinguished by subscript: $n_{\text{total}}$ is the total number of cases, $n_R$ is the number of cases per row, $n_C$ is the number of cases per columns, and $n_{\text{cell}}$ is the number of cases per cell.

**$SS_{\text{total}}$**
sum of the squared deviations from the grand mean;
$$\sum_{\substack{\text{all} \\ \text{scores}}} (X - \overline{\overline{X}})^2$$

1. *Total sum of squares:* $SS_{\text{total}}$. This is identical to $SS_{\text{total}}$ in the one-way design. It is a measure of total variation present in our data and is generated from the squared deviations of the individual scores from the grand mean of all scores:

> TOTAL SUM OF SQUARES:
> DEVIATION-SCORE FORMULA
>
> $$SS_{\text{total}} = \sum_{\substack{\text{all} \\ \text{scores}}} (X - \overline{\overline{X}})^2 \qquad (21.1a)$$

> TOTAL SUM OF SQUARES:
> RAW-SCORE FORMULA
>
> $$SS_{\text{total}} = \sum_{\substack{\text{all} \\ \text{scores}}} X^2 - \frac{\left(\displaystyle\sum_{\substack{\text{all} \\ \text{scores}}} X\right)^2}{n_{\text{total}}} \qquad (21.1b)$$

**$SS_{\text{wc}}$**
sum of the squared deviations within cells (analogous to $SS_{\text{within}}$ in the single-factor ANOVA),
$$\sum_{\substack{\text{all} \\ \text{scores}}} (X - \overline{X}_{\text{cell}})^2$$

2. *Within-cells sum of squares:* $SS_{\text{wc}}$ (sometimes called $SS_{\text{error}}$). This would be the same as $SS_w$ (within-groups) in the one-way design if each cell were considered a group. It is based on the squared deviations of the individual scores from their cell means:

> WITHIN-CELLS SUM OF SQUARES:
> DEVIATION-SCORE FORMULA
>
> $$SS_{\text{wc}} = \sum_{\substack{\text{all} \\ \text{scores}}} (X - \overline{X}_{\text{cell}})^2 \qquad (21.2a)$$

> WITHIN-CELLS SUM OF SQUARES:
> RAW-SCORE FORMULA
>
> $$SS_{\text{wc}} = \sum_{\substack{\text{all} \\ \text{cells}}} \left[ \sum X^2 - \frac{\left(\sum X\right)^2}{n_{\text{cell}}} \right] \qquad (21.2b)$$

or

> WHEN EQUAL *n* PER CELL
>
> $$SS_{\text{wc}} = \sum_{\substack{\text{all} \\ \text{scores}}} X^2 - \frac{\displaystyle\sum_{\substack{\text{all} \\ \text{cells}}} \left(\sum_{}^{\text{cell}} X\right)^2}{n_{\text{cell}}} \qquad (21.2c)$$

**$SS_R$**
sum of the
squared devia-
tions for rows
(one factor);
$\sum\limits_{\substack{\text{all}\\\text{rows}}} n_R(\overline{X}_R - \overline{\overline{X}})^2$

**3.** *Row sum of squares:* $SS_R$. This is analogous to $SS_{bet}$ in the one-way design where each row is considered a group. It is based on the squared deviations of the row means from the grand mean:

> ROW SUM OF SQUARES: DEVIATION-SCORE FORMULA
>
> $$SS_R = \sum\limits_{\substack{\text{all}\\\text{rows}}} n_R(\overline{X}_R - \overline{\overline{X}})^2 \tag{21.3a}$$
>
> ROW SUM OF SQUARES: RAW-SCORE FORMULA
>
> $$SS_R = \left[ \frac{\left(\sum X_{R_1}\right)^2}{n_{R_1}} + \frac{\left(\sum X_{R_2}\right)^2}{n_{R_2}} + \cdots \right] - \frac{\left(\sum\limits^{\substack{\text{all}\\\text{scores}}} X\right)^2}{n_{\text{total}}} \tag{21.3b}$$

or

> WHEN EQUAL $n$ PER ROW
>
> $$SS_R = \left[ \frac{\left(\sum X_{R_1}\right)^2 + \left(\sum X_{R_2}\right)^2 + \cdots}{n_R} \right] - \frac{\left(\sum\limits^{\substack{\text{all}\\\text{scores}}} X\right)^2}{n_{\text{total}}} \tag{21.3c}$$

**$SS_C$**
sum of the
squared deviations
for columns
(other factor)
$\sum\limits_{\substack{\text{all}\\\text{columns}}} n_C(\overline{X}_C - \overline{\overline{X}})^2$

**4.** *Column sum of squares:* $SS_C$. The analogy to $SS_{bet}$ holds here as well, except now the columns become the groups. $SS_C$ is generated from the squared deviations of the column means from the grand mean:

> COLUMN SUM OF SQUARES: DEVIATION-SCORE FORMULA
>
> $$SS_C = \sum\limits_{\substack{\text{all}\\\text{columns}}} n_C(\overline{X}_C - \overline{\overline{X}})^2 \tag{21.4a}$$
>
> COLUMN SUM OF SQUARES: RAW-SCORE FORMULA
>
> $$SS_C = \left[ \frac{\left(\sum X_{C_1}\right)^2}{n_{C_1}} + \frac{\left(\sum X_{C_2}\right)^2}{n_{C_2}} + \cdots \right] - \frac{\left(\sum\limits^{\substack{\text{all}\\\text{scores}}} X\right)^2}{n_{\text{total}}} \tag{21.4b}$$

or

> WHEN EQUAL $n$ PER COLUMN
>
> $$SS_C = \left[ \frac{\left(\sum X_{C_1}\right)^2 + \left(\sum X_{C_2}\right)^2 + \cdots}{n_C} \right] - \frac{\left(\sum\limits^{\substack{\text{all}\\\text{scores}}} X\right)^2}{n_{\text{total}}} \tag{21.4c}$$

**$SS_{R \times C}$**
interaction sum
of squares;
$SS_{total} - (SS_{wc} +$
$SS_R + SS_C)$

**5.** *Interaction sum of squares:* $SS_{R \times C}$ (read: row by column sum of squares). This is the new element. $SS_{R \times C}$ is generated from the squared deviations of the cell means from what would be predicted were there no interaction. Because the several components ($SS_{wc}$, $SS_R$, $SS_C$, and $SS_{R \times C}$) sum to $SS_{total}$, we may find $SS_{R \times C}$ most easily by subtraction:

INTERACTION SUM OF SQUARES

$$SS_{R \times C} = SS_{total} - (SS_{wc} + SS_R + SS_C) \tag{21.5}$$

Be sure to check your calculations; an error anywhere along the line will also cause an error in $SS_{R \times C}$. Remember also that a negative sum of squares is impossible; it results from an error in calculation.

As an example, refer again to Table 21.1. We will calculate the various sums of squares in our Alcohol $\times$ Expectation example. We start, as in one-way ANOVA, by obtaining $\Sigma X$ and $\Sigma X^2$ for each group—in this case for each cell. These are the basic building blocks from which all other computations flow.

|  | $C_1$ | $C_2$ |
|---|---|---|
| $R_1$ | $\sum X = 6 + 8 + \cdots + 5 = 64$ <br> $\sum X^2 = 36 + 64 + \cdots + 25 = 432$ | $\sum X = 6 + 3 + \cdots + 3 = 40$ <br> $\sum X^2 = 36 + 9 + \cdots + 9 = 176$ |
| $R_2$ | $\sum X = 5 + 7 + \cdots + 6 = 60$ <br> $\sum X^2 = 25 + 49 + \cdots + 36 = 380$ | $\sum X = 5 + 3 + \cdots + 4 = 35$ <br> $\sum X^2 = 25 + 9 + \cdots + 16 = 130$ |

Although we would not use a table like this in practice, it *is* a good idea to record the values of $\Sigma X$ and $\Sigma X^2$ obtained in an appropriate cell diagram of the two-way design, as shown in the following table:

| | | $C_1$ | $C_2$ | |
|---|---|---|---|---|
| $n_{cell} = 10$ | $R_1$ | $\sum X = 64$ | $\sum X = 40$ | $\sum X_{R_1} = 104$ |
| $n_R = 20$ | | $\sum X^2 = 432$ | $\sum X^2 = 176$ | |
| $n_C = 20$ | $R_2$ | $\sum X = 60$ | $\sum X = 35$ | $\sum X_{R_2} = 95$ |
| | | $\sum X^2 = 380$ | $\sum X^2 = 130$ | |
| $n_{total} = 40$ | | $\sum X_{C_1} = 124$ | $\sum X_{C_2} = 75$ | $\overset{\text{all scores}}{\sum} X = 199$ |
| | | | | $\overset{\text{all scores}}{\sum} X^2 = 1{,}118$ |

From the diagram, it is a simple matter to obtain the necessary quantities for use in the raw-score formulas. First, for row 1 we add values of $\Sigma X$ across the row to obtain $\Sigma X_{R_1} = 104$; we then do the same for the remaining row(s). Second, for column 1 we add the values of $\Sigma X$ down through the rows to obtain $\Sigma X_{C_1} = 124$; we then do the same for the remaining column(s). Third, we add the values of $\Sigma X$ and $\Sigma X^2$ for all cells to obtain

$$\overset{\substack{\text{all} \\ \text{scores}}}{\sum} X = 199 \quad \text{and} \quad \overset{\substack{\text{all} \\ \text{scores}}}{\sum} X^2 = 1{,}118.$$

Now we have the appropriate values to substitute in the raw-score formulas:

$$SS_{\text{total}} = \overset{\substack{\text{all} \\ \text{scores}}}{\sum} X^2 - \frac{\left(\overset{\substack{\text{all} \\ \text{scores}}}{\sum} X\right)^2}{n_{\text{total}}} = 1{,}118 - \frac{199^2}{40} = 127.98$$

$$SS_{\text{wc}} = \overset{\substack{\text{all} \\ \text{scores}}}{\sum} X^2 - \frac{\overset{\substack{\text{all} \\ \text{cells}}}{\sum}\left(\overset{\text{cell}}{\sum} X\right)^2}{n_{\text{cell}}} = 1{,}118 - \frac{64^2 + 40^2 + 60^2 + 35^2}{10} = 65.9$$

$$SS_{\text{R}} = \left[\frac{\left(\sum X_{R_1}\right)^2 + \left(\sum X_{R_2}\right)^2}{n_R}\right] - \frac{\left(\overset{\substack{\text{all} \\ \text{scores}}}{\sum} X\right)^2}{n_{\text{total}}} = \frac{104^2 + 95^2}{20} - \frac{199^2}{40} = 2.02$$

$$SS_{\text{C}} = \left[\frac{\left(\sum X_{C_1}\right)^2 + \left(\sum X_{C_2}\right)^2}{n_C}\right] - \frac{\left(\overset{\substack{\text{all} \\ \text{scores}}}{\sum} X\right)^2}{n_{\text{total}}} = \frac{124^2 + 75^2}{20} - \frac{199^2}{40} = 60.02$$

$$SS_{R \times C} = SS_{\text{total}} - (SS_{\text{wc}} + SS_{\text{R}} + SS_{\text{C}})$$

$$= 127.98 - (65.9 + 2.02 + 60.02)$$

$$= .04$$

## 21.5 Degrees of Freedom

Just as with one-way ANOVA, the total degrees of freedom is divided into components associated with each sum of squares:

**$df_{\text{total}}$**
$n_{\text{total}} - 1$

$$df_{\text{total}} = df_{\text{wc}} + df_C + df_R + df_{R \times C}$$

As before, $df_{\text{total}} = n_{\text{total}} - 1$. In counting degrees of freedom for the other sources of variation, we shall let $C$ equal the number of columns, $R$ equal the number of rows, and $n_{\text{wc}}$ equal the number of scores within each cell. Because there are $C$ deviations involved in the computation of $SS_C$, $df_C = C - 1$; similarly, $df_R = R - 1$. In computing $SS_{\text{wc}}$, we consider the deviation of each score in the cell from the cell mean. Consequently, each cell contributes $n_{\text{wc}} - 1$ degrees of freedom, and

**$df_R$**
$R - 1$

**$df_C$**
$C - 1$

**$df_{\text{wc}}$**
$\overset{\substack{\text{all} \\ \text{cells}}}{\sum}(n_{\text{wc}} - 1)$

$$df_{\text{wc}} = \overset{\substack{\text{all} \\ \text{cells}}}{\sum}(n_{\text{wc}} - 1)$$

**$df_{R \times C}$**
$(R - 1)(C - 1)$

Finally, $df_{R \times C} = (R - 1)(C - 1)$.

In our example (Table 21.1), we calculate the degrees of freedom as follows:

$$df_{total} = 40 - 1 = 39$$
$$df_C = 2 - 1 = 1$$
$$df_R = 2 - 1 = 1$$
$$df_{R \times C} = (2 - 1)(2 - 1) = 1$$
$$df_{wc} = (10 - 1) + (10 - 1) + (10 - 1) + (10 - 1) = 36$$

## 21.6 Variance Estimates and *F* Tests

$s_{wc}^2$
the within-cells variance estimate; an estimate of inherent variance only;
$\dfrac{SS_{wc}}{df_{wc}}$

To calculate an unbiased estimate of the population variance, you recall, we must divide the sum of squares by its degrees of freedom (Section 13.9). We can calculate four variance estimates by dividing $SS_{wc}$, $SS_R$, $SS_C$, and $SS_{R \times C}$ by their respective degrees of freedom.

$$s_{wc}^2 = \frac{SS_{wc}}{df_{wc}} \xrightarrow{\text{estimates}} \text{inherent variance } (\sigma^2)$$

As in the single-factor analysis, the within–cells value is an estimate of inherent variance $(\sigma^2)$ only and is sometimes called the *error variance*. It is unaffected by row, column, or interaction effects. The inherent variation is assumed to be equal across all populations (cells)—see Section 21.10.

$s_R^2$
the rows variance estimate; an estimate of inherent variance plus main effect for the row factor;
$\dfrac{SS_R}{df_R}$

$$s_R^2 = \frac{SS_R}{df_R} \xrightarrow{\text{estimates}} \text{inherent variance } + \text{ main effect for the row factor}$$

If $\mu_{R_1} = \mu_{R_2} = \ldots$, then the variation among the row means ($\overline{X}_{R_1}, \overline{X}_{R_2}, \ldots$) will reflect only inherent variation. Under these circumstances, $s_R^2$ will estimate the same quantity estimated by $s_{wc}^2$. If there is a difference among the levels of the row factor, $s_R^2$ will tend to be larger than $s_{wc}^2$. It is therefore analogous to $s_{bet}^2$ in one-way ANOVA.

$s_C^2$
the columns variance estimate; an estimate of inherent variance plus main effect for the column factor;
$\dfrac{SS_C}{df_C}$

$$s_C^2 = \frac{SS_C}{df_C} \xrightarrow{\text{estimates}} \text{inherent variance } + \text{ main effect for the column factor}$$

If the independent variable represented in the columns has no effect, then $\mu_{C_1} = \mu_{C_2} = \ldots$, and the variation among the column means ($\overline{X}_{C_1}, \overline{X}_{C_2}, \ldots$) will reflect only inherent variation. It is therefore just like $s_R^2$, except that it is sensitive to column effect rather than to row effect.

$s_{R \times C}^2$
the interaction variance estimate; an estimate of inherent variance plus interaction effect;
$\dfrac{SS_{R \times C}}{df_{R \times C}}$

$$s_{R \times C}^2 = \frac{SS_{R \times C}}{df_{R \times C}} \xrightarrow{\text{estimates}} \text{inherent variance } + \text{ interaction effect}$$

If there is no interaction in the populations, $s_{R \times C}^2$ will be responsive only to inherent variation and will estimate the same quantity estimated by $s_{wc}^2$. If interaction is present, $s_{R \times C}^2$ will respond to it and will therefore tend to be larger.

In one-way ANOVA, we created an *F* ratio by dividing $s_{bet}^2$ by $s_w^2$, each an estimate of inherent variation if the null hypothesis is true. Here, we have three *F* ratios calculated by dividing $s_C^2$, $s_R^2$, and $s_{R \times C}^2$ by $s_{wc}^2$. As before, we organize our calculations into a *summary table,* as shown in Table 21.2. We obtain the critical values of *F* from

**TABLE 21.2**    *General Form and Example of the Two-Factor ANOVA Summary Table*

| SOURCE | SS | df | $s^2$ | $F_{\text{calc}}$ |
|---|---|---|---|---|
| Rows | Formulas 21.3a, 21.3b, or 21.3c | $R - 1$ | $\dfrac{SS_R}{df_R}$ | $\dfrac{s_R^2}{s_{\text{wc}}^2}$ |
| Columns | Formulas 21.4a, 21.4b, or 21.4c | $C - 1$ | $\dfrac{SS_C}{df_C}$ | $\dfrac{s_C^2}{s_{\text{wc}}^2}$ |
| Rows × Columns | Formula 21.5 | $(R - 1)(C - 1)$ | $\dfrac{SS_{R \times C}}{df_{R \times C}}$ | $\dfrac{s_{R \times C}^2}{s_{\text{wc}}^2}$ |
| Within cells | Formula 21.2a, 21.2b, or 21.2c | $\displaystyle\sum_{}^{\substack{\text{all} \\ \text{cells}}} (n_{\text{wc}} - 1)$ | $\dfrac{SS_{\text{wc}}}{df_{\text{wc}}}$ | |
| Total | $SS_{\text{wc}} + SS_R + SS_C + SS_{R \times C}$ | $n_{\text{total}} - 1$ | | |

| SOURCE | SS | df | $s^2$ | $F_{\text{calc}}$ |
|---|---|---|---|---|
| Rows | 2.02 | 1 | 2.02 | 1.10 |
| Columns | 60.02 | 1 | 60.02 | 32.80 |
| Rows × Columns | .04 | 1 | .04 | .02 |
| Within cells | 65.90 | 36 | 1.83 | |
| Total | 127.98 | 39 | | |

**F ratios**

$$\frac{s_R^2}{s_{\text{wc}}^2}, \; \frac{s_C^2}{s_{\text{wc}}^2}, \; \frac{s_{R \times C}^2}{s_{\text{wc}}^2};$$

$$\frac{\text{inherent}}{\text{variance}} + \frac{\text{treatment}}{\text{effect}}$$

*inherent variance,*

when there is no treatment effect, the ratio should approximate 1.0

Table E of Appendix E to learn what magnitude we must reach or exceed to declare significance.

In our example, all three *F* ratios have 1 *df* associated with the numerator and 36 *df* associated with the denominator. Thus the critical value of *F* is the same for all three, 4.11 ($\alpha = .05$). Only the obtained value of *F* for the column effect exceeds its critical value; consequently, we reject the null hypothesis that $\mu_{C_1} = \mu_{C_2}$. These results do, in fact, mimic those found by Lang's research team in their study.

## 21.7 Studying the Outcome of Two-Factor Analysis of Variance

It is ironic that the two forms of ANOVA that we have studied are fundamentally tests about means and their relationships, yet it is possible to complete the *F* tests without ever calculating a single mean (and some research reports actually do omit this computation). Calculation of cell and marginal means ought to be a routine part of ANOVA. If any of the three *F* tests is significant, for example, you should always organize the cell means in table or group form. Always look carefully at the means and their relationship to one another to see if the results make sense. If they do not, the first step is to hunt for possible computational error.

For the present problem, a graph of the four cell means would look almost exactly like Figure 21.1b. This figure shows that the male social drinkers who expected alcohol gave higher intensity shocks than did those who did not expect alcohol, regardless of actual alcohol consumption. There was no significant effect for Alcohol, and the nonsignificant interaction component is reflected by the fact that the two lines are reasonably parallel. Thus the main effect of Expectation is generalizable to both levels of alcohol consumption used in the experiment.

If one or both of our main effects prove to be significant, we may then use Tukey's HSD test (or another *post hoc* test) to determine which levels of a factor differ from others:

**Tukey's HSD test**
a commonly used *post hoc* test; critical *HSD* value = $q\sqrt{\dfrac{s^2_{wc}}{n}}$

**TUKEY'S HSD TEST FOR FACTORIAL DESIGNS**

$$HSD = q\sqrt{\frac{s^2_{wc}}{n}} \qquad (21.6)$$

*where:*  $n$ = the number of cases per row or per column.
   $q$ = depends on the number of levels for the factor being tested.

**q**
studentized range statistic

Of course, we would use a *post hoc* test only if there are more than two levels. If we find a significant main effect for a factor with only two levels, as in our example, we already know that the two levels are different.

When the interaction is significant, we must also analyze it. This is not as easy as many people think. In fact, a survey of published research articles found that 99% of investigators who employed factorial designs had not interpreted their interaction effect in an unequivocally correct manner (Rosnow & Rosenthal, 1989b). To interpret interactions correctly, we must do more than just look at original cell means because these reflect main effects as well as interaction. We must instead look at the "corrected" cell means—the cell means *after* the main effects have been removed (Rosnow & Rosenthal, 1991, 1995).

As an example, consider the following four original cell means of a 2 × 2 design:

|  |  | Factor B $B_1$ | Factor B $B_2$ | Row means |
|---|---|:---:|:---:|:---:|
| Factor A | $A_1$ | 5 | 5 | 5 |
|  | $A_2$ | 7 | 9 | 8 |
| Column means |  | 6 | 7 | $\overline{\overline{X}} = 6.5$ |

If we were to interpret the interaction by looking only at the differences among the original cell means, as many researchers do, we would wind up with a rank ordering of $A_2B_2 > A_2B_1 > A_1B_1 = A_1B_2$. However, to look at the interaction only, we must first subtract the other influences:

**CORRECTED CELL MEANS FOR
INTERPRETING INTERACTION**

$$\textit{cell mean} - (\textit{row effect} + \textit{column effect} + \overline{\overline{X}}) \qquad (21.7)$$

*where:*   *row effect* = the row mean minus the grand mean ($\overline{\overline{X}}$).
   *column effect* = the column mean minus the grand mean.

Let us now make the corrections for the cell means:

$$A_1B_1: 5 - [(5 - 6.5) + (6 - 6.5) + 6.5] = +0.5$$
$$A_1B_2: 5 - [(5 - 6.5) + (7 - 6.5) + 6.5] = -0.5$$
$$A_2B_1: 7 - [(8 - 6.5) + (6 - 6.5) + 6.5] = -0.5$$
$$A_2B_2: 9 - [(8 - 6.5) + (7 - 6.5) + 6.5] = +0.5$$

In this example, a graphic representation of just the interaction effect is X-shaped, but the effect is small. If the main effects were large, the effect of one factor would vary only slightly across the two levels of the other.

## 21.8 Effect Size

Just as with $t$ or one-way ANOVA, we can (and should) measure the magnitude of experimental effect. First, review Section 20.11. Recall that two measures of effect size used with one-way ANOVA are eta-squared ($\eta^2$) and omega-squared ($\hat{\omega}^2$). These two measures are generally used with the factorial design as well.

**eta-squared ($\eta^2$)**
an *r* family measure of effect size

**Eta-squared** is the easier of the two—all we do is divide the sum of squares by the total sum of squares. This provides us with the proportion of variance in the dependent variable accounted for by the main and interaction effects:

FORMULAS FOR ETA-SQUARED

$$\eta^2_{\text{rows}} = \frac{SS_R}{SS_{\text{total}}}$$

$$\eta^2_{\text{columns}} = \frac{SS_C}{SS_{\text{total}}}$$    (21.8)

$$\eta^2_{R\times C} = \frac{SS_{R\times C}}{SS_{\text{total}}}$$

**partial omega-squared ($\hat{\omega}^2$)**
an *r* family measure of effect size; the degree of association between the dependent variable and the experimental effect for each factor

In our example (Table 21.2), $\eta^2_R = .016$, $\eta^2_C = .469$, and $\eta^2_{R\times C} = .000$. Thus, there was a strong effect for columns (Expectations) and weak effects for rows (Alcohol) and interaction.

Eta-squared is frequently used, and it is easy to calculate, but recall from Section 20.11 that this measure is also biased. A better measure of effect size is called **partial omega-squared** (Keren & Lewis, 1979). Effect size as calculated by $\hat{\omega}^2$ is not influenced by the other experimental design effects. The general formula for $\hat{\omega}^2$ is as follows:

$$\hat{\omega}^2 = \frac{\textit{Estimated variance (For R, C, or R} \times \textit{C)}}{\textit{Estimated variance (for R, C, or R} \times \textit{C) + Estimated variance within cells}}$$

The computational formulas are as follows:

COMPUTATIONAL FORMULAS FOR
PARTIAL OMEGA-SQUARED

$$\hat{\omega}_R^2 = \frac{(R-1)(F_R - 1)}{(R-1)(F_{R-1}) + n_{cell}\, RC}$$

$$\hat{\omega}_C^2 = \frac{(C-1)(F_C - 1)}{(C-1)(F_C - 1) + n_{cell}\, RC} \tag{21.9}$$

$$\hat{\omega}_{R \times C}^2 = \frac{(R-1)(C-1)(F_{R \times C} - 1)}{(R-1)(C-1)(F_{R \times C} - 1) + n_{cell}\, RC}$$

*where:*   $R$ = number of rows.
$C$ = number of columns.
$F_R$ = value of $F$ for rows.
$F_C$ = value of $F$ for columns.
$F_{R \times C}$ = value of $F$ for interaction.

Partial omega-squared provides us with the degree of association between the dependent variable and the experimental effect for each factor. In our example (Table 21.2), $\hat{\omega}_R^2 = .002$, $\hat{\omega}_C^2 = .443$, and $\hat{\omega}_{R \times C}^2 = .000$.

## 21.9 Planned Comparisons

**planned (*a priori*) comparisons**
tests used in place of ANOVA when the researcher knows in advance which comparisons are of interest

We do not wish to discourage the comparing and ranking of the original cell means. In fact, the investigator may be primarily concerned with these individual comparisons. As with the one-way design, if theory or logic suggests that particular comparisons are important, then **planned comparisons** are better than omnibus tests of significance such as $F$ (see Section 20.15).

Planned comparisons, you recall, are the most powerful tests the investigator can use to discover a difference, if one exists. In a $2 \times 2$ factorial design, in which there are four treatment groups, we could use the contrasts $(1, 1, -1, -1)$, $(1, -1, 1, -1)$, and $(1, -1, -1, 1)$. These could be described as providing "row," "column," and "interaction" effects, respectively. Be sure to review Section 20.15 and the Point of Controversy in Chapter 20 carefully.

## 21.10 Assumptions of the Two-Factor Design and the Problem of Unequal Numbers of Scores

The assumptions for the two-factor ANOVA are the same as for one-way ANOVA: independence of the samples in the cells, random sampling, homogeneity of variance ($\sigma^2$ is the same for all cells), and normality of the cell populations (Section 20.10). Violations of the latter two assumptions generally have little effect when there are equal numbers of cases for each level.

In one-way ANOVA, we were able to assign a different number of subjects to the several levels of the treatment variable without serious consequences. However, keeping the number of cases equal is more critical in two-way ANOVA. *The procedures in this chapter assume an equal number of subjects.* If the number of cases per cell is unequal, adjustments have to be made to the data before proceeding. These adjustments, which may reduce power or require some new assumptions that cannot easily be verified, are beyond the scope of this book. Should you need to use these procedures, see Keppel (1991) or Winer, Brown, and Michels (1991).

## 21.11  Summary

In this chapter, we extended the notions of ANOVA to situations involving two treatment variables. The two variables are called factors, and the various conditions of each are referred to as levels. One advantage of the two-way design is that we can use the same subjects to examine the effects of both variables simultaneously. A second advantage is that our conclusions can be broader—we can make conclusions about each variable for all the conditions (levels) of the other.

In the two-factor ANOVA with independent groups, we test three null hypotheses about the means of various populations: (1) the hypothesis of no difference among the levels of the row factor, (2) the hypothesis of no difference among the levels of the column factor, and (3) the hypothesis of no interaction between the row and column factors. For the first two, a significant *F* ratio is referred to as a main effect—a finding of differences among the levels of that factor *averaged* across the levels of the other factor. Thus, the *F* test for a main effect is analogous to a one-way ANOVA.

Interaction refers to the joint effect of the two independent variables (factors) on the dependent variable. A significant interaction effect indicates that the effect of one factor differs from level to level of the second factor, and vice versa. If interaction is present, the main effect of a factor can be misleading, for it will not apply equally at all levels of the other factor. The ability to examine interaction is the third important advantage of the two-way design over the one-way design.

## Key Terms, Concepts, and Symbols

| | | |
|---|---|---|
| factor   (424) | ordinal interaction   (427) | $SS_{R \times C}$   (433) |
| two-factor analysis of variance design   (425) | disordinal interaction   (427) | $df_{total}$, $df_{wc}$, $df_R$, $df_C$, $df_{R \times C}$   (434) |
| levels   (425) | null hypothesis of no interaction   (429) | $\sigma^2$   (435) |
| cell   (425) | simple effect   (429) | $s^2_{wc}$, $s^2_R$, $s^2_C$, $s^2_{R \times C}$   (435) |
| main effect   (426) | $SS_{total}$   (431) | Tukey's HSD test   (437) |
| main effect null hypothesis   (426) | $SS_{wc}$   (431) | $\eta^2$   (438) |
| interaction   (426) | $SS_R$   (432) | partial omega-squared   (438) |
| | $SS_C$   (432) | $\hat{\omega}^2$   (438) |
| | | planned comparisons   (408, 439) |

# Problems

☐ *c* 8, 9

1. Suppose an educational psychologist is carrying out an experiment in which grade-school children hear one of four stories: (1) a stereotypical (and sexist) story in which a boy is the active hero while a girl just passively watches him, (2) a reverse-stereotype story in which a girl is active while a boy just watches, (3) a story in which both a boy and a girl are active, or (4) a story in which both a boy and a girl are passive. Of the children who hear a given story, 15 are male and 15 female. After hearing the story (whichever of the four kinds it is), each subject is given an opportunity to work at the mildly frustrating task of using long-handled spoons to rearrange a terrarium in a narrow-necked jar. The psychologist observes how long the subject persists at the task. This experiment has which kind of design? (a) A one-way design in which type of story is the treatment variable. (b) A one-way design in which sex of subject is the treatment variable. (c) A two-way design in which type of story and sex of subject are the treatment variables. (d) A two-way design in which type of story and persistence at the task are the treatment variables. Explain.

2. (a) In the experiment described in Problem 1, how many levels does the factor Type of Story have? (b) How many cells are there? (c) Explain what a finding of main effect for Type of Story means here.

3. Which of the following outcomes for the experiment described in Problem 1 would indicate interaction between Type of Story and Sex of subject for the samples on hand? (a) The mean persistence score for all boys equals the mean persistence score for all girls. (b) The mean persistence score for all children who hear a given story is the same for all four stories. (c) The mean persistence score for all boys is 18.3 sec longer than the mean persistence score for all girls. (d) The mean persistence score for boys is greater than that for girls when the story the child just heard featured an active male character, but it is lower than the mean persistence

score for girls when the story featured an active female character. Explain.

4. "A good way to begin the computation of a two-way ANOVA is to find for each cell the number of raw scores, the sum of them, and the sum of their squares." Would you agree with this statement? Explain.

5. An experimenter wishes to evaluate the effectiveness of four teaching methods among three kinds of students. The study is conducted as a two-way ANOVA, and each combination of method and type of student is represented by five subjects. (a) What $df$ characterizes each of the $SS$'s that will be calculated? (b) If the tests are conducted at the 5% level of significance, what is the critical value of $F$ for testing difference among methods? For testing difference among types of students? For testing interaction?

## DATA 21A

| SOURCE | df | $s^2$ | F |
|---|---|---|---|
| Columns | 4 | 18.0 | |
| Rows | 3 | 36.0 | |
| Columns × rows | | 30.0 | |
| Within cells | — | 12.0 | |
| Total | | | |

6. Relative to Data 21A, suppose that 5 subjects had been assigned to each cell. (a) State the values of $df_{R\times C}$, $df_{wc}$, and $df_{total}$. (b) Make the possible $F$ tests, using $\alpha = .05$. (c) What can we say about the meaning of the outcome of the test for row effect?

7. Examine the graphs of the cell means from three 2 × 3 analyses of variance and one 3 × 3 ANOVA shown in Figure 21.3. Suppose that in each case all three $F$ tests (row, column, and interaction) proved to be significant. (a) Which interactions are ordinal and which are disordinal? (b) In which case(s) would conclusions based on a main effect for row factor alone be misleading? Explain.

8. An experiment was designed to test the relative effectiveness of a computer-taught

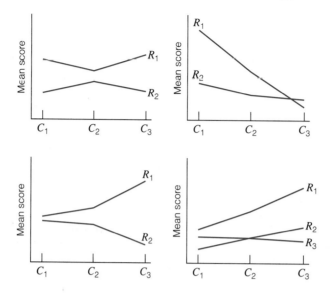

**FIGURE 21.3**

method of instruction as compared with a conventional lecture method. Two samples of three subjects each were selected from among students of good aptitude and assigned to the two methods of instruction, as shown in Data 21B. Two samples of the same size were selected from among students of ordinary ability and assigned to the same methods of instruction (also shown in Data 21B). In the test trial, the 12 students earned the scores shown in Data 21B. (a) Find $df_{\text{total}}$, $df_C$, $df_R$, $df_{\text{wc}}$, $df_{R \times C}$. (b) Find $SS_{\text{total}}$, $SS_C$, $SS_R$, $SS_{\text{wc}}$, and $SS_{R \times C}$. (c) Calculate the several variance estimates appropriate to a two-way ANOVA, and present the results thus far developed in an analysis of variance table. (d) Calculate the $F$'s required to test the main effects and the interaction effect. Draw the statistical conclusions appropriate when $\alpha = .05$ and $\alpha = .01$. (e) Calculate the effect size, $\hat{\omega}^2$. (f) Construct a graph of the cell

### DATA 21B

|                  | Computer-taught | Lecture method |
|------------------|-----------------|----------------|
| *Bright students*   | 5, 7, 9         | 10, 11, 15     |
| *Ordinary students* | 5, 10, 9        | 4, 8, 6        |

means in the manner of Figure 21.1. (g) In the light of the statistical outcome (d) and the graph (e), what appears to be the essential outcome of the study?

9. In a learning experiment, we want to know whether there is a difference in performance among three kinds of motivation and also whether there is a difference between two conditions of practice. The table below shows the 12 scores that might be obtained in such a study, if two subjects were assigned at random to each of the six possible combinations of motivation and condition of practice. (a) Complete the two-way ANOVA with summary table. (b) Calculate the effect sizes; $\hat{\omega}^2$. (c) Construct a graph of the cell means.

|                     |       | Kind of motivation |        |         |
|---------------------|-------|--------------------|--------|---------|
|                     |       | $C_1$              | $C_2$  | $C_3$   |
| *Condition of practice* | $R_1$ | 4, 4            | 2, 3   | 8, 6    |
|                     | $R_2$ | 6, 8               | 5, 4   | 10, 13  |

10. For Data 21B (Problem 8), calculate the corrected cell means necessary to interpret the interaction effect.

# Chapter $22$

## Some (Almost) Assumption-Free Tests

When you have finished studying this chapter, you should be able to:

- Understand that parametric tests, such as $t$ and $F$, make the assumption that the population(s) from which we draw our sample(s) is normally distributed;

- Explain why, when sample size is small, violations of this assumption may lead to incorrect conclusions when using $t$ or $F$;

- Understand that assumption-freer tests (e.g., randomization tests, rank-order tests) do not make assumptions about the underlying population(s), and are more powerful than parametric tests when the population is not normally distributed and sample size is small; and

- Calculate the Mann-Whitney $U$ test, the sign test, the Wilcoxon signed-ranks test, the Kruskal-Wallis test, and Friedman's rank test.

The inferential statistical techniques that we have considered up to this point—$t$, $F$, and $\chi^2$—are widely used, but they require assumptions about population distributions that may be incorrect in a lot of cases. For example, the $t$ and $F$ tests of the difference between (among) means of independent samples assume normality of the group

**nonparamet-
ric statistics**

tests that do not
test hypotheses
about popula-
tion parameters

**distribution-
free methods**

tests that do not
make any as-
sumptions about
the shape of the
population(s)
from which the
sample is (are)
drawn

**assumption-
freer tests**

tests that make
fewer assump-
tions than the
traditional para-
metric tests
such as *t* or *F*

populations and homogeneity of variance. However, as you have learned, many real-world variables are distributed in a manner that differs substantially from normality (Micceri, 1989; see Point of Controversy in Chapter 7). Moderate departures from normality (and even substantial departures from homogeneity of variance) may not seriously invalidate these tests when sample size is moderate to large, but the problem of violation of assumptions is of great concern when sample size is small (<25). Why?

Recall from Section 12.4 that even when the population distribution greatly departs from normality, the central limit theorem states that the sampling distribution of $\overline{X}$ will nevertheless approach a normal distribution as sample size increases (and will resemble a normal curve when $n = 25$). Unless the population distribution is normal in shape, the use of samples with $n < 25$ is risky, and more so the greater the population deviates from normality.

In this chapter, we introduce some alternative procedures for testing hypotheses that make less restrictive assumptions about the population distributions. These procedures are often referred to as **nonparametric statistics** because the statistical hypotheses that are tested are not about parameters, such as $\mu$, or as **distribution-free methods** if the procedure does not make any assumptions about the shape of the population. These two terms are often used interchangeably, but they do have different meanings. Consequently, Ury (1967) suggested an alternative, more descriptive name—**assumption-freer tests.** "Freer" emphasizes that the tests are not completely free of assumptions; it is just that the assumptions are less restrictive than for *t*, *F*, or $\chi^2$. (Many people call chi-square a nonparametric test, but it does in fact assume the central limit theorem; see Bradley, 1968.)

## 22.1  The Null Hypothesis in Assumption-Freer Tests

The *t* and *F* tests focus on the mean of a distribution or the difference between means of two (or more) distributions. The techniques described here are less specific. *The usual hypothesis is simply that the distributions are not different in any respect,* rather than that there is no difference among the distributions with regard to the mean. This suggests (correctly) that "significance" could result from some unknown combination of differences in central tendency (location), variability, and symmetry. However, if distributions are not of greatly differing shape, most are indeed good tests of location (even though they do not specifically refer to a particular measure of central tendency) and may, in fact, be the preferred procedures with small sample sizes.

## 22.2  Randomization Tests

Our text follows a decades-old tradition in its focus on inferential techniques based on the statistics *t*, *F*, and $\chi^2$. One of the assumptions of these tests is that each batch of observations under analysis comes from a normally distributed population through sampling at random. In many experiments, however, the assumption of random sampling is not met. Researchers typically obtain subjects through an informal process, taking whoever is convenient. They usually introduce randomness into their investigation only in choosing which condition a subject will serve in.

In an experiment investigating the effect of aerobic exercise on depression, for example, we might enroll the next 30 female students who come to our college's health center for treatment of depression. We might then flip a coin to determine whether each participant will be subjected to the experimental treatment (a thrice-weekly aerobics class, say) or simply put on a waiting list for therapy (design from McCann & Holmes, 1984). This process is called *random assignment* or *randomization* (see Sections 15.12 and 15.13).

Statisticians have developed tests that are free of the assumptions of normality and homogeneity of variance in the parent population, and most do not require random sampling (May, Masson, & Hunter, 1997). They do require that scores or pairs of scores be independent of each other, but this is achieved by random assignment rather than random sampling. **Randomization tests** directly address the question of whether the batches of observations differ only because of chance. The essential insight from which randomization tests derive is Sir Ronald Fisher's (1935).

**randomization tests**
tests that use random assignment and compare obtained results with all possible combinations of scores

To conduct a randomization test for an experiment like the one on aerobics and depression, we start with the observations on hand, collecting them into one bunch. We then assign each observation at random to one of the two conditions. Think of the conditions as a pair of boxes resting side by side in front of us. In effect, we are tossing each score at the boxes blindly so that the scores have an equal chance to land in each box. When all scores are assigned (randomly) between the two boxes, we find the mean for each box and then the difference between the means.

Now we repeat the process. From the undifferentiated batch of scores—the actual scores that we obtained when measuring the subjects for depression—we again pull them out, one at a time (the order doesn't matter) and toss them blindly at those boxes. Again we summarize the result as the difference between the means of the two batches so created. Because of the randomness, it is unlikely that we will find the same difference that occurred the first time.

We continue to repeat the process until we have generated *all possible combinations of scores*. With many scores in each group, this may mean thousands, perhaps millions, of different combinations. Such calculations were not possible before computers, but the modern computer can do this work for us quickly. What we now have is an *actual* (not theoretical) distribution of the differences between means, each difference the result of the randomization of the scores *of our particular experiment*. We know this distribution through observation; we generated it, and we can directly look at it.

As a simple example, suppose we have six subjects that we randomly assign to one of two groups of three, and that when the study is over they have scores of 1, 2, 3, 4, 5, and 6. How many ways could the study have turned out? Look at Table 22.1. It shows that there are 20 possible outcomes (determined by $6!/(6 - 3)!3!$). However, when we compare the difference between the means of the two groups, we see that there are 10 possible outcomes, some more probable than others.

Now we simply compare the difference between the two means that turned up in our experiment with the distribution we generated. Suppose our difference proves to be small compared to most in the distribution, say, $-0.33$ or $+0.33$. This is a quite ordinary difference, one that was not included among the 5% most extreme outcomes. It is therefore plausible that the difference is due only to randomization, so we have no grounds for concluding that anything systematic caused the scores in the two conditions to differ.

Do you recognize the logic of hypothesis testing here? The null hypothesis says that our subjects' depression scores are unaffected by which condition of the experiment

TABLE 22.1 *All Possible Outcomes of Random Assignment of Six Scores to Two Groups of Three*

| OUTCOME | X | Y | $\overline{X} - \overline{Y}$ |
|---|---|---|---|
| 1 | 1, 2, 3 | 4, 5, 6 | −3.00 |
| 2 | 1, 2, 4 | 3, 5, 6 | −2.34 |
| 3 | 1, 3, 4 | 2, 5, 6 | −1.66 |
| 4 | 1, 2, 5 | 3, 4, 6 | −1.66 |
| 5 | 1, 2, 6 | 3, 4, 5 | −1.00 |
| 6 | 1, 3, 5 | 2, 4, 6 | −1.00 |
| 7 | 2, 3, 4 | 1, 5, 6 | −1.00 |
| 8 | 1, 3, 6 | 2, 4, 5 | −0.33 |
| 9 | 1, 4, 5 | 2, 3, 6 | −0.33 |
| 10 | 2, 3, 5 | 1, 4, 6 | −0.33 |
| 11 | 2, 3, 6 | 1, 4, 5 | +0.33 |
| 12 | 2, 4, 5 | 1, 3, 6 | +0.33 |
| 13 | 1, 4, 6 | 2, 3, 5 | +0.33 |
| 14 | 1, 5, 6 | 2, 3, 4 | +1.00 |
| 15 | 2, 4, 6 | 1, 3, 5 | +1.00 |
| 16 | 3, 4, 5 | 1, 2, 6 | +1.00 |
| 17 | 2, 5, 6 | 1, 3, 4 | +1.66 |
| 18 | 3, 4, 6 | 1, 2, 5 | +1.66 |
| 19 | 3, 5, 6 | 1, 2, 4 | +2.34 |
| 20 | 4, 5, 6 | 1, 2, 3 | +3.00 |

they served in. According to this null hypothesis, the two batches of scores differ only because of randomization. Because our obtained difference between the means is one of those that would be common when only randomization is at work, we retain the null hypothesis.

But perhaps the actual difference will prove to be unusual when compared to the others that constitute our distribution of such quantities. Suppose the mean for the experimental condition is so much lower than the mean for the control condition that the difference is among the most rare 5%. Now it seems implausible that the difference between the two batches is due only to randomization. Now we are justified in rejecting the null hypothesis. We may conclude that something systematic was at work. What's the risk that we are making an error? It's 5%—so we tested the null hypothesis at the .05 level of significance.

The familiar logic of hypothesis testing thus underlies a randomization test. We can employ a directional or a nondirectional alternative hypothesis, and we can choose any level of significance and thereby set our risk of a Type I error.

As the example shows, a randomization test leads directly to a conclusion of the kind an experimenter seeks: Is the difference between the batches of scores due only to chance or to something systematic? Had we drawn samples at random from the population of interest, then statistics would have also proved a basis for making generalizations to the population. However, when the groups are formed by random assignment of available subjects, the inferential statistics do not pretend to generalize

BIZARRE SEQUENCE OF COMPUTER-GENERATED RANDOM NUMBERS

© 2002 by Sidney Harris

beyond these scores. *Without random sampling (whether using parametric or assumption-freer tests), generalizations require judgment based on knowledge of the subject matter and on the similarity of new circumstances to those that characterize the previous studies of the topic* (see Sections 15.12 and 15.13).

## 22.3 Rank-Order Tests

**rank-order tests**

tests in which original scores are first transformed into ranks

Most of the assumption-freer tests you will learn to use in this chapter are called **rank-order tests**. Original scores are transformed into ranks according to magnitude. Rank-order tests make no assumption about the shape of the distribution. In fact, if there are no ties in ranks, the distribution is known—rectangular (one score at each rank). Converting original scores to ranks has another advantage in that it effectively eliminates outliers. Recall that an outlier is an anomaly, a score that is very different from the others in the distribution. An outlier or two can often eliminate the possibility of obtaining a significant difference when using a parametric test (e.g., $t$ or $F$).

After the scores are placed into ranks, we evaluate the outcome by the randomization procedures you learned in the previous section (Edgington, 1987). In essence then, these tests are really *rank-order randomization tests.* You have already been introduced to one of them. Look again at Spearman's rank-order correlation coefficient from Chapter 8. The first four statistical tests that we discuss in this chapter were all derived from randomization tests. If you are interested in how these tests were derived, see Edgington (1987). For an introduction to many other different randomization tests, see May, Masson, and Hunter (1997).

Most rank-order tests assume that the underlying variable is continuous. However, recall that many dependent variables in psychology and education are discrete variables. This can result in identical scores, which will lead to ties in ranks. Ties in ranks will usually not cause a problem until one-third of the scores result in ties. Look at Section 8.9 to review how to assign ranks to tied scores.

When the assumption of normality is met, the parametric tests (e.g., $t$ and $F$) are more powerful than the assumption-freer tests. However, when the assumptions are *not* met (which is often the case), the assumption-freer methods are more powerful. That is, they are more likely than $t$ or $F$ to give a significant result when the null hypothesis is false.

## 22.4 The Bootstrap Method of Statistical Inference

The key problem in inferential statistics is how to infer the value of a population parameter from a sample drawn from that population. Conventional statistical methods, developed between 1800 and 1930, rely on mathematical equations, such as those for $z$, $t$, and $F$, that had to be calculated by hand. (The intervention of calculators sped up the process somewhat.) As we've seen, these techniques compare an obtained sample with other samples that could be generated from the population (if the null hypothesis is true). To generate these samples, the methods generally assume that the population data are distributed normally.

**bootstrap method**
a testing technique that compares an obtained sample with (usually billions of) samples computer-generated from the original sample

In 1977, Bradley Efron, a statistician at Stanford University, invented a new method of statistical inference that takes advantage of high-speed computers (see Efron, 1979). In fact, the technique would not be possible without them. Efron's **bootstrap method** generates new samples from the original sample and requires no assumptions about the distribution of scores in the population.

To see how the bootstrap method works, let us suppose that we have randomly drawn a sample of 15 scores from a population of scores. Each of the 15 scores is copied by a computer a large number of times (a billion is not unreasonable with computers), and the 15 billion copies that result are thoroughly mixed. Thousands of additional samples, called *boot-strap samples*, of size 15 are then randomly sampled (with replacement) by the computer from this pool.

For each new sample, some of the 15 values might be drawn more than once and others not at all. The resulting range of values provides an index of the amount of variation in the statistic under examination (such as the mean). The statistical accuracy of the original sample statistic depends on the width of the interval associated with a particular percentage of all the samples. For example, if 95% of the calculated values of $\overline{X}$ are between 101 and 105, we would probably judge an original $\overline{X}$ of 103 to be highly accurate. If 95% of the $\overline{X}$'s are between 88 and 115, on the other hand, we would place less faith in our original sample statistic. The method is called the bootstrap method because "the data, in a sense, pull themselves up by their own bootstraps by generating new data sets through which their reliability can be determined" (Kolata, 1988).

How accurate is this new method? If the population from which the original sample is drawn is normally distributed, the bootstrap method and conventional methods produce the same answer. When the population deviates from normality, the bootstrap method is superior. This has been empirically demonstrated many times by drawing samples from populations with known characteristics. See Diaconis and Efron (1983) for some easy-to-understand examples.

It is probably safe to say that had inferential statistics been invented in this era of computers, its methods would be quite different from those presented in this text. New ideas take time to be accepted, but computer-intensive techniques may soon dominate statistics, and the techniques taught in this book may be relegated to a special box on "historical points of interest."

## 22.5 An Assumption-Freer Alternative to the *t* Test of a Difference between Two Independent Groups: The Mann-Whitney *U* Test

**Mann-Whitney U test**
a rank-order test of a difference between two independent groups

The **Mann-Whitney** *U* **test** is a popular alternative to the *t* test of the difference between means of two *independent* samples. We should consider using it when our measurements are weaker than interval scaling (see Section 2.3) or even with interval scale measurements when our samples are small and we have serious doubts about the distributional assumptions necessary for the *t* test.

The null hypothesis is that the two samples come from populations with the same *distribution*. If the two population distributions are of even moderately similar shape and variability, the Mann-Whitney *U* test is also an excellent test of central tendency. Because the test is on ranks, the most closely corresponding measure of central tendency is the median. Keep this in mind when evaluating the outcome of the test. (See Section 5.6 for properties of the median.)

The test is sometimes referred to as the *Wilcoxon rank-sum test*, in honor of the man who first thought of the basic idea (Wilcoxon, 1945). However, to use the rank-sum test, sample size should be at least 10 for both groups. Mann and Whitney (1947) offered a variant of the same test that we may use when sample sizes are smaller (or greater) than 10 and gave it the name *U*. We will refer to the test by their names to avoid the confusion that might result from the fact that another test described in this chapter is usually known by Wilcoxon's name (Section 22.7).

The Mann-Whitney *U* test is easy to understand at an intuitive level. Suppose there are two groups with distributions as shown in Figure 22.1*a*; we see that they overlap to a substantial extent. Suppose that we combined the two distributions and ranked all scores from 1 (the lowest score) to $n_X + n_Y$ (the highest score). If the distributions

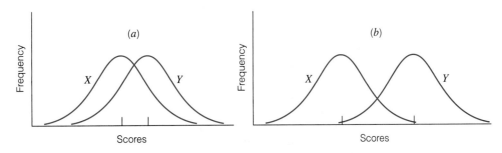

**FIGURE 22.1**  Distributions that overlap by different amounts.

overlapped perfectly, and we then summed the ranks of the $X$ scores and the ranks of the $Y$ scores, we would expect the weighted sum (in the case of unequal $n$) of the ranks to be the same for each group. However, for the distributions in Figure 22.1$a$ the ranks of the scores in the $X$ group will tend to be somewhat lower than those of the scores in the $Y$ group; consequently, the sum of the ranks of the $X$ group ($\Sigma R_X$) will tend to be lower than the sum of the ranks of the $Y$ group ($\Sigma R_Y$). If the two groups are more widely separated, as shown in Figure 22.1$b$, the discrepancy between $\Sigma R_X$ and $\Sigma R_Y$ will be even greater. The Mann-Whitney $U$ test is based on exactly this discrepancy. It derives from the probability of obtaining a sum of ranks for one distribution that differs from the expected sum of ranks (under the hypothesis of equality of the two distributions) by more than a given amount.

> $\Sigma R_X, \Sigma R_Y$
> symbols for the sum of the ranks of the $X$ and $Y$ groups

To conduct the test, we follow these procedures:

**Step 1:** Label the two groups $X$ and $Y$; *if one group contains fewer cases than the other, it must be labeled* $X$.

**Step 2:** Combine all the scores into one distribution of $n_X + n_Y$ cases. Then assign the rank of 1 to the lowest score, 2 to the next lowest, and so on, until all scores are ranked.

**Step 3:** Find $\Sigma R_X$, the sum of the ranks of all scores in the $X$ distribution.

**Step 4:** Calculate $U_X$ as follows:

> $(n_X)(n_Y) + \dfrac{n_X(n_X + 1)}{2} - \sum R_X$
>
> formula for the Mann-Whitney $U$ test

FORMULA FOR THE
MANN-WHITNEY $U$

$$U_X = (n_X)(n_Y) + \frac{n_X(n_X + 1)}{2} - \sum R_X \qquad (22.1)$$

When submitting research reports, it is necessary to provide the obtained value of $U$. However, for convenience, we provide Table J in Appendix E, which gives critical values of $\Sigma R_X$ corresponding to one-tailed probabilities of .005, .01, .025, and .05 for $n_X$ values from 3 to 15 and $n_Y$ values from 3 to 15.

**Step 5:** Locate the row of entries in Table J that corresponds to $n_X$ and $n_Y$. Then follow procedure (a), (b), or (c), depending on our alternative hypothesis:

  **a.** The alternative hypothesis, $H_A$, states only that the two population *distributions* are different in *some* way. Find the pair of numbers corresponding to the column heading equal to $\alpha/2$. (If $\alpha = .05$, use the reading designated .025.) Reject $H_0$ if $\Sigma R_{X\text{calc}}$ equals or falls below the lower number *or* if it equals or exceeds the higher number.

  **b.** $H_A: X < Y$. Find the pair of numbers corresponding to the column heading equal to $\alpha$. (If $\alpha = .05$, use the heading designated .05.) Reject $H_0$ if $\Sigma R_{X\text{calc}}$ equals or falls below the lower number.

  **c.** $H_A: X > Y$. Find the pair of numbers corresponding to the column heading equal to $\alpha$. (If $\alpha = .05$, use the heading designated .05.) Reject $H_0$ if $\Sigma R_{X\text{calc}}$ equals or exceeds the higher number.

As sample size increases, the distribution of $U$ comes to resemble a normal curve. Thus, when sample sizes are too large to use Table J, we can calculate the Mann-Whitney $U$ test statistic and use the normal-curve table (Table A):

$$\frac{U - \frac{(n_X n_Y)}{2}}{\sqrt{\dfrac{n_X n_Y (n_X + n_Y + 1)}{12}}}$$

*z formula for the Mann-Whitney U test with large samples*

MANN-WHITNEY $U$ TEST STATISTIC
FOR LARGER SAMPLES

$$z = \frac{U - \frac{(n_X n_Y)}{2}}{\sqrt{\dfrac{n_X n_Y (n_X + n_Y + 1)}{12}}} \qquad (22.2)$$

Negative values of $z$ imply $X < Y$, and positive values imply $X > Y$.

**Example**   Suppose that we gave nine children an arithmetic achievement test and record their scores. They then receive daily practice on arithmetic problems. At the end of each practice session, their papers are marked by a teacher's aide, who praises them for the number they got right and states that she thinks they might do even better in the next few days. We treat eight other children the same except for the statements of the teacher's aide. For these children, she points out the problems they missed and tells them that they should be able to do better than that. At the end of 2 weeks, we retest all children on a parallel form of the arithmetic achievement test and calculate their "gain scores" over the 2-week period:

$$\text{Criticism } (X): \quad -3 \quad -2 \quad 0 \quad 0 \quad 2 \quad 5 \quad 7 \quad 9$$
$$\text{Praise } (Y): \quad 0 \quad 2 \quad 3 \quad 4 \quad 10 \quad 12 \quad 14 \quad 19 \quad 21$$

**Solution**   When we examine these scores we see that they are skewed positively. Because the samples are fairly small, we decide to use the Mann-Whitney $U$ test rather than the $t$ test for independent means to test the null hypothesis of no difference between the population distributions. We decide to conduct a two-tailed test at the .05 level of significance.

We must first rank the scores according to Step 2 of the procedures. Note that some scores will be tied in rank. We assign ranks for these scores according to the procedure explained in Section 8.9. We then sum the $X$ ranks:

$$\text{Criticism } (X): \quad 1 \quad 2 \quad 4 \quad 4 \quad 6.5 \quad 10 \quad 11 \quad 12$$
$$\text{Praise } (Y): \quad 4 \quad 6.5 \quad 8 \quad 9 \quad 13 \quad 14 \quad 15 \quad 16 \quad 17$$

$$\sum R_X = 50.5$$

We enter Table J with $n_X = 8$, $n_Y = 9$, and $\alpha = .05$ (for a two-tailed test, we look in the column headed .025). We find that the critical values of $\Sigma R_X$ are 51 and 93. Because our obtained $\Sigma R_X = 50.5$ falls below the lower critical value, we reject the null hypothesis. The low value of $\Sigma R_X$ indicates that the gains of the criticized group generally fell below those of the praised group. This is confirmed when we note the median of the gains of the criticized group is 1, whereas that of the praised group is 10.

# Point of Controversy

## A Comparison of the *t* Test and Mann-Whitney *U* Test with Real-World Distributions

The *t* test was a notable advance in science. It has allowed researchers to apply the precise, objective methods of statistics to small samples of observations that can be gathered quickly and cheaply. Recall, however, that one of the underlying assumptions of the *t* test is that the population from which the sample(s) was drawn be normally distributed. What if the population is not normal in shape?

The traditional answer has been that the *t* test holds up well against violations of the assumption of normality. (Statisticians refer to this as *robustness*.) This conclusion was based largely on work by Boneau (1960), who examined the behavior of the *t* statistic when applied to smooth, continuous nonnormal distributions derived from mathematical models. Although others expressed some serious reservations about use of the *t* test when distributions differed more radically from those studied by Boneau (e.g., Bradley, 1978; Freedman, Pisani, & Purves, 1978, p. A20; Wilkinson, 1988, p. 717), their warnings went unheeded because there was little evidence that real-world distributions differed substantially from normality.

Recall that Micceri (1989), in a study of 440 large, real-world data sets from the social and behavioral sciences, found that none of the distributions were normal in shape, and that very few could even be described as smooth and continuous (see Point of Controversy in Chapter 7). Most distributions of data in psychology and education were multimodal, lumpy, and/or skewed. How well does the *t* test hold up in these real-world situations?

Sawilowsky and Blair (1992) examined the robustness of the independent-samples *t* test with samples drawn from distributions like those found by Micceri. Overall, the *t* test was reasonably robust *to Type I error* when (a) sample sizes were equal (or nearly so), (b) sample sizes were fairly large (25–30), and (c) tests were two-tailed. Discrepancies between nominal and actual alpha levels were usually of a conservative nature. These results agree with those by Boneau (1960). The one notable exception was when distributions were extremely skewed. In this case, the *t* test was nonrobust to Type I error.

But what about robustness to Type II error and power? Earlier studies had found that nonparametric tests were often more robust and provided greater power than the *t* test when samples were drawn from nonnormal populations (Chernoff & Savage, 1958; Neave & Granger, 1968). Sawilowsky and Blair (1992) compared the power for the *t* test and Mann-Whitney *U* test with small samples (5, 15) drawn from a very asymmetric distribution. The Mann-Whitney *U* test was clearly more powerful.

The *t* test has been in wide use for many decades and researchers will no doubt continue to use it, for traditions end slowly. This text thus devotes considerable attention to the *t* test—but you are now apprised of its limitations. When you must choose a test for comparison of small samples and have doubts about the shape of the population distribution, keep in mind the following conclusion by Sawilowsky and Blair (1992):

Researchers should not overlook robust nonparametric competitors that are often more powerful than the *t* test when its underlying assumptions are violated.

If, instead of using Table J, we figure the outcome from Formulas 22.1 and 22.2, we have:

$$U = (8)(9) + \frac{8(9)}{2} - 50.5 = 57.5$$

$$z = \frac{57.5 - \frac{(8)(9)}{2}}{\sqrt{\frac{(8)(9)(8 + 9 + 1)}{12}}} = -2.07$$

This value falls just below $z = -1.96$, the critical value of normally distributed $z$ corresponding to $\alpha = .05$ for a two-tailed test.

The Mann-Whitney $U$ test has only two assumptions: (1) independence of samples and (2) continuous scores. With a continuous variable, the possibility of ties is very low. However, the scores recorded in behavioral science research are often discrete rather than continuous, thus creating the possibility of ties. The existence of tied ranks *across* groups reduces the power of the test (i.e., makes it *more* difficult to reject $H_0$ when it is false). Fortunately, as in the example illustrated, a moderate number of tied ranks does not substantially disturb the outcome.

What about effect size? The appropriate measure for the $U$ test is the **Glass rank biserial correlation coefficient**, $r_g$:

**Glass rank biserial correlation coefficient, ($r_g$)**
a measure of effect size for $U$

FORMULA FOR $r_g$

$$r_g = \frac{2(\overline{R}_X - \overline{R}_Y)}{n_X + n_Y} \qquad (22.3)$$

*where:* $\overline{R}_X$ = the mean rank for $X$
$\overline{R}_Y$ = the mean rank for $Y$

In our example,

$$r_g = \frac{2(6.31 - 11.39)}{8 + 9}$$

$$= -.60$$

The Glass rank biserial correlation coefficient shows the strength of the relationship between $X$ and $Y$ and can take on values between $-1.00$ and $+1.00$. Thus, we interpret it much like Pearson's $r$.

## 22.6 An Assumption-Freer Alternative to the $t$ Test of a Difference between Two Dependent Groups: The Sign Test

The sign test and the Wilcoxon signed-ranks test are commonly used to test for a difference in location between two *dependent* samples. Both are assumption-freer alternatives for the $t$ test for dependent means, but each has an important advantage that the other does not. We present the sign test in this section and the Wilcoxon signed-ranks test in the next.

The **sign test** is very useful for analyzing results of studies in which the scale of measurement is ordinal, such as rating degrees of sociability or other aspects of personality. Its name comes from the use of plus or minus signs rather than quantitative measurements (the sign test is *not* a rank-order test).

**Example**

Suppose that a social psychologist is interested in whether a short course in human relations can enhance an individual's tolerance of people of other ethnic groups. The psychologist worries, however, that intelligence and tolerance of others are correlated variables, so she decides to match 20 pairs of subjects on the basis of their scores on an intelligence test. One member of each pair then takes the course and the other does not (decided randomly). All 40 subjects are then interviewed and rated for their tolerance of others on a 30-point scale. Let us suppose that the results are those shown in Table 22.2 in the columns under "Tolerance score."

**Solution**

The sign test is appropriate here because the measurement scale is ordinal at best. To use the test, the psychologist assigns a plus sign (+) to a pair of observations when the member who took the course received a higher tolerance score and a minus sign (−) when the opposite was the case, as shown in Table 22.2 in the column labeled "Difference."

If the course made no difference, we would expect there to be as many "pluses" as "minuses," within the limits of sampling variation. In other words, the null

**sign test**
an assumption-freer test of a difference between two dependent groups (for use when the scale of measurement is ordinal)

TABLE 22.2 *Testing the Difference between Two Dependent Groups: The Sign Test*

| MATCHED PAIR | TOLERANCE SCORE | | DIFFERENCE |
| | *Took course* | *No course* | |
|---|---|---|---|
| 1 | 23 | 21 | + |
| 2 | 17 | 10 | + |
| 3 | 15 | 17 | − |
| 4 | 30 | 24 | + |
| 5 | 25 | 18 | + |
| 6 | 18 | 12 | + |
| 7 | 10 | 9 | + |
| 8 | 24 | 20 | + |
| 9 | 16 | 17 | − |
| 10 | 30 | 27 | + |
| 11 | 15 | 9 | + |
| 12 | 20 | 18 | + |
| 13 | 25 | 20 | + |
| 14 | 22 | 17 | + |
| 15 | 20 | 21 | − |
| 16 | 16 | 12 | + |
| 17 | 20 | 17 | + |
| 18 | 28 | 24 | + |
| 19 | 30 | 28 | + |
| 20 | 24 | 21 | + |

hypothesis is that the proportions of pluses and minuses in the population are equal. We can apply chi-square to this type of question. The expected and observed frequencies of plus and minus are as follows:

|         | $(-)$ | $(+)$ |
|---------|-------|-------|
| $f_o$   | 3     | 17    |
| $f_e$   | 10    | 10    |

We calculate chi-square as described in Section 19.2:

$$\chi^2 = \frac{(f_{o+} - f_{e+})^2}{f_{e+}} + \frac{(f_{o-} - f_{e-})^2}{f_{e-}}$$

$$= \frac{(17 - 10)^2}{10} + \frac{(3 - 10)^2}{10}$$

$$= 9.80$$

With 1 degree of freedom, $\chi^2$ must reach or exceed 3.84 to be significant at the 5% level and 6.64 to be significant at the 1% level. (These values are determined from Table I in Appendix E for a nondirectional test.) The psychologist's $\chi^2$ surpasses both of these critical values, so it appears that the pluses predominate because of some systematic process—perhaps the human-relations course resulted in increased understanding of others.

If you use the sign test, a difference will occasionally be zero and cannot therefore be categorized as a plus or minus. We may solve this dilemma in one of several ways. Probably the simplest is to ignore such cases, reduce *n* accordingly, and proceed with the test on the remaining values.

Evaluation of the sign test by $\chi^2$ will give reasonable accuracy for 10 or more pairs of scores. *With fewer than 10 pairs, we should use the binomial test in place of chi-square.*

An assumption required for the sign test is that no difference is exactly zero. The use of the method as described here will be reasonably satisfactory provided the number of zeros is small.

The special advantages of the sign test are its ease of application and assumptions that are less restrictive than those for the Wilcoxon signed-ranks test. Its main disadvantage is that it is less sensitive because it disregards some information that the other takes into account. In our example, each plus simply indicates that the subject who completed the human-relations course is more tolerant than the paired subject who did not take the course, but *no account is taken of how much more.*

## 22.7 Another Assumption-Freer Alternative to the *t* Test of a Difference between Two Dependent Groups: The Wilcoxon Signed-Ranks Test

The **Wilcoxon signed-ranks test** is an alternative to the sign test (and also to the *t* test of the difference between two dependent means). It is more powerful than the sign test because it weighs the size of a difference between pairs of scores. However, it demands an assumption that we may not be willing to make (more about this later).

**Wilcoxon signed-ranks test**

*a rank-order test of a difference between two dependent groups*

Suppose we are studying the effect of a drug on the performance of mental operation—for example, on the speed and accuracy of the addition and subtraction of figures. We form 10 pairs of subjects, matched according to their pretest score earned on similar arithmetic problems, and then randomly assign members of each pair to two treatments: the drug and a placebo. At an appropriate time after ingesting the substance (active or inert), the subjects take the test. Their scores are recorded in the columns labeled "Placebo $(X)$" and "Drug $(Y)$" in Table 22.3. We wish to know whether the drug made a difference in performance; we decide to conduct a two-tailed test at $\alpha = .05$ and to use the Wilcoxon signed-ranks test. We describe the procedure below and show the calculations in Table 22.3.

**Step 1:**   Record the paired scores in two columns. In the table these appear under the column headings "Placebo $(X)$" and "Drug $(Y)$." See ①.

**Step 2:**   Obtain the difference between members of each pair $(X - Y)$. See ②.

**Step 3:**   If any difference is zero, disregard it in subsequent calculations and reduce *n,* the number of pairs of scores, accordingly.

**Step 4:**   *Disregard the sign of the difference obtained,* and then supply ranks to the absolute magnitude of the differences, assigning a rank of 1 to the smallest of the differences, 2 to the next smallest, and so forth. Ties in rank are handled as described in Section 8.9. The outcome is shown in the column headed "Rank of $|X - Y|$." See ③.

**$T$**

*the sum of the ranks with a negative sign $(R_-)$ or the sum of the ranks with a positive sign $(R_+)$, whichever is smaller*

**Step 5:**   Next, resupply the appropriate sign of the differences to the rank of the differences. We show this in the column labeled "Signed Rank of $X - Y$." See ④.

**Step 6:**   The test statistic, $T$, will be the sum of the ranks with a negative sign or the sum of the ranks with a positive sign, *whichever is smaller.* We will call the former $R_-$ and the latter $R_+$. Often it will be obvious which to calculate; for purposes of completeness, we show both in Table 22.3. See ⑤.

**TABLE 22.3**   *Testing the Difference between Two Dependent Samples: The Wilcoxon Signed-Ranks Test*

| PAIR | ①<br>PLACEBO<br>$(X)$ | ①<br>DRUG<br>$(Y)$ | ②<br>$\|X - Y\|$ | ③<br>RANK OF<br>$\|X - Y\|$ | ④<br>SIGNED<br>RANK OF<br>$X - Y$ | $R_+$ | ⑤ | $R_-$ |
|------|---------|------|---------|----------|-----------|-------|---|-------|
| 1 | 24 | 28 | 4 | 2 | −2 | | | 2 |
| 2 | 39 | 29 | 10 | 6.5 | +6.5 | 6.5 | | |
| 3 | 29 | 34 | 5 | 3.5 | −3.5 | | | 3.5 |
| 4 | 28 | 21 | 7 | 5 | +5 | 5 | | |
| 5 | 25 | 28 | 3 | 1 | −1 | | | 1 |
| 6 | 32 | 15 | 17 | 10 | +10 | 10 | | |
| 7 | 31 | 17 | 14 | 8 | +8 | 8 | | |
| 8 | 33 | 28 | 5 | 3.5 | +3.5 | 3.5 | | |
| 9 | 31 | 16 | 15 | 9 | +9 | 9 | | |
| 10 | 22 | 12 | 10 | 6.5 | +6.5 | 6.5 | | |
| | | | $\sum\|X - Y\| = 55$ | | | $R_+ = 48.5$ | | $R_- = 6.5$ |
| | | | $= n(n + 1)/2$ | | | $T = 6.5$ | | |

**Step 7:** In Table K in Appendix E you will find critical values for one- and two-tailed tests at the usual levels of significance. We compare the obtained value of $T$ (*disregarding the sign*) with the entry in the table corresponding to $n$ (the number of pairs), $\alpha$, and the nature of our alternative hypothesis. For a two-tailed test, we reject the null hypothesis if the calculated value *equals or is less than the tabulated value.* For a one-tailed test, we must also take the sign of the test statistic into account. A positive sign means that $X$ is greater than $Y$; a negative sign means the opposite. However, because our test statistic is the smaller of the two sums, rejecting the null hypothesis for a very small sum of negative ranks means that positive ranks predominate and that therefore $X > Y$. Similarly, if the test statistic is positive, it indicates that $X < Y$.

In our example, $R_-$ is smaller than $R_+$ and is therefore the test statistic. According to Table K (in Appendix E), the critical value for a two-tailed test at $\alpha = .05$ with 10 pairs of scores is 8. Because the absolute value of $R_-$ is smaller, we reject the null hypothesis and conclude that the drug resulted in reduced performance.

When the sample size is too large to use Table K, the statistic $z$ is approximately normally distributed:

$z$ STATISTIC FOR THE WILCOXON
SIGNED-RANKS TEST

$$z = \frac{R_+ - .25n(n + 1)}{\sqrt{\dfrac{n(n + 1)(2n + 1)}{24}}} \qquad (22.4)$$

**$z$ formula for the Wilcoxon signed-ranks test with large samples**

$$\frac{R_+ - .25n(n + 1)}{\sqrt{\dfrac{n(n + 1)(2n + 1)}{24}}}$$

If it is more convenient, substitute $R_-$ (again, disregarding its sign) for $R_+$ in the formula.

You can see why the Wilcoxon signed-ranks test is more sensitive than the sign test. The sign test responds only to the direction of the difference between a pair of scores, whereas the Wilcoxon test uses additional information about the size of the difference. For useful interpretation of the outcome of the Wilcoxon test, we must assume not only that the scores are from an ordinal scale of measurement but also that the *differences between pairs of scores can be placed in rank order.* In behavioral science, this may often be a hazardous assumption. Is it true that the difference between scores of 20 and 25 is the same as that between scores 40 and 45? This depends on the scale properties of the measure, which are often unknown. See Section 2.4 for further comment on this matter.

Other assumptions for the test are the random assignment of treatment condition to members of a pair (with independent assignment among different pairs), no differences of zero, and no ties in rank.

To calculate effect size, we use the **matched-pairs rank biserial correlation coefficient,** $r_C$:

**matched-pairs rank biserial correlation coefficient, ($r_C$)**
a measure of effect size for the Wilcoxon signed-ranks test

FORMULA FOR $r_C$

$$r_C = \frac{4\left| T - \left(\dfrac{R_+ + R_-}{2}\right) \right|}{n(n + 1)} \qquad (22.5)$$

In our example,

$$r_C = \frac{4\left|6.5 - \left(\dfrac{48.5 + 6.5}{2}\right)\right|}{10(11)}$$

$$= .76$$

We calculate the magnitude of $r_C$ the same way we do $r$.

## 22.8 An Assumption-Freer Alternative to the One-Way ANOVA for Independent Groups: The Kruskal-Wallis Test

**Kruskal-Wallis test**

a rank-order test of a difference among three or more independent groups

Look again at the assumptions associated with the one-way ANOVA (Section 20.10). The **Kruskal-Wallis test** is an alternative to ANOVA (with independent samples) for situations in which measurements are on an ordinal scale or when we have doubts about the distributional assumptions associated with the $F$ test. You may think of it as an extension of the Mann-Whitney $U$ test to more than two groups. As with the Mann-Whitney test, the null hypothesis concerns the identity of the population distributions rather than the identity of some particular measure of central tendency for the populations. Under ordinary circumstances, however, it is a good test for location. (Again the median is probably the best statistic to use when examining a significant outcome.)

Suppose we combine the scores from $k$ groups and rank all scores from 1 (the lowest score) to $n_1 + n_2 + \cdots + n_k$ (the highest score). Look at Section 8.9 if you need to review how to rank scores. After separating the groups again, we find the mean rank of each and then compare them. The basic logic involves determining whether the mean ranks ($\Sigma R/n$) for the groups differ more than would be expected due to random sampling variation alone. If the samples all came from identical populations, we would expect the mean ranks of the groups to vary to some extent (due to random variation) around the overall rank mean. If, however, the samples come from different populations, we would expect the mean ranks of the groups to vary more widely. The Kruskal-Wallis test examines the magnitudes of the $k$ discrepancies between mean rank of each group and the overall mean rank and finally compares the total magnitude of the discrepancies with what might be expected by chance. Note the similarity of the rationale for the one-way ANOVA and the rationale here. (Figures 20.1 and 20.2 are worth studying again because they present pictorially the essence of the argument developed here.)

**H**

the test statistic for the Kruskal-Wallis test

The test statistic, $H$, for the Kruskal-Wallis test is:

THE KRUSKAL-WALLIS TEST STATISTIC, $H$

$$H = -3(n_{\text{total}} + 1) + \frac{12}{n_{\text{total}}(n_{\text{total}} + 1)}\left[\frac{\left(\sum R_1\right)^2}{n_1} + \frac{\left(\sum R_2\right)^2}{n_2} + \cdots \frac{\left(\sum R_k\right)^2}{n_k}\right] \quad (22.6)$$

**$\Sigma R_1$**

sum of the ranks in group 1

*where:*   $\Sigma R_1$ = the sum of the ranks in group 1, and so forth.
            $n_1$ = the number of cases in group 1, and so forth.
            $n_{\text{total}}$ = the number of cases in all the groups combined.

When $H_0$ is true, the sampling distribution of $H$ approximates the chi-square distribution (Chapter 19). With three groups and five or more cases per group, we may use the chi-square distribution to evaluate $H$ with good approximate results. (With more than three groups, some groups can have as few as two or three cases.) We compare our $H_{calc}$ with the critical values of $\chi^2$ in Table I in Appendix E for $df = k - 1$, where $k$ is the number of groups. Because $H$ reflects the magnitude of the discrepancies and is not sensitive to their direction, the region of rejection lies entirely in the upper tail of the $\chi^2$ distribution. If we consult the column of Table I headed by .05, for example, it supplies the critical value of $\chi^2$ (or $H$) for a nondirectional test at $\alpha = .05$. We reject the null hypothesis for $H_{calc}$ that equals or exceeds the tabulated value.

One assumption of the Kruskal-Wallis test is that there are no ties in rank. As with the Mann-Whitney $U$ test for two independent groups, the effect of ties in rank is not great unless there are many of them.

**Example**

Suppose we study three brands of computer printers, A, B, and C, for their legibility. We sample six Brand A printers, six Brand B, and five Brand C. The legibility scores of the 17 printers sampled are shown in Table 22.4.

**Solution**

Using the Kruskal-Wallis test to examine possible differences, the first step (①) is to combine the $6 + 6 + 5 = 17$ scores into a single distribution and to assign the scores ranks beginning with 1 for the lowest score and ending with 17 for the highest. Note that the score of 26 appears three times, so we assign the mean of the three ranks available for these scores (8) to each (Section 8.9). We calculate $\Sigma R$, the sum of the ranks for each group, and record it below the body of the table (step ②). We check the assignment of ranks (step ③) using the fact that

$$\sum_{}^{all} R = \frac{n_{total}(n_{total} + 1)}{2}$$

This is shown, immediately below the sum of the ranks for the groups. Next we calculate $H$, which yields a value of 9.96 (step ④). Using the chi-square distribution to evaluate $H$, $df = k - 1 = 3 - 1 = 2$ (step ⑤). For $\alpha = .05$ and $df = 2$, Table I in Appendix E gives $\chi^2_{crit} = 5.99$ (step ⑥). Our $H_{calc} = 9.96$ falls beyond that value, so we reject the null hypothesis (step ⑦).

We are not limited to the overall test of significance; as with analysis of variance, we can make multiple comparisons if our $H$ proves to be significant (Dunn, 1964). To make comparisons of all possible pairs of mean ranks, use the Mann-Whitney $U$ test. However, we must use a revised alpha level to account for the increased chance of a Type I error. Dunn suggests that we use *alpha/# pairs of mean ranks tested*. In our example there are three possible comparisons (A versus B, A versus C, B versus C), so our revised alpha level is $.05/3 = .017$.

**epsilon-squared ($E_R^2$)**
a measure of effect size for the Kruskal-Wallis test

An appropriate measure of effect size for the Kruskal-Wallis test is **epsilon-squared, $E_R^2$**:

FORMULA FOR EPSILON-SQUARED

$$E_R^2 = \frac{H}{(n_{total}^2 - 1)/(n_{total} + 1)} \tag{22.7}$$

**TABLE 22.4** *Examination of the Difference in Legibility of Three Brands of Computer Printers Using the Kruskal-Wallis Test*

| PRINTER A ① | | PRINTER B ① | | PRINTER C ① | |
|---|---|---|---|---|---|
| *Score* | *Rank* | *Score* | *Rank* | *Score* | *Rank* |
| 22 | 3 | 26 | 8 | 23 | 4 |
| 24 | 5 | 36 | 16 | 30 | 12 |
| 21 | 2 | 27 | 10 | 29 | 11 |
| 17 | 1 | 37 | 17 | 26 | 8 |
| 26 | 8 | 33 | 15 | 31 | 13 |
| 25 | 6 | 32 | 14 | | |
| $n_1 = 6$ | | $n_2 = 6$ | | $n_3 = 5$ | |
| | $\sum R_1 = 25$ | | $\sum R_2 = 80$ | | $\sum R_3 = 48$ |

Calculations:

② $\displaystyle\sum^{\text{all}} R = 25 + 80 + 48 = 153$

③ $\displaystyle\sum^{\text{all}} R = \frac{n_{\text{total}}(n_{\text{total}} + 1)}{2} = \frac{17(17 + 1)}{2} = 153 \quad \text{(check)}$

④ $H = -3(n_{\text{total}} + 1) + \dfrac{12}{n_{\text{total}}(n_{\text{total}} + 1)}\left[\dfrac{\left(\sum R_1\right)^2}{n_1} + \dfrac{\left(\sum R_2\right)^2}{n_2} + \dfrac{\left(\sum R_k\right)^2}{n_k}\right]$

$\quad = -3(17 + 1) + \dfrac{12}{17(17 + 1)}\left[\dfrac{(25)^2}{6} + \dfrac{(80)^2}{6} + \dfrac{(48)^2}{5}\right]$

$\quad = -54 + .0392(1631.63)$

$\quad = 9.96$

⑤ $df = k - 1 = 3 - 1 = 2$

⑥ $\chi^2_{\text{crit}} = 5.99$ for $\alpha = .05$

*Decision*:

⑦ $H_0$ is rejected at $\alpha = .05$.

Epsilon-squared can have values between 0 (no relationship) and 1.00 (indicating a perfect relationship between the independent and dependent variables). In our example,

$$E^2_R = \frac{9.96}{(17^2 - 1)/(17 + 1)}$$

$$= \frac{9.96}{288/18}$$

$$= .623$$

# 22.9 An Assumption-Freer Alternative to ANOVA for Repeated Measures: Friedman's Rank Test for Correlated Samples

**Friedman's rank test**
a rank-order test of a difference among three or more dependent groups

$\chi_F^2$
statistic for Friedman's rank test

$\dfrac{12\sum R_j^2}{Nk(k+1)} -$

$3N(k+1)$
formula for Friedman's rank test for correlated samples

If you want to use a repeated-measures design, and you have serious doubts about the distributions in the populations from which you have drawn your samples, an assumption-freer alternative to ANOVA is **Friedman's rank test** ($\chi_F^2$) for correlated samples. Friedman's test (named after economist Milton Friedman, who developed it) may be used when there are at least three levels in the repeated-measures design and when scores are in the form of ranks:

$$\chi_F^2 = \frac{12\sum R_j^2}{Nk(k+1)} - 3N(k+1) \tag{22.8}$$

*where:* $\chi_F^2$ = a statistic with a sampling distribution that closely resembles the chi–square distribution with $k - 1$ degrees of freedom.
$R_j^2$ = the sum of the ranks in the *j*th condition.
$N$ = sample size.
$k$ = number of conditions.

To use Friedman's test, you must first rank the scores *for each subject across all conditions.* When there are ties in scores, assign the mean rank to both. As an example, suppose we were interested in knowing the effects of stress on the ability to solve problems. Twelve subjects are recruited and asked to solve problems under each of three conditions—after a pretest period of no stress, mild stress, or moderate stress. We counterbalance the three conditions to ensure that the order of presentation does not affect our results, and the problems are graded on a 100-point scale. Hypothetical results are presented in Table 22.5, accompanied by their ranks. Look, for

**TABLE 22.5**  *Data, Ranks, and Initial Calculations for Friedman's Test*

| SUBJECT | NO STRESS | MILD STRESS | MODERATE STRESS |
|:---:|:---:|:---:|:---:|
| 1 | 65 (3) | 60 (2) | 50 (1) |
| 2 | 80 (2) | 85 (3) | 70 (1) |
| 3 | 75 (3) | 60 (1) | 65 (2) |
| 4 | 40 (3) | 35 (2) | 20 (1) |
| 5 | 60 (2) | 65 (3) | 50 (1) |
| 6 | 70 (1) | 75 (2) | 80 (3) |
| 7 | 90 (2) | 95 (3) | 70 (1) |
| 8 | 55 (3) | 40 (2) | 25 (1) |
| 9 | 85 (2) | 90 (3) | 75 (1) |
| 10 | 85 (1) | 90 (2) | 95 (3) |
| 11 | 35 (3) | 30 (2) | 15 (1) |
| 12 | 75 (3) | 65 (2) | 60 (1) |
| | $R_1 = 28$ | $R_2 = 27$ | $R_3 = 17$ |

example, at subject 1. His or her scores of 65 after no stress, 60 after mild stress, and 50 after moderate stress correspond to ranks of 3, 2, and 1, respectively.

The null hypothesis is that the scores under each condition are from identical populations. If this were true, the rankings within each condition would be random, and any differences across conditions would be due to chance. Let us now solve for $\chi_F^2$:

$$\chi_F^2 = \frac{12(28^2 + 27^2 + 17^2)}{12(3)(4)} - 3(12)(4)$$

$$= \frac{12(1802)}{144} - 144$$

$$= \frac{21,624}{144} - 144$$

$$= 150.17 - 144$$

$$= 6.17$$

To evaluate the outcome at $\alpha = .05$, look in Table I of Appendix E for $k - 1 = 2df$. The critical value is 5.99. Our calculated value of 6.17 exceeds this, so we reject the null hypothesis and conclude that ability to solve problems is affected by stress. As with ANOVA, once $\chi_F^2$ is found to be significant we may make multiple comparisons (Dunn, 1964). Use the Wilcoxon signed-ranks test, but to account for the increased possibility of Type I errors the alpha level should be revised by *alpha/# pairs rank sum tested*. In our example, alpha is $.05/3 = .017$.

**concordance coefficient (W)**
a measure of effect size for Friedman's rank test

To measure effect size, calculate the **concordance coefficient, W**:

FORMULA FOR THE CONCORDANCE COEFFICIENT

$$W = \frac{\chi_F^2}{N(k - 1)} \tag{22.9}$$

In our example,

$$W = \frac{6.17}{12(2)} = .257$$

The concordance coefficient takes on values between 0 and 1.00, and in this case indicates a moderate effect.

## 22.10 Summary

To use *t*, *F*, or $\chi^2$, we must make assumptions about the underlying population distributions. The two most important assumptions are that the populations are normally distributed and that there is homogeneity of variance. With moderate to large samples, these "parametric" tests are reasonably accurate (because of the central limit theorem) even when the assumptions are violated. The major problem comes with the use of small samples, for which violation of the assumptions can lead to considerable inaccuracy.

Assumption-freer tests make no assumption about the underlying distribution and are more powerful than parametric tests when sample size is small and the population distribution is normal. Most of the assumption-freer tests introduced in this chapter are rank-order tests in which original scores are converted to ranks. The rank-order tests were derived from randomization tests that compare the obtained outcome with the distribution of outcomes from all possible combination of scores.

The Mann-Whitney $U$ test is commonly used in place of the $t$ test for independent samples. With more than two groups, we can use the Kruskal-Wallis test in place of one-way ANOVA. Although the null hypothesis for these tests is that the population distributions are the same, we can use them for detecting differences in central tendency if we are relatively certain that differences in variability and shape are not pronounced.

The sign test and Wilcoxon's signed-ranks test are popular alternatives to the $t$ test for dependent samples. Wilcoxon's test is the more powerful of the two, but it assumes that the differences between pairs of scores can be placed in rank order. With more than two groups, we can use Friedman's rank test in place of repeated-measures ANOVA.

# Key Terms, Concepts, and Symbols

nonparametric statistics   (444)

distribution-free methods   (444)

assumption-freer tests   (444)

randomization tests   (445)

rank-order tests   (447)

bootstrap method   (448)

Mann-Whitney $U$ test   (449)

$\Sigma R_X, \Sigma R_Y$   (450)

$U$   (450)

Glass rank biserial correlation coefficient   (453)

$r_g$   (453)

sign test   (454)

Wilcoxon signed-ranks test   (456)

$T$   (456)

$R_+, R_-$   (456)

matched-pairs rank biserial correlation coefficient   (457)

$r_C$   (457)

Kruskal-Wallis test   (458)

$H$   (458)

$\Sigma R_1, \Sigma R_2$   (458)

epsilon-squared   (459)

$E_R^2$   (459)

Friedman's rank test   (461)

$\chi_F^2$   (461)

concordance coefficient   (462)

$W$   (462)

# Problems

$\boxed{c}$  7, 9, 10, 11, 12, 13, 14, 15, 16, 17

1. Explain the differences between the terms *parametric test, nonparametric test, distribution-free test,* and *assumption-freer test.*

2. (a) Why might a researcher choose to use assumption-freer methods? (b) Would sample size influence his or her decision? (c) Are the assumption-freer methods truly assumption-free? Explain.

3. How does the sampling distribution of a randomization test differ from the sampling distributions of $t$, $F$, and $\chi^2$?

4. What is the difference between the null hypothesis tested by parametric tests (e.g., $t$) and

the null hypothesis tested by assumption-freer tests?

**5.** With regard to outliers, explain the advantage of using a rank-order test.

**6.** Place the following scores in rank order: 97, 105, 110, 92, 90, 100, 105, 135, 102, 96. If you need to review, look at Section 8.9.

**7.** In a large class, 14 students required a make-up examination. The instructor gave the same test to everyone but because of circumstances could find a quiet environment for only 6 of the students. The other 8 had to take their test in a noisy environment. Assignment to testing environment can be considered random. The scores of the two groups were

Noisy environment: 55 38 46 63 35 61 56 47
Quiet environment: 62 56 47 65 59

Is the difference in performance significant according to a two-tailed test using $\alpha = .05$? Use the Mann-Whitney $U$ test to solve the problem. Interpret the outcome using appropriate descriptive statistics.

**8.** Rework Problem 7 using the large sample ($z$) approach.

**9.** *Androgyny* sometimes refers to the ability of an individual to fill both "masculine" and "feminine" gender roles. An androgynous male, for example, would have no difficulty helping his female partner clean house or do the cooking. A sex-stereotyped male, on the other hand, might refuse to engage in these activities. Suppose that a marriage counselor believes that androgyny is a characteristic that helps lead to long-lasting relationships. To test this, she administers a test to measure androgyny (higher scores indicate greater androgyny) to men whose marriages broke up within 3 years and to men whose marriages have lasted at least 10 years. Suppose the scores were as follows:

Less than 3: 4 6 2 5 8 3 1
More than 10: 9 11 7 6 14 13 12 10

Apply the Mann-Whitney $U$ test to evaluate these results. What can the counselor conclude?

**10.** Suppose we had doubts about the normality of the two distributions of scores in Problem 15.7. Rework the problem using the

Mann-Whitney $U$ test with $\alpha = .05$. Did you get the same outcome?

**11.** In two equivalent problem situations, 12 children are praised on one occasion and blamed on another. Their reactions toward others subsequent to the problem situations are judged for aggressiveness. Ratings of aggressive behavior are as follows:

| Child: | A | B | C | D | E | F | G | H | I | J | K | L |
|---|---|---|---|---|---|---|---|---|---|---|---|---|
| Praise: | 6 | 8 | 2 | 1 | 4 | 5 | 6 | 9 | 8 | 7 | 7 | 3 |
| Blame: | 7 | 11 | 4 | 5 | 3 | 7 | 9 | 8 | 9 | 11 | 9 | 6 |

Examine, by the sign test, the hypothesis of no difference between the two treatments. Use $\alpha = .05$ and $\alpha = .01$.

**12.** Eleven pipe smokers were blindfolded and given a pipe of tobacco to smoke. At a later session, the same subjects were again blindfolded and given a pipe to smoke. This time the pipe contained a heated coil rather than tobacco, so the subjects drew in nothing but warm air. At both sessions blood pressure was measured before and after puffing the pipe. Below is a record of change in blood pressure during each session (a positive number represents an increase, a negative number a decrease):

| Subject: | A | B | C | D | E | F | G | H | I | J | K |
|---|---|---|---|---|---|---|---|---|---|---|---|
| First session (tobacco): | 12 | 4 | 6 | 17 | 14 | 4 | 20 | 7 | 0 | 10 | 7 |
| Second session (warm air): | 14 | 4 | 6 | 14 | 6 | 5 | 11 | 2 | −4 | 3 | 7 |

(a) Test for a difference between scores at the first session and those at the second. Use the sign test to make a two-tailed test at the 5% significance level. (b) What appears to be interesting about the data aside from the result of the comparison you made in (a)? (c) What comments do you have about the way the study was conducted?

**13.** Eleven male subjects responded to an attitude questionnaire designed to evaluate their tendency to view females in stereotypic roles. A month later they were shown a film that illustrated the ways in which women have often been treated unfairly relative to men. Four months later the subjects again responded to the attitude questionnaire. The subjects' scores on the questionnaire (the higher the score, the greater the bias) before and after were as follow:

| Subject: | A | B | C | D | E | F | G | H | I | J | K |
|----------|---|---|---|---|---|---|---|---|---|---|---|
| Before: | 21 | 25 | 31 | 26 | 21 | 31 | 28 | 24 | 27 | 24 | 22 |
| After: | 13 | 26 | 35 | 24 | 17 | 24 | 22 | 27 | 17 | 19 | 18 |

(a) Conduct a nondirectional test for a difference in response between the two sets of data. Use the Wilcoxon signed-ranks test and the 5% significance level. (b) Calculate effect size. (c) Do you feel that the way the study was conducted was adequate? Explain.

**14.** Rework Problem 13 (a) using the large-sample ($z$) Wilcoxon approach.

**15.** (a) Repeat Problem 12(a), but evaluate the outcome with the Wilcoxon signed-ranks test. (b) Calculate effect size.

**16.** Fifteen applicants to the Better Ways Corporation were randomly assigned to one of three new training programs. After completing the programs, all were placed in the same type of job. Six weeks later a supervisor rated each of them on their job performance. Suppose the ratings were as shown in Data 22A. Apply the appropriate nonparametric test to evaluate these results. What can the Better Ways Corporation conclude?

## DATA 22A

| GROUP 1 | GROUP 2 | GROUP 3 |
|---------|---------|---------|
| 2 | 20 | 10 |
| 4 | 18 | 17 |
| 3 | 14 | 16 |
| 1 | 8 | 12 |
| 6 | 15 | 13 |

**17.** You are interested in knowing if morning eating habits affect energy levels later in the day. Nine subjects are tested under three conditions in a counterbalanced design: no breakfast, coffee only, or juice plus cereal. The following are hypothetical self-ratings taken at 2 p.m. The scale ranges from 1 (very little energy) to 5 (very energetic). Use Friedman's test to evaluate the results and compute effect size.

## DATA 22B

| SUBJECT | NO BREAKFAST | COFFEE | JUICE + CEREAL |
|---------|--------------|--------|----------------|
| 1 | 1 | 2 | 4 |
| 2 | 2 | 1 | 3 |
| 3 | 3 | 3 | 5 |
| 4 | 4 | 2 | 3 |
| 5 | 1 | 3 | 2 |
| 6 | 2 | 1 | 5 |
| 7 | 3 | 5 | 4 |
| 8 | 1 | 2 | 4 |
| 9 | 2 | 3 | 5 |

# EPILOGUE
## The Realm of Statistics

We developed an outline of the role of applied statistics early in this book (Section 1.5). There we considered the difference between a research question (for example, Do children learn better with spaced practice or massed practice?) and a statistical question (Does $\mu_{spaced} = \mu_{massed}$?) and the difference between a statistical conclusion and a research conclusion. We also explained how statistical procedures were only an intermediate part of an investigation. Now that you have learned so much more about the nature of statistical procedures, it is time to return to that overall picture and examine it at a more sophisticated level than was possible earlier.

Figure E.1 shows the typical steps in the development of an inquiry in behavioral science. The square boxes on the left show the progression in general terms, from the real world of knowledge at the beginning to the real world of knowledge again at the end. To the right of each of these boxes (connected by a straight line) is an example of that phase for a hypothetical study of learning and retention.

Between the square boxes are representative descriptions of the kinds of actions we must take to progress from one box to the next. We list these by numbers: ① through ⑤. Notice the word *representative*; it is not possible to list all the considerations that investigators must take into account. Many of the statements or questions

467

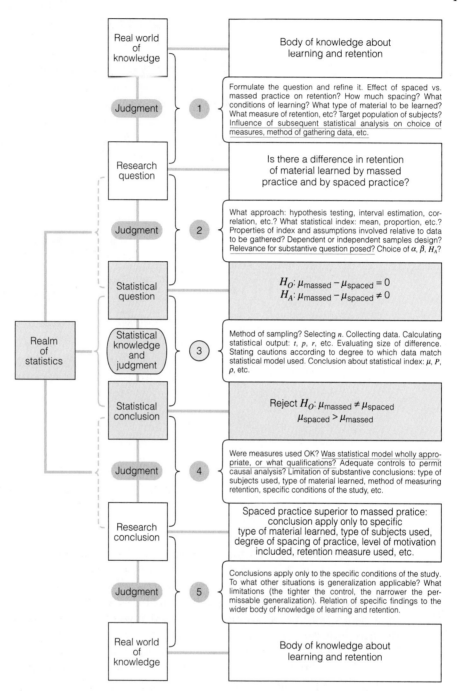

**FIGURE E.1**   The steps of an inquiry in behavioral science.

we identify here involve not just a single step but the interaction between factors characterizing one step and those pertaining to another. In some cases, we have underlined statements or questions. These identify considerations that particularly demonstrate the interplay of statistical and research questions.

Next, note that between the square boxes there is a reminder that some form of judgment is required at each step. Statistical calculations, once one has learned how to do them, follow a "formula" that can be laid out in a simple sequence of cookbook instructions. But at its very best, this only gets us from the statistical question to the statistical conclusion. In all the other steps in the progression (and to some extent in the one just mentioned), judgment based on knowledge of the research discipline enters in most importantly. This reminds us that statistical procedures do not carry automatic authority but serve as merely one step in the chain.

> Distinguishing statistical significance from theoretical significance (Kirk, 1996) will help the entire research community publish more substantial results. . . . Good theories and intelligent interpretation advance a discipline more than rigid methodological orthodoxy. . . . Statistical methods should guide and discipline our thinking but should not determine it. (Wilkinson and the Task Force on Statistical Inference, 1999)

We have indicated the realm of statistics at the extreme left of the figure. Its central domain (shown in blue) begins with the formulation of the statistical question and ends with the statistical conclusion. Nevertheless, we should take statistical considerations into account when moving from the research question to the statistical question and again when moving from the statistical conclusion to the research conclusion.

**statistical conclusion**
a conclusion about a numerical property of the data

**research conclusion**
a conclusion about the subject matter

The move from the statistical conclusion to the research conclusion is a particularly important matter. Suppose, for example, that we wish to compare the performance of two groups. In the statistical conclusion of the study, we may be informed that mean performance is different for the two groups. But in moving to the research conclusion, we want to know *why* that difference occurred. To what do we attribute causality? The fact that a difference has occurred does not inform us as to the reason for it. It will not be clear that the difference in experimental conditions we imposed on the two groups is responsible for the difference *unless adequate controls* were used. The discussion about controls in Sections 15.13 and 15.14 and that concerning causation in Section 8.11 are particularly important here.

After we have made a conclusion about causality, we must then concern ourselves with generalizations (Sections 14.12 and 15.12). As indicated by ⑤ in Figure E.1, research conclusions apply, strictly speaking, only to the *particular* circumstances that

PEANUTS © United Feature Syndicate. Reprinted by permission.

characterize the study. See ① in the figure for examples of such specification. The problem in generalizing to other types of subjects, kinds of material learned, and conditions of learning is serious because (again strictly speaking) it is necessary to demonstrate that any differences between the characteristics of the situation in which the study was conducted and those of the situation to which we wish to generalize would have no effect—a tall order indeed. This is where great experience with the variables concerned can be most important in suggesting what can be safely ventured and what cannot.

The general (and ideal) model for the two group (or more) comparisons developed in this book is founded on the concept of drawing two (or more) random samples from a fully defined population and treating one group one way and the other another. In practice we are seldom so blessed but must instead take a convenient group at hand and randomly assign these subjects to two (or more) treatment groups. Now *both* random sampling and random assignment serve the purpose of experimental control, as we described in Section 15.13. Whereas we may properly generalize the result of random sampling to the defined target population, the outcome of a study using random assignment applies *only* to the kind of subjects represented in the study. This is not to say that we cannot make generalizations, only that statistics does not provide a basis for making those generalizations.

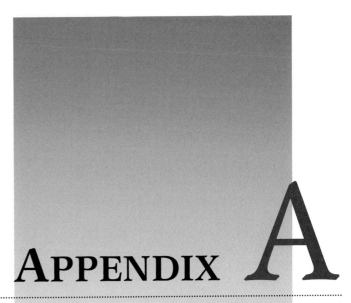

# Appendix A

# Review of Basic Mathematics

## A.1 Introduction

This appendix offers information about basic skills that are useful in an introductory course in statistics. It is not intended to be a comprehensive compendium, nor should it be considered an initial unit of instruction for those who have no knowledge of the subject. It is intended primarily as a reminder of principles formerly learned but possibly covered with mental cobwebs.

A pretest follows that covers many (*but not all*) of the principles stated in the remaining sections. If you can answer all of these questions correctly, you would do well to skim the subsequent sections, looking for principles that seem unfamiliar. Questions are keyed to particular sections in this appendix, so if you miss a question you will know where to look to review the principles involved. Answers to the pretest questions are given at the end of this appendix.

## A.2 Pretest of Mathematical Skills

**Reference for Questions 1–4: Section A.3.**

1. What symbol, inserted between 3 and 2, indicates that 3 is greater than 2?

_____

   **2.** The reciprocal of 2/3 is                                   _____
   **3.** $|-8| = ?$                                                 _____
   **4.** Write $(ab)^2$ another way                                 _____

## Reference for Questions 5–11: Section A.4.

   **5.** $2 - (-4) = ?$                                             _____
   **6.** $(3)(-4) = ?$                                              _____
   **7.** $(-3)(-4) = ?$                                             _____
   **8.** $(2)(-3)(-2)(-2) = ?$                                      _____
   **9.** $(2)(-3)(0)(-1) = ?$                                       _____
   **10.** $2 - 4(3/4) = ?$                                          _____
   **11.** $-4/-2 = ?$                                               _____

## Reference for Questions 12–18: Section A.5.

   **12.** Does $(abc)^2 = abc^2$?                                   _____
   **13.** Does $a^2 + b^2 = (a + b)^2$?                             _____
   **14.** Does $\dfrac{a^2}{b^2} = \left(\dfrac{a}{b}\right)^2$?    _____
   **15.** Does $\sqrt{4b} = 2\sqrt{b}$?                             _____
   **16.** Does $\sqrt{a^2 + b^2} = a + b$?                          _____
   **17.** Does $\sqrt{\dfrac{a^2}{b^2}} = \dfrac{a}{b}$?            _____
   **18.** The square of $\sqrt{a} = ?$                              _____

## Reference for Questions 19–23: Section A.6.

   **19.** $3/12 = $ what percent?                                  _____
   **20.** Simplify: $\dfrac{2ab^2}{a}$                             _____
   **21.** Simplify: $\dfrac{\frac{a}{ab}}{c}$                      _____
   **22.** Does $\dfrac{a - b}{c} = \dfrac{a}{c} - \dfrac{b}{c}$?   _____
   **23.** Does $12/15 = 4/5$?                                       _____

## Reference for Questions 24–29: Section A.7.

   **24.** $a - (b - a) = ?$                                         _____
   **25.** $a(X + Y) = ?$                                            _____
   **26.** $2ab^2 - 2b$ may be expressed as the product of what two
   quantities?                                                      _____
   **27.** $(X + 4)(Y - 2) = ?$                                      _____
   **28.** $(X - Y)^2 = ?$                                           _____
   **29.** $\left\{20 - 3\left[3 + \left(\dfrac{12}{4}\right)\right]\right\}^2 = ?$   _____

**Reference for Questions 30–36: Section A.8.**

**30.** $Y - 3 = 2$ \hfill $Y =$ _____

**31.** $2Y = -6$ \hfill $Y =$ _____

**32.** $(3/4)Y = 12$ \hfill $Y =$ _____

**33.** $\dfrac{2}{Y} = 3$ \hfill $Y =$ _____

**34.** $2(Y - 2) = 4$ \hfill $Y =$ _____

**35.** $3Y - 3 = 2Y + 5$ \hfill $Y =$ _____

**36.** $\sqrt{Y^2 - 9} = k$ \hfill $Y =$ _____

**Reference for Questions 37–44: Section A.9.**

**37.** The graph of a linear function is what kind of line? \hfill _____

**38.** Among the following, which are linear equations? Write the *letters* corresponding to those equations that are linear functions on the line provided at the end of this question.

   (a)   $Y = 3X - 4$        (e)   $Y^2 = 3X + 2$

   (b)   $3Y = 4X + 2$       (f)   $\sqrt{Y} = X - 3$

   (c)   $Y - 3 = (7 + 2X)/3$     (g)   $Y = X^2 - 2X + 1$

   (d)   $Y/2 = 20 - 4(X - 1)$    (h)   $Y = -4$ \hfill _____

*Score Question 38 correct only if all parts are correct.*

If $Y = bX + a$, what are the values of $b$ and $a$ for

**39.** $Y = -X + 20$ \hfill $b =$ _____ ; $a =$ _____

**40.** $Y = 3X - 14$ \hfill $b =$ _____ ; $a =$ _____

**41.** $Y = -7X$ \hfill $b =$ _____ ; $a =$ _____

**42.** $Y = -3$ \hfill $b =$ _____ ; $a =$ _____

*Score Questions 39–42 correct only if both parts of each question are correct.*

If $Y = 2X - 30$, then

**43.** When $X = 20$, $Y = ?$ \hfill _____

**44.** When $X = 10$, $Y = ?$ \hfill _____

**Reference for Questions 45–46: Section A.10.**

$100^2 = 10{,}000$ and $102^2 = 10{,}404$. If we assumed that change in the square proceeded at the same rate as change in the number to be squared, we would estimate that:

**45.** $101^2 = ?$ \hfill _____

**46.** $(100.5)^2 = ?$ \hfill _____

*Questions 47–50 are to be answered without the aid of tables.*

**Reference for Questions 47 and 48: Section A.11.**

**47.** $800^2 = ?$ \hfill _____

**48.** $.8^2 = ?$ \hfill _____

**Reference for Questions 49 and 50: Section A.12.**

**49.** $\sqrt{90{,}000} = ?$ \hfill _____

**50.** $\sqrt{1.44} = ?$ \hfill _____

# A.3 Symbols and Their Meanings

| Symbol | Meaning |
|---|---|
| $X \neq Y$ | $X$ is not equal to $Y$. |
| $X \sim Y$ or $X \approx Y$ | $X$ is approximately equal to $Y$. |
| $X > Y$ | $X$ is greater than $Y$. |
| $X < Y$ | $X$ is less than $Y$. |
| $X \geq Y$ | $X$ is equal to or greater than $Y$. |
| $X < W < Y$ | $W$ is greater than $X$ but less than $Y$. |
| $X \leq W \leq Y$ | $W$ is not less than $X$ nor greater than $Y$ |
| $X \pm Y$ | As used in this book, it always identifies two limits: $X + Y$ and $X - Y$. |
| $\lvert X \rvert$ | The *magnitude* of $X$ without regard to its sign; e.g., $\lvert +3 \rvert = 3$ and $\lvert -3 \rvert = 3$. |
| $XY$ or $(X)(Y)$ | The product of $X$ and $Y$; $X$ times $Y$. |
| $\dfrac{X}{Y}$ or $X/Y$ | Alternative ways of indicating $X$ divided by $Y$. |
| $\dfrac{Y}{X}$ | The *reciprocal* of $\dfrac{X}{Y}$. |
| $\dfrac{1}{Y}$ | The *reciprocal* of $Y\left(\text{reciprocal of } \dfrac{Y}{1}\right)$. |
| $(X)\left(\dfrac{1}{Y}\right)$ | The product of $X$ and the reciprocal of $Y$; an alternative way of writing $X/Y$. |
| $(XY)^2$ | The square of the product of $X$ and $Y$. |
| $X^2Y^2$ | The product of $X^2$ and $Y^2$; it is the same as $(XY)^2$. |
| $XY^2$ | The product of $X$ and $Y^2$; the *"square" sign modifies Y but not X.* |
| $\infty$ | Infinity; a number indefinitely large. |
| 4 or +4 | When a *specific* number is written without a sign in front of it, a positive number is intended. Negative numbers are so indicated, e.g., $-4$. |

# A.4 Arithmetic Operations Involving Positive and Negative Numbers

| Problem | Comment |
|---|---|
| $3 - 12 = -9$ | To subtract a larger number from a smaller one, subtract the smaller from the larger and reverse the sign. |
| $3 + (-12) = -9$ | Adding a negative number is the same as subtracting the number.[1] |

---

[1] An equivalent instruction is: "When a positive sign precedes parentheses, the parentheses may be removed without changing the sign of the terms within, but when a negative sign precedes, reverse the signs of these terms." See Section A.7.

| Problem | Comment |
|---|---|
| $3 - (-12) = 15$ | Subtracting a negative number is the same as adding it.[1] |
| $-3 - 12 = -15$ | The sum of two negative numbers is the negative sum of the two numbers. |
| $(3)(-12) = -36$ | The product of two numbers is negative when *one* of the two is negative. |
| $(-3)(-12) = 36$ | The product of two numbers is positive when *both* are negative. |
| $(-2)^2 = 4$ | The square of a negative number is positive, since to square is to multiply a number by itself. |
| $(-2)(3)(-4) = 24$ | The product of more than two numbers is obtained by finding the product of any two of them, multiplying that product by one of the remaining numbers, and continuing this process as needed. Thus, $(-2)(3) = -6$ and $(-6)(-4) = 24$. |
| $(2)(0)(4) = 0$ | The product of several terms is zero if any one of them is zero. |
| $2 + 3(-4) = 2 - 12 = -10$ | In an additive sequence, reduce each term before summing. In the example, obtain the product *first,* then add it to the other term. |
| $\dfrac{-4}{2} = -2$ | When *one* of the numbers in a fraction is negative, the quotient is negative. |
| $\dfrac{-4}{-2} = 2$ | When *both* numbers in a fraction are negative, the quotient is positive. |

# A.5 Squares and Square Roots

| Problem | Comment |
|---|---|
| $[(2)(3)(4)]^2 = (2^2)(3^2)(4^2)$ <br> $24^2 = (4)(9)(16)$ <br> $576 = 576$ | The square of a product equals the product of the squares. |
| $(2 + 3 + 4)^2 \neq 2^2 + 3^2 + 4^2$ <br> $9^2 \neq 4 + 9 + 16$ <br> $81 \neq 29$ | The square of a sum does *not* equal the sum of the squares. |
| $\left(\dfrac{4}{16}\right)^2 = \dfrac{4^2}{16^2}$ <br> $\left(\dfrac{1}{4}\right)^2 = \dfrac{16}{256}$ <br> $1/16 = 1/16$ | The square of a fraction equals the fraction of the squares. |

| **Problem** | **Comment** |
|---|---|
| $\sqrt{(4)(9)(16)} = \sqrt{4}\,\sqrt{9}\,\sqrt{16}$ <br> $\sqrt{576} = (2)(3)(4)$ <br> $24 = 24$ | The square root of a product equals the product of the square roots. |
| $\sqrt{9 + 16} \neq \sqrt{9} + \sqrt{16}$ <br> $\sqrt{25} \neq 3 + 4$ <br> $5 \neq 7$ | The square root of a sum does not equal the sum of the square roots. |
| $\sqrt{\dfrac{4}{16}} = \dfrac{\sqrt{4}}{\sqrt{16}}$ <br> $\sqrt{\dfrac{1}{4}} = \dfrac{2}{4}$ <br> $\dfrac{1}{2} = \dfrac{1}{2}$ | The square root of a fraction equals the fraction of the square roots. |
| $(\sqrt{4})^2 = 4$ <br> $2^2 = 4$ <br> $4 = 4$ | The square of a square root is the same quantity found under the square root sign. Another example: $\sqrt{(x^2 - c)^2} = x^2 - c$. |

## A.6 Fractions

| **Problem** | **Comment** |
|---|---|
| $\dfrac{1}{4} = .25$ | To convert the ratio of two numbers to a decimal fraction, divide the numerator by the denominator. |
| $.25 = (100)(.25)\%$ <br> $= 25\%$ | To convert a decimal fraction to percent, multiply by 100. |
| $\left(\dfrac{3}{5}\right)(16) = \dfrac{(3)(16)}{5}$ <br> $= \dfrac{48}{5}$ <br> $= 9.6$ | To multiply a quantity by a fraction, multiply the quantity by the numerator of the fraction and divide that product by the denominator of the fraction. |
| $\dfrac{16}{4} = \left(\dfrac{1}{4}\right)(16) = 4$ | To divide by a number is the same as multiplying by its reciprocal. |
| $\dfrac{16}{\dfrac{4}{5}} = \left(\dfrac{5}{4}\right)(16) = 20$ | To divide by a fraction, multiply by its reciprocal. |

| **Problem** | **Comment** |
|---|---|
| $$\frac{3+4-2}{8} = \frac{3}{8} + \frac{4}{8} - \frac{2}{8}$$ $$= \frac{5}{8}$$ | When the numerator of a fraction is a sum, the numerator may be separated into component additive parts, each divided by the denominator. |
| $$\frac{3}{8} + \frac{4}{8} - \frac{2}{8} = \frac{3+4-2}{8}$$ $$= \frac{5}{8}$$ | When the several terms of a sum are fractions having a common denominator, the sum may be expressed as the sum of the numerators divided by the common denominator. |
| $$\frac{(3)(15)}{5} = \frac{(3)(3)(\cancel{5})}{\cancel{5}}$$ $$= 9$$ | When the numerator and/or denominator of a fraction is the product of two or more terms, identical terms appearing in the numerator and denominator may be canceled. |
| $$\left(\frac{1}{5}\right)\left(\frac{2}{7}\right)\left(\frac{3}{11}\right) = \frac{(1)(2)(3)}{(5)(7)(11)}$$ $$= \frac{6}{385}$$ | The product of several fractions equals the product of the numerators divided by the product of the denominators. |

## A.7 Operations Involving Parentheses

| **Problem** | **Comment** |
|---|---|
| $2 + (4 - 3 + 2)$ $= 2 + 4 - 3 + 2$ $= 5$ | When a positive sign precedes parentheses, the parentheses may be removed without changing the signs of the terms within. |
| $2 - (4 - 3 + 2)$ $= 2 - 4 + 3 - 2$ $= -1$ | When a negative sign precedes parentheses, they may be removed if the signs of the terms within are reversed. |
| $a(b + c) = ab + ac$ A numerical example: $2(3 + 4) = 2(3) + 2(4)$ $2(7) = 6 + 8$ $14 = 14$ | When a quantity within parentheses is to be multiplied by a number, *each* term within the parentheses must be so multiplied. |
| $2a + 4ab^2 = (2a)(1) + (2a)(2b^2)$ $= 2a(1 + 2b^2)$ A numerical example: $(6 + 8) = (2)(3) + (2)(4)$ $14 = 2(3 + 4)$ $14 = (2)(7) = 14$ | When all terms of a sum contain a common multiplier, that multiplier may be factored out as a multiplier of the remaining sum. |

| **Problem** | **Comment** |
|---|---|
| $3 + (1 + 2)^2 = 3 + 3^2$<br>$\qquad = 3 + 9 = 12$ | When parentheses are modified by squaring or some other function, take account of the modifier before combining with other terms. |

$$\left[100 - 40\left(\frac{20}{10}\right)\right] + \left[\frac{20}{10} + (40 - 30)\right]$$
$$= [100 - 40(2)] \; + [2 + 10]$$
$$= [100 - 80] \qquad + 12$$
$$= 20 \qquad\qquad\; + 12$$
$$= 32$$

When an expression contains nesting parentheses, *perform those operations required to remove the most interior parentheses first.* Simplify the expression by working outward.

$(a + b)(c - d) = ac - ad + bc - bd$

A numerical example:

$(2 + 3)(5 - 4)$
$= (2)(5) + (2)(-4) + (3)(5) + (3)(-4)$
$= \quad 10 \; - \quad 8 \quad + \quad 15 \; - \quad 12$
$= 5$

The product of two sums may be obtained by multiplying each element of one term by each element of the other term.

$(a - b)^2 = a^2 - 2ab + b^2$

A numerical example:

$(2 - 4)^2 = 2^2 + 2(2)(-4) + (-4)^2$
$(-2)^2 \quad = 4 - \quad 16 \quad + \quad 16$
$4 \qquad = 4$

The square of a binomial equals the square of the first term plus two times the product of the two terms plus the square of the second term.

## A.8 Equations in One Unknown

To solve an equation in an unknown, we must work to isolate the unknown, unmodified and by itself, on one side of the equation, and everything else on the other side of the equation. In working toward this goal, one side of the equation may be altered if the other side is altered in the *same* way. Alteration by adding, subtracting, multiplying, dividing, squaring, taking the square root, or taking the reciprocal may each be useful, depending on circumstances. *In each of the following problems, we shall suppose that it is required to solve for Y.*

| **Problem** | **Comments** |
|---|---|
| $Y + 3 = 4$<br>*Operation:* subtract 3 from both sides<br>$Y = 1$ | Subtracting 3 isolates $Y$ on one side of the equation. |
| $3Y = 12$<br>*Operation:* divide both sides by 3<br>$Y = 4$ | Dividing by 3 isolates $Y$. |

**Problem**

$$\frac{Y}{3} = 4$$

*Operation:* multiply both sides by 3

$$Y = 12$$

**Comments**

Multiplying by 3 isolates $Y$.

Many problems require two or more successive operations to isolate the unknown. Several examples follow. The order of operations is generally important, although sometimes there is more than one economical solution. Steps in a solution should be thought out in advance, as if it were a chess game.

**Problem**

$$\frac{3}{Y} = 4$$

*First operation:* take the reciprocal of both sides

$$\frac{Y}{3} = \frac{1}{4}$$

*Second operation:* multiply both sides by 3

$$Y = \frac{3}{4}$$

**Comment**

$Y$ must be dug out of the denominator, and taking the reciprocal is one way to do it. Can you think of another way?

$$2Y - 4 = 8$$

*First operation:* add 4 to both sides

$$2Y = 12$$

*Second operation:* divide both sides by 2

$$Y = 6$$

In this problem, the two operations could be performed in reverse order with no loss of efficiency.

$$2(4 - Y) = 12$$

*First operation:* perform the indicated multiplication

$$8 - 2Y = 12$$

*Second operation:* subtract 8 from both sides

$$-2Y = 4$$

*Third operation:* divide both sides by $-2$

$$Y = -2$$

There is another way to isolate $Y$; can you think of it?

$$5Y - 3 = Y + 5$$

*First operation:* subtract $Y$ from both sides

$$4Y - 3 = 5$$

*Second operation:* add 3 to both sides

$$4Y = 8$$

*Third operation:* divide both sides by 4

$$Y = 2$$

Like terms must be collected in solving an equation.

Sometimes it is required to solve an equation for an unknown when the constants are expressed by letters rather than numbers (e.g., *A, B, C,* etc.). The same principles hold. Here are two examples (we are to solve for *Y*):

$$\frac{C}{Y + K} = A$$

*First operation:* take the reciprocal of both sides

$$\frac{Y + K}{C} = \frac{1}{A}$$

*Second operation:* multiply both sides by *C*

$$Y + K = \frac{C}{A}$$

*Third operation:* subtract *K* from both sides

$$Y = \frac{C}{A} - K$$

A different solution is possible.

$$\sqrt{Y^2 - C^2} = A$$

*First operation:* square both sides

$$Y^2 - C^2 = A^2$$

*Second operation:* add $C^2$ to both sides

$$Y^2 = A^2 + C^2$$

*Third operation:* take the square root of both sides

$$Y = \sqrt{A^2 + C^2}$$

This problem becomes a nightmare unless the first operation is to square both sides.

## A.9 The Linear Function: An Equation in Two Variables

The equation $Y = 2X + 20$ is really a sentence expressing the functional relation between two variables. It states: "If *X* is . . . , then *Y* is . . ." Table A.1 shows several ways in which that sentence may be completed, each of which is in agreement with the equation.

TABLE A.1    *Values of* Y *Corresponding to Particular Values of* X *When* Y = 2X + 20

| IF *X* IS | THEN *Y* IS |
|:---:|:---:|
| +20 | +60 |
| +15 | +50 |
| +10 | +40 |
| +5 | +30 |
| 0 | +20 |
| −5 | +10 |
| −10 | 0 |
| −15 | −10 |
| −20 | −20 |

When the graph of an equation is a straight line, the equation is said to express a *linear function*. The equation $Y = 2X + 20$ is an equation of a straight line, so we may say that $Y$ is a linear function of $X$. It is easy to tell when an equation describes a straight line; the variables in such an equation are always expressed as an additive (but not multiplicative) function of "just plain $X$ and $Y$." Thus, the following equations on the left are linear functions, whereas those on the right are not:

| Linear functions | Nonlinear functions |
|---|---|
| $Y - 3X = 12$ | $Y - 3X^2 = 12$ |
| $\dfrac{2Y + 3}{4} = 16X$ | $\dfrac{2Y + 3}{4} = 16\sqrt{X}$ |
| $2Y + 1 = \dfrac{2X - 3}{7}$ | $\dfrac{4}{5(2Y - 3)} = \dfrac{2 \log X - 3}{7}$ |
| $Y = 4$ | $2XY = 3$ |

The equation at the bottom on the left is of special importance. Although it does not contain the variable $X$, it is still the equation of a straight line. If we think of it as a sentence relating $X$ and $Y$, it says: "$Y$ has the value $+4$ for any and all values of $X$." Its graph would be a horizontal line lying 4 units above the intersection of the two axes.

A linear function expressing the relation between two variables can always be reduced to the form $Y = bX + a$, where $a$ and $b$ are constants and $X$ and $Y$ are *variables*. In the equation $Y = 2X + 20$, $b = +2$, and $a = +20$. Here are several other linear functions, together with the values of $a$ and $b$:

| Equation | Values of $a$ and $b$ |
|---|---|
| $Y = -3X - 20$ | $b = -3,\ a = -20$ |
| $Y = -X + 2$ | $b = -1,\ a = +2$ |
| $Y = 4$ | $b = 0,\ a = +4$ |
| $Y = 3X$ | $b = +3,\ a = 0$ |

In elementary statistics, we encounter linear functions that are not initially expressed in this simplest form. In statistical computation, it is often required to simplify the expression and put it in this form:

$$X_n = \left(\frac{S_n}{S_o}\right)X_o + \overline{X}_n - \left(\frac{S_n}{S_o}\right)\overline{X}_o$$

where $X_n$ and $X_o$ are variables and the other symbols stand for constants. If the values of the constants are

$$\overline{X}_o = 70 \qquad S_o = 10$$
$$\overline{X}_n = 100 \qquad S_n = 20$$

the equation becomes

$$X_n = \left(\frac{20}{10}\right)X_o + 100 - \left(\frac{20}{10}\right)(70)$$
$$X_n = 2X_o + 100 - 140$$
$$X_n = 2X_0 - 40$$

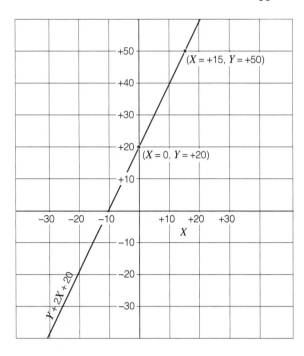

**FIGURE A.1**   Graph of the linear function $Y = 2X + 20$.

It is now apparent that the equation is in the form $Y = bX + a$, where $b = +2$ and $a = -40$. The constants $b$ and $a$ have particular meanings that help to interpret a given linear function. This aspect is explored in Section 10.4.

Because two points determine a straight line, the graph of a linear function is easy to construct. Let $X$ be any convenient numerical value, substitute that value in the equation, and determine the corresponding numerical value of $Y$. The pair of numerical values of $X$ and $Y$ identify one point on the line. Repeat this operation, using another convenient value for $X$. These values identify a second point on the line. Find the location of each point on the graph, and draw a straight line through them.

This process may be illustrated with the equation $Y = 2X + 20$, described at the beginning of this section. Referring to Table A.1, we find that when $X = 0$, $Y = +20$. The point thus identified is shown in Figure A.1. When $X = +15$, $Y = +50$; this point is also shown in Figure A.1. In practical work, it is a good idea to find a third point as a check on computational accuracy. If the third point does not lie on the line drawn through the other two, a mistake has been made. Compare other pairs of values appearing in Table A.1 with the graph. For example, Table A.1 states that when $X = -15$, $Y = -10$. Does this point fall on the line?

## A.10  Linear Interpolation

Suppose Johnny is 64 in. tall on his 16th birthday and 68 in. tall on his 17th birthday. If we wish to establish how tall he was at 16 and a half, we might assume that growth proceeded at a constant rate during the year and conclude that he was probably 66 in. tall at that time. If we wish to estimate his height at age 16 and three-quarters, we would proceed on the assumption that three-quarters of the growth had taken place when three-quarters of the time interval had passed. His height at that time is therefore estimated to be 64 in. + (3/4)(4 in.) = 67 in.

The method of estimating Johnny's height just described is called *linear interpolation*. The term *interpolation* implies that values exterior to the one desired are known, and that this knowledge is used to help estimate the desired value. The adjective *linear* tells us that the rate of change is assumed to be constant. If it is, the equation relating the variable used to assist in prediction to the variable being predicted is one that describes a straight line. In the example here, it is assumed that age and stature are linearly related.

In evaluating this procedure, we must focus on the assumption that the relationship is really linear. As with the height–age relationship, it is often known that it is not. *This will not matter much if the relation is close to a linear one, or if the two values between which interpolation takes place are close together.*

## A.11 Answers to Pretest Questions

| | | | | | |
|---|---|---|---|---|---|
| **1.** | $>$ | **18.** | $a$ | **35.** | 8 |
| **2.** | $3/2$ | **19.** | 25 | **36.** | $\sqrt{k^2 + 9}$ |
| **3.** | 8 | **20.** | $2b^2$ | **37.** | Straight line |
| **4.** | $a^2 b^2$ | **21.** | $c/b$ | **38.** | $a, b, c, d,$ and $h$ |
| **5.** | 6 | **22.** | Yes | **39.** | $b = -1, a = 20$ |
| **6.** | $-12$ | **23.** | Yes | **40.** | $b = 3, a = -14$ |
| **7.** | 12 | **24.** | $2a - b$ | **41.** | $b = -7, a = 0$ |
| **8.** | $-24$ | **25.** | $aX + aY$ | **42.** | $b = 0, a = -3$ |
| **9.** | Zero | **26.** | $2b$ and $(ab - 1)$ | **43.** | 10 |
| **10.** | $-1$ | **27.** | $XY + 4Y - 2X - 8$ | **44.** | $-10$ |
| **11.** | 2 | **28.** | $X^2 - 2XY + Y^2$ | **45.** | 10,202 |
| **12.** | No | **29.** | 4 | **46.** | 10,101 |
| **13.** | No | **30.** | 5 | **47.** | 640,000 |
| **14.** | Yes | **31.** | $-3$ | **48.** | .64 |
| **15.** | Yes | **32.** | 16 | **49.** | 300 |
| **16.** | No | **33.** | $2/3$ | **50.** | 1.2 |
| **17.** | Yes | **34.** | 4 | | |

# Appendix B

## Summation Rules

In the algebraic transformation of statistical equations, there are three basic rules of summation that come into frequent play. The first is

**Rule 1:** *When a quantity that is itself a sum or difference is to be summed, the summation sign may be distributed among the separate terms of the sum. That is,*

$$\sum (X + Y) = \sum X + \sum Y \qquad \text{(B.1)}$$

Proof of this proposition is

$$\sum (X + Y) = (X_1 + Y_1) + (X_2 + Y_2) + \cdots + (X_n + Y_n)$$

$$= (X_1 + X_2 + \cdots + X_n) + (Y_1 + Y_2 + \cdots + Y_n)$$

$$= \sum X + \sum Y$$

By extension of the proof, it follows that

$$\sum (X + Y + W + \cdots) = \sum X + \sum Y + \sum W + \cdots$$

The second rule is

**Rule 2:** ***The sum of a constant equals the product of the constant and the number of times the constant appears.*** **That is,**

$$\sum a = na \tag{B.2}$$

Proof of this proposition is apparent from the consequences of Proposition B.1:

$$\sum (X + a) = (X_1 + a) + (X_2 + a) + \cdots + (X_n + a)$$
$$= (X_1 + X_2 + \cdots + X_n) + (a + a + \cdots + a)$$
$$= \sum X + \sum a$$

Because the number of $a$'s to be summed is the same as the number of scores to be summed, it is clear that there are $n$ of them and that $\sum a = na$.

The third rule is

**Rule 3:** ***The sum of the product of a constant and a variable is equivalent to the product of the constant and the sum of the variable.*** **That is,**

$$\sum aX = a \sum X \tag{B.3}$$

Proof of this proposition is

$$\sum aX = aX_1 + aX_2 + \cdots + aX_n$$
$$= a(X_1 + X_2 + \cdots + X_n)$$
$$= a \sum X$$

These three rules can be combined and extended. Several illustrations follow, with the rules involved listed at the right. In the illustrations, $a$ and $b$ represent constants, and $X$ and $Y$ are variables:

| | | |
|---|---|---|
| **1.** | $\Sigma(X + 2) = \Sigma X + 2n$ | B.1, B.2 |
| **2.** | $\Sigma(X^2 - 1) = \Sigma X^2 - n$ | B.1, B.2 |

*Note:* If $X$ is a variable, so is $X^2$.

| | | |
|---|---|---|
| **3.** | $\Sigma 2a = 2an$ | B.2 |
| **4.** | $\Sigma ab^2 XY^2 = ab^2 \Sigma XY^2$ | B.3 |
| **5.** | $\Sigma a(Y + 3)^2 = a\Sigma(Y + 3)^2$ | B.3 |

*Note:* If $Y$ is a variable, so is $(Y + 3)^2$.

| | | |
|---|---|---|
| **6.** | $\Sigma(2X - 3) = 2\Sigma X - 3n$ | B.1, B.2, B.3 |
| **7.** | $\Sigma(Y - a)^2 = \Sigma(Y^2 - 2aY + a^2)$ | |
| | $\qquad = \Sigma Y^2 - 2a\Sigma Y + na^2$ | B.1, B.2, B.3 |

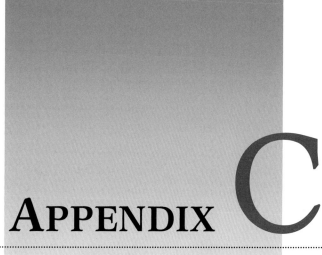

# APPENDIX C

## List of Symbols

Symbols used in this book are identified below. Numbers in parentheses indicate the page on which each symbol is introduced and defined and where pronunciation is given for Greek letters.

## Greek Letter Symbols

| | | |
|---|---|---|
| $\alpha$ | level of significance, probability of a Type I error | (234) |
| $\beta$ | probability of a Type II error | (271) |
| $1 - \beta$ | power of a test | (272) |
| $\mathrm{E}_R^2$ | epsilon squared | (459) |
| $\eta$ | correlation ratio | (146) |
| $\eta^2$ | eta-squared, a measure of effect size for $F$ | (404, 418) |
| $\mu, \mu_X$ | mean of a population | (68) |
| $\mu_{\overline{X}}$ | mean of the sampling distribution of means | (218) |

| | |
|---|---|
| $\mu_{\bar{X}-\bar{Y}}$ | mean of the sampling distribution of $\bar{X} - \bar{Y}$ (290) |
| $\rho_{XY}$ | population Pearson correlation coefficient (332) |
| $\Sigma$ | the sum of (68) |
| $\sigma, \sigma_X$ | standard deviation of a population (88) |
| $\sigma^2, \sigma_X^2$ | variance of a population (86) |
| $\sigma_r$ | standard error of $r$ (332) |
| $\sigma_{\bar{X}}$ | standard error of the mean (219) |
| $\sigma_{\bar{X}-\bar{Y}}$ | standard error of the difference between two means (293) |
| $\phi$ | phi coefficient (380), Cramer's phi (381) |
| $\chi^2$ | chi-square (368) |
| $\chi_F^2$ | test statistic for Friedman's rank test (461) |
| $\hat{\omega}$ | measure of effect size for $\chi^2$ (367) |
| $\hat{\omega}^2$ | omega-squared, a measure of effect size for $F$ (405, 438) |

# English Letter Symbols

| | |
|---|---|
| $a$ | $Y$ intercept of a line (178) |
| $b$ | slope of a line (179) |
| $C$ | confidence coefficient (346) |
| $D$ | differences between paired scores (322) |
| $\bar{D}$ | mean difference between paired scores (322) |
| $d$ | (1) discrepancy between an hypothesized value and the true value; (2) effect size (267, 302) |
| $df$ | degrees of freedom (247) |
| $F$ | variance ratio (396) |
| $f$ | frequency (30) |
| $f_e$ | expected frequency (367) |
| $f_o$ | observed frequency (367) |
| $g$ | effect size (267, 302) |
| $H$ | test statistic for the Kruskal–Wallis test (458) |
| $H_A$ | alternative hypothesis (234) |
| $H_0$ | null hypothesis (233) |
| $i$ | class interval width (29) |
| $K$ | a comparison (410) |
| $k$ | number of groups (367, 389) |
| $k^2$ | coefficient of nondetermination (185) |
| $Mdn$ | median (66) |
| $Mo$ | mode (66) |
| $MS$ | mean square, or variance estimate (396) |

| | |
|---|---|
| $N$ | number of cases in a population   (30) |
| $n$ | number of cases in a sample   (30) |
| $n_i$ | number of cases in the $i$th subgroup   (393) |
| $\tilde{n}$ | harmonic mean   (407) |
| $P$ | population value of a proportion   (366) |
| $p$ | sample value of a proportion   (372) |
| $P_j$ | $j$th percentile   (36) |
| $Pr$ | probability   (196) |
| $q$ | Studentized range statistic   (406) |
| $Q$ | semi-interquartile range   (84) |
| $R_+, R_-$ | sum of the ranks with a positive or negative sign   (456) |
| $r$ | (1) sample Pearson's correlation coefficient   (131); (2) effect size   (303) |
| $r^2$ | coefficient of determination   (187) |
| $r_c$ | matched-pairs rank biserial correlation coefficient   (457) |
| $r_g$ | Glass rank biserial correlation coefficient   (453) |
| $r_s$ | Spearman's rank order correlation coefficient   (138) |
| $S, S_X$ | standard deviation of a sample   (88) |
| $S^2, S_X^2$ | variance of a sample   (86) |
| $S_{Y'}^2$ | variance of predicted scores   (186) |
| $S_{YX}$ | standard error of estimate   (162) |
| $S_{YX}^2$ | variance of obtained scores about their predicted scores   (186) |
| $s, s_X$ | estimate of a population standard deviation   (244) |
| $s^2, s_X^2$ | unbiased estimate of a population variance   (244) |
| $s_{\text{bet}}^2$ | between-groups variance estimate   (396) |
| $s_C^2$ | column variance estimate   (435) |
| $s_{\overline{D}}$ | estimate of the standard error of the mean of difference scores   (322) |
| $s_k$ | standard error of a comparison   (408) |
| $s_p^2$ | pooled estimate of the population variance   (294) |
| $s_{\text{resid}}^2$ | residual variance estimate   (415) |
| $s_R^2$ | row variance estimate   (435) |
| $s_{R \times C}^2$ | row by column interaction variance estimate   (435) |
| $s_w^2$ | within-groups variance estimate   (396) |
| $s_{\text{wc}}^2$ | within-cell variance estimate   (435) |
| $s_{\overline{X}}$ | estimate of the standard error of the mean   (245) |
| $s_{\overline{X}-\overline{Y}}$ | estimate of the standard error of the difference between two means   (294) |
| $SS$ | sum of squares   (86) |

| | | |
|---|---|---|
| $T$ | test statistic for the Wilcoxon signed-ranks test | (456) |
| $t$ | Student's $t$ statistic | (245) |
| $t_p$ | $t$ beyond which a given proportion of values fall | (346) |
| $U$ | test statistic for the Mann-Whitney test | (449) |
| $W$ | concordance coefficient | (462) |
| $w$ | maximum desired discrepancy between sample and population characteristic in an interval estimate | (357) |
| $X$ | raw scores | (68) |
| $\overline{X}$ | mean of a sample | (68) |
| $\overline{\overline{X}}$ | mean of all scores, or grand mean | (392) |
| $Y$ | raw scores | (288) |
| $\overline{Y}$ | mean of a sample | (290) |
| $Y'$ | predicted raw score | (156) |
| $z$ | $z$ score, or standard score | (95) |
| $z'_Y$ | predicted $z$ score | (159) |
| $z'$ | Fisher's logarithmic transformation of $r$ | (334) |

# APPENDIX D
## Answers to Problems

### CHAPTER 1

**1.** (a) First    (b) Both    (c) Second
(d) First   (e) First

**3.** (a) inferential    (b) relationship and prediction    (c) inferential   (d) descriptive
(e) descriptive    (f) relationship and prediction

**5.** Yes; a statistical conclusion is a conclusion about the data only. A research conclusion derives partly from the statistical conclusion, but other factors must also be considered, such as the adequacy of the experimental design. As an example, review the executive monkey experiment (Section 1.5).

**7.** The statistical conclusion was about the data: The number of rats that developed bladder tumors when given saccharin was so much greater than for rats not given saccharin that it was unlikely that chance alone could account for the difference. (b) One possible research conclusion was that the use of saccharin might increase the chance of bladder tumors in humans. (c) Several questions might be raised about the research conclusion stated in (b). Can we generalize from rats to humans? After all, the same dosage of saccharin did not cause tumors in mice. Also, the rats were fed the human equivalent of 1,000 packets a day, whereas the average human would probably consume just a few packets. Last, do the risks posed by taking saccharin negate the benefits gained by not using sugar (e.g., fewer cases of diabetes)? Once again, keep in mind that statistics is just a middle step in the investigation of a research question.

### CHAPTER 2

**1.** (a) Choice of major of all this year's entering freshmen at our university. (b) Choice of major of the 10% of freshmen surveyed. (c) A descriptive index of all the entering freshmen's recorded choice of major. (d) A descriptive index of the recorded choice of major obtained from the 10% of freshmen surveyed. (e) Qualitative and discrete; only certain classifications (major) are possible.

**3.** It is better not to treat them so. In the best statistical sense, the population is the set of test scores in the first instance and the set of heights in the second.

**5.** (a) The sexual behavior of all adult Americans. (b) The sexual behavior of the 100,000+ readers who responded to the questionnaire. (c) A descriptive index of the population (for example, a proportion). (d) A descriptive index of the sample (for example, a proportion). (e) No; the sample is not a random sample and may be biased (review the example of the *Literary Digest*).

**7.** Type and difficulty of material to be studied; physical study conditions (light, noise, etc.), length of study period.

**9.** Ordinal

**11.** Yes; because a given numerical interval has the same meaning at any point along the scale, an interval of 20 points is twice one of 10 points no matter where the two intervals are located. Note of caution: This is not the same as saying that a score of 20 is twice as big as a score of 10.

**13.** (a) No; the true zero is no longer called zero. (b) Yes; zero remains zero, and although any interval is magnified by 10, all similar intervals are also so magnified and so remain equal.

**15.** (a) Continuous   (b) Continuous (c) Discrete   (d) Discrete   (e) Discrete (f) Continuous (the underlying variable is continuous)   (g) Continuous (h) Continuous

**17.** (a) No; the accuracy of measurement was only to the nearest tenth of a pound. (b) Yes (c) No; the investigators must have been in-terested in weight to the nearest tenth of a pound; otherwise, they would not have measured with that degree of accuracy.

# CHAPTER 3

**1.** (a)

| ACADEMIC STANDING | FREQUENCY |
|---|---|
| Graduate | 2 |
| Senior | 6 |
| Junior | 6 |
| Sophomore | 8 |
| Freshman | 2 |

(b) Ordinal   (c) Yes; they should be placed in order of rank.

**3.**

| | INTERVAL WIDTH | REAL LIMITS | APPARENT LIMITS OF NEXT HIGHER INTERVAL | REAL LIMITS OF NEXT HIGHER INTERVAL |
|---|---|---|---|---|
| (a) | 5 | 4.5–9.5 | 10–14 | 9.5–14.5 |
| (b) | 10 | 39.5–49.5 | 50–59 | 49.5–59.5 |
| (c) | 0.5 | 1.95–2.45 | 2.5–2.9 | 2.45–2.95 |
| (d) | 20 | 55–75 | 80–90 | 75–95 |
| (e) | .25 | 1.745–1.995 | 2.00–2.24 | 1.995–2.245 |

**5.** If two persons use different intervals to construct frequency distributions of the same data, the two frequency distributions will convey different information (although both may be correct). The difference between the two will become even greater if the interval widths differ.

**7.** (a) Intervals are not continuous (scores of 32–37 are omitted); top interval is open-ended. (b) Not all intervals are of the same width. (c) Not all intervals are of the same width; highest scores should be at top. (a–c) In most situations, between 10 and 20 intervals would be better.

**9.**

| SCORE | FREQUENCY | SCORE | FREQUENCY |
|-------|-----------|-------|-----------|
| 62 | 1 | 40 | 1 |
| 61 | 0 | 39 | 1 |
| 60 | 0 | 38 | 12 |
| 59 | 1 | 37 | 3 |
| 58 | 1 | 36 | 1 |
| 57 | 1 | 35 | 5 |
| 56 | 2 | 34 | 2 |
| 55 | 0 | 33 | 2 |
| 54 | 1 | 32 | 3 |
| 53 | 0 | 31 | 1 |
| 52 | 1 | 30 | 1 |
| 51 | 1 | 29 | 6 |
| 50 | 1 | 28 | 0 |
| 49 | 1 | 27 | 0 |
| 48 | 5 | 26 | 4 |
| 47 | 3 | 25 | 0 |
| 46 | 0 | 24 | 2 |
| 45 | 0 | 23 | 1 |
| 44 | 3 | 22 | 0 |
| 43 | 2 | 21 | 0 |
| 42 | 1 | 20 | 2 |
| 41 | 8 | | |

**15.**  (a)

| | REF $f$ (%) | |
|---|---|---|
| | Good mood | Bad mood |
| SCORE | (A) | (B) |
| 155–159 | | 2.0 |
| 150–154 | 1.33 | 4.0 |
| 145–149 | 2.67 | 14.0 |
| 140–144 | 4.67 | 24.0 |
| 135–139 | 8.00 | 20.0 |
| 130–134 | 9.33 | 14.0 |
| 125–129 | 16.67 | 8.0 |
| 120–124 | 15.33 | 6.0 |
| 115–119 | 12.00 | 0 |
| 110–114 | 13.33 | 4.0 |
| 105–109 | 8.00 | 2.0 |
| 100–104 | 5.33 | 0 |
| 95–99 | 2.00 | 2.0 |
| 90–94 | 1.33 | |
| | 99.99 | 100.0 |

(b) Relative frequency distributions are more meaningful for comparing two distributions in which the number of cases differ because they put both distributions on the same basis.

**11.**

| STEM | LEAF |
|------|------|
| 2 | 0 0 3 4 4 6 6 6 6 9 9 9 9 9 9 |
| 3 | 0 1 2 2 2 3 3 4 4 5 5 5 5 5 6 7 7 7 8 8 8 8 8 8 8 8 8 8 9 |
| 4 | 0 1 1 1 1 1 1 1 1 2 3 3 4 4 4 7 7 7 8 8 8 8 9 |
| 5 | 0 1 2 4 6 6 7 8 9 |
| 6 | 2 |

**13.**  (a) .37   (b) .563   (c) .042   (d) .0921
(e) .004   (f) .0085   (g) .0002

**17.** (From Problem 10a)

| SCORE | (a)<br>CUM $f$ | (b)<br>CUM % |
|---|---|---|
| 62–64 | 80 | 100.00 |
| 59–61 | 79 | 98.75 |
| 56–58 | 78 | 97.50 |
| 53–55 | 74 | 92.50 |
| 50–52 | 73 | 91.25 |
| 47–49 | 70 | 87.50 |
| 44–46 | 61 | 76.25 |
| 41–43 | 58 | 72.50 |
| 38–40 | 47 | 58.75 |
| 35–37 | 33 | 41.25 |
| 32–34 | 24 | 30.00 |
| 29–31 | 17 | 21.25 |
| 26–28 | 9 | 11.25 |
| 23–25 | 5 | 6.25 |
| 20–22 | 2 | 2.50 |

(From Problem 15a)

| SCORE | (a)<br>CUM $f$ | (b)<br>CUM % |
|---|---|---|
| 155–159 | 150 | 100.00 |
| 150–154 | 150 | 100.00 |
| 145–149 | 148 | 98.67 |
| 140–144 | 144 | 96.00 |
| 135–139 | 137 | 91.33 |
| 130–134 | 125 | 83.33 |
| 125–129 | 111 | 74.00 |
| 120–124 | 86 | 57.33 |
| 115–119 | 63 | 42.00 |
| 110–114 | 45 | 30.00 |
| 105–109 | 25 | 16.67 |
| 100–104 | 13 | 8.67 |
| 95–99 | 5 | 3.33 |
| 90–94 | 2 | 1.33 |

**19.** (a) Yes; a percentile is a score *point* on the measurement scale below which a specified percentage of the scores in the distribution fall—it may have any value that the scores may have. (b) Yes; same as (a). (c) No; percentile ranks may take values only between zero and 100. (d) No; same as (c).

**21.** (a) Range = $99 - 52 = 47$

$$\left.\begin{array}{l} 47/10 = 4.7 \\ 47/20 = 2.35 \end{array}\right\} \quad i = 3 \text{ or } 4$$

| SCORE | (a)<br>FREQUENCY | (b)<br>CUM $f$ | (c)<br>CUM % |
|---|---|---|---|
| 97–100 | 2 | 50 | 100 |
| 93–96 | 2 | 48 | 96 |
| 89–92 | 5 | 46 | 92 |
| 85–88 | 7 | 41 | 82 |
| 81–84 | 9 | 34 | 68 |
| 77–80 | 5 | 25 | 50 |
| 73–76 | 4 | 20 | 40 |
| 69–72 | 8 | 16 | 32 |
| 65–68 | 2 | 8 | 16 |
| 61–64 | 2 | 6 | 12 |
| 57–60 | 2 | 4 | 8 |
| 53–56 | 1 | 2 | 4 |
| 49–52 | 1 | 1 | 2 |
| | $n = 50$ | | |

(d) $100\left[\dfrac{34 + \left(\dfrac{3.5}{4} \times 7\right)}{50}\right]$

$= 100\left[\dfrac{40.125}{50}\right]$

$= 80.25$

*Note:* For this example, we chose to ignore guideline #7 (Section 3.3) and have 100 as our upper apparent limit for the highest interval. We could have begun with 96–99, but that would have excluded the highest possible score of 100. A frequency distribution with $i = 3$ was also possible.

## CHAPTER 4

1. Graphs of widely differing appearance may be constructed from the same distribution; under some circumstances, the graphic representation may be misleading. However, salient features of the data may be more visible in graphic representation.

3.

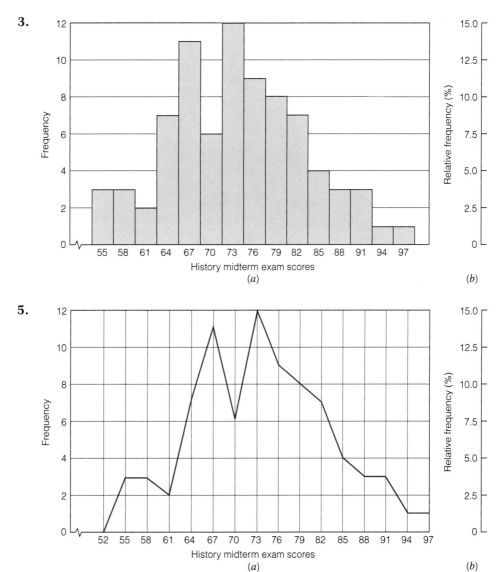

**7.**

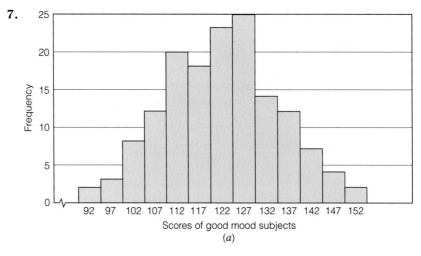

(a)

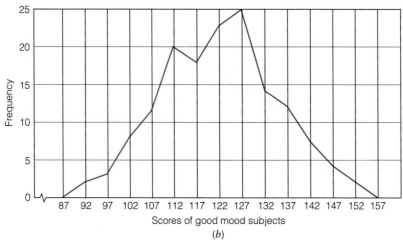

(b)

**9.**

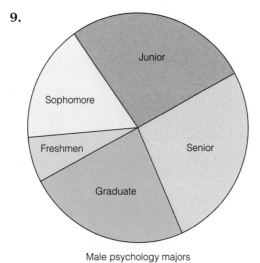

Male psychology majors

**11.**

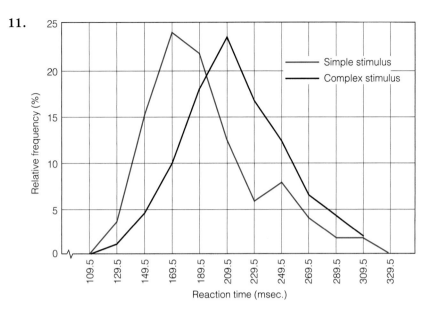

Conclusion: The spread of reaction times under the two conditions is similar, but a greater proportion of subjects react more quickly to the simple stimulus.

**13.**

| SCORE FOR GOOD MOOD SUBJECTS | FREQUENCY | (a) CUM $f$ | (b) CUM % |
|---|---|---|---|
| 150–154 | 2 | 150 | 100.0 |
| 145–149 | 4 | 148 | 98.7 |
| 140–144 | 7 | 144 | 96.0 |
| 135–139 | 12 | 137 | 91.3 |
| 130–134 | 14 | 125 | 83.3 |
| 125–129 | 25 | 111 | 74.0 |
| 120–124 | 23 | 86 | 57.3 |
| 115–119 | 18 | 63 | 42.0 |
| 110–114 | 20 | 45 | 30.0 |
| 105–109 | 12 | 25 | 16.7 |
| 100–104 | 8 | 13 | 8.7 |
| 95–99 | 3 | 5 | 3.3 |
| 90–94 | 2 | 2 | 1.3 |

(c–d)

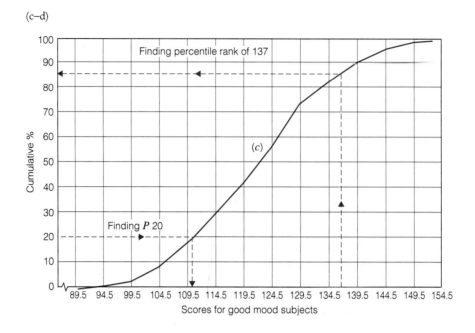

Scores for good mood subjects

**15.** (a)

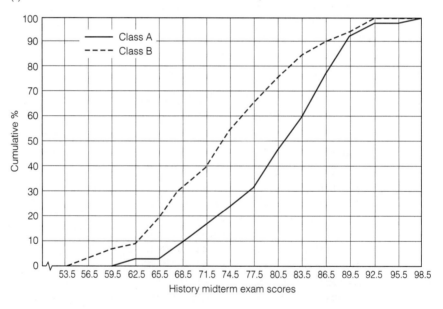

History midterm exam scores

(b) Distribution A falls to the right of distribution B. (c) The horizontal space occupied by distribution B is greater. (d) The cumulative curves are smoother. (e) The noncumulated distribution shows the frequency of a particular score or range of scores; the cumulative distribution shows the frequency of scores below a particular score point and is better for identifying the position of a score relative to the group.

**17.** (a) Rises quickly at first, then less rapidly. (b) Rises more slowly at first, then quickly. (c) Rises at uniform rate. (d) Center shows less rapid rise than portions immediately preceding or following.

## CHAPTER 5

**1.** (a) Median = 12.5; mean = 12.25
(b) Median = 12; mean = 12    (c) Median = 11; mean = 11    (d) Median = 10; mean = 9.67    (e) Median = 8; mean = 7.17    (f) Median = 6; mean = 6.5    (g) Median = 7.17; mean = 6.5    (h) Median = 3.83; mean = 3.5    (i) Median = 2; mean = 2.62

**3.** (a) Mean = 55.0; *Mdn* = 55.2; *Mo* = 57; (b) Mean = 55.6; *Mdn* = 55.5; *Mo* = 56.5.

**5.** Yes; the mode is 9 because no other score can have a frequency of 3 or more.

**7.** No; the mean is the sum of *all* the scores in a distribution.

**9.** (a) +    (b) 0    (c) −    (d) +    (e) −

**11.** (a) For example, a bimodal distribution. (b) The mean will equal the median.

**13.** Negatively skewed.

**15.** The distribution is positively skewed.

**17.** Median; the distribution is open-ended, so we cannot calculate the mean without making assumptions.

**19.** (a) *Mo* = 12    (b) *Mdn* = 14.5
(c) $\overline{X}$ = 14.75    (d) Median

**21.** Yes; if "average" refers to $\overline{X}$, in a positively skewed distribution the *Mdn* will be less than $\overline{X}$, and thus more than half earn less than the mean income.

**23.** $\overline{X}_C = \dfrac{n_1\overline{X}_1 + n_2\overline{X}_2 + \cdots}{n_1 + n_2 + \cdots}$

## CHAPTER 6

**1.** (a) Semi-interquartile range (b) Range (c) Standard deviation (d) Standard deviation (e) Range (f) Semi-interquartile range (g) Standard deviation (h) Semi-interquartile range (i) Standard deviation

**3.** Simple stimulus: (a) 199, (b) 25.4    Complex stimulus: (a) 199, (b) 25.4    (c) Variability of the two in terms of range and *Q* is equal.

**5.** (a) 85    (b) 68    (c) 80

**7.** 15, 12, 11, 2, and 10

**9.** (a) $S^2 = 10.44$    (b) $S = 3.23$

**11.** (a) Inches²    (b) Inches

**13.** (a) 9    (b) 3    (c) 9    (d) 3    (e–f) Because the *Y* scores are obtained by adding a constant (2) to each *X* score; adding a con-

stant to each score in a distribution does not affect the variance or standard deviation.

**15.** (a) No; the variance is obtained by squaring scores and thus cannot have a negative value. (b) No; the standard deviation is the square root of the variance, which always is a positive value.

**17.** (a) 38    (b) 42    (c) 42    (d) When we calculate deviations from the mean, the sum of squares is smaller than when deviations are taken about any other point.

**19.** (a) 40,000    (b) 12,437

**21.** Dividing each score by 1,000, calculating *S*, and then multiplying the obtained value of *S* by 1,000 would make the calculation of *S* less cumbersome.

**23.** (a) +1.00    (b) +2.00    (c) −2.00
(d) 0.00    (e) −1.33    (f) −0.33
(g) +0.53    (h) −0.87    (i) +1.47

**25.** Nothing; a score is uninterpretable without a frame of reference (such as the mean and standard deviation).

**27.** Robin; her score is 1.5 *z* scores (standard deviations) greater than the mean for her exam, whereas Susan's score is 1.17 *z* scores greater than the mean for her exam.

**29.** −1.11, −1.51, +1.71, +0.91, +0.50, +0.10, +0.10, and −0.71. The shape of the distribution has not changed because to calculate each *z* score we first subtract a constant (the mean) and then divide by another constant (the standard deviation).

## CHAPTER 7

**1.** The normal curve is a mathematical abstraction having a particular defining equation. No real variable is exactly normally distributed, but the normal curve does offer a convenient and reasonably accurate *description* of a number of distributions (especially the hypothetical distributions that we will encounter in inferential statistics).

**3.** (a) .8413    (b) .50    (c) .9772    (d) .8023

**5.** (a) .2957    (b) .1359    (c) .0215

**7.** (a) .3085    (b) .1587    (c) .2119
(d) .9332    (e) .3023    (f) .8716
(g) .0934    (h) .3056

**9.** (a) +1.64 (b) +1.96 (c) +2.33    (d) +2.58

**11.** .8944

**13.** 31.68 and 48.32 (*z* scores of ±1.04)

**15.** (a) About .0004    (b) 72,000

## CHAPTER 8

**1.** (a) Positive    (b) Close to zero
(c) Negative    (d) Positive

**3.** (a)

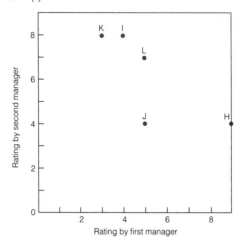

The relationship is negative.
(b) $\Sigma X = 26$; $\Sigma Y = 31$; $\Sigma X^2 = 156$;
$\Sigma Y^2 = 209$; $\Sigma XY = 147$; $r = -.76$
(c) $S_X = 2.04$; $S_Y = 1.83$
(d) Agreement

**5.** (a) $\Sigma X = 381$; $\Sigma Y = 775$; $\Sigma X^2 = 14{,}699$;
$\Sigma Y^2 = 60{,}281$;   $\Sigma XY = 29{,}664$;   $r = .68$
(b) They offer moderately strong evidence
that the test is valid.

**7.** (a) Nations    (c) Positive and moderate
in strength.    (e) $\Sigma X = 6620$; $\Sigma Y = 2230$;
$\Sigma X^2 = 5{,}436{,}400$; $\Sigma Y^2 = 590{,}100$; $\Sigma XY = 1{,}672{,}300$; $r = .74$

**9.** (a) $r_S = +.60$

**11.** (a)

| $R_X$ | $R_Y$ |
|-------|-------|
| 1 | 1 |
| 2 | 2 |
| 3 | 3 |
| 4 | 5.5 |
| 5.5 | 5.5 |
| 5.5 | 8 |
| 7 | 4 |
| 8 | 9 |
| 9 | 10 |
| 10 | 11 |
| 11 | 7 |
| | $r_s = .83$ |

(b) No; because differences between adjacent scores are not proportional to differences between adjacent ranks, and because of ties in ranks.

**13.** Start with a set of original (untransformed) scores. For each find the transformed score according to any of the so-called linear transformations. In a two-dimensional plot, where the $X$ axis shows the original and the $Y$ axis the transformed score, each point whose coordinates are an original and the corresponding transformed score will lie on the same straight line.

**15.** (a) Positive    (b) A correlation between two variables cannot by itself prove a causal relationship between them. (c) A third variable or a complex of additional variables may influence both smoking and lung cancer, causing them to covary. For example, certain temperaments may predispose people both to smoke and to develop lung cancer. Or the third variable may be socioeconomic status; lower-class people are generally heavier smokers than middle-class people, and they generally live where air pollution is worse. (d) Besides the simple correlational findings, other evidence includes sophisticated correlational findings in which third variables are ruled out as alternative explanations, experiments in which laboratory animals are exposed to tobacco smoke, and biological research showing exactly how smoking damages the tissues and cells of the lungs.

**17.** (a) Positive (b) No; a correlation between two variables cannot by itself prove a causal relationship between them. (c) A third variable influences both the quantity of ice cream sold and the number of murders, causing them to covary: the temperature. On hotter days, people buy more ice cream, and on hotter days murders become more likely—perhaps because the heat brings extra irritability or because it raises testosterone levels. (d) "c"

**19.** The conclusion may be correct, but it doesn't warrant much confidence; the values of $r$ may differ only because of sampling variation (sampling error), or only because of restricted variability among the men in mathematical ability or in exam score.

**21.** The tests of extraversion may differ. The measures of leadership ability may differ. The range of talent on either or both variables may differ. The kinds of officers sampled may differ. The relationship between the two variables may be curvilinear in the navy. Or everything could be the same between the army's study and the navy's, and the different values of $r$ could have arisen merely from sampling variation (sampling error).

**23.** (a) $\Sigma X = 552, \Sigma Y = 1,183, \Sigma X^2 = 11,598,$ $\Sigma Y^2 = 48,459, \ \Sigma XY = 22,742, \ r = .6037$
(b) $S_X = 6.9311 \ S_Y = 7.7661$

---

# CHAPTER 9

**1.** When the relationship between $X$ and $Y$ is linear, and when the data are a sample from a population rather than the population itself.

**3.** No; the discrepancies between predicted and actual values would appear as horizontal line segments, and minimizing the squares of these horizontal discrepancies usually requires a different line. See Figure 10.3.

**5.** Zero. When $r = -1.00$, all data points lie on a (straight) line, and this is the line of best fit. Thus $Y' = Y$ for each case, $d_Y = 0$ for each case, $d_Y^2 = 0$ for each case, and $\Sigma d_Y^2 = 0$.

**7.** (a) $z_X = 0.00, z_Y' = 0.00, Y' = 500$
(b) $z_X = 1.00, z_Y' = 0.50, Y' = 550$
(c) $z_X = 2.00, z_Y' = 1.00, Y' = 600$
(d) $z_X = -1.00, z_Y' = -0.50, Y' = 450$
(e) $z_X = -2.00, z_Y' = -1.00, Y' = 400$
(f) $z_X = 3.00, z_Y' = 1.50, Y' = 650$
(g) $z_X = -3.00, z_Y' = -1.50, Y' = 350$

**9.** No; here $X = \overline{X}$ and $Y' = \overline{Y}$, but no matter what the value of $r$, $Y' = \overline{Y}$ if $X = \overline{X}$.

**11.** The least-squares criterion calls for minimizing $\Sigma d_Y^2$, which is $\Sigma(Y - Y')^2$. When $r = 0.00$, $Y' = \overline{Y}$ for all values of $X$, so $\Sigma d_Y^2 = \Sigma(Y - \overline{Y})^2$, and this sum is lower than the sum of the squared deviations about any quantity other than the mean of the $Y$ scores.

**13.** $Y' = 3.333X + 166.667$ (a) For $X = 100, Y' = 3.333(100) + 166.667 = 500$
(c) For $X = 130, Y' = 3.333(130) + 166.667 = 433.290 + 166.667 = 600$
(e) For $X = 70, Y' = 3.333(70) + 166.667 = 233.310 + 166.667 = 400$

**15.** (a)

(b) $Y' = .74X + 49.306$ (c) See graph. (d) 70.0 (e) 77.4 (f) 84.1

**17.** (a) $-77.74$ lb. (b) The weight is impossible, and thus the regression equation fails to work for low values of $X$. It is valid only for adult heights like those in the data that generated the equation.

**19.** (a) 86.6 (b) 13.73

**21.** (a) $Y' = .00233X + 1.343$ (b) 2.475 and 3.000 (c) Linearity of regression (d) .30311 (e) $z = .58$ for the mean of 2.65; proportion = .2810 (f) $z = -1.57$ for a GPA of 2.0; proportion = .0582 (g) 1.88 and 3.07 (h) $z = -1.65$ for a GPA of 2.5; proportion = .9505 (i) $z = .00$ for a GPA of 3.0; proportion = .5000 (j) $z = \pm 0.67$; 2.80 and 3.20 (k) Linearity of regression, homoscedasticity, and normality of the distribution of $Y$ values for both values of $X$.

**23.** For (e) through (g), we would have overestimated the variability around the $Y'$ of 2.475. For (h) through (j), we would have underestimated the variability around the $Y'$ of 2.999.

---

# CHAPTER 10

**1.** $S_{YX}^2 = S_Y^2(1 - r^2) = S_Y^2 - S_Y^2 r^2$

$S_Y^2 r^2 = S_Y^2 - S_{YX}^2$

$r^2 = \dfrac{S_Y^2 - S_{YX}^2}{S_Y^2} = 1 - \dfrac{S_{YX}^2}{S_Y^2}$

$r = \sqrt{1 - \dfrac{S_{YX}^2}{S_Y^2}}$

**3.** Because all the persons in the group are highly creative, the range of talent on this variable is small. The two variables would probably correlate more substantially in a random sample of the general population.

**5.** There is likely to be less variability among currently employed workers than among job applicants, so we expect a lower correlation for the employed.

**7.** For the sample of ninth and twelfth graders because of the discontinuities in the heights and in the weights resulting from the removal of the students in the intermediate grades.

**9.** (a)

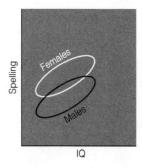

(b) No; it will be lower in the pooled data. The spelling means differ between the two sexes, but the IQ means are about the same, so the regression line fitted to the pooled data will lie between the two distributions such that the ratio of $S_{YX}^2$ to $S_Y^2$ will be larger than that for either sample alone.

**11.** (a) No; the regression coefficient here is 2; for a regression equation in standard-score form, the regression coefficient is $r$, and $r$ cannot be greater than 1. One can also tell that this is not a standard-score form for the reason given in answer 12(a). (b) The correlation is positive, and on average $Y$ increases by 2 units for each unit of increase in $X$, but we cannot tell how strong the correlation is.

**13.** Yes; the $Y$ intercept here is 0, which means that when $X = 0$, $Y' = 0$ and the regression line for the raw scores passes through the origin of the graph. This state of affairs can happen by coincidence.

**15.** (a) .00125 (b) The slope is .00125. This very small value signifies a line that is nearly flat (horizontal); it slopes only gradually from lower left to upper right.

**17.** (a) $Y' = .102X + 54.215$ (b) .102 (c) Height increases .102 inches, on average, for every 1-pound increase in weight.

**19.** To assess the effects of the praise and the rebukes, we need more data. The observations cited could have been due entirely to regression on the mean. To disentangle the effects of the teacher's words from the effects of regression, we should create control conditions. We could randomly assign students who did well to an experimental condition in which they receive praise or to a control condition in which the teacher says something neutral. Similarly, we could randomly assign students who did poorly to an experimental condition in which they receive rebukes or to a control condition in which the teacher says something neutral. For each kind of student, we would then compare the average examination scores of the two conditions to isolate the effects of the teacher's praise or rebukes.

**21.** The safety course may have been beneficial, but because of regression toward the mean, one would expect improvement even if the course were useless.

**23.** (a) .94 (b) The errors in predicting GPAs from SAT scores are on average 94% as great as those that would occur in the worst possible case (obtained when the correlation is zero for the two variables and our prediction for each student's GPA is the mean). (c) .12 (d) Of the variation in GPA among the freshmen, 12% is associated with differences in their SAT scores.

**25.** (a) Zero (b) See the answers to Problems 4 and 5 for Chapter 9.

**27.** When $Y' = Y$, for each case, which occurs when $r = \pm 1$.

**29.** (a) The proportion of correct placements would be .50 + .11 = .61. (b) .50 correct (c) The bivariate data are normally distributed.

**31.** (a) The predictive error relative to the worst possible case has improved from .97 to .87. (b) The proportion of variation in common between the two variables has increased from .06 to .25. (c) The proportion of correct placements has increased from .58 to .67. (d) No; the increase in the proportion of correct placements in excess of .50, the chance level, is approximately a doubling, but that is only a coincidence. In general, a doubling in the absolute value of *r* does not signify a doubling in the strength of the relation between the two variables.

## CHAPTER 11

1. (a) .25 (b) 25

3. (a) $(1/6) \times (1/6) = 1/36$ (b) $(1/6) \times (1/6) = 1/36$ (c) $[(1/6) \times (1/6)] + [(1/6) \times (1/6)] = 2/36 = 1/18$

5. (a) $(1/52) \times (1/52) = 1/2704$
(b) $(4/52) \times (4/52) = 16/2704 = 1/169$
(c) $(13/52) \times (13/52) = 169/2704 = 1/16$ (d) $(4/52) \times (4/52) = 16/2704 = 1/169$ (e) $[(4/52) \times (4/52)] + [(4/52) \times (4/52)] = 32/2704 = 2/169$

7. Odds against event A = (Total number of outcomes − Number of outcomes favoring A) to Number of outcomes favoring A

9. (a) Die #1: 1 1 1 1 1 1 2 2 2 2 2 2
Die #2: 1 2 3 4 5 6 1 2 3 4 5 6

Die #1: 3 3 3 3 3 3 4 4 4 4 4 4
Die #2: 1 2 3 4 5 6 1 2 3 4 5 6

Die #1: 5 5 5 5 5 5 6 6 6 6 6 6
Die #2: 1 2 3 4 5 6 1 2 3 4 5 6

(b) Sum of points: 2 3 4 5 6 7
Relative *f*: 1/36 2/36 3/36 4/36 5/36 6/36

Sum of points: 8 9 10 11 12
Relative *f*: 5/36 4/36 3/36 2/36 1/36

(c) 1/36 (d) 3/36 or 1/12 (e) 6/36 or 1/6
(f) 15/36 or 5/12; 30/36 or 5/6 (g) 1/36; 1/1296

11. (a) .0032 (b) .0916 (c) .0139
(d) .1509

13. (a) .0005 (b) .0171 (c) .1333
(d) .8491 (e) .1509

15. .6634

17. $(30/3,000,000) \times (30/3,000,000) = 1/10,000,000,000 = 1/10^{10}$ (one in 10 billion). Diaconis and Mosteller calculated the probability that *any one* of the millions of the people who enter two lotteries within 4 months will win both. The probability of this event is much higher because there are millions of chances for it to occur—one chance for each of the people who enter two lotteries. Your friend has only one of those chances.

## CHAPTER 12

1. A person in the population will have an unfairly large chance to get into your sample if the person speaks fluent English, has an opinion on the issue, and is not in a hurry. Bias may also arise because you prefer people of a certain age or gender or ethnic group.

3. One should assign to each score a unique number; the conventional choices would be the two-digit integers 01–30. In the table of random numbers, one should arbitrarily select a starting location and a direction in which to read out successive numbers, two at a time. One should choose for the sample those scores designated by the first 10 selections from the table that lie within the range 01 to 30.

5. $\mu_X = 5.0; \sigma_X = 3.63$

| (b) Samples | (c) $\overline{X}$ | (d) $\overline{X}$ | *f* |
|---|---|---|---|
| 1,1 | 1.0 | 1.0 | 1 |
| 1,2 | 1.5 | 1.5 | 2 |
| 1,4 | 2.5 | 2.0 | 1 |
| 1,7 | 4.0 | 2.5 | 2 |
| 1,11 | 6.0 | 3.0 | 2 |
| 2,1 | 1.5 | 4.0 | 3 |
| 2,2 | 2.0 | 4.5 | 2 |
| 2,4 | 3.0 | 5.5 | 2 |
| 2,7 | 4.5 | 6.0 | 2 |
| 2,11 | 6.5 | 6.5 | 2 |
| 4,1 | 2.5 | 7.0 | 1 |
| 4,2 | 3.0 | 7.5 | 2 |
| 4,4 | 4.0 | 9.0 | 2 |
| 4,7 | 5.5 | 11.0 | 1 |
| 4,11 | 7.5 | | |
| 7,1 | 4.0 | | |
| 7,2 | 4.5 | | |
| 7,4 | 5.5 | | |
| 7,7 | 7.0 | | |
| 7,11 | 9.0 | | |
| 11,1 | 6.0 | | |
| 11,2 | 6.5 | | |
| 11,4 | 7.5 | | |
| 11,7 | 9.0 | | |
| 11,11 | 11.0 | | |

(e) $\mu_{\overline{X}} = 5.0$, $\sigma_{\overline{X}} = 2.57$ (f) $\sigma_{\overline{X}} = 2.57$
(g) Yes, 5 (h) Yes, 2.57 (i) No; however it is more like the normal curve than is the population of 5 scores. This is in accord with the central limit theorem.

7. (a) .19 (b) .32

**9.** (a) 159.3 (b) 139.7–160.3

**11.** (a) 153.2 (b) 145.9–154.1

**13.** $\mu_{\bar{X}} = 100$ and $\sigma_{\bar{X}} = 1.5$ (a) .0004 (b) .0004 (c) $z = \pm 1.96$. The limits are 97.1 and 102.9. (d) Sample means show less variation as sample size increases.

**15.** (a) 2.5% (b) 5.1% (c) 29.2%

---

# CHAPTER 13

**1.** (a) No (b) No (c) No (d) No (e) No (f) Yes (g) No (h) No

**3.** (a) $H_0$: $\mu = 82$, $H_A$: $\mu \neq 82$ (b) $H_0$: $\mu = 210$, $H_A$: $\mu < 210$ (c) $H_0$: $\mu = 24$, $H_A$: $\mu > 24$

**5.** If interest is *only* in a difference in a particular direction, a one-tailed test is appropriate. If, however, we are interested in discovering a difference in either direction, we should conduct a two-tailed test, even if we expect the outcome to be in just one of those directions.

**7.** Rejecting $H_0$ means that we have found a statistic to be so deviant that its probability of occurrence when $H_0$ is true is rare enough for us to conclude that it is not reasonable to believe $H_0$. Retaining $H_0$ means that we do not have sufficient evidence to reject it, and this conclusion does not imply that it is true—only that it *could* be true. The two conclusions, reject and retain, thus differ in the confidence that they warrant: Rejecting the null deserves more confidence than retaining the null.

**9.** No; the .05 is the probability of rejecting $H_0$ when $H_0$ is true. There is no way to turn an alpha level into a number indicating the degree of confidence warranted by the conclusion about the null hypothesis.

**11.** (a) $p > .05$ (b) $p < .01$ (c) $p < .001$ (d) $p > .05$

**13.** $z = \dfrac{87.1 - 85.0}{10/\sqrt{100}} = +2.1$

Dr. Brown would conclude that students in her school district perform better on that particular mathematics achievement test.

**15.** (a) $z_{obt} = +2.50$, $z_{crit} = \pm 1.96$; reject $H_0$ (b) $z_{obt} = +2.50$, $z_{crit} = \pm 2.58$; retain $H_0$ (c) .0062 (d) .0124

**17.** $z_{obt} = +2.50$, $z_{crit} = -1.64$; retain $H_0$

**19.** (a) $+2.602$ (b) $-1.341$

**21.** (a) .10 (b) .90 (c) .05 (d) .75 (e) .95 (f) .925

**23.** (a) Retain $H_0$; $t_{crit} = \pm 2.262$ (b) Reject $H_0$; $t_{crit} = \pm 2.093$ (c) Reject $H_0$: $t_{crit} = +1.833$

**25.** (a) $H_0$: $\mu_X = 18.9$, $H_A$: $\mu_X \neq 18.9$ (b) $t_{crit} = \pm 2.064$ (c) $t_{obt} = -2.69$ (d) Students at your school perform worse on the English component of the ACT than do students nationally.

**27.** (a) $H_A$: $\mu_X < 98$ (b) We would have to retain the null hypothesis because the result is opposite the direction stated by the alternative hypothesis.

**29.** (a) $t_{obt} = +12.22$ (b) $t_{crit} = \pm 2.064$; reject $H_0$ and conclude that the advertisement is correct. (c) The increase in $n$ results in a smaller value of $s_{\bar{X}}$; thus, it takes less of a difference between $\mu_{hyp}$ and $\mu_{obt}$ to reject the null hypothesis. In addition, the critical value of $t$ is smaller.

**31.** (a) $\sqrt{5.0} = 2.24$ (b) 0, 1.41, 2.83, 4.24, 1.41, 0, 1.41, 2.83, 2.83, 1.41, 0, 1.41, 4.24, 2.83, 1.41, 0 (c) 1.77 (d) No; although $s^2$ is an unbiased estimator of $\sigma^2$, $s$ still tends to underestimate $\sigma$ because a square root is not a linear transformation

---

# CHAPTER 14

**1.** $r^2$ appears small, but it is important to examine the effect size. As it turned out, the effect size for this study revealed that $r = .32$, which meant that 66 of 100 subjects receiving psychotherapy improved, whereas only 34 of 100 subjects not receiving psychotherapy improved.

**3.** $\dfrac{104 - 100}{20} = .2$

**5.** (a) 0.64 (b) 2.44

**7.** (a) .92; .08 (b) .83; .17

**9.** (a) .83; .17 (b) .48; .52

**11.** (a) $H_0$: $\mu_X = 3.1$ $H_A$: $\mu_X \neq 3.1$ (b) $d = .09/.30 = .30$, so $n$ should be slightly less than 100.

**13.** 70

**15.** (a) .094 (b) .314 (c) .656 (d) There is not a good chance of detecting a difference.

**17.** The authors of the study properly generalized their results only to coeds at Brown University, whereas the newspaper improperly generalized the results to all college women; nationally, college women may or may not behave similarly to those attending Brown.

---

## CHAPTER 15

**1.** No; because of the variability introduced by random sampling, we would expect two samples to yield different means even if the two groups had been treated alike. We can only conclude that the memory pill works if the difference between the two sample means is so great that it could not reasonably be accounted for by chance variation when the population means are the same.

**3.** (a) $H_0$: $\mu_X - \mu_Y = 0$, $H_A$: $\mu_X - \mu_Y \neq 0$ (b) 1.03 (c) $-9.71$ (d) In both cases, reject $H_0$ and conclude that $Y$ is greater than $X$.

**5.** .25; —

**7.** (a) $H_0$: $\mu_E - \mu_{NE} = 0$, $H_A$: $\mu_E - \mu_{NE} \neq 0$ (b) $t = -4.98$ ($s_{\bar{E}-\bar{NE}} = 2.91$); reject $H_0$ (c) No (d) $g = 2.42$, $r = +.79$

**9.** (a) $H_0$: $\mu_{ABZ} - \mu_{placebo} = 0$ $H_A$: $\mu_{ABZ} - \mu_{placebo} \neq 0$ (b) sample (c) $t = 4.97$ ($s_{\overline{ABZ}-\bar{p}} = 14.8$, $t_{crit} = 2.878$, reject $H_0$ and conclude that ABZ increases the CD4+ cell count. (d) $g = 2.22$, $r = +.76$ (e) No; the researcher would have to randomly assign available subjects. For most situations in which groups are formed by random assignment, use of the random sampling model will lead to the same statistical conclusion as would result from use of the proper model.

**11.** (a) $H_0$: $\mu_X - \mu_Y = 0$ $H_A$: $\mu_X - \mu_Y \neq 0$ (b) $t = +1.32$ ($s_{\bar{X}-\bar{Y}} = 3.02$, $t_{crit} = 2.101$), retain $H_0$ (c) No; retaining $H_0$ means that we do not have sufficient evidence to reject $H_0$—it does not mean that $H_0$ is probably true, but only that it *could* be true. (d) $g = 0.59$, $r = .30$

**13.** (a) $H_0$: $\mu_{notice} - \mu_{no\ notice} = 0$ $H_A$: $\mu_{notice} - \mu_{no\ notice} \neq 0$ (b) $d = .25$, $n =$ approximately 500

**15.** (a) .39 × 50 replications = 19 or 20 (b) .66 × 50 = 33 (c) .96 × 50 = 48 (d) .999 × 50 = 50

**17.** (a) .31 (b) .95 (c) .99+ (d) Better chance of detecting a difference than in Problem 16.

**19.** (a) 400 (b) Approximately 66 (c) 25 (d) 13

---

## CHAPTER 16

**1.** Only in that the sign of the obtained $t$ would be different. (b) No; the difference between the two means is still the same. (c) Because students were matched in terms of intellectual ability, forming 15 pairs.

**3.** (a) $H_0$: $\mu_X - \mu_Y = 0$, $H_A$: $\mu_X - \mu_Y \neq 0$ (b) $s_{\bar{X}-\bar{Y}} = 1.80$ (c) $t = +1.67$; retain $H_0$ at both levels

**5.** (a) $\overline{D} = 2.2$; $s_{\overline{D}} = .86$ (b) $t = +2.56$; same (c) At $\alpha = .05$, retain $H_0$; at $\alpha = .01$, retain $H_0$ (d) $g = 1.15$

**7.** (a) $H_0$: $\mu_E - \mu_I = 0$, $H_A$: $\mu_E - \mu_I \neq 0$ (b) $t_{obt} = +2.43$ ($s_{\overline{D}} = 1.54$); reject $H_0$ and conclude that twins raised in an enriched environment have higher IQs than their counterparts raised in an impoverished environment. (c) Twins are biologically matched. (d) No; only that environment plays a role. (e) $g = 0.70$ (f) No; the researcher must be careful about making generalizations to the intended population—this can be done, but statistics alone does not provide the basis for it.

---

## CHAPTER 17

**1.** (a) .878 (b) .632 (c) .396 (d) .505 (e) .337 (f) .197 (g) .062

**3.** (a) $r_{crit} = \pm.374$, reject $H_0$ (b) $r_{crit} = \pm.590$, retain $H_0$ (c) $r_{crit} = -.360$, reject $H_0$ (d) $r_{crit} = -.337$, retain $H_0$

**5.** $r = .75$ suggests a strong relationship, but with the small sample we find it is not great enough to reject the null hypothesis that $\rho = 0$ at $\alpha = .05$

**7.** (a) Yes; the coefficient must be $< .062$ (two-tailed test), and therefore it is probably not an important relationship. (b) No; the size of the relationship could be substantial or small enough to be unimportant.

**9.** (a) $df = 4$, $r_{crit} = .811$, retain $H_0$ (b) $n$ is too small for proper evaluation by Table G.

## CHAPTER 18

1. (a) $C[60.62 \leq \mu_X \leq 65.38] = .95$
   (b) $C[59.85 \leq \mu_X \leq 66.15] = .99$

3. (a) $C[109.04 \leq \mu_X \leq 124.96] = .95$
   (b) $C[106.44 \leq \mu_X \leq 127.56] = .99$

5. $d = .41$; only moderately precise: $\mu_X$ should be within .41 $\sigma_X$ of $\overline{X}$.

7. (a) $C[-19.75 \leq (\mu_X - \mu_Y) \leq -.25] = .95$
   (b) $C[-22.93 \leq (\mu_X - \mu_Y) \leq +2.93] = .99$

9. $d = .43$; only moderate precision: $\mu_X - \mu_Y$ should be within .436 of $\overline{X} - \overline{Y}$.

11. $d = .33$; $\mu_X - \mu_Y$ should be within .336 of $\overline{X} - \overline{Y}$, moderately precise

13. (a) Retain $H_0$    (b) Reject $H_0$    (c) A confidence interval contains all those values that if hypothesized would be retained.

15. (a) $+5$    (b) retain $H_0$

17. $C[-8.3 \leq (\mu_X - \mu_Y) \leq -20.7] = .95$

19. $C[32.33 \leq (\mu_X - \mu_Y) \leq 40.97] = .99$

21. $C[-0.19 \leq (\mu_X - \mu_Y) \leq 4.59] = .95$

23. $C[-1.03 \leq (\mu_X - \mu_Y) \leq 8.53] = .99$

25. 96

27. (a) 69    (b) 42

29. (a) $C[.03 \leq \rho \leq .91] = .95$
    (b) $C[.29 \leq \rho \leq .85] = .95$
    (c) $C[.43 \leq \rho \leq .80] = .95$
    (d) $C[.50 \leq \rho \leq .76] = .95$

## CHAPTER 19

1. Because all discrepancies are squared, both positive and negative discrepancies make a positive contribution to the value of $\chi^2$. Only large positive values are possibly indicative of nonchance discrepancies.

3. It would be necessary to assume that each of the 50 trials is independent of the others, which is almost certainly wrong.

5. (a) $\chi^2 = 6.93$, for $df = 2$, $\chi^2_{0.5} = 5.99$, so we reject $H_0$; $\chi^2_{.01} = 9.21$, so we retain $H_0$. When $\chi^2$ is significant, we can conclude only that $H_0$ is untrue in some (any) way.    (b) .29    (c) Medium

7. On statistical grounds, it is possible to generalize the inferential outcome of a test *only* to the population from which the observations may be considered to be a random sample. The sample in Problem 5 is not random.

9. (a) Observed frequencies—40 correct, 60 incorrect; (b) expected frequencies—20 correct, 80 incorrect (c) $H_0$: $P = .20$ (d) $\chi^2 = 25$ ($\chi^2_{.05} = 3.84$); reject $H_0$ and conclude that $P > .20$ (i.e., some students must know the answer) (e) $H_A$: $P > .20$ (f) There are only two possibilities in this problem; there were five possibilities in Problem 8.

11. (a) $H_0$: $P_R = 1/4$, $P_B = 1/4$, $P_P = 1/2$ (b) $\chi^2 = 6.32$ ($\chi^2_{.05} = 5.99$); reject $H_0$—the results tend to disprove the theory. (c) .23

13. (a) $\chi^2_{\text{calc}} = 21.97$, for $df = 4$, $\chi^2_{.05} = 9.49$; reject $H_0$

    (b)

|  |  | 30–49 | 50–69 | 70 AND ABOVE |
|---|---|---|---|---|
| OBSERVED | UNSKILLED | .33 | .50 | .17 |
| CELL | SEMISKILLED | .12 | .50 | .38 |
| PROPORTIONS | SKILLED | .14 | .29 | .57 |
| EXPECTED | UNSKILLED | .20 | .46 | .34 |
| CELL | SEMISKILLED | .20 | .46 | .34 |
| PROPORTIONS | SKILLED | .20 | .46 | .34 |

The three classes of workers are dissimilar with regard to mechanical aptitude. It appears that aptitude level is higher with higher skill classification of workers, though this conclusion goes beyond the overall $\chi^2$ test. (c) .25 (d) .35

15. (a) The responses are independent of sex. (b) $\chi^2 = 11.21$ ($df = 1$, $\chi^2_{0.5} = 3.84$, reject $H_0$ (c) .09 (d) Because it is a $2 \times 2$ table, the phi coefficient is equivalent to $\hat{\omega}$.

17. (a) Attitudes toward the bond issue are independent of political affiliation. (b) $\chi^2 = 97.62$ ($df = 4$, $\chi^2_{0.5} = 9.49$) (c) Reject $H_0$ (d) $\phi = .40$, $\hat{\omega} = .57$ (e) Because the observations are independent of one another

## CHAPTER 20

1. 1 *v.* 2, 1 *v.* 3, 1 *v.* 4, 1 *v.* 5, 1 *v.* 6, 1 *v.* 7, 2 *v.* 3, 2 *v.* 4, 2 *v.* 5, 2 *v.* 6, 2 *v.* 7, 3 *v.* 4, 3 *v.* 5, 3 *v.* 6, 3 *v.* 7, 4 *v.* 5, 4 *v.* 6, 4 *v.* 7, 5 *v.* 6, 5 *v.* 7, 6 *v.* 7. With so many tests, there is an increased likelihood of committing at least one Type I error—that is, of obtaining a "significant difference" when no true difference exists.

**3.** Only a large value of $F$ is evidence for rejecting $H_0$. When $H_0$ is true $s_{bet}^2 / s_w^2 = $ unity. When treatment effect exists, $s_{bet}^2$ grows larger, but $s_w^2$ is unaffected.

**5.** (a) 4, 22, 87 (b) $F_{crit,.05} = 2.72$, $F_{crit,.01} = 4.04$, $F_{obt} = 3.4$; difference is significant at the .05 level but not at the .01 level.

**7.** $SS_w = 24$, $SS_{bet} = 56.01$, $SS_{total} = 80.01$; yes (b) $df_w = 6$, $df_{bet} = 2$, $df_{total} = 8$; yes (c) $s_w^2 = 4.00$, $s_{bet}^2 = 28.00$ (e) $F = 28.00/4.00 = 7.00$; $F_{.05} = 5.14$; reject $H_0$

(d)

| SOURCE | SS | df | $s^2$ | F |
|---|---|---|---|---|
| Between groups | 56.01 | 2 | 28.00 | 7.00 |
| Within groups | 24 | 6 | 4.0 | |
| Total | 80.01 | 8 | | |

**9.** (a) The means of groups $A$, $C$, and $D$ appear similar, and that of B is higher. (b) That the mean of at least one of the groups differs from the others. (c) Make *post hoc* comparisons.

**11.** (a)

| | $\overline{X}_1 = $ 14.5 | $\overline{X}_2 = $ 11.5 | $\overline{X}_3 = $ 19.0 | $\overline{X}_4 = $ 18.1 | $\overline{X}_5 = $ 12.0 |
|---|---|---|---|---|---|
| $\overline{X}_1 = 14.5$ | 0 | −3.0 | 4.5 | 3.6 | −2.5 |
| $\overline{X}_2 = 11.5$ | | 0 | 7.5 | 6.6 | 0.5 |
| $\overline{X}_3 = 19.0$ | | | 0 | −0.9 | 3.0 |
| $\overline{X}_4 = 18.1$ | | | | 0 | −6.1 |
| $\overline{X}_5 = 12.0$ | | | | | 0 |

(b) $HSD = 5.75$; $\mu_2 < \mu_3$, $\mu_2 < \mu_4$, $\mu_5 < \mu_4$ (c) $HSD = 7.01$; $\mu_2 < \mu_3$

**13.** Planned comparisons

**15.** (a) $H_0: \mu_D = \mu_{DW} = \mu_{DR}$

(b)

| SOURCE | SS | df | $s^2$ | F |
|---|---|---|---|---|
| Between groups | 156 | 2 | 78 | 11.03 |
| Within groups | 106 | 15 | 7.07 | |
| Total | 262 | 17 | | |

(c) $HSD_{.05} = 3.98$ (d) Dieting in combination with either a walk or a run lowers cholesterol more effectively than does dieting alone. There is no evidence to support that running is better than walking. (e) $\eta^2 = .60$, $\hat{\omega}^2 = .53$

**17.** (a) $H_0: \mu_A = \mu_B = \mu_C$

(b)

| SOURCE | SS | df | $s^2$ | F |
|---|---|---|---|---|
| Subjects | 5.98 | 7 | .85 | — |
| Between groups | 15.25 | 2 | 7.62 | 7.19 |
| Residual | 14.77 | 14 | 1.06 | |
| Total | 36 | 23 | | |

(c) $HSD_{.05} = 1.35$ (d) $\mu_C > \mu_A$ and $\mu_B$
(e) $\eta^2 = .29$

# CHAPTER 21

**1.** c A two-way design in which type of story and sex of subjects are the treatment variables

**3.** d

**5.** (a) $df_{methods} = 3$, $df_{students} = 2$, $df_{wc} = 48$, $df_{methods \times students} = 6$, $df_{total} = 59$ (b) Methods, $F_{crit} = 2.80$; students, $F_{crit} = 3.19$; interaction, $F_{crit} = 2.30$

**7.** (a) The interaction in the second graph is disordinal. The interactions in the other three graphs are ordinal. In the fourth graph, $R_2$ and $R_3$ cross, but the interaction is still ordinal because $R_1$ is greater than $R_2$ or $R_3$ at all levels of $C$. (b) In all four graphs, the main effect for rows shows a higher overall mean for row 1, yet such a conclusion does not apply at $C_3$ in the second graph or $C_1$ in the third graph (and it may not hold for $C_2$ in the first and third graphs and $C_1$ in the fourth graph).

**9.** (a)

| SOURCE | SS | df | $s^2$ | F | $\hat{\omega}^2$ |
|---|---|---|---|---|---|
| Columns | 68.17 | 2 | 34.09 | 21.58 | .782 |
| Rows | 30.09 | 1 | 30.09 | 19.04 | .613 |
| Columns × rows | 3.16 | 2 | 1.58 | 1.00 | 0 |
| Within cells | 9.50 | 6 | 1.58 | | |
| Total | 110.92 | 11 | | | |

(b)

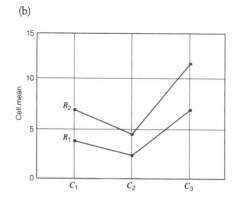

## CHAPTER 22

1. Parametric tests evaluate hypotheses about population parameters, whereas nonparametric tests do not. Distribution-free tests do not make any assumptions about the shape of the population. The terms *nonparametric test* and *distribution-free* test do not mean the same thing. Assumption-freer tests do not make the usual assumption about population distributions, but the tests are not completely free of assumptions.

3. The sampling distribution of a randomization test is derived empirically, whereas the sampling distribution of $t$ is derived through theory.

5. Converting original scores to ranks effectively eliminates outliers (a score that is very different from others in the distribution). For example, when ranked the scores 6, 8, 9, 10, 100 become 1, 2, 3, 4, 5. The presence of an outlier can often eliminate the possibility of obtaining a significant result with a parametric test.

7. No; $\Sigma R_X = 45$, which is within the critical values 21–49 for the Mann-Whitney $U$ test. $Mdn_{quiet} = 59$, $Mdn_{noisy} = 51$; those in the quiet environment performed better, but the difference was not significant.

9. $\Sigma R_X = 30.5$; critical values for a two-tailed test at the .01 level are 34–78, so the null hypothesis is rejected. Androgyny appears to be predictive of longer-lasting relationships.

11. $\chi^2_{calc} = 4.08$, $df = 1$; $\chi^2_{.05} = 3.84$, reject $H_0$; $\chi^2_{.01} = 6.63$, retain $H_0$.

13. (a) $R_- = 9$, $R_{crit} = 10$, reject $H_0$ (b) $r_c = .73$ (c) No; factors other than the firm may have been operative; it is not clear that the film was responsible for the difference.

15. (a) $R_- = 3$, $R_{crit} = 3$, reject $H_0$. (b) $r_c = .83$

17. $\chi^2_F = 6.5$, at $\alpha = .05$ and 2 $dF$, reject $H_0$; $W = .36$

# APPENDIX E

## Statistical Tables

**TABLE A**   *Areas under the Normal Curve Corresponding to Given Values of z*

Column 2 gives the proportion of the area under the entire curve that is between the mean ($z = 0$) and the positive value of $z$. Areas for negative values of $z$ are the same as for positive values because the curve is symmetrical.

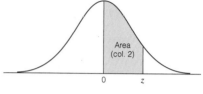

Column 3 gives the proportion of the area under the entire curve that falls beyond the stated positive value of $z$. Areas for negative values of $z$ are the same because the curve is symmetrical.

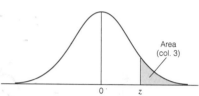

| $z$ 1 | AREA BETWEEN MEAN AND $z$ 2 | AREA BEYOND $z$ 3 | $z$ 1 | AREA BETWEEN MEAN AND $z$ 2 | AREA BEYOND $z$ 3 |
|---|---|---|---|---|---|
| 0.00 | .0000 | .5000 | 0.25 | .0987 | .4013 |
| 0.01 | .0040 | .4960 | 0.26 | .1026 | .3974 |
| 0.02 | .0080 | .4920 | 0.27 | .1064 | .3936 |
| 0.03 | .0120 | .4880 | 0.28 | .1103 | .3897 |
| 0.04 | .0160 | .4840 | 0.29 | .1141 | .3859 |
| 0.05 | .0199 | .4801 | 0.30 | .1179 | .3821 |
| 0.06 | .0239 | .4761 | 0.31 | .1217 | .3783 |
| 0.07 | .0279 | .4721 | 0.32 | .1255 | .3745 |
| 0.08 | .0319 | .4681 | 0.33 | .1293 | .3707 |
| 0.09 | .0359 | .4641 | 0.34 | .1331 | .3669 |
| 0.10 | .0398 | .4602 | 0.35 | .1368 | .3632 |
| 0.11 | .0438 | .4562 | 0.36 | .1406 | .3594 |
| 0.12 | .0478 | .4522 | 0.37 | .1443 | .3557 |
| 0.13 | .0517 | .4483 | 0.38 | .1480 | .3520 |
| 0.14 | .0557 | .4443 | 0.39 | .1517 | .3483 |
| 0.15 | .0596 | .4404 | 0.40 | .1554 | .3446 |
| 0.16 | .0636 | .4364 | 0.41 | .1591 | .3409 |
| 0.17 | .0675 | .4325 | 0.42 | .1628 | .3372 |
| 0.18 | .0714 | .4286 | 0.43 | .1664 | .3336 |
| 0.19 | .0753 | .4247 | 0.44 | .1700 | .3300 |
| 0.20 | .0793 | .4207 | 0.45 | .1736 | .3264 |
| 0.21 | .0832 | .4168 | 0.46 | .1772 | .3228 |
| 0.22 | .0871 | .4129 | 0.47 | .1808 | .3192 |
| 0.23 | .0910 | .4090 | 0.48 | .1844 | .3156 |
| 0.24 | .0948 | .4052 | 0.49 | .1879 | .3121 |

*Source:* From Appendix 2 of R. Clarke, A. Coladarci, and J. Caffrey, *Statistical Reasoning and Procedures,* Charles E. Merrill Books, with permission of the author.

TABLE A *(continued)*

| z<br>1 | AREA<br>BETWEEN<br>MEAN AND z<br>2 | AREA<br>BEYOND<br>z<br>3 | z<br>1 | AREA<br>BETWEEN<br>MEAN AND z<br>2 | AREA<br>BEYOND<br>z<br>3 |
|---|---|---|---|---|---|
| 0.50 | .1915 | .3085 | 0.90 | .3159 | .1841 |
| 0.51 | .1950 | .3050 | 0.91 | .3186 | .1814 |
| 0.52 | .1985 | .3015 | 0.92 | .3212 | .1788 |
| 0.53 | .2019 | .2981 | 0.93 | .3238 | .1762 |
| 0.54 | .2054 | .2946 | 0.94 | .3264 | .1736 |
| 0.55 | .2088 | .2912 | 0.95 | .3289 | .1711 |
| 0.56 | .2123 | .2877 | 0.96 | .3315 | .1685 |
| 0.57 | .2157 | .2843 | 0.97 | .3340 | .1660 |
| 0.58 | .2190 | .2810 | 0.98 | .3365 | .1635 |
| 0.59 | .2224 | .2776 | 0.99 | .3389 | .1611 |
| 0.60 | .2257 | .2743 | 1.00 | .3413 | .1587 |
| 0.61 | .2291 | .2709 | 1.01 | .3438 | .1562 |
| 0.62 | .2324 | .2676 | 1.02 | .3461 | .1539 |
| 0.63 | .2357 | .2643 | 1.03 | .3485 | .1515 |
| 0.64 | .2389 | .2611 | 1.04 | .3508 | .1492 |
| 0.65 | .2422 | .2578 | 1.05 | .3531 | .1469 |
| 0.66 | .2454 | .2546 | 1.06 | .3554 | .1446 |
| 0.67 | .2486 | .2514 | 1.07 | .3577 | .1423 |
| 0.68 | .2517 | .2483 | 1.08 | .3599 | .1401 |
| 0.69 | .2549 | .2451 | 1.09 | .3621 | .1379 |
| 0.70 | .2580 | .2420 | 1.10 | .3643 | .1357 |
| 0.71 | .2611 | .2389 | 1.11 | .3665 | .1335 |
| 0.72 | .2642 | .2358 | 1.12 | .3686 | .1314 |
| 0.73 | .2673 | .2327 | 1.13 | .3708 | .1292 |
| 0.74 | .2704 | .2296 | 1.14 | .3729 | .1271 |
| 0.75 | .2734 | .2266 | 1.15 | .3749 | .1251 |
| 0.76 | .2764 | .2236 | 1.16 | .3770 | .1230 |
| 0.77 | .2794 | .2206 | 1.17 | .3790 | .1210 |
| 0.78 | .2823 | .2177 | 1.18 | .3810 | .1190 |
| 0.79 | .2852 | .2148 | 1.19 | .3830 | .1170 |
| 0.80 | .2881 | .2119 | 1.20 | .3849 | .1151 |
| 0.81 | .2910 | .2090 | 1.21 | .3869 | .1131 |
| 0.82 | .2939 | .2061 | 1.22 | .3888 | .1112 |
| 0.83 | .2967 | .2033 | 1.23 | .3907 | .1093 |
| 0.84 | .2995 | .2005 | 1.24 | .3925 | .1075 |
| 0.85 | .3023 | .1977 | 1.25 | .3944 | .1056 |
| 0.86 | .3051 | .1949 | 1:26 | .3962 | .1038 |
| 0.87 | .3078 | .1922 | 1.27 | .3980 | .1020 |
| 0.88 | .3106 | .1894 | 1.28 | .3997 | .1003 |
| 0.89 | .3133 | .1867 | 1.29 | .4015 | .0985 |

*continued*

**TABLE A** (*continued*)

| z 1 | AREA BETWEEN MEAN AND z 2 | AREA BEYOND z 3 | z 1 | AREA BETWEEN MEAN AND z 2 | AREA BEYOND z 3 |
|---|---|---|---|---|---|
| 1.30 | .4032 | .0968 | 1.65 | .4505 | .0495 |
| 1.31 | .4049 | .0951 | 1.66 | .4515 | .0485 |
| 1.32 | .4066 | .0934 | 1.67 | .4525 | .0475 |
| 1.33 | .4082 | .0918 | 1.68 | .4535 | .0465 |
| 1.34 | .4099 | .0901 | 1.69 | .4545 | .0455 |
| 1.35 | .4115 | .0885 | 1.70 | .4554 | .0446 |
| 1.36 | .4131 | .0869 | 1.71 | .4564 | .0436 |
| 1.37 | .4147 | .0853 | 1.72 | .4573 | .0427 |
| 1.38 | .4162 | .0838 | 1.73 | .4582 | .0418 |
| 1.39 | .4177 | .0823 | 1.74 | .4591 | .0409 |
| 1.40 | .4192 | .0808 | 1.75 | .4599 | .0401 |
| 1.41 | .4207 | .0793 | 1.76 | .4608 | .0392 |
| 1.42 | .4222 | .0778 | 1.77 | .4616 | .0384 |
| 1.43 | .4236 | .0764 | 1.78 | .4625 | .0375 |
| 1.44 | .4251 | .0749 | 1.79 | .4633 | .0367 |
| 1.45 | .4265 | .0735 | 1.80 | .4641 | .0359 |
| 1.46 | .4279 | .0721 | 1.81 | .4649 | .0351 |
| 1.47 | .4292 | .0708 | 1.82 | .4656 | .0344 |
| 1.48 | .4306 | .0694 | 1.83 | .4664 | .0336 |
| 1.49 | .4319 | .0681 | 1.84 | .4671 | .0329 |
| 1.50 | .4332 | .0668 | 1.85 | .4678 | .0322 |
| 1.51 | .4345 | .0655 | 1.86 | .4686 | .0314 |
| 1.52 | .4357 | .0643 | 1.87 | .4693 | .0307 |
| 1.53 | .4370 | .0630 | 1.88 | .4699 | .0301 |
| 1.54 | .4382 | .0618 | 1.89 | .4706 | .0294 |
| 1.55 | .4394 | .0606 | 1.90 | .4713 | .0287 |
| 1.56 | .4406 | .0594 | 1.91 | .4719 | .0281 |
| 1.57 | .4418 | .0582 | 1.92 | .4726 | .0274 |
| 1.58 | .4429 | .0571 | 1.93 | .4732 | .0268 |
| 1.59 | .4441 | .0559 | 1.94 | .4738 | .0262 |
| 1.60 | .4452 | .0548 | 1.95 | .4744 | .0256 |
| 1.61 | .4463 | .0537 | 1.96 | .4750 | .0250 |
| 1.62 | .4474 | .0526 | 1.97 | .4756 | .0244 |
| 1.63 | .4484 | .0516 | 1.98 | .4761 | .0239 |
| 1.64 | .4495 | .0505 | 1.99 | .4767 | .0233 |

*continued*

TABLE **A** (*continued*)

| z 1 | AREA BETWEEN MEAN AND z 2 | AREA BEYOND z 3 | z 1 | AREA BETWEEN MEAN AND z 2 | AREA BEYOND z 3 |
|------|------|------|------|------|------|
| 2.00 | .4772 | .0228 | 2.35 | .4906 | .0094 |
| 2.01 | .4778 | .0222 | 2.36 | .4909 | .0091 |
| 2.02 | .4783 | .0217 | 2.37 | .4911 | .0089 |
| 2.03 | .4788 | .0212 | 2.38 | .4913 | .0087 |
| 2.04 | .4793 | .0207 | 2.39 | .4916 | .0084 |
| 2.05 | .4798 | .0202 | 2.40 | .4918 | .0082 |
| 2.06 | .4803 | .0197 | 2.41 | .4920 | .0080 |
| 2.07 | .4808 | .0192 | 2.42 | .4922 | .0078 |
| 2.08 | .4812 | .0188 | 2.43 | .4925 | .0075 |
| 2.09 | .4817 | .0183 | 2.44 | .4927 | .0073 |
| 2.10 | .4821 | .0179 | 2.45 | .4929 | .0071 |
| 2.11 | .4826 | .0174 | 2.46 | .4931 | .0069 |
| 2.12 | .4830 | .0170 | 2.47 | .4932 | .0068 |
| 2.13 | .4834 | .0166 | 2.48 | .4934 | .0066 |
| 2.14 | .4838 | .0162 | 2.49 | .4936 | .0064 |
| 2.15 | .4842 | .0158 | 2.50 | .4938 | .0062 |
| 2.16 | .4846 | .0154 | 2.51 | .4940 | .0060 |
| 2.17 | .4850 | .0150 | 2.52 | .4941 | .0059 |
| 2.18 | .4854 | .0146 | 2.53 | .4943 | .0057 |
| 2.19 | .4857 | .0143 | 2.54 | .4945 | .0055 |
| 2.20 | .4861 | .0139 | 2.55 | .4946 | .0054 |
| 2.21 | .4864 | .0136 | 2.56 | .4948 | .0052 |
| 2.22 | .4868 | .0132 | 2.57 | .4949 | .0051 |
| 2.23 | .4871 | .0129 | 2.58 | .4951 | .0049 |
| 2.24 | .4875 | .0125 | 2.59 | .4952 | .0048 |
| 2.25 | .4878 | .0122 | 2.60 | .4953 | .0047 |
| 2.26 | .4881 | .0119 | 2.61 | .4955 | .0045 |
| 2.27 | .4884 | .0116 | 2.62 | .4956 | .0044 |
| 2.28 | .4887 | .0113 | 2.63 | .4957 | .0043 |
| 2.29 | .4890 | .0110 | 2.64 | .4959 | .0041 |
| 2.30 | .4893 | .0107 | 2.65 | .4960 | .0040 |
| 2.31 | .4896 | .0104 | 2.66 | .4961 | .0039 |
| 2.32 | .4898 | .0102 | 2.67 | .4962 | .0038 |
| 2.33 | .4901 | .0099 | 2.68 | .4963 | .0037 |
| 2.34 | .4904 | .0096 | 2.69 | .4964 | .0036 |

*continued*

TABLE A   (continued)

| $z$ 1 | AREA BETWEEN MEAN AND $z$ 2 | AREA BEYOND $z$ 3 | $z$ 1 | AREA BETWEEN MEAN AND $z$ 2 | AREA BEYOND $z$ 3 |
|---|---|---|---|---|---|
| 2.70 | .4965 | .0035 | 3.00 | .4987 | .0013 |
| 2.71 | .4966 | .0034 | 3.01 | .4987 | .0013 |
| 2.72 | .4967 | .0033 | 3.02 | .4987 | .0013 |
| 2.73 | .4968 | .0032 | 3.03 | .4988 | .0012 |
| 2.74 | .4969 | .0031 | 3.04 | .4988 | .0012 |
| 2.75 | .4970 | .0030 | 3.05 | .4989 | .0011 |
| 2.76 | .4971 | .0029 | 3.06 | .4989 | .0011 |
| 2.77 | .4972 | .0028 | 3.07 | .4989 | .0011 |
| 2.78 | .4973 | .0027 | 3.08 | .4990 | .0010 |
| 2.79 | .4974 | .0026 | 3.09 | .4990 | .0010 |
| 2.80 | .4974 | .0026 | 3.10 | .4990 | .0010 |
| 2.81 | .4975 | .0025 | 3.11 | .4991 | .0009 |
| 2.82 | .4976 | .0024 | 3.12 | .4991 | .0009 |
| 2.83 | .4977 | .0023 | 3.13 | .4991 | .0009 |
| 2.84 | .4977 | .0023 | 3.14 | .4992 | .0008 |
| 2.85 | .4978 | .0022 | 3.15 | .4992 | .0008 |
| 2.86 | .4979 | .0021 | 3.16 | .4992 | .0008 |
| 2.87 | .4979 | .0021 | 3.17 | .4992 | .0008 |
| 2.88 | .4980 | .0020 | 3.18 | .4993 | .0007 |
| 2.89 | .4981 | .0019 | 3.19 | .4993 | .0007 |
| 2.90 | .4981 | .0019 | 3.20 | .4993 | .0007 |
| 2.91 | .4982 | .0018 | 3.21 | .4993 | .0007 |
| 2.92 | .4982 | .0018 | 3.22 | .4994 | .0006 |
| 2.93 | .4983 | .0017 | 3.23 | .4994 | .0006 |
| 2.94 | .4984 | .0016 | 3.24 | .4994 | .0006 |
| 2.95 | .4984 | .0016 | 3.30 | .4995 | .0005 |
| 2.96 | .4985 | .0015 | 3.40 | .4997 | .0003 |
| 2.97 | .4985 | .0015 | 3.50 | .4998 | .0002 |
| 2.98 | .4986 | .0014 | 3.60 | .4998 | .0002 |
| 2.99 | .4986 | .0014 | 3.70 | .4999 | .0001 |

TABLE B   *The Binomial Distribution*

| N | NUMBER OF P OR Q EVENTS | P or Q | | | | | | | | | |
|---|---|---|---|---|---|---|---|---|---|---|---|
| | | .05 | .10 | .15 | .20 | .25 | .30 | .35 | .40 | .45 | .50 |
| 1 | 0 | .9500 | .9000 | .8500 | .8000 | .7500 | .7000 | .6500 | .6000 | .5500 | .5000 |
| | 1 | .0500 | .1000 | .1500 | .2000 | .2500 | .3000 | .3500 | .4000 | .4500 | .5000 |
| 2 | 0 | .9025 | .8100 | .7225 | .6400 | .5625 | .4900 | .4225 | .3600 | .3025 | .2500 |
| | 1 | .0950 | .1800 | .2550 | .3200 | .3750 | .4200 | .4550 | .4800 | .4950 | .5000 |
| | 2 | .0025 | .0100 | .0225 | .0400 | .0625 | .0900 | .1225 | .1600 | .2025 | .2500 |
| 3 | 0 | .8574 | .7290 | .6141 | .5120 | .4219 | .3430 | .2746 | .2160 | .1664 | .1250 |
| | 1 | .1354 | .2430 | .3251 | .3840 | .4219 | .4410 | .4436 | .4320 | .4084 | .3750 |
| | 2 | .0071 | .0270 | .0574 | .0960 | .1406 | .1890 | .2389 | .2880 | .3341 | .3750 |
| | 3 | .0001 | .0010 | .0034 | .0080 | .0156 | .0270 | .0429 | .0640 | .0911 | .1250 |
| 4 | 0 | .8145 | .6561 | .5220 | .4096 | .3164 | .2401 | .1785 | .1296 | .0915 | .0625 |
| | 1 | .1715 | .2916 | .3685 | .4096 | .4219 | .4116 | .3845 | .3456 | .2995 | .2500 |
| | 2 | .0135 | .0486 | .0975 | .1536 | .2109 | .2646 | .3105 | .3456 | .3675 | .3750 |
| | 3 | .0005 | .0036 | .0115 | .0256 | .0469 | .0756 | .1115 | .1536 | .2005 | .2500 |
| | 4 | .0000 | .0001 | .0005 | .0016 | .0039 | .0081 | .0150 | .0256 | .0410 | .0625 |
| 5 | 0 | .7738 | .5905 | .4437 | .3277 | .2373 | .1681 | .1160 | .0778 | .0503 | .0312 |
| | 1 | .2036 | .3280 | .3915 | .4096 | .3955 | .3602 | .3124 | .2592 | .2059 | .1562 |
| | 2 | .0214 | .0729 | .1382 | .2048 | .2637 | .3087 | .3364 | .3456 | .3369 | .3125 |
| | 3 | .0011 | .0081 | .0244 | .0512 | .0879 | .1323 | .1811 | .2304 | .2757 | .3125 |
| | 4 | .0000 | .0004 | .0022 | .0064 | .0146 | .0284 | .0488 | .0768 | .1128 | .1562 |
| | 5 | .0000 | .0000 | .0001 | .0003 | .0010 | .0024 | .0053 | .0102 | .0185 | .0312 |
| 6 | 0 | .7351 | .5314 | .3771 | .2621 | .1780 | .1176 | .0754 | .0467 | .0277 | .0156 |
| | 1 | .2321 | .3543 | .3993 | .3932 | .3560 | .3025 | .2437 | .1866 | .1359 | .0938 |
| | 2 | .0305 | .0984 | .1762 | .2458 | .2966 | .3241 | .3280 | .3110 | .2780 | .2344 |
| | 3 | .0021 | .0146 | .0415 | .0819 | .1318 | .1852 | .2355 | .2765 | .3032 | .3125 |
| | 4 | .0001 | .0012 | .0055 | .0154 | .0330 | .0595 | .0951 | .1382 | .1861 | .2344 |
| | 5 | .0000 | .0001 | .0004 | .0015 | .0044 | .0102 | .0205 | .0369 | .0609 | .0938 |
| | 6 | .0000 | .0000 | .0000 | .0001 | .0002 | .0007 | .0018 | .0041 | .0083 | .0156 |
| 7 | 0 | .6983 | .4783 | .3206 | .2097 | .1335 | .0824 | .0490 | .0280 | .0152 | .0078 |
| | 1 | .2573 | .3720 | .3960 | .3670 | .3115 | .2471 | .1848 | .1306 | .0872 | .0547 |
| | 2 | .0406 | .1240 | .2097 | .2753 | .3115 | .3177 | .2985 | .2613 | .2140 | .1641 |
| | 3 | .0036 | .0230 | .0617 | .1147 | .1730 | .2269 | .2679 | .2903 | .2918 | .2734 |
| | 4 | .0002 | .0026 | .0109 | .0287 | .0577 | .0972 | .1442 | .1935 | .2388 | .2734 |
| | 5 | .0000 | .0002 | .0012 | .0043 | .0115 | .0250 | .0466 | .0774 | .1172 | .1641 |
| | 6 | .0000 | .0000 | .0001 | .0004 | .0013 | .0036 | .0084 | .0172 | .0320 | .0547 |
| | 7 | .0000 | .0000 | .0000 | .0000 | .0001 | .0002 | .0006 | .0016 | .0037 | .0078 |
| 8 | 0 | .6634 | .4305 | .2725 | .1678 | .1001 | .0576 | .0319 | .0168 | .0084 | .0039 |
| | 1 | .2793 | .3826 | .3847 | .3355 | .2670 | .1977 | .1373 | .0896 | .0548 | .0312 |
| | 2 | .0515 | .1488 | .2376 | .2936 | .3115 | .2965 | .2587 | .2090 | .1569 | .1094 |
| | 3 | .0054 | .0331 | .0839 | .1468 | .2076 | .2541 | .2786 | .2787 | .2568 | .2188 |

**TABLE B**   *(continued)*

| N | NUMBER OF P OR Q EVENTS | P or Q .05 | .10 | .15 | .20 | .25 | .30 | .35 | .40 | .45 | .50 |
|---|---|---|---|---|---|---|---|---|---|---|---|
| 8 | 4 | .0004 | .0046 | .0185 | .0459 | .0865 | .1361 | .1875 | .2322 | .2627 | .2734 |
|   | 5 | .0000 | .0004 | .0026 | .0092 | .0231 | .0467 | .0808 | .1239 | .1719 | .2188 |
|   | 6 | .0000 | .0000 | .0002 | .0011 | .0038 | .0100 | .0217 | .0413 | .0703 | .1094 |
|   | 7 | .0000 | .0000 | .0000 | .0001 | .0004 | .0012 | .0033 | .0079 | .0164 | .0312 |
|   | 8 | .0000 | .0000 | .0000 | .0000 | .0000 | .0001 | .0002 | .0007 | .0017 | .0039 |
| 9 | 0 | .6302 | .3874 | .2316 | .1342 | .0751 | .0404 | .0277 | .0101 | .0046 | .0020 |
|   | 1 | .2985 | .3874 | .3679 | .3020 | .2253 | .1556 | .1004 | .0605 | .0339 | .0176 |
|   | 2 | .0629 | .1722 | .2597 | .3020 | .3003 | .2668 | .2162 | .1612 | .1110 | .0703 |
|   | 3 | .0077 | .0446 | .1069 | .1762 | .2336 | .2668 | .2716 | .2508 | .2119 | .1641 |
|   | 4 | .0006 | .0074 | .0283 | .0661 | .1168 | .1715 | .2194 | .2508 | .2600 | .2461 |
|   | 5 | .0000 | .0008 | .0050 | .0165 | .0389 | .0735 | .1181 | .1672 | .2128 | .2461 |
|   | 6 | .0000 | .0001 | .0006 | .0028 | .0087 | .0210 | .0424 | .0743 | .1160 | .1641 |
|   | 7 | .0000 | .0000 | .0000 | .0003 | .0012 | .0039 | .0098 | .0212 | .0407 | .0703 |
|   | 8 | .0000 | .0000 | .0000 | .0000 | .0001 | .0004 | .0013 | .0035 | .0083 | .0176 |
|   | 9 | .0000 | .0000 | .0000 | .0000 | .0000 | .0000 | .0001 | .0003 | .0008 | .0020 |
| 10 | 0 | .5987 | .3487 | .1969 | .1074 | .0563 | .0282 | .0135 | .0060 | .0025 | .0010 |
|   | 1 | .3151 | .3874 | .3474 | .2684 | .1877 | .1211 | .0725 | .0403 | .0207 | .0098 |
|   | 2 | .0746 | .1937 | .2759 | .3020 | .2816 | .2335 | .1757 | .1209 | .0763 | .0439 |
|   | 3 | .0105 | .0574 | .1298 | .2013 | .2503 | .2668 | .2522 | .2150 | .1665 | .1172 |
|   | 4 | .0010 | .0112 | .0401 | .0881 | .1460 | .2001 | .2377 | .2508 | .2384 | .2051 |
|   | 5 | .0001 | .0015 | .0085 | .0264 | .0584 | .1029 | .1536 | .2007 | .2340 | .2461 |
|   | 6 | .0000 | .0001 | .0012 | .0055 | .0162 | .0368 | .0689 | .1115 | .1596 | .2051 |
|   | 7 | .0000 | .0000 | .0001 | .0008 | .0031 | .0090 | .0212 | .0425 | .0746 | .1172 |
|   | 8 | .0000 | .0000 | .0000 | .0001 | .0004 | .0014 | .0043 | .0106 | .0229 | .0439 |
|   | 9 | .0000 | .0000 | .0000 | .0000 | .0000 | .0001 | .0005 | .0016 | .0042 | .0098 |
|   | 10 | .0000 | .0000 | .0000 | .0000 | .0000 | .0000 | .0000 | .0001 | .0003 | .0010 |
| 11 | 0 | .5688 | .3138 | .1673 | .0859 | .0422 | .0198 | .0088 | .0036 | .0014 | .0005 |
|   | 1 | .3293 | .3835 | .3248 | .2362 | .1549 | .0932 | .0518 | .0266 | .0125 | .0054 |
|   | 2 | .0867 | .2131 | .2866 | .2953 | .2581 | .1998 | .1395 | .0887 | .0513 | .0269 |
|   | 3 | .0137 | .0710 | .1517 | .2215 | .2581 | .2568 | .2254 | .1774 | .1259 | .0806 |
|   | 4 | .0014 | .0158 | .0536 | .1107 | .1721 | .2201 | .2428 | .2365 | .2060 | .1611 |
|   | 5 | .0001 | .0025 | .0132 | .0388 | .0803 | .1231 | .1830 | .2207 | .2360 | .2256 |
|   | 6 | .0000 | .0003 | .0023 | .0097 | .0268 | .0566 | .0985 | .1471 | .1931 | .2256 |
|   | 7 | .0000 | .0000 | .0003 | .0017 | .0064 | .0173 | .0379 | .0701 | .1128 | .1611 |
|   | 8 | .0000 | .0000 | .0000 | .0002 | .0011 | .0037 | .0102 | .0234 | .0462 | .0806 |
|   | 9 | .0000 | .0000 | .0000 | .0000 | .0001 | .0005 | .0018 | .0052 | .0126 | .0269 |
|   | 10 | .0000 | .0000 | .0000 | .0000 | .0000 | .0000 | .0002 | .0007 | .0021 | .0054 |
|   | 11 | .0000 | .0000 | .0000 | .0000 | .0000 | .0000 | .0000 | .0000 | .0002 | .0005 |
| 12 | 0 | .5404 | .2824 | .1422 | .0687 | .0317 | .0138 | .0057 | .0022 | .0008 | .0002 |
|   | 1 | .3413 | .3766 | .3012 | .2062 | .1267 | .0712 | .0368 | .0174 | .0075 | .0029 |
|   | 2 | .0988 | .2301 | .2924 | .2835 | .2323 | .1678 | .1088 | .0639 | .0339 | .0161 |

*continued*

**TABLE B** *(continued)*

| N | NUMBER OF P OR Q EVENTS | .05 | .10 | .15 | .20 | .25 | .30 | .35 | .40 | .45 | .50 |
|---|---|---|---|---|---|---|---|---|---|---|---|
| 12 | 3 | .0173 | .0852 | .1720 | .2362 | .2581 | .2397 | .1954 | .1419 | .0923 | .0537 |
| | 4 | .0021 | .0213 | .0683 | .1329 | .1936 | .2311 | .2367 | .2128 | .1700 | .1208 |
| | 5 | .0002 | .0038 | .0193 | .0532 | .1032 | .1585 | .2039 | .2270 | .2225 | .1934 |
| | 6 | .0000 | .0005 | .0040 | .0155 | .0401 | .0792 | .1281 | .1766 | .2124 | .2256 |
| | 7 | .0000 | .0000 | .0006 | .0033 | .0115 | .0291 | .0591 | .1009 | .1489 | .1934 |
| | 8 | .0000 | .0000 | .0001 | .0005 | .0024 | .0078 | .0199 | .0420 | .0762 | .1208 |
| | 9 | .0000 | .0000 | .0000 | .0001 | .0004 | .0015 | .0048 | .0125 | .0277 | .0537 |
| | 10 | .0000 | .0000 | .0000 | .0000 | .0000 | .0002 | .0008 | .0025 | .0068 | .0161 |
| | 11 | .0000 | .0000 | .0000 | .0000 | .0000 | .0000 | .0001 | .0003 | .0010 | .0029 |
| | 12 | .0000 | .0000 | .0000 | .0000 | .0000 | .0000 | .0000 | .0000 | .0001 | .0002 |
| 13 | 0 | .5133 | .2542 | .1209 | .0550 | .0238 | .0097 | .0037 | .0013 | .0004 | .0001 |
| | 1 | .3512 | .3672 | .2774 | .1787 | .1029 | .0540 | .0259 | .0113 | .0045 | .0016 |
| | 2 | .1109 | .2448 | .2937 | .2680 | .2059 | .1388 | .0836 | .0453 | .0220 | .0095 |
| | 3 | .0214 | .0997 | .1900 | .2457 | .2517 | .2181 | .1651 | .1107 | .0660 | .0349 |
| | 4 | .0028 | .0277 | .0838 | .1535 | .2097 | .2337 | .2222 | .1845 | .1350 | .0873 |
| | 5 | .0003 | .0055 | .0266 | .0691 | .1258 | .1803 | .2154 | .2214 | .1989 | .1571 |
| | 6 | .0000 | .0008 | .0063 | .0230 | .0559 | .1030 | .1546 | .1968 | .2169 | .2095 |
| | 7 | .0000 | .0001 | .0011 | .0058 | .0186 | .0442 | .0833 | .1312 | .1775 | .2095 |
| | 8 | .0000 | .0000 | .0001 | .0011 | .0047 | .0142 | .0336 | .0656 | .1089 | .1571 |
| | 9 | .0000 | .0000 | .0000 | .0001 | .0009 | .0034 | .0101 | .0243 | .0495 | .0873 |
| | 10 | .0000 | .0000 | .0000 | .0000 | .0001 | .0006 | .0022 | .0065 | .0162 | .0349 |
| | 11 | .0000 | .0000 | .0000 | .0000 | .0000 | .0001 | .0003 | .0012 | .0036 | .0095 |
| | 12 | .0000 | .0000 | .0000 | .0000 | .0000 | .0000 | .0000 | .0001 | .0005 | .0016 |
| | 13 | .0000 | .0000 | .0000 | .0000 | .0000 | .0000 | .0000 | .0000 | .0000 | .0001 |
| 14 | 0 | .4877 | .2288 | .1028 | .0440 | .0178 | .0068 | .0024 | .0008 | .0002 | .0001 |
| | 1 | .3593 | .3559 | .2539 | .1539 | .0832 | .0407 | .0181 | .0073 | .0027 | .0009 |
| | 2 | .1229 | .2570 | .2912 | .2501 | .1802 | .1134 | .0634 | .0317 | .0141 | .0056 |
| | 3 | .0259 | .1142 | .2056 | .2501 | .2402 | .1943 | .1366 | .0845 | .0462 | .0222 |
| | 4 | .0037 | .0349 | .0998 | .1720 | .2202 | .2290 | .2022 | .1549 | .1040 | .0611 |
| | 5 | .0004 | .0078 | .0352 | .0860 | .1468 | .1963 | .2178 | .2066 | .1701 | .1222 |
| | 6 | .0000 | .0013 | .0093 | .0322 | .0734 | .1262 | .1759 | .2066 | .2088 | .1833 |
| | 7 | .0000 | .0002 | .0019 | .0092 | .0280 | .0618 | .1082 | .1574 | .1952 | .2095 |
| | 8 | .0000 | 0000 | .0003 | .0020 | .0082 | .0232 | .0510 | .0918 | .1398 | .1833 |
| | 9 | .0000 | .0000 | 0000 | .0003 | .0018 | .0066 | .0183 | .0408 | .0762 | .1222 |
| | 10 | .0000 | .0000 | .0000 | .0000 | .0003 | .0014 | .0049 | .0136 | .0312 | .0611 |
| | 11 | .0000 | .0000 | .0000 | .0000 | .0000 | .0002 | .0010 | .0033 | .0093 | .0222 |
| | 12 | .0000 | .0000 | .0000 | .0000 | .0000 | .0000 | .0001 | .0005 | .0019 | .0056 |
| | 13 | .0000 | .0000 | .0000 | .0000 | .0000 | .0000 | .0000 | .0001 | .0002 | .0009 |
| | 14 | .0000 | .0000 | .0000 | .0000 | .0000 | .0000 | .0000 | .0000 | .0000 | .0001 |
| 15 | 0 | .4633 | .2059 | .0874 | .0352 | .0134 | .0047 | .0016 | .0005 | .0001 | .0000 |
| | 1 | .3658 | .3432 | .2312 | .1319 | .0668 | .0305 | .0126 | .0047 | .0016 | .0005 |

*continued*

TABLE **B**    *(continued)*

| N | NUMBER OF P OR Q EVENTS | P or Q | | | | | | | | | |
|---|---|---|---|---|---|---|---|---|---|---|---|
| | | .05 | .10 | .15 | .20 | .25 | .30 | .35 | .40 | .45 | .50 |
| 15 | 2 | .1348 | .2669 | .2856 | .2309 | .1559 | .0916 | .0476 | .0219 | .0090 | .0032 |
| | 3 | .0307 | .1285 | .2184 | .2501 | .2252 | .1700 | .1110 | .0634 | .0318 | .0139 |
| | 4 | .0049 | .0428 | .1156 | .1876 | .2252 | .2186 | .1792 | .1268 | .0780 | .0417 |
| | 5 | .0006 | .0105 | .0449 | .1032 | .1651 | .2061 | .2123 | .1859 | .1404 | .0916 |
| | 6 | .0000 | .0019 | .0132 | .0430 | .0917 | .1472 | .1906 | .2066 | .1914 | .1527 |
| | 7 | .0000 | .0003 | .0030 | .0138 | .0393 | .0811 | .1319 | .1771 | .2013 | .1964 |
| | 8 | .0000 | .0000 | .0005 | .0035 | .0131 | .0348 | .0710 | .1181 | .1647 | .1964 |
| | 9 | .0000 | .0000 | .0001 | .0007 | .0034 | .0116 | .0298 | .0612 | .1048 | .1527 |
| | 10 | .0000 | .0000 | .0000 | .0001 | .0007 | .0030 | .0096 | .0245 | .0515 | .0916 |
| | 11 | .0000 | .0000 | .0000 | .0000 | .0001 | .0006 | .0024 | .0074 | .0191 | .0417 |
| | 12 | .0000 | .0000 | .0000 | .0000 | .0000 | .0001 | .0004 | .0016 | .0052 | .0139 |
| | 13 | .0000 | .0000 | .0000 | .0000 | .0000 | .0000 | .0001 | .0003 | .0010 | .0032 |
| | 14 | .0000 | .0000 | .0000 | .0000 | .0000 | .0000 | .0000 | .0000 | .0001 | .0005 |
| | 15 | .0000 | .0000 | .0000 | .0000 | .0000 | .0000 | .0000 | .0000 | .0000 | .0000 |

## TABLE C   *Random Numbers*

| | | | | | | | | | |
|---|---|---|---|---|---|---|---|---|---|
| 11339 | 19233 | 50911 | 14209 | 39594 | 68368 | 97742 | 36252 | 27671 | 55091 |
| 96971 | 19968 | 31709 | 40197 | 16313 | 80020 | 01588 | 21654 | 50328 | 04577 |
| 07779 | 47712 | 33846 | 84716 | 49870 | 59670 | 46946 | 71716 | 50623 | 38681 |
| 71675 | 95993 | 08790 | 13241 | 71260 | 16558 | 83316 | 68482 | 10294 | 45137 |
| 32804 | 72742 | 16237 | 72550 | 10570 | 31470 | 92612 | 94917 | 48822 | 79794 |
| 14835 | 56263 | 53062 | 71543 | 67632 | 30337 | 28739 | 17582 | 40924 | 32434 |
| 15544 | 14327 | 07580 | 48813 | 30161 | 10746 | 96470 | 60680 | 63507 | 14435 |
| 92230 | 41243 | 90765 | 08867 | 08038 | 05038 | 10908 | 00633 | 21740 | 55450 |
| 33564 | 93563 | 10770 | 10595 | 71323 | 84243 | 09402 | 62877 | 49762 | 56151 |
| 84461 | 55618 | 40570 | 72906 | 30794 | 49144 | 65239 | 21788 | 38288 | 29180 |
| 91645 | 42451 | 83776 | 99246 | 45548 | 02457 | 74804 | 49536 | 89815 | 74285 |
| 78305 | 63797 | 26995 | 23146 | 56071 | 97081 | 22376 | 09819 | 56855 | 97424 |
| 97888 | 55122 | 65545 | 02904 | 40042 | 70653 | 24483 | 31258 | 96475 | 77668 |
| 67286 | 09001 | 09718 | 67231 | 54033 | 24185 | 52097 | 78713 | 95910 | 84400 |
| 53610 | 59459 | 89945 | 72102 | 66595 | 02198 | 26968 | 88467 | 46939 | 52318 |
| 52965 | 76189 | 68892 | 64541 | 02225 | 09603 | 59304 | 38179 | 75920 | 80486 |
| 25336 | 39735 | 25594 | 50557 | 96257 | 59700 | 27715 | 42432 | 27652 | 88151 |
| 73078 | 44371 | 77616 | 49296 | 55882 | 71507 | 30168 | 31876 | 28283 | 53424 |
| 31797 | 52244 | 38354 | 47800 | 48454 | 43304 | 14256 | 74281 | 82279 | 28882 |
| 47772 | 22798 | 36910 | 39986 | 34033 | 39868 | 24009 | 97123 | 59151 | 27583 |
| 54153 | 70832 | 37575 | 31898 | 39212 | 63993 | 05419 | 77565 | 73150 | 98537 |
| 93745 | 99871 | 37129 | 55032 | 94444 | 17884 | 27082 | 23502 | 06136 | 89476 |
| 81676 | 51330 | 58828 | 74199 | 87214 | 13727 | 80539 | 95037 | 73536 | 16862 |
| 79788 | 02193 | 33250 | 05865 | 53018 | 62394 | 56997 | 41534 | 01953 | 13763 |
| 92112 | 61235 | 68760 | 61201 | 02189 | 09424 | 24156 | 10368 | 26527 | 89107 |
| 87542 | 28171 | 45150 | 75523 | 66790 | 63963 | 13903 | 68498 | 02981 | 25219 |
| 37535 | 48342 | 48943 | 07719 | 20407 | 33748 | 93650 | 39356 | 01011 | 22099 |
| 95957 | 96668 | 69380 | 49091 | 90182 | 13205 | 71802 | 35482 | 27973 | 46814 |
| 34642 | 85350 | 53361 | 63940 | 79546 | 89956 | 96836 | 81313 | 80712 | 73572 |
| 50413 | 31008 | 09231 | 46516 | 61672 | 79954 | 01291 | 72278 | 55658 | 84893 |
| 53312 | 73768 | 59931 | 55182 | 43761 | 59424 | 79775 | 17772 | 41552 | 45236 |
| 16302 | 64092 | 76045 | 28958 | 21182 | 30050 | 96256 | 85737 | 86962 | 27067 |
| 96357 | 98654 | 01909 | 58799 | 87374 | 53184 | 87233 | 55275 | 59572 | 56476 |
| 38529 | 89095 | 89538 | 15600 | 33687 | 86353 | 61917 | 63876 | 52367 | 79032 |
| 45939 | 05014 | 06099 | 76041 | 57638 | 55342 | 41269 | 96173 | 94872 | 35605 |
| 02300 | 23739 | 68485 | 98567 | 77035 | 91533 | 62500 | 31548 | 09511 | 80252 |
| 59750 | 14131 | 24973 | 05962 | 83215 | 25950 | 43867 | 75213 | 21500 | 17758 |
| 21285 | 53607 | 82657 | 22053 | 29996 | 04729 | 48917 | 72091 | 57336 | 18476 |
| 93703 | 60164 | 19090 | 63030 | 88931 | 84439 | 94747 | 77982 | 61932 | 21928 |
| 15576 | 76654 | 19775 | 77518 | 43259 | 82790 | 08193 | 63007 | 68824 | 75315 |

*Source:* Reprinted from *A Million Random Digits with 100,000 Normal Deviates,* RAND (New York: The Free Press, 1955). Copyright © 1955 and 1983 by RAND. Used by permission.

TABLE C   (*continued*)

| | | | | | | | | | |
|---|---|---|---|---|---|---|---|---|---|
| 12752 | 33321 | 69796 | 03625 | 37328 | 75200 | 77262 | 99004 | 96705 | 15540 |
| 89038 | 53455 | 93322 | 25069 | 88186 | 45026 | 31020 | 52540 | 10838 | 72490 |
| 62411 | 56968 | 08379 | 40159 | 27419 | 12024 | 99694 | 68668 | 73039 | 87682 |
| 45853 | 68103 | 38927 | 77105 | 65241 | 70387 | 01634 | 59665 | 30512 | 66161 |
| 84558 | 24272 | 84355 | 00116 | 68344 | 92805 | 52618 | 51584 | 75964 | 53021 |
| 45272 | 58388 | 69131 | 61075 | 80192 | 45959 | 76992 | 19210 | 27126 | 45525 |
| 68015 | 99001 | 11832 | 39832 | 80462 | 70468 | 89929 | 55695 | 77524 | 20675 |
| 13263 | 92240 | 89559 | 66545 | 06433 | 38634 | 36645 | 22350 | 81169 | 97417 |
| 66309 | 31466 | 97705 | 46996 | 69059 | 33771 | 95004 | 89037 | 38054 | 80853 |
| 56348 | 05291 | 38713 | 82303 | 26293 | 61319 | 45285 | 75784 | 50043 | 44438 |
| 93108 | 77033 | 68325 | 10160 | 38667 | 62441 | 87023 | 94372 | 06164 | 30700 |
| 28271 | 08589 | 83279 | 48838 | 60935 | 70541 | 53814 | 95588 | 05832 | 80235 |
| 21841 | 35545 | 11148 | 34775 | 17308 | 88034 | 97765 | 35959 | 52843 | 44895 |
| 22025 | 79554 | 19698 | 25255 | 50283 | 94037 | 57463 | 92925 | 12042 | 91414 |
| 09210 | 20779 | 02994 | 02258 | 86978 | 85092 | 54052 | 18354 | 20914 | 28460 |
| 90552 | 71129 | 03621 | 20517 | 16908 | 06668 | 29916 | 51537 | 93658 | 29525 |
| 01130 | 06995 | 20258 | 10351 | 99248 | 51660 | 38861 | 49668 | 74742 | 47181 |
| 22604 | 56719 | 21784 | 68788 | 38358 | 59827 | 19270 | 99287 | 81193 | 43366 |
| 06690 | 01800 | 34272 | 65497 | 94891 | 14537 | 91358 | 21587 | 95765 | 72605 |
| 59809 | 69982 | 71809 | 64984 | 48709 | 43991 | 24987 | 69246 | 86400 | 29559 |
| 56475 | 02726 | 58511 | 95405 | 70293 | 84971 | 06676 | 44075 | 32338 | 31980 |
| 02730 | 34870 | 83209 | 03138 | 07715 | 31557 | 55242 | 61308 | 26507 | 06186 |
| 74482 | 33990 | 13509 | 92588 | 10462 | 76546 | 46097 | 01825 | 20153 | 36271 |
| 19793 | 22487 | 94238 | 81054 | 95488 | 23617 | 15539 | 94335 | 73822 | 93481 |
| 19020 | 27856 | 60526 | 24144 | 98021 | 60564 | 46373 | 86928 | 52135 | 74919 |
| 69565 | 60635 | 65709 | 77887 | 42766 | 86698 | 14004 | 94577 | 27936 | 47220 |
| 69274 | 23208 | 61035 | 84263 | 15034 | 28717 | 76146 | 22021 | 23779 | 98562 |
| 83658 | 14204 | 09445 | 41081 | 49630 | 34215 | 89806 | 40930 | 97194 | 21747 |
| 78612 | 51102 | 66826 | 40430 | 54072 | 62164 | 68977 | 95583 | 11765 | 81072 |
| 14980 | 74158 | 78216 | 38985 | 60838 | 82836 | 42777 | 85321 | 90463 | 11813 |
| 63172 | 28010 | 29405 | 91554 | 75195 | 51183 | 65805 | 87525 | 35952 | 83204 |
| 71167 | 37984 | 52737 | 06869 | 38122 | 95322 | 41356 | 19391 | 96787 | 64410 |
| 78530 | 56410 | 19195 | 34434 | 83712 | 50397 | 80920 | 15464 | 81350 | 18673 |
| 98324 | 03774 | 07573 | 67864 | 06497 | 20758 | 83454 | 22756 | 83959 | 96347 |
| 55793 | 30055 | 08373 | 32652 | 02654 | 75980 | 02095 | 87545 | 88815 | 80086 |
| 05674 | 34471 | 61967 | 91266 | 38814 | 44728 | 32455 | 17057 | 08339 | 93997 |
| 15643 | 22245 | 07592 | 22078 | 73628 | 60902 | 41561 | 54608 | 41023 | 98345 |
| 66750 | 19609 | 70358 | 03622 | 64898 | 82220 | 69304 | 46235 | 97332 | 64539 |
| 42320 | 74314 | 50222 | 82339 | 51564 | 42885 | 50482 | 98501 | 02245 | 88990 |
| 73752 | 73818 | 15470 | 04914 | 24936 | 65514 | 56633 | 72030 | 30856 | 85183 |

*continued*

TABLE C    (*continued*)

| | | | | | | | | | |
|---|---|---|---|---|---|---|---|---|---|
| 97546 | 02188 | 46373 | 21486 | 28221 | 08155 | 23486 | 66134 | 88799 | 49496 |
| 32569 | 52162 | 38444 | 42004 | 78011 | 16909 | 94194 | 79732 | 47114 | 23919 |
| 36048 | 93973 | 82596 | 28739 | 86985 | 58144 | 65007 | 08786 | 14826 | 04896 |
| 40455 | 36702 | 38965 | 56042 | 80023 | 28169 | 04174 | 65533 | 52718 | 55255 |
| 33597 | 47071 | 55618 | 51796 | 71027 | 46690 | 08002 | 45066 | 02870 | 60012 |
| 22828 | 96380 | 35883 | 15910 | 17211 | 42358 | 14056 | 55438 | 98148 | 35384 |
| 00631 | 95925 | 19324 | 31497 | 88118 | 06283 | 84596 | 72091 | 53987 | 01477 |
| 75722 | 36478 | 07634 | 63114 | 27164 | 15467 | 03983 | 09141 | 60562 | 65725 |
| 80577 | 01771 | 61510 | 17099 | 28731 | 41426 | 18853 | 41523 | 14914 | 76661 |
| 10524 | 20900 | 65463 | 83680 | 05005 | 11611 | 64426 | 59065 | 06758 | 02892 |
| 93815 | 69446 | 75253 | 51915 | 97839 | 75427 | 90685 | 60352 | 96288 | 34248 |
| 81867 | 97119 | 93446 | 20862 | 46591 | 97677 | 42704 | 13718 | 44975 | 67145 |
| 64649 | 07689 | 16711 | 12169 | 15238 | 74106 | 60655 | 56289 | 74166 | 78561 |
| 55768 | 09210 | 52439 | 33355 | 57884 | 36791 | 00853 | 49969 | 74814 | 09270 |
| 38080 | 49460 | 48137 | 61589 | 42742 | 92035 | 21766 | 19435 | 92579 | 27683 |
| 22360 | 16332 | 05343 | 34613 | 24013 | 98831 | 17157 | 44089 | 07366 | 66196 |
| 40521 | 09057 | 00239 | 51284 | 71556 | 22605 | 41293 | 54854 | 39736 | 05113 |
| 19292 | 69862 | 59951 | 49644 | 53486 | 28244 | 20714 | 56030 | 39292 | 45166 |
| 79504 | 40078 | 06838 | 05509 | 68581 | 39400 | 85615 | 52314 | 83202 | 40313 |
| 64138 | 27983 | 84048 | 42631 | 58658 | 62243 | 82572 | 45211 | 37060 | 15017 |

**TABLE D**   *Student's t Distribution*

The first column identifies the specific *t* distribution according to its number of degrees of freedom. Other columns give the proportion of the area under the entire curve that falls beyond the tabled positive value of *t*. Areas for negative values of *t* are the same because the curve is symmetrical.

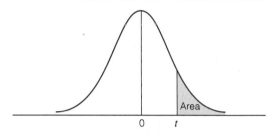

| | | | AREA IN ONE TAIL | | | |
|---|---|---|---|---|---|---|
| *df* | .25 | .10 | .05 | .025 | .01 | .005 |
| 1 | 1.000 | 3.078 | 6.314 | 12.706 | 31.821 | 63.657 |
| 2 | 0.816 | 1.886 | 2.920 | 4.303 | 6.965 | 9.925 |
| 3 | 0.765 | 1.638 | 2.353 | 3.182 | 4.541 | 5.841 |
| 4 | 0.741 | 1.533 | 2.132 | 2.776 | 3.747 | 4.604 |
| 5 | 0.727 | 1.476 | 2.015 | 2.571 | 3.365 | 4.032 |
| 6 | 0.718 | 1.440 | 1.943 | 2.447 | 3.143 | 3.707 |
| 7 | 0.711 | 1.415 | 1.895 | 2.365 | 2.998 | 3.500 |
| 8 | 0.706 | 1.397 | 1.860 | 2.306 | 2.896 | 3.355 |
| 9 | 0.703 | 1.383 | 1.833 | 2.262 | 2.821 | 3.250 |
| 10 | 0.700 | 1.372 | 1.812 | 2.228 | 2.764 | 3.169 |
| 11 | 0.697 | 1.363 | 1.796 | 2.201 | 2.718 | 3.106 |
| 12 | 0.696 | 1.356 | 1.782 | 2.179 | 2.681 | 3.054 |
| 13 | 0.694 | 1.350 | 1.771 | 2.160 | 2.650 | 3.012 |
| 14 | 0.692 | 1.345 | 1.761 | 2.145 | 2.624 | 2.977 |
| 15 | 0.691 | 1.341 | 1.753 | 2.132 | 2.602 | 2.947 |
| 16 | 0.690 | 1.337 | 1.746 | 2.120 | 2.584 | 2.921 |
| 17 | 0.689 | 1.333 | 1.740 | 2.110 | 2.567 | 2.898 |
| 18 | 0.688 | 1.330 | 1.734 | 2.101 | 2.552 | 2.878 |
| 19 | 0.688 | 1.328 | 1.729 | 2.093 | 2.540 | 2.861 |
| 20 | 0.687 | 1.325 | 1.725 | 2.086 | 2.528 | 2.845 |
| 21 | 0.686 | 1.323 | 1.721 | 2.080 | 2.518 | 2.831 |
| 22 | 0.686 | 1.321 | 1.717 | 2.074 | 2.568 | 2.819 |
| 23 | 0.685 | 1.320 | 1.714 | 2.069 | 2.500 | 2.807 |
| 24 | 0.685 | 1.318 | 1.711 | 2.064 | 2.492 | 2.797 |
| 25 | 0.684 | 1.316 | 1.708 | 2.060 | 2.485 | 2.787 |
| 26 | 0.684 | 1.315 | 1.706 | 2.056 | 2.479 | 2.779 |
| 27 | 0.684 | 1.314 | 1.703 | 2.052 | 2.473 | 2.771 |
| 28 | 0.683 | 1.312 | 1.701 | 2.048 | 2.467 | 2.763 |
| 29 | 0.683 | 1.311 | 1.699 | 2.045 | 2.462 | 2.756 |
| 30 | 0.683 | 1.310 | 1.697 | 2.042 | 2.457 | 2.750 |
| 31 | 0.682 | 1.310 | 1.696 | 2.040 | 2.453 | 2.744 |
| 32 | 0.682 | 1.309 | 1.694 | 2.037 | 2.449 | 2.738 |
| 33 | 0.682 | 1.308 | 1.692 | 2.034 | 2.445 | 2.733 |

*continued*

**TABLE D** *(continued)*

| df | .25 | .10 | .05 | .025 | .01 | .005 |
|---|---|---|---|---|---|---|
| | | | AREA IN ONE TAIL | | | |
| 34 | 0.682 | 1.307 | 1.691 | 2.032 | 2.441 | 2.728 |
| 35 | 0.682 | 1.306 | 1.690 | 2.030 | 2.438 | 2.724 |
| 36 | 0.681 | 1.306 | 1.688 | 2.028 | 2.434 | 2.720 |
| 37 | 0.681 | 1.305 | 1.687 | 2.026 | 2.431 | 2.715 |
| 38 | 0.681 | 1.304 | 1.686 | 2.024 | 2.429 | 2.712 |
| 39 | 0.681 | 1.304 | 1.685 | 2.023 | 2.426 | 2.708 |
| 40 | 0.681 | 1.303 | 1.684 | 2.021 | 2.423 | 2.704 |
| 45 | 0.680 | 1.301 | 1.679 | 2.014 | 2.412 | 2.690 |
| 50 | 0.679 | 1.299 | 1.676 | 2.009 | 2.403 | 2.678 |
| 55 | 0.679 | 1.297 | 1.673 | 2.004 | 2.396 | 2.668 |
| 60 | 0.679 | 1.296 | 1.671 | 2.000 | 2.390 | 2.660 |
| 70 | 0.678 | 1.294 | 1.667 | 1.994 | 2.381 | 2.648 |
| 80 | 0.678 | 1.292 | 1.664 | 1.990 | 2.374 | 2.639 |
| 90 | 0.677 | 1.291 | 1.662 | 1.987 | 2.368 | 2.632 |
| 100 | 0.677 | 1.290 | 1.660 | 1.984 | 2.364 | 2.626 |
| 120 | 0.676 | 1.289 | 1.658 | 1.980 | 2.358 | 2.617 |
| 150 | 0.676 | 1.287 | 1.655 | 1.976 | 2.352 | 2.609 |
| 200 | 0.676 | 1.286 | 1.652 | 1.972 | 2.345 | 2.601 |
| 300 | 0.675 | 1.284 | 1.650 | 1.968 | 2.339 | 2.592 |
| 400 | 0.675 | 1.284 | 1.649 | 1.966 | 2.336 | 2.588 |
| 500 | 0.675 | 1.283 | 1.648 | 1.965 | 2.334 | 2.586 |
| 1000 | 0.675 | 1.282 | 1.646 | 1.962 | 2.330 | 2.581 |
| ∞ | 0.674 | 1.282 | 1.645 | 1.960 | 2.326 | 2.576 |

*Source:* Owen, *Handbook of Statistical Tables* p. 28–30. © 1962 by Addison-Wesley Publishing Company. Copyright renewal © 1990. Reprinted by permission of Pearson Education, Inc.

## TABLE E  *The F Distribution*

The specific *F* distribution must be identified by the number of degrees of freedom characterizing the numerator and the denominator of *F*. The values of *F* corresponding to 5% of the area in the upper tail are shown in roman type. Those corresponding to 1% are in boldface type.

$F_{.05}$  $F_{.01}$  Area = .05  Area = .01

**DEGREES OF FREEDOM: NUMERATOR** — $df_{bet}$

| Den. df | Area | 1 | 2 | 3 | 4 | 5 | 6 | 7 | 8 | 9 | 10 | 11 | 12 | 14 | 16 | 20 | 24 | 30 | 40 | 50 | 75 | 100 | 200 | 500 | ∞ |
|---|---|---|---|---|---|---|---|---|---|---|---|---|---|---|---|---|---|---|---|---|---|---|---|---|---|
| 1 | .05 | 161 | 200 | 216 | 225 | 230 | 234 | 237 | 239 | 241 | 242 | 243 | 244 | 245 | 246 | 248 | 249 | 250 | 251 | 252 | 253 | 253 | 254 | 254 | 254 |
| | .01 | **4052** | **4999** | **5403** | **5625** | **5764** | **5859** | **5928** | **5981** | **6022** | **6056** | **6082** | **6106** | **6142** | **6169** | **6208** | **6234** | **6258** | **6286** | **6302** | **6323** | **6334** | **6352** | **6361** | **6366** |
| 2 | .05 | 18.51 | 19.00 | 19.16 | 19.25 | 19.30 | 19.33 | 19.36 | 19.37 | 19.38 | 19.39 | 19.40 | 19.41 | 19.42 | 19.43 | 19.44 | 19.45 | 19.46 | 19.47 | 19.47 | 19.48 | 19.49 | 19.49 | 19.50 | 19.50 |
| | .01 | **98.49** | **99.00** | **99.17** | **99.25** | **99.30** | **99.33** | **99.34** | **99.36** | **99.38** | **99.40** | **99.41** | **99.42** | **99.43** | **99.44** | **99.45** | **99.46** | **99.47** | **99.48** | **99.48** | **99.49** | **99.49** | **99.49** | **99.50** | **99.50** |
| 3 | .05 | 10.13 | 9.55 | 9.28 | 9.12 | 9.01 | 8.94 | 8.88 | 8.84 | 8.81 | 8.78 | 8.76 | 8.74 | 8.71 | 8.69 | 8.66 | 8.64 | 8.62 | 8.60 | 8.58 | 8.57 | 8.55 | 8.54 | 8.54 | 8.53 |
| | .01 | **34.12** | **30.82** | **29.46** | **28.71** | **28.24** | **27.91** | **27.67** | **27.49** | **27.34** | **27.23** | **27.13** | **27.05** | **26.92** | **26.83** | **26.69** | **26.60** | **26.50** | **26.41** | **26.35** | **26.27** | **26.23** | **26.18** | **26.14** | **26.12** |
| 4 | .05 | 7.71 | 6.94 | 6.59 | 6.39 | 6.26 | 6.16 | 6.09 | 6.04 | 6.00 | 5.96 | 5.93 | 5.91 | 5.87 | 5.84 | 5.80 | 5.77 | 5.74 | 5.71 | 5.70 | 5.68 | 5.66 | 5.65 | 5.64 | 5.63 |
| | .01 | **21.20** | **18.00** | **16.69** | **15.98** | **15.52** | **15.21** | **14.98** | **14.80** | **14.66** | **14.54** | **14.45** | **14.37** | **14.24** | **14.15** | **14.02** | **13.93** | **13.83** | **13.74** | **13.69** | **13.61** | **13.57** | **13.52** | **13.48** | **13.46** |
| 5 | .05 | 6.61 | 5.79 | 5.41 | 5.19 | 5.05 | 4.95 | 4.88 | 4.82 | 4.78 | 4.74 | 4.70 | 4.68 | 4.64 | 4.60 | 4.56 | 4.53 | 4.50 | 4.46 | 4.44 | 4.42 | 4.40 | 4.38 | 4.37 | 4.36 |
| | .01 | **16.26** | **13.27** | **12.06** | **11.39** | **10.97** | **10.67** | **10.45** | **10.27** | **10.15** | **10.05** | **9.96** | **9.89** | **9.77** | **9.68** | **9.55** | **9.47** | **9.38** | **9.29** | **9.24** | **9.17** | **9.13** | **9.07** | **9.04** | **9.02** |
| 6 | .05 | 5.99 | 5.14 | 4.76 | 4.53 | 4.39 | 4.28 | 4.21 | 4.15 | 4.10 | 4.06 | 4.03 | 4.00 | 3.96 | 3.92 | 3.87 | 3.84 | 3.81 | 3.77 | 3.75 | 3.72 | 3.71 | 3.69 | 3.68 | 3.67 |
| | .01 | **13.74** | **10.92** | **9.78** | **9.15** | **8.75** | **8.47** | **8.26** | **8.10** | **7.98** | **7.87** | **7.79** | **7.72** | **7.60** | **7.52** | **7.39** | **7.31** | **7.23** | **7.14** | **7.09** | **7.02** | **6.99** | **6.94** | **6.90** | **6.88** |
| 7 | .05 | 5.59 | 4.74 | 4.35 | 4.12 | 3.97 | 3.87 | 3.79 | 3.73 | 3.68 | 3.63 | 3.60 | 3.57 | 3.52 | 3.49 | 3.44 | 3.41 | 3.38 | 3.34 | 3.32 | 3.29 | 3.28 | 3.25 | 3.24 | 3.23 |
| | .01 | **12.25** | **9.55** | **8.45** | **7.85** | **7.46** | **7.19** | **7.00** | **6.84** | **6.71** | **6.62** | **6.54** | **6.47** | **6.35** | **6.27** | **6.15** | **6.07** | **5.98** | **5.90** | **5.85** | **5.78** | **5.75** | **5.70** | **5.67** | **5.65** |
| 8 | .05 | 5.32 | 4.46 | 4.07 | 3.84 | 3.69 | 3.58 | 3.50 | 3.44 | 3.39 | 3.34 | 3.31 | 3.28 | 3.23 | 3.20 | 3.15 | 3.12 | 3.08 | 3.05 | 3.03 | 3.00 | 2.98 | 2.96 | 2.94 | 2.93 |
| | .01 | **11.26** | **8.65** | **7.59** | **7.01** | **6.63** | **6.37** | **6.19** | **6.03** | **5.91** | **5.82** | **5.74** | **5.67** | **5.56** | **5.48** | **5.36** | **5.28** | **5.20** | **5.11** | **5.06** | **5.00** | **4.96** | **4.91** | **4.88** | **4.86** |
| 9 | .05 | 5.12 | 4.26 | 3.86 | 3.63 | 3.48 | 3.37 | 3.29 | 3.23 | 3.18 | 3.13 | 3.10 | 3.07 | 3.02 | 2.98 | 2.93 | 2.90 | 2.86 | 2.82 | 2.80 | 2.77 | 2.76 | 2.73 | 2.72 | 2.71 |
| | .01 | **10.56** | **8.02** | **6.99** | **6.42** | **6.06** | **5.80** | **5.62** | **5.47** | **5.35** | **5.26** | **5.18** | **5.11** | **5.00** | **4.92** | **4.80** | **4.73** | **4.64** | **4.56** | **4.51** | **4.45** | **4.41** | **4.36** | **4.33** | **4.31** |
| 10 | .05 | 4.96 | 4.10 | 3.71 | 3.48 | 3.33 | 3.22 | 3.14 | 3.07 | 3.02 | 2.97 | 2.94 | 2.91 | 2.86 | 2.82 | 2.77 | 2.74 | 2.70 | 2.67 | 2.64 | 2.61 | 2.59 | 2.56 | 2.55 | 2.54 |
| | .01 | **10.04** | **7.56** | **6.55** | **5.99** | **5.64** | **5.39** | **5.21** | **5.06** | **4.95** | **4.85** | **4.78** | **4.71** | **4.60** | **4.52** | **4.41** | **4.33** | **4.25** | **4.17** | **4.12** | **4.05** | **4.01** | **3.96** | **3.93** | **3.91** |
| 11 | .05 | 4.84 | 3.98 | 3.59 | 3.36 | 3.20 | 3.09 | 3.01 | 2.95 | 2.90 | 2.86 | 2.82 | 2.79 | 2.74 | 2.70 | 2.65 | 2.61 | 2.57 | 2.53 | 2.50 | 2.47 | 2.45 | 2.42 | 2.41 | 2.40 |
| | .01 | **9.65** | **7.20** | **6.22** | **5.67** | **5.32** | **5.07** | **4.88** | **4.74** | **4.63** | **4.54** | **4.46** | **4.40** | **4.29** | **4.21** | **4.10** | **4.02** | **3.94** | **3.86** | **3.80** | **3.74** | **3.70** | **3.66** | **3.62** | **3.60** |

*continued*

524

TABLE E (continued)

|  | | DEGREES OF FREEDOM: NUMERATOR | | | | | | | | | | | | | | | | | | | | | | |
|---|---|---|---|---|---|---|---|---|---|---|---|---|---|---|---|---|---|---|---|---|---|---|---|---|
| DEGREES OF FREEDOM: DENOMINATOR | 1 | 2 | 3 | 4 | 5 | 6 | 7 | 8 | 9 | 10 | 11 | 12 | 14 | 16 | 20 | 24 | 30 | 40 | 50 | 75 | 100 | 200 | 500 | ∞ |
| 12 | 4.75 | 3.88 | 3.49 | 3.26 | 3.11 | 3.00 | 2.92 | 2.85 | 2.80 | 2.76 | 2.72 | 2.69 | 2.64 | 2.60 | 2.54 | 2.50 | 2.46 | 2.42 | 2.40 | 2.36 | 2.35 | 2.32 | 2.31 | 2.30 |
|  | **9.33** | **6.93** | **5.95** | **5.41** | **5.06** | **4.82** | **4.65** | **4.50** | **4.39** | **4.30** | **4.22** | **4.16** | **4.05** | **3.98** | **3.86** | **3.78** | **3.70** | **3.61** | **3.56** | **3.49** | **3.46** | **3.41** | **3.38** | **3.36** |
| 13 | 4.67 | 3.80 | 3.41 | 3.18 | 3.02 | 2.92 | 2.84 | 2.77 | 2.72 | 2.67 | 2.63 | 2.60 | 2.55 | 2.51 | 2.46 | 2.42 | 2.38 | 2.34 | 2.32 | 2.28 | 2.26 | 2.24 | 2.22 | 2.21 |
|  | **9.07** | **6.70** | **5.74** | **5.20** | **4.86** | **4.62** | **4.44** | **4.30** | **4.19** | **4.10** | **4.02** | **3.96** | **3.85** | **3.78** | **3.67** | **3.59** | **3.51** | **3.42** | **3.37** | **3.30** | **3.27** | **3.21** | **3.18** | **3.16** |
| 14 | 4.60 | 3.74 | 3.34 | 3.11 | 2.96 | 2.85 | 2.77 | 2.70 | 2.65 | 2.60 | 2.56 | 2.53 | 2.48 | 2.44 | 2.39 | 2.35 | 2.31 | 2.27 | 2.24 | 2.21 | 2.19 | 2.16 | 2.14 | 2.13 |
|  | **8.86** | **6.51** | **5.56** | **5.03** | **4.69** | **4.46** | **4.28** | **4.14** | **4.03** | **3.94** | **3.86** | **3.80** | **3.70** | **3.62** | **3.51** | **3.43** | **3.34** | **3.26** | **3.21** | **3.14** | **3.11** | **3.06** | **3.02** | **3.00** |
| 15 | 4.54 | 3.68 | 3.29 | 3.06 | 2.90 | 2.79 | 2.70 | 2.64 | 2.59 | 2.55 | 2.51 | 2.48 | 2.43 | 2.39 | 2.33 | 2.29 | 2.25 | 2.21 | 2.18 | 2.15 | 2.12 | 2.10 | 2.08 | 2.07 |
|  | **8.68** | **6.36** | **5.42** | **4.89** | **4.56** | **4.32** | **4.14** | **4.00** | **3.89** | **3.80** | **3.73** | **3.67** | **3.56** | **3.48** | **3.36** | **3.29** | **3.20** | **3.12** | **3.07** | **3.00** | **2.97** | **2.92** | **2.89** | **2.87** |
| 16 | 4.49 | 3.63 | 3.24 | 3.01 | 2.85 | 2.74 | 2.66 | 2.59 | 2.54 | 2.49 | 2.45 | 2.42 | 2.37 | 2.33 | 2.28 | 2.24 | 2.20 | 2.16 | 2.13 | 2.09 | 2.07 | 2.04 | 2.02 | 2.01 |
|  | **8.53** | **6.23** | **5.29** | **4.77** | **4.44** | **4.20** | **4.03** | **3.89** | **3.78** | **3.69** | **3.61** | **3.55** | **3.45** | **3.37** | **3.25** | **3.18** | **3.10** | **3.01** | **2.96** | **2.89** | **2.86** | **2.80** | **2.77** | **2.75** |
| 17 | 4.45 | 3.59 | 3.20 | 2.96 | 2.81 | 2.70 | 2.62 | 2.55 | 2.50 | 2.45 | 2.41 | 2.38 | 2.33 | 2.29 | 2.23 | 2.19 | 2.15 | 2.11 | 2.08 | 2.04 | 2.02 | 1.99 | 1.97 | 1.96 |
|  | **8.40** | **6.11** | **5.18** | **4.67** | **4.34** | **4.10** | **3.93** | **3.79** | **3.68** | **3.59** | **3.52** | **3.45** | **3.35** | **3.27** | **3.16** | **3.08** | **3.00** | **2.92** | **2.86** | **2.79** | **2.76** | **2.70** | **2.67** | **2.65** |
| 18 | 4.41 | 3.55 | 3.16 | 2.93 | 2.77 | 2.66 | 2.58 | 2.51 | 2.46 | 2.41 | 2.37 | 2.34 | 2.29 | 2.25 | 2.19 | 2.15 | 2.11 | 2.07 | 2.04 | 2.00 | 1.98 | 1.95 | 1.93 | 1.92 |
|  | **8.28** | **6.01** | **5.09** | **4.58** | **4.25** | **4.01** | **3.85** | **3.71** | **3.60** | **3.51** | **3.44** | **3.37** | **3.27** | **3.19** | **3.07** | **3.00** | **2.91** | **2.83** | **2.78** | **2.71** | **2.68** | **2.62** | **2.59** | **2.57** |
| 19 | 4.38 | 3.52 | 3.13 | 2.90 | 2.74 | 2.63 | 2.55 | 2.48 | 2.43 | 2.38 | 2.34 | 2.31 | 2.26 | 2.21 | 2.15 | 2.11 | 2.07 | 2.02 | 2.00 | 1.96 | 1.94 | 1.91 | 1.90 | 1.88 |
|  | **8.18** | **5.93** | **5.01** | **4.50** | **4.17** | **3.94** | **3.77** | **3.63** | **3.52** | **3.43** | **3.36** | **3.30** | **3.19** | **3.12** | **3.00** | **2.92** | **2.84** | **2.76** | **2.70** | **2.63** | **2.60** | **2.54** | **2.51** | **2.49** |
| 20 | 4.35 | 3.49 | 3.10 | 2.87 | 2.71 | 2.60 | 2.52 | 2.45 | 2.40 | 2.35 | 2.31 | 2.28 | 2.23 | 2.18 | 2.12 | 2.08 | 2.04 | 1.99 | 1.96 | 1.92 | 1.90 | 1.87 | 1.85 | 1.84 |
|  | **8.10** | **5.85** | **4.94** | **4.43** | **4.10** | **3.87** | **3.71** | **3.56** | **3.45** | **3.37** | **3.30** | **3.23** | **3.13** | **3.05** | **2.94** | **2.86** | **2.77** | **2.69** | **2.63** | **2.56** | **2.53** | **2.47** | **2.44** | **2.42** |
| 21 | 4.32 | 3.47 | 3.07 | 2.84 | 2.68 | 2.57 | 2.49 | 2.42 | 2.37 | 2.32 | 2.28 | 2.25 | 2.20 | 2.15 | 2.09 | 2.05 | 2.00 | 1.96 | 1.93 | 1.89 | 1.87 | 1.84 | 1.82 | 1.81 |
|  | **8.02** | **5.78** | **4.87** | **4.37** | **4.04** | **3.81** | **3.65** | **3.51** | **3.40** | **3.31** | **3.24** | **3.17** | **3.07** | **2.99** | **2.88** | **2.80** | **2.72** | **2.63** | **2.58** | **2.51** | **2.47** | **2.42** | **2.38** | **2.36** |
| 22 | 4.30 | 3.44 | 3.05 | 2.82 | 2.66 | 2.55 | 2.47 | 2.40 | 2.35 | 2.30 | 2.26 | 2.23 | 2.18 | 2.13 | 2.07 | 2.03 | 1.98 | 1.93 | 1.91 | 1.87 | 1.84 | 1.81 | 1.80 | 1.78 |
|  | **7.94** | **5.72** | **4.82** | **4.31** | **3.99** | **3.76** | **3.59** | **3.45** | **3.35** | **3.26** | **3.18** | **3.12** | **3.02** | **2.94** | **2.83** | **2.75** | **2.67** | **2.58** | **2.53** | **2.46** | **2.42** | **2.37** | **2.33** | **2.31** |
| 23 | 4.28 | 3.42 | 3.03 | 2.80 | 2.64 | 2.53 | 2.45 | 2.38 | 2.32 | 2.28 | 2.24 | 2.20 | 2.14 | 2.10 | 2.04 | 2.00 | 1.96 | 1.91 | 1.88 | 1.84 | 1.82 | 1.79 | 1.77 | 1.76 |
|  | **7.88** | **5.66** | **4.76** | **4.26** | **3.94** | **3.71** | **3.54** | **3.41** | **3.30** | **3.21** | **3.14** | **3.07** | **2.97** | **2.89** | **2.78** | **2.70** | **2.62** | **2.53** | **2.48** | **2.41** | **2.37** | **2.32** | **2.28** | **2.26** |
| 24 | 4.26 | 3.40 | 3.01 | 2.78 | 2.62 | 2.51 | 2.43 | 2.36 | 2.30 | 2.26 | 2.22 | 2.18 | 2.13 | 2.09 | 2.02 | 1.98 | 1.94 | 1.89 | 1.86 | 1.82 | 1.80 | 1.76 | 1.74 | 1.73 |
|  | **7.82** | **5.61** | **4.72** | **4.22** | **3.90** | **3.67** | **3.50** | **3.36** | **3.25** | **3.17** | **3.09** | **3.03** | **2.93** | **2.85** | **2.74** | **2.66** | **2.58** | **2.49** | **2.44** | **2.36** | **2.33** | **2.27** | **2.23** | **2.21** |

*continued*

TABLE E (continued)

DEGREES OF FREEDOM: NUMERATOR

| DEGREES OF FREEDOM: DENOMINATOR | 1 | 2 | 3 | 4 | 5 | 6 | 7 | 8 | 9 | 10 | 11 | 12 | 14 | 16 | 20 | 24 | 30 | 40 | 50 | 75 | 100 | 200 | 500 | ∞ |
|---|---|---|---|---|---|---|---|---|---|---|---|---|---|---|---|---|---|---|---|---|---|---|---|---|
| 25 | 4.24 | 3.38 | 2.99 | 2.76 | 2.60 | 2.49 | 2.41 | 2.34 | 2.28 | 2.24 | 2.20 | 2.16 | 2.11 | 2.06 | 2.00 | 1.96 | 1.92 | 1.87 | 1.84 | 1.80 | 1.77 | 1.74 | 1.72 | 1.71 |
|  | **7.77** | **5.57** | **4.68** | **4.18** | **3.86** | **3.63** | **3.46** | **3.32** | **3.21** | **3.13** | **3.05** | **2.99** | **2.89** | **2.81** | **2.70** | **2.62** | **2.54** | **2.45** | **2.40** | **2.32** | **2.29** | **2.23** | **2.19** | **2.17** |
| 26 | 4.22 | 3.37 | 2.98 | 2.74 | 2.59 | 2.47 | 2.39 | 2.32 | 2.27 | 2.22 | 2.18 | 2.15 | 2.10 | 2.05 | 1.99 | 1.95 | 1.90 | 1.85 | 1.82 | 1.78 | 1.76 | 1.72 | 1.70 | 1.69 |
|  | **7.72** | **5.53** | **4.64** | **4.14** | **3.82** | **3.59** | **3.42** | **3.29** | **3.17** | **3.09** | **3.02** | **2.96** | **2.86** | **2.77** | **2.66** | **2.58** | **2.50** | **2.41** | **2.36** | **2.28** | **2.25** | **2.19** | **2.15** | **2.13** |
| 27 | 4.21 | 3.35 | 2.96 | 2.73 | 2.57 | 2.46 | 2.37 | 2.30 | 2.25 | 2.20 | 2.16 | 2.13 | 2.08 | 2.03 | 1.97 | 1.93 | 1.88 | 1.84 | 1.80 | 1.76 | 1.74 | 1.71 | 1.68 | 1.67 |
|  | **7.68** | **5.49** | **4.60** | **4.11** | **3.79** | **3.56** | **3.39** | **3.26** | **3.14** | **3.06** | **2.98** | **2.93** | **2.83** | **2.74** | **2.63** | **2.55** | **2.47** | **2.38** | **2.33** | **2.25** | **2.21** | **2.16** | **2.12** | **2.10** |
| 28 | 4.20 | 3.34 | 2.95 | 2.71 | 2.56 | 2.44 | 2.36 | 2.29 | 2.24 | 2.19 | 2.15 | 2.12 | 2.06 | 2.02 | 1.96 | 1.91 | 1.87 | 1.81 | 1.78 | 1.75 | 1.72 | 1.69 | 1.67 | 1.65 |
|  | **7.64** | **5.45** | **4.57** | **4.07** | **3.76** | **3.53** | **3.36** | **3.23** | **3.11** | **3.03** | **2.95** | **2.90** | **2.80** | **2.71** | **2.60** | **2.52** | **2.44** | **2.35** | **2.30** | **2.22** | **2.18** | **2.13** | **2.09** | **2.06** |
| 29 | 4.18 | 3.33 | 2.93 | 2.70 | 2.54 | 2.43 | 2.35 | 2.28 | 2.22 | 2.18 | 2.14 | 2.10 | 2.05 | 2.00 | 1.94 | 1.90 | 1.85 | 1.80 | 1.77 | 1.73 | 1.71 | 1.68 | 1.65 | 1.63 |
|  | **7.60** | **5.42** | **4.54** | **4.04** | **3.73** | **3.50** | **3.33** | **3.20** | **3.08** | **3.00** | **2.92** | **2.87** | **2.77** | **2.68** | **2.57** | **2.49** | **2.41** | **2.32** | **2.27** | **2.19** | **2.15** | **2.10** | **2.06** | **2.03** |
| 30 | 4.17 | 3.32 | 2.92 | 2.69 | 2.53 | 2.42 | 2.34 | 2.27 | 2.21 | 2.16 | 2.12 | 2.09 | 2.04 | 1.99 | 1.93 | 1.89 | 1.84 | 1.79 | 1.76 | 1.72 | 1.69 | 1.66 | 1.64 | 1.62 |
|  | **7.56** | **5.39** | **4.51** | **4.02** | **3.70** | **3.47** | **3.30** | **3.17** | **3.06** | **2.98** | **2.90** | **2.84** | **2.74** | **2.66** | **2.55** | **2.47** | **2.38** | **2.29** | **2.24** | **2.16** | **2.13** | **2.07** | **2.03** | **2.01** |
| 32 | 4.15 | 3.30 | 2.90 | 2.67 | 2.51 | 2.40 | 2.32 | 2.25 | 2.19 | 2.14 | 2.10 | 2.07 | 2.02 | 1.97 | 1.91 | 1.86 | 1.82 | 1.76 | 1.74 | 1.69 | 1.67 | 1.64 | 1.61 | 1.59 |
|  | **7.50** | **5.34** | **4.46** | **3.97** | **3.66** | **3.42** | **3.25** | **3.12** | **3.01** | **2.94** | **2.86** | **2.80** | **2.70** | **2.62** | **2.51** | **2.42** | **2.34** | **2.25** | **2.20** | **2.12** | **2.08** | **2.02** | **1.98** | **1.96** |
| 34 | 4.13 | 3.28 | 2.88 | 2.65 | 2.49 | 2.38 | 2.30 | 2.23 | 2.17 | 2.12 | 2.08 | 2.05 | 2.00 | 1.95 | 1.89 | 1.84 | 1.80 | 1.74 | 1.71 | 1.67 | 1.64 | 1.61 | 1.59 | 1.57 |
|  | **7.44** | **5.29** | **4.42** | **3.93** | **3.61** | **3.38** | **3.21** | **3.08** | **2.97** | **2.89** | **2.82** | **2.76** | **2.66** | **2.58** | **2.47** | **2.38** | **2.30** | **2.21** | **2.15** | **2.08** | **2.04** | **1.98** | **1.94** | **1.91** |
| 36 | 4.11 | 3.26 | 2.86 | 2.63 | 2.48 | 2.36 | 2.28 | 2.21 | 2.15 | 2.10 | 2.06 | 2.03 | 1.98 | 1.93 | 1.87 | 1.82 | 1.78 | 1.72 | 1.69 | 1.65 | 1.62 | 1.59 | 1.56 | 1.55 |
|  | **7.39** | **5.25** | **4.38** | **3.89** | **3.58** | **3.35** | **3.18** | **3.04** | **2.94** | **2.86** | **2.78** | **2.72** | **2.62** | **2.54** | **2.43** | **2.35** | **2.26** | **2.17** | **2.12** | **2.04** | **2.00** | **1.94** | **1.90** | **1.87** |
| 38 | 4.10 | 3.25 | 2.85 | 2.62 | 2.46 | 2.35 | 2.26 | 2.19 | 2.14 | 2.09 | 2.05 | 2.02 | 1.96 | 1.92 | 1.85 | 1.80 | 1.76 | 1.71 | 1.67 | 1.63 | 1.60 | 1.57 | 1.54 | 1.53 |
|  | **7.35** | **5.21** | **4.34** | **3.86** | **3.54** | **3.32** | **3.15** | **3.02** | **2.91** | **2.82** | **2.75** | **2.69** | **2.59** | **2.51** | **2.40** | **2.32** | **2.22** | **2.14** | **2.08** | **2.00** | **1.97** | **1.90** | **1.86** | **1.84** |
| 40 | 4.08 | 3.23 | 2.84 | 2.61 | 2.45 | 2.34 | 2.25 | 2.18 | 2.12 | 2.07 | 2.04 | 2.00 | 1.95 | 1.90 | 1.84 | 1.79 | 1.74 | 1.69 | 1.66 | 1.61 | 1.59 | 1.55 | 1.53 | 1.51 |
|  | **7.31** | **5.18** | **4.31** | **3.83** | **3.51** | **3.29** | **3.12** | **2.99** | **2.88** | **2.80** | **2.73** | **2.66** | **2.56** | **2.49** | **2.37** | **2.29** | **2.20** | **2.11** | **2.05** | **1.97** | **1.94** | **1.88** | **1.84** | **1.81** |
| 42 | 4.07 | 3.22 | 2.83 | 2.59 | 2.44 | 2.32 | 2.24 | 2.17 | 2.11 | 2.06 | 2.02 | 1.99 | 1.94 | 1.89 | 1.82 | 1.78 | 1.73 | 1.68 | 1.64 | 1.60 | 1.57 | 1.54 | 1.51 | 1.49 |
|  | **7.27** | **5.15** | **4.29** | **3.80** | **3.49** | **3.26** | **3.10** | **2.96** | **2.86** | **2.77** | **2.70** | **2.64** | **2.54** | **2.46** | **2.35** | **2.26** | **2.17** | **2.08** | **2.02** | **1.94** | **1.91** | **1.85** | **1.80** | **1.78** |
| 44 | 4.06 | 3.21 | 2.82 | 2.58 | 2.43 | 2.31 | 2.23 | 2.16 | 2.10 | 2.05 | 2.01 | 1.98 | 1.92 | 1.88 | 1.81 | 1.76 | 1.72 | 1.66 | 1.63 | 1.58 | 1.56 | 1.52 | 1.50 | 1.48 |
|  | **7.24** | **5.12** | **4.26** | **3.78** | **3.46** | **3.24** | **3.07** | **2.94** | **2.84** | **2.75** | **2.68** | **2.62** | **2.52** | **2.44** | **2.32** | **2.24** | **2.15** | **2.06** | **2.00** | **1.92** | **1.88** | **1.82** | **1.78** | **1.75** |
| 46 | 4.04 | 3.20 | 2.81 | 2.57 | 2.42 | 2.30 | 2.22 | 2.14 | 2.09 | 2.04 | 2.00 | 1.97 | 1.91 | 1.87 | 1.80 | 1.75 | 1.71 | 1.65 | 1.62 | 1.57 | 1.54 | 1.51 | 1.48 | 1.46 |
|  | **7.21** | **5.10** | **4.24** | **3.76** | **3.44** | **3.22** | **3.05** | **2.92** | **2.82** | **2.73** | **2.66** | **2.60** | **2.50** | **2.42** | **2.30** | **2.22** | **2.13** | **2.04** | **1.98** | **1.90** | **1.86** | **1.80** | **1.76** | **1.72** |

*continued*

**TABLE E** (*continued*)

DEGREES OF FREEDOM: NUMERATOR

| DEGREES OF FREEDOM: DENOMINATOR | 1 | 2 | 3 | 4 | 5 | 6 | 7 | 8 | 9 | 10 | 11 | 12 | 14 | 16 | 20 | 24 | 30 | 40 | 50 | 75 | 100 | 200 | 500 | ∞ |
|---|---|---|---|---|---|---|---|---|---|---|---|---|---|---|---|---|---|---|---|---|---|---|---|---|
| 48 | 4.04 | 3.19 | 2.80 | 2.56 | 2.41 | 2.30 | 2.21 | 2.14 | 2.08 | 2.03 | 1.99 | 1.96 | 1.90 | 1.86 | 1.79 | 1.74 | 1.70 | 1.64 | 1.61 | 1.56 | 1.53 | 1.50 | 1.47 | 1.45 |
|  | **7.19** | **5.08** | **4.22** | **3.74** | **3.42** | **3.20** | **3.04** | **2.90** | **2.80** | **2.71** | **2.64** | **2.58** | **2.48** | **2.40** | **2.28** | **2.20** | **2.11** | **2.02** | **1.96** | **1.88** | **1.84** | **1.78** | **1.73** | **1.70** |
| 50 | 4.03 | 3.18 | 2.79 | 2.56 | 2.40 | 2.29 | 2.20 | 2.13 | 2.07 | 2.02 | 1.98 | 1.95 | 1.90 | 1.85 | 1.78 | 1.74 | 1.69 | 1.63 | 1.60 | 1.55 | 1.52 | 1.48 | 1.46 | 1.44 |
|  | **7.17** | **5.06** | **4.20** | **3.72** | **3.41** | **3.18** | **3.02** | **2.88** | **2.78** | **2.70** | **2.62** | **2.56** | **2.46** | **2.39** | **2.26** | **2.18** | **2.10** | **2.00** | **1.94** | **1.86** | **1.82** | **1.76** | **1.71** | **1.68** |
| 55 | 4.02 | 3.17 | 2.78 | 2.54 | 2.38 | 2.27 | 2.18 | 2.11 | 2.05 | 2.00 | 1.97 | 1.93 | 1.88 | 1.83 | 1.76 | 1.72 | 1.67 | 1.61 | 1.58 | 1.52 | 1.50 | 1.46 | 1.43 | 1.41 |
|  | **7.12** | **5.01** | **4.16** | **3.68** | **3.37** | **3.15** | **2.98** | **2.85** | **2.75** | **2.66** | **2.59** | **2.53** | **2.43** | **2.35** | **2.23** | **2.15** | **2.06** | **1.96** | **1.90** | **1.82** | **1.78** | **1.71** | **1.66** | **1.64** |
| 60 | 4.00 | 3.15 | 2.76 | 2.52 | 2.37 | 2.25 | 2.17 | 2.10 | 2.04 | 1.99 | 1.95 | 1.92 | 1.86 | 1.81 | 1.75 | 1.70 | 1.65 | 1.59 | 1.56 | 1.50 | 1.48 | 1.44 | 1.41 | 1.39 |
|  | **7.08** | **4.98** | **4.13** | **3.65** | **3.34** | **3.12** | **2.95** | **2.82** | **2.72** | **2.63** | **2.56** | **2.50** | **2.40** | **2.32** | **2.20** | **2.12** | **2.03** | **1.93** | **1.87** | **1.79** | **1.74** | **1.68** | **1.63** | **1.60** |
| 65 | 3.99 | 3.14 | 2.75 | 2.51 | 2.36 | 2.24 | 2.15 | 2.08 | 2.02 | 1.98 | 1.94 | 1.90 | 1.85 | 1.80 | 1.73 | 1.68 | 1.63 | 1.57 | 1.54 | 1.49 | 1.46 | 1.42 | 1.39 | 1.37 |
|  | **7.04** | **4.95** | **4.10** | **3.62** | **3.31** | **3.09** | **2.93** | **2.79** | **2.70** | **2.61** | **2.54** | **2.47** | **2.37** | **2.30** | **2.18** | **2.09** | **2.00** | **1.90** | **1.84** | **1.76** | **1.71** | **1.64** | **1.60** | **1.56** |
| 70 | 3.98 | 3.13 | 2.74 | 2.50 | 2.35 | 2.23 | 2.14 | 2.07 | 2.01 | 1.97 | 1.93 | 1.89 | 1.84 | 1.79 | 1.72 | 1.67 | 1.62 | 1.56 | 1.53 | 1.47 | 1.45 | 1.40 | 1.37 | 1.35 |
|  | **7.01** | **4.92** | **4.08** | **3.60** | **3.29** | **3.07** | **2.91** | **2.77** | **2.67** | **2.59** | **2.51** | **2.45** | **2.35** | **2.28** | **2.15** | **2.07** | **1.98** | **1.88** | **1.82** | **1.74** | **1.69** | **1.62** | **1.56** | **1.53** |
| 80 | 3.96 | 3.11 | 2.72 | 2.48 | 2.33 | 2.21 | 2.12 | 2.05 | 1.99 | 1.95 | 1.91 | 1.88 | 1.82 | 1.77 | 1.70 | 1.65 | 1.60 | 1.54 | 1.51 | 1.45 | 1.42 | 1.38 | 1.35 | 1.32 |
|  | **6.96** | **4.88** | **4.04** | **3.56** | **3.25** | **3.04** | **2.87** | **2.74** | **2.64** | **2.55** | **2.48** | **2.41** | **2.32** | **2.24** | **2.11** | **2.03** | **1.94** | **1.84** | **1.78** | **1.70** | **1.65** | **1.57** | **1.52** | **1.49** |
| 100 | 3.94 | 3.09 | 2.70 | 2.46 | 2.30 | 2.19 | 2.10 | 2.03 | 1.97 | 1.92 | 1.88 | 1.85 | 1.79 | 1.75 | 1.68 | 1.63 | 1.57 | 1.51 | 1.48 | 1.42 | 1.39 | 1.34 | 1.30 | 1.28 |
|  | **6.90** | **4.82** | **3.98** | **3.51** | **3.20** | **2.99** | **2.82** | **2.69** | **2.59** | **2.51** | **2.43** | **2.36** | **2.26** | **2.19** | **2.06** | **1.98** | **1.89** | **1.79** | **1.73** | **1.64** | **1.59** | **1.51** | **1.46** | **1.43** |
| 125 | 3.92 | 3.07 | 2.68 | 2.44 | 2.29 | 2.17 | 2.08 | 2.01 | 1.95 | 1.90 | 1.86 | 1.83 | 1.77 | 1.72 | 1.65 | 1.60 | 1.55 | 1.49 | 1.45 | 1.39 | 1.36 | 1.31 | 1.27 | 1.25 |
|  | **6.84** | **4.78** | **3.94** | **3.47** | **3.17** | **2.95** | **2.79** | **2.65** | **2.56** | **2.47** | **2.40** | **2.33** | **2.23** | **2.15** | **2.03** | **1.94** | **1.85** | **1.75** | **1.68** | **1.59** | **1.54** | **1.46** | **1.40** | **1.37** |
| 150 | 3.91 | 3.06 | 2.67 | 2.43 | 2.27 | 2.16 | 2.07 | 2.00 | 1.94 | 1.89 | 1.85 | 1.82 | 1.76 | 1.71 | 1.64 | 1.59 | 1.54 | 1.47 | 1.44 | 1.37 | 1.34 | 1.29 | 1.25 | 1.22 |
|  | **6.81** | **4.75** | **3.91** | **3.44** | **3.14** | **2.92** | **2.76** | **2.62** | **2.53** | **2.44** | **2.37** | **2.30** | **2.20** | **2.12** | **2.00** | **1.91** | **1.83** | **1.72** | **1.66** | **1.56** | **1.51** | **1.43** | **1.37** | **1.33** |
| 200 | 3.89 | 3.04 | 2.65 | 2.41 | 2.26 | 2.14 | 2.05 | 1.98 | 1.92 | 1.87 | 1.83 | 1.80 | 1.74 | 1.69 | 1.62 | 1.57 | 1.52 | 1.45 | 1.42 | 1.35 | 1.32 | 1.26 | 1.22 | 1.19 |
|  | **6.76** | **4.71** | **3.88** | **3.41** | **3.11** | **2.90** | **2.73** | **2.60** | **2.50** | **2.41** | **2.34** | **2.28** | **2.17** | **2.09** | **1.97** | **1.88** | **1.79** | **1.69** | **1.62** | **1.53** | **1.48** | **1.39** | **1.33** | **1.28** |
| 400 | 3.86 | 3.02 | 2.62 | 2.39 | 2.23 | 2.12 | 2.03 | 1.96 | 1.90 | 1.85 | 1.81 | 1.78 | 1.72 | 1.67 | 1.60 | 1.54 | 1.49 | 1.42 | 1.38 | 1.32 | 1.28 | 1.22 | 1.16 | 1.13 |
|  | **6.70** | **4.66** | **3.83** | **3.36** | **3.06** | **2.85** | **2.69** | **2.55** | **2.46** | **2.37** | **2.29** | **2.23** | **2.12** | **2.04** | **1.92** | **1.84** | **1.74** | **1.64** | **1.57** | **1.47** | **1.42** | **1.32** | **1.24** | **1.19** |
| 1000 | 3.85 | 3.00 | 2.61 | 2.38 | 2.22 | 2.10 | 2.02 | 1.95 | 1.89 | 1.84 | 1.80 | 1.76 | 1.70 | 1.65 | 1.58 | 1.53 | 1.47 | 1.41 | 1.36 | 1.30 | 1.26 | 1.19 | 1.13 | 1.08 |
|  | **6.66** | **4.62** | **3.80** | **3.34** | **3.04** | **2.82** | **2.66** | **2.53** | **2.43** | **2.34** | **2.26** | **2.20** | **2.09** | **2.01** | **1.89** | **1.81** | **1.71** | **1.61** | **1.54** | **1.44** | **1.38** | **1.28** | **1.19** | **1.11** |
| ∞ | 3.84 | 2.99 | 2.60 | 2.37 | 2.21 | 2.09 | 2.01 | 1.94 | 1.88 | 1.83 | 1.79 | 1.75 | 1.69 | 1.64 | 1.57 | 1.52 | 1.46 | 1.40 | 1.35 | 1.28 | 1.24 | 1.17 | 1.11 | 1.00 |
|  | **6.64** | **4.60** | **3.78** | **3.32** | **3.02** | **2.80** | **2.64** | **2.51** | **2.41** | **2.32** | **2.24** | **2.18** | **2.07** | **1.99** | **1.87** | **1.79** | **1.69** | **1.59** | **1.52** | **1.41** | **1.36** | **1.25** | **1.15** | **1.00** |

*Source:* Reproduced by permission from *Statistical Methods*, 5th ed., by George W. Snedecor. Copyright © 1956 by Iowa State University Press.

**TABLE F**  *The Studentized Range Statistic*

| $df_W$ | $\alpha$ | k = NUMBER OF GROUPS | | | | | | | | |
|---|---|---|---|---|---|---|---|---|---|---|
| | | 2 | 3 | 4 | 5 | 6 | 7 | 8 | 9 | 10 |
| 5 | .05 | 3.64 | 4.60 | 5.22 | 5.67 | 6.03 | 6.33 | 6.58 | 6.80 | 6.99 |
| | .01 | 5.70 | 6.98 | 7.80 | 8.42 | 8.91 | 9.32 | 9.67 | 9.97 | 10.24 |
| 6 | .05 | 3.46 | 4.34 | 4.90 | 5.30 | 5.63 | 5.90 | 6.12 | 6.32 | 6.49 |
| | .01 | 5.24 | 6.33 | 7.03 | 7.56 | 7.97 | 8.32 | 8.61 | 8.87 | 9.10 |
| 7 | .05 | 3.34 | 4.16 | 4.68 | 5.06 | 5.36 | 5.61 | 5.82 | 6.00 | 6.16 |
| | .01 | 4.95 | 5.92 | 6.54 | 7.01 | 7.37 | 7.68 | 7.94 | 8.17 | 8.37 |
| 8 | .05 | 3.26 | 4.04 | 4.53 | 4.89 | 5.17 | 5.40 | 5.60 | 5.77 | 5.92 |
| | .01 | 4.75 | 5.64 | 6.20 | 6.62 | 6.96 | 7.24 | 7.47 | 7.68 | 7.86 |
| 9 | .05 | 3.20 | 3.95 | 4.41 | 4.76 | 5.02 | 5.24 | 5.43 | 5.59 | 5.74 |
| | .01 | 4.60 | 5.43 | 5.96 | 6.35 | 6.66 | 6.91 | 7.13 | 7.33 | 7.49 |
| 10 | .05 | 3.15 | 3.88 | 4.33 | 4.65 | 4.91 | 5.12 | 5.30 | 5.46 | 5.60 |
| | .01 | 4.48 | 5.27 | 5.77 | 6.14 | 6.43 | 6.67 | 6.87 | 7.05 | 7.21 |
| 11 | .05 | 3.11 | 3.82 | 4.26 | 4.57 | 4.82 | 5.03 | 5.20 | 5.35 | 5.49 |
| | .01 | 4.39 | 5.15 | 5.62 | 5.97 | 6.25 | 6.48 | 6.67 | 6.84 | 6.99 |
| 12 | .05 | 3.08 | 3.77 | 4.20 | 4.51 | 4.75 | 4.95 | 5.12 | 5.27 | 5.39 |
| | .01 | 4.32 | 5.05 | 5.50 | 5.84 | 6.10 | 6.32 | 6.51 | 6.67 | 6.81 |
| 13 | .05 | 3.06 | 3.73 | 4.15 | 4.45 | 4.69 | 4.88 | 5.05 | 5.19 | 5.32 |
| | .01 | 4.26 | 4.96 | 5.40 | 5.73 | 5.98 | 6.19 | 6.37 | 6.53 | 6.67 |
| 14 | .05 | 3.03 | 3.70 | 4.11 | 4.41 | 4.64 | 4.83 | 4.99 | 5.13 | 5.25 |
| | .01 | 4.21 | 4.89 | 5.32 | 5.63 | 5.88 | 6.08 | 6.26 | 6.41 | 6.54 |
| 15 | .05 | 3.01 | 3.67 | 4.08 | 4.37 | 4.59 | 4.78 | 4.94 | 5.08 | 5.20 |
| | .01 | 4.17 | 4.84 | 5.25 | 5.56 | 5.80 | 5.99 | 6.16 | 6.31 | 6.44 |
| 16 | .05 | 3.00 | 3.65 | 4.05 | 4.33 | 4.56 | 4.74 | 4.90 | 5.03 | 5.15 |
| | .01 | 4.13 | 4.79 | 5.19 | 5.49 | 5.72 | 5.92 | 6.08 | 6.22 | 6.35 |
| 17 | .05 | 2.98 | 3.63 | 4.02 | 4.30 | 4.52 | 4.70 | 4.86 | 4.99 | 5.11 |
| | .01 | 4.10 | 4.74 | 5.14 | 5.43 | 5.66 | 5.85 | 6.01 | 6.15 | 6.27 |
| 18 | .05 | 2.97 | 3.61 | 4.00 | 4.28 | 4.49 | 4.67 | 4.82 | 4.96 | 5.07 |
| | .01 | 4.07 | 4.70 | 5.09 | 5.38 | 5.60 | 5.79 | 5.94 | 6.08 | 6.20 |
| 19 | .05 | 2.96 | 3.59 | 3.98 | 4.25 | 4.47 | 4.65 | 4.79 | 4.92 | 5.04 |
| | .01 | 4.05 | 4.67 | 5.05 | 5.33 | 5.55 | 5.73 | 5.89 | 6.02 | 6.14 |
| 20 | .05 | 2.95 | 3.58 | 3.96 | 4.23 | 4.45 | 4.62 | 4.77 | 4.90 | 5.01 |
| | .01 | 4.02 | 4.64 | 5.02 | 5.29 | 5.51 | 5.69 | 5.84 | 5.97 | 6.09 |
| 24 | .05 | 2.92 | 3.53 | 3.90 | 4.17 | 4.37 | 4.54 | 4.68 | 4.81 | 4.92 |
| | .01 | 3.96 | 4.55 | 4.91 | 5.17 | 5.37 | 5.54 | 5.69 | 5.81 | 5.92 |
| 30 | .05 | 2.89 | 3.49 | 3.85 | 4.10 | 4.30 | 4.46 | 4.60 | 4.72 | 4.82 |
| | .01 | 3.89 | 4.45 | 4.80 | 5.05 | 5.24 | 5.40 | 5.54 | 5.65 | 5.76 |
| 40 | .05 | 2.86 | 3.44 | 3.79 | 4.04 | 4.23 | 4.39 | 4.52 | 4.63 | 4.73 |
| | .01 | 3.82 | 4.37 | 4.70 | 4.93 | 5.11 | 5.26 | 5.39 | 5.50 | 5.60 |
| 60 | .05 | 2.83 | 3.40 | 3.74 | 3.98 | 4.16 | 4.31 | 4.44 | 4.55 | 4.65 |
| | .01 | 3.76 | 4.28 | 4.59 | 4.82 | 4.99 | 5.13 | 5.25 | 5.36 | 5.45 |
| 120 | .05 | 2.80 | 3.36 | 3.68 | 3.92 | 4.10 | 4.24 | 4.36 | 4.47 | 4.56 |
| | .01 | 3.70 | 4.20 | 4.50 | 4.71 | 4.87 | 5.01 | 5.12 | 5.21 | 5.30 |
| ∞ | .05 | 2.77 | 3.31 | 3.63 | 3.86 | 4.03 | 4.17 | 4.29 | 4.39 | 4.47 |
| | .01 | 3.64 | 4.12 | 4.40 | 4.60 | 4.76 | 4.88 | 4.99 | 5.08 | 5.16 |

*Source:* Abridged from Table 29, E. Pearson and H. Hartley, *Biometrika Tables for Statisticians,* vol. 1, 3d ed., University Press, Cambridge, 1966, with permission of the Biometrika Trustees.

**TABLE G**  *Values of the Correlation Coefficient Required for Different Levels of Significance When* H$_0$: $\rho = 0$

| | LEVELS OF SIGNIFICANCE FOR A ONE-TAILED TEST | | | |
| --- | --- | --- | --- | --- |
| | .05 | .025 | .01 | .005 |
| | LEVELS OF SIGNIFICANCE FOR A TWO-TAILED TEST | | | |
| *df* | .10 | .05 | .02 | .01 |
| 1 | .988 | .977 | .9995 | .9999 |
| 2 | .900 | .950 | .980 | .990 |
| 3 | .805 | .878 | .934 | .959 |
| 4 | .729 | .811 | .882 | .917 |
| 5 | .669 | .754 | .833 | .874 |
| 6 | .622 | .707 | .789 | .834 |
| 7 | .582 | .666 | .750 | .798 |
| 8 | .549 | .632 | .716 | .765 |
| 9 | .521 | .602 | .685 | .735 |
| 10 | .497 | .576 | .658 | .708 |
| 11 | .476 | .553 | .634 | .684 |
| 12 | .458 | .532 | .612 | .661 |
| 13 | .441 | .514 | .592 | .641 |
| 14 | .426 | .497 | .574 | .623 |
| 15 | .412 | .482 | .558 | .606 |
| 16 | .400 | .468 | .542 | .590 |
| 17 | .389 | .456 | .528 | .575 |
| 18 | .378 | .444 | .516 | .561 |
| 19 | .369 | .433 | .503 | .549 |
| 20 | .360 | .423 | .492 | .537 |
| 21 | .352 | .413 | .482 | .526 |
| 22 | .344 | .404 | .472 | .515 |
| 23 | .337 | .396 | .462 | .505 |
| 24 | .330 | .388 | .453 | .496 |
| 25 | .323 | .381 | .445 | .487 |
| 26 | .317 | .374 | .437 | .479 |
| 27 | .311 | .367 | .430 | .471 |
| 28 | .306 | .361 | .423 | .463 |
| 29 | .301 | .355 | .416 | .456 |
| 30 | .296 | .349 | .409 | .449 |
| 32 | .287 | .339 | .397 | .436 |
| 34 | .279 | .329 | .386 | .424 |
| 36 | .271 | .320 | .376 | .413 |
| 38 | .264 | .312 | .367 | .403 |
| 40 | .257 | .304 | .358 | .393 |
| 42 | .251 | .297 | .350 | .384 |
| 44 | .426 | .291 | .342 | .376 |

*continued*

TABLE **G** (*continued*)

| df | LEVELS OF SIGNIFICANCE FOR A ONE-TAILED TEST | | | |
|---|---|---|---|---|
| | .05 | .025 | .01 | .005 |
| | LEVELS OF SIGNIFICANCE FOR A TWO-TAILED TEST | | | |
| | .10 | .05 | .02 | .01 |
| 46 | .240 | .285 | .335 | .368 |
| 48 | .235 | .279 | .328 | .361 |
| 50 | .231 | .273 | .322 | .354 |
| 55 | .220 | .261 | .307 | .339 |
| 60 | .211 | .250 | .295 | .325 |
| 65 | .203 | .240 | .284 | .313 |
| 70 | .195 | .232 | .274 | .302 |
| 75 | .189 | .224 | .265 | .292 |
| 80 | .183 | .217 | .256 | .283 |
| 85 | .178 | .211 | .249 | .275 |
| 90 | .173 | .205 | .242 | .267 |
| 95 | .168 | .200 | .236 | .260 |
| 100 | .164 | .195 | .230 | .254 |
| 120 | .150 | .178 | .210 | .232 |
| 150 | .134 | .159 | .189 | .208 |
| 200 | .116 | .138 | .164 | .181 |
| 300 | .095 | .113 | .134 | .148 |
| 400 | .082 | .098 | .116 | .128 |
| 500 | .073 | .088 | .104 | .115 |
| 1000 | .052 | .062 | .073 | .081 |

*Source:* Table V.A of Fisher, *Statistical Methods for Research Workers,* by permission of Oxford University Press. Supplementary values were calculated at San Jose State University by K. Fernandes.

TABLE **H**    *Values of Fisher's z' for Values of* r

| r | z' | r | z' | r | z' | r | z' | r | z' |
|---|----|---|----|---|----|---|----|---|----|
| .000 | .000 | .200 | .203 | .400 | .424 | .600 | .693 | .800 | 1.099 |
| .005 | .005 | .205 | .208 | .405 | .430 | .605 | .701 | .805 | 1.113 |
| .010 | .010 | .210 | .213 | .410 | .436 | .610 | .709 | .810 | 1.127 |
| .015 | .015 | .215 | .218 | .415 | .442 | .615 | .717 | .815 | 1.142 |
| .020 | .020 | .220 | .224 | .420 | .448 | .620 | .725 | .820 | 1.157 |
| .025 | .025 | .225 | .229 | .425 | .454 | .625 | .733 | .825 | 1.172 |
| .030 | .030 | .230 | .234 | .430 | .460 | .630 | .741 | .830 | 1.188 |
| .035 | .035 | .235 | .239 | .435 | .466 | .635 | .750 | .835 | 1.204 |
| .040 | .040 | .240 | .245 | .440 | .472 | .640 | .758 | .840 | 1.221 |
| .045 | .045 | .245 | .250 | .445 | .478 | .645 | .767 | .845 | 1.238 |
| .050 | .050 | .250 | .255 | .450 | .485 | .650 | .775 | .850 | 1.256 |
| .055 | .055 | .255 | .261 | .455 | .491 | .655 | .784 | .855 | 1.274 |
| .060 | .060 | .260 | .266 | .460 | .497 | .660 | .793 | .860 | 1.293 |
| .065 | .065 | .265 | .271 | .465 | .504 | .665 | .802 | .865 | 1.313 |
| .070 | .070 | .270 | .277 | .470 | .510 | .670 | .811 | .870 | 1.333 |
| .075 | .075 | .275 | .282 | .475 | .517 | .675 | .820 | .875 | 1.354 |
| .080 | .080 | .280 | .288 | .480 | .523 | .680 | .829 | .880 | 1.376 |
| .085 | .085 | .285 | .293 | .485 | .530 | .685 | .838 | .885 | 1.398 |
| .090 | .090 | .290 | .299 | .490 | .536 | .690 | .848 | .890 | 1.422 |
| .095 | .095 | .295 | .304 | .495 | .543 | .695 | .858 | .895 | 1.447 |
| .100 | .100 | .300 | .310 | .500 | .549 | .700 | .867 | .900 | 1.472 |
| .105 | .105 | .305 | .315 | .505 | .556 | .705 | .877 | .905 | 1.499 |
| .110 | .110 | .310 | .321 | .510 | .563 | .710 | .887 | .910 | 1.528 |
| .115 | .116 | .315 | .326 | .515 | .570 | .715 | .897 | .915 | 1.557 |
| .120 | .121 | .320 | .332 | .520 | .576 | .720 | .908 | .920 | 1.589 |
| .125 | .126 | .325 | .337 | .525 | .583 | .725 | .918 | .925 | 1.623 |
| .130 | .131 | .330 | .343 | .530 | .590 | .730 | .929 | .930 | 1.658 |
| .135 | .136 | .335 | .348 | .535 | .597 | .735 | .940 | .935 | 1.697 |
| .140 | .141 | .340 | .354 | .540 | .604 | .740 | .950 | .940 | 1.738 |
| .145 | .146 | .345 | .360 | .545 | .611 | .745 | .962 | .945 | 1.783 |
| .150 | .151 | .350 | .365 | .550 | .618 | .750 | .973 | .950 | 1.832 |
| .155 | .156 | .355 | .371 | .555 | .626 | .755 | .984 | .955 | 1.886 |
| .160 | .161 | .360 | .377 | .560 | .633 | .760 | .996 | .960 | 1.946 |
| .165 | .167 | .365 | .383 | .565 | .640 | .765 | 1.008 | .965 | 2.014 |
| .170 | .172 | .370 | .388 | .570 | .648 | .770 | 1.020 | .970 | 2.092 |
| .175 | .177 | .375 | .394 | .575 | .655 | .775 | 1.033 | .975 | 2.185 |
| .180 | .182 | .380 | .400 | .580 | .662 | .780 | 1.045 | .980 | 2.298 |
| .185 | .187 | .385 | .406 | .585 | .670 | .785 | 1.058 | .985 | 2.443 |
| .190 | .192 | .390 | .412 | .590 | .678 | .790 | 1.071 | .990 | 2.647 |
| .195 | .198 | .395 | .418 | .595 | .685 | .795 | 1.085 | .995 | 2.994 |

*Source:* From *Statistical Methods,* 2d ed., by Allen L. Edwards. Copyright © 1954, 1967 by Allen L. Edwards. Reprinted by permission of Allen L. Edwards.

# TABLE I The $\chi^2$ Distribution

The first column identifies the specific $\chi^2$ distribution according to its number of degrees of freedom.[*] Other columns give the proportion of the area under the entire curve that falls above the tabled value of $\chi^2$.

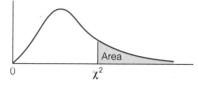

## AREA IN THE UPPER TAIL

| df | .995 | .99 | .975 | .95 | .90 | .10 | .05 | .025 | .01 | .005 |
|---|---|---|---|---|---|---|---|---|---|---|
| 1 | .000039 | .00016 | .00098 | .0039 | .016 | 2.71 | 3.84 | 5.02 | 6.63 | 7.88 |
| 2 | .010 | .020 | .051 | .10 | .21 | 4.61 | 5.99 | 7.38 | 9.21 | 10.60 |
| 3 | .072 | .11 | .22 | .35 | .58 | 6.25 | 7.81 | 9.35 | 11.34 | 12.84 |
| 4 | .21 | .30 | .48 | .71 | 1.06 | 7.78 | 9.49 | 11.14 | 13.28 | 14.86 |
| 5 | .41 | .55 | .83 | 1.15 | 1.61 | 9.24 | 11.07 | 12.83 | 15.09 | 16.75 |
| 6 | .68 | .87 | 1.24 | 1.64 | 2.20 | 10.64 | 12.59 | 14.45 | 16.81 | 18.55 |
| 7 | .99 | 1.24 | 1.69 | 2.17 | 2.83 | 12.02 | 14.07 | 16.01 | 18.48 | 20.28 |
| 8 | 1.34 | 1.65 | 2.18 | 2.73 | 3.49 | 13.36 | 15.51 | 17.53 | 20.09 | 21.96 |
| 9 | 1.73 | 2.09 | 2.70 | 3.33 | 4.17 | 14.68 | 16.92 | 19.02 | 21.67 | 23.59 |
| 10 | 2.16 | 2.56 | 3.25 | 3.94 | 4.87 | 15.99 | 18.31 | 20.48 | 23.21 | 25.19 |
| 11 | 2.60 | 3.05 | 3.82 | 4.57 | 5.58 | 17.28 | 19.68 | 21.92 | 24.72 | 26.76 |
| 12 | 3.07 | 3.57 | 4.40 | 5.23 | 6.30 | 18.55 | 21.03 | 23.34 | 26.22 | 28.30 |
| 13 | 3.57 | 4.11 | 5.01 | 5.89 | 7.04 | 19.81 | 22.36 | 24.74 | 27.69 | 29.82 |
| 14 | 4.07 | 4.66 | 5.63 | 6.57 | 7.79 | 21.06 | 23.68 | 26.12 | 29.14 | 31.32 |
| 15 | 4.60 | 5.23 | 6.26 | 7.26 | 8.55 | 22.31 | 25.00 | 27.49 | 30.58 | 32.80 |
| 16 | 5.14 | 5.81 | 6.91 | 7.96 | 9.31 | 23.54 | 26.30 | 28.85 | 32.00 | 34.27 |
| 17 | 5.70 | 6.41 | 7.56 | 8.67 | 10.09 | 24.77 | 27.59 | 30.19 | 33.41 | 35.72 |
| 18 | 6.26 | 7.01 | 8.23 | 9.39 | 10.86 | 25.99 | 28.87 | 31.53 | 34.81 | 37.16 |
| 19 | 6.84 | 7.63 | 8.91 | 10.12 | 11.65 | 27.20 | 30.14 | 32.85 | 36.19 | 38.58 |
| 20 | 7.43 | 8.26 | 9.59 | 10.85 | 12.44 | 28.41 | 31.41 | 34.17 | 37.57 | 40.00 |
| 21 | 8.03 | 8.90 | 10.28 | 11.59 | 13.24 | 29.62 | 32.67 | 35.48 | 38.93 | 41.40 |
| 22 | 8.64 | 9.54 | 10.98 | 12.34 | 14.04 | 30.81 | 33.92 | 36.78 | 40.29 | 42.80 |
| 23 | 9.26 | 10.20 | 11.69 | 13.09 | 14.85 | 32.01 | 35.17 | 38.08 | 41.64 | 44.18 |
| 24 | 9.89 | 10.86 | 12.40 | 13.85 | 15.66 | 33.20 | 36.42 | 39.36 | 42.98 | 45.56 |
| 25 | 10.52 | 11.52 | 13.12 | 14.61 | 16.47 | 34.38 | 37.65 | 40.65 | 44.31 | 46.93 |
| 26 | 11.16 | 12.20 | 13.84 | 15.38 | 17.29 | 35.56 | 38.89 | 41.92 | 45.64 | 48.29 |
| 27 | 11.81 | 12.88 | 14.57 | 16.15 | 18.11 | 36.74 | 40.11 | 43.19 | 46.96 | 49.64 |
| 28 | 12.46 | 13.56 | 15.31 | 16.93 | 18.94 | 37.92 | 41.34 | 44.46 | 48.28 | 50.99 |
| 29 | 13.12 | 14.26 | 16.05 | 17.71 | 19.77 | 39.09 | 42.56 | 45.72 | 49.59 | 52.34 |
| 30 | 13.79 | 14.95 | 16.79 | 18.49 | 20.60 | 40.26 | 43.77 | 46.98 | 50.89 | 53.67 |
| 40 | 20.71 | 22.16 | 24.43 | 26.51 | 29.05 | 51.81 | 55.76 | 59.34 | 63.69 | 66.77 |
| 50 | 27.99 | 29.71 | 32.36 | 34.76 | 37.69 | 63.17 | 65.50 | 71.42 | 76.15 | 79.49 |
| 60 | 35.53 | 37.48 | 40.48 | 43.19 | 46.46 | 74.40 | 79.08 | 83.30 | 88.38 | 91.95 |
| 70 | 43.28 | 45.44 | 48.76 | 51.74 | 55.33 | 85.53 | 90.53 | 95.02 | 100.42 | 104.22 |
| 80 | 51.17 | 53.54 | 57.15 | 60.39 | 64.28 | 96.58 | 101.88 | 106.63 | 112.33 | 116.32 |
| 90 | 59.20 | 61.75 | 65.65 | 69.13 | 73.29 | 107.56 | 113.14 | 118.14 | 124.12 | 128.30 |
| 100 | 67.33 | 70.06 | 74.22 | 77.93 | 82.36 | 118.50 | 124.34 | 129.56 | 135.81 | 140.17 |
| 120 | 83.85 | 86.92 | 91.58 | 95.70 | 100.62 | 140.23 | 146.57 | 152.21 | 158.95 | 163.64 |

[*]When $df > 30$, the critical value of $\chi^2$ may be found by the following approximate formula: $\chi^2 = df[1 - (2/9df) + z\sqrt{2/9\ df}\ ]^3$, where $z$ is the normal deviate above which lies the same proportionate area in the normal curve. For example, to find the value of $\chi^2$ that divides the upper 1% of the distribution from the remainder when $df = 30$, we calculate: $\chi^2 = 30(1 - .00741 + 2.3263\sqrt{.0074074})^3 = 50.91$, which compares closely with the tabled value of 50.89.

*Source:* Modified from Table 8, E. Pearson and H. Hartley, *Biometrika Tables for Statisticians,* vol. 1, 3d ed., University Press, Cambridge, 1966, with permission of the Biometrika Trustees.

**TABLE J**  *Critical One-Tail Values of $\sum R_X$ for the Mann-Whitney U Test*

| | $n_X = 3$ | | | | | $n_X = 4$ | | | |
|---|---|---|---|---|---|---|---|---|---|
| $n_Y$ | .005 | .01 | .025 | .05 | $n_Y$ | .005 | .01 | .025 | .05 |
| 3 | | | | 6–15 | 4 | | | 10–26 | 11–25 |
| 4 | | | | 6–18 | 5 | | 10–30 | 11–29 | 12–28 |
| 5 | | | 6–21 | 7–20 | 6 | 10–34 | 11–33 | 12–32 | 13–31 |
| 6 | | | 7–23 | 8–22 | 7 | 10–38 | 11–37 | 13–35 | 14–34 |
| 7 | | 6–27 | 7–26 | 8–25 | 8 | 11–41 | 12–40 | 14–38 | 15–37 |
| 8 | | 6–30 | 8–28 | 9–27 | 9 | 11–45 | 13–43 | 14–42 | 16–40 |
| 9 | 6–33 | 7–32 | 8–31 | 10–29 | 10 | 12–48 | 13–47 | 15–45 | 17–43 |
| 10 | 6–36 | 7–35 | 9–33 | 10–32 | 11 | 12–52 | 14–50 | 16–48 | 18–46 |
| 11 | 6–39 | 7–38 | 9–36 | 11–34 | 12 | 13–55 | 15–53 | 17–51 | 19–49 |
| 12 | 7–41 | 8–40 | 10–38 | 11–37 | 13 | 13–59 | 15–57 | 18–54 | 20–52 |
| 13 | 7–44 | 8–43 | 10–41 | 12–39 | 14 | 14–62 | 16–60 | 19–57 | 21–55 |
| 14 | 7–47 | 8–46 | 11–43 | 13–41 | 15 | 15–65 | 17–63 | 20–60 | 22–58 |
| 15 | 8–49 | 9–48 | 11–46 | 13–44 | | | | | |

| | $n_X = 5$ | | | | | $n_X = 6$ | | | |
|---|---|---|---|---|---|---|---|---|---|
| $n_Y$ | .005 | .01 | .025 | .05 | $n_Y$ | .005 | .01 | .025 | .05 |
| 5 | 15–40 | 16–39 | 17–38 | 19–36 | 6 | 23–55 | 24–54 | 26–52 | 28–50 |
| 6 | 16–44 | 17–43 | 18–42 | 20–40 | 7 | 24–60 | 25–59 | 27–57 | 29–55 |
| 7 | 16–49 | 18–47 | 20–45 | 21–44 | 8 | 25–65 | 27–63 | 29–61 | 31–59 |
| 8 | 17–53 | 19–51 | 21–49 | 23–47 | 9 | 26–70 | 28–68 | 31–65 | 33–63 |
| 9 | 18–57 | 20–55 | 22–53 | 24–51 | 10 | 27–75 | 29–73 | 32–70 | 35–67 |
| 10 | 19–61 | 21–59 | 23–57 | 26–54 | 11 | 29–80 | 30–78 | 34–74 | 37–71 |
| 11 | 20–65 | 22–63 | 24–61 | 27–58 | 12 | 30–84 | 32–82 | 35–79 | 38–76 |
| 12 | 21–69 | 23–67 | 26–64 | 28–62 | 13 | 31–89 | 33–87 | 37–83 | 40–80 |
| 13 | 22–73 | 24–71 | 27–68 | 30–65 | 14 | 32–94 | 34–92 | 38–88 | 42–84 |
| 14 | 22–78 | 25–75 | 28–72 | 31–69 | 15 | 33–99 | 36–96 | 40–92 | 44–88 |
| 15 | 23–82 | 26–79 | 29–76 | 33–72 | | | | | |

| | $n_X = 7$ | | | | | $n_X = 8$ | | | |
|---|---|---|---|---|---|---|---|---|---|
| $n_Y$ | .005 | .01 | .025 | .05 | $n_Y$ | .005 | .01 | .025 | .05 |
| 7 | 32–73 | 34–71 | 36–69 | 39–66 | 8 | 43–93 | 45–91 | 49–87 | 51–85 |
| 8 | 34–78 | 35–77 | 38–74 | 41–71 | 9 | 45–99 | 47–97 | 51–93 | 54–90 |
| 9 | 34–84 | 37–82 | 40–79 | 43–76 | 10 | 47–105 | 49–103 | 53–99 | 56–96 |
| 10 | 37–89 | 39–87 | 42–84 | 45–81 | 11 | 49–111 | 51–109 | 55–105 | 59–101 |
| 11 | 38–95 | 40–93 | 44–89 | 47–86 | 12 | 51–117 | 53–115 | 58–110 | 62–106 |
| 12 | 40–100 | 42–98 | 46–94 | 49–91 | 13 | 53–123 | 56–120 | 60–116 | 64–112 |
| 13 | 41–106 | 44–103 | 48–99 | 52–95 | 14 | 54–130 | 58–126 | 62–122 | 67–117 |
| 14 | 43–111 | 45–109 | 50–104 | 54–100 | 15 | 56–136 | 60–132 | 65–127 | 69–123 |
| 15 | 44–117 | 47–114 | 52–109 | 56–105 | | | | | |

*continued*

TABLE J    (*continued*)

| $n_Y$ | .005 | .01 | .025 | .05 |
|---|---|---|---|---|
| | | $n_X = 9$ | | |
| 9 | 56–115 | 59–112 | 62–109 | 66–105 |
| 10 | 58–122 | 61–119 | 65–115 | 69–111 |
| 11 | 61–128 | 63–126 | 68–121 | 72–117 |
| 12 | 63–135 | 66–132 | 71–127 | 75–123 |
| 13 | 65–142 | 68–139 | 73–134 | 78–129 |
| 14 | 67–149 | 71–145 | 76–140 | 81–135 |
| 15 | 69–156 | 73–152 | 79–146 | 84–141 |

| $n_Y$ | .005 | .01 | .025 | .05 |
|---|---|---|---|---|
| | | $n_X = 10$ | | |
| 10 | 71–139 | 74–136 | 78–132 | 82–128 |
| 11 | 73–147 | 77–143 | 81–139 | 86–134 |
| 12 | 76–154 | 79–151 | 84–146 | 89–141 |
| 13 | 79–161 | 82–158 | 88–152 | 92–148 |
| 14 | 81–169 | 85–165 | 91–159 | 96–154 |
| 15 | 84–176 | 88–172 | 94–166 | 99–161 |

| $n_Y$ | .005 | .01 | .025 | .05 |
|---|---|---|---|---|
| | | $n_X = 11$ | | |
| 11 | 87–166 | 91–162 | 96–157 | 100–153 |
| 12 | 90–174 | 94–170 | 99–165 | 104–160 |
| 13 | 93–182 | 97–178 | 103–172 | 108–167 |
| 14 | 96–190 | 100–186 | 106–180 | 112–174 |
| 15 | 99–198 | 103–194 | 110–187 | 116–181 |

| $n_Y$ | .005 | .01 | .025 | .05 |
|---|---|---|---|---|
| | | $n_X = 12$ | | |
| 12 | 105–195 | 109–191 | 115–185 | 120–180 |
| 13 | 109–203 | 113–199 | 119–193 | 125–187 |
| 14 | 112–212 | 116–208 | 123–201 | 129–195 |
| 15 | 115–221 | 120–216 | 127–209 | 133–203 |

| $n_Y$ | .005 | .01 | .025 | .05 |
|---|---|---|---|---|
| | | $n_X = 13$ | | |
| 13 | 125–226 | 130–221 | 136–215 | 142–209 |
| 14 | 129–235 | 134–230 | 141–223 | 147–217 |
| 15 | 133–244 | 138–239 | 145–232 | 152–225 |

| $n_Y$ | .005 | .01 | .025 | .05 |
|---|---|---|---|---|
| | | $n_X = 14$ | | |
| 14 | 147–259 | 152–254 | 160–246 | 166–240 |
| 15 | 151–269 | 156–246 | 164–256 | 171–249 |

| $n_Y$ | .005 | .01 | .025 | .05 |
|---|---|---|---|---|
| | | $n_X = 15$ | | |
| 15 | 171–294 | 176–289 | 184–281 | 192–273 |

*Source:* Adaptation of Table 1, L. R. Verdooren, "Extended Tables of Critical Values for Wilcoxon's Test Statistic," *Biometrika,* **50,** 177–186 (1963), with permission of the author and the Biometrika Trustees.

**TABLE K**   *Critical Values for the Smaller of* $R_+$ *or* $R_-$ *for the Wilcoxon Signed-Ranks Test*

| | LEVELS OF SIGNIFICANCE FOR A ONE-TAILED TEST | | | |
| | .05 | .025 | .01 | .005 |
| | LEVELS OF SIGNIFICANCE FOR A TWO-TAILED TEST | | | |
| NUMBER OF PAIRS | .10 | .05 | .02 | .01 |
|---|---|---|---|---|
| 4 | — | | | |
| 5 | 0 | — | | |
| 6 | 2 | 0 | — | |
| 7 | 3 | 2 | 0 | — |
| 8 | 5 | 3 | 1 | 0 |
| 9 | 8 | 5 | 3 | 1 |
| 10 | 10 | 8 | 5 | 3 |
| 11 | 13 | 10 | 7 | 5 |
| 12 | 17 | 13 | 10 | 7 |
| 13 | 21 | 17 | 12 | 10 |
| 14 | 25 | 21 | 16 | 13 |
| 15 | 30 | 25 | 19 | 16 |

# REFERENCES

ABELSON, R. P. (1997). On the surprising longevity of flogged horses: Why there is a case for the significance test. *Psychological Science, 8,* 12–15.

ADAMS, E. W. (1966). On the nature and purpose of measurement. *Synthese,* 16, 125–129.

AMERICAN PSYCHOLOGICAL ASSOCIATION. (2001). *Publication Manual of the American Psychological Association.* Washington, DC: American Psychological Association.

AMERICAN PSYCHOLOGICAL ASSOCIATION TASK FORCE ON STATISTICAL INFERENCE. (1996). Preliminary report. Washington, DC: American Psychological Association.

ATOR, N. A. (1999). Statistical inference in behavior analysis: Environmental determinants? *Behavior Analyst, 22,* 93–97.

BANDURA, A., ROSS, D. A., & ROSS, S. A. (1963). Imitation of film-mediated aggressive models. *Journal of Abnormal and Social Psychology, 66,* 3–11.

BAYES, T. (1763). An essay towards solving a problem in the doctrine of chances. *Philosophical Transactions of the Royal Society, 53,* 370–418.

BERGER, J. D., & BERRY, D. A. (1988). Statistical analysis and the illusion of objectivity. *American Scientist, 76,* 159–165.

BEST, J. (2001). *Damned Lies and Statistics.* Berkeley, CA: University of California Press.

BEST, J. B. (1979). Item difficulty and answer changing. *Teaching of Psychology, 6,* 228–230.

BOIK, R. J. (1987). The Fisher-Pitman permutation test: A non-robust alternative to the normal theory *F* when variances are heterogeneous. *British Journal of Mathematical and Statistical Psychology, 40,* 26–42.

BOLLES, R. C. (1988). Why you should avoid statistics. *Biological Psychiatry, 23,* 79–85.

BONEAU, C. A. (1960). The effects of violations of assumptions underlying the *t* test. *Psychological Bulletin, 57,* 49–64.

BOWERS, T. G., & CLUM, G. A. (1988). Relative contribution of specific and nonspecific treatment effects: Meta-analysis of placebo-controlled behavior therapy research. *Psychological Bulletin, 103,* 315–323.

BRADLEY, J. V. (1968). *Distribution-Free Statistical Tests.* Englewood Cliffs, NJ: Prentice Hall.

BRADLEY, J. V. (1978). Robustness? *British Journal of Mathematical and Statistical Psychology, 31,* 144–152.

BRADY, J. V., PORTER, R. W., CONRAD, D. G., & MASON, J. W. (1958). Avoidance behavior and the development of gastroduodenal ulcers. *Journal of the Experimental Analysis of Behavior, 1,* 69–72.

BROWN, K. S. (1995). Testing the most curious subject—oneself. *Scientist, 9* (24), 1.

BYRNE, W. L., ET AL. (1966). Memory transfer. *Science, 153,* 658–659.

CAMILLI, G., & HOPKINS, K.D. (1978). Applicability of chi-square to 2 × 2 contingency tables with small expected cell frequencies. *Psychological Bulletin, 85,* 163–167.

CHATTERJEE, S., & YILMAZ, M. (1992). A review of regression diagnostics for behavioral research. *Applied Psychological Measurement, 16,* 209–227.

CHERNOFF, H., & SAVAGE, I. R. (1958). Asymptotic normality and efficiency of certain nonparametric test statistics. *Annals of Mathematical Statistics, 29,* 972–999.

CHOW, S. L. (1998). Précis of statistical significance: Rationale, validity, and utility. *Behavioral and Brain Sciences, 21,* 169–239.

CLEVELAND, W. S. (1995). *Visualizing Data.* Summit, NJ: Hobart Press.

CLEVELAND, W. S., & MCGILL, R. (1985). *The Elements of Graphing Data.* Belmont, CA: Wadsworth.

COHEN, J. (1962). The statistical power of abnormal-social psychological research: A review. *Journal of Abnormal and Social Psychology, 65,* 145–153.

COHEN, J. *(1965).* Some statistical issues in psychological research. In B. B. Wolman (Ed.), *Handbook of Clinical Psychology* (pp. 95–121). New York: McGraw-Hill.

COHEN, J. (1988). *Statistical Power Analysis for the Behavioral Sciences* (2nd ed.). Hillsdale, NJ: Lawrence Erlbaum Associates.

COHEN, J. (1990). Things I have learned (so far). *American Psychologist, 45,* 1304–1312.

COHEN, J. (1992). A power primer. *Psychological Bulletin, 112,* 155–159.

COHEN, J. (1994). The earth is round ($p < .05$). *American Psychologist, 49,* 997–1003.

COHEN, P. (1988). Are statistics necessary? *Biological Psychiatry, 23,* 1–2.

COHEN, S., & WILLIAMSON, G. (1988). Perceived stress in a probability sample of the United States. In S. Spacapan & S. Oskamp (Eds.), *The Social Psychology of Health* (pp. 31–67). Newsbury Park, CA: Sage.

COLE, K. C. (1985). Is there such a thing as scientific objectivity? *Discover, 6*(9), 98–99.

CONOVER, W. J. (1974). Some reasons for not using the Yates continuity correction on 2 × 2 contingency tables. *Journal of the American Statistical Association, 69,* 374–376.

CORMACK, R. S., & MANTEL, N. (1990). Doubt and certainty in statistics. *Journal of the Royal Society of Medicine, 83,* 136–137.

CURRAN-EVERETT, D. (2000). Multiple comparisons: philosophies and illustrations. *American Journal of Physiology, 279,* R1–R8.

DAVISON, M. L., & SHARMA, A. R. (1988). Parametric statistics and levels of measurement. *Psychological Bulletin, 104,* 137–144.

DAVISON, M. L., & SHARMA, A. R. (1990). Parametric statistics and levels of measurement: Factorial designs and multiple regression. *Psychological Bulletin, 107,* 394–400.

DAWES, R. B. (1975). Graduate admission variables and future success. *Science, 187,* 721–723.

DEBUONO, B. A., ZINNER, S. H., DAAMEN, M., & MCCORMACK, W. M. (1990). Sexual behavior of college women in 1975, 1986, and 1989. *New England Journal of Medicine, 322,* 821–825.

DELUCHHI, K. L. (1983). The use and misuse of chi-square: Lewis and Burke revisited. *Psychological Bulletin, 94,* 166–176.

DENENBERG, V. H. (1984). Some statistical and experimental considerations in the use of the analysis-of-variance procedure. *American Journal of Physiology, 246,* R403–R408.

DEWES, P. B. (1955). Studies on behavior. I. Differential sensitivity to pentobarbital of pecking performance in pigeons depending on the schedule of reward. *Journal of Pharmacology and Experimental Therapeutics, 113,* 393–401.

DIACONIS, P., & EFRON, B. (1983). Computer-intensive methods in statistics. *Scientific American, 248,* 116–130.

DIACONIS, P., & MOSTELLER, F. (1989). Methods for studying coincidences. *Journal of the American Statistical Association, 84,* 853–861.

DOLL, R. (1955). Etiology of lung cancer. *Advances in Cancer Research, 3,* 1–50.

DREW, B., & WATERS, J. (1985). Video games: Utilization of a novel strategy to improve perceptual-motor skills in non-institutionalized elderly. *Proceedings and Abstracts of the Eastern Psychological Association, 5,* 56.

DUNN, O. J. (1964). Multiple comparisons using rank sums. *Technometrics, 6,* 241–252.

EDGINGTON, E. S. (1987). *Randomization Tests* (2nd ed.). New York: Marcel Dekker.

EFRON, B. (1979). Bootstrap methods: Another look at the jackknife. *Annals of Statistics, 7,* 1–26.

ENGEL, R., & BENSON, R. C. (1968). Estimate of conceptual age by evoked response activity. *Biologia Neonatorum, 12,* 201–213.

EPSTEIN, J. L., & McPARTLAND, J. M. (1976). The concept and measurement of the quality of school life. *American Educational Research Journal, 13,* 15–50.

FISCHL, M. A., ET AL. (1987). The efficacy of azidothymidine (AZT) in the treatment of patients with AIDS and AIDS-related complex. *New England Journal of Medicine, 317,* 185–191.

FISHER, R. A. (1935). The logic of inductive inference. *Journal of the Royal Statistical Society, 98,* 39–54.

FISHER, R. A. (1949). *The Design of Experiments* (5th ed.). London: Oliver & Boyd.

FISHER, R. A. (1960). *The Design of Experiments* (7th ed.). Edinburgh, Scotland: Oliver & Boyd.

FLEISS, J. L. (1969). Estimating the magnitude of experimental effects. *Psychological Bulletin, 72,* 273–276.

FLEISS, J. L. (1981). *Statistical Methods for Rates and Proportions.* New York: Wiley.

FLETCHER, R. (1991). *Science, Ideology, and the Media: The Cyril Burt Scandal.* New Brunswick, NJ: Transaction Publishers.

FOLLMAN, J. (1984). Cornucopia of correlations. *American Psychologist, 39,* 701–702.

FOLTZ, E. L., & MILLETT, F. E. (1964). Experimental psychosomatic disease states in monkeys. 1. Peptic "ulcer-executive" monkeys. *Journal of Surgical Research, 4,* 445–453.

FRANKLIN, R. D., ALLISON, D. B., & GORMAN, B. S. (Eds.) (1997). *Design and Analysis of Single-Case Research.* Mahwah, NJ: Erlbaum.

FREEDMAN, D., PISANI, R., & PURVES, R. (1978). *Statistics.* New York: Norton.

GALTON, F. (1889). *Natural Inheritance.* London: Macmillan.

GARFIELD, E. (1991). Meta-analysis and the metamorphosis of the scientific literature review. *Current Contents, 43* (Oct. 28), 5–8.

GEARY, R. C. (1947). Testing for normality. *Biometrika, 34,* 209–242.

GELMAN, A. (1998). Some class-participation demonstrations for decision theory and Bayesian statistics. *American Statistician, 52,* 167–174.

GIGERENZER, G. (1987). Probabilistic thinking and the fight against subjectivity. In L. Kruger, G. Gigerenzer, & M. S. Morgan (Eds.), *The Probabilistic Revolution* (vol. 2, pp. 11–33). Cambridge, MA: Bradford/MIT Press.

GLASS, G. V. (1976). Primary, secondary, and meta-analysis of research. *Educational Research, 5,* 3–8.

GLASS, G. V., & HOPKINS, K. D. (1996). *Statistical Methods in Education and Psychology* (3rd ed.). Boston, MA: Allyn and Bacon.

GLASS, G. V., PECKHAM, P. D., & SANDERS, J. R. (1972). Consequences of failure to meet assumptions underlying the fixed effects analysis of variance and covariance. *Review of Educational Research, 42,* 237–288.

GREENHOUSE, S. W. (1990). Comment. *Statistics in Medicine, 9,* 371–372.

GUTTMACHER, A. F. (1973). *Pregnancy, Birth, and Family Planning.* New York: New American Library.

HAGAN, R. L. (1997). In praise of the null hypothesis statistical test. *American Psychologist, 52,* 15–24.

HARRIS, R. J. (1997). Significance tests have their place. *Psychological Science, 8,* 8–11.

HARTWIG, F., & DEARING, B. E. (1979). Exploratory data analysis. In J. L. Sullivan (Ed.), *Quantitative Applications in the Social Sciences.* Beverly Hills, CA: Sage.

HAUCK, W. W., & ANDERSON, S. (1986). A proposal for interpreting and reporting negative studies. *Statistics in Medicine, 5,* 203–209.

HAVILAND, M. G. (1990). Yates' correction for continuity and the analysis of 2 × 2 contingency tables. *Statistics in Medicine, 9,* 363–367.

HAYS, W. L. (1994). *Statistics* (5th ed.). New York: Holt, Rinehart, & Winston.

HEARNSHAW, L. S. (1979). *Cyril Burt, Psychologist.* Ithaca, NY: Cornell University Press.

HEDGES, L. V. (1981). Distributional theory for Glass's estimator of effect size and related estimators. *Journal of Educational Statistics, 6,* 107–128.

HEDGES, L. V., & OLKIN, I. (1985). *Statistical Methods for Meta-Analysis.* New York: Academic.

HEDGES, L.V., & VEVEA, J. L. (1996). Estimating effect size under publication bias: Small sample properties and robustness of a random effects selection model. *Journal of Educational and Behavioral Statistics, 21,* 299–332.

HOAGLIN, D. C., MOSTELLER, F., & TUKEY, J. W. (2000). *Understanding Robust and Exploratory Data Analysis.* New York: John Wiley.

HOPKINS, B. L., COLE, B. L., & MASON, T. L. (1998). A criticism of the usefulness of inferential statistics in applied behavior analysis. *Behavior Analyst, 21,* 125–137.

HOPKINS, K. D., GLASS, G. V., & HOPKINS, B. R. (1987). *Basic Strategies for the Behavioral Sciences* (2nd ed.). Englewood Cliffs, NJ: Prentice Hall.

HOWSON, C., & URBACH, P. (1991). Bayesian reasoning in science. *Nature, 350,* 371–374.

HUFF, D. (1993). *How to Lie with Statistics.* New York: Norton.

HUNTER, J. E. (1997). Needed: A ban on the significance test. *Psychological Science, 8,* 3–7.

JASIENSKI, M. (1996). Wishful thinking and the fallacy of single-subject experimentation. *Scientist,* March 4, 10.

JOYNSON, R. B. (1989). *The Burt Affair.* London: Routledge.

KAGAN, D. M., & SQUIRES, R. L. (1984). Compulsive eating, dieting, stress, and hostility among college students. *Journal of College Student Personnel, 25,* 213–219.

KAPLAN, R. M., & SACCUZZO, D. P. (1989). *Psychological Testing: Principles, Applications, and Issues* (2nd ed.). Pacific Grove, CA: Brooks/Cole.

KEPPEL, G. (1991). *Design and Analysis: A Researcher's Handbook* (3rd ed.). Englewood Cliffs, NJ: Prentice Hall.

KEREN, G., & LEWIS, C. (1979). Partial omega squared for ANOVA designs. *Educational and Psychological Measurement, 39,* 119–128.

KING, B. M. & ANDERSON, P. B. (1994). A failure of HIV education: Sex can be more important than a long life. *Journal of Health Education, 25,* 13–18.

KIRK, R. E. (1990). *Statistics: An Introduction.* Fort Worth, TX: Holt.

KIRK, R. E. (1996). Practical significance: A concept whose time has come. *Educational and Psychological Measurement, 56,* 746–759.

KITCHEN, I. (1987). Letter. *Trends in Pharmacological Science, 8,* 252–253.

KOLATA, G. (1988). Theorist applies computer power to uncertainty in statistics. *New York Times,* Nov. 11, C1, C6.

KRUEGER, J. (2001). Null hypothesis significance testing: On the survival of a flawed method. *American Psychologist, 56,* 16–26.

LANG, A. R., GOECKNER, D. J., ADESSO, V. I., & MARLATT, G. A. (1975). Effects of alcohol and aggression in male social drinkers. *Journal of Abnormal Psychology, 84,* 508–518.

LOFTUS, G. R. (1993). A picture is worth a thousand *p* values: On the irrelevance of hypothesis testing in the microcomputer age. *Behavior Research Methods, Instruments & Computers, 25,* 250–256.

LOFTUS, G. R. (1996). Psychology will be a much better science when we change the way we analyze data. *Current Directions in Psychological Science, 5,* 161–171.

MACKINTOSH, N. J. (Ed.) (1995). *Cyril Burt: Fraud or Framed?* Oxford: Oxford University Press.

MAHONEY, M. J. (1976). *Scientist as Subject. The Psychological Imperative.* Cambridge, MA: Ballinger.

MANN, C. (1990). Meta-analysis in the breech. *Science, 249,* 476–480.

MANN, H. B., & WHITNEY, D. R. (1947). On a test of whether one or two random variables is stochastically larger than the other. *Annals of Mathematical Statistics, 18,* 50–60.

MANTEL, N. (1990). Comment. *Statistics in Medicine, 9,* 369–370.

MANTEL, N., & GREENHOUSE, S. W. (1968). What is the continuity correction? *American Statistician, 22,* 27–30.

MATARAZZO, J. D. (1972). *Wechsler's Measurement and Appraisal of Adult Intelligence: Fifth and Enlarged Edition.* New York: Oxford University Press.

MAXWELL, S. E., & DELANEY, H. D. (1985). Measurement scales and statistics: An examination of variable validity. *Psychological Bulletin, 97,* 85–93.

MAY, R. B., MASON, M. E. J., & HUNTER, M. A. (1997). *Application of Statistics in Behavioral Research* (2nd ed.). New York: Harper Row.

McCALL, R. B. (1977). Childhood IQ's as predictors of adult educational and occupational status. *Science, 197,* 482–483.

McCANN, I. L., & HOLMES, D. S. (1984). Influence of aerobic exercise on depression. *Journal of Personality and Social Psychology, 46,* 1142–1147.

MCHUGH, R. B. (1963). Comment on "Scales and statistics: parametric and non-parametric." *Psychological Bulletin, 60*, 350–355.

MICCERI, T. (1989). The unicorn, the normal curve, and other improbable creatures. *Psychological Bulletin, 105*, 156–166.

MICHAEL, W. B. (1966). An interpretation of the coefficients of predictive validity and of determination in terms of the proportions of correct inclusions or exclusions in cells of a fourfold table. *Educational and Psychological Measurement, 26*, 419–424.

MILLIGAN, G. W., WONG, D. S., & THOMPSON, P. A. (1987). Robustness properties of nonorthogonal analysis of variance. *Psychological Bulletin, 101*, 464–470.

MINIUM, E. W., & CLARKE, R. B. (1982). *Elements of Statistical Reasoning.* New York: John Wiley.

MOHER, D., DULBERG, C. S., & WELLS, G. A. (1994). Statistical power, sample size, and their reporting in randomized controlled trials. *Journal of the American Medical Association, 272*, 122–124.

MOHER, D., & PHAM, B. (1999). Meta-analysis: An adolescent in need of evidence and a watchful eye. *Annals of Medicine, 31*, 153–155.

MORGAN, D. L., & MORGAN, R. K. (2001). Single-participant research design. Bringing science to managed care. *American Psychologist, 56*, 119–127.

NATELSON, B. (1976). The "executive" monkey revisited. Paper presented at the Symposium on Nerves and the Gut, Philadelphia.

NEAVE, H. R., & GRANGER, C. W. J. (1968). A Monte Carlo study comparing various two-sample tests for differences in mean. *Technometrics, 10*, 509–522.

NELDER, J. A. (1988). Response to Berger and Berry. *American Scientist, 76*, 431–432.

NEWMAN, J., & PEARSON, E. (1928a). On the use and interpretation of certain test criteria for purposes of statistical inference: Part I. *Biometrika, 20A*, 175–240.

NEYMAN, J., & PEARSON, E. (1928b). On the use and interpretation of certain test criteria for purposes of statistical inference: Part II. *Biometrika, 20A*, 263–294.

NISBETT, R. E., & ROSS, L. (1980). *Human Inference: Strategies and Shortcomings of Social Judgment.* Englewood Cliffs, NJ: Prentice Hall.

NOLAN, E. G., BRAM, P., & TILLMAN, K. (1963). Attitude information in high school seniors: A study of values and attitudes. *Journal of Educational Research, 57*, 185–188.

NUNNALLY, J. C. (1978). *Psychometric Theory.* New York: McGraw Hill.

PERONE, M. (1999). Statistical inference in behavior analysis: Experimental control is better. *Behavior Analyst, 22*, 109–116.

PILIAVIN, I. M., RODIN, J., & PILIAVIN, J. A. (1969). Good Samaritan: An underground phenomenon. *Journal of Personality and Social Psychology, 13*, 289–299.

PLOMIN, R., DEFRIES, J. C., & ROBERTS, M. K. (1977). Assortative mating by unwed biological parents of adopted children. *Science, 196*, 449–450.

POLANYI, M. (1961). The unaccountable element in science. *Transactions of the Bose Research Institute, 24*, 175–184.

PRUZEK, R. M. (1997). An introduction to Bayesian inference and its applications. In L. Harlow, S. A. Mulaik, & J. Steigen (Eds.), *What If There Were No Significance Tests?* (pp. 285–316). Hillsdale, NJ: Erlbaum.

ROGAN, J. D., & KESELMAN, H. J. (1977). Is the ANOVA *F*-test robust to variance heterogeneity when sample sizes are equal? An investment via a coefficient of variation. *American Educational Research Journal, 14*, 493–498.

ROGERS, J. L., HOWARD, K. I., & VESSEY, J. T. (1993). Using significance tests to evaluate equivalence between two experimental groups. *Psychological Bulletin, 113*, 553–565.

ROMAN, M. B. (1988). When good scientists turn bad. *Discover,* April, 50–58.

ROSCOE, J. T., & BYERS, J. A. (1971). An investigation of the restraints with respect to sample size commonly imposed on the use of the chi-square statistic. *Journal of the American Statistical Association, 66*, 755–759.

ROSENTHAL, R. (1991). Cumulating psychology: An appreciation of Donald C. Campbell. *Psychological Science, 2*, 213–221.

ROSENTHAL, R., & DIMATTEO, M. R. (2001). Meta-analysis: Recent developments in quantitative methods for literature reviews. *Annual Review of Psychology, 52*, 59–82.

ROSNOW, R. L., & ROSENTHAL, R. (1989a). Definition and interpretation of interaction effects. *Psychological Bulletin, 105*, 143–146.

ROSNOW, R. L., & ROSENTHAL, R. (1989b). Statistical procedures and the justification of knowledge in psychological science. *American Psychologist, 44*, 1276–1284.

ROSNOW, R. L., & ROSENTHAL, R. (1991). If you're looking at cell means, you're looking at only the interaction (unless all main effects are zero). *Psychological Bulletin,* 110, 574–576.

ROSNOW, R. L., & ROSENTHAL, R. (1995). "Some things you learn aren't so": Cohen's paradox, Asch's paradigm, and the interpretation of interaction. *Psychological Science,* 6, 3–9.

ROSNOW, R. L., ROSENTHAL, R., & RUBIN, D. B. (2000). Contrasts and correlations in effect-size estimation. *Psychological Science,* 11, 446–453.

ROSSI, J. S. (1990). Statistical power of psychological research: What have we gained in 20 years? *Journal of Consulting and Clinical Psychology,* 58, 646–656.

ROTTON, J., & KELLY, I. (1985). Much ado about the full moon: a meta-analysis of lunar-lunacy research. *Psychological Bulletin,* 97, 286–306.

ROZEBOOM, W. W. (1966). Scaling theory and the nature of measurement. *Synthese,* 16, 170–233.

SAMELSON, F. (1996). He didn't? Yes, he did (probably)! *Contemporary Psychology,* 41, 1177–1179.

SAN JOSE, B., VAN DE MHEEN, H., VAN OERS, J. A. M., MACKENBACH, J. P., & GARRETSEN, H. F. L. (1999). The U-shaped curve: Various health measures and alcohol drinking patterns. *Journal of the Study of Alcohol,* 60, 725–731.

SAWILOWSKY, S. S., & BLAIR, R. C. (1992). A more realistic look at the robustness and Type II error properties of the *t* test to departures from population normality. *Psychological Bulletin,* 111, 352–360.

SCARR, S. (1985). Constructing psychology: Making facts and fables for our times. *American Psychologist,* 40, 499–512.

SCHMIDT, F. L. (1992). What do data really mean? Research findings, meta-analysis, and cumulative knowledge in psychology? *American Psychologist,* 47, 1173–1181.

SCHMIDT, F. L. (1996). Statistical significance testing and cumulative knowledge in psychology: Implications for the training of researchers. *Psychological Methods,* 1, 115–129.

SEDLMEIER, P., & GIGERENZER, G. (1989). Do studies of statistical power have an effect on the power of studies? *Psychological Bulletin,* 105, 309–316.

SHADISH, W. R., & RAGSDALE, K. (1996). Random versus nonrandom assignment in controlled experiments: Do you get the same answer? *Journal of Consulting and Clinical Psychology,* 64, 1290–1305.

SHAPIRO, S. (1994). Meta-analysis/shmeta-analysis. *American Journal of Epidemiology,* 140, 771–778.

SIDMAN, M. (1960). *Tactics of Scientific Research.* New York: Basic Books.

SIEGEL, S. S., & CASTELLAN, N. J. (1988). *Nonparametric Statistics for the Behavioral Sciences* (2nd ed.). New York: McGraw Hill.

SINCLAIR, J. D. (1988). Multiple *t*-tests are appropriate in science. *Trends in Pharmacological Science,* 9, 12–13.

SKINNER, B. F. (1966). What is the experimental analysis of behavior? *Journal of the Experimental Analysis of Behavior,* 9, 213–218.

SLACK, W. V., & PORTER, D. (1980). The Scholastic Aptitude Test: A critical appraisal. *Harvard Educational Review,* 50, 154–175.

SMITH, D., BEST, L. A., CYLKE, V. A., & STUBBS, D. A. (2000). Psychology without *p* values: Data analysis at the turn of the 19th century. *American Psychologist,* 55, 260–263.

SMITH, M. L., & GLASS, G. V. (1977). Meta-analysis of psychotherapy outcome studies. *American Psychologist,* 32, 752–760.

STEERING COMMITTEE PHYSICIANS' HEALTH STUDY RESEARCH GROUP (1988). Preliminary report: Findings from the aspirin component of the ongoing physicians' health study. *New England Journal of Medicine,* 318, 262–264.

STERLING, T. D. (1959). Publication decisions and their possible effects on inferences drawn from tests of significance—or vice versa. *Journal of the American Statistical Association,* 54, 30–34.

STEVENS, S. S. (1946). On the theory of scales of measurement. *Science,* 103, 677–680.

STINE, W. W. (1989). Meaningful inference: The role of measurement in statistics. *Psychological Bulletin,* 105, 147–155.

TAYLOR, H., & RUSSELL, J. (1939). The relationship of validity coefficients to the practical effectiveness of tests in selection: Discussion and tables. *Journal of Applied Psychology,* 23, 565–578.

TAYLOR, S. E. (1991). *Health Psychology.* New York: Random House.

TOMARKEN, A. J., & SERLIN, R. C. (1986). Comparison of ANOVA alternatives under variance heterogeneity and specific noncentrality structures. *Psychological Bulletin,* 99, 90–99.

TOWNSEND, J. T., & ASHBY, F. G. (1984). Measurement scales and statistics: The misconception misconceived. *Psychological Bulletin,* 96, 394–401.

TUKEY, J. W. (1977). *Exploratory Data Analysis.* Reading, MA: Addison-Wesley.

TVERSKY, A., & KAHNEMAN, D. (1971). Belief in the law of small numbers. *Psychological Bulletin,* 76, 105–110.

URY, H. (1967). In response to Noether's letter, "Needed—a new name." *American Statistician,* 21, 53.

VAUGHAN, G. M., & CORBALLIS, M. C. (1969). Beyond tests of significance: Estimating strength of effects in selected ANOVA designs. *Psychological Bulletin,* 72, 204–223.

WACHTER, K. W. (1988). Disturbed by meta-analysis? *Science,* 241, 1407–1408.

WAINER, H. (1999). One cheer for null hypothesis significance testing. *Psychological Methods,* 4, 212–213.

WEISS, D. J. (1989). An experiment in publication: Advance publication review. *Applied Psychological Measurement,* 13, 1–7.

WEISS, J. M. (1971). Effects of coping behavior with and without a feedback signal on stress pathology in rats. *Journal of Comparative and Physiological Psychology,* 77, 22–30.

WESTLAKE, W. J. (1981). Bioequivalence testing—A need to rethink. *Biometrics,* 37, 591–593.

WESTLAKE, W. J. (1988). In K. E. Peace (Ed.), *Biopharmaceutical Statistics for Drug Development* (pp. 329–352). New York: Marcel Dekker.

WHITLEY, B. E. JR. (1992). Units of analysis, measurement scales, and statistics: A comment on Kerwin and Shaffer. *Personality and Social Psychology Bulletin,* 18, 680–684.

WHITNEY, E., & NUNNELLEY, E. (1987). *Understanding Nutrition* (4th ed.). St. Paul, MN: West.

WILCOXON, F. (1945). Individual comparisons by ranking methods. *Biometrics Bulletin,* 1, 80–83.

WILCOXON, F. (1947). Probability tables for individual comparisons by ranking methods. *Biometrics,* 3, 119–122.

WILKINSON, L. (1988). *SYSTAT: The System for Statistics.* Evanston, IL: SYSTAT.

WILKINSON, L., AND THE TASK FORCE ON STATISTICAL INFERENCE. (1999). Statistical methods in psychology journals. Guidelines and explanations. *American Psychologist,* 54, 594–604.

WILLIAMS, M., LECLUYSE, K., & ROCK-FAUCHEUX, A. (1992). Effective interventions for reading disabilities. *Journal of the American Optometric Association,* 63, 411–417.

WINER, B. J., BROWN, D. R., & MICHELS, K. M. (1991). *Statistical Principles in Experimental Design* (3rd ed.). New York: McGraw Hill.

YATES, F. (1934). Contingency tables involving small numbers and the $\chi^2$ test. *Journal of the Royal Statistical Society* (supplement), 1, 217–235.

ZIVIN, J. A., & BARTKO, J. J. (1976). Statistics for disinterested scientists. *Life Science,* 18, 15–26.

# INDEX

# USEFUL FORMULAS

Here are some of the computing formulas that appear in the book. The reference is to the section number where each formula is introduced and defined.

| | | |
|---|---|---|
| Confidence Interval for $\mu_X$ | $\overline{X} \pm t_p s_{\overline{X}}$ | Sec. 18.2 |
| Confidence Interval for $\mu_X - \mu_Y$ | $(\overline{X} - \overline{Y}) \pm t_p s_{\overline{X} - \overline{Y}}$ | Sec. 18.7 |
| Chi-Square: General Formula | $\chi^2 = \sum \left[ \dfrac{(f_o - f_e)^2}{f_e} \right]$ | Sec. 19.2 |
| Within-Groups Sum of Squares | $SS_w = \overset{\substack{\text{all}\\\text{scores}}}{\sum} (X - \overline{X})^2$ | Sec. 20.3 |
| | $= \overset{\substack{\text{all}\\\text{scores}}}{\sum} X^2 - \left[ \dfrac{\left(\sum X_A\right)^2}{n_A} + \dfrac{\left(\sum X_B\right)^2}{n_B} + \cdots \right]$ | Sec. 20.9 |
| Between-Groups Sum of Squares | $SS_{bet} = \overset{k}{\sum} n_i (\overline{X}_i - \overline{\overline{X}})^2$ | Sec. 20.3 |
| | $= \left[ \dfrac{\left(\sum X_A\right)^2}{n_A} + \dfrac{\left(\sum X_B\right)^2}{n_B} + \cdots \right] - \dfrac{\left(\overset{\substack{\text{all}\\\text{scores}}}{\sum} X\right)^2}{n_{\text{total}}}$ | Sec. 20.9 |
| Total Sum of Squares | $SS_{\text{total}} = \overset{\substack{\text{all}\\\text{scores}}}{\sum} (X - \overline{\overline{X}})^2$ | Sec. 20.3 |
| | $= \overset{\substack{\text{all}\\\text{scores}}}{\sum} X^2 - \dfrac{\left(\overset{\substack{\text{all}\\\text{scores}}}{\sum} X\right)^2}{n_{\text{total}}}$ | Sec. 20.9 |
| Within-Groups Degrees of Freedom | $df_w = n_{\text{total}} - k$ | Sec. 20.4 |
| Between-Groups Degrees of Freedom | $df_{bet} = k - 1$ | Sec. 20.4 |
| Within-Groups Variance Estimate | $s_w^2 = \dfrac{SS_w}{df_w}$ | Sec. 20.5 |
| Between Groups Variance Estimate | $s_{bet}^2 = \dfrac{SS_{bet}}{df_{bet}}$ | Sec. 20.5 |